T0228024

IET SECURITY SERIES 16

Machine Learning, Blockchain Technologies and Big Data Analytics for IoTs

Other volumes in this series:

Machine Learning, Blockchain Technologies and Big Data Analytics for IoTs

Methods, technologies and applications

Edited by
Amit Kumar Tyagi, Ajith Abraham, Farookh Khadeer Hussain, Arturas Kaklauskas and R. Jagadeesh Kannan

The Institution of Engineering and Technology

Published by The Institution of Engineering and Technology, London, United Kingdom

The Institution of Engineering and Technology is registered as a Charity in England & Wales (no. 211014) and Scotland (no. SC038698).

© The Institution of Engineering and Technology 2022

First published 2022

The Institution of Engineering and Technology
Futures Place
Kings Way, Stevenage
Hertfordshire, SG1 2UA, United Kingdom

www.theiet.org

British Library Cataloguing in Publication Data
A catalogue record for this product is available from the British Library

ISBN 978-1-83953-339-6 (hardback)
ISBN 978-1-83953-340-2 (PDF)

Typeset in India by MPS
Printed in the UK by CPI Group (UK) Ltd, Croydon

Contents

11 Blockchain network with artificial intelligence—DeFi affair management   235

R. Vedhapriyavadhana, S.L. Jayalakshmi, R. Girija and Ninoslav Marina

12 Vulnerabilities of smart contracts and solutions   257

Roshni Nawaz, Amit Kumar Tyagi and M. Shamila

23   Knowledge extraction from abnormal stock returns: evidence from Indian stock market   517

Molla Ramizur Rahman, Anirudh Bharadwaj and Pabitra Mitra

24   Impact of influence analysis of social media fake news—a machine learning perspective   537

V. Kakulapati and S. Mahender Reddy

About the Editors

Amit Kumar Tyagi is an assistant professor and senior researcher at the School of Computer Science and Engineering, Vellore Institute of Technology (VIT), Chennai Campus, Chennai, Tamil Nadu, India. His current research focuses on machine learning with big data, blockchain technology, data science, cyber physical systems, smart & secure computing and privacy. He has contributed to several projects such as "AARIN" and "P3-Block" to address some of the open issues related to the privacy breaches in vehicular applications (such as parking) and medical cyber physical systems. He is a member of the IEEE. He received his PhD from Pondicherry Central University, India.

Ajith Abraham is the director of Machine Intelligence Research Labs (MIR Labs), Australia. MIR Labs are a not-for-profit scientific network for innovation and research excellence connecting industry and academia. His research focuses on real world problems in the fields of machine intelligence, cyber-physical systems, Internet of things, network security, sensor networks, Web intelligence, Web services, and data mining. He is the Chair of the IEEE Systems Man and Cybernetics Society Technical Committee on Soft Computing. He is editor-in-chief of *Engineering Applications of Artificial Intelligence* (EAAI) and serves on the editorial board of several international journals. He received his PhD in Computer Science from Monash University, Melbourne, Australia.

Farookh Khadeer Hussain is an associate professor with the School of Software, University of Technology Sydney, Australia. He is also an associate member of the Advanced Analytics Institute and a core member of the Centre for Artificial Intelligence. His key research interests include trust-based computing, cloud of things, blockchains, and machine learning. He has published widely in these areas in top journals, such as *FGCS*, the *Computer Journal, JCSS, IEEE Transactions on Industrial Informatics*, and *IEEE Transactions on Industrial Electronics*. He holds a PhD from Curtin University, Perth, Australia.

Arturas Kaklauskas is a professor at Vilnius Gediminas Technical University, Lithuania. His areas of interest include affective computing, Internet of Things, Big Data and text analytics, intelligent event prediction, opinion mining, intelligent decision support systems, neuro-marketing, intelligent tutoring systems, massive open online courses (MOOCS), smart built environment, energy and resilience management. He is editor-in-chief of the *Journal of Civil Engineering and*

Management, editor of *Engineering Applications of Artificial Intelligence,* and associate editor of *Ecological Indicators Journal.* His publications include nine books. The Belarusian State Technological University (Minsk, Belarus) has awarded him an Honorary Doctorate.

R. Jagadeesh Kannan is a professor at the School of Computer Science and Engineering, Vellore Institute of Technology, Chennai, Tamil Nadu, India. His research focuses on semantic web, network security, software engineering, and artificial intelligence. He is an active member of the Indian Society for Technical Education (ISTE), Computer Society of India (CSI), Software Process Improvement Network (SPIN), International Association of Engineers (IAENG), Association of Computer Electronics & Electrical & Engineers (ACEEE), International Association of Computer Science & Information Technology (IACSIT), Research GATE—Scientific Network, Society of Digital Information and Wireless Communications (SDIWC), Computer Science Teachers Association (CSTA), and the International forum of Researchers Students and Academician (IFRSA). He received a PhD from Anna University, Tamil Nadu, India in 2011.

Foreword

I am happy to hear that Institution of Engineering & Technology is writing a book on Machine Learning, Blockchain Technologies and Big Data Analytics for IoTs. These emerging technologies are already finding their footing in the learning industry. The application of emerging technology trends will lead to a transformation of educational models and completely reimagine the way students approach learning.

The Ministry of Electronic and Information Technology (MeitY) is instrumental in creation of ecosystem and integration of emerging technology in education sector in India. MeitY is entrusted to enhance the learning process of students for the ultimate objective of building knowledge economy in India. Leveraging machine learning, blockchain technologies, and Big Data Analytics and IoTs in education sector highlight the objective of revolutionizing the learning process for students. It promises to help students capture their imaginations with the sole aim of improving learning process and to be ready for a technology-based future.

The Government of India introduced National Education Policy (NEP) that emphasizes of technology in education. The objective is to further the reach of quality education to corners of Indian geography. With increased penetration of Internet, and wider digitization India is well placed on the path of making quality education available to all parts of the country.

With emerging technologies finding their way into the education sector, it's time to bid adieu to traditional methods of teaching and learning. The augmented reality and virtual reality technology are redefining how teachers deliver the content. The adaptive learning systems are redefining how learning is designed. The new emerging technologies are likely to change the face of education in the forthcoming years. The interactive technology is going to change the face of teacher–student medium of interaction.

There are various initiatives taken by Government of India in this field. On September 17, 2021, Mr Ashwini Vaishnaw, the Minister of Railways, Communications, Electronics and Information Technology, launched Rail Kaushal Vikas Yojana, a program under the aegis of Pradhan Mantri Kaushal Vikas Yojana (PMKVY), in Rail Bhavan to empower youth by providing entry-level training in industry relevant skills through railway training institutes as part of 75 years of Azadi ka Amrit Mahotsav.

Emerging technologies are going to revolutionize learning process of students. They have the potential to enhance the way teachers and student interact. Some of the technologies and their impact are noted below:

(i)   Augmented reality and simulation: It has the potential to change the face of interaction of students and teachers. It is going to revolutionize the mode of collaboration.

(ii) Adaptive learning: It is the technology that is going to define the learning activities based on the need of the learner. The plan adapts as per the need of the learner and help them adapt a learning path as per their interest and learning ability

(iii) AI in education: AI has the potential to reshape education. In its current form, it is going to augments the knowledge of the human in making decisions bases of previous learning from available data.

(iv) Automation: Automation is set to support students by customizing the contentment delivery based on adaptive learning plan.

(v)   Learning analytics: It will help students and teachers to track and measure learning goals and find gaps that need attention. It will be clubbed with adaptive learning modules to enhance the learning plan and delivery plans as per the requirement.

In conclusion, education is set to experience a huge level of future reshaping with the help of emerging technologies. Increasing exposure to technology from a young age will go a long way in helping future generations lead the way to a new world of innovation and creativity.

I extend my best wishes to the authors of the book and look forward to a grand success.

Smt. Kavita Bhatia
Scientist F, eGovernance and Emerging Technologies
Division, MeitY, Government of India, India

Preface

We are moving into a smart era where Internet of Things (IoTs) and smart devices will be used at a large scale. In fast-developing applications such as healthcare, transportation, education, retail, etc., the storing of information (generated by IoT devices) and its access will require secure mechanisms. Blockchain is designed specifically to accelerate and simplify the process of how transactions are made without any intermediary. They can be recorded transparently as a completely decentralized system. Blockchain technologies and concepts will help support decentralized services to end users by providing reliable, full-proof services using ledger functionality, and it will likely be used in many future applications.

Moreover, both industry and academic researchers are now looking at transforming applications into automated applications using machine learning and deep learning. The next generation of automated applications will command machines to do tasks better and more efficiently. To enhance security, machine learning (ML) methodologies and technologies will be used to build better models by taking advantage of the decentralized nature of blockchain (that encourage data sharing) and to govern the chain. The combination of blockchain (or Distributed Ledger Technology (DLT)), Big Data analytics, and machine learning could be a game changer in many sectors and for many future applications including the financial and insurance industries as they can be used to identify fraud and bogus users inside systems and networks. With such enhancements, blockchain will provide new opportunities for building cutting-edge next-generation Artificial Intelligence-based business applications.

But the advent of these new technologies also brings unrealistically high expectations to industries, organizations, and users. The decrease of computing costs, the improvement of data integrity in blockchain, and the verification of transactions using machine learning are becoming essential goals. We can imagine a decentralized marketplace where no intermediary is needed to buy and sell things and to do tasks. But there are serious issues such as security interoperability (as there will probably be multiple Blockchains) and regulations that will require efficient solutions and the attention of researchers from around the world.

This book will cover challenges and opportunities related to machine learning, Big Data analytics, and blockchain technologies and applications for IoTs. The aim is to provide a broad coverage of research and technology innovations, and emerging trends and concepts in the field, and to introduce applications in communication, healthcare, transportation, manufacturing, and financial services.

Editors:
- Amit Kumar Tyagi
- Ajith Abraham
- Farookh Khadeer Hussain
- Habil Arturas Kaklauskas
- R. Jagadeesh Kannan

Acknowledgment

First of all, we would to extend our gratitude to our family members, friends, and supervisors, which stood with us as an advisor in completing this book. Also, we would like to thanks our almighty "God" who makes us to write this book. We also thank IET Publishers (who has provided their continuous support during this COVID-19 pandemic) and our colleagues with whom we have work together inside the college/university and others outside of the college/university who have provided their continuous support toward completing this book on machine learning, blockchain technologies, etc., for IoTs.

Also, we would like to thank our Respected Madam, Prof. G. Aghila, Prof. Siva Sathya, our Respected Sir Prof. N. Sreenath and Prof. Aswani Kumar Cherukuri, for giving their valuable inputs and helping us in completing this book.

-Dr Amit Kumar Tyagi and other Editors

Glossary

Machine learning	Machine learning is a computational algorithm which builds a mathematical model to make decisions based on experience rather than developing explicit programs to meet a task. It uses data known as "training data" to build a sample algorithm and tests the built algorithm with "test data" to make predictions and arrive at a conclusion.
Blockchain technologies	Blockchain is a system which is tamper evident digital ledger that allows secure transactions to take place within a community without any central authority or bias such that the published transaction or information cannot be changed and is stored in a block permanently.
Big Data analytics for Internet of Things	The information collected from various sensors associated with the Internet of Things (IoT) system contains huge volumes of data and requires proper analytical methods to process them. Big Data analytics is a technology that is used to analyze the data and provide different insights using algorithms like descriptive analytics, prescriptive analytics, predictive analytics, etc.
Advanced data analytics	Advanced data analytics is a sub set of data analytics that is used to process more huge and complex data sets and provide more deeper insights using machine learning algorithms, Artificial Intelligence, and semi or complete automation processes.
Recent trends in IoT-based applications	IoT-based automation or number of connected devices available in the market has experienced a boom due to the advancement in 5G technologies. Wearable and self-monitoring health devices have witnessed a sudden growth in sales in the post pandemic

world due to the fear of people to visit hospitals. Since it involves exchange of huge volumes of data, it has led to concerns due to cybersecurity. This has created more opportunities and need to protect the data.

AI in healthcare—from data to Intelligence

Huge and unstructured data flowing in the health-care industry can be streamlined and put to proper medical use and analysis with the help of Artificial Intelligence that helps to detect, classify the unorganized healthcare data to a meaningful and structured information.

AI technologies and machine learning for smart applications

AI and machine learning algorithms are widely used in smart applications to analyze and categorize the data and then take decisions in a smarter way. Smart applications mainly involve natural language processing, sentiment analysis, robotic process automation, AI optimized hardware, etc.

Automated machine learning

Automated machine learning is a technique using which solutions to real world problems are completely automated using various machine learning algorithms that collects the raw data, develops the model, and tests the model to provide suitable outcomes.

Automated systems for smart applications

Automated systems are majorly embedded applications that are integrated with various sensors to monitor the ambient conditions, movement, etc. and perform actions using appropriate actuators to completely automize the process to simplify human activities such as automated door openers in homes, buses, garage etc., and watering systems, etc.

Autonomous Intelligent vehicles

Autonomous intelligent vehicles are the next-generation vehicles that percept the ambient data and control the vehicle accordingly. It detects road signs, objects, human beings, signal and plan the path and control the speed accordingly.

Autonomous vehicles

Autonomous intelligent vehicles are the next-generation vehicles that percept the ambient data and control the vehicle accordingly. It detects road signs, objects, human beings, signal and plan the path and control the speed accordingly.

Big Data analytics in IoT-based smart applications	Big data analytics deals with the categorization and classification of the data collection from sensors incorporated in various smart applications developed using IoT. The data is converted to digestible databases that can be utilized by companies to streamline their processes or perform particular actions.
Big Data applications in smart city	Big Data applications aid in collecting various information regarding the vehicle congestion, traffic, etc. from intelligent transportation systems or energy consumptions from smart grids, environment morning data, etc. and analyze them using suitable methods to minimize energy consumptions, promote a sustainable environment or optimize traffic, etc.
Cognitive science and computing	Cognitive computing is a stream of computer science that is used to study the human brain in areas like neuroscience, neuro health-related domains, psychology, philosophy, etc. to provide deep insights and simplify the process of analyzing humans with mind or brain related illness.
Computational intelligence	Computational intelligence are computational algorithms developed motivated to mimic biological responses of human brain namely neural networks, evolutionary computation, and fuzzy control systems.
Computer vision systems	Computer vision is oriented with the use of artificial and machine learning algorithms to analyze systems consisting of majorly images, videos, and other visual inputs and to provide resourceful outcomes based on the analyses.
Hybridized machine learning-deep learning framework	Hybridized machine learning and deep learning framework is a combination of two two machine learning like supervised and reinforcement learning or a machine learning and a deep learning algorithm like neural network to improve the complexity and efficiency by taking in the best features of two algorithms and using them for different purposes like clustering, classification etc.
Intelligent information system and retrieval	Information retrieval systems are used to process information in a smarter way using neural networks and other complex computational

	processes and use it to come to conclusions based on strong evidence gathered from the knowledge gained.
Intelligent systems for smart applications	Intelligent systems are technically advanced machines that are programmed to integrate and handle data, technology and people to provide automated solutions based on trained programs through a faster and smarted approach.
Knowledge management in medical informatics	Knowledge management system allows healthcare providers to gather information from various patients regarding symptoms and cure for various diseases. This helps to gather knowledge regarding various issues and further use them to classify outcomes based on the learning simultaneously maintain the privacy of the patient.
Semantic technology	Semantic technology is a process that helps the machines understand the information and language similar to the way understood by humans and this is achieved through a variety of tools and technologies.
Adversarial search	It is a type of search which generally consists of two players where they take turns to produce different outcomes and the state of the problem keeps changing every turn. It follows perfect rules and the scope of the system is fully observable and the number of unique outcomes is limited.
AI accelerator	AI accelerator is more hardware-oriented implementation of machine learning, artificial intelligence, and sensor-related tasks keeping in mind the limited availability of resources and developing an approach with lesser computational capability and more memory efficient algorithms.
Ambient Intelligence	Ambient intelligence is the future of artificial intelligence where the need for explicit input and output devices is eliminated and is replaced by smarter sensors to observe ambient data in devices used every day and act seamlessly.
Applied machine learning	The application of machine learning to a specific data-related problem is known as applied machine learning. It can entail either supervised

	models, in which an algorithm develops itself based on labeled training data, or unsupervised models, in which the inferences and analyses are obtained from unlabeled data. The application of statistical algorithms and techniques to make sense of, categorize, and alter data characterizes applied machine learning in general.
Quantum machine learning	Quantum machine learning (QML) is a new discipline that blends quantum computing and machine learning algorithms to address issues that are extremely difficult to answer in traditional ways. Quantum machine learning is a type of machine learning that employs quantum computers to train machine learning models. Quantum computers use quantum bits (qubits) instead of the traditional bits used by classical digital computers to process data in a unique way. Due to the present challenges with massive data processing, quantum machine learning has developed. Quantum computing can speed up the training of machine learning models. Furthermore, enormous spaces can be searched for approximation functions utilizing quantum methods.
Artificial narrow intelligence (ANI)	Artificial narrow intelligence is a sort of AI that we have been able to successfully develop and execute up to this point. It is a goal-oriented, limited rangeability perspective that performs specific concentrated tasks without the ability to self-expand machines that are dedicated to a single purpose are subjected to a certain set of constraints and limitations. Narrow AI, on the other hand, does not reproduce true human intelligence; rather, it replicates human behavior based on a limited set of criteria.
Augmented intelligence	Augmented intelligence works by finding and expanding on human capabilities using smart algorithms to produce near-real-time and data-driven insights. Humans would find it easier to recognize patterns that work, unlock strategic opportunities, examine their functions, and even turn data into action if they had access to these insights. It should not be

seen solely as a tool for automating tasks. It is more than that because its main objective is to improve people's cognitive capacities, and that is where the true beauty of it lies. It uses previous data to assist humans in making forecasts, but the final decision is still made by humans.

Backward chaining

Backward chaining is a useful strategy for teaching humans a complex sequence of behaviors. Although it has been utilized with people who are usually developing, it has primarily been used to educate people with developmental impairments fundamental daily life tasks. Backward chaining is defined as teaching a series of behaviors in reverse order, beginning with the last step in the behavioral sequence. Although it is unknown whether backward chaining is more effective than other chaining techniques, one advantage is that the terminal reinforcer is always supplied as the individual completes each phase.

Cognitive automation

Cognitive automation is a type of automation that uses software to add intelligence to data-intensive processes. It is frequently related with robotic process automation (RPA), which is a combination of AI and cognitive computing. Cognitive automation extends and improves the range of actions typically associated with RPA by leveraging Artificial Intelligence technologies, resulting in cost savings and improved customer satisfaction, as well as increased accuracy in complex business processes involving the use of unstructured data.

Robotic process automation (RPA)

Robotic process automation is a technology used to maintain entire robotic systems process right from gathering data, analyzing, performing actions and manage robot software's more strategically across multiple fields like industrial manufacturing, finance, supply chain, etc.

Cognitive robotic process automation

Cognitive robotic process automation majorly deals with the use of optical or visual AI technologies such as text identification, image classification, and sentiment analysis

	to extend it to perform robotic operations based on the outcomes observed from the cognitive computing parameters used to study the environment etc.
Connected devices	Smart electronics devices are connected to each other as well as other mechanical or electrical devices through wired or wireless communication network to exchange information and perform actions simultaneously without any manual intervention. They are widely used in home automation, industrial automation, etc. to command multiple units from a single or multiple sources.
Convolutional neural network	Convolutional neural network is special type of neural network that is mainly utilized to study and analyze visual content. It involves a mathematical algorithm called convolution which uses two variables/inputs and provide a third variable (outcome) as the convolution product of the two inputs and helps in comparing the similarity between the two images.
Embedded vision	Embedded vision is a category of computer vision that involves processors and physical cameras to capture visual images and further analyze them using various computer vision algorithms in a similar manner to human brain processing.
Generative adversarial network (GAN)	A GAN is a type of construct in neural network technology that offers a lot of potential in the world of artificial intelligence. A generative adversarial network is composed of two neural networks: a generative network and a discriminative network. These work together to provide high-level simulation of conceptual tasks.
Granular computing	Granular computing is a study that deals with processing of information accumulated & represented at a granular level by different individual entities. Granulation of information at entity level helps in many ways to use the data effectively.
Hyper-automation	Hyper-automation is an advanced automation process with an additional layer consisting of artificial intelligence and machine learning

	concepts to quicken the automation process compared to traditional methods. It is widely used in many business researches and information technology sectors.
Industry 4.0	It involves the collaboration of the latest cutting-edge technologies such as cyber physical systems, Internet of Things, robotics and automation, special learning algorithms to develop smarter and quicker manufacturing processes that maximize quality and productivity with minimal effort.
Society 5.0	Society 5.0 represents a smarter society that integrates nature, technology, and humans to provide solutions to society's technological problems with smart Artificial Intelligent data systems.
Intelligent agent	Intelligent agent is a subset of artificial intelligence that studies its environment and gathers knowledge regarding it and takes actions autonomously based on the historical and continuous learning.
Intelligent character recognition (ICR)	ICR is an image processing technique applied to study various styles of handwriting and gather information about them to improve the system accuracy and recognition capability to identify the text correctly.
Knowledge engineering	Knowledge engineering is a process that helps to expedite the decision-making process for complex problems by simulating the human thought process combining human behavior and computer programming techniques.
Knowledge representation	It is the representation of information about the entire world, what we know and how to solve a particular problem so that this information can be utilized by any machine using artificial intelligence techniques to solve any complex problem.
Knowledge-based system	Knowledge-based system is a very wide concept used to develop computational algorithms to solve problems with the help of human knowledge. It also consists of interactive interface for users to question the

	system such as doubt clarification in online tutoring and get responses.
Machine intelligence	Machine intelligence is a synonym for artificial intelligence that involves the collaboration of machine learning, deep learning, and natural language processing to build interactive chatbots or robots to mimic human behavior using cognitive computing.
Machine teaching	Machine teaching is a technology where the machine not only learns from the data provided but also tries to gather knowledge from human beings to solve tasks efficiently. It is highly useful than machine learning algorithms when proper labeling of data is not available.
Machine translation	Machine translation is a software developed to automatically translate the text from one language to another without human interaction. The base language can be studied using computational algorithms and can be converted to one or more target languages.
Machine-to-machine (M2M)	M2M communication involves the exchange of data between two electronic or mechanical devices over wired/wireless medium which ultimately reduces human intervention and results in faster transfer rate with more accuracy.
Natural language processing (NLP)	NLP is a method in which the computer understands the human language and enables interaction that can be used to manipulate data or analyze and classify the. It is widely used to text identification and automation processes.
Near field communication (NFC)	Near field communication is a wireless short distance communication protocol that enables exchange of information between two electronic devices. It is mainly used for transactions between consumers and retailers through smart phones without the exchange of paper money.
Neural network	A neural network consists of multiple nodes that are interconnected to each other mimicking the neuron connections in a human brain and also adopt a similar procedure for studying the data to recognize patterns, correlations and classify the outcomes accordingly.

Predictive modeling	Predictive modeling is a type of data mining that studies the historical data, analyze them to develop a particular model or algorithm that describes the pattern of outcome and use it to predict the future outcomes.
Reinforcement learning	Reinforcement learning is a machine learning technique in which the intelligent AI agent interacts with the environment directly to understand the resulting positive and negative rewards based on different actions and improves the performance to achieve maximum positive results.
Robotics	Robotics is a branch of science that requires the knowledge of computer science, electronics, and mechanics to build machines known as robots that mimic the actions performed by humans and are used to assist them. They are also used to control various machines autonomously.
Self-supervised learning	Self-supervised uses artificial neural network that uses unlabeled data to retrieve labels. It is more advantageous as it reduces the effort to manually label data. It is more similar to method adopted by humans to classify objects.
Sentiment analysis	Sentiment analysis is a method of natural language processing (NLP) that is used to identify the emotions behind a text mainly as positive, negative or neutral. It is highly useful in understanding the customers review or opinion about a product and categorizes them accordingly.
Spatial computing	Spatial computing is a technology where the environment including the objects and humans present in it are completely digitalized in order to enable interaction with a digital world by being present in it and take perform actions. It mainly involves virtual reality, augmented reality and mixed reality.
Theory of computation	It is the development of algorithms that involve either mathematical or logical models to solve a particular problem and also analyze the degree of efficiency of the algorithm in solving the problem.
Deep learning	A feedback-based learning, a subset/ type of machine learning technique.

Chapter 1

Introduction to machine learning, blockchain technologies, and Big Data analytics for IoTs: concepts, open issues, and critical challenges

Amit Kumar Tyagi[1], Ajith Abraham[2], Farookh Khadeer Hussain[3], Habil Arturas Kaklauskas[4] and R. Jagadeesh Kannan[1]

Abstract

Today a plethora of applications are trying to shift toward using the Internet of Things (IoT) or Internet Connected Things. IoTs can be used in many applications such as Healthcare, Agriculture, Transportation, and Logistics. These devices can help healthcare professionals take care of patients in real time. However, there are several issues around smart devices such as security, privacy, and trust. Blockchain is the most secured technology today. It is a novel concept to provide a decentralized and distributed structure and is based on a distributed ledger concept. This chapter discusses IoT and its uses in smart AI-based applications with the integration of blockchain.

Keywords: Machine learning; Internet of Things (IoT); Blockchain; Big Data analytics

1.1 Introduction

IoT devices can share data on a cloud that is public, private, or hybrid depending on the organization's requirement and complexity [1,2]. These technologies can be introduced below as:

- **Artificial Intelligence (AI):** AI is used to interpret and process data in IoT applications, including intelligent machine-to-human decision-making capabilities.

[1]School of Computer Science and Engineering, Vellore Institute of Technology, Chennai, India
[2]Machine Intelligence Research Labs (MIR Labs), USA
[3]Discipline (Software Engineering), University of Technology, Sydney, Australia
[4]Construction Economics and Property Management, Vilnius Gediminas Technical University, Lithuania

AI is a method using which a machine can complete a series of tasks or learn from data in a more intelligent way. As AI is applied to the Internet of Things (IoT), these machines can interpret data, make decisions, and act on that data without human intervention.

- **IoT:** IoT is an emerging technique in which the hardware devices called sensors are equipped to collect real-time data and transmitted to a cloud storage through gateway. For quite some time, the main components needed for IoT have existed but they are now mature, such as inexpensive sensors required to convert analog to digital, reliable transmission networks, and the processing and decision-making of intelligent analytics. It is this whole stack coming together that has made it possible for IoT to become possible.

- **Blockchain:** Blockchain is used for providing a decentralized and distributed platform for IoT applications. By setting up a harmonized digital network for IoT data open to multiple parties, blockchain technology may promote data standardization. Data is stored in an encrypted form on blockchain networks using hash functions. This ensures that the data is more secure and stored in standard manner.

- **Cloud computing:** Cloud computing, also simply referred to as the "Cloud," is a collection of Internet-connected servers and computers that create a vast distributed system that can provide on-demand Internet services on a pay-for-use basis. Most cloud computing services can be classified into three major categories: IaaS (Infrastructure-as-a-Service), PaaS (Platform-as-a-Service), and SaaS (Software-as-a-Service).

AI alludes to computers which are intended to think and emulate humans. These techniques can likewise be applied to any frameworks that show qualities connected to the human psyche, for example, learning and critical thinking. By studying the patterns of human actions, computers can solve problems at a quicker rate, while reducing human involvement. Several experiments on the subject are ongoing to find out how computers and machines can mimic human behaviors. These humans and AI are wired using the cross-disciplinary approach. Previous accomplishments in the field are obsolete. There is so much scope in this area that we have not even reached the starting line [3]. Figure 1.1 depicts various frameworks of AI.

Creating/building humanoid is a very difficult task and requires a lot of efforts and analyses. AI is a man-made reasoning innovation or a type of digital intelligence that enables frameworks to take in and understand and respond in a smarter way without being customized explicitly. AI focuses on patterns in which computer programs can learn and process. There is a learning cycle for every model and each one has different patterns for taking a decision, such as models, direct insights, or directions. The principal goal is that computers or machines should work without the help of humans. Machine Learning (ML) is the child of AI. ML methods [4] include the following:

- Supervised learning
  It is an algorithm using which the outputs of a system are obtained from inputs based on input output pairs. It trains the data and helps in predicting new examples.

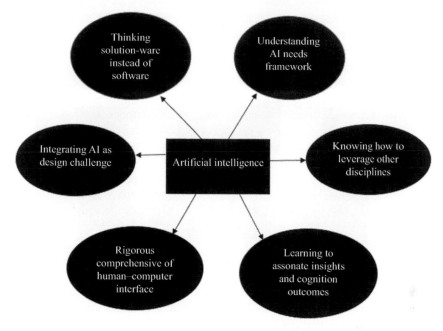

Figure 1.1   AI frameworks

- Unsupervised learning
    It is a method in which the system identifies naturally occurring patterns to learn and train the data rather than any preassigned labels or scores.
- Semi-supervised learning
    Semi-supervised learning is a ML technique that involves training using a small amount of labeled data and a big amount of unlabeled data. Semi-supervised learning is the middle ground between unsupervised and supervised learning. It is a unique case of weak supervision.
- Reinforcement learning
    The training of ML models to make a series of judgments is known as reinforcement learning. In an uncertain, potentially complex environment, the agent learns to achieve a goal. An AI meets a game-like circumstance in relevance feedback.

ML allows the analysis of major pieces of data, based on mathematical principles of s, to give accurate results in less time. In the processing of large volumes of knowledge, combining ML with cognitive technology will make it even more efficient. A system program is said to profit by experience (E) according to some undertaking (T) and some yield measure (P) if its exhibition on T, as estimated by P, increments with experience E. In the accompanying circumstances, we need ML: human information is missing (for instance Mars exploration), people cannot depict their insights (for instance, recognition for voice), changes in the solution with time (e.g., controlling a temperature). ML, by definition, is an area of computer science that emerged from AI with the study of pattern recognition and computational learning theory. It is the

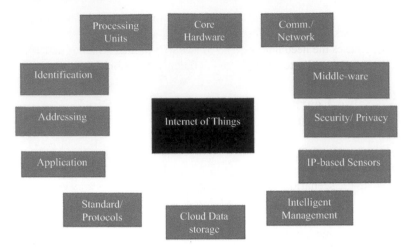

Figure 1.2   IoT components

learning and creation of algorithms from which data sets can learn from and make predictions. To settle on information-driven expectations or choices instead of following firm static program arranges, these strategies work by building a model from model data sources. Using these algorithms, a robust system is built which makes it the future of all technologies. A sub-branch of ML known as deep learning.

Figure 1.2 depicts the various components of IoT and its components. The IoTs integrating the digital and physical worlds make the fabric of the world around us smarter and more sensitive. The IoT alludes to the billion [5] of connected gadgets which assemble and trade data all over the world. Alexa, for example, connects every part of your home, you are only one command away. Everything and anything can be turned into an IOT system and can be linked to the internet to and create connectivity and become part of a network. The IoT is always progressing, and the variety is even greater. The planet is becoming one large network that uses the IoT principle to link to each other via smartphones, sensors, personal computers, and smart objects. By utilizing decentralization and cryptographic hashing, blockchain [6], which is alluded to as a Distributed Ledger Technology (DLT), makes the historical backdrop of any computerized resource that can unalterable. A model is taken and offering it with clustered individuals for guessing the neighbor or making them realize that the record entered are not duplicated, so these are solved by placing a decentralized dissemination chain that permits everyone admittance to the report simultaneously. Blockchain is an innovation that is profoundly energizing and inventive because it limits hazard, gets rid of misrepresentation, and gets responsibility for different utilizations in a saleable way. The resource is decentralized, empowering full continuous access. Changes are made up till the validity of records and so as building trust among resources is also taken place. Blockchain keeps a permanent record that takes into consideration when decentralized exchanges occur. Applications dependent on blockchain are arising, covering different fields, including monetary administrations, the standing framework, and IoT. In a blockchain network, the public records are exchanged in dedicated mechanism and stored in blocks, put away in top-notch blocks. This chain develops as new blocks are continuously added to that. This increases the need and demand for security of data which is achieved using asymmetric cryptography to encrypt the data before it is stored in the ledger.

1.2   Machine Learning, blockchain, IoT, and Big Data analytics – a useful overview

AI, ML, blockchain, IoT, and cloud computing are emerging technologies and are used today almost in every application. This section describes in detail how ML-based blockchain scenarios could potentially help sectors such as Aerospace, the Military, Satellite Communication, and nuclear energy, and many more.

Constraints in IoT devices possible uses: Consensus mechanisms need exhaustive processing power and consume intensive energy. Hence, they cannot operate with IoT devices which have limited resources in terms of memory, processing power, and energy. For instance, smart meters have low battery power, limited storage, and low computing. Moreover, as discussed earlier, the storage capacity is among the major issues of blockchain. The total size of Bitcoin and Ethereum blockchains are around 150 and 400 gigabytes, respectively. IoT devices generate data in Zettabytes. Therefore, blockchain is not suitable for storing IoT data. Possible solution is the integration of cloud computing with IoT and blockchain to resolve the resource constraints of IoT objects. The main issue is how to integrate a centralized cloud computing with blockchain to provide an efficient technology.

Aerospace applications: AI plays an important role in cost reduction, design cycle time reduction, modeling, prototyping, optimization, maintenance, manufacturing, and product updating, all of which are expected to drive aerospace industry innovations in the next 15 years. AI developments could help aerospace businesses optimize their production processes. In the aviation industry, however, there is a restricted acceptance of ML techniques, and the key reason is the lack of access to high-quality data, the increased reliability of simple models compared to complex models, and a lack of qualified staff and collaborators to effectively implement them. But AI can be a revolutionary technology with the right partners that will affect aerospace companies' performance, productivity as well as speed, and innovation. The application of ML in the aerospace industry will ensure cost-effectiveness and safety. Here are example areas where ML is effectively applied in the aerospace industry today:

- Control of smart compromises
- The management of smart repairs
- Global positioning system/geo position automatic portion
- DMU or assembly line recognition
- Device for NC documentation
- Engineering dependent on experience
- Alternative range fastener
- Aircraft components for predictive maintenance
- Aircraft part sizing

- Engineering in reverse
- In-service damage prediction for aircraft based on their area of activity
- Construction of smart plants
- Repeated non-engineering operations

In the medium term, real-time data analytics with an interactive display/graphical user interface (GUI) will have greater penetration, which will give vendors opportunities to expand. Solution providers are encouraged to incorporate these innovations into their solutions, with airlines adopting the capabilities of next-generation technologies such as AI and ML. Vendors are encouraged to develop solutions to resolve airline disruption problems, especially in the areas of re-accommodation and compensation for passengers. The use of big data systems will streamline airline operations and reduce costs and time.

Military application: AI has penetrated almost all civilian industries. It has transformed the way individuals and businesses work, and now it is quickly making its way to becoming a critical part of modern warfare. In some of the most developed nations, investment in the military sector is the highest as compared to other sectors. A major part of this investment goes towards rigorous research and the development of modern technologies such as AI in military applications. AI-equipped military systems are capable of handling volumes of data more efficiently. In addition, such systems have improved self-control, self-regulation, and self-actuation due to their superior computing and decision-making capabilities.

Nuclear applications: When applied to nuclear science, AI has the potential to advance cancer staging in nuclear medicine and cancer treatment, accelerate progress towards the realization of fusion energy production, as well as to help protect global water resources from overexploitation and contamination, and more. In the past decade, many experts/researchers delivered insights into key areas of AI applications in nuclear science and answered questions from online participants.

Healthcare applications: It is generally believed that AI tools will facilitate and enhance work and not replace the work of physicians and other healthcare staff. AI can support healthcare personnel with a variety of tasks from administrative workflow to clinical documentation and patient outreach as well as specialized support such as in image analysis, medical device automation, and patient monitoring. There are different opinions on the most beneficial applications of AI for healthcare purposes. Forbes stated in 2018 that the most important areas would be administrative workflows, image analysis, robotic surgery, virtual assistants, and clinical decision support. In 2018, a report by Accenture mentioned the same areas and also included connected machines, dosage error reduction, and cybersecurity. A 2019 report from McKinsey states important areas being connected and cognitive devices, targeted and personalized medicine, robotics-assisted surgery, and electroceuticals.

1.2.1   Securing the IoTs-based applications using AI

The manufacturing of smart gadgets with detection and acting capacities makes the IoT structure possible. A lot of information is created by the large number of gadgets associated with a network. In an IoT climate, it is a moving position to

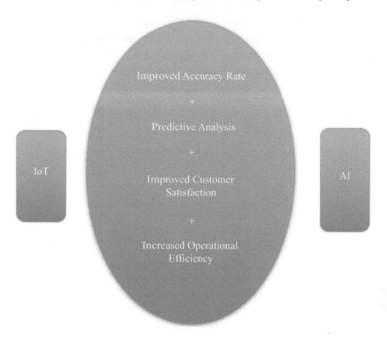

Figure 1.3   Benefit of IoTs and AI in combination

measure and complete figuring. AI combined with other innovations can address IoT security issues. As furnished in Figure 1.3, IoT and AI will join to improve the examination of a framework, upgrade operational execution and improve the exactness rate. The creators clarified in [7] that AI could permit IoT to gauge gigantic amounts, unstructured information, continuous heterogeneous information, making the framework useful. The creators propose the procedure of wide edge cosine assessment [7–10] to distinguish an IoT-empowered adversary.

In the near future, we will see many developments based on the integration of AI, IoT, and blockchain in many useful, and critical applications such as nuclear, military, healthcare and transportation.

1.2.2   Advantages of blockchain solutions

- **Ensuring trust (data integrity):** Blockchain information is reliable because it went through a cycle of confirmation that ensures its precision. It additionally considers responsibility, as it is conceivable to follow occasions and exchanges occurring on a blockchain network. This utilization of blockchain to recognize counterfeit reports and structures was exhibited by Lenovo a year ago. To check actual archives that are inserted with advanced marks, PC goliaths utilized blockchain. PCs measure the advanced marks and the report's legitimacy is checked using a blockchain record. At the point when data of the sources and cooperation are encompassing information, blocks are put away on the block-chain and consequently checked (or approved) before it may be followed up on. This way, information honesty is frequently guaranteed.

- **Preventing vindictive exercises:** It is far-fetched for a solitary unit to represent a threat to the information network since blockchain utilizes agreement calculation to approve the transaction. We can without much of a stretch recognize and cancel from the organization, a hub (or unit) that begins to carry on unusually. Since the network is so conveyed, it makes it practically unimaginable for a solitary gathering to create adequate computational capacity to change the approval prerequisites and empower the framework to give undesirable information. A greater part of hubs should be pooled together to agree to change the blockchain rules. A solitary agitator would not have the option to do this.

- **Predictive analysis:** Blockchain data can be investigated to uncover valuable bits of knowledge into mentalities, designs and accordingly, can be utilized to estimate future execution, much like different sorts of information. Furthermore, blockchain offers coordinated information from individuals or individual gadgets. Information researchers rely on wide informational collections in prescient examination to survey the result of get-together, for example, shopper wants, client lifetime esteem, unstable expenses, and stir rates as they apply to network with great precision. Be that as it may, this is not restricted to showcase bits of knowledge, likewise with the correct information examination, regardless of whether it is social feelings or venture markers, pretty much every event can be anticipated. Furthermore, even in more modest associations, information researchers can perform exhaustive prescient investigation undertakings given the dispersed idea of the blockchain and the massive figuring assets accessible through it. The registering intensity of a few thousand PCs connected on a blockchain organization can be utilized by these information researchers as cloud-based support of examinations social outcomes on a scale that would not have been conceivable something else.

- **Real-time data analysis:** Blockchain offers continuous cross-fringe moves, as observed in monetary and installment frameworks. A few banks and fintech trend-setters are currently analyzing blockchain because paying little mind to geographic limits, gives quick, ongoing settlement of huge sums. Similarly, associations that need enormous scope continuous information investigation will require a blockchain-empowered system to achieve it. Banks and different associations can notice information changes continuously with blockchain, permitting quick choices to be made, regardless of whether to impede a dubious exchange or track sporadic exercises.

- **Manage data sharing:** Data gathered from information studies can be put away in a blockchain network in this regard. Along these lines, project groups do not repeat information examination previously performed by different groups or reuse information that has just been utilized unjustly. A blockchain stage can likewise help information researchers to adapt their work, likely by trading the aftereffects of examination put away on the stage.

1.2.3   *Others*

- Securing IoT-based cloud platforms using blockchain
- IoT-blockchain integration for smart environment

- Development of decentralized applications using IoTs for ensuring transparency
- Ensuring privacy, trust, and security of IoT devices

1.3   AI, Machine Learning, blockchain for the IoT: critical challenges and opportunities for future

As discussed in [10–12], we can find out that the integration of these emerging technologies definitely will change the way of living, working in the next decade. But together these technologies get serious challenges like leaking of personal information, habits by IoT devices, require high energy for ML to refine big data, require more storage in cloud computing and many data center to store this data, security of this data by blockchain and providing authentication process to these integrated (AI+blockchain+IoT) systems, and many more. In [1,11], authors have provided several benefits and important uses of these technologies in many sectors like healthcare, agriculture, retail, transportation, etc. Further, in [11,8], authors have provided important extensions and uses of these technologies in day-to-day work. Hence, this section discusses few faced critical challenges in the integration of these technologies as:

1.3.1   Critical challenges in the integration of AI and IoT

Few challenges in the integration of AI and IoT can be discussed as:

(a) **Connecting gadgets**: We have the assignment of connecting the PCs and gadgets around us to the web these days. Fundamental gadgets including lights and temperature sensors convey over Bluetooth or ZigBee, yet both are guidelines that do not work on the web. Further developed mechanical machines conceivably impart through OPC or exclusive attachment inter-changes, however, with all their multifaceted nature, these gadgets can in any case not associate with the web. Organizations creating IoT gadgets are tending to this obstruction by utilizing doors, otherwise called edge-based registering, to interface with cloud-based IoT stages. This makes it workable for systems to communicate information to the web. Be that as it may, interfacing systems is not as simple as refreshing programming; all things considered, it is an interest in retrofitting old gadgets, supplanting existing gear, and empowering a labor force to use this hardware. As current HVAC frameworks from Honeywell and Johnson controls are putting doors close to their current M2M arrangements and web-based information to the web using MQTT, we see this simply starting to occur in numerous structures today. It is an advancement, over numerous years, not a quick redesign.

(b) **Data understanding**: The test of connecting products to the web has shrou-ded the way that the data passed on by their machines has not yet been gotten a handle on by a few organizations. A gadget that persistently streams vol-tage, temperature, battery, and erosion data is significant if the information cannot be deciphered (and to be perceived, information should be organized so it tends to be placed into a comprehended space model). Moreover, the information is futile without the opportunity to recognize results. This infers that we need information on how machines break down before we can chart what is happening. In the wake of interfacing hardware and sending information to an information lake, we need to stand by and see what's going on. This is the place where we can impact topic specialists, as they might have the option to give us more data. A PC with a lot of vibration, for instance, will before long breakdown. We additionally endeavoured to apply prescient support, which is the thing that we have achieved, to connected entryways. In doing as such, we found that dampness and temperature among information focus, for example, engine temperature, RPMs, utilization every day, amperage load, stickiness, commotion decibels, opening velocity, geolocation, air particles, a season of the day, and encompassing temperature might be the best indicators of future issues. This equitable shows that understanding our piles of information requests that we utilize our inside abilities when preparing AI.

(c)   **Training AI**: When we have acquired enough information to start actualizing AI, we show up at a preparation stage. This is extraordinary to each machine, representing variables, for example, the particular model, sorts of information, and potential impacts. To discover relations among data sources and results, we would then be able to utilize measurable methods with this data. No single model is appropriate for all cases of utilization; information researchers need to test different models to perceive what works. The impact of preparing guarantees that the calculations that work best to anticipate our system conduct are known to us. Shockingly, they will in any case be one-sided by this underlying arrangement of seed information. Thus, we need to accomplish more on the off chance that we truly need to gain from systems. To accomplish genuine AI, we should represent more instances of machines working in genuine conditions, add new sensors for new data sources, and record new sorts of results. We need to re-run this model investigation again and again, endlessly, with each new case helping the AI models adjust and improve. For instance, we made a structure for understanding MRI checks and their ensuing conclusion. It has complex likelihood tables and numerical calculations with input factors and information to permit patients to be analyzed and treated all the more productively by doctors and radiologists. It at that point proceeds to take and case and figure out how to upgrade the probabilities when new factors, for example, offices and specialists are presented.

1.3.2   *Challenges in the integration of blockchain and IoT*

Blockchain stockpiling limit and adaptability are as yet under discussion, as expressed; however, in the feeling of IoT applications, the character limit, and versatility impediments make these difficulties a lot more prominent. In this sense, blockchain may appear to be wrong to IoT applications, yet there are manners by which it is conceivable to completely ease or departure these limitations. This limitation is a significant snag to its consolidation into the IoT blockchain, where gadgets can create ongoing Gigabytes (GBs) of information. It is realized that some current blockchain usage can uphold only a couple of exchanges for every second, so this could be a likely bottleneck for the IoT. Moreover, the object of blockchain is not to store tremendous measures of data, for example, those created in the IoT. By joining these innovations, these worries can be managed. Presently, a ton of IoT information is put away and just a little part is valuable for separating data and creating activity. To decrease them, different methods have been recommended in the writing for separating, normalizing, and compacting IoT information. Inserted PCs, correspondences, and target administrations (blockchain, cloud) are remembered for the IoT, countless layers can profit by reserve funds in the measure of information produced by the IoT. The high volume of IoT information produced by transmission, handling assignments, and capacity can be facilitated by information pressure. Typical practices do not generally need extra, fundamental data, in contrast to odd information. To wrap things up, as the instance of Bitcoin-NG illustrates, blockchain could likewise be adjusted to expand data transmission and abatement the dormancy of its exchanges and, specifically, its agreement convention that causes its bottleneck, consequently empowering a smoother move to the IoT. Few popular challenges in the integration of blockchain and IoT will be:

- **Security:** IoT frameworks need to determine security issues at various stages, however, with extra multifaceted nature because of an absence of execution and raised heterogeneity of the stage. Moreover, the IoT situation includes a bunch of properties that influence wellbeing, for example, versatility, remote correspondence, or size. A careful IoT security investigation is past the extent of this chapter, anyway, thorough reviews can be found. The expanding number of IoT network assaults and their genuine ramifications make fabricating an IoT with more modern security unmistakably more fundamental. To give the genuinely necessary IoT security updates, blockchain is seen by numerous specialists as a key innovation [1,13,14]. Notwithstanding, one of the vital difficulties of incorporating the IoT with the blockchain is the dependability of the information produced by the IoT. In any case, if data in the blockchain is as of now bad, blockchain can guarantee the information in the chain is perpetual and can recognize their changes. Degenerate IoT information may emerge from numerous conditions, aside from vindictive ones. The prosperity of the IoT design is influenced by a few components, for example, the climate, members, defacing, and the disappointment of the structures. Some of the time, the machines themselves and their sensors and actuators battle to work appropriately from the beginning. This condition would not be known until the gadget being referred to has been checked or it frequently works appropriately for some time and changes its conduct for reasons unknown (cut off, customized out of date quality, etc.).

  Notwithstanding these cases, there are a few perils, for example, listening, trying to claim ignorance of administration, or force that can influence the IoT. Hence, IoT gadgets should be completely tried before their reconciliation with blockchain, and they should be put and epitomized in the perfect spot to stay away from actual harm, notwithstanding giving strategies to recognize framework disappointments when they happen. These gadgets are bound to be undermined because their constraints oblige firmware refreshes, keeping them from following up on potential bugs or breaks of security. Moreover, refreshing gadgets individually is additionally troublesome, as in worldwide IoT usage. Consequently, run-time refreshing and reconfiguration components should be situated in the IoT to keep it running over the long haul. Organization and firmware refreshes are permitted over the long haul by activities, for example, GUITAR and REMOWARE and are important to guarantee that the IoT is safely incorporated with the blockchain over the long haul. IoT and blockchain incorporation would likewise affect IoT correspondences. To give secure interchanges, for example, Transport Layer Security (TLS) or DTLS, IoT application conventions, for example, CoAP and MQTT right now utilize other security conventions. These safe conventions are mind-boggling and incredible, notwithstanding requiring brought together control and administration of key foundation, by and large with PKI. In the blockchain network, each IoT gadget will have its Global Unique Identifier (GUID) and an unbalanced key pair introduced before it is associated with the organization. This will rearrange existing security conventions that as of now need to trade PKI endorsements and permit them to be utilized in lower-ability gadgets. "Filament" is a critical IoT venture with the execution of a blockchain regarding security. Fiber is a product and equipment arrangement that gives Bitcoin-based installments and shrewd agreements with IoT highlights. Fiber frameworks have inserted crypto-processors that help five conventions: block name, tele-hash and savvy contracts running, and extra Penny back and Bit-torrent conventions. Square name handles client character, while Tele-hash, the open-source execution of Kademlia DHT, offers securely encoded correspondences, and brilliant agreements characterize how a framework can be utilized.

• **Anonymity and privacy of data:** The issue of information security and secrecy, for example, in the e-health situation, is significant for some IoT applications to manage touchy information, when the gadget is connected to an individual. Blockchain is viewed as the ideal answer for tending to the administration of IoT character, yet there may be executions where, likewise with Bitcoin, protection should be ensured. This is the situation of a wearable with the capacity to veil the character of the individual while sending individual subtleties or keen vehicles that secure the protection of the courses of clients. The issue of information security in open and public blockchains has just been handled alongside the absolute most recent arrangements. Be that as it may, greater intricacy is associated with the issue of information security in IoT gadgets, as it begins with information assortment and proceeds to the correspondence and application levels. Frameworks need to be ensured so that information is secured and not reached by a third party without authorization, as it includes the reconciliation of cryptographic security programming into the gadget. These progressions should consider the limitations on machine assets and restrictions on monetary reasonability. A few frameworks have been utilized to make sure about correspondences utilizing encryption (IPsec, SSL/TLS, and DTLS). To implement these security instruments, for example, entryways, limitations on IoT gadgets regularly make it conceivable to utilize less confined gadgets [15]. Utilizing cryptographic equipment could accelerate cryptographic exercises and forestall the over-burdening of confounded ensured programming conventions. Information security and protection are key worries for IoT, and the issue of personality on the board in IoT can be lightened utilizing blockchain innovation. Another fundamental IoT work is a certainty, where blockchain joining can assume a job. The significance of trust in IoT frameworks is distinguished as one of the primary objectives to guarantee its viability. Information respectability procedures are another option in contrast to guaranteeing information access simultaneously, as they forestall the blockchain from over-burdening with the huge measure of IoT information created. This can bring about open administrations, yet with viable and confined admittance controls. MuR-DPA conveys dynamic information cautions and effective checks through open review confirmation. To wrap things up, there are information security laws, for example, the EU Data Protection Directives (EU-DPA), which should be modified to cover the new models that innovation makes conceivable. To guarantee information security in consistence with the law, these laws can be overwhelmed by actualizing the blockchain as a lawful structure.

- **Legal issues:** The possibility of an unregulated blockchain is significant for its plan and mostly liable for Bitcoin's prevalence. As observed, blockchain, particularly in the feeling of virtual monetary standards, has carried with it a Himalayan deal of debate about legitimateness. The need, or possibility, to add control components over the organization has come as acknowledged, private and consortium blockchains. The IoT area, for example, the Data Protection Directive, is likewise influenced by the information security laws or guidelines of a nation. The greater part of these guidelines is getting out of date and should be refreshed, particularly with the rise of new troublesome innovations, for example, blockchain. Growing new laws and guidelines would make it simpler to ensure the security highlights of gadgets and in this manner, help to assemble the IoT network that is generally secure and trusted. Information security and information taking care of laws are as yet a gigantic obstruction to be handled in IoT in this unique circumstance and will likewise be a much more serious issue whenever utilized in blend with blockchain. As characterized, the non-appearance of guidelines makes drawbacks, as private key recovery or reset instruments or exchange inversion are not possible. Some IoT executions conceive a worldwide, remarkable blockchain for gadgets, yet it is indistinct if this sort of organization is proposed to be controlled by producers or accessible to clients. For this situation, it is normal that it would require a legitimate investigation. The fate of blockchain and IoT might be affected by these laws and, accordingly, the decentralized and free embodiment of blockchain could hypothetically be undermined by presenting a controlled, incorporated part.

- **Agreement:** With regard to IoT applications, the restricted asset nature of gadgets makes them unacceptable for direct support in agreement measures, for example, PoW. As expressed, there is a wide assortment of propositions for agreement conventions, yet they are beginning by and large and have not been tried satisfactorily. Asset necessities rely upon the specific sort of agreement convention in the blockchain network. Arrangements regularly expect to designate these assignments to passages or some other unconstrained unit equipped for giving this usefulness. While there are endeavors to coordinate total blockchain hubs into IoT gadgets, mining is as yet a critical test in the IoT on account of its constraints, the users might be upheld by alternatively off-chain arrangements that move information outside the blockchain to lessen the high inertness in the blockchain. The IoT generally comprises of asset obliged applications, however, the IoT worldwide has a conceivably colossal figuring power, considering that by 2020 the quantity of gadgets in it is required to reach between 20 billion and 50 billion. Examination endeavors should zero in on this district and exploit the appropriated idea of the IoT and the worldwide limit of the IoT agreement to adjust.
- **Energy:** Energy is a big concern for both technologies, i.e., for verifying blocks in blockchain (by miners) and making communications of IoTs for a long time, we want energy/ power for running these integrated systems for a long time.

1.4   Our motivation

The motto of this book is to incorporate AI and blockchain technologies that could theoretically assist the IoT in different aspects, such as healthcare, agriculture, and military. This often brings challenges when implementing them into real-life circumstances. Most importantly, the study aims to enlighten their futuristic minds to bring out new and ground breaking future approaches that could theoretically assist in the respective fields.

1.5   Organization of this work

In this book, chapters on AI, blockchain, ML, Big Data analytics, and the IoT have been written keeping in mind the technical necessity of the future. All chapters have been designed/written in such a way that readers are beneficial through this book, enlighten themselves and generate new thoughts for emerging technologies.

Disclaimer: The paper cited on Machine Learning/Deep learning, etc., by the Editors in this introduction section are only given as examples for future reference (for readers/researchers). To leave any citation or link is not intentional.

References

[1] A.K. Tyagi, M.M. Nair, S. Niladhuri, and A. Abraham, Security, privacy research issues in various computing platforms: a survey and the road ahead, *Journal of Information Assurance & Security* 2020;15(1):1–16.

[2] A.K. Tyagi and M.M. Nair, Internet of Everything (IoE) and Internet of Things (IoT): threat analyses, possible opportunities for future, *Journal of Information Assurance & Security* 2020;15(4):194–218.

[3] N. Silaparasetty, An Overview of Artificial Intelligence. In: *Machine Learning Concepts with Python and the Jupyter Notebook Environment.* Berkeley, CA: Apress, 2020. https://doi.org/10.1007/978-1-4842-5967-2_1

[4] A.K. Tyagi, and M.M. Nair, Internet of Everything (IoE) and Internet of Things (IoTs): threat analyses, possible opportunities for future, *Journal of Information Assurance & Security (JIAS)*, Vol. 15 Issue 4, 2020;15(4):194–218.

[5] Z. Zheng, S. Xie, H. Dai, X. Chen, and H. Wang, An overview of blockchain technology: architecture, consensus, and future trends, IEEE International Congress on Big Data (BigData Congress), Honolulu, HI, USA, 2016.

[6] J. Frankenfield, Website: https://www.investopedia.com/terms/a/artificial-intelligence ai

[7] A.K. Tyagi, A. Abraham, A. Kaklauskas, *Intelligent Interactive Multimedia Systems for e-Healthcare Applications*, Springer 2022.

[8] A.K. Tyagi, *Data Science and Data Analytics: Opportunities and Challenges*, London: CRC Press, 2021.

[9] A.K. Tyagi, G. Rekha, and N. Sreenath (Eds.). (2021). *Opportunities and Challenges for Blockchain Technology in Autonomous Vehicles*. IGI Global. http://doi:10.4018/978-1-7998-3295-9

[10] A.K. Tyagi (Ed.). (2021). *Multimedia and Sensory Input for Augmented, Mixed, and Virtual Reality*. IGI Global. http://doi:10.4018/978-1-7998-4703-8

[11] A.K. Tyagi and A. Abraham, *Recent Trends in Blockchain for Information Systems Security and Privacy*, London: CRC Press, 2021. https://doi.org/10.1201/9781003139737

[12] M.M. Nair, A.K. Tyagi, and N. Sreenath, The future with industry 4.0 at the core of society 5.0: open issues, future opportunities and challenges. *2021 International Conference on Computer Communication and Informatics (ICCCI)*, 2021;1–7. doi: 10.1109/ICCCI50826.2021.9402498.

[13] A.K. Tyagi, T.F. Fernandez, S. Mishra, and S. Kumari, Intelligent automation systems at the core of industry 4.0. In: A. Abraham, V. Piuri, N. Gandhi, P. Siarry, A. Kaklauskas, A. Madureira (eds.) *Intelligent Systems Design and Applications (ISDA) 2020. Advances in Intelligent Systems and Computing*, vol. 1351. Springer, Cham; 2021. https://doi.org/10.1007/978-3-030-71187-0_1

[14] R. Varsha, S.M. Nair, A.K. Tyagi, S.U. Aswathy, and R. RadhaKrishnan, The future with advanced analytics: a sequential analysis of the disruptive technology's scope. In: A. Abraham, T. Hanne, O. Castillo, N. Gandhi, T. Nogueira Rios, T.P. Hong (eds.) *Hybrid Intelligent Systems (HIS) 2020.*

Advances in Intelligent Systems and Computing, vol. 1375. Springer, Cham; 2021. https://doi.org/10.1007/978-3-030-73050-5_56

[15]   A.K. Tyagi, A. Abraham, A. Kaklauskas, N. Sreenath, G. Rekha, and S. Malik (eds.). *Security and Privacy-Preserving Techniques in Wireless Robotics*, 1st edn. CRC Press, New York; 2022. https://doi.org/10.1201/9781003156406

Chapter 2

Image enhancement on low-light and dark images for object detection using Artificial Intelligence for field practitioners

Vivek Kumar Varma Nadimpalli[1] and Gopichand Agnihotram[1]

Abstract

In recent times, there is a lot of demand for Artificial Intelligence solutions based on computer vision in various fields. Many solutions like object detection, fault detection, environment description, and scene prediction are helping to solve many real-life problems. But these solutions are dependent on vision-based computations. Generally, all these computations are designed in such a way that environment in each frame is visible and computation performed with data captured from the frame is in visible condition. But in the case of dark condition, the photons count that a camera capture decreases drastically, and the environment may not be visible. In this scenario, the system will fail to compute all the tasks that are dependent on visibility of environment. With the increase in Artificial Intelligence solutions using vision data, it is important to process low-light/dark images and draw intelligence from them. The information and subsequent intelligence available during low-light scenarios can be extracted wisely by our proposed deep learning architecture. The algorithm will process the raw data taken from the camera sensor and provides you the enhanced JPEG images. These enhanced images will be used to train the object detection using TensorFlow lite to detect the objects in the frames. The entire solution will be ported into the mobile devices for capturing the raw data to enhance images and detect the objects on the enhanced images. The proposed chapter will also explain how this solution will be used in the field assistance where user can be able to see the objects in the scene clearly with the enhanced images and detect the objects for machine repair and maintenance of various tasks.

Keywords: Object detection; Artificial Intelligence; Image enhancement; Smart and optimal solutions

[1]Wipro CTO Office, Wipro Technology Limited, India

2.1   Introduction

Field assistance technology enables in bridging the gap between the field agent of the machine and the expert of the machine. The rise in digital era led to increase in machines around the world but this led to increase the demand of field assistance and created a challenge for field assistants to have complete knowledge of the machine. For example, few maintenances or repair works cannot be done by the field agent alone and may requires assistance from the off-field experts. Many companies are facing the same issues to provide on field expert assistance for maintenance or repair of the machines. This is probably due to rise in demand for machines and experts are located at various countries from the country of origin and providing field assistance is highly difficult. These challenges made the remote field assistance technology by experts as relevant and many companies are presently adapting and developing these technologies to carry on different tasks. Recently, due to the ongoing pandemic and lockdown of countries, the companies saw a rise in repair and maintenance works with remote assistance, which led to an increase in research and development to improve the existing solution and to increase innovation in the remote assistance domain.

There are many existing systems that help the field agents to perform the various tasks on the machine. Few include object detection that helps user to know the various parts of the machine, machine state prediction which predicts the machine's state based on the various actions performed on the machine. But these systems work on the basis that the images are trained and tasks are performed on well-lighted conditions. In case of low-light conditions, all the field assistance tasks based on computer vision algorithms that assist the field agents will fail. To overcome these challenges in the existing field assistance systems, the images need to be enhanced in such a way that it will allow the computer vision-based intelligent systems to perform a required field assistance task. Also, the field agents may need to perform tasks on many critical locations like underground task where lightening conditions and Internet connectivity are very low. Therefore, the whole application needs to be developed in such a way that the applications need to work on a single device like a smartphone or a tablet from enhancement of images to object detection.

Generally, computer vision-based intelligence systems such as object detection and action prediction take the pixels in each image and compute the output based on the trained model. Thus, the noise in the images which may not be visible to naked eye will result in wrong outputs. Therefore, in case of low light, image enhancement should result in smooth images with low noise and detect the objects with good amount of accuracy. There are many methods to enhance the images in low-light conditions. Initially, the images are processed to adjust the contrast levels that makes the images visible, but these methods also increase the noise levels in the images. Next, the low-light images were treated with various filtering methods for denoising [1–4] to enhance the images. Even though these methods could denoise images, the natural low-light images still contain the noise that will impact on object detection and action prediction modules. Later many methods evolved in the field of low-light image enhancement like multi-layer perceptions, wavelet transform, Retinex models, convolutional neural networks, and auto encoder decoder models. For low-light image enhancements, the auto encoder decoder model is trained to take the low-light image as the input and compute the enhanced images as the output. The output of the enhanced images is smooth and the noise is low. It is very challenging to extract the information from the low-light images as the low-light images are very noisy. The object detection model performance improves with the information from input images which are very high. Therefore, the raw images which capture the high information from the camera sensors are chosen over traditional images like JPEG/PNG which comprise raw images. In this chapter, the model is trained on raw images and the datasets are collected by taking short exposure images in low-light conditions in raw format and corresponding long exposure images as the ground truth images. The auto encoder decoder model was trained based on the prepared dataset, which will learn the necessary features to predict the enhanced images from low-light images. Once the images from real-time stream are enhanced, the object detection methods will be used to detect the objects on enhanced images. These models are converted into mobile accessible models which can capture the raw images in real time and enhance the images to predict the objects on the images. Using the detected objects, the field-related activities such as repair or maintenance can be done easily with the help of expert assistance.

The field agent may not be knowing entirely about the device, i.e., every part of the equipment repair/periodic maintenance procedures of the device. Hence, there is a need for remote expert assistance where field agent will contact the expert about device repair and maintenance tasks remotely. This requires the object detection of the video streaming where field agent will consult the expert remotely for device assistance. Hence, for the field agent, the object detection will help in finding the various parts of the devices and the fault parts in the device which can be streamed to the expert for assistance. Over the object detection, augmented description of the parts will be added that will help the field agent to identify the solution for repair or maintenance task on the device. Also, video augmentation can be added to guide the field agent to perform specific tasks on the device. The approach for image enhancement and object detection module was to train mobile accessible models on device data for image enhancement and object detection on smartphones (mobiles). We have trained various single shot detection (SSD) models with the device data of the Arduino robot data. The trained models are further processed to convert them into mobile accessible models and are ported into the mobile application. We compared these models based on different metrics such as inference time, precision, and recall values. The final model was chosen based on trade-off between accuracy and performance (time taken for detection). The image enhancement, object detection, augmentation module will be integrated to form the complete field assistance solution and ported into smartphones. We have built the mobile applications for both Android and iOS mobile devices using android studio and Xcode, respectively.

This chapter is organized as follows: Section 2.2 explains the related work on different models available for image enhancement and object detection. Section 2.3 and its subsections discuss about the solution approach for low-light image enhancement with examples. Section 2.4 and its subsections discuss about the different object detection models on enhanced images and also discuss the porting of these trained models on mobile devices along with the performance accuracy of different models. One of the subsections also discusses the augmentation on detected objects with the examples. Section 2.5 explains the application in oil and gas field where the lighting conditions are not optimum and the proposed solution will help the field user to perform the field activities. Section 2.6 describes the conclusions and future enhancements followed by References.

2.2   Related work

This section discusses the different methods used for low-light image enhancement and different models used for object detection.

There are different methods of image enhancements on digital images such as various filtering approaches, adjusting various parameters, and removing the noise from the images. Gilboa *et al.* [5] described a method to enhance and denoise an image using forward and backward diffusion process. In this method, the various image features will be enhanced by adjusting the nonlinear diffusion coefficient. This will result in enhancement of the features and smoother regions of the images using denoised forward and backward adaptive diffusion process. Dabov *et al.* [6] proposed a denoising method by transforming image into 3D and applying the Weiner filtering method. In this method, the 2D fragments are converted into 3D data. Various transformations are applied on the 3D data that will enhance the minute features in the images. Li *et al.* [7] developed a framework for both contrast enhancement and noise reduction. The noise levels are obtained from local standard deviation and local gradients of the image. Based on noise level and various filtering processes like BM3D, smoother images are obtained with reduced noise. These images are further processed to improve the contrast of the images.

Chen *et al.* [8] discussed preparing a low-light dataset and training an end-to-end neural network. The procedure consists of end-to-end trainable Retinex with parameters picked for illumination and decomposition and two models that are Decom-net that decomposes the low-light images and Enhance-net that adjusts the illumination images along with denoising operation to produce the output. Shen *et al.* [9] described a method to enhance low-light images using convolutional neural network and Retinex theory. They implemented end-to-end convolutional neural network named MSR-net that learns to map various features between dark and bright images. Ren *et al.* [10] described a Retinex model that will perform decomposition image features into sequence. The authors also discussed the procedures to utilize the weight matrices into decomposition process which will result in improvement in image contrast by reducing the noise. Also, the illumination layer is adjusted based on the generated reflectance and illumination map.

Gwn Lore *et al.* [11] proposed a deep autoencoder approach to enhance the images in low light. They prepared a dataset by adding synthetic noise and darkness and trained stacked sparse denoising encoder. Even though, synthetic noise and darkness were present in the dataset, the model could generalize to natural low-light images. Chen *et al.* [12] discussed image enhancement by building an end-to-end trainable auto encoder model. In this method, raw images of long and short exposure are collected to train an end-to-end model that will learn to predict the long exposure image. The papers also highlighted the advantages of usage of RAW images from camera sensor over traditional JPEG/PNG images for image enhancement. Shifeng *et al.* [13] described filter out negative anchors to reduce search space for the classifier, and coarsely adjust the locations and sizes of anchors to provide better initialization for the subsequent regressor. Authors designed a transfer connection block to transfer the features in the anchor refinement module to predict locations, sizes, and class labels of objects in the object detection module.

Howard, Andrew *et al.* [14] proposed a method based on a streamlined archi-tecture that uses depth-wise separable convolutions to build light weight deep neural networks for object detection. The authors also discussed two simple global hyper-parameters that efficiently trade-off between latency and accuracy. The hyper-parameters allow the model builder to choose the right-sized models for their application based on the constraints of the problem. To improve the accuracy on SSD MobileNet, the MobileNet FPNs can be trained for object detection. Kirillov *et al.* [15] exploited the inherent multi-scale, pyramidal hierarchy of deep con-volutional networks to construct feature pyramids with marginal extra cost. It proposes a top-down architecture with lateral connections which is developed for building high-level semantic feature maps at all scales. To further improve the performance, ResNet50 has been used [16] for object detection. Kaiming *et al.* [16] presented a residual learning framework to ease the training of networks that are substantially deeper. This method explicitly reformulates the layers as learning residual functions with reference to the layer inputs, instead of learning unrefer-enced functions.

2.3   Solution approach for image enhancement

The proposed approach uses auto encoder decoder model for low-light image enhancement from raw images and deep learning approaches used for object detection of the device that helps the field agents to complete repair and main-tenance tasks. There are four stages in the solution approach as mentioned in the architecture diagram in Figure 2.1. In the first stage, the camera sensor is exposed to the natural environment and the video stream will be passed to the low-light recommender system which will predict whether the low-light conditions are pre-sent or not. This recommender recommends the user to switch to low-light mode if the low-light conditions are present. The recommender is a classifier model built on bright and low-light images to predict whether the class of low-light conditions are present or not. Once the low-light mode is switched on, the application will start

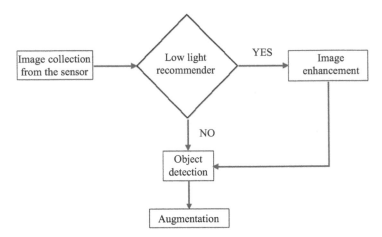

Figure 2.1   The field assistance solution architecture

collecting the raw images from the camera sensor in a video stream that will be sent to the next stage for image enhancement. The advantages of raw images over traditional images are also discussed in the next subsection. In the second stage, the raw images are processed and passed to the encoder–decoder model which is trained on the dataset of short exposure raw image and corresponding long exposure image as the ground truth. The output of the model will be the smooth enhanced image that will be sent to third stage for further computations. The details of the raw image's dataset and training of encoder–decoder model are explained in the following subsections.

Once the low-light image is enhanced, the image can be used to detect various parts of the device. For the demonstration, Arduino robot images are taken with five labels. Around 700 images were annotated for the five labels using LabelImg [17] tool and created XML files in Pascal VOC format. The collected data is trained with SSD models that can be ported to mobile devices using transfer learning methods. The details related to datasets and training are mentioned in the following subsections. The object tracking and augmentation module is built over object detection module that will help the field agent in performing a repair and maintenance work on the device. ARKit libraries have been used for the augmentation in iOS devices and ARCore libraries are used for the augmentation in Android devices. The details of augmentation module will be explained in further subsections.

2.3.1   Raw data from camera sensors

In this subsection, we will discuss the raw data and its role in enhancing the images for detection. Unlike a JPEG file, RAW format is uncompressed and is not an image file. In fact, RAW files are a collection of data from camera's sensor that are saved on camera. Software like Adobe Photoshop or Adobe Lightroom will allow to view the Raw data as images and edit the RAW files. Though the standard format on digital cameras is a JPEG file, most professional photographers prefer to shoot in RAW. The advantages for considering the raw images are given below:

- RAW format is that the camera captures absolutely all the data it receives from the camera sensors. This means that no information from the images are removed or discarded (which is often happens with the JPEGs). With the RAW format, the camera is collecting everything it can see and storing the information in the device so that one can process these details easily. This means one can have high-quality data files to work with during processing and with that data the best images can be created.
- The RAW format contains a lot more colors than JPEG files around 68 billion more colors, to be exact. A 12-bit RAW image contains thousands of shades of red, green, and blue, while a 14-bit RAW file contains trillions of possible colors. Shooting RAW ensures capturing as many colors in an image as possible, creating photos with a higher color range and color depth. Therefore, a brightly colored landscape or a vibrant fashion scene with a range of shades and tones will likely turn out better if one shoots in RAW vs. JPEG. RAW photography is very forgiving and end up having to correct the light in an image. These files have a very high dynamic range, so they can capture a lot of lights and shadows. Having all this data in the image will make it easier to correct underexposed images.

The disadvantages of working with the raw data are given below:

- Collecting the raw data from camera can consume a significant amount of space. The Raw files are not compressed and they take up more memory on camera. Due to the high size of the file, transferring the raw data for processing have challenges. The data transfer has a lot of challenges like bandwidth, speed, security, and reliability.
- RAW vs. JPEG-wise, RAW files give more freedom to adjust and edit images. But processing an image does take a significant amount of time, especially when we are working on image by image and new to photo editing. Shooting RAW vs. JPEG means one must set aside time after a project to upload the images to editing software and tweak them so that the images look their best.
- Unlike JPEGs, RAW files are not designed to work across different manufacturers. So, if you have a Canon digital camera, and Canon RAW files, one cannot use Nikon software to open it. Always check that the software is using to open and edit RAW files designed by the same manufacturer of digital camera, i.e., Canon software for Canon RAW files. If someone has a newer digital camera, one has to wait for some time for software companies to update their software to open RAW files using their platform.

However, Adobe has recently developed an open-source RAW format called Digital Negative (DNG). We can use Lightroom to convert RAW files into open-source DNG files. This procedure is an extra step, but it will ensure that the files are readable and accessible as needed. Many camera manufacturers are starting to offer an option to shoot in DNG format, and soon this open-source format will likely to be common for manufacturers moving forward which will make it easier to all to access RAW files.

The first stage in the demonstration includes capturing the environment in the low-light situations from the camera sensors. The low-light environment contains very less information due to low pixel count. Therefore, it is necessary to maximize the information while capturing the environment as it will help to improve the results on detection in further stages. Thus, the RAW images are captured as the initial part of the demonstration. One of the major disadvantages of the RAW format was the size of the images which makes the images transferred to online GPU server for further processing difficult. Hence, we process these Raw images in mobile devices itself to avoid transferring into remote servers for processing. Here, the DNG format has been chosen as it can be captured through mobile phone and processed in the same mobile devices. In this chapter, DNG captured from the iPhone has been chosen to create datasets for training in the next stages and also in the final application demonstration.

2.3.2   Image enhancement on low-light images

In this subsection, we will discuss image enhancement on low-light conditions and how these enhanced images can be used subsequently for object detection. The raw image taken from the camera in low-light condition is the input to the model and enhanced images will be the output of the model. The enhanced image is such that the objects in that environment can be detected by the next stage in the demonstration. As found in the literature, most of the image enhancement techniques such as adding various filers on the images or various noise reduction techniques on images but the output of the image has still a lot of noise that will hamper the traditional object detection algorithms. The output of the image enhancement model needs to be smooth with low noise for better results of object detection module.

In this chapter, we will be using U-net architecture for image enhancement on low-light image (refer the paper [12]). Here, the model input is preprocessed raw images data taken in low-light conditions and where output is enhanced images such that the objects are visible in JPEG/PNG format. The auto encoder–decoder models which are used in the U-net architecture as input and output model are in different format. With the given input data, the model is trained end-to-end to enhance the images from low-light conditions. The model needs to learn the various boundaries in the images and also the colors for each object in the images similar to image segmentation problem.

Initially, the U-net architecture was used in image segmentation problems for Bio medical images [18]. Later the method extended to various major applications like pan sharpening remote sensing images using pixel wise regression [19]. The regression relationship between multi-resolution image features and target image pixel values is obtained from the model that will volumetrically segment and learned from sparsely annotated data [20]. One of the major wide used applications of U-net architecture was the image segmentation as described in TernausNet [21].

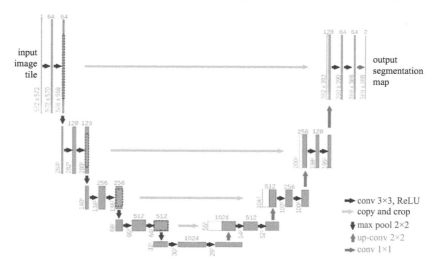

Figure 2.2   U-net architecture

The U-net architecture generally consists of the shrinking path for encoder region typically a convolutional neural network with ReLU, Max Pooling operations and symmetric expanding path for decoder region typically consisting of transposed Convolutional neural networks, which gives a "U" shape as given Figure 2.2. Thus, it is an end-to-end fully convolutional.

2.3.3   Datasets setup for training the U-net architecture

The datasets for training the deep learning models required an input type for the model, based on which the trained model will predict and compute the output. In our approach, the input for the model will be an image taken in low-light conditions which will be sent into encoder–decoder model and output from the model will be an enhanced image which will have enough features to detect objects in the image. Therefore, we have collected the image data for training the model in dark conditions and corresponding ground truth images. The main challenge for this procedure was to collect the ground truth images. We have gone through various literatures and research work on obtaining the ground truths for low-light images. The See In the Dark (SID) dataset [12] approach where the images are taken in dark using short exposure time and corresponding ground truth is obtained by taking the long exposure time as it can be utilized for the end-to-end auto encoder–decoder model. Here, the collection of ground truth images is relatively simpler.

In photography, the exposure is the amount of light per unit area (the image plane illuminance times the exposure time) reaching a frame of photographic film or the surface of an electronic image sensor, as determined by shutter speed, lens aperture, and scene luminance. In case of short exposure, the shutter speed is very high, allowing light to come into the frame for very few seconds of times (less than 1 s usually). Generally, in video, which are a sequence of individual frames, the frames are captured using short exposure but major disadvantage is in low-light condition. The sensor is not exposed for enough time, making the objects in low-light invisible. Figures 2.3 and 2.4 describe the short exposure images captured at different frame rates such as 1/200, 1/100, and 1/10 sec.

In the case of long exposure photography, the shutter speed will be low, allowing more light to come into the sensor and brighter images can be captured. The major disadvantage of long exposure images is that if there is a movement of object, blurriness, or obscurity issue may arise. In our case, the dataset was captured for only static images by nullifying the blurriness issue (refer Figure 2.5).

| 1/200 | 1/100 | 1/10 | 1/5 | 1/2 |

Figure 2.3   Short exposure images in seconds

| 1/200 | 1/100 | 1/10 | 1/5 | 1/2 |

Figure 2.4   Short exposure time in seconds

Figure 2.5   Long exposure images

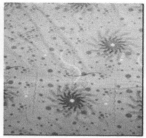

Figure 2.6   Ground truth images (long exposure images) at different conditions

The SID dataset contains 424 distinct reference images and for each reference image, the ground truths are given based on different long exposure images of the same reference images. The dataset contains images under moon and street lights, and also images in indoor conditions with lights off. On exploring and evaluating the dataset, for better results and generalizing in normal conditions which are different from the dataset we wanted to expand for training. Majorly, we created new 40 distinct reference images for indoor conditions that were captured in low light by turning off the lights and allowing slight reflection of combination of natural light and room lights from different locations on objects (refer Figure 2.6).

Also, further 15 distinct reference images were added that were taken in night condition under moon light and slight street light reflection (refer Figure 2.7). The images were added to balance the dataset in most possible low-light conditions. The new images were captured in iPhone X using the Adobe Lightroom App in DNG format. The DNG images are further preprocessed and added to the already existing dataset and pushed for training the U-net architecture.

2.3.4   Training with U-net architecture

This subsection discusses the model training with U-net architecture. The training model takes the input as the processed raw image and corresponding ground truth form the dataset, i.e., the long exposure images will be the desired output. From the initial training model, the least absolute deviation loss is computed from random initialization and corresponding ground truth for input. Further, the loss will be used to update the weights of the network using back propagation. Here, the Adam optimizer is used to find the local minimum for loss efficiently. The system hardware consists of 64 GB ram and Nvidia Gtx 1080 for faster computation. The model was trained for 4,000 epochs. The final training model will be used to obtain the enhanced JPEG images by processing the raw input data to the model. Once the images are enhanced, these images will be used for object detection as explained in the following section.

Figure 2.7   Ground truth images (long exposure images) at different conditions

2.4   Object detection with the enhanced images

This section discusses the different models trained for object detection and the models' comparisons on enhanced images. Once the low-light images are enhanced, we need to predict the location of the various objects from the enhanced images that will help the user to perform various assigned tasks. The enhanced

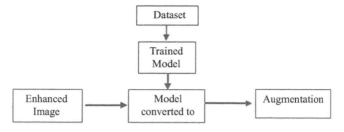

Figure 2.8   Object detection using TFLite

images will be input to the object detection model and the image will be passed through a pre-trained deep learning model which will detect the object and predict the locations of the different objects in the device using TFLite model (refer Figure 2.8). Here, we have set up the training model with a large dataset consisting of images and the labeled annotations which needs to be predicted at detection time. Once the dataset is created, training the deep learning model will be a major challenge and building the training model from scratch is very heavy computing and time-consuming process. Therefore, we will be using pre-trained model on COCO dataset and perform a transfer learning on our labeled dataset. The processing time and accuracy will vary depending upon the architecture of the data which we choose. Hence, few different models are trained and final model will be chosen based on tradeoff between accuracy and inference time. In the whole demonstration, we need to detect the objects on mobile devices for performing the repair or maintenance activities. Here we are converting the mobile trained models to TFLite files which will be compatible with mobile devices for detection. With the help of TFLite files, the models will be ported into both Android and iOS devices (refer Figure 2.9). The inference time will be calculated on the mobile devices and comparisons are computed on various models. The augmentation as given in Figure 2.8 will help to augment the device information on top of each object and also the procedure related to the repair or maintenance. We will be using ARCore or ARKit-based augmentation to know the device information after object detection.

2.4.1   Dataset preparation for object detection

The input data required for training the object detection models are explained in this subsection. The object detection model will take an image as the input and if the target labels are present in the input image, the model will able to predict the label in the input image and also its location (Region of Interest (ROI)) in the image. To train deep learning models for object detection, the dataset should contain information of image of label and also the location details of the label in input image. We need to prepare datasets for training model as images of the object needs to be collected and each image needs to be annotated such that it contains the location information of the target labels in the input image.

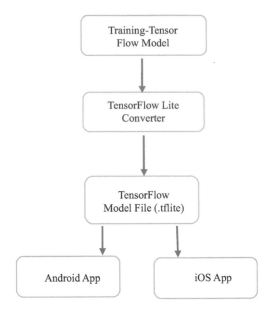

Figure 2.9   Model porting in Android and iOS devices

The requirements of dataset for object detection are a challenging task, as the data should contain images of different objects. Also, the dataset should be annotated and annotated images should provide the information of the location of each label in the object. For the demonstration purpose, we have illustrated the object detection stage with the Arduino robot datasets with few annotated labels in it. For better performance of the model, the images of robot to be well distributed and every possible angle needs to be incorporated in the model. We can also capture the video of the Arduino robot and from video we extract the sequence of image frames. In this way, multiple videos of the Arduino robot kit were taken in different background, lighting, orientations, and each individual frame is extracted from the recorded video. We have taken six videos of Arduino robot in various situation, each video consisting of 120 sec with 30 fps frame rate. The consecutive frames are very similar and we will be discarding the consecutive frames from the dataset. So, one image in every 30 frames (1 sec of video) is collected and stored in the dataset. Approximately, 720 images were collected from 6 videos and after removing blurred, out focused images without the full object in the frame, 700 images have been extracted from all the multiple recorded videos and these images were sent for annotation.

For annotating the labels in the collected images, LabelImg [17] tool was used (refer Figures 2.10 and 2.11). There are five labels which are annotated such as right wheel, left wheel, circuit, sensor, and chassis for training the deep learning model. In each image, rectangle annotations are taken on the labels.

Figure 2.10   Annotating the Arduino Robot data using LabelImg Tool

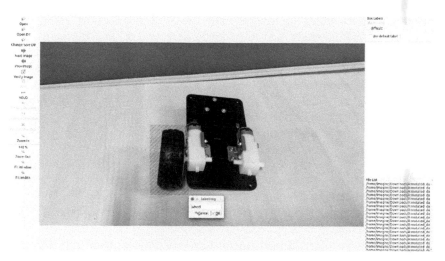

Figure 2.11   Annotating the Arduino robot data wheel using LabelImg Tool

2.4.2   Training the object detection models

This subsection discusses the different models used for trained the object detection models. The data collected is divided into 80% for training the deep learning model, 10% for validation of tuning the hyper parameters, and 10% for testing the model with the input data. The trained models will be converted into mobile accessible models and these models are efficient even in low computation power environments. The SSD models were chosen since these models are computation lite models and good on accuracy when trained on COCO dataset. These models are easy to convert into the mobile accessible versions. As per the use case, the trade-off of accuracy and inference time should be computed to select a preferable model. We chose SSD MobilenetV2, SSD MobileNet FPN, and SSD Resnet50 models, and we have trained Arduino robot data using these models. We have also chosen the best model which is suitable for our datasets. Alternatively, we have also tried various values for hyperparameters like learning rate, batch size, momentum to achieve the best model with the datasets.

In general, machine data will be used for training the deep learning models. But the trained deep learning model will require heavy computation power and making it difficult to run the trained model on all devices. Most of the smartphones do not have the necessary resources to run the model except few high-end phones. These high-end phones will run the model, but the time taken for the computation will not be suitable for the remote assistance use case. Therefore, the deep learning model is converted to mobile accessible models for detecting the objects faster. This conversion will result in decreasing the accuracy slightly, but the model will be more efficient even with low resources in the smart phones. Hence, there is a reasonable trade-off to take for porting a deep learning model into the mobile app directly. The trained TensorFlow model further optimized and converted into TensorFlow model file .tflite using TFLite. The .tflite file is ported into Android mobile using Android studio and iOS mobile devices the .tflite file ported using Xcode (see in Figure 2.4). The converted model file (.tflite) will be deployed on the streaming API at user side and expert side to view the device and objects information. The images streaming module on both sides of user and expert will able to coordinate with each other for ROIs and class label prediction. This information will help the expert to assist the user at field side.

The model works as a function as described

$$y_1 = f_1(x_1)$$

x_1 – base 64 encoded data of the image

f_1 – the trained deep learning model

y_1 – list of ROIs – [[label_1, $x_1$min, $y_1$min, $x_1$max, $y_1$max], [label_2, $x_1$min, $y_1$min, $x_1$max, $y_1$max]]

In this way, the object detection works on local devices with faster and better predictions. Once the object detection is completed, the augmentation module will be built using ARCore and ARKit over the object detection module. We will use the ROIs and detected labels to perform augmentation that will help the expert to guide the user on various tasks and helps the expert with the description of all the detected labels. The different models trained on Arduino robot data and the performance metric of different models are given in Tables 2.1 and 2.2.

In Table 2.1, the mobile accessible deep learning models that is, the SSD MobileNetV2 model on Arduino robot data was performing good with low inference speed, but the accuracy when compared to other models was significantly low. The SSD MobileNetV1 FPN has better accuracy than MobileNetV2 but the inference time was increased. The SSD ResNet was theoretically thought to be best performing as it has better mAP value than MobilenetV1 FPN when trained on

Table 2.1   Models comparisons MobileNetV2 vs. MobileNetV1 FPN vs. ResNet50

	MobileNetV2	MobileNetV1 FPN	ResNet50
mAP@ .75IOU	0.57	0.71	0.69
mAP@ .5IOU	0.79	0.88	0.87
Average Recall	0.54	0.7	0.67
Steps for convergence	40,000	80,000	60,000
Loss at convergence	1.8	0.41	0.42

Table 2.2   Approach 2, Android vs. iOS devices detection time

	MobileNetV2	MobileNetV1 FPN	ResNet50
Android (Redmi k20)	250 ms	1,250 ms	1,800 ms
iOS (iPhone XR)	50 ms	650 ms	1,050 ms

COCO dataset, but on the Arduino robot datasets, the SSD ResNet was having mAP values slight lower than the MobileNetV1 FPN but inference time was more. Another observation is that these models performed well on iOS device than on Android devices as seen in Table 2.2. For the Arduino robot data, MobileNetV1 FPN was chosen for the object detection and real-time guiding of user with the expert help on machine repair and maintenance activities. In general, these models are chosen based on accuracy and inference time between MobileNetV2 and MobileNetV1 FPN. Note that "SqueezeNet and MobileNet are two network architectures that are well suited for mobile phones and achieve impressive accuracy levels above AlexNet".

2.4.3   Testing object detection on low-light-enhanced images

This subsection discusses the result of the tests of object detection of Arduino robot in low-light conditions. We have taken raw images of Arduino robot in natural low-light and artificial low-light conditions and sent for image enhancement module. The enhanced images are further sent to object detection module and then evaluated. The results are shown in Figure 2.12.

The left row is object detection on enhanced images taken in outdoor low-light conditions and the right row is the object detection on enhanced images taken in indoor low-light conditions. The images show the detection of various parts like Arduino kit, complete robot kit, robot neck from the enhanced images. On the object-detected images, we have tested performance by comparing them to manually annotated data on enhanced image and found mAP@ 0.5 IOU value to be 0.76.

2.4.4   Augmentation

The augmentation is the last step on the remote assistance system where the information about the device will be augmented and shown to the user and expert.

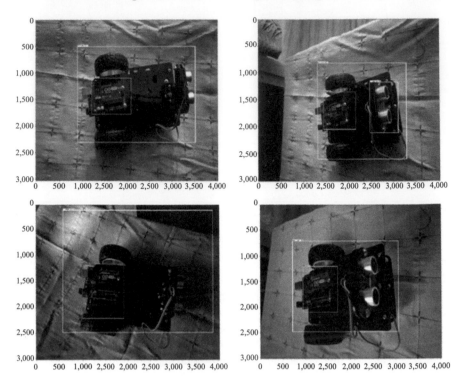

Figure 2.12   Object detection on enhanced images at outdoor vs. indoor

Initially, the information that needs to be augmented is the description of the labels (machine parts) and device information. In our application, the information about the Arduino robot and its parts must be stored in the database and this information can be leverage along with object detection module. In the object detection module, the last or lower layer will predict the labels of the data and its location (ROIs) and this information will be sent to the augmentation module. Based on the ROIs, the augmentation module will augment the description that has been stored in the database. These augmentations will help expert and user as they have the description of the labels and location of the objects. The augmented information can also include the periodic maintenance details and repair details such as which part has anomaly or which part has to be repaired. Figure 2.13 shows the augmentation on Arduino robot device for illustration purpose.

For Android devices, ARCore libraries and for iOS devices, ARKit libraries are used for augmentation. Using the libraries, we have imported a 3D arrow figure which is designed in unity to provide the information about the devices and its parts. Once the ROIs from object detection module are received, the arrow will be augmented on the device with the label name that is predicted. If user or expert needs to know more information about those labels, they will click on the arrow which will augment the description of device that is stored in the database. Once the objects are detected, the labels' information will be shown to the user as

Figure 2.13   Augmentation on Arduino robot device

augmented features using ARCore and ARKit libraries. These augmentation features will be tracked throughout the object and therefore, even if the orientation changes, the augmentation will still be visible and help the user with the repair or maintenance of device.

2.5   Application on low-light machine activities

In this section, we discuss the application for low-light image enhancement in natural conditions for assistance of field agents in various tasks. We have taken an application in oil and natural gas, where the equipment will be located underground (refer Figures 2.14 and 2.15) with minimum light conditions. The equipment in underground will need various tasks to be performed by the field agents like installation of the device, maintenance work on the device and if necessary repair and replacing the few parts in the device. The field agents performing the tasks may require assistance to complete the work without any errors. The object detection of the device will locate various parts of the device and with the help of augmentation it will guide the user to perform the tasks on the device. But, in our application, the images of the device are taken in low light and due to the less pixel information in low-light images object detection module and augmentation module will fail. Therefore, the low-light images need to be enhanced in such a way that the object detection and augmentation module works on the enhanced images.

The system demonstrated in the previous sections for image enhancement and object detections will be utilized to overcome the challenges of low-light conditions in the oil and natural gas application. As those maintenance activities of oil and gas pipelines needs to be carried out in low-light conditions. The field agent will be provided with a device that consists a sensor to capture the raw images. A stream of raw images is taken by the camera and based on the processing speed, for every certain interval, a raw image frame is collected and sent to further module. The collected raw image will be pre-processed and sent to the encoder decoder

Figure 2.14   Oil and gas pipe installation

Figure 2.15   Oil and gas maintenance work

model that was trained using the manually prepared low-light images dataset. The output of the encoder–decoder model will be an enhanced image in JPEG format with low noise. In the similar way, the stream of the raw images for a fixed interval will be sent to the model, and stream of enhanced images will be generated from the model. As the model enhances the images from raw data and output generated consist of low noise, this will help the object detection and augmentation modules from failing in the low-light conditions that are prevalent in oil and natural gas application (device in underground). The enhanced images stream will be sent to the object detection module. The object detection module will take the enhanced image as the input and if the image consists of the device on which the object detection module was trained, then it will detect the various parts of the device and location of the parts based on the trained model. Based on the object detection, the field agent will be able to locate the various parts of the device. Once the various parts of the device are being displayed on the device of field agent, the agent will select the required part that will enable the augmentation on the detected parts. The augmentation consists of the explanations to perform certain tasks on the specific part. Thus, the augmentation module will guide the field agents in performing the tasks on the device. In this way, the field agent will be able to perform various tasks on the device in the underground and in low-light conditions. The field tasks can check the leak or burst of the pipeline which may be due to corrosion defects or dents of the pipeline. The field agent will continuously monitor those defects physically with the help of enhanced images. There may be a case where field agent wants to change the screw or clamp at joints of pipeline at segment level, network, or line level. This requires identifying the clamp and screw of the pipeline in dark conditions. The above modules demonstrated in Sections 2.3 and 2.4 will help in enhancing the dark images and identifying the objects such as screw and clamp on the enhanced images. Once the objects are identified in real time, the field agent will perform the maintenance tasks such as replacing the clamp, screws (Figures 2.16 and 2.17), and checking the corroded pipeline.

We have developed the whole oil and gas maintenance application in iOS and tested the application on iPhone XR device and observed that the processing time for image enhancement from raw images is approximately 5 sec. The enhancement speed may increase in mobile due to better neural engine computation powers. Due to the processing speed and not to create bottleneck of raw images for processing, 5 sec is chosen as the fixed interval for which each raw image from stream will be sent to the image enhancement model. The encoder–decoder model is trained on the low-light images and then converted into ML model. This will be used in creating the application for iOS using CoreML library. In the next module, the object detection model was trained on 3,000 images of different labels of the device such as screw, clamp, an pipe segment using annotation from LabelImg [17] tool. The tensor flow object detection API was used to train the model and converted into TFLite file that was ported into the iOS application. The object detection will be followed by augmentation which was ported into the same device using the ARKIT library in iOS. Hence, the end-to-end solution from image enhancement to augmentation will help the field expert for underground maintenance tasks.

Figure 2.16   Corroded pipe after image enhancement

Figure 2.17   Removing the rusted bold/clamp

2.6   Conclusions and future works

The solution provided in this chapter discusses assistance systems for field agent in low-light conditions. The method will capture a stream of raw data from the camera sensor and send the images for enhancement at regular intervals. The image enhancement module will process the raw images using the trained encoder–decoder model and compute the enhanced image in JPEG format. The chapter discusses collecting the dataset and architecture design along with procedure for training the model. The enhanced image is then sent to the object detection module, where various parts of the device will be detected along with location with the help of trained model. Various models were trained using Arduino robot data and comparisons were provided for accuracy and performance. Final model was chosen based on tradeoff between accuracy and performance. The final stage of the solution was the Augmentation, which will enable the necessary augmentations that will be projected on the specific device which will help the field agent to perform the task. We will be using ARCore and ARKit libraries for augmentations. All these modules were built, integrated, and ported into iOS devices to assist the field agents.

In future works, the end-to-end solution will be extended to Android device which can capture the raw images. Also, the action and scene prediction on images can be added to the object detection intelligence which will point out the anomalies or errors of machine. We will also fuse the sensor information along with the image information for better action prediction. We will port the complete solution on hands-free devices such as head-mounted devices (HMD) like Google glass, HoloLens, etc. This solution can also be extended to other domains like remote training where the user will be learning practically about the device from the expert. It can also be extended to consultancy in healthcare, retail, and e-commerce domain.

References

[1]   Thivakaran, T. K. and Chandrasekaran, R. M. "Nonlinear filter based image denoising using AMF approach," (2010), arXiv preprint arXiv:1003.1803.

[2]   Kervrann, C. and Boulanger, J. "Optimal spatial adaptation for patch-based image denoising," *IEEE Transactions on Image Processing*, 15(10), 2866–2878 (2006), doi: 10.1109/TIP.2006.877529.

[3]   Yinxue, Z., Xuemin, T., and Ren P. "An adaptive bilateral filter based framework for image denoising," *Neurocomputing,* 140, 299–316 (2014), ISSN 0925-2312, https://doi.org/10.1016/j.neucom.2014.03.008.

[4]   Teng, L., Li, H., and Yin, S. "Modified pyramid dual tree direction filter-based image denoising via curvature scale and nonlocal mean multigrade remnant filter," *International Journal of Communication Systems*, 31, e3486 (2018), https://doi.org/10.1002/dac.3486.

[5]   Gilboa, G., Sochen, N., and Zeevi, Y. Y. "Forward-and-backward diffusion processes for adaptive image enhancement and denoising," *IEEE Transactions on Image Processing*, 11(7), 689–703 (2002), doi: 10.1109/TIP.2002.800883.

[6]   Dabov, K., Foi, A., Katkovnik, V., and Egiazarian, K. "Image denoising by sparse 3-d transform-domain collaborative filtering," *IEEE Transactions on Image Processing*, 16(8), 2080–2095 (2007), doi: 10.1109/TIP.2007.901238.

[7]   Li, L., Wang, R., Wang, W., and Gao, W. "A low-light image enhancement method for both denoising and contrast enlarging," IEEE International Conference on Image Processing (ICIP), Quebec City, QC, pp. 3730–3734 (2015), doi: 10.1109/ICIP.2015.7351501.

[8]   Chen, W., Wenjing, W., Wenhan, Y., and Jiaying, L. "Deep Retinex decomposition for low-light enhancement," (2018), https://arxiv.org/abs/1808.04560.

[9]   Shen, L., Zihan, Y., Quan, C., and Fan, F. "Msr-net: low-light image enhancement using deep convolutional network," (2017), https://arxiv.org/abs/1711.02488.

[10] Ren, X., Li, M., Cheng, W., and Liu, J. "Joint enhancement and denoising method via sequential decomposition," IEEE International Symposium on Circuits and Systems (ISCAS), Florence, pp. 1–5 (2018), doi: 10.1109/ISCAS.2018.8351427.

[11] Gwn Lore, K., Akintayo, A., and Soumik, S. "LLNet: a deep autoencoder approach to natural low-light image enhancement," *Pattern Recognition*, 61, 650–662 (2017), ISSN 0031-3203, https://doi.org/10.1016/j.patcog.2016.06.008.

[12] Chen, C., Qifeng, C., Jia, X., and Vladlen, K. "Learning to see in the dark," (2018), arXiv, arXiv preprint arXiv:1805.01934.

[13] Shifeng, Z., Longyin, W., Xiao, B., Zhen L., and Stan, Z. Single-shot refinement neural network for object detection. *Proceedings of the IEEE Conference on Computer Vision and Pattern Recognition (CVPR)*, pp. 420–4212 (2018).

[14] Howard, A. G., Menglong, Z., Bo, C., *et al.* "Mobilenets: efficient convolutional neural networks for mobile vision applications," (2017), arXiv preprint arXiv:1704.04861.

[15] Kirillov, A., Ross, G., Kaiming, H., and Piotr, D. "Panoptic feature pyramid networks," Proceedings of the IEEE Conference on Computer Vision and Pattern Recognition, pp. 6399–6408 (2019).

[16] Kaiming, H., Xiangyu, Z., Shaoqing, R., and Jian, S. "Deep residual learning for image recognition," Proceedings of the IEEE Conference on Computer Vision and Pattern Recognition, pp. 770–778 (2016).

[17] Tzutalin. LabelImg. Git Code (2015). https://github.com/tzutalin/labelImg

[18] Ronneberger, O., Philipp, F., and Thomas B. "U-net: convolutional networks for biomedical image segmentation," International Conference on Medical Image Computing and Computer-Assisted Intervention, Cham: Springer (2015).

[19]   Wei, Y., Zhigang, Z., Cheng, L., and Huiming, Tang. "Pixel-wise regression using U-Net and its application on pan sharpening," *Neurocomputing*, 312, 364–371 (2018), ISSN 0925-2312.

[20]   Özgün, C., Ahmed, A., Soeren, S., Thomas, B., and Olaf, R. "3D U-Net: learning dense volumetric segmentation from sparse annotation," International Conference on Medical Image Computing and Computer-Assisted Intervention, Cham: Springer (2016).

[21]   Iglovikov, V. and Alexey, S. "Ternausnet: U-net with vgg11 encoder pre-trained on imagenet for image segmentation," (2018), arXiv preprint arXiv:1801.05746.

Chapter 3

Cache memory architecture for the convergence of machine learning, Internet of Things (IoT), and blockchain technologies

Reeya Agrawal¹, Sangeeta Singh² and Kamal Sharma³

Abstract

This chapter describes the need for cache memory architecture for the convergence of machine learning (ML), the Internet of Things (IoTs), and blockchain technologies with a brief introduction of cache memory and its types. Furthermore, this chapter implements cache memory design for single-bit architecture (CMDSBA). Single-bit architecture comprises six transistors static random access memory cell (SRAMC), a CWD, and latch sense amplifier (LSA) such as voltage latch type sense amplifier, and current latch type sense amplifier that has been implemented and compared on different values of resistance. Results depicted that cache memory design for single-bit six transistor SRAMC (STSRAMC) voltage LSA architecture consumes 14.32 μW of power. Apart from it, to optimize the consumption of power, power reduction sleep transistor technique, power reduction sleepy stack technique, and power reduction dual sleep technique are applied over different blocks of cache memory designed for single-bit architecture and the conclusion arises that single-bit STSRAMC with sleep transistor technique CLSA with sleep stack technique in architecture consumes 9.38 μW of power with 40 number of transistors.

Keywords: Six transistor static random access memory cell (STSRAMC); Voltage latch sense amplifier (VLSA); Current latch sense amplifier (CLSA); Power reduction techniques (TPR); Cache memory design for single-bit architecture (CMDSBA); Circuit of write driver (CWD); Latch sense amplifier (LSA)

3.1 Introduction

Data (information) and program (command sequence) of computers are permanently or temporarily stored in certain physical devices. Stored material depends on

¹Department of Computer Science and Applications Engineering, GLA University, Mathura, India
²Department of Electronics and Communication Engineering, NIT Patna, India
³Department of Mechanical Engineering, GLA University, Mathura, India

the program on other computers or time calculations. For big files, magnetic storage would have to be accessible permanently in the future. Runtime information is contained in semiconductor memory [1,2]. Six transistor static random access memory cell (STSRAMC) is a random-access memory of six transistors, which ensures that its contents can be accessed from anywhere on the memory. Data is saved in cells and fixed addresses are allocated to all storage cell locations to access data randomly. STSRAMCs are volatile so that after power shutdown, their storage data is destroyed. It can also be used in computer systems to store runtime data. STSRAMC serves for quicker execution of software in a computer system as a registry and cache memory. STSRAMCs are constructed from the same resources as process sources and are thus fully compliant with the processor and their speed corresponds to the current speed of the processor [3,4]. Therefore, during writing, it stores data quickly, STSRAMC is made up of a cross-coupled inverter latch with a positive feedback loop. It uses the sense amplifier circuit, which increases the difference in small voltage between lines. The memories are quicker than other types of memories and the read and write speed is the fastest at STSRAMC. By using effective circuit methods, the power dissipation for STSRAMC can be minimized. Leakage power dissipation is an overarching challenge to VLSI circuit engineers for the latest CMOS feature sizes.

The International Disposal of Leakage Power Planning states that total energy consumption will prevail. Dynamic and static elements are the power consumption of CMOS. As transistors convert and the transistor switches absorb static power, dynamic power is absorbed. The earliest challenge for low-power chip producers (at 0.18μ and above technology) was dynamic power consumption, with dynamic power accounting for 90% or more of their total chip capabilities. Many strategies, including voltage and frequency scaling, have previously been suggested hence based on dynamic lowering control. However, as the feature size decreases, e.g., 0.09μ and 0.065μ, static control, for existing and future technology, has become a major challenge. The power failure in the CMOS circuit has several causes. Recently STSRAMC's high-speed architecture and implementation have received considerable attention as a result of the exceptional need to include cache memory that plays a critical role in knowledge management and advanced mobile devices such as PDA and mobile phones [5]. Each chip area decreases, however, with submicron technology decreasing chip density. This method of scaling leads to various problems, such as power dissipation and resilience. The latch sense amplifier (LSA) is the main system to read the saved memory data. The efficiency influences the length of time it takes to store and dissipate [6].

Latch sense enhancer circuit is used in two configurations: voltage latch sense enhancer and current latch sense enhancer. The sensory voltage amplification used in memories leads to speed constraints due to high bit line capacity. Present sensor amplifiers, however, specifically fuel cell current, exhibit substantial speed improvements relative to the traditional sensory amplifier voltage mode [7]. The sensor amplifier for load transfer provides high efficiency and low power solutions. It also helps reduce the energy of the bit line than the amplification latch voltage.

This results in a lower-bit line swing. In proposed work/implementation of cache memory design for single-bit STSRAMC LSA architecture with different types of LSAs is to optimize the consumption of power and number of transistors in architecture using cadence virtuoso [8]. As with stand-alone STSRAMC, the table is usually wide and the grid occupies 60–70% of the entire size of a chip and it is around 50% for high-end embedded STSRAMC. A new implementation of the switched hierarchical bit belt greatly reduced the variance and the magnitude of bit line voltages and produced complex energy savings of 33% using a typical STSRAMC without changing the memory voltage [9]. One of the most important peripheral essential circuits of the CMOS memories is LSAs. Its output greatly affects both memory access time and total dissipation of memory power. CMOS memories, like other ICs today, are needed to speed up, increase capability and keep dissipation of the power down [10]. The aims of memory sensory-amplifier architecture are somewhat contradictory. Typically, the ability of the bit line parasite is increased with increased memory. This increases the capacity of the bit line, which in turn delays the sensing of voltage and makes it costly to change the energy voltage, resulting in sluggish, hunger memories. Sensor amplifiers have become a very broad class of circuits, because of their great significance in the memory output. Its key feature is that the data processing from a read-selected memory cell is sensed or detected [11].

3.1.1 Literature review

Habeeb and Salahuddin [12] describe many VLSI chips that now have 6TSRAMCs, which are fast and low power. Simultaneously, increasing integration and operation speeds have made power dissipation an essential concern. As a result, a lot of work has gone into employing circuit and architectural approaches to reduce the power consumption of CMOS RAM chips. This study describes a design that uses a hierarchical split bit-line method to reduce active power and access time in 6TSRAMCs by 40–50% and 5–10%, respectively, as compared to conventional 6TSRAMCs.

S.N. Panda *et al.* [13] describe that 6TSRAMC has a few benefits over DRAM. That is why SRAM is commonly chosen, and the major advantage is that 6TSRAMC does not require regular periodic refreshing, meaning that whatever is stored in a 6TSRAMC will last until the power is turned on. However, in the case of DRAM, it is necessary to refresh it regularly. As a result, 6TSRAMC is commonly used. Again, 6TSRAMC is divided into many categories, such as 4TSRAMC, 6TSRAMC, and 8TSRAMC, based on the number of MOSFETs, it includes, i.e., 4TSRAMC containing 4 MOSFETs, 6TSRAMC containing 6 MOSFETs, 8TSRAMC containing 8 MOSFETs, and so on. 6TSRAMC is the most commonly utilized of these due to its benefits over the others. Because there are fewer MOSFETs in 4TSRAMC, it takes up less chip space, but the voltage swing is quite significant, thus 4TSRAMC is rejected from a stability standpoint. Now, if we consider the 8TSRAMC, it is quite stable, but it uses more chip area owing to the increased number of MOSFETs, therefore, the 8TSRAMC is rejected from an area consumption standpoint.

Bhaskar *et al.* [14] describe that the power consumption, write delay, and write power delay product of low-power 6TSRAMC devices were investigated in this study. The power consumption of the 6TSRAMC has been reduced using gated V_{DD} and MTCMOS design methods. These designs are compared using the 6TSRAMC standard. In terms of power consumption and write latency, the MTCMOS-based 6TSRAMC outperforms the competition. It consumes 38.1% less energy than a traditional 6TSRAMC. Furthermore, the MTCMOS-based 6TSRAMC outperforms the regular 6TSRAMC by 18.18%. The gated V_{DD} 6TSRAMC also outperforms the traditional 6TSRAMC, using 16.8% less power and running 13.3% quicker.

Kumar *et al.* [15] describe that because of the quicker memory operations and lower power consumption, embedded 6TSRAMC has become an essential element of current SoCs. As CMOS devices become smaller, there will be a slew of side effects, such as short channel effects, that will wreak havoc on device performance. FinFET technology is a technique for overcoming the impacts of short channel effects and improving the performance of 6TSRAMC circuit designs by providing improved gate control over the channel.

Lokesh *et al.* [16] describe how, as technology advances, devices shrink in size, resulting in a reduction in the length of the MOSFET's channel, with the speed of operation becoming more important. The goal of this chapter is to build a 6TSRAMC, as well as its READ and WRITE operations that function at a high speed while using less power. The 6TSRAMC is simulated, and graphs for reading and writing operations, as well as their associated power results, are shown.

Tripti *et al.* [17] describe that in today's world, the electronics sector has a serious problem with standby leakage current in most electronic equipment. As the speed of the CPU increases, so does the requirement for high-speed cache memory. Because SRAM is primarily utilized for cache memory design, a variety of low-power methods are employed to decrease leakage current. For most digital circuits, full CMOS 6TSRAMC is the best option. The MTCMOS method is used to construct a 6T CMOS SRAM cell, and simulation results demonstrate a substantial decrease in leakage during standby mode.

Rath and Panda [18] describe that 6TSRAMC is a key component of the embedded cache memory found in portable digital devices. Because of its high storage density and quick access time, the 6TSRAMC has become a popular data storage device. The need for low-voltage low-power 6TSRAMC has increased because of the exponential rise of low-power digital devices. 6TSRAMC's performance has been assessed in terms of latency, power, and static noise margin (SNM).

P. Shubham *et al.* [19] describe that memory is a critical component in current VLSI system design, and it must be extensively examined in terms of space, power, and performance before manufacturing. Due to the ever-increasing need for data processing, 6TSRAMC is a key contender in the design of memory, and it is receiving a lot of attention. The performance of traditional CMOS devices is harmed by submicron scaling due to short channel effects, and circuits become unstable. FinFET is suggested to be the greatest feasible alternative for CMOS technology below the sub-32nm domain. The author of this work constructed and studied the performance of CMOS and FinFET-based 6TSRAMCs at 22 nm technology, comparing performance parameters. While both circuits provide stable SNM at 1 V, the FinFET-based 6TSRAMC outperforms the other in terms of reading and write performance due to its great process variation tolerance.

V. Singh *et al.* [20] describe that traditional scaling tendencies, which involve shrinking the essential dimensions of the transistor, have long benefited CMOS technology. 6TSRAMC, which has typically been used as cache memory, has also benefitted from downsizing. Because memory components such as SRAM take up the bulk of silicon space in a typical integrated circuit, such optimization is important for key criteria such as portability, operating speed, and power consumption reduction.

Sphurti *et al.* [21] explain that researchers have been shrinking CMOS circuits for the last five decades to achieve successful execution in terms of speed, power blow-out, size, and unchanging quality. Our goal is to make common electronics, such as computers, smaller in size, faster, and consume less power. The scaling of CMOS is done to achieve speed and reduce memory size. 6TSRAMC is a data storage format that may be utilized in a variety of devices. 6TSRAMC is now preferred over 8T and 9T SRAM because it has a very low latency when compared to 8T and 9T SRAM and its power dissipation is half that of 8T and 9T SRAM.

Lakshmi *et al.* [22] describe that nowadays every gadget has a high-capacity memory to meet all of the demands of clients. Power consumption and latency are two more characteristics that play a vital part in determining the device's performance. Memory is an essential component of many widgets, and its size shrinks as the device's size shrinks. As a result, every computerized gadget has low-power consumption and high speed is a top priority. In today's environment, 6TSRAMC is frequently utilized for 6TSRAMC-based memory architectures since it is more beneficial than other cells. Low-power consumption is a crucial problem in today's electronics industry, with static and dynamic power dissipation being the two essential characteristics to consider. High bandwidth, low power, and high-speed consuming storage are also necessary to fulfill customer demands. The major focus of this study is on lowering the power dissipation of 6TSRAMC. The digital industry's key problems are power reduction and delay reduction. Connecting two CMOS inverters back-to-back is a simple and beneficial SRAM cell arrangement. The noise immunity of this setup is excellent.

Janniekode *et al.* [23] describe that 6TSRAMC takes up 60% of the space of SoCs. The MOSFET experiences numerous short channel effects under nanoscale CMOS technology at lower supply voltages and technology nodes, and the design of the SRAM cell becomes increasingly complex due to higher leakage power consumption and decreased data stability. As a result, overcoming those restrictions and improving its performance is critical. This chapter describes the design of a 6TSRAMC that incorporates modern technologies like FinFET, CNTFET, and GNRFET at various nodes to increase leakage power and stability.

3.1.2   Role of cache memory design in IoT

A standard IoT sensor has four main sensor devices: an MCU, Bluetooth, WiFi, LoRa, and STSRAMC [24]. The sensor is also equipped with four main sensor devices. Because sensor nodes run at low data rates and low power, devices interconnect through a serial bus such as the SPI or IC communication protocol (I$_2$C). The MCU is the IoT node's main controller through which all transfers between devices can be negotiated [25]. The wireless computer sends sensor data to the closest gateway and receives gateway control instructions. The sensor tests the environmental parameters (temperature, humidity, etc.) and the data are digitalized through the serial contact bus SPI/I$_2$C [26]. When no gateway is available for communication, STSRAMC is used for storing local data. This chapter describes the concept and execution of a 0.6 μm CMOS technology for low-power SPI-accessible STSRAMC [27]. The invention of this project is the creation and control, without the use of internal clocks, of all the signals needed by STSRAMC that draw all the control signals from the SPI, rendering the system a simple and scalable system that consumes very little power with slower access times [28].

3.1.3   Need of cache memory for convergence of machine learning (ML)

Memory remains one of the most critical technologies for enabling continued advances in artificial intelligence (AI)/ML processing. From the rapid development of PCs in the 1990s to the explosion of gaming in the 2000s and the emergence of mobile and cloud computing in the 2010s, memory has played an integral role in enabling these new computing paradigms. The memory industry has responded to the needs of the industry over the last 30 years and is being called upon again to continue innovating as we enter a new age of AI/ML [29]. PCs drove an increase in memory bandwidth and capacity, as users processed growing amounts of data with applications like Word, Excel, and PowerPoint. Graphical user interfaces, the Web, and gaming pushed performance even higher. This gave rise to a new type of memory called graphics DDR (GDDR), designed to meet increased bandwidth demands. Mobile phones and tablets ushered in a new era with on-the-go computing, and the need for long battery life drove the memory industry to create new Mobile-specific memories to meet the needs of these markets [30]. Today, cloud computing continues to drive increases in capacity and performance to tackle larger workloads from connected devices. Looking forward, AI/ML applications are driving the need for better memory performance, capacity, and power efficiency, challenging memory system designers on multiple fronts all at the same time [31]. AI/ML models and training sets are growing in size as well, with the largest models now exceeding 170 billion parameters and even larger models on the horizon. While part of the improvement in performance and model size has been driven by silicon improvements due to Moore's Law, the challenge is that Moore's Law is slowing [32]. This makes it harder to continue achieving these types of performance increases. In addition to silicon improvements, another crucial part of the gains in system performance has been due to improved memory systems. When discussing the role of memory, it is important to understand that AI/ML applications are composed of two tasks, training and inference, and each has its requirements driving the choice of the best memory solutions for each.

Training is the process of "teaching" tasks to a neural network and often requires large data sets to be presented to the neural network so that it can comprehend its task. This sometimes takes place over days or weeks, so that it can become proficient [33]. The inference is the use of trained neural networks on data that it has not seen before, with inference accuracy determined by how well the neural network was trained. Cloud computing infrastructure allows the training of neural network models to be split across multiple servers, each running in parallel, to improve training time and to handle extremely large training sets [34]. Additionally, because of the value created through these training workloads, a powerful "time-to-market" incentive makes completing training runs a priority. Moving data to the AI model can become a bottleneck, driving the need for higher memory bandwidth. Because this training is taking place in data centers that are facing increasing space and power constraints, there is an increased need for power-efficient and compact solutions to reduce cost and improve ease of adoption [35]. Once an AI/ML model has been successfully trained, it can be deployed either in the data center, at the network edge, or increasingly in IoT devices. AI/ML inferencing requires memory to have both high bandwidth and low latency to produce answers in real-time. Because inferencing is appearing in an increasingly wide range of devices, cost becomes more of a priority for this hardware than for hardware intended for data center applications. There are also market-specific needs that must be addressed. In the case of advanced driver-assistance system (ADAS) applications, the memory needs to meet stringent automotive qualification requirements to be tolerant of extreme temperatures which could otherwise potentially lead to dangerous failures. As 5G continues its rollout and autonomous cars move closer toward deployment, the market will witness an increase in the number of AI-powered devices performing complicated inferencing [36]. AI/ML solutions typically choose between three types of memory depending on their needs: on-chip memory, high bandwidth memory (HBM), and GDDR memory. HBM and GDDR memory are the two highest-performing external memories and have evolved over multiple generations to continue meeting the needs of the most demanding applications.

On-chip memory is the fastest memory available and has the best power efficiency, but is severely limited in capacity by comparison. On-chip memory is typically a good choice for systems with smaller neural networks that only do inferencing. HBM is ideally positioned for training, and GDDR6 is well suited for both training and inference for large neural network models and training sets [27]. Introduced in 2013, HBM is a high-performance, 3D-stacked DRAM architecture, which provides the needed high bandwidth and capacity in a very small footprint. Furthermore, by keeping data rates low and the memory closer to the processor, overall system power efficiency is improved. The newest version of HBM memory, HBM2E, is compelling for many applications but is more complex and pricier compared to more traditional DRAMs like GDDR [37]. For many systems, this unmatched combination of capabilities outweighs other concerns, making HBM a great solution for AI/ML training. GDDR STSRAMC, which was originally designed for the gaming and graphics market, gradually evolved since it was originally introduced over two decades ago [38]. The current generation, GDDR6, supports data rates of up to 16 Gbps, allowing a single DRAM device to achieve 64 GB/s of bandwidth. While HBM can provide better performance and power efficiency for AI/ML, GDDR6 can reduce cost and implementation complexities, as it leverages existing infrastructure and processes. The main challenge for GDDR6 implementations is maintaining good signal integrity at much higher data rates used to transfer data between the SoC and the DRAM [39].

For AI/ML inferencing in IoT devices (such as autonomous vehicles), GDDR6 offers a strong combination of performance, power efficiency, capacity, cost, and reliability, while also maintaining the more familiar and cheaper implementation approach. It is still the early days in this next chapter of the AI/ML revolution, and there are no signs of slowing in the demand for more computing performance [40]. Improvements to every aspect of computing hardware and software will be needed to maintain the historic improvements we have witnessed over the past 5 years. Memory will continue to be critical to achieving continued performance gains. For AI/ML training and inference, HBM2E and GDDR6 provide best-in-class performance for training and inference, and the memory industry is continuing to innovate to meet the future needs of these systems.

3.1.4   Need of cache memory for convergence of blockchain technologies

PUFs, or physical unclonable functions, employ device-specific random patterns to distinguish semiconductors. PUFs, especially STSRAMC PUFs, are made to be hard to reproduce, clone, or forecast [41]. To take advantage of the unpredictability in their behavior, PUFs are actively stimulated and executed. A PUF may be thought of as a device fingerprint [42]. The system additionally takes advantage of the noisy behavior of this device fingerprint. To generate robust, independent random numbers with high entropy, the noise entropy is gathered. In all sorts of cryptographic protocols, strong independent random number generators are required, and they are frequently the weakest link in a cryptographic implementation. The most secure and robust technique to incorporating PUF in integrated circuits is intrinsic-STSRAMC ID's PUF technology [43]. The STSRAMC PUF makes use of the device STSRAMC memory's unique properties deep inside the transistors. The physical attributes of a gadget cannot be reproduced or cloned because these process variances are uncontrolled during production. It is difficult to develop a gadget with a certain electronic fingerprint on purpose [44]. Figure 3.1 shows the benefits of IoT and blockchain, and Figure 3.2 offers applications of IoT and blockchain.

3.1.5   Cache memory

Specific high-speed memory is cache memory. It is used for high-speed CPU acceleration and synchronization [45]. The memory cache is less than the main memory or disc, but less than the background of the CPU. A memory cache between RAM and CPU is a highly fast, buffer-based memory. It also includes necessary data and commands, so that the CPU is automatically accessible when

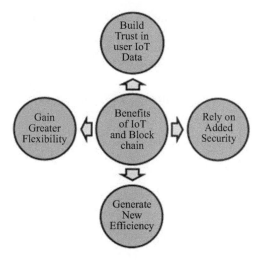

Figure 3.1   Benefits of IoT and blockchain

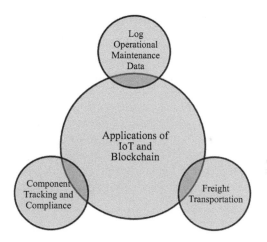

Figure 3.2   Applications of IoT and blockchain

necessary [46]. The entire main memory entry is reduced with cache memory. The cache is a smaller and faster-caching device with backups of data from commonly used storage sites. A CPU incorporates several different caches to store data and instructions [47]. Cache memory is a chip component built on a device to allow for more convenient data retrieval from computer memory [48]. It serves as a readily accessible temporary storage area for the user. This temporary cache storage region is simpler to processors than the principal computer's memory source, normally a DRAMC [49]. Cache memory is commonly called CPU memory since it is usually built into a CPU chip or on a special CPU chip

Table 3.1   Difference between SRAMC and DRAMC

DRAMC	SRAMC
High-density equipment is the DRAMC	Low-density computers are SRAMCs
This is included in key memories	This is found in memories in a cache
DRAMCs are instruments of high density	This is costly
Slow access speeds are provided for DRAMC	In comparison to DRAMC, SRAMC is quicker
To store data longer, the condenser contents must be regularly refreshed	Therefore, refreshments are not required capacitors
Data is stored in DRAMC with capacitors	Transistors are used in SRAMC to store information

that has a separate bus connection [50]. Thus, when physically next to the processor, the processor can handle and function easier. The cache memory should be far smaller than the main memory to be near the CPU. It also has less room for storage. It is much more costly because the chip performs better than the main storage [51]. DRAMC is the main memory hardware of the computer [52]. The cache memory for the wider cache name should not be confused. There are two kinds of cache memory [53] (Table 3.1):

- Static random access memory cell (SRAMC)
- Dynamic random access memory cell (DRAMC)

3.1.5.1   SRAMC

Transistors store data and require a steady power flow. SRAMC does not have to be refreshed to recall the data stored because of the continuous capacity. SRAMC is called static when no modification or intervention is required, i.e., to maintain data stable, refreshing is not needed. It is used in-memory cache [54].

Merit: Faster connection rates and lower power consumption.

Demerit: Low memory capacity and high production costs.

3.1.5.2   DRAMC

In condensers, data is stored. Data storage capacitors are steadily discharging energy in DRAMC, no energy is lost to data. To run, a regular power refresh is needed. The DRAMC is referred to as dynamic, i.e., the data must be maintained or updated continuously. It is used to implement main memory [55].

Merit: Low cost of output and increased memory.

Demerit: High power consumption and low link speed.

In this chapter in the Introduction, a small brief about IoT, need of cache memory, literature survey and what is cache memory as well as the type of cache memory, need of cache memory for convergence of blockchain technologies, role of cache memory design in IoT, and need of cache memory for convergence of ML has been described. In Section II, single-bit STSRAMC LSA architecture has been described with circuit of write driver (CDW), STSRAMC, and SA (such as VLSA and CLSA). Section III describes single-bit STSRAMC VLSA architecture and power reduction techniques. Section IV describes results and discussion and comparison tables. Section V describes the conclusion and future scope.

3.2 Single-bit STSRAMC SA architectures

3.2.1 Single-bit STSRAMC LSA architecture

STSRAMC is a form of volatile semiconductor memory which means that it stores data while it is operated. STSRAMC uses a transistor-bistable latching circuit to store any bit. STSRAMC does not have a condenser to store the data so STSRAMC functions without refreshing unlike DRAMC [32]. As a memory cache, STSRAMC is typically used. Single-bit STSRAMC LSA architecture block diagram shown in Figure 3.3 includes CWD, LSA, and STSRAMC [56,57].

3.2.1.1 CWD

The CWD lowers the written margin of the STSRAMC from the complete PCH by unloading the bit lines voltage. Figure 3.2 reveals that the information sought is entered on the bit lines by loading [58]. If WE = tall, the data pin value is saved on bit lines (i.e., WE are enabled). The voltage of the bit lines would then be sent to the transistors and the voltage in the form of data in the memory cell [59].

3.2.1.2 Six transistor static random access memory cell (STSRAMC)

STSRAMC has named six random access cell transistors. It has a data storage property even before power is delivered [60]. The STSRAMC consists of a single-bit STSRAMC, two CMOS-logged reverse inverters with two additional transistor units, each dependent on the data stored on the two inverters. Two other access transistors are also available [61]. As seen in Figure 3.3, STSRAMC provides data access via the bit lines. The high strength and the lowest static dissipation of it is

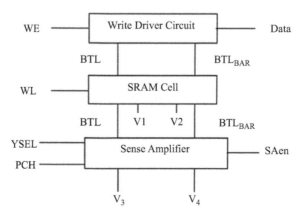

Figure 3.3   Single bit STSRAMC LSA architecture block diagram

the most typical memory cell [62]. Permission to write and read transistors in cell-bit lines (WL = high) WL permission. The expression static is extracted from the lack of refreshment as dynamic RAM [63]. The STSRAMC cycle time is significantly shorter than the DRam cycle because the accesses do not need to stop. STSRAMC is very costly but hungry faster than DRAMC and considerably less fuel [64].

STSRAMC write operation
BTL will be loaded to V_{DD} in a written process, and BTL_{BAR} will be charged to 0 V, now a word line will be allowed and transistors will be switched on and information will be stored in the STSRAMC. After the writing process has been completed, access transistors switch on OFF, and read data is stored.

STSRAMC read operation
During the reading process, both BTL and BTL_{BAR} are preloaded to V_{DD} and WL = high. It is common knowledge that the driver is more powerful than the driving force since a bit line is drawn from a transistor in the memory cell [65]. The input is also detected on bit lines by the amplifier. The diameter of the transistor should be equal and high for any column of the proposed architecture. The transistor width should be equal and high [66].

3.2.1.3   LSA

A sense amplifier is used while data is read out of the memory; its function in sensing the low power signals from a bit line representing a data bit (1 or 0) in the memory cell, and amplifying the tiny voltage swing to recognizable logic values to better interpret the data outside the memory with the logic required [67].

- The sense amplifier type lock is also separated from bit line capacity due to its high speed and performance.
- The disadvantage of the latch-type sense amplifier is the errors due to the input voltage and high power usage caused by inadequate sensing margin.
- A basic structure of this sensory amplifier, quick access speed, and an easy-to-build interface size of this system.

  LSA of two types:

- Voltage LSA
- Current-LSA

Voltage LSA
VLSA uses four MOS transistors i.e., PM_1, PM_2, NM_1, and NM_2 are seen in Figure 3.4 from the inverters which fix differential stress on the bit lines to a complete swing [68]. This design's internal nodes are pre-laden by bit bars. The circuit architecture is dependent on the voltage difference produced by the input bit lines on its internal nodes. The NM_3 is OFF and the PM_3 and PM_4 transfer transistors ON as the Word line (i.e., WL) are switched on and the priors to the

amplifier are triggered [69]. As the void in the bit lines expands, the internal nodes of the sensory amplifier are voltage enough. As the SA_{EN} sense amplifier signal is strengthened, the interconnector inverter comprising PM_1, PM_2, NM_1, and PM_2 extends this differential voltage to its full swing output [70].

Current LSA (CLSA)

To achieve a low-performance and automatic power-saving system in Figure 3.5, the currently operated sensor amplifier is built [71]. In a reading cycle, the cell data appears on the bit lines as a slight difference (BTL and BTL_{BAR}). The 2-gate NM_1

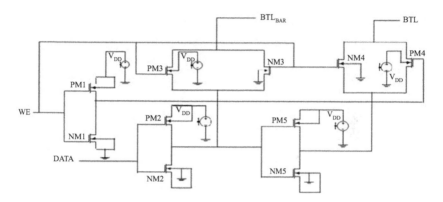

Figure 3.4   CWD schematic

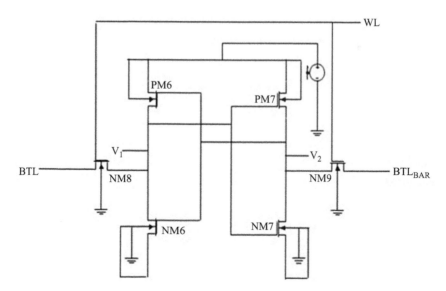

Figure 3.5   STSRAMC schematic

and NM_2 (i.e., BTL and BTL_{BAR}) are related. Two NMOS current flow regulates the serial latch circuit. A minor variation between the current and two NMOS transforms into a significant voltage [72]. Sense amplifier signal (SA_{EN}) continues to use NM_3 to initiate the sensory process. SA_{EN} is then enabled; when output nodes are transited, the running current flows. And when the lock sensor amplifier is switched this current flows [73]. The current flow then stops automatically in the amplifier and this sensor amplifier does not dissipate static power during a read process. Furthermore, the flow of the locking circuit is restricted since the latched sensing amplifier does not specifically drive the BTL and BTL_{BAR} high load capacity [74].

3.3 Description of proposed architectures and techniques of power reduction

3.3.1 Single-bit STSRAMC VLSA architecture

Figure 3.6 shows the single-bit STSRAMC VLSA architecture schematic comprised of CWD, STSRAMC, and VLSA as shown in the figure. Three of the circuits are connected via bit lines.

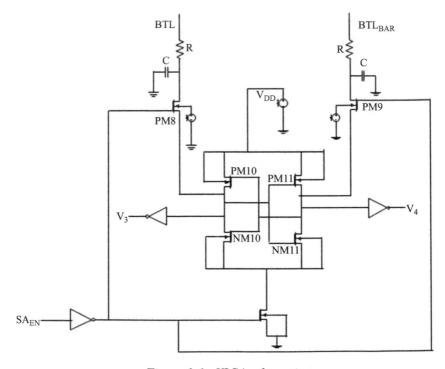

Figure 3.6   VLSA schematic

3.3.1.1   Single-bit STSRAMC CLSA architecture

Figure 3.7 shows the single-bit STSRAMC CLSA architecture schematic comprised of CWD, STSRAMC, and CLSA as shown in the figure. Three of the circuits are connected via bit lines.

3.3.2   Techniques of power reduction

The fundamental operational approach for leakage power reduction methods is covered in this section, such as power reduction sleep transistor technique, power reduction dual sleep technique, and power reduction sleep stack technique, which have been used to analyze various parameters in the STSRAMC [75]:

3.3.3   Power reduction sleep transistor technique

Reduction of force most widely used method of power reduction is sleep transistor technology. The sleep transistor strategy diagram is shown in Figure 3.8. The sleep transistor process connects V_{DD} with the pull-up network in the PMOS circuit and (ii) connects the pull-down network to GND in the NMOS circuit [76].

3.3.4   Power reduction sleep stack technique

The stacking method forces a stack effect by dismantling one current transistor in two half-size transistors, as shown in Figure 3.9, which is another technique for reducing strength. The caused reverse bias between the two transistors, when simultaneously deactivated, results in a reduced sub-threshold of the current.

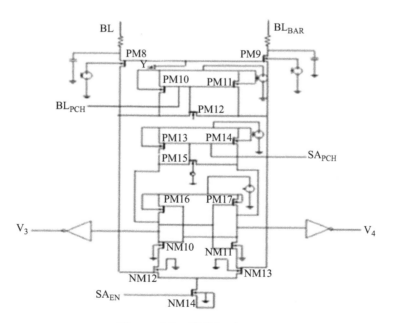

Figure 3.7   CLSA schematic

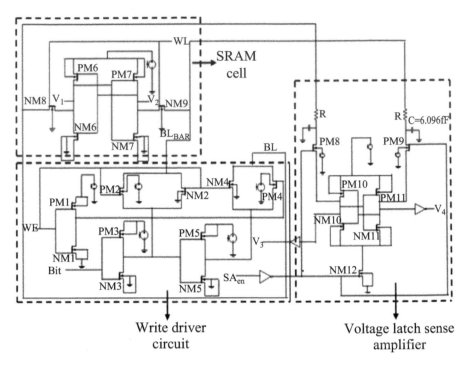

Figure 3.8   Single bit STSRAMC VLSA architecture schematic

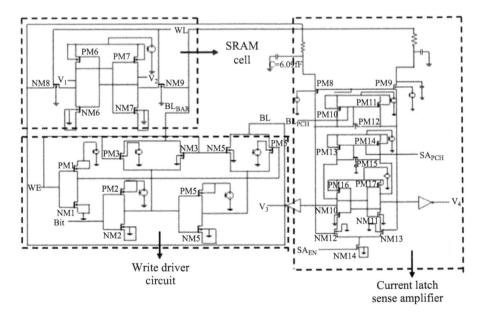

Figure 3.9   Single bit STSRAMC CLSA architecture schematic

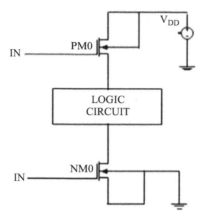

Figure 3.10   Power reduction sleep transistor technique

3.3.5   Power reduction dual sleep technique

Four transistors, two NMOS (NM_0 and NM_1) and two PMOS (PM_0 and PM_1), optimize the field requirements for this technique. The two additional pull-ups and pull-down transistors were used in sleep mode in either an OFF/ON state. As seen in Figure 3.10, a specific logic circuit requires fewer transistors [77].

3.4   Simulated resulted of proposed architecture with discussion

3.4.1   Results and discussion

In this chapter, discussion on methodology and discussion of results has been done. This thesis work will be done on cadence tools at 90 nm technology. As the technology and number of transistors on a single chip, both are increasing and keep on increasing. To design the circuit, a designer needs to select the appropriate tool and technology. As the feature size of technology decreases the threshold voltage of MOS decreases, because of the scale down the threshold voltage MOS transistor is turned on at a lower voltage so the delay of the circuit decreases, and the power dissipation as the supply voltage decreases. In-circuit design, the tool plays a very important part. The configuration of the circuit also relies on the tool in which the schematic simulation time is designed. The tool is used to find the parameters and characteristics of the circuit. CADENCE TOOL is used for the design of STSRAMC, different types of LSAs.

3.4.2   Simulation of CWD

Figure 3.11 shows the WDC output waveform and connects the STSRAMC with BTL and BTL_{BAR} bit lines, WL = H (i.e., activated WL). Those outputs are stored in the memory cell. The SA_{EN} sense amplifier signal is used for the reading process, while the SA_{EN} = H amplifier starts to work (i.e., SA_{EN} is enabled). When

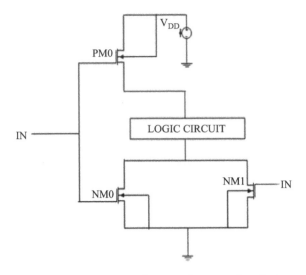

Figure 3.11   Power reduction sleep stack technique

WE are switched on, the data is contained in BTL, and the BTL_{BAR} complements the data. BTL has written memory cell data and similarly BTL_{BAR} when WE are disabled (e.g., WE = L).

The output waveform of the WDC describes four cases that occur, where H is denoted High and L denotes Low:

Case 1: Bit = L and WE = L BTL = H and BTL_{BAR} = H,
Case 2: Bit = L WE = H, BTL = L and BTL_{BAR} = H/2,
Case 3: Bit = H WE = L so, BTL = L and BTL_{BAR} = H/2
Case 4: Bit = H WE= H, BTL = H and BTL_{BAR} = L.

3.4.3   Simulation of STSRAMC:

STSRAMC may be divided into synchronous STSRAMC and asynchronous STSRAMC depending on how a clock is used. All inward flags and timing in synchronous STSRAMC are controlled by the clock edge [78]. Information in, control movements, and placement are all tied to the clock signal, hence it is mostly used as a cache memory, whereas asynchronous STSRAMC is clock-independent. Asynchronous STSRAMC is useful as primary memory for cache-less embedded processors that are used as part of current hardware, an estimate of frameworks, and arranging hardware due to its short access time [79]. The functioning of the STSRAMC may be divided into three modes. The first is standby mode, in which the word line is not begun and the address and data lines are maintained removed from STSRAMC memory cells. In this mode, the power consumption is the lowest. Reading data from cells is the second manner of action [80]. The read cycle starts with pre-charging the bit line and bit line bar, following which the word line is triggered by a specific row address and one of the bit lines begins discharging via

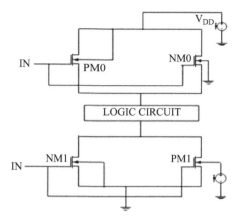

Figure 3.12   Power reduction dual sleep technique

the cell. If the bit line voltage is higher than the bit line, bar voltage, the sense amplifier's output is logic 1, indicating a read 1 operation [81,82]. Similarly, if the bit line voltage is lower than the bit line bar voltage, the sense amplifier's output indicates read 0 operations. Because it detects the slight difference between voltages on bit lines, the presence of a SA speeds up memory operation.

Figure 3.12 shows the output waveform of STSRAM which holds two operations:

- Write operation
- Hold operation

There are six transistors in STSRAMC which are called: (i) access transistors (NM8 and NM9), (ii) pull-up transistors (PM6 and PM7), and (iii) pull-down transistors (NM6 and NM7).

3.4.4   Simulation of LSA

Sense amplifiers are used in reading circuitry and it amplifies the signal. There are different types of LSA circuits. Here is shown a simulation of two types of sense amplifiers: (i) voltage LSA and (ii) CLSA.

Figures 3.13 and 3.14 show the output waveform of VLSA and CLSA, respectively. The internal nodes are preloaded using the bit lines of this architecture. The circuit architecture works directly from its internal reference bit-line nodes depending on the voltage differential.

3.4.5   Comparison table

From Table 3.2, conclusions arise that single-bit STSRAMC VLSA architecture consumes 36.57 μW with 29 number transistors, whereas single-bit STSRAMC CLSA architecture consumes 26.78 μW with 35 number of transistors at R= 42.3 Ω. Figure 3.14 shows the graphical representation of Table 3.2.

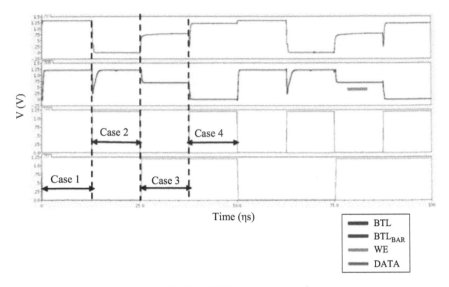

Figure 3.13   CWD output waveform

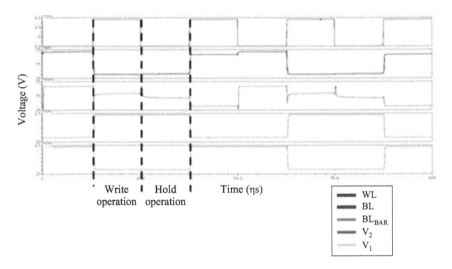

Figure 3.14   STSRAMC output waveform

Table 3.2   *Single-bit STSRAMC LSA architecture ADP at* R = 42.3 Ω

S. no.	Single-bit STSRAMC LSA architecture	Consumption of power	Number of transistors	Delay in sensing
1.	Single-bit STSRAMC VLSA architecture	36.57 μW	29	13.50 ηs
2.	Single-bit STSRAMC CLSA architecture	73.92 μW	35	18.68 ηs

From Table 3.3, conclusions arise that single-bit STSRAMC VLSA architecture consumes 14.32 μW with 29 number transistors, whereas single-bit STSRAMC CLSA architecture consumes 26.78 μW with 35 number of transistors at $R=$ 42.3 kΩ. Figure 3.15 shows the graphical representation of Table 3.3.

From Table 3.4, conclusions arise that single-bit STSRAMC CLSA with sleep stack technique in architecture consume 13.4 μW of power with 38 transistors which is the lowest as compared to other as shown in the table: 4 at $R=$42.3 kΩ on applying TPR over LSA in architecture. Figure 3.16 shows the graphical representation of Table 3.4.

From Table 3.5, conclusions arise that single-bit STSRAMC with sleep transistor technique CLSA in architecture consume 10.27 μW of power with 37 number of transistors which is lowest as compared to others as shown in Table 3.5 at $R=$42.3 kΩ on applying TPR over STSRAM in architecture. Figure 3.17 shows the graphical representation of Table 3.5.

From Table 3.6, conclusions arise that single-bit STSRAMC with sleep stack technique and CLSA with sleep stack techniques consume 11.56 μW of power with

Table 3.3 Single-bit STSRAMC LSA architecture ADP at R = 42.3 kΩ

S. no.	Single-bit STSRAMC LSA architecture	Consumption of power	Number of transistors	Delay in sensing
1.	Single-bit STSRAMC VLSA architecture	14.32 μW	29	13.50 ηs
2.	Single-bit STSRAMC CLSA architecture	26.78 μW	35	18.68 ηs

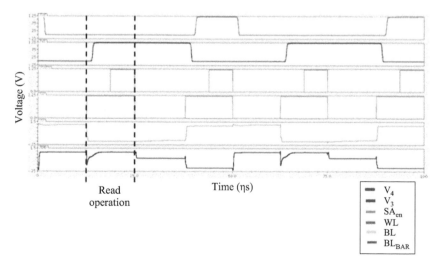

Figure 3.15 VLSA output waveform

Table 3.4   Single-bit STSRAMC LSA architecture power consumption at R = 42.3
kΩ on applying TPR over LSA

Techniques used	Single-bit STSRAMC VLSA architecture		Single-bit STSRAMC CLSA architecture	
	Consumption of power	Number of transistors	Consumption of power	Number of transistor
Sleep transistor	13.58 μW	31	25.89 μW	37
Sleep stack	13.67 μW	32	13.4 μW	38
Dual sleep	13.57 μW	33	25.9 μW	39

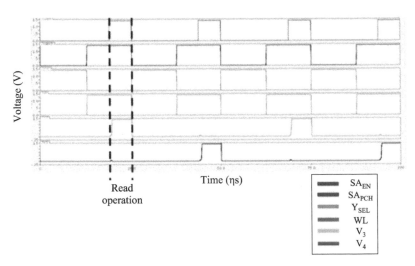

Figure 3.16   CLSA output waveform

Table 3.5   Single-bit STSRAMC LSA architecture power consumption at R = 42.3
kΩ on applying TPR over STSRAMC in architecture

Technique used	Single-bit STSRAMC VLSA architecture		Single-bit STSRAMC CLSA architecture	
	Consumption of power	Number of transistor	Consumption of power	Number of transistor
Sleep transistor	12.21 μW	31	10.27 μW	37
Sleep stack	13.36 μW	32	11.38 μW	38
Dual sleep	12.82 μW	33	11.15 μW	39

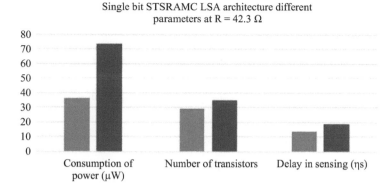

Figure 3.17   *Single bit STSRAMC LSA architecture ADP (architecture different parameters) at R= 42.3Ω*

Table 3.6   *Single-bit STSRAMC LSA architecture power consumption at R = 42.3 kΩ on applying TPR over STSRAMC and LSA in architecture*

Techniques used	Single-bit STSRAMC VLSA architecture		Single-bit STSRAMC LSA architecture	
	Consumption of power	**Number of transistor**	**Consumption of power**	**Number of transistor**
Sleep transistor	11.62 μW	33	24.62 μW	39
Sleep stack	12.69 μW	36	11.56 μW	42
Dual sleep	11.71 μW	37	24.64 μW	43

42 number transistors which are the lowest as compared to others. Figure 3.18 shows the graphical representation of Table 3.6.

From Tables 3.4 and 3.5, conclusion arises that single-bit STSRAMC with sleep transistor technique VLSA with dual sleep technique in architecture consume 11.48 μW with 35 number of transistors and single-bit STSRAMC with sleep transistor technique CLSA with sleep stack technique in architecture consume 9.38 μW of power with 40 number of transistors.

From Table 3.7, conclusions arise that single-bit STSRAMC with power reduction sleep transistor technique VLSA with power reduction dual sleep technique in architecture consume 11.48 μW of power with 35 transistors, whereas single-bit STSRAMC with power reduction sleep transistor technique CLSA with power reduction sleep stack technique in architecture consume 9.38 μW of power with 40 transistors.

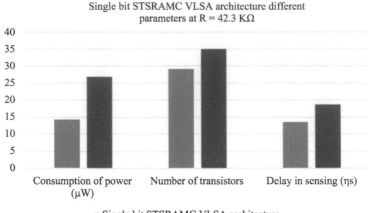

Figure 3.18   Single bit STSRAMC LSA architecture ADP at R=42.3KΩ

Table 3.7   Single-bit STSRAMC LSA architecture power consumption at R=42.3
kΩ on applying TPR over STSRAMC and LSA in architecture

Architecture	Consumption of power	Number of transistors
Single-bit STSRAMC with power reduction sleep transistor technique VLSA with power reduction dual sleep technique architecture	11.48 μW	35
Single-bit STSRAMC with power reduction sleep transistor technique CLSA with sleep stack technique architecture	9.38 μW	40

Note: Table 3.7 concludes that there is always a tradeoff b/w power and area.

3.5   Conclusion and future scope

3.5.1   Conclusion

In the proposed work, cache memory design for single-bit STSRAMC LSA architecture has been implemented and compared at different values of resistance. Single-bit STSRAMC VLSA architecture and single-bit STSRAMC CLSA architecture have been implemented over a tool and the consumption of power of each architecture has been calculated with several transistors. Furthermore, techniques of power reduction have been applied over different blocks of architecture such as power reduction sleep transistor technique, power reduction sleep stack technique, and power reduction dual sleep technique over STSRAMC and LSA in architecture. The conclusion arises that single-bit sleep transistor technique STSRAMC CLSA sleep stack technique architecture consumes 9.38 μW of power with 35 number transistors.

3.5.2 Future scope

As conclusion arise that single-bit sleep transistor technique STSRAMC CLSA sleep stack technique architecture consumes 9.38 μW of power. So, in cache memory design for single bit STSRAMC LSA architecture array, researchers can use these amplifiers, and consumption of power through architecture can be further reduced by using other techniques of power reduction. And the researcher also implemented STSRAMC with power reduction technique in array architecture, so that less power consumption is there in architecture.

References

[1] Madhava Rao, K. and M. Tiwari. "Local Bitline 8T Differential SRAM Architecture Based on 22 Nm FinFET for Low Power Operation." *Annals of the Romanian Society for Cell Biology* 25 (2021): 3404–3418.

[2] Sheu, M. H., S. M. S. Morsalin, C.-M. Tsai, *et al.* "Stable Local Bit-Line 6 T SRAM Architecture Design for Low-Voltage Operation and Access Enhancement." *Electronics* 10(6) (2021): 685.

[3] Kumar, J. R. Dinesh, C. Ganesh Babu, V. R. Balaji, and S. P. Karthi. "Performance Investigation of Various SRAM Cells for IoT Based Wearable Biomedical Devices." In *Inventive Communication and Computational Technologies*, Springer, Singapore, 2021, pp. 573–588.

[4] Shiba, K., T. Omori, M. Hamada, and T. Kuroda. "A 3D-Stacked SRAM Using Inductive Coupling Technology for AI Inference Accelerator in 40-nm CMOS." Proceedings of the 26th Asia and South Pacific Design Automation Conference, 2021.

[5] Simopoulos, T., G. Ph. Alexiou, L. Spyridopoulos, and N. Konofaos. "Simultaneous Accessing of Multiple SRAM Subregions Forming Configurable and Automatically Generated Memory Fields." *International Journal of Circuit Theory and Applications* 49 (2021): 2238–2254.

[6] Pasuluri, B., *et al.* "Design of CMOS 6T and 8T SRAM for Memory Applications." Proceedings of Second International Conference on Smart Energy and Communication, Springer, Singapore, 2021.

[7] Gong, Y.-H. "Monolithic 3D-Based SRAM/MRAM Hybrid Memory for an Energy-Efficient Unified L2 TLB-Cache Architecture." *IEEE Access* 9 (2021): 18915–18926.

[8] Lv, J., Z. Wang, M. Huang, and Y. He. "A Read-Disturb-Free and Write-Ability Enhanced 9T SRAM with Data-Aware Write Operation." *International Journal of Electronics* 109 (2022): 23–37.

[9]   Lin, Z., H. Zhan, Z. Chen, *et al.* "Cascade Current Mirror to Improve Linearity and Consistency in SRAM In-Memory Computing." *IEEE Journal of Solid-State Circuits* 56(8) (2021): 2550–2562.

[10]   Kim, H., T. Yoo, T. T. -H. Kim, *et al.* "Colonnade: A Reconfigurable SRAM-Based Digital Bit-Serial Compute-In-Memory Macro for Processing Neural Networks." *IEEE Journal of Solid-State Circuits* 56 (2021): 2221–2233.

[11]   Bazzi, H., A. Harb, H. Aziza, M. Moreau, and A. Kassem. "RRAM-Based Non-Volatile SRAM Cell Architectures for Ultra-Low-Power Applications." *Analog Integrated Circuits and Signal Processing* 106.2 (2021): 351–361.

[12]   Habeeb, M. S. and S. Md. "Design of Low Power SRAM using Hierarchical Divided Bit-line Approach in 180-nm Technology."

[13]   Panda, S. N., S. Padhi, V. Phanindra, U. Nanda, S. K. Pattnaik, and D. Nayak. "Design and Implementation of SRAM Macro Unit." 2017 International Conference on Trends in Electronics and Informatics (ICEI), 2017, pp. 119–123, IEEE.

[14]   Bhaskar, A. "Design and Analysis of Low Power SRAM Cells." 2017 Innovations in Power and Advanced Computing Technologies (i-PACT), 2017, pp. 1–5, doi: 10.1109/IPACT.2017.8244888.

[15]   Kumar, A. A. and A. Chalil. "Performance Analysis of 6T SRAM ell on Planar and FinFET Technology." 2019 International Conference on Communication and Signal Processing (ICCSP), IEEE, 2019.

[16]   Lokesh, S. B. and K. Megha Chandana. "Design of Reading and Write Operations for 6T SRAM Cell." *IOSR Journal of VLSI and Signal Processing (IOSR-JVSP)* 8(1) (2018): 43–46.

[17]   Tripathi, T., S. K. Singh, D. S. Chauhan, and S. V. Singh, "Implementation of Low-Power 6T SRAM Cell Using MTCMOS Technique." *Advances in Computer and Computational Sciences*, Springer, Singapore, 2017, pp. 475–482.

[18]   Rath, S. and S. Panda. "Analysis of 6T SRAM Cell in Different Technologies." Proceedings of the 2nd National Conference of Mechatronics Comput. Signal Process. (MCSP-2017), 2017, pp. 7–10.

[19]   Sanjana S. R., S. Balaji Ramakrishna, Samiksha, R. Banu, and P. Shubham. "Design and Performance Analysis of 6T SRAM Cell in 22nm CMOS and FINFET Technology Nodes." 2017 International Conference on Recent Advances in Electronics and Communication Technology (ICRAECT), 2017, pp. 38–42, doi: 10.1109/ICRAECT.2017.65.

[20]   Singh, V., S. K. Singh, and R. Kapoor. "Static Noise Margin Analysis of 6T SRAM." 2020 IEEE International Conference for Innovation in Technology (INOCON), 2020, pp. 1–4, doi: 10.1109/INOCON50539. 2020.9298431.

[21]   Shukla, S., S. Singh, K. Bansal, P. Tyagi, and S. K. Singh. "Design of 6T SRAM Cell on Different Technology Nodes." *Smart Computing*, CRC Press, London, 2021, pp. 599–605.

[22] Venkat Lakshmi, T. and M. Kamaraju. "Implementation of High-Performance 6T-SRAM Cell." *Journal of Physics: Conference Series* 1804 (1) (2021): 012185 (IOP Publishing).

[23] Janniekode, U. M., R. P. Somineni, and C. D. Naidu. "Design and Performance Analysis of 6T SRAM Cell in Different Technologies and Nodes." *International Journal of Performability Engineering* 17(2) (2021): 167–177.

[24] Kim, Y., S. Patel, H. Kim, N. Yadav, and K. K. Choi. "Ultra-Low Power and High-Throughput SRAM Design to Enhance AI Computing Ability in Autonomous Vehicles." *Electronics* 10(3) (2021): 256.

[25] Fritsch, A., R. Joshi, S. Chakraborty, *et al.* "24.1 A 6.2 GHz Single-Ended Current Sense Amplifier (CSA) Based Compileable 8T SRAM in 7nm FinFET Technology." 2021 IEEE International Solid-State Circuits Conference (ISSCC), IEEE, 2021.

[26] Duari, C., S. Birla, and A. K. Singh. "A 4x4 8T-SRAM Array with Single-Ended Read and Differential Write Scheme for Low Voltage Applications." *Semiconductor Science and Technology* 36 (2021): 065013.

[27] Kneip, A. and D. Bol. "Impact of Analog Non-Idealities on the Design Space of 6T-SRAM Current-Domain Dot-Product Operators for In-Memory Computing." *IEEE Transactions on Circuits and Systems I: Regular Papers* 68 (2021): 1931–1944.

[28] Wang, H., Y. Wang, and W. Wang. "Impact of TMR Design Layouts on Single Event Tolerance in SRAM-Based FPGAs." *Microelectronics Reliability* 120 (2021): 114113.

[29] Jhang, C., C. -X. Xue, J. -M. Hung, *et al.* "Challenges and Trends of SRAM-Based Computing-In-Memory for AI Edge Devices." *IEEE Transactions on Circuits and Systems I: Regular Papers* 68 (2021): 1773–1786.

[30] Lin, Z., Z. Tong, J. Zhang, *et al.* "Two-Direction In-Memory Computing Based on 10T SRAM with Horizontal and Vertical Decoupled Read Ports." *IEEE Journal of Solid-State Circuits* 56 (2021): 031401.

[31] Nag, A., K. Ruchira Reddy, N. Majumder, E. Debbarma, and S. N. Pradhan. "A Novel NOR Gate-Based Dynamic Power Gating Technique in SRAM." Proceedings of the Fourth International Conference on Microelectronics, Computing and Communication Systems, Springer, Singapore, 2021.

[32] Choi, J. H., Y.-H. Gong, and S. W. Chung. "A System-Level Exploration of Binary Neural Network Accelerators with Monolithic 3D Based Compute-in-Memory SRAM." *Electronics* 10(5) (2021): 623.

[33] Radhika, K., Y. M. Mohan Babu, and S. Mishra. "Design and Implementation of Low Power High-Speed Robust 10T SRAM." 2021 International Conference on Emerging Smart Computing and Informatics (ESCI), IEEE, New York, NY, 2021.

[34] Dounavi, H. M., Y. Sfikas, and Y. Tsiatouhas. "Aging Prediction and Tolerance for the SRAM Memory Cell and Sense Amplifier." *Journal of Electronic Testing* 99 (2021): 1–18.

[35] Zhang, Z., W. Wang, P. Yu, *et al.* "Cache Performance of NV-STT-MRAM with Scale Effect and Comparison with SRAM." *International Journal of Electronics* 109 (2021): 391–409. Accepted for publication.

[36] Murali Mohan Babu, Y., S. Mishra, and K. Radhika. "Design Implementation and Analysis of Different SRAM Cell Topologies." 2021 International Conference on Emerging Smart Computing and Informatics (ESCI), IEEE, 2021, pp. 678–682.

[37] Kumar, R. M. and P. V. Sridevi. "Design of 1kb SRAM array using enhanced stability 10T SRAM cell for FPGA based applications."

[38] Singh, R. and S. Jain. "Efficient Deblocking Filter with SRAM using 22nm FinFET Technology." 2021 International Conference on Artificial Intelligence and Smart Systems (ICAIS), IEEE, 2021.

[39] Gupta, N., A. Makosiej, H. Shrimali, A. Amara, A. Vladimirescu, and C. Anghel. "Tunnel FET Negative-Differential-Resistance Based 1T1C Refresh-Free-DRAM, 2T1C SRAM and 3T1C DRAM." *IEEE Transactions on Nanotechnology* 20 (2021): 270–277.

[40] Kumar, P. D., R. K. Kushwaha, and P. Karuppanan. "Design and Analysis of Low-Power SRAM." *Advances in VLSI, Communication, and Signal Processing*, Springer, Singapore, 2021, pp. 41–56.

[41] Lin, Z., L. Li, X. Wu, *et al.* "Half-Select Disturb-Free 10T Tunnel FET SRAM Cell with Improved Noise Margin and Low Power Consumption." *IEEE Transactions on Circuits and Systems II: Express Briefs* 68 (2021): 2628–2632.

[42] Lakshmi Priya, G., M. Venkatesh, N. B. Balamurugan, and T. S. Arun Samuel. "Triple Metal Surrounding Gate Junctionless Tunnel FET based 6T SRAM Design for Low Leakage Memory System." (2021).

[43] Li, X., H. Lou, and Z. Jin. "A Fault-tolerant Method of SRAM FPGA Based on Processor Scrubbing." 2021 IEEE 5th Advanced Information Technology, Electronic and Automation Control Conference (IAEAC), Vol. 5, IEEE, New York, NY, 2021.

[44] Hu, S., *et al.* "Image Recognizing Based on the Architecture Integrated with CIM and CIS." 2021 IEEE 5th Advanced Information Technology, Electronic and Automation Control Conference (IAEAC), Vol. 5, IEEE, New York, NY, 2021.

[45] Raj, M., L. Gopalakrishnan, and S.-B. Ko. "Reliable SRAM using NAND-NOR Gate in beyond-CMOS QCA technology." *IET Computers & Digital Techniques* 15(3) (2021): 202–213.

[46] Kim, J.-H., J. Lee, J. Lee, *et al.* "Z-PIM: A Sparsity-Aware Processing-in-Memory Architecture With Fully Variable Weight Bit-Precision for Energy-Efficient Deep Neural Networks." *IEEE Journal of Solid-State Circuits* 56 (4) (2021): 1093–1104.

[47] Agrawal, R. "Analysis of Low-Power Cache Memory Design for Single Bit Architecture." In: *Technology Innovation in Mechanical Engineering* 2022, pp. 161–170. Springer, Singapore.

[48] Prasad, G., B. C. Mandi, and M. Ali. "Low Power and Write-Enhancement RHBD 12T SRAM Cell for Aerospace Applications." *Analog Integrated Circuits and Signal Processing* 107.2 (2021): 377–388.

[49] Tiwari, N., V. Sankath, A. Upadhyay, *et al.* "Modelling and Design of 5T, 6T and 7T SRAM Cell Using Deep Submicron CMOS Technology." Proceedings of Second International Conference on Smart Energy and Communication, Springer, Singapore, 2021.

[50] Mandal, S., A. Chakrabarti, and S. Bodapati. "Clustered Error Resilient SRAM based Reconfigurable Computing Platform." *IEEE Transactions on Aerospace and Electronic Systems* 57(3) (2021): 1768–1779.

[51] Cho, D. "A Study on Improvement of Low-Power Memory Architecture in IoT/Edge Computing." *Journal of the Korean Society of Industry Convergence* 24(1) (2021): 69–77.

[52] Al-O., F. A. Asad, and F. A. Mohammadi. "A Power-Aware Hybrid Cache for Chip-Multi Processors Based on Neural Network Prediction Technique." *International Journal of Parallel Programming* 49 (2021): 1–21.

[53] Garzón, E., R. De Rose, F. Crupi, *et al.* "Exploiting STT-MRAMs for Cryogenic Non-Volatile Cache Applications." *IEEE Transactions on Nanotechnology* 20 (2021): 123–128.

[54] Wilson, A. E., S. Larsen, C. Wilson, *et al.* "Neutron Radiation Testing of a TMR VexRiscv Soft Processor on SRAM-based FPGAs." *IEEE Transactions on Nuclear Science* 68 (2021): 1054–1060.

[55] Banbury, C., C. Zhou, I. Fedorov, *et al.* "Micronets: Neural Network Architectures for Deploying Tinyml Applications on Commodity Microcontrollers." *Proceedings of Machine Learning and Systems* 3 (2021).

[56] Nisha, O. S. "Architecture for an Efficient MBIST Using Modified March-y Algorithms to Achieve Optimized Communication Delay and Computational Speed." *International Journal of Pervasive Computing and Communications* 17 (2021): 135–147.

[57] Zhang, R., K. Yang, Z. Liu, *et al.* "A Comprehensive Framework for Analysis of Time-Dependent Performance-Reliability Degradation of SRAM Cache Memory." *IEEE Transactions on Very Large-Scale Integration (VLSI) Systems* 29 (2021): 857–870.

[58] Cannon, J. M., T. D. Loveless, R. Estrada, *et al.* "Electrical Measurement of Cell-to-Cell Variation of Critical Charge in SRAM and Sensitivity to Single-Event Upsets by Low-Energy Protons." *IEEE Transactions on Nuclear Science* 68(5) (2021): 815–822.

[59] Agrawal, R., N. Faujdar, P. Kumar, and A. Kumar. "Security and Privacy of Blockchain-Based Single-Bit Cache Memory Architecture for IoT Systems." *IEEE Access* 10 (2022): 35273–35286.

[60] Satyanarayana, B. V. V. and M. D. Prakash. "Design Analysis of GOS-HEFET on Lower Subthreshold Swing SOI." *Analog Integrated Circuits and Signal Processing* 109 (2021): 1–12.

[61]   Prada-Delgado, M. A. and I. Baturone. "Behavioral and Physical Unclonable Functions (BPUFs): SRAM Example." *IEEE Access* 9 (2021): 23751–23763.

[62]   Do Park, K., D. G. Kim, Y. G. Pu, *et al.* "10.76 TOPS/W CNN Algorithm Circuit using Processor-In-Memory with 8T-SRAM." 2021 IEEE International Conference on Big Data and Smart Computing (BigComp), IEEE, New York, NY, 2021.

[63]   Shrivastava, A., A. Gatherer, T. Sun, S. Wokhlu, and A. Chandra. "SLAP: A Split Latency Adaptive VLIW Pipeline Architecture Which Enables on-the-Fly Variable SIMD Vector-Length." arXiv preprint arXiv:2102.13301 (2021).

[64]   Shim, W. and S. Yu. "Ferroelectric Field-Effect Transistor-based 3D NAND Architecture for Energy-Efficient On-chip Training Accelerator." *IEEE Journal on Exploratory Solid-State Computational Devices and Circuits* 7 (2021): 1–9.

[65]   Su, J. -W., *et al.* "16.3 A 28nm 384kb 6T-SRAM Computation-in-Memory Macro with 8b Precision for AI Edge Chips." 2021 IEEE International Solid-State Circuits Conference (ISSCC), Vol. 64. IEEE, 2021.

[66]   Soniya, T., I. Ragasudha, and P. N. Valli. "Routing Architecture and Applications of FPGA: A Survey." *Journal of Physics: Conference Series* 1717(1) (2021): 012025. IOP Publishing.

[67]   Maddela, V., S. K. Sinha, and M. Parvathi. Open Defect Fault Analysis in Single Cell SRAM Using R, and C Parasitic Extraction Method. No. 5132. EasyChair, 2021.

[68]   Liu, H., L. Fan, J. Luo, and G. Feng. "Embedded Multiport Data Buffer for a Solid-State Drive Controller." *IEICE Electronics Express* 18 (2021): 20210132.

[69]   Krishnaraj, R., B. Soundarya, S. Mythili, and N. Vikram. "Design of a Memory Array Using Tail Transistor and Sleep Transistor Based 7T SRAM with Low Short Circuit and Standby Power." IOP Conference Series: Materials Science and Engineering, Vol. 1084. No. 1. IOP Publishing, 2021.

[70]   Gonzalez, C., and H. Liu. "F5: Enabling New System Architectures with 2.5 D, 3D, and Chiplets." 2021 IEEE International Solid-State Circuits Conference (ISSCC), Vol. 64. IEEE, 2021.

[71]   Bol, D., M. Schramme, L. Moreau, and D. Flandre "SleepRunner: A 28-nm FDSOI ULP Cortex-M0 MCU with ULL SRAM and UFBR PVT Compensation for 2.6-3.6-µW/DMIPS 40-80-MHz Active Mode and 131-NW/kB Fully Retentive Deep-Sleep Mode." *IEEE Journal of Solid-State Circuits* (2021).

[72]   Sakakibara, Y., K. Nakamura, and H. Matsutani. "An FPGA NIC Based Hardware Caching for Blockchain." Proceedings of the 8th International Symposium on Highly-Efficient Accelerators and Reconfigurable Technologies, 2017.

[73]   Sharma, V., I. You, D. N. Jayakody, D. G. Reina, and K. K. Choo. "Neural-Blockchain-Based Ultrareliable Caching for Edge-Enabled UAV Networks." *IEEE Transactions on Industrial Informatics* 15(10) (2019): 5723–5736.

[74] Javed, M. U., M. Rehman, N. Javaid, A. Aldegheishem, N. Alrajeh, and M. Tahir. "Blockchain-Based Secure Data Storage for Distributed Vehicular Networks." *Applied Sciences* 10(6) (2020): 2011.

[75] Zhang, R., F. Richard Yu, and R. Yang. "Deep Reinforcement Learning (DRL)-Based Device-to-Device (D2D) Caching with Blockchain and Mobile Edge Computing." *IEEE Transactions on Wireless Communications* 19(10) (2020): 6469–6485.

[76] Guo, S., X. Hu, S. Guo, X. Qiu, and F. Qi. "Blockchain Meets Edge Computing: A Distributed and Trusted Authentication System." *IEEE Transactions on Industrial Informatics* 16(3) (2019): 1972–1983.

[77] Zhu, Y., Z. Zhang, C. Jin, A. Zhou, and Y. Yan. "SEBDB: Semantics Empowered Blockchain Database." *2019 IEEE 35th International Conference on Data Engineering (ICDE)*, IEEE, 2019, pp. 1820–1831.

[78] Rehman, M., N. Javaid, M. Awais, M. Imran, and N. Naseer. "Cloud Based Secure Service Providing for IoTs Using Blockchain." *2019 IEEE Global Communications Conference (GLOBECOM)*, IEEE, 2019, pp. 1–7.

[79] Sanka, A. I., and R. C. Cheung. "Efficient High Performance FPGA Based NoSQL Caching System for Blockchain Scalability and Throughput Improvement." *2018 26th International Conference on Systems Engineering (ICSEng)*, IEEE, 2018, pp. 1–8.

[80] Sakakibara, Y., S. Morishima, K. Nakamura, and H. Matsutani. "A Hardware-Based Caching System on FPGA NIC for Blockchain." *IEICE Transactions on Information and Systems* 101(5) (2018): 1350–1360.

[81] Cui, H., Z. Chen, N. Liu, and B. Xia. "Blockchain-Driven Contents Sharing Strategy for Wireless Cache-Enabled D2D Networks." *2019 IEEE International Conference on Communications Workshops (ICC Workshops)*, IEEE, 2019, pp. 1–5.

[82] Moghimi, A., J. Wichelmann, T. Eisenbarth, and B. Sunar. "MemJam: A False Dependency Attack Against Constant-Time Crypto Implementations." *International Journal of Parallel Programming* 47(4) (2019): 538–570.

Chapter 4

Machine learning algorithms for Big Data analytics including deep learning

Shaveta Malik[1], Amit Kumar Tyagi[2] and Rohit Sahoo[1]

Abstract

Owing to recent development in technology, major changes have been noticed in human being's life. Today's lives of human being are becoming more convenient (i.e., in terms of living standard). In current real-world applications, we have shifted our attention from wired devices to wireless devices. As a result, we moved into the era of smart technology, where a lot of Internet devices are connected together in a distributed and decentralized manner. Such Internet-connected devices (ICDs) or Internet of Things (IoTs) engender tremendous data (i.e., via communicating other smart devices). With the tremendous increase in the amount of data, there is a higher requirement to process this huge amount of data (generated through billions of ICDs) using efficient machine learning (ML) algorithms.

In the past decade, we refer data mining algorithms to make some decision from collected data-sets. But, due to increasing data on a large scale, data mining fail to handle this data. So, as substitute of data mining algorithms and to refine this information in an efficient manner, we require tradition analytics algorithms, i.e., ML or data mining algorithms. In current scenario, some of the ML algorithms (available to analysis this data) are supervised (used with labeled data), unsupervised (used with unlabelled data) and semi-supervised (work as reward-based learning). Supervised learning algorithms are like linear regression, classification and k-nearest neighbor (KNN), etc. Whereas, unsupervised learning algorithms are clustering, k-means, etc. In general, ML focuses on building the systems that learn and hence improves with the knowledge and experience. Being the heart of artificial intelligence (AI) and data science, ML is gaining popularity day by day. Several algorithms have already been developed (in the past decade) for processing of data, although this field focuses on developing new learning algorithm for big data computability with minimum complexity (i.e., in terms of time and space). ML algorithms are not only applicable to computer science field but also extend to medical, psychological, marketing, manufacturing, automobile, etc.

[1]Department of Computer Engineering, Terna Engineering College, India
[2]School of Computer Science and Engineering, Vellore Institute of Technology, Chennai, India

On another side, Big Data including deep learning are the two primary and highly demandable fields of data science. A subset of ML, computer vision or AI, deep learning is used here. The large (or massive) amount of data related to a specific domain which forms Big Data (in form of 5 V's like velocity, volume, value, variety, and veracity) contains valuable information related to various fields like marketing, automobile, finance, cyber security, medical, fraud detection, etc. Such real-world applications are creating a lot of information every day. The valuable (i.e., needful or meaningful) information are required to be processed (or retrieved) from analysis of this unstructured/ large amount of data for further processing of the data for future use (or for prediction). Big organizations have to accord with the tremendous volume of data for prediction, classification, decision making, etc. The use of ML algorithms for big data analytics, which extracts the high-level semantics from the valuable (meaningful) information form the data. It uses hierarchical process for efficient processing and retrieving the complex abstraction from the data.

Hence, this chapter discusses several algorithms of ML, to analysis of Big Data. Also, the subset AI like ML algorithms, deep learning algorithms are being discussed here (i.e., to analysis this Big Data for efficient prediction). Later, this chapter focuses on benefits of ML, deep learning algorithms in analyzing tremendous volume of data (i.e., in unsupervised or unstructured form) for numerous complex problems like information retrieval, medical diagnosis, cognitive science, indexing using semantic analysis, data tagging, speech recognition, natural language processing, etc. Also, weakness, raised issues, and challenges (during analysis big data) using (in) ML or deep learning have been discussed in detail. In other words, research gaps in using ML, deep learning algorithms for big data will also be discussed (covering future research aspects/trends). Finally, this chapter discusses the significance of the smart era, computational intelligence, and AI in depth.

Keywords: Machine learning algorithms; Big Data analytics; Real-world problems; Advanced analytics

4.1   Introduction

In recent decades, because of advancements in Web technology, social networking sites, and phone and computing devices, data is now exploding at an unparalleled pace. Twitter, for instance, handles more than 70 million tweets each day, resulting in a daily data volume of more than 8 terabytes. In areas as diverse as medical services, engineering, logistics, digital marketing, energy storage, and banking, Big Data has immense potential in terms of business impact. Data analytics aims to find underlying functional trends and give insights to help with choice and performance improvement. Machine Learning (ML), on the other hand, adds techniques to big data analytics that allow computers to dynamically extract meaningful connections and learn and develop from previous experiences in order to foresee the future without being explicitly programmed. According to the McKinsey Global Institute, ML will be a crucial driver in the Era of technological revolution of big data [1].

Advanced analytical techniques must be applied to tremendous, compound data sets in order to engender valuable analysis and insights. Big Data analysis is a rapidly expanding field of research which involves capturing, storing, and analyzing tremendous data sets in order to find previously undiscovered patterns, as well as other pertinent information. Big Data research allows us to classify data that will be critical in strategic business decisions. Banks and insurance providers, as well as medical services, education, social networking sites, media, and bioinformatics, will all benefit from big data research. Managing massive data with standard data processing software is a significant challenge. The majority of traditional ML methods were created for data sets that could be completely stored in memory [2]. As the volume of data expands by the day, many efficient learning algorithms are being used to deliver solutions to big data predictive analytics problems.

4.1.1   Machine Learning (ML)

Even if you are not aware of it, ML is being utilized in your daily life. The quantity of data arriving will not diminish, and being able to make sense of all this data will be a vital ability for individuals working in a data-driven business. In ML, you look at the data instance. Each data instance is made up of many characteristics. Classification, a well-known and important ML job, is used to place an unknown piece of data for which you know the class. This information is referred to as your training set. People will be able to receive treatment more quickly if we develop software that can mimic a human doctor. Better weather forecasting might lead to fewer water shortages and a more plentiful food supply. There are several such scenarios in which ML could be useful.

ML is a subpart of Artificial Intelligence (AI). There are a number of applications of ML in day-to-day life. Due to its integration in various applications, ML has reached almost every research field and has significantly influenced science and human development [3]. ML application learns through experience; it has the capability to familiarize with new data independently. The application learns from past experiences, and the ML algorithm recognizes patterns to produce the output. For example, in [4], Google utilizes ML algorithms to process enormous amounts of unstructured data acquired from the Web for Google Assistant, Google Image Search, Google Maps, and Google Translate. Unsupervised learning, supervised learning, and reinforcement learning are the three forms of ML.

4.1.1.1   Types of ML

The types are divided into the two categories clustering and classification (refer Figure 4.1).

(a) *Supervised learning:* It is based on the classification technique which classifies the data. It is based on the labels. It uses the past data or previous experience for prediction, in which output data is known. As the name

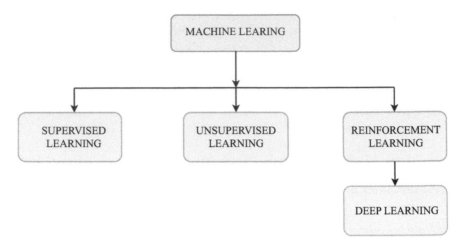

Figure 4.1   ML categories

suggests, it indicates the supervision or teacher, in which we train the machine with labels then supervised learning algorithm analyses the training data and produces the output. For example.

- If you have a basket of fruit and you have number of fruits then train the machine with different kinds of fruit with label data.
- If the shape of the fruit is round and color is red then it is labeled as Apple.
- If the object is long curve and cylindrical and its color is green yellow then it is Banana.

Machine will classify the data or fruits with different size, shape, and color and machines learn from training data and then apply what they have learned to test data.

Supervised learning is divided into two types:

- Classification
- Regression

Each term can be discussed as:

- *Classification*: It is based on classifying the data into the category e.g., disease and non-disease. The classification method is a feature that allows the dataset to be divided into groups according to various parameters. The training dataset is used in classification categorizes the data into different groups. The classifying algorithm aims to find the mapping to map the input (x) to the distinct output variable (y). Example: E-mail spam detection is the best example for understanding the classification problem. The model is trained based on millions of e-mails with various parameters, and it can identify whether the e-mails are spam or not until a new email is received. If spam is an e-mail, it is transferred to the spam folder.

- *Regression:* It is a technique for determining the connections between dependent and independent variables. It aids in the forecasting of continuous variables. Regression predictive modeling is the process of estimating a mapping function (f) from input variables (x) to a continuous output variable (y). To forecast the weather, for example, use the regression method. When it comes to weather prediction, the model is trained on past data and, once completed, it can anticipate the weather for the following few days correctly.

(b) *Unsupervised leaning*: It is based on the technique of clustering patterns which makes cluster based on the patterns and no label data is present in it. No supervision or teacher is provided and no training is provided to the machine. It deals with finding the pattern in a collection of uncategorized data. For example, suppose we have data of dog and cat and machine has no idea about the features of dog and cat or about the data and in this we cannot categorize into cat and dog. The data categorize into the similarities and patterns.

(c) *Reinforcement learning:* It is basically based on the reward or criticism. Initially this technique is developed for the machines to learn for games that is based on the moves when the move is right then the machine is rewarded else it may be reprimanded. Machine will start differentiating the right and left move. To improve the accuracy, increase the number of iterations, it will also help to learn the machine more precisely. For example, if we are going to train a pet or dog to catch the ball and bring a ball to us, if the dog or pet brings the ball to us then we will give reward to dog and if the dog not does not do the right job, then we will not give the reward to dog. Slowly the dog learns that if he is doing the right thing then we give him reward otherwise we are not giving him reward.

4.1.2 Deep learning

Deep learning a subdivision of ML and it is built on the artificial neural network (ANN) that is convolutional neural network and it is poised of many layers. It extracts the higher-level features. Deep learning is a technology behind the driverless car that can identify the signs, etc., in which the number of the layers will be more and it can classify the data through classification whether it is text, images or sound. Deep learning model will train with large dataset or labeled data and with large number of layers.

Why deep learning is useful?

- Due to greater processing power, it necessitates GPUs, which are potent for deep learning, and when combined with cloud computing, the time is reduced from weeks to hours or even minutes.
- It requires large amount of data or labeled data.

How deep learning works?

It works on neural network architecture, most of the deep learning methods uses neural network architectures. The term "deep" in deep learning refers to a network's hidden layers. It can be of 100 or 150 or more, in which we do not need to extract or give features separately. In neural network architecture, features can be easily extracted. In CNN or Conv Net that is the popular deep learning model in which features can be extracted automatically, CNN learns features from input data. So, there is no need to extract features manually. Automatically feature extraction is more prominent and efficient and that also makes the model definite for computer vision task being recognition, object detection, etc.

How deep learning differs from ML?

- In ML, features are manually retrieved from pictures, but deep learning is only useful when features are automatically extracted. In both cases, classification may be used to categorize the data.
- The deep learning model has the benefit of continually improving accuracy as the size of the data rises.
- In deep learning, the pictures are automatically sorted and the features are extracted, whereas in ML, the images are manually sorted and the features are extracted.
- Deep learning does not require the structure or labeled data of the picture to categorize, but ML does.

In terms of deciding between ML and deep learning, if you have GPUs and a significant amount of labeled data, deep learning should be used; otherwise, ML techniques should be used.

4.1.3   Big Data

It requires large specialized technique to gather, analyze and implement because it is a large amount of the data which is huge in size and eventually growing day by day. Researchers all across the globe use the term "big data," which alludes to astounding datasets. Big data cannot be directed by conventional database systems. Sensors, transactional software, and social networking sites, among other outlets, provide a massive amount of data sets. The importance of Big Data is determined not by the bulk of data collected but by whether it can be processed to improve savings. New product developments and wise judgments can result from solutions [5]. To create and analyze Big Data, technologies such as Spark and Hadoop, as well as methodologies such as data mining, ML, and many others, are employed [6]. To derive accurate results from data analysis is critical for making correct and valuable decisions in a variety of fields.

Big Data refers to enormous quantities of unorganized and organized complicated data that conventional computer systems are incapable of managing. Its goal is to uncover hidden information, and it has encouraged a transition from a framework to an information approach [7]. Gartner describes explicitly the essential characteristics of Big Data [8]. According to its definition, Big Data is a massive amount, elevated, and diverse data resource. This involves new forms of management to enable better decision-making and information sharing. ML and deep learning algorithm can be applied to increase the efficiency and accuracy of the data.

Vs. of Big Data:

- *Volume:* The pile of data that is collected.
- *Velocity:* The pace at which information is processed.
- *Variety:* Data of many types can be collected and processed.
- *Veracity:* The coherence and nature of the data.

1. Volume:

   The "amount" of data generated is described by big data volume. The data volume or size currently exceeds terabytes and petabytes [9]. The size of the data affects its importance. Data is now produced in a variety of formats, both structured and unstructured, from a variety of sources. Word and Excel files, PDFs and reports, as well as media information in the form of images or videos, are examples of data types. Data is increasingly being generated in such large chunks due to the data explosion created by digital and social media has made it difficult for businesses to store and process it using traditional business intelligence and analytics methods.

2. Velocity:

   The pace at which information is produced, processed, analyzed is referred to as velocity. Data is constantly transmitted through many channels, such as computers, networks, social networking sites, and smartphones. These data can be collected in real-time, making the correct data accessible at the right time. Timely and precise business decisions are affected by the speed at which data can easily be accessed.

3. Variety:

   Although data volume and velocity are essential factors in adding value to a company, Big Data often means processing various data types from a variety of sources. Inconsistency and data quality issues are directly related to veracity [10]. Big Data is divided into three categories: structured, semi-structured, and unstructured data. Semi-structured data could only partially comply to a certain data format, whereas structured data has a defined format, length, and volume. Unorganized data is data that does not adhere to conventional data formats. Unstructured data includes photos, videos, tweets, and other data engendered by digital and social media.

4. Veracity:

   The veracity of big data, also known as validity, is a guarantee of the exactitude or legitimacy of the acquired data. Because big data is so enormous and encompasses so many sources of information, it's conceivable that not all of the data obtained is of decent value or reliable. As a result, while working with big data sets, it is necessary to double-check the data's provenance before proceeding.

Big Data analytics tools:

(a) *Apache Hadoop:*

   It is a distributed open-source platform for accumulating and processing tremendous data volumes. Hadoop allows for the parallel processing of

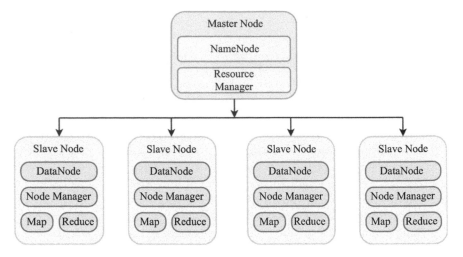

Figure 4.2   Hadoop architecture

massive data sets in a distributed fashion. Hadoop is a low-cost method for storing vast amounts of data that does not require any format.

Hadoop architecture: Hadoop architecture is a master–slave architecture (refer Figure 4.2). The NameNode is the master, and DataNodes are the slaves. The NameNode manages clients' access to the data. The DataNodes are in charge of data management on the active nodes. Hadoop divides the data across one or more blocks, which are then stored in DataNodes. To ensure Hadoop's high availability, each data block is distributed across several DataNodes. The JobTracker is in charge of arranging customer work. JobTracker generates a map, reduces assignments, and assigns them to data nodes (TaskTrackers). TaskTrackers is a program that operates on DataNodes. TaskTracker's role is to run the map and minimize the task allocated by NameNode and communicate the task's status to the NameNode.

The hardware implementation of the master/slave Apache framework includes the following components:

1.   Hadoop common: It includes Hadoop libraries that are utilized by other Hadoop modules.
2.   HDFS: It is referred to as Hadoop Distributed File System. It is a java-based distributed file system for storing massive amounts of data.
3.   Hadoop YARN: It offers resource control and a central forum for Hadoop clusters to provide coherent processes, stability, and governance resources.
4.   MapReduce: It is a computational method for large-scale data collection and analysis.

(b) *Apache Spark:*

Apache spark has been developed for rapid computing, fast lightning technology. The article was posted by the AMPLab at the University of California, Berkeley [11] in April 2012 (first studies were carried out as early as 2010) presenting the concept of the Spark Framework, which is an implementation of RDD. It is based on Hadoop MapReduce and improves the MapReduce architecture to allow for more competent and expeditious computations.

Spark enables Hadoop clusters to accomplish programs 100 times expeditiously in RAM and ten times speedier on disc. Spark would do this by decreasing the number of reading and writing discs required. The data from the transitional processing is kept in memory. It uses the resilient distributed dataset (RDD) approach, which allows it to maintain data in memory discreetly and preserve it on disc only when necessary. RDD is a segmented data set, which implies that individual components of a compendium may be split and processed in parallel by cluster nodes [12]. This speed up data transmission by reducing the number of discs reads and writes, which are the most time-consuming aspects.

Apache Spark is a Hadoop-based framework that can be used as standalone or in the cloud. It can also get data from various places, such as HDFS, Cassandra, HBase, and S3. The primary feature of Apache Spark is in-memory cluster computing, which accelerates the processing performance of an application. Spark is a programming framework that allows whole programming clusters to have innate data parallelism and fault tolerance.

ML applications for big data: There are several applications of machine learning exists which can be listed here as:

- *Web scraping*

  Consider what a designer of kitchen appliances can derive from a retailer's quarterly surveys on industry dynamics and consumer loyalty trends. The producer decides to web-scrape the vast volume of current data about online user comments and product ratings to figure out what the papers may have missed. The maker learns how to refine and better explain its goods by aggregating this data and feeding it into a deep-learning algorithm. This leads to improved revenue.

- *Systems for a mixed-initiative approach*

  The Netflix recommendation engine, which offers movies on your profile page, uses collaborative filtering: machine-learning algorithms are used to predict what you should watch subsequently, and big data is being used to map your (and everyone else's) experience. This example shows how big data and ML collide in the realm of mixed-initiative schemes or human–computer encounters whose outcomes are determined by whether humans or machines take the initiative.

  In the ML-based systems that power the cars of smart-car manufacturers Big Data and deep learning are utilized as well. Tesla vehicles, for example, use data to make algorithm-based decisions to interact with their drivers and respond to external stimuli.

Now the organization of this work is as follows:
This chapter is organized further as:

Section 4.2 will discuss about the related work.
Section 4.3 will discuss the motivation behind this chapter.
Section 4.4 will discuss the importance of Big Data in near future.
Section 4.5 will discuss the benefits of ML and deep learning in Big Data analytics.
Section 4.6 will discuss about the weaknesses of ML, deep learning algorithms during Big Data analysis.
Section 4.7 will discuss critical issues in Big Data analytics.
Section 4.8 will discuss challenges faced by the users and organization.
Section 4.9 will discuss the future research directions in Big Data analytics.
Section 4.10 will discuss about the conclusion of the chapter.

4.2   Related work

Data mining

Data mining is based primarily on the application of methods and algorithms for discovering and extracting patterns from stored data, but data must be pre-processed before this stage [13].

The word "data mining" was coined in the 1990s, but data mining is the progression of a long-standing industry. Two early techniques for identifying patterns in outcomes include the Bayes theorem (from the 1700s) and the evolution of regression (1800s). Computer science's creation and rising efficiency has enhanced data gathering, retention, and exploitation as data sets have expanded in size and complexity. Passive, automated data processing, as well as other ML breakthroughs such as neural networks, clustering, evolutionary algorithms (in the 1950s), decision trees (in the 1960s), and supporting vector machines, have steadily enhanced comprehensive practical data study (1990s).

ML-based analytics

People are increasingly waking up to the reality that robots can now implement complex mathematical computations to domains such as big data at a far rapid pace. Google Car, for example, is mainly based on the core of AI. Another major use of ML may be seen in the frequent suggestions made by firms such as Netflix and Amazon – an application of ML in daily situations. Following that, ML may be coupled with the development of language rules. Twitter has adopted this application, and we will be able to see what consumers are saying about us.

Figure 4.3 describes scenarios from previous century to current century of ML.

Deep learning-based analytics

Moreover this, deep learning is being popular post 2000s/twentieth century in many applications. Today's deep learning use has been increased in many useful and critical applications like biomedical imaging, HealthCare for disease detection, etc.

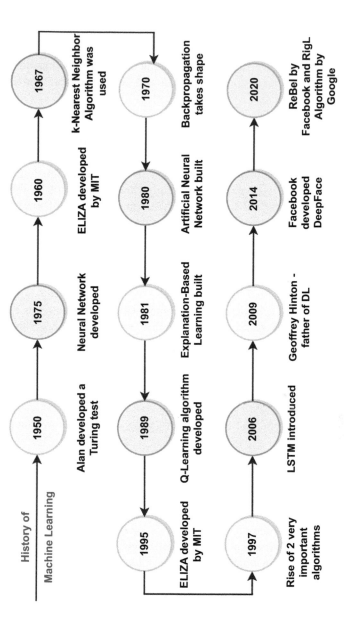

Figure 4.3   History of ML

Automotive Big Data analytics

It is a type of AI-based data analytics, which will be a trend in near future.

4.3 Motivation

The scope of this work/chapter is beyond traditional and modern big data analytics process. This chapter provides a complete detail and comprehensive knowledge about future data analytics also.

4.4 Importance of Big Data analytics in near future

These days, data is growing exponentially not only in the same dimension but in multiple dimensions. There will be Big Data everywhere which will be there to gather the insight from it and hence help everyone in their field of work be it doctors, engineers, scientists, military, etc. Big data analyst will be looking for the feature abstractions from the big data to make the representations for the predictive outcomes for the same. Hence, big data processing can be used in various applications which can be discussed as stated in the following sections:

(a) In the public sector:

Ministries, regardless of nation, are confronted with massive amounts of data on a regular basis. This is due to the fact that they must maintain track of numerous documents and databases pertaining to their population, their growth, natural resources, geographical studies, and many other things. All of this information contributes to big data. With the impact of Big Data technology on society acknowledged, governments all over the world are increasingly investing heavily in Big Data programs [14]. As a result, effective research and analysis of this data benefits governments in a plethora of ways. Here are a few examples:

Welfare programs
1. Making quicker and more accurate judgments on various political initiatives.
2. Identifying issues that require quick attention.
3. Keeping track of all available property and cattle in order to stay current in the agricultural sector.
4. To solve societal issues such as unemployment, insurgency, and the development of renewable energy sources, among others.

Cyber security
1. Big Data is often utilized in the detection of deception.
2. It is also utilized to catch tax cheats or money launderers.
3. In the field of security, analytics help in collecting large volumes of online data in order to examine, interpret, and develop conclusions that might help detect and prevent cyber threats.

Defense

1. The capacity to analyze, integrate, and act on the revelations big data may give turns into tactical expertise that saves lives during actual battle.
2. The advantages of obtaining and analyzing pictures and video recorded by aerial (drone) sensing devices that can track and conduct surveillance over vast regions, such as metropolitan zones, are enormous.

(b) In the world of entertainment and media:

With people having access to various digital gadgets, generation of large amount of data is inevitable and this is the main cause of the rise in big data in media and entertainment industry. The primary business issues that media companies are exploring Big Data are the need to minimize operational costs in the increasingly competitive environment and, at the same time, to increase revenue from content and data delivery through different product platforms [15].

Some of the benefits extracted from Big Data in the media and entertainment industry are given below:

1. Predicting what audiences are interested in.
2. In digital entertainment marketplaces, optimized or on-demand scheduling of streaming services.
3. Obtaining information from customer reviews.
4. Advertisements that are effectively targeted.
5. Businesses can predict when consumers are likely to see material and what platform they will use to do it.
6. Firms can design the best marketing and merchandise campaigns to grow and keep customers by leveraging Big Data to understand why people buy and cancel.

(c) In the field of medicine:

Healthcare is yet another industry which is bound to generate a huge amount of data. Big Data analysis may play an essential role in solving the problems associated with mining knowledge in the area of treatment, emphasizing improvements to make medical treatments healthy, quick, cost-effective, and reliable [16].

Some of the ways in which Big Data has contributed to healthcare:

1. Big Data lowers medical expenses because it eliminates the need for unneeded diagnostics.
2. It aids in the prediction of contagious diseases as well as the determination of countermeasures that might be implemented to mitigate the consequences of the very same.
3. It aids in the prevention of avoidable diseases by recognizing them in their early phases.
4. It keeps them from becoming severe, making therapy easier and more effective.
5. Patients can be given scientific proof medication that has been identified and recommended by doing study on previous medical findings.

(d)   In the transportation industry

Since the rise of Big Data, it has been used in various ways to make transportation more efficient and easier.

Some of the areas where Big Data contributes to transportation.

1.   *Route selection:*

Big Data may be utilized to analyze and predict users' demands on various routes and means of transportation, and then route selection could also be used to decrease their waiting period.

2.   *Congestion control and traffic management:*

Real-time assessment of massive traffic patterns is now feasible because to Big Data. People, for instance, are utilizing Google Maps to find the least congested ways to reach destination.

3.   *The traffic safety level:*

Using real-time big data processing and predictive analytics to identify crash-prone locations can assist in reducing fatalities and increasing road safety.

(e)   In logistics

Companies, including the logistics sector, need to use dedicated tools called Big Data analytics, for the efficient and rapid management and analysis of large data to deal with the large data generated by road and vehicle sensors, GPS devices, customer applications, and websites [17].

Some of the areas where Big Data analytics contribute to logistics:

1.   *Visibility of the supply chain*

Data analytics is one such technique that aids in the real-time tracking of goods and equipment. One can control and monitor automobiles and keep track of shipments from the manufacturing process to the last mile delivery of products—continuous system tracking results in enhanced distribution and shipment status.

2.   *Predictive analytics*

One of the significant implications of data analytics in logistics is predicted to be predictive analysis. Companies can now research and analyze computer behavior patterns, which can then be used to identify anomalies. Organizations have control over the changes in behavior that prevent computers from working correctly. This means that businesses can use predictive analysis to help detect and react to events such as weather changes.

3.   *Route optimization*

The route optimization method is used to find the most efficient path from site a to site b. This reduces the time required to deliver a package while improving the efficiency of the system. The same can be said for logistics route optimization. Obtaining information from a variety of sources resulted in a large amount of data. The GPS, climate, fleet details, and timely delivery contribute to the system that predicts the best delivery path.

(f)   Energy and utilities

The energy and utility industry are generally made up of power plants that produce energy, which is subsequently transferred over cables and eventually distributed to households and workplaces via transmission lines.

The energy and utility industries are witnessing a massive revolution as a result of technology such as data analytics. Grids are becoming intelligent with each day, thanks to advanced analytics. Power generation sources are becoming healthier, and users have more options for receiving electricity. The rise of Big Data technologies, which play critical roles in the business, has become one of the technical forces that has influenced this.

Some of the ways in which Big Data has contributed to energy and utilities:

1.   *Power generation planning:*

Utility companies may use analytics to improve power planning and generation. In electricity production, there are two main decision-making processes—energy planning and economical loading. When all data is obtained from many sources, several models will be used to produce power planning on top of these data. This ensures that electricity demand is matched with the optimum grid power supply by cost-saving delivery over a given period.

2.   *Efficient and precise forecasts*:

Data analysis contributes to a precise forecast of energy consumption, which is essential for generating dynamic pricing. Similarly, it plays a crucial role in forecasting energy generation, notably for renewable energy sources from solar and wind sources affected by the changing climate. Data collected from weather systems can be used for predictive analysis.

3.   *Load management that is smart:*

E&U businesses must strategically and intelligently align electricity demand with optimum power supply in a given period to effectively handle energy load. With the aid of distributed energy sources, automated control systems, and end-use applications, they will cover the end-to-end network management needs, including demand and energy sources, with an intelligent load management framework.

(g)   In the retail business

Through means of forecasting analytics, retailers have benefited in comparison to those companies which do not employ marketing and additional sales by 75% and the "retail sector" is now active and vibrant among company which perform predictive analysis to identify new customers purchasing trends [18].

Some of the ways in which Big Data has contributed to retail industry:

1.   *Making recommendations:*

Based on past orders, retailers can predict what a customer will buy next. Retailers may make specific recommendations using ML models that have been trained on historical data.

2. *Policymaking:*
   Businesses should combine data to make intelligent business decisions based on a single, accurate product and customer information source. Business dashboards can provide a high standard picture of key competitive performance metrics such as promotion of price and movement of catalogues.
3. *Trend foreseeing:*
   Retailers can consider how economic and demographic factors are used to meet consumer demands.
4. *Use of market basket analysis:*
   The consumer basket study, a standard methodology used by retailers, helps determine what items consumers are most likely to buy together. Retailers can now evaluate additional data using Hadoop.
5. *Pricing optimization:*
   Big stores, such as Walmart, spend much money on retail merchandising programs. Walmart is now operating a private cloud that monitors millions of transactions every day. Stocks, rivals, and demand can be tracked, and market shifts can be automatically responded to.
6. *Trends forecast:*
   Marketers use what is known as feeling research to predict trends. Advanced ML algorithms are used to assess the context. The collected data can then be used to forecast best-selling products for a specific category.
7. *Consumer experience improvement:*
   Retail analyses are now used to predict customer demand and deliver a smooth customer experience. This would increase the experience and loyalty of the customer.

(h) In finance/banking sector
   The amount of data in the banking sector is skyrocketing every second. According to GDC prognosis, this data is estimated to grow 700% by the end of the next year. Analysts in the financial sector identify Big Data as a means to enable an enterprise in a specific period of creating, manipulating, and managing very massive datasets and storing data to accommodate a range, amount, and speed of data [19]. Proper study and analysis of this data can help detect any and all illegal activities that are being carried out such as:
1. *Insights on the stock market in real time:*
   Analytics is transforming commerce and investing. Rather than studying stock prices, Big Data may now consider economic and societal factors that may affect the stock market. Analytics tracks patterns in real time, making analysts able to gather and analyze relevant reports and process informed judgments.
2. *Investigation and avoidance of fraud:*
   Advanced analytics, powered by Big Data, plays a key role in fraud identification and avoidance. Bank account security threats have been

reduced through analysis tools that evaluate purchasing trends. When sensitive and critical credit card account is hacked, banks can immediately suspend the card and transactions and warn the consumer of security risks.

3. *Risk assessment that is precise:*
   Large financial choices, such as commercial loans, are now based on impartial advanced analytics. Predictive analytics-based choices consider from the economy, market characteristics, and company finance to detect possible hazards like as speculative investments or debtors.

(i) In education:
   Some of the sectors in the educational business that are being altered by advanced analytics innovations include as follows:
   1. Personalized and adaptive teaching programs: Using information acquired from each learner's studying experience, personalized programs and strategies to assist specific learners may be built. This massively increases learner performance.
   2. Re-forming course content: Re-forming the lesson plan based on insights obtained over what a learners know and to what degree real-time tracking of lesson elements is helpful to learners.
   3. Assessment algorithms: As a consequence of effective advanced analytics, new improvements in assessment algorithms have been created to prevent deception.
   4. Profession prognosis: Thorough examination and research of each individual's data will aid in understanding each person's development, skills, limitations, passions, and other characteristics. This would also aid in choosing which professional path might be best for the individual in the class. By adding to e-learning options, advanced analytics-based applications have given a remedy to more serious flaws in the educational system: the general-purpose academic setup.

   According to International Data Corporation (IDC), businesses who engage in these technologies and achieve the ability to evaluate huge volumes of data rapidly and retrieve relevant insights may gain an additional 430 billion dollars in efficiency advantages over their competition. As a result, this article examines the relevance of data analytics in the near future, with examples such as looking at the people on Netflix or online gaming platform. The next part will go through some of the most important and beneficial advantages of ML and deep learning algorithms in Big Data analytics.

4.5 Benefits of Machine Learning and deep learning algorithms in Big Data analytics

The term of Big Data is generally defining the large volume of data that is growing exponentially. Among various data building all possible relations data analytics generally extract the useful information such as hidden patterns, market trends, etc.

Big Data simply manages huge data, and ML is used to train machines by providing datasets, which aids in prediction and problem solving, decision making, etc.

ML algorithms have the ability to learn from experience and past (with human intervention) and make learning better and better for future generations. So various benefits of ML in the twenty-first century will be like fraud detection in banks, consumption or demand of a product over a season or by a particular area, detecting cyber vulnerabilities, suggesting various innovative and creative applications for making people life easier and longer to live.

Benefits of ML in Big Data analytics

As stated in previous section, Big Data has many uses nowadays in a variety of sectors. Among the applications include social media analytics, banking and utilities, and so on.

- Future trends marketing: ML algorithm helps in to analyze the big data or large amount of data and predict the future trends. ML make the machines interconnected with large data and acquire things on their own. For example, Geyser manufacturing company may analyze the future sale or demand in next year by using the Big Data and ML algorithm for prediction. Based on current data, required number of fridge or geyser will be in particular numbers (approximately).
- Workforce improvement: By using the big data analytics and ML algorithm, we are decreasing the workforce as most of the work is done by the AI machines and robot but still, we need the humans because machines have lack of sentiments and emotions. Human can also analyze the market trends or market condition in various parts of the world.
- Big Data in healthcare: There is sample data in the healthcare. Through big data and ML algorithm we can predict the disease at early stage and recognize or predict the disease through past health reports or lab reports. The impact of data cannot be ignored as the data is increasing day by day eventually, we are managing the data but we have to manage more in future. By analyzing the data, we are predicting the adopting the new strategy and ML algorithms are managing data and help in grow business.
- Deep learning algorithms on Big Data analytics: Analysis and learning of large amount of data or unsupervised data make it an appreciated tool for big data and that is a benefit of deep learning. Deep learning is used in many big data problems, for example, extracting complex patterns from large amount of data, information. Deep learning algorithms are used on big data to learn from large amount of data using unsupervised learning in faster and efficient manner.

In Big Data analytics, decision making and prediction with large dataset are very precarious, there are some challenges such as fast-moving streaming data and imbalanced input data.

- Semantic Indexing: In massive data analytics, retrieving information and storing it efficiently is a major issue. For example, textual, imagery, multimedia, and sound. Semantic indexing is a useful approach for enabling data analysis and making search engines more effective and quicker.

- Conducting discriminative task: In big data analytics, learning algorithm permits to extract the non-linear features and while extracting feature with deep learning can add non-linearly to the data analysis, it is more efficient computationally and it is beneficial for big data because the complicated task because easily such as object recognition, image comprehension.
- Semantic image and video tagging: Deep learning is used in semantic tagging and it is a process which can simplifies segmentation and mark complex image scene. It uses independent variant analysis. This approach is used in discriminative task a data of video and image.

As a result, the benefits of ML in Big Data analytics are discussed in this section. Now next section will discuss about weaknesses identified in ML techniques.

4.6 Weaknesses identified in (of) Machine Learning, deep learning algorithms during analysis of Big Data

Categorizing or classifying the ML algorithm is tricky, there are many reasonable approaches and grouped into descriptive and non-descriptive and parametric and non-parametric, supervised and unsupervised and so on.

ML: It is difficult to choose the algorithm to specific problem, we cannot say which algorithm is best for any specific problem, not one algorithm is best for every problem.

Neural network is not best for every problem, we cannot say neural network is best as compared to decision tree, etc., because there are number of factors like size of dataset, etc. So, you should try different algorithm for different problem to evaluate the performance.

We will cover the difficulties and discuss what are the problems we are facing. Few weaknesses are listed here as:

1. Regression
2. Classification
3. Clustering

1. *Regression:*
    It does not perform well when non-linear relation will follow and it is not comfortable and flexible to solve many complex patterns. So, if the number of interactions is more than it can be trickier and time consuming. For example, regression tree. The individual tree keeps branches and it is easily prone to over fitting problem for example, random forest, decision tree.
    - Deep learning:
        For general purpose, algorithm deep learning algorithms are not suitable because they need large amount of data. They require more expert to train, for example, architecture.
    - K-NN (nearest neighbor):
        Due to high-dimensional data, these algorithms cannot work because it requires a distance function to find out the similarity.

2. *Classification:*

It is supervised task or technique, for example, e-mail-spam, final fraud, etc.

- Logistic regression:

It is not capable to handle multiple relationship or more complex relationship, for example, non-linear decision boundaries.

- Deep learning:

It is very well in classifying audio, images and text but it requires lot of data to train.

- Support vector machine (SVM):

It does not scale on large scale of dataset, it is trickier to adjust because of the selection of right kernel.

- Naïve Bayes:

This algorithm is difficult to beat by properly trained algorithm as compared to previously used algorithm.

3. *Clustering:*

It is based on the unsupervised learning and it is for finding and grouping, for example clusters.

- K-means clustering:

In which user can define the cluster but sometimes it is not easy every time, sometime it may produce bad clusters.

The difficulties of deep learning with Big Data:

1. Non-stationary data: Dealing with streaming data and extracting usable information from it, such as fraud detection, is a major issue in big data analytics. Here the deep learning algorithm is helpful in solving these kinds of problems as deep learning work on hidden layers and can extract the features automatically.
2. High-dimensional data: Most of the deep learning algorithm gives a degraded performance while dealing with high dimensional data due to slow learning such as images, etc. The high dimensionality of the data increases the volume of the data to multi-folds.
3. Large-scale models: Most of the algorithms fail to extract the features from the large volume of data they can utilize the large-scale models with a number of GPU, etc., to do a parallel processing and hence can be able to extract a large number of features

Hence, this section describes the weaknesses of ML, deep learning algorithms during Big Data analysis.

4.7   Critical issues raised during Big Data analytics

As discussed earlier, Big Data analytics effectively assists businesses in becoming more successful. This contributes to the company's earnings increasing. Big Data analytics solutions such as Hadoop aid in lowering storage costs. This improves the operational productivity even more. On the other side, there are several critical issues towards Big Data analytics:

- *Lack of resources*: The size of business organizations is increasingly increasing. As companies and major business organizations have expanded, the amount of data produced has skyrocketed. Keeping track of such a large amount of data is becoming a significant challenge for everyone. Data lakes and warehouses are common storing data solutions for maintaining huge amounts of unstructured and structured data in its native format. Data redundancy, inaccurate data, logical incompatibilities, and superfluous data can cause data accuracy challenges when a data lake or warehouse seeks to aggregate unstructured and dispersed information from diverse sources.
- *Lack of skilled people:* Data processing is essential for making sense of the vast amount of data produced every minute. With the exponential development in data, the industry desperately needs big data scientists and analysts. Since a data scientist's job is multidisciplinary, companies must hire someone with diverse skills. A shortage of professionals familiar with Big Data analytics is another major problem that businesses face. In comparison to the large amount of data produced, data scientists are in short supply.
- *Data is too large*: Among the biggest serious issues with Big Data is properly handling all of these huge amounts of data. The amount of data stored in storage systems and corporate databases is growing drastically. The management of large data sets gets increasingly difficult as they grow significantly with duration. The great majority of data is unstructured and originates from a multitude of different, including documents, pictures, sound, text documents, and other content. Unexpectedly, data is increasing with each day. This implies that firms should engage with a large amount of data on a daily basis. The quantity and diversity of data available today will confound any data engineer.
- *Data protection and confidentiality:* When a business understands about using data analytics, it opens up a whole new realm of opportunities and prospects. Nevertheless, it also includes the potential dangers associated with massive data of data safety and security. Big Data tools are processed and information are stored from diverse sources. As a result, the danger of data exposure is considerably increased, making it vulnerable. As a corollary, the rising amounts of information raises concerns about confidentiality.

Privacy and trust will be the biggest challenge in near future, with almost every applications/ technology.

4.8 Challenges faced by Users/Organization (with respect to Big Data Analytics)

Big data faces a variety of problems in addition to the four Vs. Validation, data cleaning, data consistency, feature optimization, high-throughput data sampling, data visualization, distributed and parallel data collection, real-time monitoring, decision making, data discovery, and heterogeneous data integration are just a few of the significant issues.

The premise behind ML is that algorithms can understand more from much more data and provide more favorable returns [20]. Enormous datasets, on the other end, provide a number of challenges since traditional algorithms are incapable of meeting such expectations. Several ML methods, for instance, were designed with the assumption that the full dataset could be stored in memory. A further assumption is that the entire dataset is accessible for computation at the data pre-processing stage. Big Data defines these expectations, making standard algorithms obsolete or significantly slowing them down [21,22]. As a corollary of the rise of Data Analytics, new technologies and enterprises arise on a daily basis. Businesses in the Advanced Analytics industry, on the other hand, present a substantial difficulty in choosing which technique is most suited to their needs without adding new issues or risks.

4.9   Future research directions (with respect to Big Data analytics, Machine Learning and deep learning algorithms)

Since the deep learning algorithms that deal with big data analytics are evolving and maturing, hence all the relevant features pertaining to big data are not captured while dealing with big data analytics. Furthermore, the main challenge that faces Big Data analysts is determining what is the proper volume of data that must be used for training of the models in order to gain the exact insight from the data that is available and to forecast the rest of the data. Criteria to obtain the good data abstraction and representation out of the volume of data.

4.10   Conclusion

We reach to a conclusion that there are several benefits of big data and its processing which are included here as:

- Gathering data from numerous sources, such as the Internet, social networking websites, online purchasing pages, and business records.
- Real-time forecasting of the company and demand.
- Identifying key points embedded in massive datasets to affect business decisions.
- Mitigating risks as much as possible by making complex decisions in the event of unexpected incidents or attacks.
- Identifying problems in real-time in applications and business processes.
- Collecting consumer information to create personalized goods, programs, offers, and discounts, among other things.
- Allowing for the rapid delivery of products/services that meet or exceed the customer's standards.
- Responding to customer requests, questions, and inquiries in real-time.
- Creating innovative business models, as well as new products and services.

References

[1] M. James, C. Michael, B. Brad, and B. Jacques, "Big Data: The Next Frontier for Innovation, Competition, and Productivity," The McKinsey Global Institute, 2011.

[2] X. W. Chen and X. Lin, "Big Data Deep Learning: Challenges and Perspectives," *IEEE Access*, 2, 514–525, 2014, doi: 10.1109/access.2014.2325029.

[3] C. Rudin and K. L. Wagstaff, "Machine Learning for Science and Society." *Mach Learn,* 95, 1–9, 2014, https://doi.org/10.1007/s10994-013-5425-9.

[4] N. Jones, "Computer Science: The Learning Machines." *Nat News,* 505 (7482), 146, 2014.

[5] S. Kumari and P. Muthulakshmi, "Transformative Effects of Big Data on Advanced Data Analytics: Open Issues and Critical Challenges." *Journal of Computer Science,* 18(6), 463–479, 2022, https://doi.org/10.3844/jcssp.2022.463.479.

[6] I. Yaqoob, I. A. T., A. Gani, *et al.,* "Big Data: From Beginning to Future." *Int J Inf Manage*, 36(6), 1231–1247, 2016.

[7] K. Taylor-Sakyi, "Understanding Big Data," arXiv.org > cs > arXiv1601.04602, January, 166, 2016.

[8] M. Beyer and D. Laney, "The Importance of 'Big Data': A Definition," Gartner, Analysis Report G00235055, 2012. [Online]. Available: https://www.gartner.com/doc/2057415/importance-big-datadefinition [Accessed: 02-Sep-2018].

[9] C. Eaton, D. Deroos, T. Deutsch, G. Lapis and P. C. Zikopoulos, *"Understanding Big Data: Analytics for Enterprise Class Hadoop and Streaming Data,"* McGraw-Hill Companies, 2012, 978-0-07-179053-6.

[10] B. Saha and D. Srivastava, "Data Quality: The Other Face of Big Data," In 2014 IEEE 30th International Conference on Data Engineering, 2014, pp. 1294–1297, doi: 10.1109/ICDE.2014.6816764.

[11] M. Zaharia, M. Chowdhury, T. Das, *et al*, "Resilient Distributed Datasets: A Fault-Tolerant Abstraction for In memory Cluster Computing," In Proceedings of the 9th USENIX Conference on Networked Systems Design and Implementation, USENIX Association, 2012, pp. 2–2. [Online]. Available: http://www.cs.berkeley.edu/~matei/papers/2012/nsdi spark.pdf

[12] B. Kupisz and O. Unold, "Collaborative Filtering Recommendation Algorithm Based on Hadoop and Spark," In 2015 IEEE International Conference on Industrial Technology (ICIT), 2015, pp. 1510–1514, doi: 10.1109/ICIT.2015.7125310.

[13] J. He, "Advances in Data Mining: History and Future," In 2009 Third International Symposium on Intelligent Information Technology Application, 2009, pp. 634–636, doi: 10.1109/IITA.2009.204.

[14] G. Pandula, "New Development: Leveraging 'big data' Analytics in the Public sector," *Public Money Manag*, 36(5), 385–390, 2016.

[15] H. Lippell, "Big Data in the Media and Entertainment Sectors." In *New Horizons for a Data-Driven Economy*, Springer, Cham, 2016, pp. 245–259.

[16]   R. Nambiar, R. Bhardwaj, A. Sethi and R. Vargheese, "A Look at Challenges and Opportunities of Big Data Analytics in Healthcare," In 2013 IEEE International Conference on Big Data, 2013, pp. 17–22, doi: 10.1109/BigData.2013.6691753.

[17]   A. Ben Ayed, M. Ben Halima and A. M. Alimi, "Big Data Analytics for Logistics and Transportation," In 2015 4th International Conference on Advanced Logistics and Transport (ICALT), 2015, pp. 311–316, doi: 10.1109/ICAdLT.2015.7136630.

[18]   N. Verma, D. Malhotra and J. Singh, "Big Data Analytics for Retail Industry Using MapReduce-Apriori Framework," *J Manag Anal*, 7(3), 424–442, 2020, doi: 10.1080/23270012.2020.1728403.

[19]   U. Srivastava and S. Gopalkrishnan, "Impact of Big Data Analytics on Banking Sector: Learning for Indian Banks." *Procedia Comput Sci*, 50, 643–652, 2015.

[20]   K. Grolinger, M. Hayes, W. A. Higashino, A. L'Heureux, D. S. Allison, and M. A. M. Capretz, "Challenges for MapReduce in Big Data." In Proceedings of the 2014 IEEE World Congress on Services (SERVICES), 2014, pp. 182–189.

[21]   A. L'Heureux, K. Grolinger, H. F. Elyamany and M. A. M. Capretz, "Machine Learning with Big Data: Challenges and Approaches," *IEEE Access*, 5, 7776–7797, 2017, doi: 10.1109/ACCESS.2017.2696365.

[22]   S. Mishra, A.K. Tyagi, "The Role of Machine Learning Techniques in Internet of Things-Based Cloud Applications." In: Pal S., De D., Buyya R. (eds) *Artificial Intelligence-based Internet of Things Systems*. Springer, Cham, pp. 105–135, 2022, https://doi.org/10.1007/978-3-030-87059-1_4.

Chapter 5

Machine learning-based blockchain technologies for data storage: challenges, and opportunities

S. Kannadhasan[1], R. Nagarajan[2] and Xiaolei Wang[3]

Abstract

Technical problems have dominated machine learning (ML) research. ML is being increasingly commonly employed in healthcare, and it is assisting patients and physicians in a variety of ways. ML is a pattern recognition technology that may be used on medical pictures. After that, the ML algorithm system determines the optimum combination of these image attributes for categorizing the picture or generating a metric for the specified image area. The goals were to promote fundamental and applied research in the application of ML methods to medical problem solving and research, to provide a forum for reporting significant results, to determine whether ML methods are capable of underpinning research and development on intelligent systems for medical applications, and to identify areas that needed more research. Several research agenda suggestions were presented, covering both technical and human-centered issues.

Keywords: Machine learning; Data storage; Applications; Artificial Intelligence

5.1 Introduction

Data analysis, such as identifying regularities in data by efficiently dealing with faulty data, interpretation of continuous data used in the Intensive Care Unit, and intelligent alerts, are all examples of how machine learning (ML) is being used to improve monitoring effectiveness and efficiency. It is proposed that the proper use of ML methods may assist in the integration of computer-based systems in the healthcare environment, enabling medical experts' work to be facilitated and improved, thus increasing the efficiency and quality of medical treatment. ML provides methods, strategies, and tools that may assist in the diagnosis and

[1]Department of Electronics and Communication Engineering, Cheran College of Engineering, India
[2]Department of Electrical and Electronics Engineering, Gnanamani College of Technology, India
[3]Electrical Engineering and Automation, Aalto University, Finland

prognosis of illnesses in a variety of medical fields. For instance, ML is being used to evaluate the usefulness of clinical indicators and their combinations for prognosis, such as disease progression prediction, as well as to collect medical data for outcomes research, treatment planning and support, and overall patient care. Some of the most significant ML applications in medicine are listed here [1–5].

Artificial Intelligence (AI) in healthcare may be defined as a collection of technologies that enable computers to observe, perceive, act, and learn in order to conduct administrative and clinical healthcare tasks, as well as research and education. Unlike earlier technologies that only complemented human skills, today's health AI has the potential to significantly expand the range of human activities. These technologies include natural language processing, intelligent agents, computer vision, ML, expert systems, chat bots, and voice recognition. These technologies may also be used to compensate for cognitive biases in doctors, such as "regency bias," which happens when a doctor permits the result of a prior case to affect the treatment of a new patient. AI is being utilized at all levels of the healthcare sector. By diverting these reports to analysis and predictive modeling, ML may be utilized to address the issue of silted electronic health records (EHRs) reporting. This technology may be utilized in public health initiatives as well. ML may be used to integrate an individual's data with data from other sources, such as EHRs, to predict the likelihood of developing an illness, which can then be addressed with timely therapies such as preventative medication [6–10].

AI addresses the issue of information overload that plagues the healthcare sector and undermines the adoption of evidence-based medicine by utilizing ML to make sense of otherwise overwhelming amounts of healthcare data. Filter failure is a term used to describe a situation in which the main problem is not a lack of information, but rather how that information is processed. Inadequate information retrieval methods for point-of-care settings, challenges locating all relevant evidence in a large landscape of information resources, and a lack of basic health information literacy are just a few examples. For instance, IBM's Watson for Oncology analyses a vast quantity of medical literature to identify the best course of treatment. Researchers used sophisticated algorithms to extract data from radiological reports housed in a collection that spans several institutions. They claim that their method "provides an effective automatic method to annotate and extract clinically significant information from a large collection of free-text radiology reports," that it can be used to help clinicians better understand these reports and priorities their review process, and that it can link radiology reports to data from other data sources like electron microscopy [11–16]. They include both public and private hospitals, such as healthcare centers, district hospitals, and general hospitals, as well as nursing homes and mid-tier and top-tier private hospitals. Hospitals in India are adopting descriptive and predictive AI, according to a review of solutions.

Bitcoin is a digital currency that is used for advanced payments and speculative reasons all over the globe. Bitcoin is decentralized in the sense that it is not owned by anybody. Bitcoin exchanges are easy since they are not tied to any country. Speculation should be available via several "bitcoin transactions," or commercial hubs. These allow people to sell and buy Bitcoins using a variety of other currencies. Mt Gox is the largest Bitcoin exchange. Bitcoins are stored in a sophisticated wallet, which functions similarly to a virtual bank account. The timestamp information and the record of a large number of transactions are stored in a place called blockchain. A square is the name given to each record in a block chain. Each square provides a link to a previous information square. The data on the blockchain has been jumbled. During exchanges, the client's identity is not revealed; just their wallet ID is revealed.

The value of Bitcoin swings similarly to that of a stock, but in an unexpected manner. For value forecasting, different calculations are used to financial exchange data. Nonetheless, the variables that influence Bitcoin are exceptional. In this way, it is critical to forecast Bitcoin's value so that the best business decisions can be made. Unlike stock exchanges, the price of Bitcoin does not depend on business events or a middleman government. As a result, we believe it is critical to utilize AI innovation to forecast the price of Bitcoin in order to predict its value [17–20].

Venture-based learning is a method of learning in which ventures drive knowledge and is used in specific topics without the addition of specialized content. This chapter discusses the design and delivery of venture-based learning in software engineering design as a major task that encourages undergraduate creativity and focuses on real-world, open-ended tasks. These exercises develop a broad range of talents, not only those related to subject knowledge or specialist skills but also everyday abilities. The goal of this innovative student project is to demonstrate how a trained machine model can predict the cost of a cryptographic currency if we provide the right amount of information and computing power. It displays a graph with the expected characteristics. The most well-known invention is a mechanical setup that may aid mankind in anticipating future events. With massive amounts of data being generated and recorded on a regular basis, we have now arrived at a point where precise predictions can be made based on accurate data. Furthermore, as the crypto advanced time has progressed, more eyes have gone to the computerized market for endeavors. This gives us the opportunity to develop a model capable of predicting digital currencies, namely Bitcoin. This may be accomplished via the use of a series of AI techniques and concepts [21–26].

5.2   Machine Learning (ML) data storage

Knowledge equals power, and knowledge equals data. In this age of information overload, data analytics has changed the way individuals think about how to solve problems in different industries. One of the potential areas where data analytics may have a major effect is healthcare. Healthcare analytics may help patients, as well as other stakeholders and key players in the healthcare industry. It can prevent disease outbreaks, detect and diagnose diseases, reduce hospital operating costs, help the government with healthcare policy, and improve overall quality of life. Researchers develop algorithms that can effectively self-learn from data in the field of ML, which is a branch of computer science. The primary aim is for computers to be able to learn on their own without the need for human intervention. Data analytics and ML go hand in hand. In this study, we looked at the literature on some of the most significant ML techniques utilized in the healthcare sector. The aim of this extensive study is to determine the applications and challenges of ML in health care. According to [27], ML is an area of study that allows computers to learn without being explicitly programmed. It involves developing or using algorithms that can learn and train on their own as a result of their own experiences. ML has lately received a lot of attention, and it now has applications in almost every area. ML is useful in circumstances where there is a lot of data and a lot of underlying patterns that need to be recognized and retrieved.

The input data (also known as training data or training set) includes clearly distinct marked values. In supervised learning, the algorithm goes through a training phase. The training will continue until reliable predictions can be made. Two kinds of supervised learning algorithms are classification and regression algorithms. We utilize unsupervised learning when the input data is unlabeled, which means we have no clue what sort of output we will get. As a general approach, probabilistic data modeling is used for training. There is a mix of labeled and unlabeled data in the input data. The model that emerges should be able to organize data and anticipate outcomes. This class of algorithms is gaining a lot of momentum since the data to be analyzed in real life is often a combination of tagged and unlabeled.

The goal is to develop a smart agent (Reinforcement Learning agent/RL-agent) that can work in a dynamic problem environment. The RL-agent, like humans, learns via trial and error. Feedback is given to the model as a reward for success and as a punishment for making bad decisions in the problem setting. By analyzing past actions for which it was rewarded, the RL-agent will learn. In supervised learning, datasets are labeled. There are two components to the data set: training and testing. The training set is used by the algorithm to determine which label the target belongs to. It generates a prediction model that may be used to anticipate the appearance of fresh data labels. The test set may be used to verify that the model is correct, and the learning process can be repeated if the output is not satisfactory. It is a simple and frequently used technique that, in the vast majority of instances, yields accurate findings. It may be used for both classification and regression. The method assembles and combines a collection of decision trees. Artificial neural networks, often known as connectionist systems, are modeled after the human central nervous system. It is a graphical depiction that uses neurons to represent computer components. Neurons are connected and organized in layers to transmit information. The input layer is the first layer to receive unprocessed data. The prediction is done by the output layers, which are the last layers.

The intermediate layers are hidden layers. Feed forward neural networks (FFNNs) were used to predict protein site-directed recombination. When categorizing data of a continuous nature, regression is employed. It is a statistical technique for generating equations to determine the relationship between variables. The equation's parameters are provided by the training set. The most often used regression models are linear regression and regularized linear regression. Regularized regression models have a finite number of coefficients. Rigid regression and Least Absolute Shrinkage and Selection Operator (LASSO) are two popular regularized regression techniques. In k-mean clustering, we start with k-random samples and use them as cluster centers, also known as cancroids. As the learning progresses, the data will be moved across clusters. The distance between data points and the centric is calculated using the Euclidian distance. A cluster center is assigned to a data point depending on its distance. The weight of the cluster center is adjusted when each data point is assigned to it. This strategy is followed until the researcher's criterion is met. As a criterion, the number of times the cluster center has been recalculated or the distance between clusters may be utilized. The efficiency of k-means clustering is governed by the value of k, which is first established since it specifies the number of clusters that will be formed. Based on their genetic profile, individuals were classified by ethnicity using k-means clustering. In unsupervised learning, the dataset is unlabeled, and the model generated works with unlabeled data. We are trying to group the data together in this instance based on some underlying similarity. The vast majority of data collected via the Internet or through automated procedures is unlabeled. In the fields of life science, large quantities of unlabeled data are generated, and extracting meaningful information from them has become a challenge.

The primary goal of this chapter is to forecast the current Bitcoin price in US dollars. The Bitcoin price should be found in the dataset's price index. The issue will be addressed with a high degree of success thanks to the use of Bayesian regression. As a contrast to deep learning models, the prominent ARIMA model for time series forecasting is used. The non-linear deep learning techniques beat the ARIMA prediction, which has a poor performance. Finally, the results of both learning models show a relatively low degree of accuracy. This section provides an overview of prediction architecture as well as a survey on Bitcoin price prediction utilizing ML algorithm methods, as well as survey papers on price prediction basis articles. In a quantifiable sense, AI is defined as the application of computerized reasoning in which readily available data is used to process or assist in the management of factual facts via computations. While AI incorporates mechanization concepts, it still needs human guidance. To create a framework that works effectively on yet unknown information events, AI requires a considerable amount of conjecture.

AI is a relatively recent control in software engineering that provides a variety of data analysis techniques. Some of these systems rely on well-established factual methods (e.g., strategic relapse and head part research), whereas others do not. Most measurable methods are based on the idea of selecting a particular probabilistic model from a group of related models that best represents observed data. Similarly, most AI systems are designed to find models that best match data (e.g., to address specific improvement problems), but these AI models are never restricted to probabilistic models.

For the first time, blockchain technology enables the development of intermediary-free, trustworthy online databases that may be used for a variety of applications requiring trust and transparency, such as financial transactions, supply chain management, and provenance validation. For example, this new digital architecture enables financial transactions between two strangers to be conducted directly without the danger of default or duplicate spending. In terms of transportation, increasing technological enabling of cars and modes improves much of the functionality; however, third-party devices and physical identification techniques may be utilized in the meantime. In practice, this means having tamper-proof timestamped documents and data storage, as well as the capacity to execute intermediary-free micropayments and maintain identification and ownership credentials.

Transportation is a huge component of the global economy, accounting for up cash flows, and there are a lot of players: shippers, carriers, customs, and businesses that supply fuel for trucks, aircraft, trains, and other vehicles. Any shipment involves a large number of transactions. Consider having to wait 60–90 days for payment from each and every person engaged in each and every phase. Instead, what if we used blockchain and smart contracts to accelerate payments. Because there is so much payment float in the global economy, this adds trust and automation, accelerating verification and removing a huge drag. Vehicles will be reinvented as information-rich devices capable of mobile payments, thanks to blockchain technology, which will be at the heart of efforts to enhance economic efficiency, quality of life, and commercial results. It has the potential to improve the efficiency of vehicle parking assets and arterial road networks.

Vehicles may send and receive payments using a cryptocurrency wallet based on real-time location information thanks to blockchain technology. Array Systems Computing, a Canadian firm, has developed a blockchain-based system dubbed "ZeroTraffic", which enables drivers and government organizations to utilize digital tokens to incentivize preferred vehicle routing to help with traffic control.

5.3   Machine Learning (ML) techniques

In this research, we looked at recent publications on ML methods that have been utilized to address problems in the healthcare industry. We have tried to give an overview of the most popular ML methods used to address issues in the healthcare industry. During our investigation, we found that the analytic method employed is almost always dependent on the data set being examined and the intended outcomes. We've also found that ML works well with Big Data. ML algorithms often need to be trained again and again, and they work best when data is stored locally. Distributed computing systems like Apache Spark and Apache Hadoop, on the other hand, can easily manage this problem. To summarize, ML is a rapidly evolving field, especially in the field of healthcare. Huge breakthroughs and new discoveries are on the horizon, with the potential to transform the healthcare industry.

The health industry has undergone considerable change as a consequence of new computer technology, which has prompted it to generate more medical data, leading in the development of new fields of research. Many efforts are undertaken to cope with the explosion of medical data, on the one hand, and to extract useful information from it, on the other hand. This encouraged academics to take use of all technology advances, such as big data analytics, predictive analytics, ML, and learning algorithms, to extract useful data and assist decision-making. Predicting the future is no longer a difficult task, due to the promises of predictive analytics in big data and the use of ML algorithms, particularly in healthcare, where diseases and treatments can now be anticipated. In this post, we will provide an overview of the rise of Big Data in the healthcare industry and apply a learning algorithm to a set of medical data. The medical field has made a significant contribution to this data because of technological innovations in the field, such as cloud computing, which has moved care tests beyond the four walls of the hospital and made them available anywhere and anytime, laparoscopic surgery and robotic surgery, which have replaced traditional surgery, and smart homes, which allow patients to self-care and mHealth.

Smart applications or software that analyze body signals using integrated sensors with the aim of monitoring are also available, as are mHealth technologies that allow for new biological, behavioral, and environmental data collection methods. Among these are sensors that provide a more precise view of the phenomenon. All of these advancements led to the explosion of medical data through expanding data sources and electronic medical records that include diagnostic pictures, lab results, and biometric information that is generated and stored. This avalanche of medical data, according to experts, has the potential to improve clinical judgments at the moment of treatment. Doctors will be able to extract relevant information for each patient, allowing them to make better decisions and achieve better results. Because the process of analysis in the medical sector goes beyond the ability to manage large databases and extends to the ability to retrieve future knowledge, which many researchers and experts encourage, the terms "analyzing medical data" and "predictive analytics" have seen a significant increase in interest in Google Trends. It has been established that the only method capable of addressing all of the medical sector's problems is Big Data analysis.

Because of the rapid growth of data on the cloud system, data mining plays a critical function. Predictive modeling is a mathematical technique for making predictions that uses statistics. The term "data mining" refers to a technique for extracting information from huge data sets that is becoming more prominent in the medical field. In order to conduct effective medical diagnosis, treatment, management, prognosis, monitoring, and screening, evaluating and extracting information from both known and unknown patterns. Data that is noisy, missing, inconsistent, imbalanced, or has a high dimensionality may be found in historical medical data. This uncomfortable data caused substantial bias in predictive modeling and harmed the efficacy of data mining techniques. Several pre-processing and ML methods and models, such as supervised learning, unsupervised learning, and reinforcement learning, have been described in recent study. As a result, the present research analyses and contrasts a range of clinical predictive modeling models, algorithms, and ML methods in order to produce high-performance results from vast quantities of medical data related to patients with a variety of diseases.

Along with the drive for more widespread use of ML in healthcare, there is a growing need for ML and AI-based systems to be regulated and held accountable. Interpretable ML models may aid in maintaining the accountability of ML systems. Healthcare offers a unique set of challenges for ML, with higher demands for explainability, model accuracy, and overall performance than in most other industries. In this research, we look at the notion of interpretability in the context of healthcare, as well as the many nuances associated with it, healthcare-specific interpretability challenges, and the future of interpretability in healthcare. Questions of accountability, fairness, and transparency of ML systems will become increasingly relevant as ML becomes more widely used in healthcare.

The bulk of predictive ML systems in healthcare just offer predictions, but many use cases which need reasoning to convince doctors to utilize the models' input. As a consequence, interpretable models with forecasts must be integrated into medical facility operations. Prediction models in general are neither pre-scriptive nor causal. In many healthcare applications, explanations are inadequate, and prescriptions or actionability are needed. We think causal explanations will be the next frontier in ML research. While interpretability is a critical component in keeping ML models accountable, it is not the sole way. Researchers have also suggested that examining the outputs of ML systems is a useful way to audit them since certain models are too complex for humans to comprehend, and auditing the outputs for fairness and bias may be a better option. Furthermore, many healthcare problems are complex, and simplifying them to simple remedies with accompanying explanations may result in subpar outcomes.

Consider the difficulty of reducing the chances of a hospital readmission. To decrease readmission risk, optimizing predictions and actionability may actually increase patients' average duration of stay in hospitals. Even though the initial formulation of the ML problem is described as such, this is a suboptimal solution that is not in the patient's best interests. As a consequence, such contexts and interdependencies should be incorporated in interpretable model problem for-mulations. There is also debate in the scientific community over whether to use post-hoc or ante-hoc prediction models. There is concern about utilizing these models in circumstances when critical decisions must be made since post-hoc model explanations do not match how the model really predicts. Current and future predictive modeling research should concentrate on anticipatory explanation models such as context explanation networks, falling rule lists, and SLIM. Scalability of interpretable ML models is another area of study that has to be looked at further. Creating explanations for models like LIME and Shapley values may take a long time. In the case of LIME, each instance that has to be explained involves the creation of a local model. This may be problematic in terms of scal-ability if there are hundreds of millions of instances for which predictions and explanations are required.

In academics, applied ML in healthcare is a popular subject. As ML models become more extensively used, they will need explanations in order to be held accountable. While there is no clear definition of interpretability in ML, researchers have discovered a number of interpretable model characteristics that may be used to create interpretable model requirements. Which interpretable models should be utilized depends on the application or use case for which explanations are required. As a consequence, a critical application like predicting a patient's end-of-life care may have far tighter explanation fidelity requirements than just calculating surgical costs, when getting the prediction right is much more important than providing explanations. In the area of interpretable models, there are still many unsolved issues, and we expect it to remain a hotspot of research for the next several years.

Blockchain is a novel platform for supporting transactional services inside a multi-party business network, with the aim of allowing substantial cost and risk savings for all parties via the development of creative new business models. Data in the distributed ledger can only be accessed by executing a smart contract (i.e., a distributed ledger stored procedure call) that specifies the rules that govern a transaction. Furthermore, the architecture of blockchain technology guarantees that no one corporate organization may alter, remove, or even add to the ledger without the consent of other business entities in the network, making the system ideal for guaranteeing the immutability of data and legal documents.

Given the aforementioned key characteristics, blockchain technology has swept the globe in recent years due to its potential to revolutionize every sector. For example, it is now being utilized in a broader variety of applications, such as the Internet of Things (IoT). IoT devices may transmit data to a shared transaction repository with tamper-resistant records, and business partners can access and provide IoT data without the need for central control and administration, thanks to blockchain technology. Blockchain for IoT may improve supply chains by monitoring items as they move through the export/import supply chain, enforcing shipping rules, and speeding up incremental payments. Blockchain technology has the potential to disrupt the insurance sector as well. It was utilized to allow the idea of pay-as-you-go insurance in a vehicle micro-insurance application.

This software enables drivers who only use their vehicles sometimes to pay insurance premiums for specific journeys rather than a large annual cost. Every participant in the insurance contract, including the driver, the insurance company, and the financial institution, may be assured that the data is tamper-proof and traceable by openly keeping all data related to the actual trip and premium payment on blockchain. This ensures that every trip-related insurance claim is handled promptly and without question, resulting in a better customer experience. Furthermore, because the micro-insurance application requires access to multiple risk analytic databases for computing premiums, such as past driving behavior statistics and past vehicle runtime statistics, a system architecture that allows for both on-chain and off-chain data maintenance and analysis was proposed.

One of the major platform-enabling technologies to monitor is blockchain. Despite the fact that there is presently no standard in the blockchain sector, there is a growing agreement that the technology is approaching a pinnacle of exaggerated expectations. The study predicted that blockchain technology will take 5–10 years to gain widespread acceptance. Furthermore, the majority of current blockchain initiatives, particularly when applied to commercial settings, are still in their infancy. The views and difficulties of blockchain research have been addressed, however they are mostly for cryptocurrencies and public blockchain settings. The moment has come for the database community to get more actively engaged in resolving outstanding issues related to data management and analytics on a permissioned blockchain network for business applications.

Because blockchain systems are built on a foundation of database, transaction, encryption, consensus, and other distributed system technologies, it is only natural to wonder if existing capabilities of mature data and information systems can be leveraged through robust integration into blockchain systems. Multi-storage and index support, innovative transaction concurrency model, scalable transaction throughput, master and reference data management, smart contract management, data security and privacy guarantees, and information leakage prevention are some of the outstanding research problems. Furthermore, although the blockchain database is helpful for transparent preservation of flowing business data, no one database solution suits all applications. While blockchain was created to store transaction data, there is an increasing interest in incorporating analytics into blockchain-based data platforms. We will focus on particular research issues in this chapter, such as built-in analytics for blockchain and data integration and analytics for on-chain and off-chain data.

5.4   Healthcare sector

Blockchain is a decentralized and public digital ledger that records transactions across several computers in such a way that no record can be changed retrospectively without affecting subsequent blocks. Each "block" in the blockchain is confirmed and connected to the one before it, making a continuous chain. After all, the name of the record is blockchain. Blockchain delivers a high level of accountability since every transaction is recorded and verified publicly. No one can change the information recorded in the blockchain after it has been entered. Its purpose is to show that the data is current and unaltered. Data is stored on networks rather than a central database in blockchain, which improves stability while also exposing its vulnerability to hacking. Blockchain provides an excellent platform for developing and competing with conventional businesses for current and innovative company models.

The blockchain technology aids marketers in keeping track of medical items. Using blockchain technology, the health and pharmaceutical industries will be able to eliminate counterfeit drugs while also allowing for the traceability of all of these products. It aids in the discovery of the source of the fabrication. Blockchain can ensure the privacy of patient records; when a medical history is created, blockchain can also keep it, and this record cannot be changed. The hospital's whole commodity hardware is connected to this decentralized network. Researchers may use the resources saved by these devices to calculate estimates for treatments, drugs, and remedies for a variety of ailments and conditions. Data analysis approaches that are quicker, more secure, and simpler to use are required by today's information systems and computerization. It is also necessary to keep data analysis efficient and accurate. As a result, ML and blockchain technology have been applied in data analysis and security in a variety of disciplines, ranging from medical to business and education to energy applications. To analyse the data, this research uses ML and blockchain approaches, as well as an assessment of selection methods, query strategies, applications, and security. Blockchain technology is used to tackle security challenges with highly protected data. Blockchain technology is quickly gaining traction in the field of data security. The healthcare sector is one of the domains of business where there is a significant level of risk, and it has drawn the attention of many technical companies. As a result, this field needs security to protect their data. The blockchain is most often used to provide protection for highly sensitive data. There are several potential for the healthcare business to accomplish and benefit by using blockchain technology. Reduced transaction costs, enhanced transparency for regulatory reporting, effective healthcare data management, universality of healthcare records, and the ability to access data from any place are just few of the benefits. In the framework of a smart healthcare system, blockchain may provide different advantages, especially from a context-aware standpoint, where people and society may get efficient and customized treatments. This study examines the link between ML and blockchain technologies in the context of a smart healthcare system. In addition, we will highlight some of the issues that may arise when establishing a ML-based safe healthcare system utilizing blockchain technology.

Each transaction performed in a block of the network is validated through a process based on the consensus distributed across all nodes (that is, the devices/users connected to the net). Blockchain technology belongs to the larger category of distributed ledger technologies, whose functioning is based primarily on a register structured in blocks linked in a network; each transaction performed in a block of the network is validated through a process based on the consensus distributed across all nodes (that is, the devices/users).

The transactions are the outcomes of the activities that take place among the network's subjects. The notion of blockchain comes from the fact that each block keeps a reference to the previous one using a cryptographic method. Blockchain is not stored on a centralized server like typical online services, but rather on network devices (computers) called nodes, each of which has a copy of the whole blockchain. From prescription production to drugstore shelves, the blockchain makes the whole prescription process public. IoT and blockchain may be used to monitor traffic congestion, freight direction, and speed. It allows for effective acquisition scheduling to avoid delays and shortages in clinics, pharmacies, and other medical institutions where a particular medicine is used. The use of blockchain-based digital frameworks might aid in preventing unauthorized changes to logistical data. It builds confidence and prohibits the unauthorized handling of data, money, and medications by a variety of persons interested in buying pharmaceuticals. The technique may successfully enhance patients' conditions while keeping finances at a low cost. In multi-level authentication, it removes all impediments and barriers. Blockchain is well suited for security applications because it can maintain an incorruptible, decentralized, and transparent record of all patient data. Furthermore, although blockchain is public, it is also private, concealing any individual's identity behind complex and secure algorithms that may protect medical data sensitive. Patients, physicians, and healthcare professionals may all communicate information quickly and securely because to the technology's decentralized nature.

Because it enables people to make their medical data available and comply with access rules, blockchain technology makes the move to interoperability driven by patients simpler. This allows patients more control over their personal data while also improving confidentiality and privacy. Quality management and enforcement are difficult to monitor and apply. Throughout the sector, blockchain applications might alleviate any of these technological challenges. The use of blockchain headlines will aid regulatory agencies with tracking legitimate pharmaceuticals and distinguishing them from counterfeits. This guarantees that all parties that have been authorized exchange digital transactions including the patient's information. Patients who change doctors may simply update a single permission form to have their entire medical data exchanged. The blockchain is a decentralized, immutable, and publicly accessible database. The blockchain idea is built on a peer-to-peer network architecture in which no one centralized organization controls transaction information. Transactions recorded in a chain of blocks are publicly available and trustworthy to all blockchain network participants. Blockchain validates the authenticity of data transfers via consensus procedures and encryption, ensuring that connected blocks are resistant to changes and alterations. Decentralization, accountability, and security are all desired properties of blockchain technology, which increase service efficiency and save operating costs. In recent years, such extraordinary qualities have boosted the use of blockchain-based applications.

Because of its enormous potential to create interesting services across a wide range of applications, IoT has become a critical component of the future Internet and has attracted increased attention from academics and industry. IoT seamlessly integrates disparate devices and things to create a physical environment in which sensing, processing, and communication functions are carried out without the need for human intervention. Due to the limited power and storage capacities of IoT devices, significant amounts of data produced from a large number of devices in existing IoT systems pose a barrier in ensuring the appropriate quality of service (QoS). Cloud computing, on the other hand, offers limitless storage and computational capacity, allowing it to deliver on-demand, powerful, and efficient services for IoT use domains. The confluence of cloud computing and IoT, in particular, prepares the door for a new paradigm known as CoT, which may benefit both worlds.

Indeed, the richness of resources accessible in the cloud is very useful to IoT systems, and cloud integration with IoT platforms may help the cloud acquire greater popularity in real-world applications. Furthermore, with minimum administration effort, high system performance, and service availability, CoT may alter existing IoT service supply models. IoT devices are used to detect and gather data from local surroundings in this hierarchy. IoT devices, on the other hand, will communicate recorded data to the cloud for data gathering owing to their limited processing capacity. However, as the usage of electronic systems for processing medical data grows, so does the volume of data that has to be processed. Medical data may be easily stolen, modified, or lost while being kept and processed, therefore researchers have created a new blockchain-based data storage system for relatively significant volumes of data. Users may utilize the system to preserve essential data indefinitely and verify for validity on a regular basis. Patient data in this research is produced in text and multimedia forms throughout the therapy process, then safeguarded against unwanted access and saved in encrypted form. This is accomplished via the use of a variety of encryption methods and file storage systems, as well as an identity information system that does not connect user identities to medical data. The data is saved in the form of transactions, which are sent to the blockchain network and then gathered and stored in blocks of a certain size. If the data in the database is then tampered with or corrupted, the blockchain may be used to access and verify the information.

Previously, secure medical record storage and distribution focused on the secure, digital storage and processing of mostly incoherent patient data (e.g., specialist diagnoses for different patients), but now it is more about the storage, processing, and, in particular, accessibility of temporal and patient-specific related data in the form of an electronic medical record. The use of medical patient files for various purposes always requires the consent of the patients, who currently grant or refuse these mostly in paper form and then have no control or overview over their files have developed a system with which patients can flexibly manage their consents and health organizations can efficiently obtain and manage these consents for various purposes have developed a system with which patients can flexibly manage their consents and health organizations can efficiently obtain and manage these consents for various purposes have developed a system with which patients can flexibly manage their consents The electronic system employs a specialized access control mechanism based on a permissioned blockchain powered by Hyperledger. All patient records, consents, and data access information are immutably kept in the blockchain and shared among the participants in this research. Furthermore, a computer code based on smart contracts, or rather chaincode, was constructed, which automates the business logic for managing patient permission, according to the researchers.

In the past, however, stringent regulation and slowness in the bureaucracy hindered the growth of electronic medical records significantly. Electronic records are gaining popularity as a result of new breakthroughs in electronic information technology. The development of a new, decentralized data management system for the treatment of patient data based on blockchain technology was prompted by new technological advancements as well as an increasing interest among patients in their personal data. Regardless of the institution or software system, the system offers patients with a full, unchangeable record and quick access to their medical data. These researchers' decentralized data system regulates authentication, trustworthiness, accountability, and data sharing using blockchain techniques including smart contracts, mining, and proof of work. It may also be linked into current local data storage systems, allowing for a data economy among patients, researchers, and government agencies.

In most cases, several hospitals acquire and keep digital data for the same patient. However, it is difficult to summarize or exchange data between institutions for security and data protection reasons. Develop a blockchain-based information management system that cryptographically processes patient information and enables a secure exchange of information. Large datasets may be safely maintained using this technology, and patients, physicians, researchers, and other third parties can easily have secure access to local databases of diverse institutions. Healthcare management encompasses a wide range of processes (e.g., managing finances, patients, legal issues, and so on) as well as medical workflows related to patient care. We created a smart contract-based management system for the intelligent and digital management of medical data in the healthcare sector, as well as the optimization of complex medical processes. During the implementation, representations of genuine medical files are developed, and data from medical work operations is stored in a blockchain decentralized. Smart contracts are then used to specify metadata access rights, permission management, and data access authorization rules. The data is encrypted and stored in a blockchain block, which is a particular, compressed format.

5.5   Various sector of Machine Learning (ML)

Healthcare is a need in most people's lives, and it must be both accessible and affordable. The healthcare industry is a complicated system with many moving components. It is expanding at a rapid pace. Simultaneously, in this industry, fraud is becoming a significant problem. One of the challenges is the misuse of medical insurance systems. It is difficult to detect fraud in the healthcare industry by hand. ML and data mining techniques have lately been used to automatically detect healthcare frauds. We want to offer an overview of healthcare frauds and strategies for detecting them in this work. The literature review looked at a variety of publicly available studies, with an emphasis on the technique used, identifying relevant sources, and elements of healthcare data. According to this research, advanced ML techniques and newly acquired sources of healthcare data will be future subjects of focus in order to make healthcare more affordable, improve the effectiveness of healthcare fraud detection, and bestow top quality on healthcare systems. Many recent research, as described in this article, have utilized ML and data mining to detect fraud in the healthcare industry. More research is required to uncover unique unusual patterns of healthcare fraud, and sophisticated ML techniques may be used to improve results.

Healthcare has always played an essential role in people's lives and will continue to do so in the future. The human body is made up of many components. As a consequence, having experts who can recognize and treat diseases in different parts of the body is essential. As a consequence, physicians use a range of treatment methods on patients with different specialties. The aim of the healthcare business is to help as many people as possible. Each treatment and service provided, however, comes with a price tag. Physicians, drug dealers, and medical staff must be paid for their time and skills, as well as receive a range of medical benefits. Patients are often unable to afford these expenses. As a consequence, insurance plans are used to distribute costs throughout the whole healthcare system while also covering the costs of essential people and equipment. The risk of misappropriation or fraud exists in any insurance program.

Healthcare fraud is increasingly being recognized as a serious social problem. The government is obviously concerned about healthcare fraud, and more effective detection methods are required. Detecting healthcare fraud requires a considerable amount of effort as well as a thorough knowledge of medical terminology. Healthcare fraud detection has traditionally depended largely on domain experts' knowledge, which is inefficient, expensive, and time-consuming. Healthcare fraud is caught manually by a few auditors who examine and identify suspicious medical insurance claims, which takes a lot of time and effort. However, recent advancements in ML and data mining techniques have improved the efficiency and automation of healthcare fraud detection. There has been a rise in interest in mining healthcare data for fraud detection in recent years. The many techniques for detecting fraudulent behavior in health insurance claim data are discussed in this chapter.

This chapter focused on healthcare fraud, types of healthcare fraud, types and sources of healthcare data, and healthcare fraud tactics. A variety of research are examined in the literature. In the healthcare industry, it has been established that "data" is a key issue. The bulk of the information comes from government and private insurance companies. The most common methods for detecting healthcare fraud are ML and data mining. There are three types of ML methodologies: supervised, unsupervised, and semi-supervised. In the vast majority of cases, many researchers use semi-supervised learning methods. New semi-supervised learning algorithms, on the other hand, may be used in a select case to more successfully detect healthcare fraud. There is, however, no one-size-fits-all method or pattern for hiding all instances of healthcare fraud. In order to make healthcare more affordable, improve the effectiveness of healthcare fraud detection, and ensure that healthcare systems are of the highest quality, this review concludes that advanced ML techniques and newly acquired sources of healthcare data will be hot topics in the near future.

The usage of big data in healthcare has expanded in recent years. A large amount of patient data is generated in our digitalized environment from a variety of sources, including wearable devices, mobile devices, EHRs, and medical centers. Medical data is both structured and unstructured, and it is increasing at an exponential pace. Patients' sensitive data is exchanged and managed by a number of sources, including insurance, prescriptions, and healthcare providers, as well as attackers, presenting a significant security concern. Cybercriminals employ phishing, data leaking, virus and Trojan horse attachment insertion, DNS spying, sniffing, and other social engineering methods. This article provides a brief overview of the different data mining and security methods utilized in healthcare data. In the area of medical expert systems, the study and its presentation in this context may be helpful in not only evaluating but also predicting chronic diseases based on stored data collected from various sources. Due to improvements in computer power and the availability of massive new datasets, deep learning, a subset of ML, has seen a stratospheric surge in popularity over the past six years. The ability of machines to interpret and alter data such as images, language, and speech has significantly improved in recent years. Deep learning in healthcare and medicine will benefit from the massive quantity of data generated, as well as the increasing expansion of medical equipment and digital record systems.

ML is distinguished from other types of computer programming in that it converts an algorithm's inputs into outputs using statistical, data-driven rules generated automatically from a large number of samples rather than being explicitly defined by humans. Creating feature extractors that transformed raw data into acceptable representations for a learning algorithm to identify patterns required domain expertise and human engineering in the past. Deep learning, on the other hand, is a kind of representation learning in which a computer is given raw data and then uses that data to create its own representations in order to identify patterns. Deep learning is made up of several representation layers. One layer's representation (beginning with the raw data input) is passed into the next layer and transformed into a more abstract representation. As data passes through the layers of the system, the input space is twisted repeatedly until data points can be differentiated. This method may be used to teach very complex functions. Deep-learning models outperform many conventional ML methods because they scale to large datasets and improve with fresh data. This is partly owing to their ability to work with specialized computer hardware. Deep learning algorithms may input data from a number of sources, which is particularly essential for healthcare data. The most common models are trained via supervised learning, which involves creating datasets with input data points and output data labels.

ML is a technique for predicting and detecting patterns in large datasets. In ML, computers are trained to learn from, analyse, and act on data without being explicitly programmed. Health informatics is the most challenging issue to tackle, while ML is the fastest-growing area in computer science. ML aims to develop algorithms that can learn and improve over time while also making predictions. It offers a variety of alerting and risk management decision-making tools targeted at improving patient safety and quality of treatment. As a consequence of the drive to reduce healthcare costs and the move toward personalized treatment, the healthcare industry faces challenges in the areas of electronic record administration, data integration, computer aided diagnostics, and disease forecasting. ML offers a range of tools, methods, and frameworks to address these problems. In this chapter, we look at a variety of ML prediction methods and tools in practice an assessment of the applications of ML prediction algorithms in several fields, with an emphasis on the healthcare industry.

ML is a revolutionary technique for rethinking everything we do. ML ideas and implementations may be found in a variety of places in our daily life, such as search, advertising, YouTube, and Play. Most companies that deal with large amounts of data recognize the benefits of ML technologies. By obtaining insights from this data, organizations may be able to operate more effectively or acquire a competitive advantage. ML algorithms, tools, and methods have been successfully utilized in a variety of areas to create novel prediction models. Information technology is helping to improve healthcare delivery and the quality of human life. Medical or health informatics is a branch of science concerned with storing, retrieving, and making the greatest use of medical data, knowledge, and information for problem solving and decision making. Health technology has advanced significantly in the areas of data collection, treatments, communications, and research throughout the years. Healthcare informatics, a multidisciplinary field, has been linked with technological advancements and data management problems because to the use of ML techniques.

Predictive analytics is a kind of advanced analytics that is used to predict future events that are unknown at the time. Data mining, statistics, modeling, ML, and AI are all used in predictive analytics to analyze current findings and create predictions about the future. Predictive analytics' most essential component is the predictor, which is described as a characteristic used to assess future behavior. The predictors are used to forecast future probability and provide highly reliable results. Predictive analytics is carried out using two kinds of methodologies: ML and regression. ML techniques have grown increasingly prominent in predictive analytics due to their outstanding performance in handling big datasets with consistent characteristics and noisy data. According to observational research, ML is effective for creating prediction models by identifying patterns from large datasets. These models are used in a variety of predictive data analytics applications, including price prediction, risk assessment, predicting customer behavior, and document classification. In a number of industrial contexts, ML techniques are important.

The transport and logistics sector will benefit from blockchain technology because it will provide secure and tamper-proof records in real time, bringing new levels of transparency and efficiency. For example, the Port of Rotterdam, Europe's largest port, has established a "BlockLab" and is using a blockchain solution to replace the paper-based "bill of lading" system used in ports with a digital system that allows tamper-proof records to be available in real time to all necessary parties in the supply chain, significantly reducing transaction costs and time.

With 94 organizations originally participating, IBM and Maersk, a Danish shipping container business, launched a combined electronic ledger for worldwide freight monitoring. Customs releases, business invoices, and cargo lists are examples of information exchanged on the blockchain, which are shared with all stakeholders immediately after they are created. The system has so far stored approximately 160 million shipping events, with about one million occurring each day. ShipChain offers a comparable Blockchain-based tracking system that monitors goods from the time they leave the factory to the time they reach the consumer. This tracking system provides for automated delivery confirmation, which implies that all parties engaged in the supply chain may be paid immediately after their portion is finished.

The New South Wales government's deployment of digital driver's licenses is being made more secure thanks to a blockchain-based platform. In November 2017, Secure Logic Group announced the introduction of their "TrustGrid" technology, which was utilized as the digital platform for a 1400-person digital driver's license trial in Dubbo, NSW. The technology is currently being utilized in Sydney's eastern suburbs as part of the first metro testing of the digital driver's license. More than 140,000 drivers will be eligible for a digital driver's license in the second pilot, which may be used for police checks and admission into pubs and clubs in the trial region.

The food sector may benefit greatly from improved product tracking enabled by blockchain technology. Walmart is presently experimenting with blockchain technology to monitor food movement from the farm to the shop. This enables Walmart to quickly identify which manufacturer is to blame in the case of poor quality or damaged food, as well as temperature sensor data from transportation areas. In 2018, the Commonwealth Bank of Australia backed an attempt to monitor an overseas shipment of almonds using blockchain technology. The implementation of an Ethereum-based blockchain proved effective in lowering administrative costs and allowing transparent monitoring of the shipment's location and quality.

In its most basic form, "AI" refers to computers' ability to not only make choices previously made by people but also to make decisions that humans are unable to make because to the complexity and amount of data. AI is an academic subject that was founded in the mid-1950s and has lately experienced a resurgence of interest due to the proliferation of computers and the increasing quantity of data accessible from all walks of life (used in Google searching, electronic home assistants, Spotify, etc.). AI, on the other hand, is concerned with creating machines that think and behave like humans, and therefore spans a variety of fields including computer science, psychology, ethics, cognitive studies, and neuroscience.

ML is an application of AI that is particularly useful in the transportation industry since it enables better use of current data to make choices, many of which are made needlessly by human operators or are not presently possible to be made due to complexity. ML may be divided into two categories.

The first is when a computer programmer creates a long piece of computer code that is intended to account for every possible scenario that the program may encounter and offers choices for each; in other words, the programmer's job is to "educate" the computer. This is referred to as "Supervised Learning," and it may also be referred to as "Programmed Learning." For instance, the code might instruct the computer to respond to a query like, "Are all of the train doors closed?" and then give two command choices. If the answer to the question is "Yes" after checking the data from the door sensor, the program can move on to the next question before the driverless train departs the station; if the answer is "No," the program may ask other pre-departure questions before returning to this one, with all requiring a "Yes" in order to depart. This method is time-consuming and restricted since it requires each event to be anticipated and a set of choices to be built into the code. This method is useful, but it works best when there are a limited number of possible choices and outcomes and the data sets are tiny.

The second kind replaces long computer code with questions and instructions with an artificial neural network that explores the connections between data and related outcomes, needing a lot of computing power and a lot of data. This is known as "unsupervised learning" or "deep learning," and it can be thought of as "Self-Learning," in which the computer makes decisions based on comparing examples from the past and associated outcomes with the current situation to estimate a likely outcome, updating itself as it goes, much like the human brain. Unlike programmed learning, this method requires a huge data collection in order for the system to learn how to understand a set of incoming data streams and make decisions as well as or better than a person.

The bulk of early attempts to use AI to transportation revolve on allowing computers to operate cars, freeing up the human driver and increasing safety and efficiency. This is most often referred to as making the car "autonomous," which means that the passenger does not need to do anything. Although the vehicle can drive itself at this point, it still needs help to refuel, recharge, pay for registration, go through the car wash, and so on, thus it is more appropriate to refer to it as a "Self-Driving" vehicle. Once self-driving cars are available, the focus will likely shift to passenger interaction, allowing passengers to talk freely to the car (much like Google Home and Amazon Alexa) and discuss routes, control vehicle functions such as temperature and music, and access information for display on internal screens. Instead of being "autonomous" and requiring no interaction from passengers, these cars will be very engaged with passengers.

Access control (AC) has been the subject of many studies in the literature. Meanwhile, in restricted settings, such as the IoT, such issues have not yet matured. This section will introduce the IoT paradigm, primarily from the perspective of an AC, and then show how security rules are handled in current AC models.

The IoT is already a reality that surrounds us and will continue to do so in the future, affecting many aspects of our life. Indeed, many studies believe the IoT to be one of the most important technological revolutions of this century, and it has progressed from a future vision to a growing commercial and research reality. In 2008, the world broke over the barrier of a single connected device per person, and by 2020, statistics predict that there will be approximately 26 smart objects for every people on the planet.

Despite what has been stated, the IoT is still developing, owing to a number of obstacles that stymie full use of the IoT, such as IoT device computation limitations, heterogeneity, identification, power supply, data storage/processing, and so on. Meanwhile, one of the most pressing of these issues is security and privacy, particularly considering the pervasiveness of smart devices in all aspects of human existence.

Unfortunately, given the constraints of IoT components, which are characterized by low capabilities in terms of both energy and computing resources, traditional security solutions are not applicable in general in the context of IoT environments. As a result, they are unable to implement complex security schemes. The most prevalent IoT exploits and vulnerabilities are identified by the OWASP IoT Project. The danger occurs, according to this research, since well-known security methods such as encryption, authentication, access control, and role-based access control have not been implemented. Existing security methods, tools, and solutions may not be readily adapted to IoT devices and systems, which is one reason for the lack of acceptance. The installed IoT services must be "smart" and operate in an open, dynamic, and fully dispersed environment to minimize these dangers. This necessitates their gaining more autonomy and decision-making power.

As the IoT grows in popularity, more devices join the network, and device capabilities improve, enhancing IoT services. Edge computing is a potential solution for today's IoT, since it may relieve cloud strain by shifting work to the edge. However, installing a large number of edge nodes across a large region would incur huge expenses. Edge resource sharing would be a solution for clouds that service IoT customers since they may have comparable requirements. The approach would not only alleviate cloud strain and reduce the cost of installing edge infrastructure, but it would also enhance the IoT user experience. To do so, the main problem would be to establish trust between edges belonging to different clouds.

Blockchain is a decentralized ledger system that may be a good fit for multi-center trust-based collaboration. In reality, several blockchain-based IoT trust solutions have been developed. However, there are many issues with existing blockchain-based approaches. First, storing all data on blockchain would be inefficient and difficult to maintain, while not sharing data would lead to trust issues; thus, a balance should be explored. Second, although research on blockchain-based trust has traditionally focused on identity verification and evidence storage, there has yet to be any study on blockchain-based trust evaluation.

Traditional cloud computing schemes suffer from a number of disadvantages when the amount of data gathered from underlying IoT devices grows. Fog computing was suggested in 2012 as a way to expand cloud capabilities and services. Edge computing was suggested shortly after to offer more easy service for IoT consumers. Then there is the combination of IoT and edge computing, which is getting a lot of attention. The majority of studies suggests deploying servers at the edge to minimize latency, however deploying additional servers is costly. Many works therefore prefer to use an edge resource: (1) using information from other entities to optimize resource allocation and (2) overloading jobs by utilizing idle resources owned by other entities. Both of these methods need collaboration with others, which necessitates the development of trust. In contrast to identity authentication in network security, trust management improves service reliability by guaranteeing the trustworthiness of all connecting devices during service collaboration. Trust management in dispersed networks, such as IoT edge networks, ad hoc networks, P2P computing, wireless sensor networks, cloud computing, and more, has received a lot of attention up to this point. However, these methods are never appropriate for the situation in question.

ML is a great option for assisting in trust assessment and generating an intelligent model from existing data via knowledge learning. Because blockchain can offer reliable data for learning, ML may perform better. ML-based algorithms have long been utilized in trust management, particularly in crowdsourcing and social media. For large-scale systems, a trust framework based on ML that uses past transactions of agents to infer their trustworthiness. In OSNs, ML techniques were used to user trust assessment situations, formalizing trust analysis as a classification issue.

IoT security problems can be solved using ML methods. Artificial neural networks are used to evaluate trust and identify IoT abnormalities. Validity of IoT data using a neural network complex learning techniques may be used since conventional trust assessment methods rely on central management. Decentralized collaboration, on the other hand, means that large amounts of data should not be exchanged and that restricted IoT devices are incapable of performing sophisticated computational tasks. As a result, we attempt to develop a ML algorithm that can be readily installed in restricted IoT devices, as well as evaluate their performance using simplified data.

5.6 Conclusion

Prediction techniques based on ML are important in solving many of the challenges that the healthcare industry confronts. According to an observational study, ML techniques and approaches are important in many disease predictions. In dealing with large quantities of diverse, scattered, varied, highly dynamic data sets and increasingly vast amounts of unstructured and non-standardized information, there are many current issues and potential challenges. One of the most tough challenges in clinical practice and biomedical research is developing and deploying new methods for the efficient integration, analysis, and interpretation of complex biological data with the aim of generating testable hypotheses and constructing accurate models. Furthermore, the algorithms must cope with data that is incomplete, noisy, or even conflicting or confusing. As a result, effective ML technologies are becoming more essential in the healthcare industry to address these problems. ML techniques have the potential to transform the healthcare industry by providing accurate insights and predictions related to symptoms, diagnosis, therapies, and treatments.

References

[1]   W. Meng, E. W. Tischhauser, Q. Wang, Y. Wang, and J. Han. When intrusion detection meets blockchain technology: a review. *IEEE Access*, 6:10179–10188, 2018.

[2]   N. Alexopoulos, E. Vasilomanolakis, N. RekaIvanko, and M. Muhlhauser. Towards blockchain-based collaborative intrusion detection systems. In G. D'Agostino and A. Scala, editors, *Critical Information Infrastructures Security*, Cham: Springer International Publishing, 2018, pp. 107–118.

[3]   Y. Xin, L. Kong, Z. Liu, *et al.* Machine learning and deep learning methods for cybersecurity. *IEEE Access*, 6:35365–35381, 2018.

[4]   Z. Zheng, S. Xie, H. Dai, X. Chen, and H. Wang. An overview of blockchain technology: architecture, consensus, and future trends. In 2017 IEEE International Congress on Big Data (BigData Congress), IEEE, 2017, pp. 557–564.

[5]   C.-F. Tsai, Y.-F. Hsu, C.-Y. Lin, and W.-Y. Lin. Intrusion detection by machine learning: a review. *Expert Systems with Applications*, 36 (10):11994–12000, 2009.

[6]   B. Dong and X. Wang. Comparison deep learning method to traditional methods using for network intrusion detection. In 2016 8th IEEE International Conference on Communication Software and Networks (ICCSN), IEEE, 2016, pp. 581–585.

[7]   A. Javaid, Q. Niyaz, W. Sun, and M. Alam. A deep learning approach for network intrusion detection system. In Proceedings of the 9th EAI

International Conference on Bio-inspired Information and Communications Technologies (Formerly BIONETICS), BICT'15, ICST, Brussels, Belgium, 2016, pp. 21–26.

[8]   S. McNally, J. Roche, and S. Caton. *Predicting the Price of Bitcoin Using Machine Learning*, Ireland, Dublin: IEEE, 2018.

[9]   T. Guo, A. Bifet, and N. A.-Fantulin. *Bitcoin Volatility Forecasting with a Glimpse into Buy and Sell Orders*, New York, NY: IEEE, 2018.

[10]   F. Andrade de Oliveira, L. Enrique Z. Ã¡rate and M. de Azevedo Reis; C. NeriNobre. The use of artificial neural networks in the analysis and prediction of stock prices. In IEEE International Conference on Systems, Man, and Cybernetics, 2011, pp. 2151–2155.

[11]   M. Daniela and A. Butoi. Data mining on Romanian stock market using neural networks for price prediction. *Informatica Economica*, 17, 2013.

[12]   R. Kalpanasonika, S. M. Sayasri, A.Vinothini, and H. Suga Priya. *Bitcoin Cost Prediction Using Deep Neural Network Technique*, IEEE, 2018.

[13]   J. Wang and X. Su. *An Improved K-Means Clustering Algorithm*, IEEE, 2017.

[14]   J. K. Jaiswal and R. Samikannu. *Application of Random Forest Algorithm on Feature Subset Selection and Classification and Regression*, IEEE, 2017.

[15]   M. Ma and F. L. G. Shi. Privacy-oriented blockchain-based distributed key management architecture for hierarchical access control in the iot scenario. *IEEE Access,* 7:34045–34059, 2019.

[16]   S. Guo and S. G. X. Q. F. Q. X. Hu. Blockchain meets edge computing: a distributed and trusted authentication system. *IEEE Transactions on Industrial Informatics,* 16(3):1972–1983, 2020.

[17]   Q. Xu and Q. Y. Z. Su. Blockchain-based trustworthy edge caching scheme for mobile cyber-physical system. *IEEE Internet of Things Journal,* 7(2): 1098–1110, 2020.

[18]   J. Kang. Blockchain for secure and efficient data sharing in vehicular edge computing and networks. *IEEE Internet of Things Journal,* 6(3):4660–4670, 2019.

[19]   B. Lee and J.-H. Lee. Blockchain-based secure firmware update for embedded devices in an internet of things environment. *Journal of Supercomputing*, 73(3):1152–1167, 2017.

[20]   X. Liu and A. D. G. Tredan. A generic trust framework for large scale open systems using machine learning. *Computational Intelligence*, 30(4): 700–721, 2014.

[21]   H. A. Haenssle, C. Fink, R. Schneiderbauer, *et al.* Man against machine: diagnostic performance of a deep learning convolutional neural network for dermoscopic melanoma recognition in comparison to 58 dermatologists. *Annals of Oncology*, 1836–1842, 2018.

[22]   J.-Z. Cheng, D. Ni, Y. -H. Chou, *et al.* Computer aided diagnosis with deep learning architecture: applications to breast lesions in us images and pulmonary nodules in CT scans. *Scientific Reports*, 6:24454, 2016.

[23] M. Cicero, A. Bilbily, E. Colak, *et al.* Training and validating a deep convolutional neural network for computer-aided detection and classification of abnormalities on frontal chest radiographs. *Investigative Radiology,* 52: 281–287, 2017.

[24] T. Kooi, G. Litjens, B. van Ginneken, *et al.* Large scale deep learning for computer aided detection of mammographic lesions. *Medical Image Analysis*, 35:303–312, 2017.

[25] C. M. Barreira, M. Bouslama, D. Haussen, *et al.* Abstract WP61: Automated large artery occlusion detection in stroke imaging-paladin study. *Stroke*, 49: AWP61, 2018.

[26] V. Gulshan, L. Peng, M. Coram, *et al.* Development and validation of a deep learning algorithm for detection of diabetic retinopathy in retinal fundus photographs. *JAMA,* 316:2402–2410, 2016.

[27] A. K. Tyagi and P. Chahal. Artificial intelligence and machine learning algorithms. In *Challenges and Applications for Implementing Machine Learning in Computer Vision*, IGI Global, 2020. DOI: 10.4018/978-1-7998-0182-5.ch008

Chapter 6

Clustering crowdsourced healthcare data from drones using Big Data analytics

Prince Appiah[1], V. Kakulapati[2], Thierry Oscar Edoh[3] and Jules Degila[4]

Abstract

Nowadays, a vast amount of data is considered for statistical analytical tools. Big Data analytics have generated an exponentially increasing variety of medical data from IoT devices such as drones. Today, the epidemiological data collection pattern in disease monitoring is gathering with drones. This includes organized, semi-structured and unstructured data, leading to drone data trawling. This chapter provides big data to increase healthcare quality by applying effective machine learning (ML) strategies for segregation and drones-compilation data. The process intends to resolve the drone's use of trawled data and provide real-time analyses of the data. The ML algorithm implemented the Apache Spark core for smoother segregated streaming from various crowd sources. Three drones were configured for the experiment. The principle will increase the accuracy of health care forecasts based on the investigation findings. This result showed that relative to hierarchical clustering and density-dependent clustering, the K-means cluster has the highest smoothness rate of real-time segregating data.

Keywords: Crowdsourced data; Drone; Machine learning; Apache Spark; Big Data analytics

6.1 Introduction

Recently, Big Data analytics has become a popular topic. It has been labeled the facto panacea for many organizations' data management challenges. Meanwhile,

[1]ITMO University, Russia
[2]Sreenidhi Institute of Science and Technology, India
[3]RFW—Universität Bonn, Germany
[4]Institute of Mathematics & Physical Science, Benin

collecting healthcare data using Crowdsensing comes with a volume, variety, and velocity of data, from a market basket, celebrations, twirling club, etc. It is, therefore, essential to control and manage this volume of data and make a meaningful insight. In contrast, epidemiological evidence collection and treatment to find hidden patterns using machine learning (ML) techniques. Computers can detect an issue too weak for a person and sighted [1]. Computers track patient medical reports and family histories and compare them to a personalized patient's needs using the scientific method. Cams, online networks, and crowdsourcing may provide potential approaches for obtaining remote sensing data on populations, circumventing the limits of conventional data utilized in community investigation.

The use of electronic health records [2] and the processing by medical professionals of data are projected to increase the quality and reliability of patients' treatment. This electronic health record now has a limitation of making accurate predictions because of the variety of patient-keeping data. The era of big data has come to improve healthcare through generating insight from data gathered from patients through various sources such as hospitals, insurers, pharmaceuticals, and researchers. Using methods in machine learning, diagnosis has improved, results are predicted, and personalised treatment has just begun to scratch the surface. Machines will not replace the physician. Nevertheless, Artificial Intelligence can help operators decide better clinically [1]. Big Data technologies integration with crowd sensing on real-time analytics for streaming data for prediction would provide quality healthcare decisions.

The healthcare system is a classic instance of where the 3 Vs of data, velocity (speed of data creation), variety, and volume, are built into the data it creates. This information is disseminated throughout health care, insurance providers, investigators, regulatory agencies, etc. Moreover, some of these information sources are partitioned and, by definition, ineffective in making them accessible for massive data integrity.

Moreover, data collected from using crowdsensing information is not well structured. About 90% of the data is in an unstructured format. Based on the limited structured data, predicting that is not accurate. The doctor's right decision becomes challenging due to the massive unstructured data from different sources captured using crowdsensing technology (Internet of drone Things). This will considerably delay the patient's personalized treatment.

In practically every sector of the industry and healthcare, data analytics have become exceedingly relevant. Data storage includes a variety of data collection systems for various data sources. Their studies [2] explained the potential safety and benefits of EMR systems. These authors mentioned using EMR for predicting patient outcomes and drug prescription. Their study limited data collected at hospitals, not considering data collected in crowdsensing for predictions in real-time. Data trawling promptly occurs in response to the drone for data collection due to the wind blow, temperature, and bird attacks. Hence, there is a need to use appropriate big data technology tools with ML algorithms to control data trawling and make an accurate prediction.

6.2   Problem statement and analysis

Several studies were developed to collect healthcare data from patients using social media, web-based, and crowdsensing technologies. IoT for collecting data leads to high data transmission velocity and different data sources aside from data volume. Moreover, these studies' findings highly focus on the opportunities of gathering data from patients without omission and error. In previous research [3], the digital discrepancy and lack of Internet networks in civilized economies have been demonstrated. Countries in Africa are seriously affected. The digital divide ensures that information technology is lacking. These studies do not offer crucial hindsight and foresight on the opportunities to apply Big Data analytics in managing real-time streaming of health conditions. The scope of this work focuses on the general application of IoT for collecting healthcare data.

Data collected using drones are easily trawling into improper segregation, but much attention has not been specified. For instance, drones are quickly attacked by winds and wild animals to capture wrong information or data. Most drones have a lifetime of at least 4 h because the battery designs are smaller and do not last more than 10 h. Hence, there is a need to provide Big Data analytics that is efficient and effective in making predictions in real-time. The study will highlight the opportunities to manage crowdsensing data using drone technology, opened up by Big Data analytics and ML techniques to control data trawling.

6.3   Technical background

6.3.1   Machine Learning

As part of our lives, although ordinarily unseen, intelligence data processing can be much more prevalent, with data availability critical for technical progress [4].

As far as computers are concerned, we might conclude in a widespread way that a computer knows when its structure, software, or data is changed (based on its inputs or external data). Some of these amendments inserted a document into a database and interpreted it easy for studying, falling in the province of other sciences. After hearing more than one voice sample, the accuracy of a speech-recognition system increases. We have reason to conclude that the apparatus has learned [5] in that situation.

ML applies typically to modifications to programs performing artificial intelligence (AI)-related tasks [6]. Duties include acknowledgment, diagnosis, preparation, robotic control, estimation, etc. The "changes" may improve existing structures or improve new techniques from an initial synthesis [5]. We display the architecture of a standard AI to be much more precise.

6.3.2   Types of learning

Generally, learning is a vast field [6]. ML has, thus, connected with diverse forms of training tasks in many sub-components. This offers an overview of learning paradigms to provide an outlook.

6.3.2.1   Supervised

Learning requires a learner–environment interaction. Different learning assignments depend on the nature of the relationship. Categorization is another term for supervised learning. The labeled instances in the training set provide monitoring in the learning. For instance, in the postal code identification task, a collection of handwriting postal address pictures and associated device interpretations are employed as training instances to monitor the classification model's performance [7]. In more abstract terms, to see the learning as a method of applying skills, "supervised learning describes an experience environment," the training example provides substantial detail that lacks in the unseen evaluation example "(s) to which the acquired knowledge is applied. The training example includes information such as spam/not spam labels. In this setting, the acquired expertise aims to predict the missing information for the test data. In such cases, we can think of the environment as a teacher that supervises" by giving additional information to the learner (labels).

6.3.2.2   Unsupervised since

The training technique is unsupervised because the source samples are not labeled with a classification. Categorization is commonly used to identify categories in datasets. For instance, the data collected of a drone may be grouped as an unsupervised learning technique using a clustering algorithm [7]. Nevertheless, because the training data are unlabeled, the trained model cannot deduce the semantic meaning of the discovered cluster. Unexpected learning, however, is no distinction between training and test data. The participant does data analysis to provide a summary or compressed version of the data. A typical example of such a job is clustering information into subgroups of related items [8].

6.3.2.3   Reinforcement learning

An intermediate learning environment is also accessible. If the training instances provide more detail than the test examples, students must also predict the test examples with more information. One can try to learn, for example, how much White's position is superior to Black's for each set of chessboards. The learner's only detail in the training period was during the real chess games, marked with the winner. Such systems of learning are primarily intentional under the title strengthening learning. Following is an AI learning system (Figure 6.1).

6.3.2.4   Deep learning

Deep learning is a subfield of ML concerned with algorithms inspired by the structure and function of the brain called artificial neural networks. If you are just starting in the field of deep learning or you had some experience with neural networks some time ago, you may be confused. I know how confused initially, and so were many of my colleagues and friends who learned and used neural networks in the 1990s and early 2000s [6].

The leaders and experts in the field have ideas of what deep learning is, and these specific and nuanced perspectives shed a lot of light on what deep learning is all about.

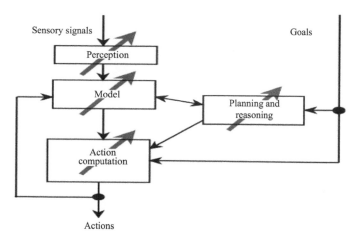

Figure 6.1   An artificial intelligent system [5]

6.3.3   Big Data analytics

It relates to the technique of studying vast sets of different data to find out the hidden patterns, trends in the market, people's preferences, and other critical information in organizations for quality decision-making [9]. With today's growing technological innovation, convectional data analysis solutions are inadequate at processing large amounts of data. Convectional software tools cannot capture or process data to retain and arrange it in human time [10]. This aspect makes the entire process tedious and quite challenging. In [10], the Big Data size ranges from dozens of Terabytes to Pet bytes per data set, continuously increasing. Thus, it is hard to visualize the data. Besides, data analytics has become quite challenging with the implementation of traditional frameworks [11].

Similarly, the traditional methods and techniques have made it difficult to store, share, search and capture the data. The reason for massive data is that enterprises are currently gathering key user details to generate data, leading to vast volumes of data being developed [11]. Russom [12] further points out that these organizations intend to analyze the data to discover new facts. Therefore, Big Data analysis requires advanced techniques to manipulate substantial data sets quickly.

6.3.3.1   Features of Big Data

Big data is characterized by diversities and scales [1]. Big Data comes with four main features known as the 4V, i.e., volume, variety, velocity, and veracity. Researchers in the field have added other features such as veracity and Value to big data features for the past half-decade.

Volume: Advanced technology such as smartphones and social network applications has led to large amounts of data from different devices and applications. This data has in yottabyte from petabytes and is exponentially increasing every second. It is quantified using sophisticated data set using the order of TB or PB [1].

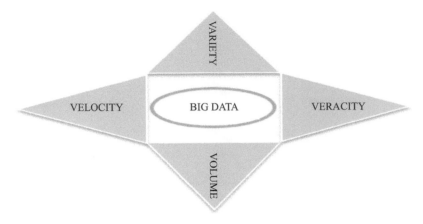

Figure 6.2   The 4V of Big Data

Variety: Considering this type of data generated for analysis is significant. The data sources also vary and could take videos, text, symbols, comments, or documents. This could take structured, semi-structured, and unstructured data stored in a traditional row–column database.

Velocity: Data is created at high speed and should be analyzed in good time to gain profitable insight. In applications such as IoT for healthcare data, the rate of generating the data is very vital than its variety. Since in the crowd preventing the spread of the disease is essential. Furthermore, businesses and companies gain a competitive advantage when accessing real-time information[13].

Veracity: The quality of data is also counting. It shows whether the information is incomplete, deceptive, ambiguous, inconsistent, active, or latent in big data. Therefore, it must be a good source for meaningful, accurate, and analyzed data within its context [14]—Figure 6.2 shows the four V.

Other research has made it 5V adding Value, which constitutes the Value impact you gain from data tripping into your repository for analysis.

6.3.3.2   Big Data technologies

There are a lot of Big Data technology tools for making predictive analytics. Some of these tools need integration with other agencies to accomplish specific tasks, while others have all in one package for data analysis. Following are some examples of Big Data technologies with brief explanations.

6.3.3.3   The Hadoop ecosystem

Hadoop is an Apache framework for distributed computing. Apache Hadoop is perhaps not as dominant as it used to be. It is not easy to speak about extensive data without referencing this open-source platform to distribute substantial data sets [15]. Forecast, "100% of all large enterprises will adopt it (Hadoop and related technologies such as Spark) for big data analytics within the next two years." Hadoop has intended to reach a whole computing community, and Hadoop is building several commercial big data solutions. Key Hadoop vendors include Cloudera, Hortonworks, and MapR, and the leading public clouds all offer services that support the technology.

6.3.4 The R

Another Open Source tool, R, is the statistics' platform and programming language. Data scientists are managed by the R Foundation and licensed under the GPL 2. Many common IDEs, like Eclipse and Visual Studio, support language [16]. Several organizations that classify the popularity of different languages state that R has become one of the world's most common languages.

6.3.5 The data lakes

Many organizations have established data lakes to facilitate their extensive data stores. Massive data warehouses capture and naturally preserve data from several different sources. This is not the case for a data warehouse that gathers, processes, and structures data for storage from diverse sources. In this scenario, the metaphors of the lake and the factory are precise. A data lake is regular and unfiltered when data is like water, whereas a data camp is more like a processed array of water bottles.

Specifically, data lakes appeal when firms want to store but don't know how to use them [15]. Many IoT data could fall into that group, and the IoT pattern is increasing in data lakes.

6.3.6 No SQL database

In structured, described columns, columns, and rows, traditional RDBMSes store information. Developers and database managers use a specific language, SQL [17], to query, process, and handle information within these RDBMSes.

NoSQL databases specialize in the stocking and fast performance of unstructured data, but they are not as consistent as RDBMS. They do. The NoSQL

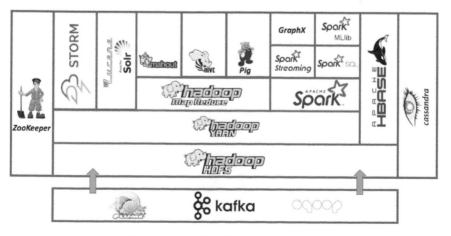

Figure 6.3   The Hadoop ecosystem

databases are expected, with MongoDB, Cassandra, Redis, Couchbase, and many more; leading Oracle and IBM RDBMS vendors now offer NoSQL databases.

6.3.7   G. Apache Spark

Apache Spark was a large-scale open-source database framework created using UC Berkeley's scala, but it merits its category. It is a large-scale data processor in Hadoop and up to a hundred times quicker than MapReduce, the standard Hadoop driver. Figure 6.4 shows the Spark ecosystem.

Twenty-five percent of respondents reported Spark had already been included in the output [18] Big Data Maturity Survey, and 33% thought the Spark ventures were in progress. Interest in the technology is sizable and growing, and many vendors with Hadoop offerings also offer Spark-based products. Other examples of big data technologies based on categories are shown in Figure 6.5. These categories are storage, mining, analytics, and visualization.

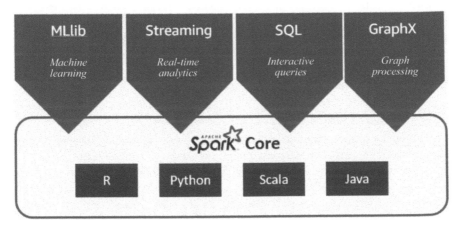

Figure 6.4   Apache Spark ecosystem

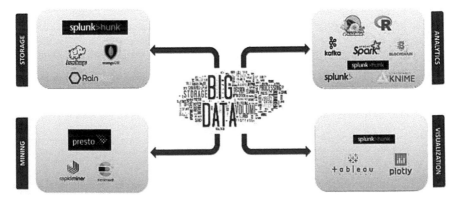

Figure 6.5   Big Data technologies [16]

6.3.8   *Crowdsensing with drone*

Crowdsensing offers many benefits of epidemiological data collection, which can help overcome the website's disadvantages. The Internet of Health Things (IoHT) provides a groundbreaking framework to monitor the disease [19]. Hybrid crowdsensing, consisting of long-distance sensors (up to 50 km) and biomedical calculations for medical details such as body temperatures and signs of diseases such as standard fiber, is part of the IoHT system.

6.3.8.1   Drone

A drone is an aircraft that flies in the sky without the pilot, either flying by itself or by remote control on land or is known as the Unmanned Aircraft Systems (UAS) or the Unmanned Aerial Vehicle (UAV) [20]. They become more popular as technology progresses rapidly. In [20], the drone is classified into three major categories: fixed, single, and multi-rotor. An example is shown in Figure 6.6.

6.3.8.2   Fixed-wing

A fixed-wing drone is made up of one stiff wing intended to look and function like an aeroplane. Fixed-wing drones differ from several other varieties in how they can

Figure 6.6   Samples of drones

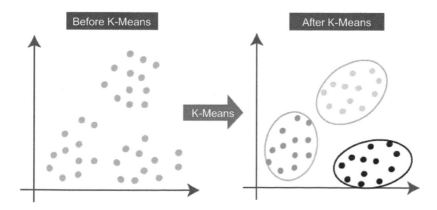

Figure 6.7   K-means clustering

hold in one spot using vertical takeoff propellers but instead drift on a pre-determined course for as long as their capacity allows. This implies that it can be far more efficient than the two other significant kinds of drones.

6.3.8.3   Single rotor

Single-rotor drones are robust and resemble helicopters in architecture and design. They feature one large propeller, similar to a revolving wing, and a tiny propeller on the rear for motion and steadiness.

6.3.8.4   Multirotor

One of the most common forms of drone for obtaining an "invisible man in the sky." This is a common choice for aerial imaging, filming, and monitoring. Both experts and enthusiasts utilize it due to its compactness and ready-to-fly abilities come equipped.

6.3.8.5   IoHT

It incorporates wellness artifacts from the digital and real-world through network synchronization. It also blends IoT and personal health technology, exploiting IoT to develop the capacity to share valuable data and enhance context sensitivity. It can also start activities based on captured and evaluated data [21]. The report of the Commission. For non-invasive glucose sensing, the benefits of using m-health things were seen [22] and mixed with m-health and IoT. mHealth supports (intelligent) healthcare defects (i.e., smartphones, etc.). In [23, 24], the IoHT is identified as the latest integrated system sensing capacity and the possibility of constantly being joined to advance patient care while decreasing costs.

6.3.8.6   Big Data in healthcare sector

Big Data leads to vast amounts of internet data and the digitization of all kinds, including medical records [13]. New large-scale data systems are committed to centralizing and processing these digital data to find patterns and forecasts.

6.3.8.7   Key element of healthcare sector

Data integrating: To learn everything, consumers and customers may use sophisticated research and computing to alter current policies. A wide range of data and company analyses are integrated. Similarly, disparate data sets must be linked to uncover emerging trends and enhance healthcare by determining the best therapy for a patient [1].

New knowledge generation: Big Data's primitive applications have become statistical methods to generate new perceptions. Patient data and their context include health and logistical data to better and correct care for the right patient. Prognosis may also help define areas for change, such as therapies, early diagnosis of more impoverished health conditions, readmission, etc.

Knowledge transformation: Data collection must be integrated, and different assessment methods to the Big Data revolution in health care apply in practice.

Big Data will reform certain clinical areas, such as comparisons, the efficacy, and statistical modeling used to diagnose, treat and provide health services to people. The data was comprehensive.

6.4   Methodology

6.4.1   Investigate objectives

This work's main objective is to apply Apache Spark and ML strategies to enhance data separation from drone-related data sources and to use extensive data analysis to forecast new ad-hoc crowds of infectious diseases as soon as possible. This approach is intended for data management trawling limitations using drone technology, which leads to a low rate of predictions.

6.4.2   Research context

The crowd is the foundation for research in the developing world. The primary explanation for this decision is the less conservative regulations on drone flight topics.

6.4.3   Investigate right consent

Authorization and written consent by both main participants and young participants' parents is to obtain written consent. The participant's permission for the analphabets is translated into the native language. The application for such a patient evaluation was reviewed and accepted by an ad hoc ethics committee at the concerned clinics.

6.4.4   Proposed framework

As a lead-up to the definition, the problem declaration (the cause of drone trawling) and its study presented in computer science and the approach to data trafficking from collecting epidemiological data using drones describing.

6.4.4.1   Crowdsensing (drone) with Apache Spark

The fundamental strategy is to address and adjust the definition accordingly any drawback of predictive analyses on epidemiological data collection systems: No real-time data streaming

(i)   High rate of data trawling
(ii)   No comprehensive analytics

The study represents innovative thoughts, which combine training techniques to reduce travel by using external high/distance temperature sensors and drones for Apache Spark crowd sensors.

6.5   Implementation

This work extends various ML algorithms' functionalities on data from the drones as a crowdsensing for data acquisition to detect and control data trawling. It further contributes to control data trawling to improve accurate prediction of real-time analytics using Apache Spark.

6.5.1   Internet of drone thing

Using drones with other gadgets like sensors for data collection is very reliable in some cases. Most data collected are not well labeled with their specific category due to the vast amount of data accumulating and the drones' life span. Applying a ML clustering algorithm to the drone's data will reduce the high rate of data trawling from various sources. Further, it improves data analytics to make accurate predictions on healthcare records.

6.5.2   Big Data analytics

The volume of data provided via the hybrid crowdsensing unit needs to be managed well with big data technology tools. Not only managing but also making predictions from the varieties of data streaming real-time to make accurate predictions. The vital collected parameters of crowd surveillance could be a good cluster or classify using ML techniques.

6.5.3   Use cases

In usability, high-risk communities and locations like the auction, ad hoc crowds, etc., are analyzed precisely with drones. Drones with crowdsensing equipment operate by the monitoring center ordered by a monitoring control center. The center aims to work the drones properly to gather and forecast epidemiological data. The steps required are:

1. Identifying the fields of interest geo-coordinate
2. Register users using communication devices such as WhatsApp and Skype
3. Endeavor, if they do not have a telephone or a GPS feature functioning, to allow their cell telephones
4. Set an alarm on the ambulance squad
5. Set up the ecosystem of Apache Spark
6. Set on the warning the ordered drones
7. Begin to flood the problem region and gather disease data
8. The drone searches for the infected person and continues with the sense of data again
9. Streaming real-time data with Apache Spark from the drones (Apache Streaming)
10. Apply ML algorithm to control data trawling
11. Predictions are complete from data while performing analytics (clustering and classification) on the participants based on their health records
12. In positive measurement, the drones automatically alert the emergency team and the monitoring center
13. The emergency team moves to the site, provides the medical attention required, isolates the infected person, and monitors any perpetrator

6.5.4   Analysis of outcomes

The concept's objective is to integrate Apache Spark real-time analysis with crowd-sensing data to track ad hoc outside crowds with a drone to monitor data trawling. Using a drone for data collection is best done with other Internet of Things tools. Drone for crowdsourcing data produces a high rate of data trawling for making real-time analytics [22].

Data coming into the innovative health system needs to be grouped into valuable data to communicate such intelligent systems. If the raw data is not a proper group, analytics becomes very difficult to make accurate predictions. Therefore, a new approach using a big data technology framework was proposed. This is completed by deploying a ML algorithm to reduce the rate of data trawling. The developmental characteristics would combine the physical and the interactive (IoT/IoHT) universe with Big Data Tools, in which objects with network connections communicate.

6.5.5   Methods description

Anticipate using Spark (MLlib) and drones (Use Cases) fitted with fiber optic sensors and infrasound cameras, as mentioned above. In this project, the infrared-equipped drones Fiber Bragg Grating Sensors and FRC will indefinitely overflow cities to gather data on the crowd in analytical applications.

Viruses generally cause common symptoms that confirm a virus's contraction: high fever, hot sweats, increased nausea, shaking, headaches, chills, and body aches. Apache Spark will manage the incoming data using the spark streaming API with real-time analytics. After collecting the data, the Spark ML library will apply cluster analysis to reduce the data trawling rate. This project's main objective is to develop a ML algorithm with a low rate of data trawling using a drone for collection from multiple sources.

The ML library of Spark comes with a different clustering algorithm. These are the partition method, hierarchical methods, and density-based method. The following techniques would be applied to the streaming data.

6.6   Clustering technique

The method of partitioning a group of data objects into subsets is cluster analysis or just clustering. Each subgroup is a cluster that is the same as a cluster but different from other cluster properties.

6.6.1   K-means clustering

It is the standard clustering method well known for partition. K-means is used to organize objects of the same set into several exclusive groups. For instance, given a dataset D, of n objects and k, the number of clusters to form. The K-means algorithm organizes the things into k partitions ($k \leq n$), where each section represents a cluster. It uses the centroid-based technique:

$$d(y, x) = \sum_{i=1}^{D} |x^i - y^i|$$

where x^i is the coordinate of x in the ith dimension.

6.6.2 Hierarchical clustering

In some cases, separating our data into groups at various levels is in a hierarchy. At the same time, partitioning methods satisfy the simple clustering criterion of grouping several objects into many separate groups [7]. By grouping data structures into a hierarchy or a cluster "tree," a hierarchical clusters approach works.

6.6.3 Grid-based method

This approach quantizes the object's space into a limited number of cells from the grid. The processing time is short and depends on the number of items. It also depends on the number of cells in the quantified space in – dimension. It works better in combination with other cluster algorithms [7].

6.6.4 Density-based methods

The clustering of objects depends on the distance in most partitioning techniques. Such approaches are limited to spherical clusters, and discovering clusters of arbitrary forms can be complex. Additional clustering methods based on the concept of density were developed [7].

6.6.5 Architectural approach

As previously described, this work anticipates using a drone to gather consumer data at a low trawling pace from crowds. The raw data compiled can be handled on edge for a long time. Therefore, this will increase data directed to be analyzed by Spark SQL for long-term analytics. These points are considered during the implementation. The incoming data will be segmented using a ML algorithm (cluster analysis) to implement analysis quickly.

Additionally, after analytics, proposed drugs are predicted to be given to the patients. The data generated are saved in the Apache Spark SQL for future classification analysis. Figure 6.8 shows the system architecture for controlling data trawling using a ML algorithm and Apache Spark.

The drone set would collect data, and through Spark streaming, the data is clustered using the clustering algorithm. In the architecture, cluster analysis is applied while streaming the data before it moves on for processing. After processing, the data gathered is stored in an SQL database for supervising analysis and prediction.

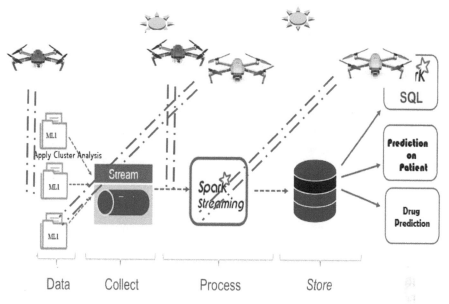

Figure 6.8   The system functional architecture

6.7   Analysis

The general definition, adequate data processing architecture, and energy usage problems are verified. A survey crowd was transferring, and participants in the trial sensed the body's temperature and, thus, some physiological anomaly observed.

Three test teams completed the collection. You performed the survey without specifying the business location of the test participants. There are ten students in each team: three pilots and three assistants. The pilots are trained to fly the drones in the specified areas efficiently. Each drone streaming data was configured based on the clustering algorithm. The first drone was configured with the Apache spark to separate the streaming data using the clustering density-based method. The second drone was configured using the Apache Spark ML algorithm K-means to reduce the rate of trawling of data-efficient healthcare prediction. Lastly, the third drone was configured with a grid-based cluster method to separate the streaming data.

Stream and interpret results list the roles and directives delegated to the team members. The three teams gathered the same demand data. The experiment was conducted simultaneously for three teams collecting data using the drone at the market. The time allocated for the teams was 3 h. The experiment started from 12 noon to 3 O'clock since malaria patient develops high fever during the afternoon.

6.7.1   Data for the study

Data for the experiment was captured using drones. The case study devices were provided to the participant to conduct the project. The monitoring team was also prepared to control and manage the data tripping into the Apache SQL.

The ML models were constructed upon the data gathered for the 3 h. The team starts the experiment at noon. Data collected were K-means clustering, hierarchical clustering, and density-based clustering. The time allocated for all the models was the same to avoid inconvenience and a low rate of predictions due to time. Table 6.1 shows the features used for predicting the malaria affection of participants for the experiment. Sample of data made is shown in Table 6.1: profuse sweating and vomiting are other factors or signs that provide pre-requisite malaria. They were additional features added to enhance predictions.

We concentrated on how body temperature primarily affects patient condition prediction compared to profuse sweating and vomiting concerning the project data.

6.7.2   Study results

This project's primary purpose is to reduce the rate of data trawling using drones for data collection from the crowd (Market). This section presents the various experiments on the data gathered using the drones from the crowd. The suggested algorithms were deployed on the streaming data to visualize reducing the trawling rate for accurate prediction to improve healthcare. Among the three algorithms selected for the experiment, hierarchical training time increased a bit balanced with time. Figure 6.9 shows each cluster algorithm's segmentation to investigate the density base, grid-based, and K-means clustering.

Table 6.1   Sample of data collected (people suffering from malaria)

Patient (at the market)	Temperature ($\geq$ 38 °C)	Profuse sweating	Vomiting
1	√	√	
2	√		√
3			√
4	√	√	√
5			
6	√	√	
7		√	
8	√		√
9	√		
10			√
11	√		
12	√		√
13	√	√	√
14	√	√	
15	√	√	√

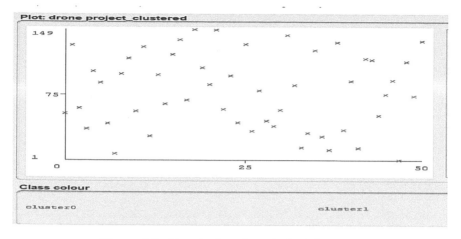

Figure 6.9 Density-based method of clustering

The density-based result (Figure 6.9) dealt with noisy data and increased the similar streaming data's sensitivity. The rate of reducing data trawling was average since it continues growing a cluster as long as the neighborhood's density exceeds the provided threshold.

The algorithm performs three iterations before clustering the streaming data, with initial starting points as random. The final cluster centroid categorized cluster patients who need attention and patients with no attention. With an average of 75% of patients needing attention, the algorithm predicted 60.73% accuracy with fitted estimators. The prior probability for clusters 0 (need attention) and 1 (no attention) were 0.5132 and 0.4868, respectively.

Forming a hierarchical data structure while streaming live requires a few other cluster techniques to work perfectly. The algorithm performed due to a few instances provided for the modeling is shown in Figure 6.10.

Since the grid-based method deals with the quantity of object space into a finite number of cells to form a grid structure, the real streaming time took a little time. Since the attribute or dimension of an object is not known at ease when steaming data. Applying a hierarchical cluster on streaming data at the early prediction point does not favor the algorithm with few attributes. Cluster 0 was considerably given attention. Meanwhile, the data streaming should not be grouped into only one group. Hence, the clustered instance for cluster 0 and cluster 1 were 98% and 2%, respectively.

The iterative relocation technique continuously improves data partition by moving objects from one group to another. On the grounds of this, the object of the same or related to each other can group. Data segmentation rate is very high using the K-means algorithm because of the iterative relocation technique. With three iterations, beginning with initial starting points as random, for the average of 75% of patients who need attention, the algorithm could predict 69.3% accurately.

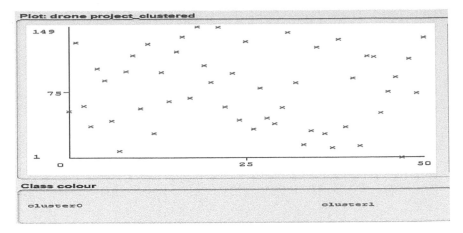

Figure 6.10   Hierarchical clustering

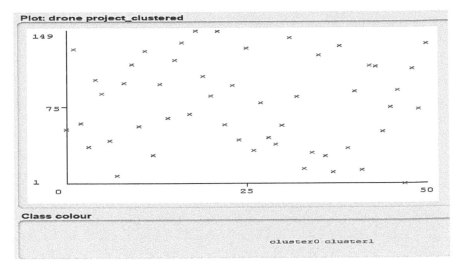

Figure 6.11   K-means clustering

The algorithm could cluster real-time streaming data of patients who need attention within the sum of squared errors (Figure 6.11) of 144.62. Data gathered with the drones could cluster more effectively than trawling.

6.8   Comparison of results

After segmenting the crowd's streaming data, the various clustering algorithms were compared using their prediction on patience. Patients with needed attention were attended to and assisted by providing them with predicted medication and treatment. As mentioned earlier, trawling's body temperature data rate is used to compare each other algorithms for justification.

Figures 6.12, 6.13, and 6.14 show the data streaming using the density-based, hierarchical, and K-means, respectively, regarding the patients' body temperature. As a normal body temperature is 38 °C, the average is high below as low and above. The hierarchical method counts all of them as "need attention" for the patients with low temperature so that the comparison will focus on density-based and K-means. Patients with average body temperature could cluster more

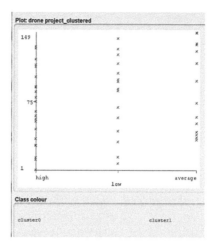

Figure 6.12   Density-based method (cluster for body temperature)

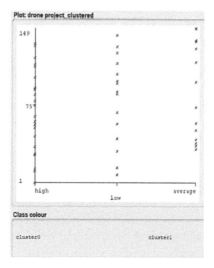

Figure 6.13   Hierarchical method (cluster for body temperature)

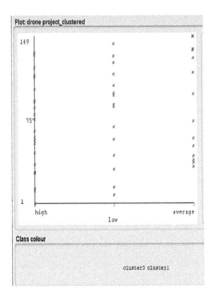

Figure 6.14   K-means method (cluster for body temperature)

accurately with K-means than density-based since the k-means clustering shows only a few patients "need attention" compared with density-based clustering. For patients with high body temperature, K-means clustering predicted 69% accuracy compared to 62% with density-based clustering. It clearly shows that real-time streaming data with drones reduced with a high data trawling rate using the K-means cluster algorithm.

6.9   Conclusion

Throughout this research, we evaluated how to control data trawling using drone technology when gathering data from the crowd by applying Big Data analytics via ML algorithms. We discuss crowdsensing data collection using drones for medical predictions, Big Data analytic tools, and the application of ML algorithms. We experiment with big data analytics tools and improve ML algorithms for controlling data trawling with a drone. On top of Apache Spark, three clustering algorithms were selected to segment the real-time data streaming: density-based, hierarchical, and K-means clustering. Three drones collect data from the crowd (market), each with different cluster algorithms with equal time. The study's result shows that drones configured with a K-means algorithm could categorize streaming data ideally compared with a density-based and hierarchical clustering algorithm. Patients suffering from severe malaria would be contacted early as possible to save their lives with big data analytics.

We look forward to applying other clustering algorithms and classification methods to control data trawling using drones to collect data. To manage and control data trawling, robust algorithms are needed to enhance predictive analytics in healthcare to save a life.

References

[1] J. Kaur and K. S. Mann, "AI-based healthcare platform for real-time, predictive and prescriptive analytics," *Communications in Computer and Information Science*, vol. 805, pp. 138–149, 2018.

[2] R. Hillestad, J. H. Bigelow, A. G. Bower, *et al.*, "Can electronic medical record systems transform health care? Potential health benefits, savings, and costs," *Health Affairs*, vol. 24, no. 5, pp. 603–617, 2017.

[3] G. Edoh and T. O. Teege, "Using information technology for an improved pharmaceutical care delivery in developing countries. Study case: Benin.," *Journal of Medical Systems*, vol. 206, pp. 623–634, 2011.

[4] European Union, *European Union Risk Assessment Report: TRIS (2-Chloroethyl) Phosphate, TCEP*, vol. I, no. July. 2009.

[5] S. Mishra, A.K. Tyagi, "The Role of Machine Learning Techniques in Internet of Things-Based Cloud Applications." In: Pal S., De D., Buyya R. (eds) Artificial Intelligence-based Internet of Things Systems. Springer, Cham, pp. 105–135, 2022, https://doi.org/10.1007/978-3-030-87059-1_4.

[6] S. Shalev-Shwartz and S. Ben-David, *Understanding machine learning: from theory to algorithms*, vol. 978607057. Cambridge University Press, 2014. Available: https://www.cs.huji.ac.il/w~shais/UnderstandingMachineLearning/.

[7] T. Edition, Data Mining Concepts, and Techniques. Available: https://doi. org/10.1016/C2009-0-61819-5.

[8] K. P. Murphy, *Machine Learning – A Probabilistic Perspective – Table-of-Contents,* Cambridge, MA: MIT Press, 2017. ISBN.

[9] S. Pouyanfar, Y. Yang, S. C. Chen, M. L. Shyu, and S. S. Iyengar, "Multimedia big data analytics: a survey," *ACM Computing Surveys*, vol. 51, no. 1, p. 18, 2018.

[10] A.K. Tyagi, M.M. Nair, S. Niladhuri, and A. Abraham, "Security, privacy research issues in various computing platforms: a survey and the road ahead," *Journal of Information Assurance & Security,* vol. 15, no. 1, pp. 1–16, 2020.

[11] J. Baseman, D. Revere, and I. Painter, "Big Data in the era of health information exchanges: challenges and opportunities for public health," *Informatics*, vol. 4, no. 4, p. 39, 2017.

[12] P. Russom, "Big Data Analytics Fourth Quarter 206 Tdwi Re Se A Rich Co-Sponsored By Big Data Analytics, Fourth Quarter 206 Tdwi Best Practices Report Introduction to Big Data Analytics," 2006.

[13] S. Dash, S. K. Shakyawar, M. Sharma, and S. Kaushik, "Big data in healthcare: management, analysis, and prospects," *Journal of Big Data*, vol. 6, p. 54, 2019.

[14] J. Kallio and M. Juhola, *Support Vector Machine and Deep Learning in Medical Application*, 2017. Available: https://trepo.tuni.fi/bitstream/handle/10024/101911/GRADU-1504009242.pdf.

[15]   Datamation, "Big Data Technologies," 2019. [Online]. Available: https://www.datamation.com/big-data/big-data-technologies.html. Accessed: 19-Oct-2019.

[16]   K. Ravi, "Big Data Tools," 2019. [Online]. Available: https://www.edureka.co/blog/top-big-data-technologies/. Accessed: 19-Oct-2019.

[17]   Apache, "Apache," 2019. [Online]. Available: www.apache.org. Accessed: 23-Sep-2019.

[18]   At Scale, "Big data technologies," 2016. [Online]. Available: www.atscale.com. Accessed: 17-Oct-2019.

[19]   L. Biswas, P., Duarte, C., Langdon, P., and Almeida, *A Multimodal End-2-End Approach to Accessible Computing*, London: Springer London, 2015.

[20]   S. Herrick, "Advantage and Disadvantage of Drowe," 2019. [Online]. Available: www.droneforgood.com.

[21]   N. Terry, "Will the Internet of Things transform healthcare?", *Vanderbilt Journal of Entertainment and Technology Law*, vol. 19, pp. 327–327, 2016.

[22]   S. Jovanović, M. Jovanović, S. Škorić, *et al.*, "A mobile crowdsensing application for hypertensive patients," *Sensors (Switzerland)*, vol. 19, no. 2, pp. 1–16, 2019.

[23]   P. A. H. Williams and V. McCauley, "Always connected: the security challenges of the healthcare Internet of Things," in 3rd World Forum on Internet of Things (WF-IoT) 2016, 2016, pp. 30–35.

[24]   A. Istepanian, R. S. H., Hu, S., Philip, N. Y., and Sungoor, "The potential of the Internet of m-health Things," Annual International Conference of the IEEE Engineering in Medicine and Biology Society, 2011, pp. 5264–5266.

Chapter 7

Authentication and authorization in cloud computing using blockchain

Geet Kiran Kaur[1], Ranjit Kaur[1] and Jaswinder Singh[1]

Abstract

Cloud computing is a technology that creates a virtual environment by configuring various computing devices. It provides software, platform as well as infrastructure as a service. Most companies have shifting or have included online operations mode along with offline mode of operation to expand business. Organizations are using cloud services to save on infrastructure and other associative costs. Most cloud services are chargeable on the basic of usage. Authentication is an important aspect of cloud computing. Various authentication algorithms which are presently in use are having some limitations. This chapter reviews various existing authentication and authorization mechanisms used for the cloud environment and will discuss how the blockchain technology with its features like transparency, immutability, traceability can be used to provide authentication in cloud environment.

Keywords: Blockchain; Cloud computing; Authentication; Authorization; Cloud services; Distributed ledger technology

7.1 Introduction

Cloud services are becoming a norm in modern world. Companies are expanding so is their client base. More and more companies are subscribing for cloud services. Gmail, Yahoo, and Amazon are deployed on cloud services to reduce operational cost. Authentication and authorization are very important for cloud services [1]. Data on the cloud is often susceptible to attacks by hackers. These cloud services are dependent on cloud providers for the authentication and authorization purpose. Cloud providers also keep account of the resources used by the different users. The existing protocol used by the cloud providers is based on the client server model. The user interacts with the client which in turn, communicates with the centralized

[1]Department of Computer Science and Engineering, College of Engineering, Punjabi University, India

server over the Internet. In this process, the user has to provide his credentials like his name, phone number, payment details, and among others. This private information of the user is saved on the centralized server across multiple data centers. Different services are hosted by separate providers. Users have to create multiple digital identities to avail those services. Research shows that users find this process very inconvenient as they need to register themselves again and again for different services. Mostly user data is saved on the centralized server which is also not safe. User data on the centralized server is prone to hacking and sometimes the user data is also misused by the service providers. For example, Yahoo an e-mail provider admitted that over one billion accounts got compromised by the hackers. LinkedIn also suffered 117 million account hacks and there are many such incidents reported by the media.

Security is one of the concern areas of cloud computing. Authentication and authorization help us in the verification of the user. There are various authentication and authorization algorithm used in cloud computing environment. Arjun [2] proposed a secure storage and access model for securing data using encryption and using RSA encryption algorithm for authentication. Meer Soheil [3] proposed location-based encryption scheme. Tawalbeh [4] proposed to achieve data security by using data classification. Mythili and Anandakumar [5] proposed a trust-based approach. The data owner enters data into the cloud. Data is converted into JAR file. The user has to authenticate himself to access the information in the jar file. Biometric-based authentication method which uses biometrics like iris scan facial features for authentication was proposed by [6, 32]. These existing algorithms were having some flaws. RSA encryption cannot cater to multipoint-to-multipoint communication. Location-specific algorithms can only be used at specific location. Classification-based method is not automatic. Biometric methods are expensive and also as the biometric information may be stored on the centralized servers it may be prone to misuse by hackers. There is scope of improvement in authentication methods for cloud.

Distributed Ledger-based blockchain is a disruptive technology [7]. Blockchain with its unique properties can be a probable candidate for the authentication in cloud environment. A blockchain is essentially a distributed database in which, all the transactions are stored in the form of blocks and different blocks are linked to each other using cryptographic hash. The key features of blockchain are immutability, transparency, decentralization, distributed, auditability. These features make blockchain suitable candidate for various financial and as well as non-financial applications. Banks no longer view blockchain as a threat to their institution. Many world banks are now looking for opportunities in this innovative technology. Many non-financial services like proof of existence of various legal documents health records, notary, software to document royalty information of the music industry are also exploring the block chain technology.

The remaining sections of this chapter are organized as follows. Introduction to cloud computing is discussed in Section 7.2. Review of various Authentication techniques is done in Section 7.3. Blockchain is introduced in Section 7.4 and various blockchain-based approaches are discussed in Section 7.6 and finally the conclusion is discussed in Section 7.7.

7.2   Cloud computing

With an increase in the usage of computer and mobile devices, enormous data is produced. Data is very important for organizations as they rely on it for their functioning. Storage on physical devices is expensive as it requires huge hardware and operational costs. Cloud computing refers to a computing infrastructure that can be accessed through Internet [8]. Data can be stored, managed, and manipulated on it without actually buying the infrastructure. Technically cloud computing refers to computer services like servers, data storage, networking, databases which are made available as a service on demand basis [9]. The main advantage of cloud computing is that it saves on hardware and operation support. On-demand services provide the facility to the user to use the resource as per the requirement. Cloud computing features also include on demand services, resource polling, broad network access, and no maintenance. Rapid elasticity and measured service. On-demand services refer to availing cloud services by the users without any interaction with service provider. Resource pooling feature of cloud computing refers to pooling of the providers' resources to serve multiple users. Cloud computing also provides broad network access as facilities that can be accessed from anywhere from the web browsers [10]. It offers rapid elasticity as the capabilities can be rapidly provisioned to scale in and scale out. It is a measured service model, that is, one has to pay for the services for the duration the services are used by the user [11]. Cloud computing offers pay as you use model so it does not incur any maintenance charges on the part of the customer.

7.2.1   Cloud computing architecture

The architecture of the cloud environment can be roughly sketched as consisting of two parts frontend and back-end (refer Figure 7.1). Visible part at the client side in

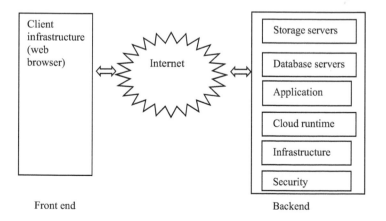

Figure 7.1   Architecture of cloud computing

the cloud computing paradigm is called the frontend. Back-end refers to the cloud environment which contains all the necessary resources that are required to provide the cloud services.

7.2.2   Deployment strategies

Cloud deployment models are classified on the basis of environmental factors like accessibility and proprietary of the infrastructure. There are four types of deployment models [12].

Public cloud: In this arrangement, server infrastructure is owned by the service providers and he manages the pooled resources. Services are available to all. It follows pay as you use model. When the security is not a concern, this model can be used. Amazon elastic compute cloud is an example of public cloud. There are many advantages of using public cloud. As infrastructure needs not to be purchased it reduces the operational cost and is managed by third party and there is no need of maintenance [10]. Cloud provides flexibility and according to the requirement more services can be sought from the provider. In spite of advantages, there are some concern areas like security, compromised reliability.

Private cloud: This is technically similar to public cloud. The difference is in the proprietorship of the infrastructure. This cloud is not open to general public. Private clouds are owned by some organizations and the access is provided to the members of the organization irrespective of the location. In view of security concerns, this model is more secure. The private cloud can be customized according to the needs of the organization [10]. Although private cloud provides more security but the disadvantage is the cost involved in setting up the infrastructure.

Community cloud: This cloud is similar to the private cloud, only difference between two of them is kind of users. In private cloud, infrastructure is owned by some organization and access is limited to the members of the organization. In cloud community, various organizations having similar concerns regarding reliability, security come up together and share infrastructure and resources. Multi-tenant architecture helps this organization to increase their efficiency. The advantages of this model are reduced cost, more reliability, and security. Disadvantages can be high cost as compared to public cloud [10].

Hybrid cloud: This model of cloud tries to incorporate the best features of the above-stated models. For example, companies can keep their mission critical projects and information on private cloud. And less critical information where the privacy requirement is less can be kept on public cloud. It improves security, privacy, reliability and also enhances scalability at reasonable rate [10]. This model can be implemented if the company is able to divide the data into critical and non-sensitive.

7.2.3   Cloud service models

To satisfy different business needs, cloud computing is offered in three service models. Following are the three service models:

SAAS: Software as a service offers web applications that are not managed by the company but the cloud service provider. All the responsibilities regarding infrastructure management, security of information, maintenance rest with the service provider. The charges are levied depending upon for how many users are there, how much data is stored and for how much time [13] and amount of transactions are processed. Applications available on Google are examples of software as a service.

PAAS: Platform as a service provides the developer various platforms where they can create, test, and develop their application. It offers accessibility; it uses virtualization technology so the resources can be scaled up and down according to requirements [13]. Examples are Windows Azure and Google apps.

IAAS: It provides infrastructure as a service. The companies can use the infrastructure/hardware over the Internet without having to purchase the same. It helps in reducing the operational cost of the company [13]. Some examples are Rackspace and Microsoft Azure.

7.2.4 Security risks of cloud computing

Cloud computing offers various advantages such as increased scalability, improved accessibility, and storage capabilities. It decreases the operation cost of companies and helps in increasing their revenue. Cloud computing has some security risks and it has been the cause for concern for the cloud computing users as well as providers.

Data security has become a major concern due to the massive growth of the cloud networks and computing. To address this concern of data security methods, it needs to be devised to protect the data from unauthorized access, phishing, and other kinds of attacks. Huge amount of data is stored on cloud servers. The users can store, update and access data from anywhere in the world. It is very important to ensure the security and privacy of data in cloud databases [1]. The insider threat is also a major threat to numerous organizations. Insider threat is when some known person inside the organization misuses his/her privilege for malicious activities. Many organizations such as Yahoo, Facebook, and Google have reported the same. The loss done by an insider is much more costly than the damage done by an outsider's threat. To safeguard the information stored on the cloud a good authentication mechanism should be implemented. The authentication techniques are based on what you know, what you have, and who you are principles. "What you know" implies that the user must know some secret password that will be asked to authenticate the user. "What you have" demands some pass code that is written on some card provided to the user. "Who you are" refers to the biometric techniques like finger print or iris scan that is unique to the user. These three have led to many authentication techniques which are used to authenticate users on the cloud.

7.3 Review of various authentication and authorization in cloud computing

Security is one of the concern areas of cloud computing, as authentication and authorization help us in the verification of the user. There are various authentication and authorization algorithms used in cloud computing environment. This section will focus on review of the various authentication and authorization algorithms and identify management access.

7.3.1 Existing authentication techniques

Various solutions provided for authentication can be classified into four categories (refer Table 7.1):

Username and password: In the traditional method of authentication, the user has to provide the password. Password is checked from the database of authenticated users and if it matches, the user is allowed to use the cloud services.

Biometric: In this mechanism, biometric information about the user is used to authenticate the user. Biometric can be physical like the retina scan, fingerprint or it can be behavioral like typing pattern, location, etc. The drawback of this technique lies in the fact that extra hardware is needed to implement. As analyzing biometric takes time, it leads to a decrease in the number of users authenticated per unit of time.

Single sign on: In this technique, the user gets authenticated on one cloud services or system and the cloud services communicate and collaborate with each other for the authentication. SSO allows users to get authenticated ones and use some other cloud services without getting authenticated again.

Multi-factor authentication: In a cloud computing paradigm, the conventional password authentication approach is not able to protect the system from various attacks. Multi-factor authentication is a reliable process. In multi-factor authentication along with username and password, another secondary element is added such as one-time password or biometric authentication (refer Figure 7.2).

7.3.2 Review of authentication methods

This section will review various authentication methods (for more details, refer Table 7.2).

Arjun [2] proposed a secure storage and access model for securing data using encryption and using RSA encryption algorithm for authentication. RSA has a smaller key size which makes it more effective. It is not able to cater to multipoint-to-multipoint communication.

Table 7.1 Existing authentication methods

Authentication	Capabilities	Limitation
User name and password	Username and password is matched with reference in centralized server	Username and password stored in centralized server prone to hacking
Multi-factor authentication using smart-phones as the token software	Generates OTP for user which user has to provide for authentication	User accessibility is not taken care of
Biometric authentication	Finger printing or iris scan is taken which is unique to user	Cost of implementation high

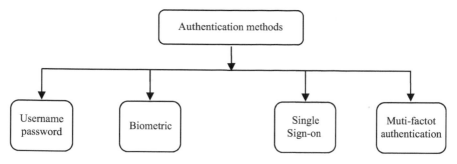

Figure 7.2   Authentication methods

Meer Soheil [3] proposed location-based encryption scheme in which location was used as a parameter while authentication. Cloud services can be accessed in a particular location. This authentication is used in institutions like banks and colleges.

Tawalbeh [4] proposed to achieve data security by using data classification. The data stored on the data will be classified into general or confidential and, based on that, authentication techniques will be used. The drawback is classification of the data is not automatic in this approach.

Mythili and Anandakumar [5] proposed a trust-based approach. The data owner enters data into the cloud. Data is converted into JAR file. The user has to authenticate to access the information in the jar file. As the registered information is copied into the jar file overhead increase.

Naveed and Batool [6] proposed a biometric-based authentication method which uses biometrics like iris scan facial features for authentication but it is hard to implement on a large scale. The cost of implementation is also high.

Bertocci *et al.* [14] introduced Cardspace where Information about the subscribers like name, passport number, credit card number, and many others are stored. User is provided with information card. When user wants to access any relying party (ex website), it is redirected to login page with info card content tag. There user selects desired digital identity and communicates with identity provider to get security token and this token is used to login into relying party services. Trustworthiness of the relying party is an important concern as it may lead to privacy violations. It has single level of authentication.

Banyal *et al.* [15] proposed a 3 factor authentication using arithmetic captcha, one time password on mobile phone and IMEI number. The Data like IMEI number is stored in a centralized server which is prone to hacking. It has complex structure.

Tang *et al.* [16] proposed multi-tenancy authorization model. It is an extension of RBAC model. It is based on building trust relationship between different tenants to perform authorization. Practical implementation was not given.

Zhou *et al.* [29] used cryptographic role-based access control in this model. This paper proposes encrypted Role-Based Access Control (RBAC). The user will encrypt the data to a role and only user who has access to that role can decrypt that data. It is a costlier model and data has to be encrypted and decrypted.

Table 7.2 Comparison of authentication methods

Name of Paper	Year of Publication	Authentication	Single Sign on	Cryptography used	IOT compatibility	Multi owner authentication	Distributed ledger used
Bertocci et al.	2007	Two factor	No	Yes	No	Yes	No
Arjun Kumar et al.	2012	PKI	No	Yes	Yes	No	No
Meer Soheil Abolghasemi et al.	2013	Geo-encryption	No	Yes	Yes	Yes	No
Mythili et al.	2013	One factor	No	No	No	Yes	No
Banyal et al.	2013	Three factor	Yes	No	Yes	Yes	No
Tang et al.	2013	Encryption	No	Yes	Yes	Yes	No
Zhou et al.	2015	Cryptography	No	Yes	Yes	Yes	No
Naveed et al.	2015	Biometric	No	No	Yes	Yes	No
Lo'aiTawalbeh et al.	2015	One factor	No	Yes	No	Yes	No
Yang et al.	2017	OpenID	Yes	No	No	Yes	No
Anakath et al.	2017	Two factor	No	No	Yes	Yes	No
Chaudhry et al.	2017	Biometric	No	Yes	Yes	Yes	No
Kumari et al.	2018	Three factor	Yes	No	Yes	Yes	No
Shajina and Varalakshmi	2017	One factor	Yes	No	No	Yes	No

Yang *et al.* [17] proposed smartcard-based approach. This is a two-factor authentication protocol which is based on openID. The data is accessed using the Diffie–Hellman algorithm. User login as well as smart card details are used in the login process. Roll-based access control is used for authorization, functional analysis, and efficiency analysis.

Kumari *et al.* [18] proposed elliptic curve cryptography-based authentication scheme. It is multi-factor authentication scheme that takes in consideration information about user, computer, and cookies. This scheme uses elliptic curve cryptography to safeguard against brute force attack. This protocol is also suitable for IOT devices.

Shajina and Varalakshmi [30] proposed dual authentication protocol. This protocol can be used for multi-owner authentication. This protocol takes multiple owners in a cloud for triple data encryption standard authentication. Community manager and service manager does the dual authentication. This protocol improves on the single sign-on protection. Primary owner can add more owners in the group and give them permissions. The certification authority checks for the owner's credentials and provides tokens for authentication for limited time.

Anakath *et al.* [19] proposed trust management-based multifactor authentication. In this model, the user information is stored in big data and is kept in encrypted form. This protocol uses ownership variable and one time password which is only accessible to the user. Awareness, ownership, and inherence are used for authentication goals.

Chaudhry *et al.* [31] proposed anonymous scheme for authentication This scheme for user authentication uses elliptic curve cryptography to enhance computing services for distributed mobile clouds. This authentication scheme enables users to use service from other cloud service providers. This authentication helps to prevent forgery attack.

Kumar *et al.* [20] proposed biometrics-based model. In this method, the facial information about the user is collected the pictures are preprocessed and facial features are extracted and stored in the database in encrypted form. It uses elliptic curve cryptography to authenticate users.

7.4   Introduction to blockchain as authentication and authorization method in cloud environment

A blockchain is essentially a distributed database in which, all the transactions are stored in the form of blocks and different blocks are linked to each other using cryptographic hash. All the participating nodes of the blockchain have the same copy of the blockchain. Every transaction has to be verified by the participating nodes before it can be put in the block. The confirmation of the transaction is done by the process called as the consensus algorithm. Blockchain works in a decentralized environment using various technologies like cryptographic hash, consensus algorithms, and digital signatures.

The key features of blockchain are immutability, transparency, decentralization, distributed, and auditability. These features make blockchain suitable candidate for various financial and well as non-financial applications. Banks no longer view blockchain as a threat to their institution. Many world banks are now looking for opportunities in this innovative technology. Many non-financial services like proof of existence of various legal documents health records, notary, software to document royalty information of the music industry are also exploring the blockchain technology. Although blockchain has the potential of becoming the new driving engine in the present digital era it has many technical issues that prove as a hindrance to the implementation and acceptance of blockchain by the industry. Scalability, interoperability, privacy, energy consumption, and selfish mining security are some of the areas of concern.

7.4.1   Blockchain technology

Blockchain is a distributed ledger technology. Distributed ledger technology existed much before the invention of Bitcoin [7]. Bitcoin was the first popular application of the blockchain technology. It was the first and most popular crypto currency in the market. It enables the owner to transfer or receive crypto currency without the intervention of the third party. In this section, working of blockchain will be discussed.

In bitcoin, every participating entity has a public–private key. Public key of the other participants of the blockchain is known to all while the private key is user to sign the transactions. Every participating entity in the blockchain is known as a node. A node initializes a transaction by digitally signing it by a private key. This transaction is then stored in the unconfirmed transactions pool and these transactions is then flooded to all the other nodes of the blockchain using gossiping protocol [21]. These nodes then verify these transactions. To verify the node needs to ensure that spender owns the transaction by verifying the digital signature and also he has enough crypto currency in his account this is done by checking every transaction in the spender's account which is registered in the blockchain. After verification, the confirmed transactions are kept in the local storage to form the candidate new block.

As the order of blockchain transaction can be different for different nodes, it can lead to double spending. To solve this issue the transaction are stored in the form of block. All the transaction in the block is assumed to have taken place at the same time [22].

All the nodes in the blockchain are eligible to create the new block. But only one block can be added to the blockchain at a particular time. So node which publishes the new node is decided by the consensus algorithm. The consensus algorithm used by the bitcoin is proof of work. The proof of work consensus model required the competing node to solve a mathematical problem. The first one to solve the puzzle gets to publish the block. The node that publishes the node to the other nodes gets rewards in the form of bitcoin. It is 12.5 bitcoin per block created.

It can be said that blockchain can be classified into four important parts namely block, consensus algorithms, smart contracts and miners (refer Figure 7.3). Now we will discuss these parts in the remaining section.

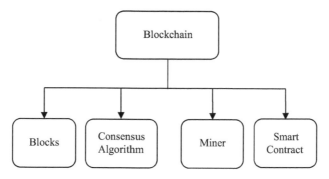

Figure 7.3   Components of blockchain

Block: It is the basic building of blockchain. Blockchain refers to blocks linked together by cryptographic hash.

The block consists of block header and body. Block header consists of block version which specifies the block number. Timestamp specifies the time at which the block was created. The next field in the header is nbits which specifies the difficulty level of the puzzle that needs to be solved in order to be published by the block and get the reward. It also consists of the parent hash. Parent hash is the field that contains hash of the block to which the present block is connected. Nonce is the value to be precise that needs to be calculated by the nodes to be able to win the contest to publish the block. The first one to find the nonce is able to publish the block. For bitcoin the mathematical problem is to find the number which when hashed along with the transaction and the blockchain header in the present block will provide a hash value that has some specific zeros preceding the hash.

Merkle root is the combined hash of all the transactions in a tree fashion. Second part is the body of the block which consists of the transactions that the part of the block along with their hash values (refer Figure 7.4).

Consensus algorithm: These are the ways or algorithms that are used to come to an agreement about which node is going to be the one to publish the block which is going to be updated on the blockchain copies of each node. There are different consensus algorithms. Blockchain variants only differ in the consensus algorithms. Some of the consensus algorithm are listed in the following sections.

In Proof of work consensus algorithm, miners compete against each other to finish network transactions and get rewarded. Users transfer digital tokens to each other on a network. All the transactions are compiled into blocks by a decentralized ledger. In order to validate the transactions and organize blocks, however, care should be taken. The main working principles are a complex mathematical puzzle and an opportunity to easily prove the solution.

Proof of Stake algorithm is a consensus algorithm in which stake in the blockchain is one parameter to qualify as the next node to publish the new block. Other factors that are considered while selecting the next node's validator include staking age and randomization.

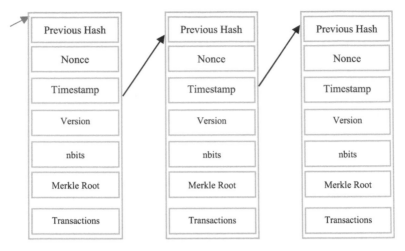

Figure 7.4   Blockchain structure

Delegated proof of stake is a consensus mechanism in which the stakeholders delegate its responsibility to some other node. This new node is responsible for taking care of the blockchain network. These nodes are responsible for creating consensus. The voting right of these nodes is directly proportional to coins owned by the user.

Leashed proof of stake is a modified version of proof of stack in this consensus algorithm. The nodes having less stake or funds in blockchain lend their fund to single stacking node. This node now can become a contender to become next block validator (refer Figure 7.5).

Miners: Miners are the complete nodes of the blockchain that compete to add new block into the blockchain. They are compensated for their effort.

Smart contracts: These are contracts which can be partially or fully executed without human intervention. Smart contracts are triggered by some events.

7.4.2   Working mechanism

In public blockchain, every node is qualified to participate in the mining procedure. Whenever some transaction takes place in the blockchain it has to pass the consensus mechanism. Every node individually checks the public key of the sender and verifies it using digital signature mechanism. After the transaction is verified by nodes, it is put in the transaction pool which every node maintains to accumulate the transaction to form a block. When sufficient transactions are collected, node competes with other nodes to add a new node. To add a new node, the competing nodes have to solve a mathematical problem, i.e., they need to find a value that when hashed together with the block will provide the hash value that is preceded by any stated number of zeros for example, 17 zeros preceding the value. The number of zeros is communicated through the difficulty level that is one field in the head of the parent block.

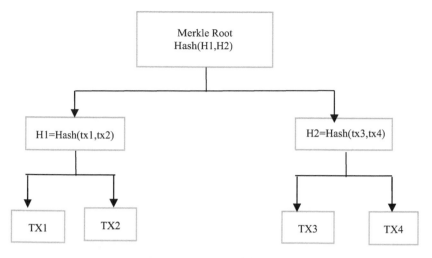

Figure 7.5 Merkle root

7.4.3 Types of blockchain

Blockchain can be classified into three types:

Public blockchain: This refers to an open blockchain. There is no restriction to enter public blockchain. All the nodes are allowed to participate in consensus algorithm as well as become validator of the next block. Examples are Bitcoin and Ethereum.

Private blockchain: Private blockchain is also referred to as private blockchain. One cannot enter private blockchain on will. Only way to enter private blockchain is through invitation, for example: Hyperledger.

Federated blockchain: Federated blockchain incorporates features of both public and private blockchain, for example: Dragonian.

7.5 Integration of cloud computing and blockchain

The most valuable asset to cloud computing environment is data. The data on the servers needs to be protected from hackers and unauthorized people. Authorization and authentication are very important aspects of cloud computing. The safety of the data on the servers depends on them. The key features of blockchain are immutability, transparency, decentralization, distributed, and audibility. These features make blockchain suitable candidate for various financial as well as non-financial applications. Blockchain can be used for authentication and authorization as well. In this section, the various requirements of cloud environment as well as how blockchain can be probable solution for the same are discussed.

Cloud computing greatly reduces infrastructure and maintenance cost. It provides high levels of scalability in less cost. This has led to its popularity. Many IT industries are using cloud computing one or the other way. Cloud computing has huge deployment which led researchers to access the associated security risks. Most of the cloud computing application has to authenticate and authorize the cloud user to provide the desired service to the cloud service user. There are some security concerns which lead to hindrance in cloud implementation [26–30]. Blockchain is a new technology that is based on cryptography and distributed databases. It is quite capable of providing the much-needed authentication and other security issues. In this section, various aspects of cloud computing and blockchain are explored.

In cloud computing environment, there are two parties mainly the cloud computing service provider and cloud computing user. In cloud environment trust and security are of utmost importance. Organization can truly benefit with the advantages of these technologies if their data and information is safe and not compromised. Mostly the responsibility of providing security is outsourced to some third party. Often information is compromised in cloud computing environment. Mostly the data is stored in some centralized server which is prone to hacking.

Blockchain is a disruptive technology that can be used for nurturing trust among the various organizations regarding various security concerns like authentication. Blockchain is a distributed ledger technology and it can provide better security than centralized database solution which provides by the existing protocols. All the transactions happening in blockchain are tamper proof. This can help in providing the much-needed security to the cloud computing scenarios. Moreover, it is peer-to-peer technology. There are no central authorities which prevents against arbitrary tampering. Blockchain can also provide transparency to the cloud users.

7.5.1 Structure of blockchain

It can be said that blockchain can be classified into four important parts: block, consensus algorithms, smart contracts and miners. Block is the basic building of blockchain. It is basically a chain of block. The block consists of header and body of the block. Header further contains hash of the previous block, timestamp, difficulty level; nonce, transaction data are stored in the body of the block (refer Table 7.3).

7.5.2 Characteristics of blockchain

The following are some of the non-functional properties of the blockchain network:

Openness: Due to the compatible existence of the nodes, blockchain is able to use and share data during a transaction.

Concurrency: In blockchain, all the nodes work concurrently.

Scalability: Blockchain is scalable as new nodes can be added or deleted simultaneously.

Fault tolerance: Fault of any node of the blockchain is visible to all the other nodes in the blockchain making it possible for the network to function properly in the event of a fault.

Transparency: Every node of the blockchain can view all transactions in the network.

Table 7.3   Components of blockchain header

Particular	Information
Block version	Contains the block number
Parent hash	Hash of the previous block to which it is attached
Timestamp	Time at which block was created
Nbits	Defines the difficulty level
Nonce	A number which when hash with block solve the consensus puzzle
Merkle root	Hash of all the transactions are hashed together to form Merkel root

Table 7.4   Mapping of cloud requirement to blockchain features

Cloud requirement	Blockchain solution
Scalability	New users can be added and deleted from blockchain
Elasticity	New resources can be added deleted from blockchain
Privacy	Encryption is used in blockchain
Computing resources	Smart contract can be used for computing resources
Pricing	Smart contract can be used for pricing
Utilization	Utilization can be adjusted by using smart contract

Security: Blockchain is a technology based on crypto graphical algorithms. It uses SHA-256.

Quality of service (QoS): The QoS in the blockchain network is measured by response time and reliability, the time taken by the transaction to completion and the dedication to provide the necessary services.

Hence, Table 7.4 provide information about the mapping of cloud requirement to blockchain features in brief.

7.5.3   Requirements of cloud

Scalability: The cloud network uses cloud resources to handle millions of users or nodes. The architecture of the blockchain is versatile in size and it is possible to scale up and scale down.

Elasticity: A proficient blockchain system can alter the workload by programmatically allocating and de-allocating resources so that all existing resources meet the current requirements at the highest feasible level at any point of time.

Privacy: Users should have control over their data.

Computing resources: Cloud provisioning services do not need to be pre-planned by the consumer.

Pricing: Various cloud software and services vary in pricing depending upon usage of resources.

Utilization: The cloud resources can be allocated to adjust to the variable load. This can be done using smart contracts.

7.6   Review of blockchain-based approaches

In this section, various blockchain based approaches are discussed and compared.

Chatterjee [32] presented a blockchain based approach for authentication in IOT devices. Five major participants of this architecture are fog nodes, IOT data hosting cloud servers, users and IOT devices. IOT devices and end users have unique Ethereum addresses but do not have any access to smart contracts. All the others have participants who have direct access to smart contracts. Admin creates smart contracts and they can add or remove users. End users are the ones asking for IoT services. Fog nodes are side nodes that contain localized storage and is used to provide access to IoT devices.

Authentication scheme works on on-chain as well as off-chain modes. Smart contracts are created in on chain mode. IoT devices are registered and mapped to the fog servers (refer Figure 7.6).

To access the IoT resources, the user has to send an authentication request to the smart contract. The smart contract checks the authentication details with the list of approved users. If the match occurs, then a token is provided to the user that is used for authentication.

Lundkvist *et al.* [23] proposed a decentralized identity called Uport. It is an open source platform. It provides identities for specific services such as e-mail and banking. It is made on top of ethereum blockchain. It has some intelligent smart contracts. It operated with the help of smart contract to provide digital identity. Uport does not have any centralized server and nodes over the Internet do not have any way to know whether the authentication claim is valid or not. It also provides a recovery option. In case the user forgets its private key or password, then some trustees are attached with the account and to replace the public key of the user the trustees have to vote.

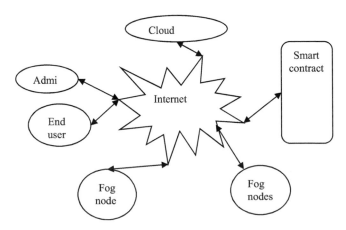

Figure 7.6   Authentication architecture using blockchain

Raifa [24] proposed EdgeMediChain. In this paper, blockchain-based authentication method for medical Intent of Things (IoT) devices is proposed. In this scheme, every patient has to register with a pair of public and private keys for his or her own MIoT devices, as well as the Ethereum patient-related accounts and devices. Information about his devices is stored in his personal nodes. The patient retrieves the hash of his Medical Internet of Things (MIoT) devices and sends it to the edge mining pool to register for transaction. Edge mining pool takes reference from the heath certificate authority data store for authentication. Medical data is collected from the MIOT devices and is stored in the blockchain in encrypted form.

Sovrin: is an open-source identity management system [33,34]. It is implemented as a permissioned blockchain. Only trusted nodes can participate in the process of consensus algorithm. Trusted nodes are like institutions and banking. Identities are written and distributed among the authorized nodes. Steward takes references for verification of identities.

Shochard: It is a blockchain-based identity provider in which identities are authenticated based on the blockchain protocol. It uses encryption to secure the identity of the consumers. Distributed ledger technology is used to link identities and attributes to user. It matches hash of the attributes of user for verification of identities

Corella [25] introduced Pemcor which is based on blockchain. It uses blockchain's distributed and decentralized features to its advantage. It stores user's information in the blockchain, instead of having a certification authority signing the certificate as in PKI, Pemcor stored user certificates in the form of hashes in the blockchain. Blockchain is controlled by authorities like banks or government. Authorities manage two databases one for generated certificates and other for revoked certificates. The verification is done taking reference from the blockchain datastore.

Guardtime: This is an authentication scheme which uses biometric information. For capturing biometric information physically non-clonable functions are used (PUF). PUF is a hardware to capture fingerprints of the user. This unique characteristic is taken in to account while generating the public and private key.

7.7 Conclusion

The most valuable asset to cloud computing environment is data. The data on the servers needs to be protected from hackers and unauthorized people. Authorization and authentication are very important aspects of cloud computing. The safety of the data on the servers depends on them. So, authentication algorithms are always updated. In this chapter, basics of cloud computing are discussed. Various authentication algorithms and how blockchain can be used to help in authentication as well as authorization process is discussed.

References

[1] Wu Z., Xu G., Lu C., Chen E., Jiang F., and Li G. An effective approach for the protection of privacy text data in the CloudDB. *World Wide Web* 2018, 21, 915–938.

[2] Kumar A, Lee BG, Lee HJ, and Kumari A. Secure storage and access of data in cloud computing. In IEEE on ICTC, 2012.

[3] Abolghasemi MS, Sefidab MM, and Atani RE. Using location based encryption to improve the security of data access in cloud computing. In IEEE Conference on Advances in Computing, Communications and Informatics, 2013.

[4] Tawalbeh L, Darwazeh NS, Al-Qassas RS, and Aldosari F. *A Secure Cloud Computing Model Based on Data Classification.* New York, NY: Elsevier, 2015.

[5] Mythili K and Anandakumar H. Trust management approach for secure and privacy data access in cloud computing. In IEEE Conference on Green Computing, Communication and Conservation of Energy, 2013.

[6] Naveed G and Batool R. Biometric authentication in cloud computing. *Journal of Biometrics and Biostatistics* 2015, 6, 258. doi:10.4172/2155-6180.1000258

[7] Nakamoto, S. and Bitcoin A. A peer-to-peer electronic cash system. *Bitcoin*, 2008. URL: https://bitcoin. org/bitcoin. pdf.

[8] Ashraf A, Hartikainen M, Hassan U, *et al.* Introduction to cloud computing technologies. In *Developing Cloud Software: Algorithms, Applications, and Tools*, vol. 60, 2013, Turku Centre for Computer Science, pp. 1–41.

[9] Patidar S, Rane D, and Jain P. A survey paper on cloud computing. In 2012 Second International Conference on Advanced Computing & Communication Technologies, 2012 Jan 7, IEEE, pp. 394–398.

[10] Xiao LQ and Zheng Q. Research survey of cloud computing. *Computer Science* 2011, 4, 008.

[11] Hussein NH and Khalid A. A survey of cloud computing security challenges and solutions. *International Journal of Computer Science and Information Security* 2016, 14(1), 52.

[12] Diaby T and Rad BB. Cloud computing: a review of the concepts and deployment models. *International Journal of Information Technology and Computer Science* 2017, 9(6), 50–58.

[13] Kumar S and Goudar RH. Cloud computing-research issues, challenges, architecture, platforms and applications: a survey. *International Journal of Future Computer and Communication* 2012, 1(4), 356.

[14] Bertocci V, Serack G, and Baker C. *Understanding Windows Cardspace: An Introduction to the Concepts and Challenges of Digital Identities,* Pearson Education, 2007.

[15] Banyal RK, Jain P, and Jain VK. Multi-factor authentication framework for cloud computing. In 2013 Fifth International Conference on Computational Intelligence, Modelling and Simulation 2013 Sep 24, IEEE, pp. 105–110.

[16] Tang B, Li Q, and Sandhu R. A multi-tenant RBAC model for collaborative cloud services. In 2013 Eleventh Annual Conference on Privacy, Security and Trust, 2013 Jul 10, IEEE, pp. 229–238.

[17] Yang TC, Lo NW, Liaw HT, and Wu WC. A secure smart card authentication and authorization framework using in multimedia cloud. *Multimedia Tools and Applications* 2017, 76, 11715–11737.

[18] Kumari S, Karuppiah M, Das AK, Li X, Wu F, and Kumar N. A secure authentication scheme based on elliptic curve cryptography for IoT and cloud servers. *Journal of Supercomputing* 2018, 74, 6428–6453.

[19] Anakath AS, Rajakumar S, and Ambika S. Privacy-preserving multi-factor authentication using trust management. *Cluster Computing* 2017, 1–7.

[20] Kumar S, Singh SK, Singh AK, Tiwari S, and Singh RS. Privacy-preserving security using biometrics in cloud computing. *Multimedia Tools and Applications* 2018, 77, 11017–11039.

[21] Zheng Z, Xie S, Dai HN, Chen X, and Wang H. Blockchain challenges and opportunities: a survey. *International Journal of Web and Grid Services* 2018, 14(4), 352–375.

[22] Li X, Jiang P, Chen T, Luo X, and Wen Q. A survey on the security of block-chain systems. *Future Generation Computer Systems* 2020, 107, 841–853.

[23] Lundkvist C, Heck R, Torstensson J, Mitton Z, and Sena M. UPort: A Platform for Self-Sovereign Identity, North York, ON, Canada: The BlockchainHub, 2016.

[24] Akkaoui R, Hei X, and Cheng W. EdgeMediChain: a hybrid edge blockchain-based framework for health data exchange. *IEEE Access* 2020, 8, 113467–113486.

[25] Corella F. "Implementing a PKI on a Blockchain," Pomcor Research in Mobile and Web Technology, October 2016, [online]. Available: https://pomcor.com/2016/10/25/implementing-a-pki-on-a-blockchain/ (accessed February 13, 2018).

[26] Ziyad S. and Rehman S. Critical review of authentication mechanisms in cloud computing. *International Journal of Computer Science Issues* 2014, 11(3), 145.

[27] Deepa P. and Haritha P. Multi factor authentication in cloud computing for data storage security. *International Journal of Advanced Research in Computer Science and Engineering* 2014, 4(8), 14–18, ISSN: 2277-128X.

[28] Ahmad A, Mustafa Hassan M, and Aziz A. A multi-token authorization strategy for secure mobile cloud computing. In IEEE Conference on Mobile Cloud Computing, Services, and Engineering, 2014.

[29] Zhou L, Varadharajan V, and Hitchens M. Trust enhanced cryptographic role-based access control for secure cloud data storage. *IEEE Transactions on Information Forensics and Security* 2015, 10(11), 2381–2395.

[30] Shajina AR and Varalakshmi P. A novel dual authentication protocol (DAP) for multi-owners in cloud computing. *Cluster Computing* 2017, 20, 507–523.

[31] Chaudhry SA, Kim IL, Rho S, Farash MS, and Shon T. An improved anonymous authentication scheme for distributed mobile cloud computing services. *Cluster Computing*. 2017.

[32] Chatterjee K. Biometric re-authentication: an approach towards achieving transparency in user authentication. *Multimedia Tools and Applications* 2019, 78, 6679–6700.

[33] Nabi AG. Comparative Study on Identity Management Methods Using Blockchain. Ph.D. Thesis, University of Zurich, Zurich, Switzerland, 2017.

[34] Dunphy P and Petitcolas FAP. A first look at identity management schemes on the blockchain. *IEEE Security & Privacy* 2018, 16, 20–29.

Chapter 8

Fundamentals of machine learning and blockchain technologies for applications in cybersecurity

Ana Carolina Borges Monteiro[1], Reinaldo Padilha França[1], Rangel Arthur[2], Yuzo Iano[1], Giulliano Paes Carnielli[2] and Henri Alves de Godoy[2]

Abstract

Artificial Intelligence (AI) as a potentially transformative and resource focused on cybersecurity aims to analyze trends in all aspects related to advances in digital threats trying to predict what lies ahead and to anticipate as much as possible these cyber threats by providing a resource through machine learning (ML) that can help companies and public agencies to protect themselves more efficiently, in an ever faster response to cyber-attacks. In addition, the AI can interpret security events to act automatically or even perform the proper screening for security specialists, already adding logs and information that will help in the analysis. AI along with other cybersecurity technologies can be used to assist in discovering the network, identifying vulnerabilities, or generating intrusion scenarios for training cyber defense teams. Another example is learning about digital security done much more quickly and effectively using ML, demonstrating that the use of AI in this process will allow implementing the best security processes without the need to mobilize large operational teams. In this scenario, improving processes and having an increasingly sophisticated base for responding to attacks can help many organizations to protect data effectively. Therefore, this chapter aims to provide an updated research background of cyber-security-related digital privacy and threats to personal data in the context of security in AI and ML, addressing fundamental concepts, showing its relationship with disruptive technologies, with a concise bibliographic background, synthesizing the potential of technology.

Keywords: Machine learning; Artificial Intelligence; IoT; Digital security; Data analysis; Malware analysis; Smart cities; Smart home; Smart transportation; Cybersecurity; Blockchain; Big Data

[1]School of Electrical and Computer Engineering (FEEC) – University of Campinas (UNICAMP), Brazil
[2]School of Technology (FT) – University of Campinas (UNICAMP), Brazil

8.1   Introduction

Cybersecurity is related to a field that protects computational devices and servers (relating to large corporations), corporations and institutions networks, mobile devices from business to mobile computing, electronic and computational systems, and even data from malicious cyber-attacks, applicable to a diversity of contexts and applications. The global virtual cyber-threat tends to evolve generate new types at an accelerated pace, with an increasing volume of data violation and breaches each year, relating medical services, e-commerce, and even public authorities are the most digitally violated. Since that, these sectors of society are more attractive to cybercriminals and digital invaders because they collect these data (mostly sensitive as financial and medical), but all companies using networks that can be the target of cyber-attacks on or even corporate espionage [1,2].

To confront the digital proliferation of malicious codes and assist in early detection, a digital structure recommends continuous and real-time digital monitoring of every electronic resource. In this sense, it is necessary to develop security technologies that can restrict potentially malicious virtual agents to a digital bubble separate from a specific network analyzing their digital behavior and learning the best way to identify and detect new digital infections [2].

Currently, cybersecurity has become essential and necessary for all organizations (from educational institutions and companies, and even the public) since the cyber-control intelligent systems and the correct methods are necessary to be undertaken and implemented to identify possible cyber-attacks and digital threats. However, increasing the employment of encryption to enhance cybersecurity, incorporating advanced tools such as the use of Artificial Intelligence (AI) (Figure 8.1) dealing with digital threats [3,4].

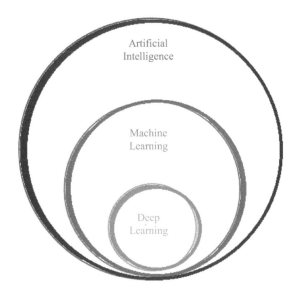

Figure 8.1   AI concept illustration

AI is a branch of information technology that allows machines and computational devices to be trained to process a huge volume of data and to identify insights and patterns. Working with the generation of intelligent machines capable of digitally learn from experience, providing it to work and perform functions like a human being. This technology has already been adopted and has revolutionized many sectors such as motorsport, healthcare, retail, and more recently cybersecurity, evaluating that knowledge engineering is an essential section of AI research, given that machines can act, understand, and even react like human beings, since that it needs a lot of information related to the outside world [5].

Assessing that AI is a technological aspect that simulates human capacity and competence with respect to problem-solving, in this aspect without any type of human intervention, through mechanisms of data collection and statistical analysis. Through the digital evolution of AI and its undertaking in cybersecurity, it was possible to identify and reveal abnormal dataset activities, and even credit card fraud, as well as digital threats such as ransomware and malware [6–8].

However, creating reasoning ability and problem-solving power-related computational intelligence in machines are a laborious and time-consuming task, considering that AI must have access to categories, objects, relationships, and properties between every data to undertake and engage knowledge engineering [6–8].

Besides, machines process huge volumes of data more readily, through secure re-mote access with greater availability, and immune to errors. However, the objective of this digital evolution is not to substitute the human being, but to enhance effectiveness at work, from human beings have cognitive skills that until then were incapable to be reproduced with the same exactitude and precision [5].

The tendency is that digital security experts and professionals, instead of dedicating and wasting a lot of time in outdated processes of protection and improvement of defenses, invest more in tools that use AI to improve security since the implementation of intelligent systems will serve as a real differential because will bring several substantial cybersecurity benefits to address attacks and protect the company [9].

With AI, it is possible to help protect a company's entire system from threats by assessing that the technology can "understand and adapt" the writing style of a person in an e-mail or even the tone of voice in instant digital messages from a user known to the target to facilitate entry to the desired system. This is the case with some AI-derived tools that utilize machine learning (ML) models to recognize the number of irregular letters utilizing optical recognition and to solve the characters utilized in digital identity verification [10]. As described in study [11], data can be extracted and the patterns could be found which aids to find various parameters the field of healthcare, entertainment, and finance [11].

Whereas, increasing the quality level of cyber-threats relates to digital data integrity and the possibility of compromising entire systems, with virtual damage to critical infrastructure. In this context, the digital hijacking of connected smart devices, given the level of connection between them and their importance for different sectors, represents unimaginable consequences with respect to cybersecurity, which would be incalculable the damage from contamination, reiterating the need for cybersecurity to increase confidence in digital technologies [12].

Or even other AI-based tools that allow automatic testing of usernames and passwords on a large number of sites can easily pass through a browser so that login attempts appear to come from many different users, which allows users and criminals access and control millions of user accounts at the same time [12–14].

Another way in which AI systems can help is by categorizing attacks based on the level of threat since confidential data is often sent via cloud systems, communicated within the web in encrypted form. In this scenario, AI tools demand to be implemented to discover and safeguard the use of encryption to mask malicious digital action. Also relating that over time, AI has the properties to automatically gain learning and enable detection of unusual patterns in web data traffic digital environments in encrypted form, that is, this will help network security defenses [12,14].

In this sense, AI can be used in the automatic investigation and identification of digital vulnerabilities, responding to cyber-threats promptly, employing this technology and its derivatives (ML) in defense processes, and even in the automation of data analysis related to cybersecurity from diverse sources [12–14].

It is also possible to employ a deep neural network, i.e., an AI technique capable of recognizing hidden patterns and correlations in raw data to automate the detection and correction of threats that, through algorithms, prevent phishing messages, for example. Considering that ML is applied to compare the data received and obtained with the standards settled in the Information Security Policy (ISP). Through intelligent techniques, such as graph analysis, demonstrating prospects from patterns identifying variations through graphical representation, i.e., unusual behavior patterns or digital actions are identified, and from classified with respect to their cybersecurity risk level, given that the solution intelligent is adapted and adjusted based on the new data and information [15].

Using AI in the security structure, it is possible to automate, by means of a process, the receipt of e-mails, which is assessed during a digital screening, which forwards high-risk files and documents for digital security analysis, before sending these data to the appropriate sector, preventing phishing cyber-attacks [12,13].

With AI, what was done manually, i.e., by human analysts (correlating and gathering data), is now accomplished by machines, that is, the gap generated by the shortage of talent in cybersecurity is filled by the effectiveness of intelligent systems and analysts use their technics and judgment skills to recognize and identify the most significant data and information, increasing the digital quality of the cybersecurity reports [1].

In this way, digital threats can be mitigated to an admissible level, where AI generates digital algorithms that identify and recognize physical and logical digital threats, reconfiguring devices to digitally protect and remedy digital vulnerabilities before it is propagated and have more complex consequences [1,4].

In addition, security teams require specific knowledge and technical conditions to employ suitable AI tools, capable of identifying threats and containing them without new digital cyber-vulnerabilities being expounded. Measuring objective cybersecurity policies is also fundamental to enhance the engagement of digital security in this regard. Or governments must regulate this process with the purpose to decrease the privacy and financial impacts of user data leaks and the employment of systems intelligent systems to combat them [16].

Investment in digital security is imperative for organizations in all sectors to be prepared to operate in the digital age and obtain all the benefits that the virtual environment offers without losing credibility and trust, providing data protection, and accelerating the identification of new one attacks exponentially [16].

Therefore, this chapter aims to provide an updated research background of cyber-security-related digital privacy and threats to personal data in the context of security in AI and ML, as well as discussing other disruptive technologies aimed at cybersecurity like Big Data analytics or even blockchain, showing its relationship with disruptive technologies, with a concise bibliographic background, featuring the potential of technology.

This chapter has motivated and focused to concede a scientific major contribution concerning the discussion of cyber-security-related digital privacy and threats, and also it is worth mentioning that this manuscript differs from the existing surveys since it is a scientific collection around the topic addressed, offering a new perspective on an element missing in the literature, while a survey or review is often employed in science describing and explaining the theoretical aspects, documenting how each discovery aggregated to the store of knowledge fitting into a theoretical model. Therefore, this type of research work is scarce in the literature, exemplifying with the most recent research, applications, and technological developments, treating with an updated discussion summarizing technological techniques, tools, and approaches focused on the topic address of this chapter.

8.2 Research method

This research was developed and endorsed on the analysis of scientific journal and scientific papers and sources referring to cyber-security-related digital privacy and threats to personal data in the context of security in AI and ML, concerning evolution and fundamental concepts of technology aiming to gather essential information regarding thematic. Thus, also enabling to boost more academic research through the background provided through this study.

In this sense, this overview is carried out on the bibliographic inspection of the main research of scientific papers related to the thematic of digital security in AI and ML, with differential focusing on the published academic material in renowned bases in the last 5 years, such as Scopus, Google Scholar, Web of Science, EI-Compendex, SciELO, IEEE Xplore, Springerlink, and more.

8.3 Cybersecurity

Cybersecurity protects stored digital information and is, in fact, a part of information security. Considering the role of cybersecurity, it prevents problems with the management of information that is done by machines, in traffic and data storage between them, i.e., it is geared toward software, hardware, and networks, that is, it takes care of the the digital infrastructure, and the system does not allow cyber-attacks. For this, cybersecurity encompasses some measures taken, such as applying antivirus on machines, having backup copies of what is on the servers, encrypting data, employing smart technologies for digital security, and even offering digital signature technology [2].

Still considering that the thematic of information security is a little more comprehensive, which is also concerned with the protection of all data. This is more directed to the physical storage of information until the data is managed by users. This consists of a set of techniques, practices, and standards that guide the protection of sensitive information, including financial and performance data, projects, stakeholder data, regardless of whether it is in a physical or digital environment. Pondering over the general precept of information security is to reduce risks and dangers to an acceptable level considering that the acceptable level needs to be as close as possible to zero incidents [17].

Still consider the existence of necessary good data protection practices such as crisis management, risk assessments, physical and logical security, security in human resources, and the awareness of employees about the importance of data protection. With this, the activities to guarantee the digital security of information are the most varied. These activities include rules for the transportation of computers and work equipment, remote access to the company's network, password exchange policy, guarantee that employees are using strong passwords and even manuals on what information can be provided to which users [18].

Reflecting on the corporate environment, companies currently operate with a large volume of data, which previously did not exist or were not obtained and stored. To accentuate, the great ease of communication between devices that increases the volume of transactions and openings to fraud is also considered. Considering these varieties of factors, it favors a scenario of cyber-attacks of many types by providing an attractive environment for cybercriminals. However, the cyber-security universe is disruptive technologies such as blockchain (applying the chain-code mechanism for virtual protection), Big Data, AI, cryptography, cloud security, use of ML to improve the process, and even the formation of secure networks [6,19].

Cybersecurity can also be considered to refer to procedures, practices, and technologies aimed at digital security against illegal practices and damage to computers, networks, programs, and data. Considering the dangers and losses that the Internet can cause on cybersecurity for users all over the world, they use connected digital systems, providing an environment for a partial or total loss of data, theft of passwords, identity, bank details, among others, bribery for the rescue of sensitive information, digital espionage, manipulation of corporate data, and even the spread of SPAM [20].

Among the main types of attacks, it is possible to quote Distributed Denial of Service (DDoS). At this moment, users are not able to access a web page or service, occurring when a server is purposely overloaded with accesses and requests to make the webpage "fall." Malware (Malicious Software) are programs used to obtain unauthorized access, capture access credentials, or monitor the user, this is a generalization of traditional and well-known viruses, spy programs, scare-ware, Trojans, and screen and keyboard captures (keyloggers). Phishing is one of the most widely used forms of cyber-attack due to the ease of expansion, usually occurring through a promotion or bank e-mail, involving the collection of data and personal information, such as credit card, through the similarity of the website legitimate where the user fails to notice the minor differences and provides their access credentials. Still consider the internal digital attacks which usually occur through confidential data or use pen drives to install malware directly on the system. This can be defined as the actions of malicious people who have physical access to systems or administrative privileges and use this advantage for their own benefit [21].

However, it is important to note that, unlike individual protection measures, cyber-security plans (whether corporate or even industrial) involve much more system protection measures, as these are environments where many people have access. It is necessary to employ an internal information security policy, which means taking legal measures to protect data with which companies or industries work and defining simple clauses such as the use of internal documents, personal storage devices, private e-mail, and so on [22].

As well as employing access control and digital invasion detection (cyberse-curity) limits physical and logical access controls, whether through digital identi-fications or even access restrictions of employees to sectors and infrastructure areas, and keep digital systems up to date detection of in-person intruders. Implementing the use of digital signatures, it is possible to have a prominent level of reliability between each signatory, consisting of a secure and advanced type of encryption and authenticity in the documents that are signed that follow cyberse-curity standards [21].

Applying connection isolation between devices and machines directly to the Internet creates an internal network free of access (Intranet) enabling the access of corporate data located in an external branch, in a secure manner, for example, by computers that are in the headquarters, that is, the intranet creates a secure direct communication channel, defining communication protocols with the external net-work (Internet). As well as monitoring systems and networks by periodically scans the digital systems for viruses, running tests, monitoring, and tracking all digital communication from end to end [23].

Finally, cybersecurity focuses especially on digital information, as well as its inter-connected processing, storage, and transmission systems, it is a specific seg-mentation of information security responsible for defining technologies and meth-odologies (using disruptive technologies) to be used for data protection in the virtual environment. This area protects all digital assets (information assets inclu-ded as a set of valuable data) whether transmitted over the network or stored in the cloud, carrying out tests to prevent potential external attacks [9,24].

Therefore, the different protocols of good practices that guarantee information security must consider the specificities of cybersecurity, and it is necessary to combat the main weaknesses in data protection, reflecting on the low rate of automation of digital processes, the absence of an efficient strategic security plan, and even effective tools.

This is because information, whether from physical or virtual media, is an organization's most asset. Considering the primary importance of investment in information security is extracted, that is, preventing (or preserving) confidential or sensitive data from the business model from becoming public, harming the company's competitiveness.

8.4 The importance of cybersecurity

With the popularization of the Internet, cybersecurity became necessary as a set of methods and actions that aim to protect and guarantee the security of equipment and systems against intrusions, consisting of activities present in information security and must cover and protect the assets in their different forms (digital, physical, among others). This topic is associated with the protection of information assets, related to the information that is processed, stored, and transported by the digital systems that are interconnected. This involves applications, software, and other assets that makeup information technology, which captures, process, and shares digital data, but are targets for attacks and threats [25].

Cybersecurity protects digital information, which in general, consists of users' personal data, e-mail history, browser cache, passwords, among others. Cybersecurity assists in digital security by reducing or preventing threats from compromising the integrity of information, avoiding types of cyber risks such as Backdoor that are like malware but, when installed, can modify the entire infected system, resulting in file deletion, installation of new programs, sending e-mails on behalf of the user and using the system perfectly, as if it were a normal user, or even spoofing by falsifying the Internet Protocol (IP), pretending to be a reliable device, and then attacking other devices through communication impaired. For Ransomware, which is one of the most common and harmful types of digital attack, hijacking computer files by blocking data, that is, to avoid such attack, ransom needs to be provided to the attacker [26].

The importance of cybersecurity becomes even greater given a scenario of digital transformation, considering that companies use data-driven business, which directs the organization's performance based on knowledge, analysis, and concrete data, and the loss of such information would compromise all processes of work. Reflecting that in a digitalized society, cybersecurity is essential for companies to keep their digital information confidential [26].

With cybersecurity, it is possible to obtain benefits related to the guarantee of data integrity, also meaning to ensure that that the information is true and reliable. This is important as it is associated with decision making based on validated data. On the other hand, it is inconsistent to use data for strategic decision making that are false or falsifiable. This also allows good management and organization of all changes made to applications or systems, informing the person responsible for the change and what has been changed. Thus, it is possible to obtain total control over publications or developments in their platforms, since when an error or threat is identified, it is also easier to locate or reverse the change that caused this error [27].

Or even with cybersecurity actions, it is possible to reduce many cyber risks, considering that the IT team does not need to dedicate so much time to monitoring the network, and being able to focus efforts on more strategic activities. Therefore, a company committed to the security of its digital information transmits the idea of responsibility and digital maturity, influencing the public's perception (competitive differentiation). Especially if the treatment of the data is related to the main activity of the business, considering that in this case, the certainty of digital security and privacy of information is even more important for the user [28].

Cybersecurity is essential for companies of all sizes and segments, although many people understand the risks and threats that digital exposure offers but are not prepared to control or reduce these digital problems. Cybersecurity helps to keep data reliable and systems always operational, reducing unavailability, establishing a security policy, minimizing potential risks, or risks that compromise business results, and investing in technological solutions that facilitate asset management [29].

8.5   Artificial Intelligence (AI) for cybersecurity

Consider that the number of mobile devices connected to the Internet continues to grow rapidly, as well as the risks of cyber-attacks to steal information from companies and individuals. Because of this, digital security strategies need to modernize their protection policies and tools used so that devices can talk to each other. In this way, it will be possible to recognize changes in the network environment and the devices themselves will be able to anticipate the new risks and even apply new policies automatically. In this sense, AI can be used as true strategic allies in cybersecurity [4,30].

AI due to its high processing capacity has been a great ally in the search for breaking patterns in networks, with properties to quickly be able to scan the system is infinitely superior to human capacity, especially with the possibility of machines expanding their learning continuously, which helps to detect unknown events and prevent them from continuing before it increases in proportion, depending less on human input of information [31].

However, AI can be used to enhance the posture of digital security, finding a balance to eliminate digital risks and threats, this allows the mitigation of complex cyber-attacks, ensuring the security of corporate information. Considering that the relationship between the importance of using robust tools such as digital security AI accelerating technological progress, about data and real-time analysis allows for improvements in asset management that also provides exponential gains in IT security, generating greater digital resilience. Thus, as advances in AI progress, new opportunities may arise to create the sophistication of cyber-attack patterns of human thought and creativity [4,30].

8.6   Machine Learning (ML) for cybersecurity

Cyber-attacks as well as the risks of privacy and digital security raise growing concerns about how to protect confidential personal and corporate data; however, one of the solutions to slow the progress of these digital attacks is the application of

AI techniques such as the use of ML to identify movements almost undetectable and data flow patterns to identify suspicious action on a large amount of content, increasingly protecting private information. In addition, the more ML works, the more it "learns," so it can deliver faster and more accurate resolutions, increasing the chances of avoiding digital losses for institutions [5].

ML has the capacity for artificial learning no longer depending on a person, focused on developing software capable of making autonomous decisions from available databases since machines can quickly learn new patterns and identify them more intuitive malicious changes on the network. This tool has been a powerful ally of information security strategies, finding the technological possibilities to develop more fully and create new possibilities for different areas such as cybersecurity [32,33].

ML is new terminology for a set of equations and algorithms based entirely on linear algebra or that defines most of the probability equations, which has properties to develop in the sense of learning alone from the suffered attacks, malware, and cyber threats. Which are malicious programs that adapt to corporate defenses? In this way, ML has characteristics for learning what was considered malicious in available binaries, since, in general, these malicious programs change parts of the code to pass for benign. ML has specifically information security, its greatest use is removing a large amount of processed information, useful, and actionable information [32,33].

ML is also geared toward the Internet of Things (IoT) cybersecurity, which is a potential technology for the development of integrated products that virtually opens a range of possibilities, such as lighting systems, sound, remotely controllable appliances among many others; however, it has opened doors to the unknown. However, precisely these little-explored networks can turn out to be open doors to criminal controllers, were once dominated, an IoT device with fragile security and can corrupt the rest of the network [33].

ML does not only advance in the field of identification and learning of pure algorithms, considering that intelligent technology is a promising front in the recognition but also in the production of automated texts that are increasingly efficient and naturalized. Still considering that it is possible to predict the malicious use of this evolution to create fraudulent e-mails (phishing), it is more difficult to detect, incorporating personalized texts, based on the victim's behavior [34].

In general, four ML skills can be the main allies of information security, i.e., regression, where the software can use past experiences to apply solutions to similar new scenarios; classification, it is possible to develop devices that can identify similarities in malicious applications to group new entries as dangerous in previously informed groups. Non-linear classification models for security feeds are treated and enriched with data volume to first establish the probability of being malicious (based on factors such as a domain, country, origin, among others) so that the statistical models have different parameters on which it is possible base predictions. Or even considering clustering, doing an operation like classification, but creating classification groups without a previous definition of the programmer, grouping the information into types of threat (phishing, botnet, ransomware, among others); and even recommendation, where the software uses previous behaviors to recommend solutions [5,33].

Whereas about digital security management, consider user tools like a personal smartphone or a sharing drive as part of their productivity. ML is a legitimate impetus protecting connected elements of operational technology, such as industrial or building equipment in cybersecurity, working together with transparent encryption mechanisms, allowing data-centric policies, i.e., passive authentication (with less attractive analyzes than passwords and confirmations), in addition to visibility of direct user connections to the cloud, being constantly renewed in security management. Considering that ML approaches and techniques are focused on protecting transactions and protecting identities by dealing with increasing volumes of phishing (attempted theft of passwords and personal information), facing increasingly covert ransomware attacks [35,36].

Thus, it is possible to use recursive feature elimination, association rules, and dimensionality reduction algorithms as principal component analysis which are important for the accuracy of the ML model. Considering that the proper choice of features is as important as the choice of the algorithm that will be used, exemplifying how relearning and performance analysis should also be in the maintenance schedule of ML models. Since once these two models have access to information from the grouped malware, it tends to achieve acceptable accuracy in detecting that is malicious, and even obtaining a drastic reduction in the amount of information that is not useful and acquiring actionable information with an extremely low probability of being a false positive [35,36].

Of course, each security strategy will use one or another ML feature with more emphasis, depending on the demands and possibilities of where the technology is being used. Highlighting the reproducibility and scale potential of cyberattacks makes it essential to constantly update strategies, however with ML's central focus on cybersecurity is to gain time and provide information for efficient decision making, it is possible to achieve systems monitoring and deep domain of the possibilities of a cyber-attack [37,38].

Anyway, the productivity gains obtained through ML with agility and scale are mandatory also because the digital hacks also have resources to automate cyber threats; however, use harmless digital traffic to learn the security models, shape the attacks, and employ other cognitive technologies are essential in ML technological solutions and cybersecurity services oriented to AI techniques. Consider that it is not just a war of intelligent algorithms, but an intelligent approach considering specialized digital supervision acting more critical, generating statistical inferences of ML and AI [37,38].

8.7 Blockchain for cybersecurity

The relationship between blockchain and cyber security (Figure 8.2) is seen in which basic structure and overview of cybersecurity tools that take advantage of blockchain concepts with a long-term perspective, or even that digital security and

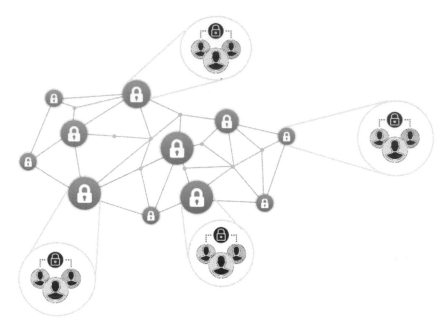

Figure 8.2   Blockchain illustration

digital communications authentication are fundamental for the Internet, given the ubiquity of electronic platforms and systems in today's world. Blockchain has been seen in the scope of cybersecurity, this is still in its initial phase, however, this can more easily see digital anomalies, since it will be recorded in the information blocks of the chain. But it has immense disruptive potential, since it records all activity permanently and transparently for the entire network, making it possible to see when a new user tries to access files that he had never accessed, for example [39,40].

Blockchain-based technology has multiple applications in many fields, it is present in IoT networks, making this technology a key element for establishing processes businesses that can even be applied in workflow management systems since this has become a fundamental component and the innovative standard for an entire range of businesses [41,42].

Through blockchains, it is possible to obtain preservation of the "CIA triad" (confidentiality, integrity, and authenticity) in relation to cybersecurity, often described as a matter of preserving these three properties. Confidentiality is present in the protection of data against unintentional, illegal, or unauthorized access, disclosure, or theft since blockchains can be used to support this by managing access rights or records (self-sovereign identity). Integrity is related to maintaining and ensuring the accuracy and consistency of data throughout its life cycle, considering that blockchain can support this through properties such as date stamp or time stamp and (document certification). Authenticity is consistent with preserving the veracity of the data, consisting of that the data received at the collection server is original and was received exactly as sent, and blockchain technology supports by providing digital credentials and ensuring digital scarcity (identity systems, tracking, and even payments) [41].

Cybersecurity areas of attention in blockchains can be seen in smart contracts, which are an interesting target due to their many vulnerabilities, i.e., it is accessible to the public, have value, and are immutable, which means that bugs/vulnerabilities, once the contract is released, it cannot be corrected. Or even code outside the chain, such as databases and APIs, with the usual security problems including security problems in databases, websites, digital key management, and even APIs [5].

In public blockchains, it is related to any node that can join the network and access/record data; and private blockchain is where the read/write operations are restricted to authorized participants. However, it is necessary to differentiate between blockchains not allowed, where any node on the network can read and write transactions, and permissioned, where one or both actions are restricted to authorized nodes. As well as it is also important to consider multilayer architecture, such as the application layer, smart contract mechanism layer, consensus layer, and even the network layer, highlighting that the consensus layer and the network layer are important for security because the two upper layers depend on them [43].

Thus, a distributed consensus protocol must guarantee security (data integrity) and liveliness (high availability of the network) in the face of different network models, different assumptions of trust between the participants, and considering the possible existence of malicious nodes. Although considering that consensus mechanisms generally have a high-level perspective, relating consensus protocols based on "lottery," such as Proof of Work (PoW) and most of the Proof of Participation (PoS), which involve a probabilistic election (encompassing the classic Byzantine fault–tolerant consensus mechanisms, however, it is highly suitable for networks allowed with a small number of nodes) by the leaders in the network (useful for public networks because it works with a large number of nodes (but are slow) [44].

Highlighting common security incidents including unsecured authentication, incorrect use of encryption, key storage exposure, software vulnerabilities, backdoors, typically created by an unsatisfied employee, among others. Also listing infrastructure vulnerabilities include node software or the network, consisting of node software, operating systems with vulnerabilities, the network itself, APIs that are "open" and even permissions not set correctly, vulnerability in node software, security operating system level host, network security, denial of service attack and even eclipse attack, among others. Since blockchains, in general, are vulnerable to an entire range of security problems related to people, from social engineering attacks, information leakage, internal attacks, including backdoors introduced by dissatisfied employees to laziness or ignorance of security procedures suitable [29].

However, it is worth considering that blockchain-based networks and applications are used in several fields; however, being a security-oriented measure, the blockchain itself may be exposed to several risks. Consider that the fact blockchains contain sensitive information about the assets and infrastructure of specific users and companies, the risks of exploits, targeted attacks, or unauthorized access can be mitigated with instant incident response and system recovery. To prevent infiltration, digital protection techniques against fraud and phishing, and user training should be employed [9,18].

In these scenarios, there are attack scenarios at the blockchain protocol level including 51% attack, associated with blockchain reorganization, and even hourly rented hash power; selfish mining is when a miner increases his chance of getting a reward for pre-mining a block. As well as the long-range attack in proof of stake consensus; bad randomness in the participation consensus test; and even dele-gate collusion in delegated proof of stake. However, it is worth noting that most cybersecurity issues faced by blockchain implementations are not directly related to technology, but to traditional cybersecurity issues that can include vulnerabilities in code outside the blockchain, such as databases and APIs, vulnerabilities in the underlying infrastructure, unsecured authentication, incorrect use of encryption or key storage exposure, among others. But, the most serious digital vulnerability is the human being, as with any type of cybersecurity [9,18].

Or even consider the risks that users of a blockchain network may be subject to phishing attacks, and in general scammers (virtual scammers with fake profiles created on social networks to seduce people on social networking sites and apply financial frauds), create fake ICOs and hubs to trick users into making payments to fake wallets. Also relating that smart contract and blockchain codes can contain bugs or even large backdoors and that can be an entry point for hackers.

Thus, configuration failures occur, as well as unprotected data storage and transfer, which can cause leaks of sensitive information. Or even control of a system can be captured due to bugs in the code, this is even more dangerous when there are components centralized on the platform. Since not all blockchain apps are decentralized, cryptocurrency exchange platforms still have strong centralized aspects, which are an attractive target for digital attackers [27].

This technology is so important that it can replace digital certificates, guaranteeing the same levels of security and with less computational resources, by decentralizing the operation (Figure 8.3). The medical record is the most sensitive

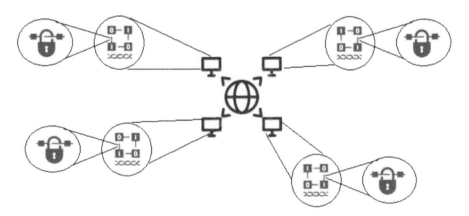

Figure 8.3   Blockchain decentralization illustration

item in relation to data protection laws because it contains personal data, sensitive data, and super-sensitive data, referring to children and people with profoundly serious illnesses. Blockchain technology can go a long way in ensuring that this type of information is protected. Or even blockchain brings the confidence built into the algorithm, in codes, which should be applied more in transactions related to contracts in the civil scope [45].

Even the logistics sector will also be another major beneficiary of the blockchain, since it is possible to apply the technology in transporting a container from Hong Kong, for example, to another part of the world going through hundreds of document steps. And in that sense, blockchain technology gains relevance due to the elevated level of confidence that this gives to transactions, executing what is written, ensuring that everything will happen exactly as it was established between the parties [18].

8.8 Discussion

The defensive capabilities of blockchain are designed with certain security elements like the distributed nature of data storage, reinforcing digital security in transactions of different natures that need to ensure the protection of personal and sensitive data. Blockchain technology is seen as a future trend for the validation and certification of contracts and negotiations of a different nature because it is a technology that simplifies processes while bringing security. Blockchain is useful and promising in terms of mitigating cyber risk due to its properties related to decentralized digital identity.

In the same sense, AI accelerates response times and optimizes security operations that suffer from scarce resources, considering that most transactional operations follow some repetitive order of events (debits and credits, records, among other aspects). And in that sense, sequence-based anomaly detection using deep learning technologies, ML-derived and successor techniques, such as recurrent neural networks, learns the specific sequence of patterns (logical operations).

As cyber-attacks increase in volume and complexity, AI is helping to analyze cybersecurity operations with scarce resources to predict threats, managing threat intelligence from instant insights to combat the noise of thousands of daily alerts, reducing response times dramatically. Considering that in the corporate environment, the search for digital innovations with the AI tendency to evaluate a large number of scenarios in which ML can generate value for the business.

This can be deployed in an existing system by adding solid tools in cybersecurity eliminating several types of attacks or malicious behavior. Consider that deep neural networks can favor the development of innovative solutions against intelligent malware that is more difficult to detect than "traditional" web-based viruses, such as Trojans, spyware, phishing, or cross-site scripting, allowing responses against threats with greater confidence and velocity.

Through AI, it is possible to eliminate time-consuming tasks and provide detailed risk analysis, reducing the time that human digital security analysts spend to make critical decisions and apply an orchestrated response to remedy the cyber threat.

Still considering the computational power automatically which investigating the danger indicators and obtaining critical insights, consolidating log events and network flow data from thousands of devices, analyzing the data and context-based benchmarking to understand security events, terminals, and applications, correlating them in single alerts, speeding up incident analysis and correction. Or even managing and automating hundreds of time-consuming, repetitive, and complicated response actions that needed human intervention in the past establish a central hub integrating a digital security infrastructure to manage the response script with speed and agility, protecting endpoints, users, applications, documents, and data, discovering endpoint vulnerabilities, with contention and identity management.

Considering that Big Data (Figure 8.4) is not only a data volume tool but also a strategic analysis mechanism, allowing the interpretation of the data obtained; it is possible to obtain important insights on various issues, since this process makes it possible to identify cybersecurity opportunities. Thus, Big Data analytics is essential to map abnormal actions, since it is characterized as a tool that, in addition to ensuring digital security, has ample capacity for collecting data from multiple sources, is customizable, and adapts to the requirements of each project.

Through Big Data and predictive analytics technologies, taking a proactive stance to understand threats before the digital attacker causes any type of virtual damage, capable of performing real-time analysis, reducing detection time, and improving the efficiency of operations around cyber-attacks may go unnoticed. This requires constant monitoring of network behavior in real-time so that threats are proactively minimized before a significant loss occurs so that irregular activities can be differentiated from normal activities. Applying predictive and behavioral analyses to all available institutional data (public or private) make it possible to estimate the potential of threats, detect attacks, and achieve advanced intelligence.

As it is also necessary to integrate the Big Data analytics platform into the core of existing security systems, improving advanced behavior analysis, to provide the market with an additional layer of security and digital detention in relation to network threats. Emphasizing that these types of effective Big Data solutions differ

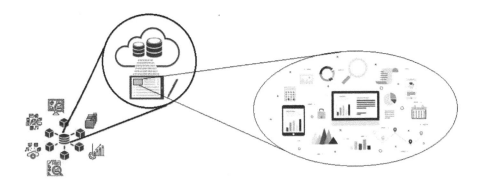

Figure 8.4   Big Data illustration

Figure 8.5   Big Data and predictive analysis illustration

from reactive "collect and analyze" methods, as they use high-performance analytics to process and evaluate billions of network transactions in real-time, to understand the business behavior in each system through inspections of correlated daily transactions in order to capture risks, identify possible threats, shortening the time to detect security threats and improve the efficiency of operations. Big Data analytics (Figure 8.5) include advanced and critical predictive analysis in advancing the cyber order, with operational risk management and cyber threats reaching the reduction of gaps and the complexity of digital channels, through advanced analytical intelligence services.

8.9   Trends

In order to try to prevent devices from being attacked and contaminating the corporate network, endpoint protection is adopted, related to digital security that ensures when the device connects to the company network, allowing to articulate the use of firewalls, antivirus and virus protection, malware, spyware on workstations and servers, encryption, network access control (NAC) and even two-point scanning to ensure the best possible protection, the server will do a full scan to ensure that it is operating within the rules of security before enabling access [46].

The Security Information and Event Management (SIEM) and ML tools will help find out who the digital attackers are who accessed company data before. Considering Security Orchestration, Automation and Response (SOAR) solutions, which allow to collect data on digital security threats and automatically respond to low-level attacks. In addition, it is important to highlight the User and Event Behavior Analytics (UEBA) solutions, which employ ML to model user behavior in corporate networks and identify the sign of a cyber-attack [47].

Deep learning analytics technology serves as a service module to make incident investigation faster and more effective, dramatically reducing false positive alarms and supporting proactive decision making and requesting faster intervention during events, accurately recognizing incidents such as digital intrusion and invasion. Given the continuing importance of cybersecurity being necessary to protect against network attacks, digital threats to organizations are too great to ignore and the consequences of failure are very damaging. Also consider that through unsupervised deep learning, it is possible to act with scalability by studying characteristics and properties of malware to identify and classify them in categories of significant threats [48].

8.10   Conclusions

All information and data are confidential (business information from companies, governments, and even users, consisting of investments, financial statements, and planning, among others) and must be protected with digital care, away from malicious people on the Internet. It is in this context that cybersecurity enters a set of actions and techniques to protect systems, programs, networks, and equipment from digital invasions, to ensure that such data is only accessible to those authorized to do so. In this way, it is possible to ensure that valuable data does not leak or be breached in cyber-attacks, which may be intended to access servers, steal passwords, hijack data, or even defraud financial transactions.

AI and ML as deep learning algorithms emerging as more prominent technologies especially with an AI revolution in cybersecurity that will make solutions more efficient. Also including natural language processing technologies, neural networks, and deep learning, consisting of trends for digital security that include advanced systems that can understand, learn, predict, adapt, and potentially even operate autonomously, identifies cyber risk and digital threats more quickly. The trend is that these systems incorporated with these disruptive technologies lead to the creation of smarter programs and devices driven by the combination of three characteristics such as greater data processing power, advanced algorithms, and the collection of large volumes of data.

AI and ML are needed in a cybersecurity solution, considering the ML ability to delve into the history of security data making the institutional environment (public and private) more secure to create an image of a specific attack based on its variables and relationships and predict the next digital attack or attempt based on that knowledge. Still considering that AI-oriented solutions can also be easily adapted to the constantly evolving cyber threat landscape based on Big Data insights, exemplifying the performance and use of AI and ML techniques in the financial sector to monitor transactions in real-time and establish predictive models capable of showing the probability of a transaction being fraudulent.

Or even relating the potential use of Big Data as an extension of the human eye that cannot see movements in the entire database, the characteristics that technology can track information, to separate data, encrypt, and prevent that non-accredited people have permission to access it. Or even relating the Blockchain technology that is suitable as a security measure, with encrypted data and separated by blocks in different "locations," aiming at the digital difficulty that an offender will be able to copy the information.

Or even Big Data analytics has the properties to identify patterns that are not common, pointing out changes and also mapping where changes were made, to ensure data security can be used in conjunction with ML, allowing machines and devices are taught to read patterns and point out when something different happens, generating alert alerts, related to the use of digital learning algorithms that help to identify cyber fraud patterns, before it occurs.

References

[1] França, R. P., A. C. B. Monteiro, R. Arthur, and Y. Iano. "The fundamentals and potential for cybersecurity of big data in the modern world." In: *Machine Intelligence and Big Data Analytics for Cyber-security Applications,* Springer, Cham, 2021, pp. 51–73.

[2] Thames, L., and D. Schaefer. *Cybersecurity for Industry 4.0,* Springer, Heidelberg, 2017.

[3] Mahdavifar, S., and A. A. Ghorbani. "Application of deep learning to cyber-security: a survey." *Neurocomputing* 347 (2019): 149–176.

[4] Li, J.-H. "Cybersecurity meets artificial intelligence: a survey." *Frontiers of Information Technology & Electronic Engineering* 19.12 (2018): 1462–1474.

[5] França, R. P., A. C. B. Monteiro, R. Arthur, and Y. Iano. "An overview of the machine learning applied in smart cities." In *Smart Cities: A Data Analytics Perspective,* 2021, 91–111.

[6] França, R. P., A. C. B. Monteiro, R. Arthur, and Y. Iano. "An overview of deep learning in big data, image, and signal processing in the modern digital age." *Trends in Deep Learning Methodologies: Algorithms, Applications, and Systems* 4 (2020): 63.

[7] Joshi, P. *Artificial Intelligence with Python,* Packt Publishing Ltd, 2017.

[8] Ciaburro, G., and B. Venkateswaran. *Neural Networks with R: Smart Models Using CNN, RNN, Deep Learning, and Artificial Intelligence Principles,* Packt Publishing Ltd, 2017.

[9] Zhang, D. "Big data security and privacy protection." In: 8th International Conference on Management and Computer Science (ICMCS 2018), Atlantis Press, 2018.

[10] Manogaran, G., C. Thota, D. Lopez, and R. Sundarasekar. "Big data security intelligence for healthcare industry 4.0." In *Cybersecurity for Industry 4.0,* Springer, Cham, 2017, pp. 103–126.

[11] Sanghvi, H. A., S. B. Pandya, P. Chattopadhyay, R. H. Patel, and A. S. Pandya. "Data science for E-Healthcare, entertainment and finance." In *2021 Third International Conference on Inventive Research in Computing Applications (ICIRCA),* IEEE, 2021, September, pp. 604–611.

[12]   Dey, N., A. E. Hassanien, C. Bhatt, A. Ashour, and S. C. Satapathy (Eds.). *Internet of things and Big Data Analytics Toward Next-Generation Intelligence*, Springer, Berlin, 2018, pp. 3–549.

[13]   Jiang, F., Fu, Y., Gupta, B. B., *et al.* "Deep learning-based multi-channel intelligent attack detection for data security." *IEEE transactions on Sustainable Computing* (2018).

[14]   Li, J. H. "Cybersecurity meets artificial intelligence: a survey." *Frontiers of Information Technology & Electronic Engineering* 19(12) (2018): 1462–1474.

[15]   McLaughlin, M.-D. and J. Gogan. "Challenges and best practices in information security management." *MIS Quarterly Executive* 17.3 (2018): 12.

[16]   Horowitz, M. C., G. C. Allen, E. Saravalle, A. Cho, K. Frederick, and P. Scharre. *Artificial Intelligence and International Security*. Center for a New American Security, 2018.

[17]   França, R. P., Y. Iano, A.C.B. Monterio, and R. Arthur. "Applying a methodology in data transmission of discrete events from the perspective of cyber-physical systems environments." In: *Artificial Intelligence Paradigms for Smart Cyber-Physical Systems*, IGI Global, 2020, pp. 278–300.

[18]   Baumann, M.-O. and W. J. Schünemann. "Introduction: privacy, data protection and cybersecurity in Europe." In: *Privacy, Data Protection and Cybersecurity in Europe,* Springer, Cham, 2017, pp. 1–14.

[19]   França, R. P., Y. Iano, A.C.B. Monterio, and R. Arthur. "Big Data and cloud computing: a technological and literary background." In: *Advanced Deep Learning Applications in Big Data Analytics*, IGI Global, 2020, pp. 29–50.

[20]   Singer, P. W. and A. Friedman. *Cybersecurity: What Everyone Needs to Know*, OUP, USA, 2014.

[21]   Zargar, S. T., J. Joshi, and D. Tipper. "A survey of defense mechanisms against distributed denial of service (DDoS) flooding attacks." *IEEE Communications Surveys & Tutorials*, 15(4) (2013): 2046–2069.

[22]   Gupta, B. B., G. M. Perez, D. P. Agrawal, and D. Gupta. *Handbook of Computer Networks and Cyber Security*, Springer Science and Business Media LLC, New York, NY, 2020.

[23]   Taylor, P. J., T. Dargahi, A. Dehghantanha, R. M. Parizi, and K. K. R. Choo. "A systematic literature review of blockchain cybersecurity." *Digital Communications and Networks* 6(2) (2020): 147–156.

[24]   Mousavinejad, E., F. Yang, Q. L. Han, and L. Vlacic. "A novel cyber-attack detection method in networked control systems." *IEEE Transactions on Cybernetics* 48(11) (2018): 3254–3264.

[25]   Farahat, I. S., A. S. Tolba, M. Elhoseny, and W. Eladrosy. "Data security and challenges in smart cities." In: Security in Smart *Cities: Models, Applications, and Challenges*, Springer, Cham, 2019, pp. 117–142.

[26]   Huang, Z, and B. Yang. "Insight of the protection for data security under selective opening attacks." *Information Sciences* 412 (2017): 223–241.

[27]   Lezzi, M., M. Lazoi, and A. Corallo. "Cybersecurity for Industry 4.0 in the current literature: a reference framework." *Computers in Industry*, 103 (2018): 97–110.

[28] Gordon, L. A. and M. P. Loeb. *Managing Cybersecurity Resources: A Cost-Benefit Analysis*, Vol. 1, McGraw-Hill, New York, NY, 2006.

[29] Thames, L. and D. Schaefer. "Industry 4.0: an overview of key benefits, technologies, and challenges." In *Cybersecurity for Industry 4.0.*, Springer, Cham, 2017, pp. 1–33.

[30] Yampolskiy, R. V. and M. S. Spellchecker. "Artificial intelligence safety and cybersecurity: a timeline of AI failures." arXiv preprint arXiv:1610.07997 (2016).

[31] Jackson, P. C. *Introduction to Artificial Intelligence*. Courier Dover Publications, 2019.

[32] Dasgupta, D., Z. Akhtar, and S. Sen. "Machine learning in cybersecurity: a comprehensive survey." *The Journal of Defense Modeling and Simulation* (2020): 1548512920951275.

[33] Buczak, A. L. and E. Guven. "A survey of data mining and machine learning methods for cybersecurity intrusion detection." *IEEE Communications Surveys & Tutorials* 18.2 (2015): 1153–1176.

[34] Boukerche, A. and R. W. L. Coutinho. "Design guidelines for machine learning-based cybersecurity in Internet of Things." *IEEE Network* 2020.

[35] Xin, Y., Kong, L., Liu, Z., *et al.* "Machine learning and deep learning methods for cybersecurity." *IEEE Access* 6 (2018): 35365–35381.

[36] Fraley, J. B. and J. Cannady. "The promise of machine learning in cyber-security." SoutheastCon 2017. IEEE, 2017.

[37] Torres, J. M., C. I. Comesaña, and P. J. García-Nieto. "Machine learning techniques applied to cybersecurity." *International Journal of Machine Learning and Cybernetics* 10.10 (2019): 2823–2836.

[38] Sarker, I. H., A.S.M. Kayes, S. Badsha, *et al.* "Cybersecurity data science: an overview from machine learning perspective." *Journal of Big Data* 7.1 (2020): 1–29.

[39] Ahram, T., A. Sargolzaei, S. Sargolzaei, *et al.* "Blockchain technology innovations." In 2017 IEEE Technology & Engineering Management Conference (TEMSCON), IEEE, 2017.

[40] Tyagi, A. K., and A. Abraham (eds.). *Recent Trends in Blockchain for Information Systems Security and Privacy*, 1st ed. CRC Press, 2021. https://doi.org/10.1201/9781003139737

[41] França, R. P., A. C. B. Monteiro, R. Arthur, and Y. Iano. "9 An overview of blockchain and its applications in the modern digital age." In *Security and Trust Issues in Internet of Things: Blockchain to the Rescue*, CRC Press, London, 2020, p. 185.

[42] de Sá, L. A. R., Y. Iano, G. G. de Oliveira, D. Pajuelo, A. C. B. Monteiro, and R. P. França. "An insight into applications of Internet of Things security from a blockchain perspective." In Brazilian Technology Symposium, Springer, Cham, 2019, October, pp. 143–152.

[43] Guegan, D. *Public Blockchain Versus Private Blockchain*, Academic Press, London, 2017.

[44] Nandwani, A., M. Gupta, and N. Thakur. "Proof-of-participation: imple-mentation of proof-of-stake through proof-of-work." International

Conference on Innovative Computing and Communications, Springer, Singapore, 2019.

[45]   Wang, L. and G. Wang. "Big data in cyber-physical systems, digital manufacturing and industry 4.0." *International Journal of Engineering and Manufacturing (IJEM)* 6.4 (2016): 1–8.

[46]   Serrao, G. J. "Network access control (NAC): An open-source analysis of architectures and requirements." 44th Annual 2010 IEEE International Carnahan Conference on Security Technology, IEEE, 2010.

[47]   Cinque, M., D. Cotroneo, and A. Pecchia. "Challenges and directions in security information and event management (SIEM)." 2018 IEEE International Symposium on Software Reliability Engineering Workshops (ISSREW), IEEE, 2018.

[48]   Deyu, M. E. N. G. and S. U. N. Lina. "Some new trends of deep learning research." *Chinese Journal of Electronics* 28.6 (2019): 1087–1090.

Chapter 9

Real-world applications of generative adversarial networks and their role in blockchain technology

*Kondreddy Rohith Sai Reddy[1], Muppaneni S.K.M. Sriniketh[1],
P. Sai Sanketh Varma[1], Kathiravan Srinivasan[2],
Aswani Kumar Cherukuri[1] and Firuz Kamalov[3]*

Abstract

This new term called "Blockchain" has come into the limelight over this decade, significantly impacting almost all major industries' development and efficiency. Blockchain is nothing but just a database. This database stores data blocks that are encrypted and chained together to form a single point of truth (SPOT) for data. Here the digital assets are not transferred or duplicated but are distributed. This creates a rigid record of assets. The asset is localised, giving public access in real-time and transparency. Document's decency is preserved via a transparent record of changes, which builds trust in the asset. A technology of this calibre when blended with another revolutionary technology called Generative Adversarial Networks (GANs) gives an outcome of utmost efficiency. GAN is the hottest topic of recent research. Since 2014, GANs have been widely studied for many years, and there are a large number of algorithms proposed by many researchers. However, very few complete studies explain the link between GAN variability and how it has evolved. In this chapter, we attempt to provide updates on the various uses of GANs in running applications. In this chapter, we discussed the way GANs are used in various real-time applications. We had reviewed various models for estimating generative models used in healthcare, Internet of Things (IoT), credit card fraud detection, and some other applications, in which GANs are used. In addition, GANs are integrated with other machine learning (ML) algorithms for specific applications, such as less supervised Learning, learning transfer, enhanced learning. This chapter compares the similarities and differences in these GAN methods. Second, theoretical issues related to GANs are being investigated. Third, the general use of

[1]School of Information Technology and Engineering, Vellore Institute of Technology, India
[2]School of Computer Science and Engineering, Vellore Institute of Technology, India
[3]Faculty of Engineering, Canadian University of Dubai, United Arab Emirates

GANs in ML, image processing, the medical field, and data science is also mentioned. Here we will be mainly focussing on real-time use of GAN such as self-driving, credit card fraud, and field medical. Also, there have been quite a few applications of GANs in blockchain, which we will be discussing in this chapter.

Keywords: Generative adversarial networks; Blockchain technology; Popular real-world applications; Deep learning techniques for smart era

9.1   Introduction

Generative adversarial networks also called GAN's are the recent trending topic in the field of research. As these were recently introduced by the reputed Ian Goodfellow and his colleagues in the year 2014, there are a lot of interesting parts to be discovered, yet in this, GAN's true potential is still not found [1].

Figure 9.1 contains the pictures that are the outcome of the model which GAN trains with all the inputs of many pictures of celebrities. Then the output is a new image out of the given input, which turned out to be the unique photos with unique facial features from the input images, overall a unique face. This would give a sample outcome of what GANs are capable of. Generative modelling is a type of unsupervised learning of machine learning (ML). In this method, the GANs should learn the new features by themselves [2]. These are a clever way of training GAN by telling the problem as a supervised method, this can be said as two models are contained in GANs (refer Figure 9.2). The generator model tries to give out the output and discriminator models categorize the examples from the database based on their features. Some of the outcomes from the GANs are so impressive that if we input the image of daylight, the model changes to a photo taken in a night light or at night. Likewise the photo from winter is converted to summer [3]. This proves that GANs are capable of many things.

Figure 9.1   This figure is the outcome of the model trained from GAN

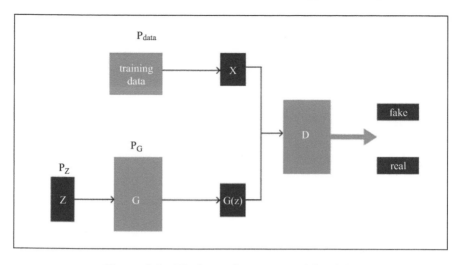

Figure 9.2   The basic functioning of the GAN

GAN contains two parts [4]:

Discriminator increases the opportunity to provide the right label for both training examples and images generated by the generator. Generator decreases the likelihood that the discriminator can predict that what you produce is not real. In simple words, we can say that the discriminator works like the police, which keeps the model in check. The improvement of GANs can be concluded that it started a year rapidly after it was introduced. As initially GAN's were hard to control and also modelling was able to fall easily, the end solution was inappropriate enough at the start [5]. Then a revolutionary improvement was proposed, using the deep convolutional GAN, which indeed made a remarkable change in the way the GANs were working. Then after this, many research scholars encouraged the study of GANs. From this, the GANs were considered good as they were started to be used in many applications. GAN's applications are in text to image conversion, image painting-like pictures, and the GANs need not be implemented alone. They can be combined with many other approaches for its implementation [6].

This review chapter studied trending topics like self-driving methods, the medical field, and credit card fraud detection fields where the approach needs to be different from the common ones. There are many limitations in this field, like the input data on which the model trains [7]. And in most cases, it would be life-threatening situations so we need a robust model. For this kind of critical situation, the GAN's implementation is made. We will discuss how the research is being done in these fields in the upcoming sections. Novice and skilful audiences looking to explore the latest trends in this field of GAN and a blockchain will find this chapter to be a perfect start for their career.

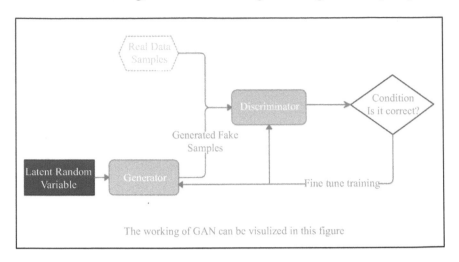

Figure 9.3   Working of GAN

Figure 9.3 provide the working structure of generative adversarial networks (GAN).

9.2   Application of Generative Adversarial Networks (GANs)

9.2.1   GAN in self-driving

Even in this largely so-called modern nation, there is something that we are still to achieve to the fullest, like a self-driving system. At first, this was achieved using the sensors, cameras, radar, ultrasonics, and Lidar [8]. First, the generic items or the objects are detected and then transformed to 2D and 3D. The traditional method to solve this problem is to build the modules independently [9], and then the end-to-end individuality is achieved. It all started with deep learning, it was the first time that had a kickstart to this stream of learning. The usually implemented deep learning models are like recurrent neural networks and convolutional neural networks, classification, and then the regression is done for this model to be built.

These traditional models try to extract the features from this training data, which are at par with the classification problem. Still, for complex scenarios like self-driving, then we need something more than the usual stuff. If we see the other options, the generative model tries to collect data distribution, the built model will have a powerful representation. The primary usage of this GAN currently is the image-to-image translation, like perfect to scenario translations, like scenes with weather lighting, etc. [10]. Even when the dataset is insufficient, we could use GANs as these require comparatively fewer data to learn things. These are mostly used in advanced data augmentation or the aspects of unsupervised and semi-supervised learning [11]. We can also do some interesting things with GANs like taking two datasets like one of cat and other of lions which both belong to a cat family [9], then we can train the dataset to make the cat images that can create an image of cat and lion mixed or coupled. We input it into the lion photos that almost resemble the lion photos of a similar format. So, from this, we can say that GANs can learn the feature set from two different places and apply them to the place which needs the knowledge set of two different sets.

9.2.1.1 Recent advancements

The newest advancement is in the training methodology of GANs where the generator and the feature set are made to learn things. This learning starts from the lower resolution, and then the new layers keep adding whenever there is specific information available to add a layer [12]. This continues till the model is learning the actual data. We can also improve the quality of the images in the [9] data sets that are lower than the required standard.

SAGAN is the short form of self-attention generative adversarial network, which uses the attention driving model for image generation and the feature set from all the training datasets. Also, the normalisation should be applied to make the accuracy of the output model better to increase the prediction rate. Also, there are few works related to posture detection [13] on the surface or the cushion of the wheelchairs, where this work can also be used in car weather to put the car in automatic parking gear when there is no human sitting in the driving seat. One more idea which would ease the parking [14] and paying system is that the vehicle is directly parked in the parking area, and then using the IoT devices, we keep track of which car is parked. Then while the vehicle exits the parking time, we also record the leaving time and calculate the total duration, which will be automatically debited from the user's account. This process saves time and human power and is also accurate. COVID-19 infection and deaths can be reduced, halted, and reversed using a variety of complementary techniques. We looked at methods for digitally enabled contact tracing and technologies, use, and network choices [15].

9.2.1.2 Data augmentation

It is a natural process or nature of GANs to do the data augmentation on the input data fed to it. It has been proved that the GANs are the best in the image-to-image translation; for example, if we take and input a black and white photo, then the most unexpected thing to a human mind is going to be the outcome [9]. We get a colour photo as the output. Not only this but we also get the opposite of the stretched images, cartoon images [16]. This gives us the possibility to enhance the existing dataset, including the pedestrians. Table 9.1 shows the applications and the model of GAN used [9].

Autonomous systems to perform driving generally require gathering and scrutinising huge amounts of training data. Using simulated environments makes the collection of data easier, but models trained on the simulated environments mostly fail to generalise on real conditions. And domain adaptation makes the ML model trained on samples from a source to generalise to a target domain to increase the model [9]. The GANs almost reduce the input by 50% less than the usually needed system [17]. Reinforcement learning is something that can be used for autonomous driving models trained in a virtual environment so that they can perform well in a natural setting (refer Figure 9.4a, b, and c).

Table 9.1   The applications as well as the model of GAN used

GAN applications	Using domains
2D synthesis	Bicycle-GAN, Pix2Pix, SRGAN, MUNIT, StarGAN, DiscoGAN, CycleGAN
3D synthesis	PrGAN, 3D-GAN, PC-GAN
Video synthesis	Video-to-video, TGAN
Object detection	Perceptual-GAN, SeGAN
Domain adaptation	GraspGAN, pixel level
Advanced data that augmentation	Placement of object instances and context-aware synthesis

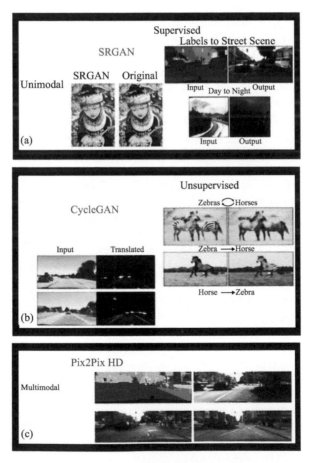

Figure 9.4   (a, b, c) Sample images that are translated using GAN

9.2.1.3 Super resolution

Autonomous driving uses lower resolution sensors. Training on the high-resolution input data representations could enhance the systems that were trained on high-resolution inputs. Considering the higher resolution from the lower resolution image is a challenging accomplishment to cope up with. GAN for image super-resolution can read the realistic photo or more like raw images four times, upscaling the model's quality. A loss function which is also an important thing to take care of, tasks that can handle the input of higher-level processing, only should be used in these conditions [9]. The learning functions can also be learned from the information and the data obtained for the data set of inputs, saying what kind of decision needs to be taken in the given scenario.

9.2.1.4 Real-life results

The problem of adverse weather conditions and the self-driving becomes a nightmare and that is a scenario that we need to handle with utmost care while designing an algorithm for self-driving. The slight disturbance to the input that we get is called the soiling categories. We can know if the weather is bad then this result can be interpreted to initiate the cleaning of the lens to get good input data at least from the next time [18]. As the input data is expensive and also problematic as this data input that we get has to be handled with utmost care as this information is about life decisions which need to be taken with perfect reasoning and safety, but the problem is that this input data has a lot of dirt or it has to undergo cleaning for it to be used for decision making. Here GANs can be used to build a model that makes the de-soiling of the soiled images which can later be used to make decisions.

9.2.1.5 Adversarial examples

Adversarial examples [9] are given as inputs given to the ML model that has been wanted to be shown to improve the accuracy of prediction. Humans do not give these minimal changes more importance, but the classifier still makes wrong decisions. However, if we use the adversarial models, we can perform checks on ML systems even in real-life examples. These kinds of checks are called Black Box attacks.

Finally, we could say that GANs are very capable of creating a high improvement in the field of autonomous driving but the research progress is not rapid in this area. There are many other uses beyond image translation applications for GANs that are yet to be discovered.

9.2.2 Credit card fraud

The mode of money transaction from solid cash has slowly transformed to a much more "digital" way after credits have been introduced. This mode of payment has been on the rise in developed countries lately thanks to the ease of use. And with the digitalisation of money, the fraudulent activities associated with it have become digital too. Credit card fraud has been on rising over the last decade leading to financial losses and the downfall of customers' trust. Therefore, efficiency in credit card fraud detection has been of utmost importance to the banking sectors.

Researchers have carried out many studies, also did they come up with some advancements in the fields of information technology [19]. Especially when it comes to data mining, researchers did fancy employing some data mining methods to resolve this issue. Researchers tried uniting pattern recognition methods like decision trees and neural networks and cognised that this does give them some scientific basis for preventing fraud or anti-fraud. These methods belong to the supervised learning category; hence, these methods do resolve the lack of knowledge attainment in the traditional systems, which are rule-based but require well-known datasets which include and differentiate normal and fraudulent transactions. And as the total fraudulent transactions are less in number when compared to normal transactions, they do not work well in fraud detection.

The majority of the credit card fraudulent actions are signature based. Hence, they are seemingly fit for binary classification [20]. Several ML methods and deep learning methods have helped researchers look into this issue and have positively helped build anti-fraud systems.

Some researchers have performed several studies and used various ML algorithms to analyse real-world credit card frauds and develop hybrid models [20]. But these studies were not quite efficient as the algorithms showed results based on the available data but could not tackle the problem of data shortage. The percentage of credit card fraud is only a tiny 0.07% of the total number of transactions. Therefore, this makes it gravely tough to detect and study frauds from the oceanic amount of transaction data resulting in a meagre dataset to be generated to evaluate. This meagre size of dataset puts a foot on the efficiency of algorithms performance resulting in a model with a deficient performance that cannot be used to predict frauds.

9.2.2.1   Recent advancement

Initially, studies have included classification methods where two or three classes of samples were made. However, we can see that one class classification has come in handy where studies are performed on one class and later differentiated from other class samples [19]. Normal transactions are first mapped into vector space using SAE, and later GAN is trained based on normal transactions to figure out if a transaction is real or fake by creating sample normal transactions [21] (refer Figure 9.5).

As mentioned above, the one-class classification method utilised on a single class for training comes in handy when we are short of fraudulent transactions datasets (in our case) or when the percentage of negative datasets is low. As discussed earlier, irregular datasets used for learning often result in low performance and cannot be compared to the one-class classification method [19]. Support vector machines (SVMs) come in very handy when dealing with one-class classification, and hence SVM is employed while using the one-class classification approach in cases like these. As mentioned earlier, imbalanced learning approaches achieve poor performance compared to one-class classification approaches. SVM is capaciously adopted into classification fields.

Another model which is slowly coming into use is that of SAE and GAN [37,39,40]. This model modifies the parameters by itself and does require human

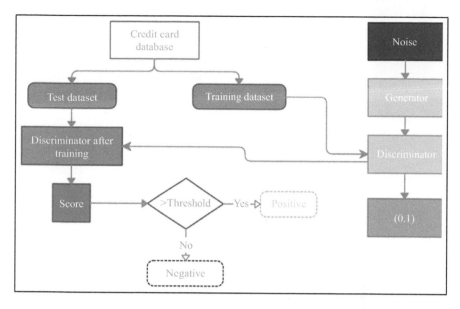

Figure 9.5   GAN credit card system

effort when dealing with one class sample [5]. The trained SAE obtains the key features and gives a hidden representation of the one-class sample transaction (normal transaction in our case) as input to the GAN [22]. The process starts when the GAN generator inputs in calm voices and creates normal fake transactions trying to match them to genuine ones to bluff the GAN discriminator [23]. The discriminator then has to identify if the transaction was genuine or not. By constant training following this process over and over, the discriminator will finally be able to differentiate the normal transactions and fake transactions.

The problem of the irregular datasets was also dealt with differently, contrary to the adversarial autoencoders discussed earlier [20]. Here a variety of GAN networks are put to work to create a sort of replica of the actual data and then ML models are trained using this data. As time passed, the generated data ominously improved and the architecture of the models was also modified to add to the performance. The GAN networks created credit card data and slowly enlarged the dataset used to train the algorithms.

Many approaches were used to tackle the irregular and imbalanced dataset problem, but the following is slightly different from the rest [24]. The uncommonly used commodities like frequency and time played an essential role in this scenario [25]. Time and frequency were new dimensions that were used to resolve the imbalanced dataset problems. Although it is a fact that the time domain did not rightly signify the transaction data. Hence taking every transaction as interval sampling data was being turned into frequency dimension. This was used to feature extraction of ML. Abnormalities in data were not a problem as they could be removed by data cleaning [24]. The dataset sample irregularity issue is dealt with

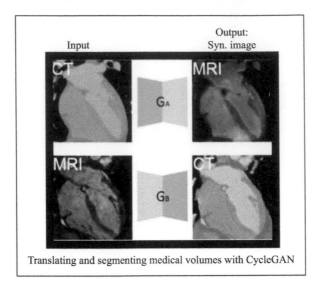

Figure 9.6   Translating and segmenting medical volumes with CycleGAN

by dividing optimisation direction in data augmentation and model optimisation. Discrete Fourier transform (DFT) is used for optimisation, which helps the samples generation process. This process successfully solves the credit card fraud dataset irregularity problem.

Hence, Figure 9.6 provides information about translating and segmenting medical volumes [38,41] with CycleGAN with a neat diagram.

9.2.3   GAN in medical field

In recent times, we have seen innovation and progress skyrocket with the introduction to ML techniques in a wide variety of fields. ML and deep learning techniques have led to the introduction of several methods to translate medical images [26]. In general, the AC prediction for a magnetic resonance image is made by merging synthetic CT patches [27]. ML-based approach KNN regression algorithm made it possible to predict pseudo-CT images by giving magnetic resonance as an input.

Local descriptors were first used to improve prediction accuracy by training them with supervised descriptor learning algorithms.

9.2.3.1   Key generative models in medical field

The medical image analysis area of study has seen a rise by the intervention of the information technology community lately. Applications like semantic segmentation, image augmentation, deep learning, and CNN have seen major developments. Hence, this has been the backbone of introducing a wide range of approaches in generating and translating images. And that brings us to the most important one of the lots – GAN [27]. To explain its primary function in simple terms, new realistic samples of original data are created or obtained from these generative models that cognise the underlying allocation of training data. These practical data samples vaguely reflect the input dataset. Also, GANs consist of a secondary adversarial network which curtails the loss function. There is contention and opposition among the two existing networks, which marks its main principle [26]. The generator, which is the first network, generates synthetic data samples but takes in arbitrary noises as input. The discriminator, the second network, differentiates between genuine training samples and fake samples, acting as a classifier.

As mentioned earlier, both the networks always run a competition among themselves during the training period. On the one hand, generators thrive on fooling the discriminator by assuming that the synthetic data samples are genuine. At the same time, the discriminator is trained to correctly maximise its classification between genuine and synthetic images.

Another variant of GAN, pix2pix GAN, introduced later in 2016, promises solutions to image-to-image translation problems [26]. Here the generator reduces the pixel reconstruction error to give the output target when given the input image from the domain [26]. At the same time, discriminator is made to discern the difference between the ground truth image and fake output provided by the generator. This variant has been updated quite a few times since its introduction to improving images' output quality. Also, a pre-trained network is used to inculcate the texture of input images on the translated images when performing one-to-many translation [5]. There are also some variants of GAN DiscoGANs that are unsupervised and do not need a paired target for training.

9.2.3.2 GAN model selection and implementation

A wide variety of GAN models were explored, and studies lately of which two models beat others hand down in synthesising authentic images in super-resolution [27].

1. CycleGAN
2. UNIT

Supervised learning is quite commonly heard in neural networks. This means that when it comes to the translation of images, both the source and objective domains are required. But our hand-out models of GAN CycleGAN and UNIT work with unsupervised training sets.

CycleGAN within itself has two variants:

1. CycleGAN
2. CycleGANs

Ground truth images included while training, in general, should produce effective results as we have a better picture of what our output should be [27]. Hence, CycleGAN underwent supervised learning/training. It was cognised with the mean absolute error between output and ground truth image.

It was also necessary to find out how cyclic loss and adversarial loss affect the model. Hence, generators were implemented. This generator is mainly contained or CycleGAN and is trained with MAE loss only in a supervised manner and is included with ground truth images but not with cycle loss nor with the adversarial loss [27]. A simple model having just two convolutional layers was implemented to evaluate at the end.

9.2.3.3   Applications in medical imaging

When it comes to applying GAN in the medical field, there are broadly two ways it can be used. The generative aspect is the first one where we focus on exploring the fundamental structure of training data and try coming up with new results. The first aspect helps in maintaining the privacy of patients and dealing with the data shortage. Next is the discriminative part. This marks the second aspect. Here, discriminator D is considered the learned former for the normal images, which later refers to when unusual results or irregular images are obtained [28].

Sometimes if diagnostic images of patients are to be used or released in the public domain, the patient's consent is necessary and may rely on institutional protocols. As GANs are quite popularly used for image synthesis, they may help in dazzling the privacy concerned with diagnostic medical image data [26]. The issue of researchers accessing the images still prevails even after collective efforts throughout many health care agencies, which thrive on making the access of large datasets open. All the information related to the patient's medical history ought to be shared by a hierarchy of users like researchers, hospital staff, and various agencies to determine the correct diagnosis [29]. Various wireless body area network sensors were used to keep a check on a patient's body functions. Translation, elastic deformation, flipping, scaling, etc. are traditional ways of expanding training datasets. However, these methods never were as successful in mentioning variations in shape, size, or location compared to standard protocols [28]. Hence, GANs are widely used courtesy of their efficient results in expanding training datasets and providing efficient outputs.

Many studies have shown that the two most efficient variants of GAN have been widely used to produce genuine magnetic resonance images, namely CycleGAN and UNIT [27]. To recreate as genuine MR images, it has been advised to run the models differently in different domains and train CycleGAN unsupervised way [11]. It can be suggested to perform GANs in the coming future for data augmentation. Doing this can also help find which is most appropriate, the model creating more genuine images or the model whose performance is effective when it comes to quantitative assessments [30]. GAN also comes in handy when it comes to nursing brain tumours. This process occurs by combining a discriminant model with a generating model, and GAN replaces CRF as a higher-order smoothing method.

9.3   Blockchain basics

9.3.1   Blockchain

Blockchain innovation is a decentralised ledger framework that can record exchanges between different users. Blockchain began as the innovation behind bitcoin however has prevalently developed into a promising moderation innovation for network protection. Blockchain can be used in any area or industry. This is because any sort of computerised resource or exchange can be embedded in the blockchain from any

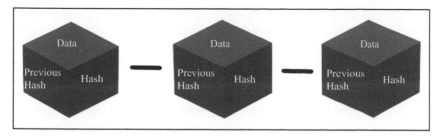

Figure 9.7   A blockchain

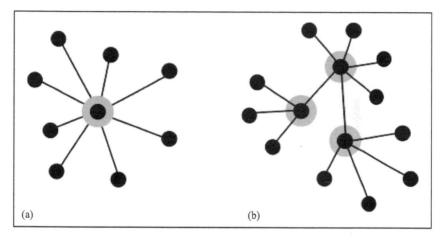

Figure 9.8   (a) Centralised and (b) decentralised

industry. The innovation is viewed as a solid network protection convention because of its ability to show any unfairness and give sureness in the uprightness of exchanges. Blockchain innovation was intended to be straightforward. Subsequently, restricting the well-known misguided judgment, blockchain offers no protection or privacy of any exchanges made through it. When named as secure, it is intended to depict the respectability of the exchanges, not its protection. Figure 9.7 is a simple blockchain and each block contains data, hash, and previous hash.

Decentralisation in blockchain (refer Figure 9.8) means transferring control from a central authority (individual, association, or gathering) to a distributed network. Decentralised organisations endeavour to decrease the degree of trust that members should put in each other and stop their capacity to apply authority or command more than each other in manners that debase the organisation's usefulness. In Figure 9.7, (a) represents centralised authority and (b) represents decentralised authority.

9.3.1.1   Security in blockchain

Blockchain technology accounts for the issues of security, safety, and trust in several ways. New blocks are always stored linearly and sequentially. That is, they are constantly added to the end of the blockchain. If you take a look at Bitcoin's blockchain, you will see that each block has a position on the chain, called a "height." As of November 2020, the block's height is above 0.65 million (656,197 blocks so far).

After a block has been added to the end of the blockchain, it is challenging to go back and change the contents of the block unless the majority reaches a consensus to do so. That is because each block contains its hash, along with the block's hash before it, as well as the previously mentioned time stamp. Hash codes are created by a math function that turns digital information into a string of numbers and letters. If that information is edited in any way, the hash code changes as well.

Suppose a hacker wants to alter the blockchain and steal Bitcoin. He has to change his single copy, it would no longer align with everyone else's copy. When everyone else cross-references their copies against each other, they would see this one copy stand out and that hacker's version of the chain would be cast away as illegitimate.

Succeeding with such an attack would require that the hacker simultaneously controls and alters 51% of the copies of the blockchain so that their new copy becomes the majority copy and, thus, the agreed-upon chain. These types of attacks are called 51% attacks. Such an attack would also require an immense amount of money and resources as they would need to redo all of the blocks because they would now have different timestamps and hash codes.

Due to the size of Bitcoin's network and how fast it is growing, the price to pull off such a feat would probably be costly. Not only would this be extremely expensive, but it is also a complete waste of resources. Doing such a thing would not go unnoticed, and as soon as network members start to see such big alterations to the blockchain, the network members would then fork off to a new version of the chain that has not been affected. Fifty-one per cent of attacks are most common in small Altcoins.

9.3.2   Security of blockchain-based wireless network

The cyber security of blockchain-based wireless networks has drawn increasing attention in the industry. One of the known dangers is blockchain-based LDDoS attacks. It was proposed in 2003 [1], which revealed that TCP's retransmission timeout mechanism can be exploited by using maliciously chosen low-rate attack flow to make TCP throughput fall to a very low rate. But in the whole Internet era, LDDoS traffic is not too big limited to traditional devices. With the emergence of blockchain-based wireless networks, those wireless devices with weak security configurations can be infected easily.

LDDoS attacks. Early in September 2016, a DDoS attack using Mirai malware hit cloud service provider OVH with 1.1 tbps at peak by about 145k hacked cameras [31]. According to CNCERT (National Computer Network Emergency Response Technical Team), the number of botnets with a scale of more than 100k were reached 39 in 2020 [5]. In the above scenarios, if using a physical test bed, the cost of large-scale wireless network simulation is too high to complete the attack verification and analysis due to limited resources. If the wireless network simulator method is used, it is challenging to build a high-fidelity simulation. Neither the process of physical testbed nor network simulator is suitable for large-scale LDDoS simulation in the era of the wireless network. Hence, it is a hot and challenging topic in academia and industry about generating datasets with low-cost and high-fidelity methods. In contrast to the above methods, we apply the LSTM-CGAN algorithm to cause LDDoS network attacks based on publicly available datasets or private small-scale datasets for blockchain-based wireless network models. The advantage of this method is not only to solve the imbalance problem of the detection model caused by insufficient attack data during the training process but also to obtain the ability to detect unknown wireless network attacks by learning these GANs evolving samples.

Discriminative models, which can also be referred to as the conditional's models, are a part of the logistical models which are helpful in regression and classification. These also help to distinguish based on the boundaries through the data that is given to it as from the dataset like a win or a loss, true or false kind of data. GANs unlike the discriminative models are very good at understanding the important links between the underlying data. Further they are very successful in data analysis [32]. In recent times, the GANs are improving with the neural networks. This consists of the two networks that are. The first one generator tries to generate the perceptually convincing points from an arbitrary distributed fashion. The second one helps in distinguishing the original and the copied sample.

In blockchain technology, we can provide security solutions without the actual need of the central or the governing body. The general protocol of the blockchain is that the user's assets that belong to him are controlled through the private key of an asymmetric key that belongs to the user. This is all a secure process, but the problem is that the person is solely responsible for his key. The current issues in handling the keys can be stated as the user does not have the best and foolproof method of storing their keys. If, by chance, the person has lost access to his private keys, then there is no efficient mechanism prevailing to recover them. Here, in this case, there are two sides to coins that need to be observed that we need to provide reasonable security to store the keys. Also, there should be some security included with biometrics or some unique way to restore the password even if he forgets the keys that he has set. One of the methods in securing the private key is that we need to exchange the secret key as a hidden image. This is where the GANs play a prominent role. This method has demonstrated reliable and efficient processes.

Blockchain-based networks are drawing increasing attention from the industry in recent times. DDoS attack [33] is something that one can look up to. This attack is called Distributed Denial-of-Service (DDoS) attack. It is a malicious attempt to disturb the regular traffic of a targeted server, service, or network by bombarding the target and its resources with a flood of Internet traffic that is not useful but to kill time that the user traffic does not serve the purpose. Each affected computer sends the request to the target's address, mostly taking the IP address as its destination. This might be easy to create, but the amount of damage it creates is vast when it is created. We can notice patterns that there will be a surge of requests in a certain interval of time, like once in 10 minutes or 20 minutes [33].

Using GAN's in key sharing, how GAN's see this problem is that it is a classification problem and blinds its real situation. Here the generator from the network creates an image from the noise as in which GANs are good at. First, the key generated is from the white noise, also called it has the equal energy of the frequency band. This generator generates the sub-images, often termed the virtual secret, which acts as the discriminator. Then this discriminates the horror percentage of the original image created before the virtual sub-image is better later. This key sharing is a popular thing in cryptography, which is to share the key among the two places. In cryptography, the primary key is divided among the users and similar to GANs. The main image is divided into sub-images or parts of it, which can then be used among the people to serve the purpose needed. Whereas in this case, we use this method to share the keys to the variable persons of the user that they trust, then even if the user forgets the key they can collect the pieces that were distributed to them and use them to authenticate and get their key back. To create these sub-images from the GANs, we change the variance and the other factors like expectations and the rounding off factors of the Gaussian noise to generate the smaller images, this by the generator governed as the discriminant network. In this way, the result that is generated is much better. This structure can also lead to adverse effects like the whole result will be diminished to a greater extinct as the result of the randomness of the dataset is not wide enough. Still, as we will be using GANs for this process, the dataset specifications can be a little compromised as GANs are good with learning to predict from the limited variety of the exposure to the data. The photographs that are the outputs of the GANs look like actual real people. This might be misleading in some concerns. Some persons might create a fake personification, which leads to potential frauds [34], thereby producing fake profiles of the persons on social media, etc., and spamming people with useless means of messages and news. There should be a governing rule set for the limit to which GAN's can be used.

Holography is a kind of technology that creates a unique photography image with no lens involved in the creation; this is also a kind of photography division that can be used in the security of the blockchain. GANs identify the hologram images from the usual ones. This is also an impressive feature that these images can be achieved clean from the hard threshold front he stained or the noisy images. These are some of the points that GANs help blockchain share the keys so that they can also recover if the user forgets their private key.

9.3.3   Applications of GAN in blockchain

In simple terms, blockchain is nothing but a database. The digital assets are dispersed rather than transferred or reproduced. This results in an inflexible asset record [32]. The asset is localised, allowing for real-time public access and transparency. Blockchain reduces risk and eliminates fraud, bringing transparency to the picture, making it a promising and thoroughgoing technology. When blended with another revolutionary technology called GANs, this technology gives an outcome of utmost efficiency. Due to its synthetic data creation abilities, GAN is one of the most underlined research fields. While there have been multiple reviews of GANs in image processing, none have focused on the review of GANs in multidisciplinary domains.

There have been quite a few applications of GANs in blockchain, of which Bitcoin is the most popular throughout the world. Let us see how GANs have lent themselves to improve the effectiveness of Bitcoin.

When it comes to the entity classification in Bitcoin, the ground-truth dataset has a considerable influence on the outcome, especially when using supervised ML techniques [35]. These datasets carry considerably more data regarding services like gambling and exchange when compared to information regarding illegal activities like mixers and services, which causes a crucial class imbalance problem. Class imbalance complicates the application of ML algorithms and lowers the quality of classification findings, particularly for demeaned but essential classes. GANs in recent years have demonstrated practical outputs in the field of image classification. Hence, this problem of Bitcoin data augmentation will be dealt with using GANs. There is no particular solution using GAN in every situation. The major problem occurs when we are set to create synthetic Bitcoin address samples for data augmentation. But this problem is solvable when we try to layout the optimiser function parameter and the batch size and dataset size parameters that act on the training of GAN. By doing this, we can ensure a significant amount of resemblance between the real and synthetic samples of a crucial Bitcoin class [35]. In this way, GANs prove to be a powerful and fast method for creating good synthetic data that closely resembles actual Bitcoin address data and hence solve the problem of class imbalance in Bitcoin address datasets.

Another application of GANs in the field of blockchain is in secret key sharing technology (refer Figure 9.9). In this application, a particular network is presented, which considers the secret key sharing process as a classification issue, while the network itself acts as a dealer [36]. During the secret key sharing process, the fundamental concept is to see the secret as an image. We can transform the user's

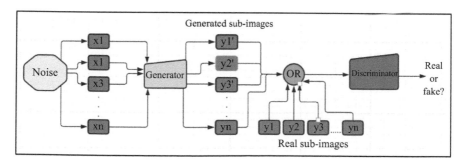

Figure 9.9   Generative adversarial secret key sharing network

private key text into an original image if the user's private key is text. We use image segmentation to break the original image into original sub-images. We next use DNA coding to encode each sub-image. And then, we lastly train the suggested network to discover the results of secret key sharing. This method shows promising results making the system more stable and also supple and well organised in communication.

9.3.3.1   GANs application in blockchain to enhance intrusion detection system (IDS)

The two critical emergent constituents of today's Internet-enabled era of technology are blockchain and the IoTs. The advantages of Blockchain (BC) is to provide trust, including security, clarity, and smart contracts, can help overcome some of the limits of the IoT environment. An IDS is a critical component of network security. The IDS seeks to detect spiteful activity or policy violations [34] instinctively. Seeing unexpected and inappropriate activities corresponding to the traffic patterns is a crucial need of a security system. In this current scenario, we will be looking at the problem of data imbalance, which occurs when the number of aberrant samples is considerably lower than the number of certain pieces. Blockchain technologies are commonly regarded as a viable alternative for enhancing data privacy, system dependability, and security. We know that blockchain is a robust tool, but it is vulnerable to assaults and security concerns. For example, a 51% attack performed on Ethereum Classic recently exposed the platform's security weaknesses.

So, to enhance the system's performance, we again come up with the revolutionary advancement in ML, GANs which will solve the class imbalance problem, and the data noise problem, which are affecting the performance of IDS.

In the context of supervised ML, which requires at least two classes, class imbalance usually refers to an unbalanced distribution of classes within a dataset. Imbalance refers to the fact that the number of data points accessible for several types differs: If there are two classes, balanced data means each class gets 50% of the points. For a real-life example of class imbalance, let us again consider the credit card fraud detection dataset, where most credit card transactions are not fraud and only a few classes are fraud transactions.

Here we will discuss the unique conditional GAN of Blockchain (BC) is to generate representative samples for minority classes to resolve the class imbalance problem in IDS (refer Figure 9.10).

Smart home technology gives homeowners protection, comfort, satisfaction, and energy savings by letting them operate smart gadgets via a smartphone or other networked device. Smart home security is a crucial topic to address since it might help people avoid various problems. If hackers gain access to a smart device, they may be able to switch off lights, as well as access doors, exposing a home vulnerable to a break-in.

Building a system detection based on blockchain technology is the greatest fit for constant monitoring of tools, making the system more dependable and secure. The system is built on a loose integration architecture, in which clients, agents, and

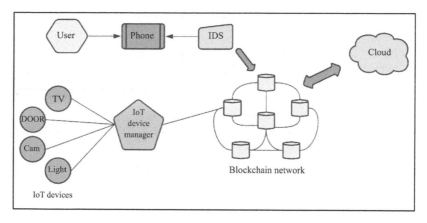

Figure 9.10   IDS with blockchain system architecture

end devices, which are classified as IoT end devices, generate all raw data such as inventory data, routing paths, and trading records.

The system is built on an open integration architecture. Clients, agents, and end devices, classified as IoT end devices, generate all raw data such as inventory data, routing paths, and trading records. The transactions are collected by the local logistics agents' network gateways and packaged as blocks for the blockchain network's further process. Blockchain records, which save data records as transactions, are shared by servers, data centres, and network gateways controlled by logistics companies. Specialised blockchain nodes store blockchain records. To increase the security of smart homes, blockchain technology was introduced to secure data from alteration and loss, but as we previously stated, this was insufficient. This is because the house contains many heterogeneous devices that rely on different protocols to communicate [34]. As a result, varied and uneven data stored on the blockchain could generate detection mistakes, resulting in many false alerts. GANs generally learn from G:z $\rightarrow$y, where z is a random noise vector, and y is random to output an image [37,39,40].

In contrast, conditional GANs (cGAN) learn a mapping from observed input x and random noise vector z, to y, G:{x,z} $\rightarrow$ y. An adversarial trained discriminator D is trained to do as well as possible at recognising the generator's "fakes." The generator G is trained to produce outputs that cannot be separated from "genuine" inputs. We create samples that look and sound like the originals, but they are a little noisy. This is where cGAN ensures by injecting actual samples with real-world noise, such as tremors and interruptions, to imitate the house's conditions at all times [34]. The samples were obtained in a predefined context that does not reflect all the reality. As a result, the model has a constrained interpretation of the information. As a result, we assume that adding noise to the data will offer a model a wide notion rather than improving its performance and reducing errors.

9.4 Conclusion

In this chapter, we swotted numerous GANs variants, which are slowly emerging to be a popular network. We also specified the popular variants of GANs, their applications, and current developments in the respective fields we undertook in this chapter. In our opinion, GANs could be one of the high potential fields in the niche area of neural networks, which is still left unexplored and has not reached full potential in research development. It could emerge to be one of the robust generative models. The work in this chapter gave us insights about blockchain and GANs working together to provide the needed results and provide insights about the GANs applications in various fields like credit card detection, self-driving, medical fields. Overall, this gives us a view of GAN's in three dimensions, opposing the blockchain, enhancing blockchain, and applications along with blockchain. Many capabilities are yet undiscovered of GANs where they make significant performance improvements.

References

[1] I. Goodfellow, J. Pouget-Abadie, M. Mirza, *et al.*, "Generative adversarial nets," in Advances in Neural Information Processing Systems 27, Montreal, Quebec, Canada, 2014, pp.2672–2680.

[2] A. Aggarwal, M. Mittal, and G. Battineni, "Generative adversarial network: an overview of theory and applications," *International Journal of Information Management Data Insights*, 1(1), 2021, 100004, ISSN 2667-0968,

[3] L. J. Ratliff, S. A. Burden, and S. S. Sastry, "Characterisation and computation of local Nash equilibria in continuous games," in Proceedings of the 51st Annual Allerton Conference on Communication, Control, and Computing (Allerton), Monticello, IL, USA, 2013, pp.917–924.

[4] A. Creswell and A. A. Bharath. "Adversarial training for sketch retrieval," in: G. Hua and H. Jégou (eds), *Computer Vision – ECCV 2016 Workshops. ECCV 2016. Lecture Notes in Computer Science*, vol. 9913, Springer, Cham, 2016.

[5] M. Önder and Y. S. Akgül, "Automatic generation of matching clothes design using generative adversarial networks," in 2020 28th Signal Processing and Communications Applications Conference (SIU), Gaziantep, Turkey, 2020, pp. 1–4, doi: 10.1109/SIU49456.2020.9302390.

[6] M. Mirza and S. Osindero, "Conditional Generative Adversarial Nets," arXiv:1411.1784v1 [cs.LG] 6 Nov 2014.

[7] A. Radford, L. Metz, and S. Chintala, "Unsupervised Representation Learning with Deep Convolutional Generative Adversarial Networks," arXiv:1511.06434v2 [cs. L.G.] 7 Jan 2016.

[8] R. Yin, "Multi-resolution generative adversarial networks for tiny-scale pedestrian detection," in 2019 IEEE International Conference on Image

Processing (ICIP), Taipei, Taiwan, 2019, pp. 1665–1669, doi: 10.1109/ICIP.2019.8803030.

[9] M. Uřičář, P. Krizek, D. Hurych, I. Sobh, S. Yogamani, and P. Denny (2019), *Yes, we GAN: Applying Adversarial Techniques for Autonomous Driving.* arXiv:1902.03442. Available at: https://doi.org/10.2352/ISSN.2470-1173.2019.15.AVM-048.

[10] E. L. Denton, S. Chintala, R. Fergus, *et al.,* "Deep generative image models using a Laplacian pyramid of adversarial networks," in Advances in Neural Information Processing Systems, 2015, pp. 1486–1494.

[11] A. Radford, L. Metz, and S. Chintala, "Unsupervised representation learning with deep convolutional generative adversarial networks," in Proceedings of ICLR, 2016.

[12] S. Hitawala, "Comparative Study on Generative Adversarial Networks", arXiv:1801.04271v1 [cs.LG] 12 Jan 2018.

[13] C. Ma, W. Li, R. Gravina, and G. Fortino, "Posture detection based on smart cushion for wheelchair users," *Sensors* 17(4), 2017, 719.

[14] A. Sant, L. Garg, P. A. Xuereb, and C. Chakraborty, "A novel green IoT-based pay-as-you-go smart parking system," *Computers, Materials & Continua* 67(3), 2021, 3523–3544, <https://www.techscience.com/cmc/v67n3/41611>, <https://www.techscience.com/cmc/>. https://doi.org/10.32604/cmc.2021.015265.

[15] L. Garg, E. Chukwu, N. Nasser, C. Chakraborty, and G. Garg, "Anonymity preserving IoT-based COVID-19 and other infectious disease contact tracing model," *IEEE Access*, 8, 2020, 159402–159414, doi: 10.1109/ACCESS.2020.3020513.

[16] D. J. Im, C. D. Kim, H. Jiang, and R. Memisevic, "Generating images with recurrent adversarial networks," 2016, arXiv preprint arXiv:1602.05110.

[17] A. Makhzani, J. Shlens, N. Jaitly, *et al.,* "Adversarial Autoencoders," Nov 2015, arXiv:1511.05644 [cs.LG].

[18] J. Donahue, P. Krähenbühl, and T. Darrell, "Adversarial Feature Learning," May 2016, arXiv:1605.09782v7 [cs.LG].

[19] J. Chen, Y. Shen, and R. Ali, "Credit card fraud detection using sparse autoencoder and generative adversarial network," in 2018 IEEE 9th Annual Information Technology, Electronics and Mobile Communication Conference (IEMCON), Vancouver, BC, 2018, pp. 1054–1059, doi: 10.1109/IEMCON.2018.8614815.

[20] A. Sethia, R. Patel, and P. Raut, "Data augmentation using generative models for credit card fraud detection," in 2018 4th International Conference on Computing Communication and Automation (ICCCA), Greater Noida, India, 2018, pp. 1–6, doi: 10.1109/CCAA.2018.8777628.

[21] D. P. Kingma and M. Welling, Auto-encoding Variational Bayes, ICLR 2014.

[22] M. Gutmann and A. Hyvärinen, "Noise-contrastive estimation: a new estimation principle for unnormalised statistical models," in Proceedings of AISTATS. Sardina, Italy, 2010.

[23] A. Ng and M. I. Jordan, "On discriminative vs. generative classifiers: a comparison of logistic regression and Naïve Bayes," in Proceedings of the

14th International Conference on Neural Information Processing Systems (NIPS'01): Natural and Synthetic, 2001, pp. 841–848.

[24]   M. Shao, N. Gu, and X. Zhang, "Credit card transactions data adversarial augmentation in the frequency domain," in 2020 5th IEEE International Conference on Big Data Analytics (ICBDA), Xiamen, China, 2020, pp. 238–245, doi: 10.1109/ICBDA49040.2020.9101344.

[25]   Y. Zhang, R. Barzilay, and T. Jaakkola, Aspect-augmented Adversarial Networks for Domain Adaptation. CoRR, 2017, arXiv:1701.00188.

[26]   K. Armanious, C. Jiang, M. Fischer, *et al.*, "MedGAN: medical image translation using GANs," *Computerized Medical Imaging and Graphics* 79, 2020,101684. doi: 10.1016/j.compmedimag.2019.101684.

[27]   P. Welander, S. Karlsson, and A. Eklund, Generative Adversarial Networks for Image-to-Image Translation on Multi-Contrast MR Images – A Comparison of CycleGAN and UNIT, 2018.

[28]   X. Yi, E. Walia, and P. Babyn, "Generative adversarial network in medical imaging: a review," *Medical Image Analysis*, 58, 2019, 101552. 10.1016/j.media.2019.101552.

[29]   G. Fortino, A. Guerrieri, F. Bellifemine, and R. Giannantonio, "Platform-independent development of collaborative wireless body sensor network applications: SPINE2," in *IEEE International Conference on Systems, Man and Cybernetics*, 2009, 3144–3150.

[30]   A. Gumaei, M. M. Hassan, M.R. Hassan, A. Alelaiwi, and G. Fortino, "A hybrid feature extraction method with regularised extreme learning machine for brain tumor classification," *IEEE Access* 7, 2019, 36266–36273.

[31]   K. Wang, C. Gou, Y. Duan, Y. Lin, X. Zheng, and F.-Y. Wang, "Generative adversarial networks: introduction and outlook," *IEEE/CAA Journal of Automatica Sinica*, 4(4), 2017, 588–598.

[32]   S. K. J. Rizvi, M. A. Azad, and M. M. Fraz, "Spectrum of advancements and developments in multidisciplinary domains for generative adversarial networks (GANs)," *Archives of Computational Methods in Engineering*, 28, 2021, 4503–4521.

[33]   Z. Liu and X. Yin, "LSTM-CGAN: towards generating low-rate DDoS adversarial samples for blockchain-based wireless network detection models," *IEEE Access*, 9, 2021, 22616–22625, doi: 10.1109/ACCESS.2021.3056482.

[34]   W. Bouzeraib, A. Ghenai, and N. Zeghib, "A Blockchain data balance using a generative adversarial network approach: application to smart house IDS," in 2020 International Conference on Advanced Aspects of Software Engineering (ICAASE), 2020, pp. 1–6, doi: 10.1109/ICAASE51408.2020.9380110.

[35]   F. Zola, J. Bruse, X. Barrio, M. Galar, and R. Urrutia, "Generative adversarial networks for bitcoin data augmentation," *Computer Science*, 2020, 10.1109/BRAINS49436.2020.9223269.

[36]   W. Zheng and K. Wang, "GAN-based key secret-sharing scheme in blockchain," *IEEE Transactions on Cybernetics*, 2020, 1–12, 10.1109/TCYB.2019.2963138.

[37] H. Zhang, I Goodfellow, D. Metaxas, and A. Odena, "Self-Attention Generative Adversarial Networks," 21 May 2018, arXiv:1805.08318v1 [stat.ML]

[38] T. Iqbal and H. Ali, "Generative adversarial network for medical images (MI-GAN)," *Journal of Medical Systems*, 42, 2018, doi:10.1007/s10916-018-1072-9.

[39] J. Li, M.-T. Luong, and D. Jurafsky, "A hierarchical neural autoencoder for paragraphs and documents," in Proceedings of the 53rd Annual Meeting of the Association for Computational Linguistics and the 7th International Joint Conference on Natural Language Processing (Volume 1: Long Papers), 2015, CoRR, arXiv:1506.01057.

[40] M. Arjovsky, S. Chintala, and L. Bottou, Wasserstein GAN, CoRR, 2017. https://arxiv.org/abs/1701.07875. Available at: https://doi.org/10.48550/arXiv.1701.07875.

[41] Z. Zhang, L. Yang, and Y. Zheng, "Translating and segmenting multimodal medical volumes with cycle- and shape-consistency generative adversarial network," *IEEE Conference Proceedings* 2018, 2018, 9242–9251. 10.1109/CVPR.2018.00963.

Chapter 10

Internet of Things (IoTs)-enabled security using artificial intelligence and blockchain technologies

Shalini Ramanathan[1], Mohan Ramasundaram[1], Hemalatha Gunasekaran[2], Hemalatha Bhujile[3] and Naresh Kumar Palanisamy[4]

Abstract

Blockchain is a private key cryptography protocol of network-to-network chain. Blockchain technology is used in many sectors since it improves the value-exchange business to an advanced level. Starting from bitcoin to healthcare, it plays a substantial role in the application. In this real-world, blockchain applications transform society to a higher level by protecting business deals, quick processes, error free, safety, and efficiency. The following are some of the protruding applications of blockchain. Blockchain healthcare is for the secure sharing of medical data. Blockchain music is for royalties tracking, transparency, and ownership rights. Blockchain asset management is a real estate processing platform used for crossborder payments. The blockchain ledger simplifies the whole process, reduces error by encrypting the records along with no intermediaries. The Internet of Things (IoT) is a peer-to-peer computing device. It transfers data without human-computer interaction. IoT with blockchain brings an improvement in the lifestyle through smart cities project. It helps to combat security breaches, and it can control devices when away from home, alert when cookies are ready, etc.

Blockchain plays an important role in supply chain and logistics monitoring. It uses sensors through that it provides location and condition transparency around the world. The supply chain is one of the application areas among blockchain. It has tremendous scope since it is an integral part of the Indian economy. Also, it is the best use-case for blockchain. Other use-cases are a charity, trading, certificate verification, digital identity, and copyright protection. Many mobile-based and

[1]National Institute of Technology, Tiruchirappalli, India
[2]University of Technology and Applied Science, IBRI, Oman
[3]SDM College of Engineering and Technology, India
[4]SNS College of Technology, India

online-based applications are available for specific processing benefits, such as Burstiq, Mediachain, Propy, Opskins, Chainalysis, Filament, Hypr, Xage Security, Civic, Evernym, Ocular, Dhl, Maersk, Madhive, Voatz, and Delaware.

Blockchain application demand is fascinating and advancing since it is a new technology. Every year, it increases the market growth. Blockchain technology and crypto economics are the heart of many growing industries. Blockchain applications are the solution to improve data integrity to the highest standards. Their technology has the potential to revolutionize big data with better security and data quality.

Keywords: Blockchain applications; Internet of Things; Security; Artificial Intelligence

10.1   Overview

Cryptocurrency is a digital or virtual currency used by social network members to purchase goods and services securely. The digital currency's security was maintained with the cryptography technique's help. One of the cryptocurrencies is bitcoin. It is also the first cryptocurrency. Bitcoin is an innovative method for payment networks or a novel kind of currency and a viable option for transactions such as betting, leveraging, and trading. It has been criticized for its use in illegal transactions, price volatility, and thefts from exchanges. Therefore, blockchain technology was introduced in the year 2008 by Satoshi Nakamoto. A blockchain is a chain of blocks linked together using cryptography. It is the best security provider for bitcoin. Satoshi's white paper titled "Bitcoin: A Peer-to-Peer Electronic Cash System" describes the world's first genuine peer-to-peer system [1]. It made a revolution in all sectors like banking, healthcare, research, industries, etc.

A Financial Institution (FI) is a company engaged in dealing with financial and money transactions such as deposits, loans, investments, and currency exchange. It is a body that collects and saves funds for future use. It also services the exchange of currency between two parties with a third party; involvement of third-party in money exchange services is at great risk for financial institutions. Not only financial institutions, other industries like real estate, supply chain, and healthcare, whoever outsourcing to third-party vendors or service providers could include access to their organization's intellectual property, data, operations, finances, customer information, and every sensitive information. All these organizations face risks such as the threat of high-profile business failure, illegal third-party actions, or regulatory enforcement for actions taken by third-parties.

Blockchain gains advantages over all these risks. Bitcoin is about electronic cash handled by the financial institution, allowing people to send their electronic money directly to another person. It is also the best solution for peer-to-peer communication without third party involvement [2]. The Internet of Things (IoT) defines the network of physical objects that are surrounded by sensors, software, and other technologies for the purpose of linking and swapping data with other devices and systems over the Internet [3]. Security is the reason for the blockchain improvement with IoT. Massive data is the treasure of the IoT network. Big Data plays a significant role here; it collects enormous real-time data through sensors and other devices. So, securing it using blockchain is very important.

Some of the available or possible ways to secure the IoT with blockchain architecture are as follows: first, it uses a tracking system for all network data to prevent replication caused by a malicious attack. Next, several IoT devices, including the distributed ledger, give awareness about device identification, data integrity, and validation. Next, blockchain usage avoids technical issues and inadequacy. Then, the absence of an intermediary reduces the operation cost. Blockchain allows IoT implementation and running costs to be minimized as there are no mediators. Lastly, blockchain architecture supports the IoT devices troubleshooting in the vast network using the history of blocks in the system [4]. This chapter gives a systematic outline based on a review of real-time blockchain technology and its applications, using the IoT with Big Data. Big Data plays a role in Cloud, IoT, Edge technologies since it must collect data and store it for use.

10.2   Blockchain technology with IoT

The IoT meets blockchain to make a revolution in all future generation technologies in the distributed environment. Blockchains benefit from the IoT, and there are multiple partners involved. The IoT appeared as a field of unbelievable influence, opportunity, and creation as intelligent cities and over 50 billion interconnected devices forecasting the future. However, it is hackable and compromises many of the IoT computers or devices. In general, these IoT products, such as smartphones, tablets, or servers, are limited in screen, store, and network resources and are thus more vulnerable to attack. IoT's key safety issues are insufficient monitoring and upgrading, Brute Force, encryption issues, malware and ransomware, blockchain botnets (mobile, Internet or cloud protection), and minor IoT attacks avoid detection, home invasions, remote access for vehicles, and unsuspecting contact. Some of the suggested futuristic solutions are as follows. The first approach is detecting botnets using profound learning, which has proved useful when detecting and preventing IoT network attacks. Second, the behavioral detection of IoT-Botnet is based primarily on the machine learning model that receives feedback, learns from your errors, and increases your prospects for zero-day assaults [5,6]. Some of the suggested futuristic solutions are as follows. The first approach is detecting botnets using profound learning, which has proved useful when detecting and preventing IoT network attacks. Second, the behavioral detection of IoT-Botnet is based primarily on the machine learning model that receives feedback, learns from your errors, and increases your prospects for zero-day assaults.

Like system verification, security analytics, utilizing shared critical infrastructure, communication defense, and network protection must be looked at ever more specifically. Unwanted offenders attack IoT devices, so implementing precautionary steps improves safety and susceptibility. This can be a guide to addressing certain IoT security issues. The IoT is maturing and becoming part of the future Internet from its infancy. While access management systems aid, they are based on centralized models that impose various technological constraints to handle them internationally, there are so many technical restrictions in IoT management.

10.2.1   Need for blockchain in IoT

Researchers, academia, and industry practitioners disrupt several IoT applications and face challenges like establishing protection and maintaining confidence. Blockchain technology protects by its architectural nature and by the concept of decentralized and distributed across peer-to-peer networks. The IoT integrates with blockchain and becomes the right security to overcome many technical hurdles like data loss, data misuse, and cyber-attacks. The growth of technologies like Cloud and Edge Computing has made the term "Big Data" a lot more interesting for academia and businesspeople [7]. Big Data has a staggering growth rate due to real-time IoTs. Big Data is defined to store, collect, group, aggregate, and process data. The processing cannot be done by traditional database methods and tools, and it needs a high-level approach and best practice.

10.2.2   Architecture

An IoT environment has many end nodes, gateways, edge computing devices, IoT devices, and cloud servers. These smart IoT devices gather information from the user and store it in the cloud environment. Examples of such IoT devices are home Voice Controllers, Dash Buttons, Doorbell Cams, Smart Locks, Mobile Robot, Smart Light Switches, Air Quality Monitors, Air Pollution Monitors, Hue Bulbs with Lighting Systems, and Smoke Alarms, shown in Figure 10.1, which send information to the cloud. Artificial intelligence (AI) techniques utilize these data to provide useful architecture and information to the end-users. It is the intellect of the devices which makes IoT intelligent. It is not only the networking but it is also the knowledge contributing to the tools. The equipment is made smart by adding sensors and actuators, which gather and transmit information to the cloud through a networking infrastructure, including Wi-Fi, Bluetooth, ZigBee, etc. It is also possible to process the data at the edge until it enters the cloud [8].

10.2.2.1   Revolutionary advantages
Build trust and security
Protection is one of blockchain's innate attributes since it can legitimize knowledge and guarantee that it comes from a trustworthy source. Blockchain is a great treasurer to provide secure communications, device authentication, and privacy agreements in the IoT environment with a huge number of devices. Secure communication involves devices and people, having a trusted ledger that transparently shows who has access, which is transacting, and a record of all those interactions. Blockchain allows to trace the past of all linked computers, detect the duplication of information in dangerous data streams in the actual environment, and provide consensus algorithms to guarantee identity and security benefits [9].

Figure 10.1   Blockchain IoT architecture

Reduce cost

It would be costly to scale a highly stable central system. Decentralization provides a more economical way of addressing the IoT data size by removing single failure points. The opportunity to minimize running costs is among the most acclaimed advantages for companies. The technology makes it available to share data peer-to-peer on an unrestricted basis, thereby reducing business costs [10]. Several third parties expect to verify every microtransaction and authenticate it to ensure the IoT network's integrity. That's a costly affair, not just a time-consuming operation. Installing the capacity of automation and eradicating reliance from third parties mitigates these problems for blockchain-based communications, smart contracts, and ecosystems.

Accelerate transaction

Bitcoin transaction accelerator called Bit Accelerator enables the unconfirmed bitcoin transactions to be verified quickly and rapidly. A transaction can inspire team members successfully to improve productivity. It provides realistic targets for people at any level. The control chain reduces uncertainty, lowers costs, increases efficiency, makes it quick and easy to follow the operation, and helps staff pick their incentives on time. To control the performance specifications of IoT, a blockchain, which can reduce the time for validating transactions by using trustworthy nodes, can manage the speed of IoT data exchange [11].

Smart accounting

Within a company, accounts will be one of the first divisions to take direct advantage of blockchain and IoT transparency. It is simply good to know entity sharing and sending money across linear time-stamped chains. In the accounting process, the blockchain creates a hard and reliable chain of transactions by eliminating the middleman, increasing the speed of transactions, and lowering costs. A typical supply chain contract takes four to five stages to verify, and it needs to pay charges for each stage. With blockchain, unstable parties can share data directly to each other, reducing the expenses involved with each stage hop [12].

10.3   Safe future with blockchain IoT

The IoT has a massive database that addresses security and privacy concerns. Enterprises such as banks and insurance providers view IoT as an environment that needs more attention. The blockchain benefits IoT to encourage the encryption of data and network equipment. The principle of decentralization and the distribution of digital ledger aims to accomplish the data security objective. IoT is becoming more prevalent in its market, and it deals with IoT systems and network data integrity, data storage, and service. It is always a challenge to produce something nice, so this community is searching for ideas or norms. The registry deployment of intelligent contracts for IoT devices and blockchain networks is a significant endeavor. Four common security-related factors are as follows:

- Secure communication

   IoT devices communicate with another through the Internet, process a business contract, and store it in a digital ledger. It creates encrypted messages for confidential communication. The sender IoT device transfers an encrypted message with the public key to the receiver. The blockchain stores the communicated encrypted message. The receiver IoT device receives the message from the digital ledger and decrypts using the private key.

- User authentication

   The user places a digital signature in the encrypted message and then sends it to the receiver as user authentication. The receiver receives the public key from the digital ledger to confirm the signature. The digital signature is created as follows:

   (a)   The transmitter determines a message hash, which is then encrypted by its private key.
   (b)   The digital signature is sent along with the message.
   (c)   The receiver decrypts the digital signature with a sender's public key kept in the ledger to get the sender hash value.
   (d)   The message shall only be valid when the calculated hash and the message's protected hash are the same.
   (e)   Ledger retains the digital signature of all the messages to improve the trust in the message.

- Legitimate IoT

  A unique IoT device added to the existing network gets a detailed report of trusted nodes in the system, registers itself in the same network, and exchanges information. The Internet functions appropriately with the help of a domain name server called DNS. Its security extension named DNSSec is used to protect the internet from certain attacks like amplification attacks and DNS cache poisoning. It also secures name resolution on main servers by avoiding spoofing attacks. All the communication is authenticated and encrypted based on the IoT device user's knowledge and by the details installed on the IoT device during network setup.

- Configuring IoT

  Blockchain technology is instrumental in setting up a safe and stable IoT system setup. The ledger holds the updated version and configuration details. Bootstrap process fetches the encrypted information from the digital catalog to prevent the discovery of IoT network properties or topologies. For every fixed interval of time, the IoT device reads the new hash value generated and updates the configuration to avoid destructive configuration attacks. The stable IoT devices network with a blockchain network decentralizes the system, in which no centralized entity can accept a transaction. Each computer has a copy of the increasing data chain. This ensures that all members of the network must verify it if someone tries to enter the computer and perform those transactions. After the confirmation is completed, the transaction is placed in a block and sent to all network nodes. This guarantees that the mechanism is protected and cannot be abused by unauthorized sources.

10.3.1 Security issues and challenges

The future will have more than 50 million IoT devices. So, the potential and impact of blockchain on IoT will be more. At present, IoT systems are habitually dependent upon a centralized architecture. The data processed using analytics and then sent back to tiny IoT devices to coordinate with all centralized systems. Information moves from the device to a proprietary cloud. In the world of complex networks, it needs much more processing and coordination happening out on the structure's edges. With coordination taking place peer-to-peer, it reduces the bottlenecks.

For centralized, security vulnerabilities need to make the decision locally, process the data locally, and share resources locally between devices on demands. Likewise, security is, of course, a massive issue with the IoT [13].

Apart from security, privacy, legal, and regulatory, ethical problems are also major issues in the blockchain, shown in Figure 10.2. There are some common issues related to security are as follows:

- The bottlenecks are formed by prevailing cloud-based IoT systems.
- The problems close to the security hazards of centralized systems.
- They are an aiding automated, dynamic resource allocation between machines.

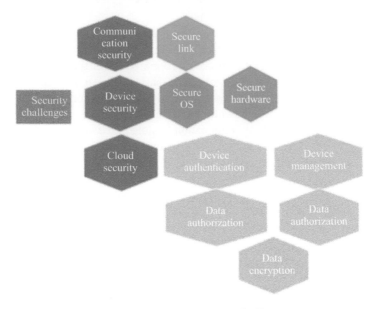

Figure 10.2   IoT security challenges

10.3.2   Security solutions with AI

Nowadays, all human actions are being automated, and everything has gone digital. AI is the ability of computers to learn and simulate the characteristics of human intelligence. It is the power of automation technology. It stands for the use of chatbots in the digital spectrum. AI is now increasingly used in all spheres.

Chatbots are doing human things. If we visit a website, the chat happened between the person from outside and the company through AI. These are all advances in technology. Blockchain is a digital ledger in the computer network. Since there are many nodes in this network, if any transaction happens at one specific node, the changes get reflected at another node. Integrating AI with blockchain avoids data misuse, data hacking, impersonation, eavesdropping, and maintains data confidentiality [14]. There are many areas where blockchain technology is being used like Pharma, HealthCare, Banking's, Agriculture, etc. Merging improves all those areas with enormous benefits on security.

- Innovative business models
  The implementation of newer industry models is another advantage of dual technology. The blockchain offers restriction-free access to all market ecosystem knowledge, with unchangeable details supplied by all stakeholders without questioning the network ownership. It would offer an AI system the possibility to get more insight into the habits, attitudes, and other variables associated with an organization's operation. And so, deliver novel business representations or models with more factually accurate decisions.

- Improved decision making

  AI and blockchain would both strengthen the mechanism of decision making by co advancing the platform. On the one side, AI algorithms can help identify any transaction or app's frauds and threats. Another side, blockchain allows boosting the accuracy of AI algorithms' data used to forecast fraud through their quick and reliable data auditing mechanism.

- Enhance personalized experiences

  Merging AI with blockchain would also improve the customers' customized experience. Though AI continues to use compassionate personal data, blockchain guarantees that the data stays intact and protected using the latest encryption technologies. In these situations, AI cannot provide consumers with the right personal experience because of intrusions or others' privacy misuse. It avoids the problem. It means that Blockchain will have encoding protection. Simultaneously, AI will give end-users more anonymity in terms of their experience using the blockchain-secured data on sites such as Netflix and Amazon.

- Advanced trust ability

  The integration of the two technologies would allow users to look at the storage, management, and use of their personal information without violating privacy and security safety. It will enable them to audit the decision-making process in every phase and promotes public confidence.

- Achieving smart contracts

  Intelligent contracts provide market worlds with different aids, such as very high speed, least to zero conflicts, and better data storage. But the difficulty of the software limits their use. AI would allow intelligent contracts to encode and verify complicated business relationships on a blockchain by incorporating blockchain. There will, therefore, be improved smart contracts. Furthermore, the contracts for self-implementation give varying service standards depending on the AI scheme's price adjustments.

- Augmented accessibility

  Coalescing blockchain and AI minimize the challenges associated with the payment system. Although cryptocurrencies rooted in blockchain could bring an end to currency and promote global trade, AI will enhance process operating performance, guarantee more excellent protection, and reduce related costs.

10.3.3   *Blockchain safety countermeasures with IoT*

The protection of blockchain is a widespread issue, arising from a variety of reasons. Blockchain's unchangeable existence offers an unmoving history of possession and development. This is important for an IP owner since it prohibits any party from disputing an ownership right. Smart blockchain contracts provide a protection net that can be used for licensing or receiving a royalty. Blockchain is also a valuable IoT strategy for preserving consumer info. Blockchain offers a way to trace possession, along with being tamper-resistant. In the block data, you can save the original copyright date. If you have challenged the possession of copyright, the data will be proof of ownership. If the prosecution is ever undertaken while third parties can access the ownership chain, the potential to track ownership will save time and money when obtaining facts. It may also be used as an indicator of the date of registration or the date of cataloging or storing of original works. In addition, blockchain allows the data to be stored anywhere, rather than simply with a national patent office. Intellectual property data can be considered as hosting IoT. Security, however, remains a big concern for IoT. More and more cyber threats are emerging, and computer security is in danger. When hosting IoT devices with a private network, security can be improved with the use of blockchain technologies and IoT. The evidence will only be changed if a device faces a cyber event if the intellectual property is stored on a blockchain [15].

Overall, blockchain is a technology to which the data recording cannot be ignored. The system has evolved from the crypto-currency implementation. In blockchain, sensitive knowledge on intellectual property for works, including copyright and patents, is now protected. The technology offers additional features with intelligent contracts and additional IoT technology protection. The above-mentioned problems can include blockchain-specific and general cybersecurity steps.

- Two-stage authentication (2SA)

  2SA is a successful strategy for access management and account protection within private and corporate security groups. It adds a layer to wallet security in blockchain technology, providing users with their wallet key and a one-time password or OTP, which is generated in real-time, in order to access their wallet currencies. To gain access to a protected network account, a cyber attacker would be required to have the pre-configured OTP device owned by the account holder.

- Anti-phishing software

  This involves systems and networks designed to explicitly recognize malicious connections, e-mail attacks, and bogus websites—leveraging software that cancels access to those services until revamped. Some tools also support legal websites and connections.

- Cold wallets

  Blockchain storage and cryptocurrency wallets are usually of the "hot" variety and are online tools that must be connected to the internet, making them vulnerable to attack. Cold wallets are hardware devices that can remain offline, introducing the possibility of physical theft, but reducing their vulnerability to hacking. These are gadgets that can be almost as minuscule as a USB stick and kept offline as the Trezor and Ledger Nano. Cold wallets are the best methods for holding cryptocurrencies because of their offline savings. Build public and private keys offline with cold storage wallet. This is the best way to store the keys when handled correctly. For example, paper wallets are a perfect way to get cold storage started. However, if these private keys are revealed to the Internet, you must not use the wallet again as you can no longer be confident that it is secure.

The common best cryptocurrency cold storage wallets are Cryptosteel, Shieldfolio, Billfodl, CypherSafe, Paper Wallet, and BalletCrypto.

(a) Cryptosteel produces multiple different stainless steel offline cold storage wallets. The wallets are designed to store data without the need for third-party involvement. These solid metal devices can survive extreme conditions and work under nearly all circumstances.

(b) Shieldfolio is a unique cold storage notebook designed with Bitcoiners in mind. The notebook is water-resistant and can be combined with a special Shieldfolio ghost pen, which hides your private keys and passwords from plain sight. The ghost pen also comes with UV light, which can be used to reveal all your hidden messages.

(c) Billfodl is a cold storage metal wallet designed for serious Bitcoin holders. The wallet comes with a bunch of letters and numbers that allows the storage of your private keys. Because Billfodl is made of stainless steel, it is also fireproof, waterproof, shockproof, and cannot destroy it, unlike paper wallets.

(d) CypherSafe cold storage products such as the CypherWheel are designed with the Bitcoin community in mind, making them easy to use, cost effective, and resistant to damage, keeping your confidential information & Bitcoin recovery seed safe from prying eyes.

(e) Paper wallet is an extremely convenient way to get started with cold storage wallets; all you do is load up a website, turn off your Internet, and print your keys on a paper. Here are some example websites you can use.

(f) BalletCrypto is a nonelectric physical offline cold storage wallet that comes with pre-printed QR code stickers, both public and private keys. Because of this, we cannot recommend Ballet for any serious cold storage holding, and it is rather more of a great gift idea.

• Threat Intelligence (TI)

TI fosters reasonable standards for TI ventures and aligns them with the corporate cybersecurity priorities and determines which TI integrations will best support the enterprise. Online information bases and databases of fraudulent initial coin offers (ICOs), phishing patterns, and known key or identity theft may provide valuable data to secure the property of citizens and organizations in the blockchain. The entire protection strategy of the company – its security mindset – is one of the most logical places to start TI. Security posture also starts with what the organization wants to defend and enforce policies and procedures. TI will help the company learn which locations are the most likely targets of business attackers and use this information to secure core properties more efficiently. For instance, a hospitality network could receive TI from a vulnerable payment card system attacking party. The chain will then create stability and contingency planning for high priority, essential priorities. This encourages TI to facilitate security intervention, such as two-factor authentication deployment or network segmentation. A company may also use TI to recognize potentially sensitive properties that were not viewed as fragile internally. Let us assume that the hospitality chain receives TI, which reveals that an assault party attempts to hack reservation systems to collect information about the location of possible victims. Reservations may previously be subjective and not a vital commodity. That does not say, of course, that TI can be the only security benchmark. It simply complements other approaches in the work of an information-security team to classify portions of a network or organization which require protection [16].

10.4   Cloud-based blockchain with IoT

The IoT has emerged as the next revolutionary technology. Its industry has expanded remarkably in the past few years. The count of IoT devices will increase to 30 million soon. Cloud computing and edge computing devices allow the exchange of data and resources to limited-resource devices like drones, smart watches, sensor devices. Recently, cloud computing and blockchain technology have generated immense interest, not only from traditional tech circles. Blockchain differs from cloud technology. Its necessary activities take place on broadly dispersed networks rather than large consolidated data centers. The potential benefits of combining cloud and blockchain technologies are more. To be specific, it can significantly improve a business' visibility into the movement of products and money around the world [17].

10.4.1   Blockchain security in cloud environment

Blockchain technology is applied in the cloud environment to improve security elements like confidentiality, integrity, authenticity, and access control. Blockchain IoT devices collect a tremendous amount of user data with the help of cloud computing. If user information discloses in the cloud computing environment, then financial and psychological damage may be caused by user sensitive information leakage. Due to these issues, the researchers concentrate on studying the security of the saving and transmitting data, such as confidentiality and integrity, in the cloud computing environment. However, data protection and secrecy studies are not enough. Blockchain is a representative anonymity technology. In tandem with the cloud storage environment, blockchain upgrades to a convenient service that provides more robust security. Cloud computing collects user details and applies blockchain to ensure user privacy. When using blockchain technologies, it is better to add an electronic wallet. If an electronic wallet is not deleted appropriately, user credentials will become an issue or risk. For devaluation of user information, use the secure bitcoin protocol to download and delete the wallet safely.

10.4.2   Blockcloud—a service-centric networking

It is a new architecture in networking. It supports the efficient delivery, discovery, and execution of distributed Internet services, it combines information at the network level and the service level. For the separation of service access (SAL), control plane, and service plane, blockcloud uses service-centered networking (SCN). The upper application layer affix to the service leads to increased mobility and scalability without applying complicated IP addresses. Besides, SCN networks improve the security level via blockchain technology. Simba Foundation Ltd introduced a term called blockcloud. It is a cloud-based blockchain with IoT. It combines security protocols of blockchain and improved Internet technology; it rebuilds the layers of technology below where existing Internet and blockchain networks operate. Blockcloud serves as the "building block" to provide constant connectivity for dynamic networks. A dynamic network is a network of nodes that can insert or remove nodes and edges when crashing or an error occurs. Dynamic network-based blockcloud enables mobility, credibility, benefits, stability, justice, and scalability in the upper layer of its architecture. By 2022, over 22 million IoT computers connect to the Internet, according to the blockcloud project's blueprint. In several industries, the impact of the IoT is being seen, such as hospitals, growing reality, autonomous automobiles, intelligent cities, and grids. Blockcloud provides an improved cloud-based IoT architecture considering connectivity failure, scalability, trust and privacy, security, and flexibility. It is the extension of the current Internet to transform it into the next generation Internet. It integrates both technologies to construct a simple network protocol in terms of "building blocks" to support seamless connectivity for dynamic networks and the interconnection of upper-layer applications securely and efficiently.

10.4.3   A dew-blockcloud model

Dewblock is a blockchain system introduced to overcome the blockchain clients' high blockchain data issues in their mobile economic devices. An independent dew client operates to perform blockchain operations and works with the cloud server to maintain the entire blockchain network's integrity. Dewblock network operates on pair connection, implements protocol with the principle of the concept system, and does all its general functions and mining operations. The cloud computing nodes and dew block nodes are connected to handle integrity, where the cloud servers supervise every node and verify through the mining activity. Naivecoin is a blockchain cryptocurrency system implemented as an open-source project concisely. Dew block reduces the client data size without disturbing the full feature of the blockchain. And its deployment is feasible and affordable since its development is on top of the naivecoin.

10.4.4   Incentive mechanism for edge servers

In all IoT devices, security is the primary concern. Due to computational resources and limited storage, the existing security solutions do not fit modern IoT devices. Applying blockchain security handling methods will help to avoid the malicious attack. In the blockchain incentive mechanism, cloud computing-based IoT devices use a cloud node to provide a secure service. Once the end-user validates the edge node with a blockchain security system, the edge server gets reward as incentives in the form of cryptocurrency. All the information gets an update in the cloud server periodically. This method is best suited for all lightweight and resource-constrained IoT devices.

10.4.5   Blockchain as a Service (BaaS)

BaaS is a technology like "software as a service." It is a third-party cloud-based infrastructure, where clients can utilize a cloud environment to host their application, use blockchain features, and code contracts. The industry provides the blockchain infrastructure with advanced implementation dealing with bandwidth control, technical issues, operational restrictions, and maintenance connected with a decentralized system. BaaS helps the end-user not to stress out among ecosystem and other performance issues. Customers' center of attention will be on utilizing the functions of blockchain. IT companies like Microsoft, Google, Amazon, IBM, R3, Oracle, and SAP provide Baas solutions with global operations. Document tracking, data storage, and contract execution are the everyday usage of BaaS in business management [18].

10.5   Blockchain IoT real-time applications

Blockchain plays a significant role in many sectors, such as supply chain management systems, healthcare, agriculture, and real estate management. It brings lots of benefits for the investors and customers by providing a decentralized distributed network, and It also creates a neutral ecosystem to grow business on common ground. Many public institutions, governments, and researchers adopted open-source blockchain technology for their specific features like traceability, data integration, trusted data exchange, and drug discovery [19]. Table 10.1, shown here, contains several examples of the real-time application of blockchain and IoT in many sectors.

For the past few years, food safety has become an unresolved issue in many countries. Subsequently, old-style agri-food logistics design cannot compete with the demands of the marketplace to any further extent; constructing an agri-food supply chain traceability system is becoming a more and more important and essential urgent need. Food safety failures are magnified, last longer, and cost more because of the lack of access to information and traceability. Food safety can profit from technology's transparency, relatively low business costs with instantaneous applications. The prevailing food traceability systems do not guarantee a high level of structural reliability, a range of capabilities, and information accuracy. A blockchain is a disseminated catalog of chronicles in the arrangement of encrypted blocks or a community ledger of all businesses or digital actions that have been performed and shared among contributing parties and can be verified at all-time in the near future [20]. This technology implemented in RFID helps the development situation to activate the new farm systems and e-agriculture schemes.

- Food management system

    Agriculture itself a network that influences from farm to plate. Blockchain across the agricultural sector provides sustainable solutions for food, farmers, and financing. SAP Ariba is an intelligent e-procurement and supply chain cloud solution for farmers. It automatically finds sourced materials that are

Table 10.1 Real-time applications of blockchain IoTs and Big Data

No.	Blockchain systems	Remarks	Industry	URL
1.	Agricultural and food management system	E-procurement and supply chain cloud solutions	SAP Ariba	https://www.ariba.com/
2.	Agricultural and food management system	Province to track the rice supply chain	Alibaba	https://www.alibaba.com
3.	Agricultural and food management system	Blockchain to trace and validate pork products	Walmart	https://www.walmart.com
4.	Agricultural and food management system	Blockchain allows tracing & validating alcohol, food, tea, and pharmaceutical	Walmart	https://corporate.jd.com/home
5.	Agricultural and food management system	It tracks fish caught by fishermen	Provenance	https://bit.ly/2LoJZp6
6.	Agricultural and food management system	Mobile application solution intended for vanishing crop value between the harvest and the point of sale.	AgriLedger	www.agriledger.io
7.	Agricultural and food management system	An intended conscience effort to enhance the associations between societies, expertise, and agriculture	AgriLedger	www.agriledger.io
8.	Agricultural and food management system	Helps the farmers to predict the weather conditions, precision farming, and access better finances	AgriLedger	www.agriledger.io
9.	Healthcare	Organized storage of medical data with a provision to access by smartphone through "Medipass" application	MediBloc	https://medibloc.org/en
10.	Healthcare	Redefine the way healthcare is accessed, delivered, managed, and paid.	Solve.Care	https://solve.care/
11.	Healthcare	To reduce the cost for long term health care of patients	Dentacoin	https://dentacoin.com/
12.	Healthcare	To securely share the patient's medical data with pharmaceutical, research, and insurance com-	Medicalchain	https://medicalchain.com/en/

(Continues)

Table 10.1 (*Continued*)

No.	Blockchain systems	Remarks	Industry	URL
		panies		
13.	Healthcare	Solution for fake drugs is done through scanning QR codes in the product application	Blockpharma	https://www.blockpharma.com/
14.	Healthcare	Provides covid-19 diagnostic kit for regulatory compliance	TataMD Check	https://healthcare-in-india.net/
15.	Supply chain management	Uses RFID chips with integrated blockchain techniques to provide smart agriculture and art industry with high data integrity and traceability	Waltonchain	https://www.waltonchain.org/
16.	Supply chain management	The mutually trusted framework ensures the origin of food and medicinal items.	Ambrosus	https://ambrosus.com/
17.	Supply chain management	Uses IoT sensors, benefit for physical medicinal products, and avoids contract management and audit	Modum	https://modum.io/
18.	Supply chain management	A public blockchain to solve the real-world economic problems through member activity	VeChain	https://www.vechain.org/
19.	Supply chain management	An ecosystem solve the real-world economic problems through member activity	Origin Trail	https://origintrail.io/
20.	Real estate	Smart contract and storage solutions with SDK and API tools; users can license it to build, publish to industries, and can earn money	Alacrity	https://www.solulab.com/portfolio-items/alacrity-blockchain/
21.	Real estate	Maintain immutable data records about buyers and sellers to provide security with cryptographic principles	DeedCoin	https://cryptoslate.com/coins/deedcoin
22.	Real estate	Real estate data providers and consumers with electronic signing rental agreements	RentBerry	https://rentberry.com
23.	Real estate	Ease the process of transfer of property, smart contracts, disintermediation	Propstory	https://propstory.com/

#	Industry	Description	Name	URL
24.	Real estate	They are preparing a legal document for the media industry with heightened transparency and speed payment.	CAMA	https://www.solulab.com/portfolio-items/collection-account-management-application/
25.	Real estate	Providing automated, low-cost property with visibility and flexibility	Atlant	https://atlant.io/
26.	Retail industry	Aws blockchain to deploy secure open -source network	Amazon block-chain	https://aws.amazon.com/
27.	Retail industry	Provides financial services to authorize their trade, compete against counterfeits.	Paytomat	https://paytomat.com/en/
28.	Retail industry	Zero platform fee marketplace, users can earn bitcoin in the conversation of goods.	OpenBazaar	https://openbazaar.org/
29.	Retail industry	To benefit growth responsibility while linking with globally	Project Provenance	https://www.provenance.org/
30.	Retail industry	To produce a more sustainable retail economy and becoming stronger by working together. Based on the value of the data, rewards are allocated to the customer.	OSA Decentralized	https://osadc.io/en/

similar and suggests the best alternative to buyers. It captures and classifies the data according to industry-standard, then enriches it with market intelligence. Alibaba tracks and authenticates rice and rice products. The firms will offer a BaaS application that is exposed to customers and supply chain companies. Every bag will have a unique identity code, which participants can scan to find out the origin of rice, seeds, and fertilizers. The authorities notify that blockchain speed up the eminence inspection and shipping procedure. In practice, this would cut the long-distance distribution delivery time from 3 to 7 days to less than two.

Walmart and JD support blockchain to build safety-driven food traceability services, which are based on Linux Foundation's Hyperledger cloth. Two proof-of-concept projects for evaluating the predominant method were assessed in collaboration with the company IBM. This method means that the time taken for monitoring the company's provenance is shortened from 7 days to 2.2 seconds in terms of performance. It also increases organizational accountability and internal obligations and helps protect the livelihoods of farmers by dismissing the small goods which could come from the affected farmland areas. The blockchain methodology helps the company and its consumers by scanning barcodes to trace the precise classification of a food product. Where there is a query, the blockchain will identify the exact position. Provenance tracks fish from shore to platform with the aid of blockchain.

Mobile blockchain technologies and intelligent marking is used for monitoring fishermen's fish with checked arguments for social sustainability. The aim was to promote solid evidence of adherence to origin and chain requirements, avoid the "double expenditure" of licensed products, and examine the ways in which these emerging technologies would serve as the foundation for a transparent framework that can provide food and other physical commodities with clarity in the face of customers. The ambition of Provence was not to show yet another digital platform but rather a solution to the serious need for data interoperability: stable, end-to-end, highly robust, but open monitoring objects without a central data management system. Blockchains have been discovered to satisfy these criteria and provide an exciting paradigm change needed to traceability in large supply chains.

- Agriculture

    For the participants in the agricultural supply chain, Agri Ledger is the best instrument. Agri Ledger focuses on digital identities, harvest records, unchangeable data, traceability, financial resources, and the preservation of revenue. Digital identity is an identifier with no formal recognition, under which a person has trouble obtaining financial care, social benefits, health facilities, education, civil and legal rights, equality between sexes, and immigration. Many farmers work at just 40% of their total knowledge power, and farmers can now prepare, harvest, and access the market more efficiently. The DLT approach offers unchangeable knowledge that gives the whole supply chain confidence and accountability. Failure to trace ensures that it is difficult to locate and remove such infected goods in the whole supply chain. Each object is traceable from seed to the customer with the DLT solution. Many agricultural suppliers lose up to 50% of their potential income without financial entry. Farmers should show their identity and profits for financial institutions to obtain admission. For improved documentation and evidence of revenue, farmers may use their digitized ledger.

• Healthcare

Blockchain applications in the field of health care help retain and defend data privacy. The latest approach in the field of healthcare is managing the medication supply chain. Patients are being enrolled in clinical trials; interoperability of IoT equipment is being enabled, and so on. The platform's ultimate aims include making access to health care open to everyone, administering health care in a more efficient way, ensures that clinicians collect compensation quickly, increases outcomes, and decreases expense. Medical chain delivers precious services to patients and health care facilities. The aim is to establish a single version of the medical records of the patient and to enable them in their network to exchange it with others.

Blockchain technology is used to unite pharmacy, investigation, and insurance providers and patients to safely access the required data. It uses smartphone devices to capture patient information immediately, to connect with physicians, and to exchange medical records. Furthermore, on the basis of online consultations, doctors can add new changes to the record. This strategy aims to improve the quality of everyday healthcare and quality of life. The bulk of blockchain healthcare initiatives are based on patients, and MediBloc is one such initiative. The organization creates a single universal distribution channel, organizing Big Data. Panacea, the blockchain from MediBloc, provides a secure and confidential method of storing medical data. Different additional clinical programs, epidemic prediction, medication production, and others will form the basis for the network [21].

McdiBloc has presently issued a patient's Medipass program for medical history and requests for benefits. It provides dental solutions, and the sound reviews give customers, welcomed by its dentists, the ability to leave detailed, confirmed, and incentivized evaluations of dental care. Dentacoin is a community of two apparently separate sectors—blockchain technology and the dental industry. Everyone gains from this—patients get incentives, and dentists get the incentive to better their jobs. DynaVox carries out market study studies and receives useful input from consumers who are paid in return for time and knowledge sharing. In the Dentacoin network, dentists, hospitals, providers, suppliers, and other businesses accept DentaCare, a smartphone app that educates children and adults on dental and oral hygiene topics. With the aid of blockchain technologies, Blockpharma works on addressing the global issue of medication falsification. The premise is simple: the user will verify the validity of the substance through the application. The program analyzes pharmaceutical company data; scanning the QR code of the drug box and extracting immediate results is the only thing you need. The TataMD CHECK test is the Latest COVID-19 standard for diagnosis—simple, accurate, and scalable. Its testing experience is easier, and results are faster using high-quality test kits assembled at its factory. The test is very effective in diagnosing the virus and provides a detailed diagnosis. More medical providers would help more patients to monitor diagnostic services to COVID easily and encourage other diagnostic centers accredited by NABL to provide test solutions to COVID-19 [22]. This test is extremely useful in quick turnaround circumstances such as airports, hospitals, colleges, and camps where rapid outcomes are crucial to minimize patient waiting times.

• Supply chain management

The first project Walton chain introduced in the field of supply chain management, incorporating the best of the real and digital environment in order to develop an effective system. It utilizes IoT RFID chips and blends them with the strength of blockchain in achieving data credibility, authenticity, confidentiality, and traceability for equal audits. It offers a structure for parents and children to bind different sectors according to their needs. They have their own chip technology that makes them in this dynamic world independent. Ambrosus seeks to protect and efficiently introduce another part of the industry across the blockchain for the powerful supply chain. Ambrosus is now a leading provider of smart farming, intelligent medical facilities, intelligent food traceability, and smart art. To build an encompassing, verifiable, and community-based framework for consistency, protection, origins of food and drug products, Ambrosus protocol incorporates high-tech sensors, blockchain tech, and intelligent contracts. These events happen through the Ambrosus protocol, fueled by Amber (AMB), and often deals with intelligent contracts. Modum is another blockchain solution for supply chain management particularly developed for the pharmaceutical industry.

Modum is headquartered in Switzerland and integrates IoT sensors with blockchain technologies to deliver data integrity for physical medicine transactions. The challenges of contract administration, security, and auditing, much needed for pharmaceuticals, can be enormously removed. The Modum sensors record environmental conditions in which goods are transported. As the products change ownership, the sensor details are reviewed in an intelligent blockchain contract under predetermined conditions. The contract confirms that the terms conform with both sender and user or regulatory requirements, causing different actions: sender and recipient notices, fees, or releases. And all of this is driven by the Modum blockchain token. VeChain is another blockchain supply chain management technology that brings tremendous potential to change the life cycle of supply chain management in several respects. However, it is good that VeChain does not limit itself to one specific area. The VeChain blockchain can have multiple user cases in Cold Chain Logistics, Vehicle, Medical Health, Luxury, Apparel, Beer, Agriculture, & Logistics industries. The IoT processors, sensors, and blockchain technologies were once again used to ensure the smooth incorporation of various companies into the supply chain management (SCM) blockchain. Trail of origin is not just a blockchain. Rather, the crypto-protocol is an agonistic blockchain supply chain management protocol. Origin Trail solves two key SCM challenges, data breakup and data centralization. It does so with the aid of the decentralized initial Trail network, which has the layers and is further driven by Tokens (the Trace token (TRAC)) such as framework layer, ODN network layer, optical distribution network (ODN) data layer, and blockchain layer.

• Real estate

DeedCoin utilizes a mobile application named dApp marketplace development; SoluLab is a dApp development company that decentralizes the financial operations to save cost by reducing middlemen intervention. The dApp developers establish a consensus between dApp and the proof of work mechanism. The open-source dApp code is easily understandable and accessible to all savvy users. Decentralized applications are built with tools that are an interface between decentralized codes in the blockchain. Unlike normal apps, decentralized applications do not require any central authority, and thus they can function with much faster efficiency and transparency. Decentralized nature provides a means to build a strong peer to peer decentralized application. dApps are open-sourced, and they are used for auditing purposes as they provide improved security features, and instead of money, users can transact using crypto coins or tokens. dApps also enhance proof of authenticity as users will be able to see the backend features too but cannot edit or manipulate them. Thus, this provides proof of transparency transactions in dApps happens instantly and faster as it is dependent on a peer-to-peer network. Rentberry is the first immobilizer that provides a fully digital leasing ride. All regular rental activities are automated to make the whole experience contactless by uploading personal records, credit reports, and rental bargaining using the personalized bid feature for virtual trips, eSigning rental agreements, and the transmission of maintenance requests. Everything can be achieved in one place, without delay, and without a touch from person to person.

Companies and Allied Matters Act (CAMA) is a legal document being prepared for the client at Union Edge, a prominent name in Media Industry. Users can develop projects at the blockchain-based platform to provide full control of the payment waterfall for film and television production with enhanced transparency, trust, analytics, and speed of payment. Speed, payout system, and producer benefits are the main theme of CAMA. Smart contracts enabled automated sales distribution process ensures no latency in payments since it dictates payment immediately upon contractual triggers and display information in doughnut charts. Users can fetch robust information about transactions and distribution data like weekly increase in gross revenue per screen, a weekly boost in several theatres, etc. All related stakeholders such as banks, law firms, sales agents, and distributors are connected to this single platform. Visual display of CAMA collection received, and collections left for next payout. Streamlined pricing and transaction costs, mitigation of legal fees, and disputes are automated through blockchain. The setting-up of the CAMA payment scheme not only serves the fund but also preserves the rights of the co-producers. Only a collection agency pays the fee to a revenue agent for a percentage of the money currently in the collection account. The advantages of the CAMA could be to manufacturers since they may outsource severe logistical responsibilities (reporting) and guarantee an unbiased third party manages revenues. And by monitoring sales also gives greater financial stability.

- Retail industry

  The Amazon Web Services (AWS), named an e-commerce giant, offers blockchain a service that uses the common open-source platform to build and deploy secure blockchain networks. Instead of wasting time and resources to set up a blockchain network, it encourages developers to concentrate on building blockchain apps. Paytomat is a payment gateway solution for merchants to embrace common encryption. It is a ready-to-install. The bars, beauty shops, and medical centers support the general population. Open security architecture (OSA) decentralized is a decentralized marketplace that provides dealers, suppliers, and customers AI-driven solutions. They gather scattered data across the whole supply chain and use the equipment for sorting, analyzing, and washing. Smart contracts aim to maintain both data suppliers' and customers' rights since they are held on blockchain to ensure they are exploited by a specific collection of PCIs, product reviews, and awards. Project Provenance works to improve retailers and suppliers' accountabilities in relations with organic customers and consumers who are mindful of human rights by creating more open product journeys for all their goods. Their hope is to fight "green-washing" practice by supplying retailers with large and blockchain-powered original solutions. OpenBazaar is a platform where users can deal with cryptocurrency on a host of products and services, which is one of the earliest entrants in the retail movement. The aim is to become a free online marketplace without platform charges where users can receive cryptocurrency in trade.

10.6 Conclusion

Blockchain is a feasible means and process for providing end-to-end applications and data integrity to prescription goods from a pharmacy to an end customer; it acts as either roadside networks or infrastructure. As well, the IoT space supports blockchain's large number of business openings. Blockchain-based Big Data is useful, which means it is organized, rich, and total and is a great source to be studied further. The Big Data created by blockchain is stable because its architecture cannot be forged.

References

[1] Nakamoto S. Bitcoin: a peer-to-peer electronic cash system. *Decentralized Business Review*. 2008; 34: 21260.
[2] Bohme R, Christin N, Edelman B, *et al.* Bitcoin: economics, technology, and governance. *Journal of Economic Perspectives*. 2015; 29(2): 213–38.
[3] Gubbi J, Buyya R, Marusic S, *et al.* Internet of Things (IoT): a vision, architectural elements, and future directions. *Future Generation Computer Systems*. 2013; 29(7): 1645–1660.

[4]   Wang Q, Zhu X, Ni Y, *et al*. Blockchain for the IoT and industrial IoT: a review. *Internet of Things*. 2020; 10: 100081.

[5]   Fakhri D and Mutijarsa K. Secure IoT communication using blockchain technology. In: 2018 International Symposium on Electronics and Smart Devices (ISESD), IEEE; 2018, pp. 1–6.

[6]   Ramanathan S and Ramasundaram M. Uncovering brain chaos with hypergraph-based framework. *International Journal of Intelligent Systems and Applications*. 2020; 12(4): 37–47.

[7]   Sharma A, Tomar R, Chilamkurti N, *et al*. Blockchain based smart contracts for internet of medical things in e-healthcare. *Electronics*. 2020; 9(10): 1609.

[8]   Wu M, Wang K, Cai X, *et al*. A comprehensive survey of blockchain: from theory to IoT applications and beyond. *IEEE Internet of Things Journal*. 2019; 6(5): 8114–8154.

[9]   Watanabe H and Fan H. A novel chip-level blockchain security solution for the Internet of Things networks. *Technologies*. 2019; 7(1): 28.

[10]   Schmidt CG and Wagner SM. Blockchain and supply chain relations: a transaction cost theory perspective. *Journal of Purchasing and Supply Management*. 2019; 25(4): 100552.

[11]   Wang Q, Wang T, Shen Z, *et al*. Re-tangle: a ReRAM-based processing-in memory architecture for transaction-based blockchain. In: 2019 IEEE/ACM International Conference on Computer-Aided Design (ICCAD), IEEE; 2019, pp. 1–8.

[12]   Schmitz J, and Leoni G. Accounting and auditing at the time of blockchain technology: a research agenda. *Australian Accounting Review*. 2019; 29(2): 331–342.

[13]   Mahmood BB, Muazzam M, Mumtaz N, *et al*. A technical review on block-chain technologies: applications, security issues & challenges. *International Journal of Computing and Communication Networks*. 2019; 1(1): 26–34.

[14]   Nassar M, Salah K, ur Rehman MH, *et al*. Blockchain for explainable and trustworthy artificial intelligence. *Wiley Interdisciplinary Reviews: Data Mining and Knowledge Discovery*. 2020; 10(1): e1340.

[15]   Zhang L, Xie Y, Zheng Y, *et al*. The challenges and countermeasures of blockchain in finance and economics. *Systems Research and Behavioral Science*. 2020; 37(4): 691–698.

[16]   Riesco R, Larriva-Novo X, and Villagra VA. Cybersecurity threat intelligence knowledge exchange based on blockchain. *Telecommunication Systems*. 2020; 73(2): 259–288.

[17]   Rehman M, Javaid N, Awais M, *et al*. Cloud based secure service providing for IoTs using blockchain. In: 2019 IEEE Global Communications Conference (GLOBECOM), IEEE; 2019. pp. 1–7.

[18]   Singh M, Nirban J, Singh S, *et al*. Blockchain as a Service for Cloud Storage (BaaS). In: *ICDSMLA 2019*, Cham: Springer; 2020, pp. 550–557.

[19]   Shalini R and Mohan R. Drugs relationship discovery using hypergraph. *International Journal of Information Technology and Computer Science*. 2018; 10: 54–63.

[20]   Ramanathan S and Ramasundaram M. Accurate computation: COVID-19 rRTPCR positive test dataset using stages classification through textual big data mining with machine learning. *The Journal of Supercomputing.* 2021; 77: 1–15.

[21]   Ramanathan S and Ramasundaram M. Hypergraph learning for fundamental shape detection. *Procedia Computer Science.* 2019; 165: 343–348.

[22]   Balakrishnan P and Ramanathan L. Test-driven development based on your own blockchain creation using javascript. In: *Blockchain, Big Data and Machine Learning*, London: CRC Press; 2020, pp. 233–264.

Chapter 11

Blockchain network with artificial intelligence—DeFi affair management

R. Vedhapriyavadhana[1], S.L. Jayalakshmi[1], R. Girija[1] and Ninoslav Marina[2]

Abstract

To create a completely decentralized exchange platform using blockchain technology that allows companies and investors to be able to tokenize real-world assets and provide them with financial services like yield farming, lending, and borrowing. Tailored commendations, announcements, and propositions can be done with decisions by artificial intelligence. Artificial intelligence plays a key role in analysis and prediction added to excellent decision-making skills on par with human intelligence. Blockchain technology proves its efficiency in high interpretability. Both blockchain and artificial intelligence compensate each other in its own feature. This chapter provides a detail description about useful topics like online education, finance, etc.

Keywords: Blockchain network; Artificial intelligence; Smart era applications; Decentralized technology

11.1 Introduction

11.1.1 Role of artificial intelligence and blockchain in various applications

The various areas where this combination is important are online education, sports, health care, agriculture, and finance.

11.1.1.1 Online education

To maintain security and privacy in the data and also the students' activities tracking and documents updating for teaching as well as learning through online. Inter- and intra-materials access by both professors and students. Across

[1]School of Computer Science and Engineering, Vellore Institute of Technology, Chennai, India
[2]University of Information Science and Technology, "St. Paul the Apostle", North Macedonia

universities and other educational institutions, assignments, and exams submitted online are finally endorsed by blockchain.

11.1.1.2 Sports

The decentralized networking is employed to maintain the athlete's data and their history. The routine progress of the athlete is especially important to track and predict his performance in the international event and take decisions based on that.

11.1.1.3 Health care

It helps good in all healthcare applications especially diagnosing the diseases, suggesting treatments, predicting the faults which aids medical practitioners, and all other healthcare personnel to take decisions accurately. In E-healthcare system, data is the most important aspect. Understanding the data for E-healthcare as explained in study [1] gives us a lot more information about the patient's health and we can find the patterns in the data using artificial intelligence. The patient details and their data base are supported with high security through which the authenticated doctors across globe can be able to view it without further delay. All these techniques really aid in life saving for many people.

11.1.1.4 Agriculture

The prediction of weather to alleviate the risk concomitant with farming and to monitor the crop wastage, pest presence sensing and precision in high irrigation technologies which will be really useful for the farmers in farming.

11.1.1.5 Finance

To take neutral decision related to customer including money transfer, account verification for which blockchain inclusion makes the process inexpensive and fast. Providing false data is very crucial and, to avoid the same, artificial intelligence with blockchain network is proposed. Among various applications, finance plays a vital role in both banking and non-banking sector.

This chapter proposes a network that acts as a bridge between blockchain and the finance space that removes the need for intermediaries like banks. This is possible with the following four phases: embraces of conceptual evidence, asset tokenization, digital stock management, and negotiators substitutes with artificial intelligence. All the companies and the users that use this platform will be able to issue digitalized assets called security tokens and these tokens are created using Ethereum smart contract that follows the ERC1400 standard. The platform also has its own token that follows the ERC20 standard which will allow the users and the companies to receive them by either staking their ether, which will allow them to yield farm these custom ERC20 tokens of the platform or they can borrow these custom ERC20 tokens by depositing a collateral amount in ether. The traditional finance market supplies numerous services from lending, borrowing, interest yielding investments, etc. This amalgamation of artificial intelligence and blockchain can aid these services which were exclusively available through established banks or financial institutes. The advancement of technology over the years has brought upon a substantial change and transformed the finance space completely, specifically blockchain technology with artificial intelligence has disrupted the finance space. The whole idea of digital currency started becoming bigger, from the introduction of Bitcoin to various new cryptocurrency that exists in the blockchain space. This expansion of the blockchain space in the finance market shifted the conversation to the concept of centralized finance also known as CeFi. Creation of blockchain application programming interface would aid the intercommunication of AI negotiators confirms the progress.

Decentralized finance also known as DeFi is introduced to blockchain finance space [2,14]. The whole operation and the functioning of the application are automated with help of smart contracts that can be deployed onto the Ethereum blockchain network, this leads to an outcome that removes the need for any financial institute needing to be involved completely aided by AI. The DeFi concept provides a very transparent and fair system with high-level security which also allows users to have complete possession of their own assets and cryptocurrency using their own wallet which is encrypted using their own private and public key. Even DeFi provides you services such as lending, borrowing, asset tokenization and provides the user with yield farming services, etc. The main ideology with DeFi is that the user will trust the technology to take care of any execution of services that are being offered to the user, instead of trusting the exchange and the other people to manage the services and the funds of the user. Storage of too sensitive data on blockchain and accessed through AI eases tailored commendations and offers apposite so that the transactions become keener and tranquil to be appraised.

11.2　Types of services in finance market

The traditional finance market provides various services from lending, borrowing, interest yielding investments etc. These services were exclusively available through established banks or financial institutes. Dominant banks have considerable knowledge with great organized data sets, characteristically of an economic nature, but must solitary newly happening to discover shapeless data. Financial data sets are analysis-ready, as they are usually composed for controlling drives and follow to commentary necessities. The advancement of technology over the years has brought upon a substantial change and transformed the finance space completely; specifically, blockchain technology has disrupted the finance space. The whole idea of digital currency started becoming bigger, from the introduction of Bitcoin to various new cryptocurrencies that exist in the blockchain space [2,3]. Further it may go into deeper of artificial intelligence. Approximately communicating machine learning includes the growth of procedures that use great volumes of data to separately conclude their individual limitations. This expansion of the blockchain and intelligence space in the finance market shifted the conversation to the concept of centralized finance also known as CeFi [4].

11.2.1　Centralized finance

Central banks also use large statistics methods to amount other features of financial action. For instance, they have used natural language meting out to create financial or rule indecision directories after written facts or to measure sentimentality in rejoinder to regulatory strategy declarations, counting those for eccentric program agencies. Centralized finance was initially adopted as the standard for trading and implements other financial services on the cryptocurrency. In CeFi, all the services implemented on the digital currency are supported through a central exchange like banks and other financial institutions in the traditional finance market. So, this concept of CeFi did not allow the users to have any access to their wallets using their private keys. Artificial intelligence algorithms are skilled to achieve in certain mistake metric. For example, the intelligence learning outline above completes the point that precincts the standards which are immaterial in greatest mechanism knowledge replicas [5,6].

11.2.2   Decentralized finance

Later a new concept was introduced to blockchain finance space which was called decentralized finance also known as DeFi [7]. The whole operation and the functioning of the application are automated with the help of smart contracts that can be deployed onto the Ethereum blockchain network, this leads to an outcome that removes the need for any financial institute needing to be involved [8]. The DeFi concept provides a very transparent and fair system with high-level security which also allows users to have complete possession of their own assets and cryptocurrency using their own wallet which is encrypted using their own private and public key. Intelligence will prospectively retain the monetary organization innocuous most of the time, greatest to be expected much improved than a virtuously human-staffed administrative organization, and we will subsequently and progressively depend on and belief on artificial intelligence. That can be together weaken the preparation and pre-emptive controlling events, though correspondingly forming an incorrect intelligence of security that might glowing terminate in a Minsky moment: apparent stumpy hazard that sources calamities [9].

11.2.2.1   Proposed system

To create a system that complements the various features that exist in the DeFi space. We will use concepts such as lending, borrowing, yield farming, and security tokens. All these various features will work cohesively to create a system that allows users to invest, earn profits, and tokenize the assets that they own. Some works and solutions are being solely done in this field to improve and grow the blockchain ecosystem. Especially when it comes to trading securities and utility tokens but it is very infrequent to find these solutions being implemented academically. Artificial intelligence made through a giant rebellion in loaning. Old-style loan guaranteeing approaches trust too deeply on credit scores providing by agencies. Though credit score confirmation is a countless chief stage in the direction of sifting out possible nonpayers, credit scores are rarely able to imprisonment multifaceted designs in loan reimbursements. The main aim of the proposed system is to create a template or a prototype that can be used to build various other applications which follow the concepts of creating ERC20 tokens that can be used with DeFi protocols like lending, borrowing, asset tokenization and provide the user with yield farming services. The architecture can be roughly sketched as a bottom sensor layer, a middle network layer, and a top application layer. One of the primary information-acquiring means at the bottom layer of the tags has found increasingly widespread applications in various business areas, with the expectation that the use of RFID tags will eventually replace the existing bar codes in all business areas.

11.2.3 Back-end

Truffle is a development environment and testing framework for creating smart contracts on the Ethereum blockchain. Truffle is also the core module of the Truffle suite, which has automated testing and automated deployment as well. Ganache is also part of the truffle suite, which allows us to create a local Ethereum blockchain that allows us to test our smart contracts. Ganache functions like a main net and ganache comes with 10 accounts that have 100 tests in each account that allows transactions, deployment, and testing possible. Solidity is the language that is used for writing the logic in the smart contracts that will be compiled to EVM bytecode. To test these smart contracts, we will be using Mocha Chai which is a JavaScript test framework that will be used to test functionalities of the smart contract that is created. Open Zeppelin contracts is a library for implementing and developing secure smart contracts. It helps in the implementation of role-based accesses and the creation of ERC20 tokens [9,10].

11.2.4 Front-end

React is a JavaScript library that is used in creating interactive user interfaces. It allows us to create components that manage their states. So this allows us to build the user interface in a modular format. Web3.js is a collection of libraries that are used to interact with the Ethereum node that is local or remote using HTTP and Web Socket. It allows the client-side application that is built with React to interact with the blockchain. Intelligence in Ethereum node has become the recognized boundary in contradiction of which practice exchanges be employed on the Ethereum blockchain. Meta Mask Wallet gives the ability to manage the accounts that exist in ganache or any other blockchain network seamlessly. Major web browsers do not directly connect to the blockchain by default, so Meta Mask solves that problem.

11.3 Decentralized bank app

This section focuses on the creation of ERC20 token using Open Zeppelin and the logic for implementing numerous services such as lending borrowing and yield farming services on the token that is written using solidity language. These services supplied incentives for other users to use the application.

11.3.1 Creation of custom ERC20 token

The ERC20 tokens are created using the Open Zeppelin library which the system inherits from. In this system instead of setting a token cap, the token will be issued or created as users deposit ether to the system or application [11,12] This token creation functionality occurs in the function mint ( ), which exists inside the Token. Sol contract. Usually, the user who deploys the smart contract will act as the minter for the tokens but in this system, the minter role is passed to the bank using the function pass MinterRole ( ) in which the minter address is changed to the bank address. The first minter address is assigned using the constructor in which the ERC20 token's name and symbol are also defined. The whole token. Sol contract only focuses on the minting of these ERC20 token as people deposit ether.

11.3.2   Creation of staking functionality

The creation of these numerous services as mentioned earlier are done completely inside the dbank.sol contract. Depositing of the ether to the application is done using the function deposit ( ) which checks whether the deposited ether is greater than 0.01 ETH. Then the ether staked by the user is taken and stored in a storage structure that points to each user's staked ether amount. The application also keeps track of when the ether is being deposited to the bank using the Ethereum current block time and this will also be stored in a storage structure like the map that will keep track of each user start deposit time. The staked status is changed to true which makes the user then only stake once and if needed to stake again then the user would have to un-stake and re-stake. When the user wishes to un-stake the amount deposited, the function withdraw ( ) will be executed and the user will earn a 10% APY on the amount staked for however long the time of staking took place. The total time of ether staked is calculated by taking the time of deposit that was stored earlier and then subtracted with the current block time of the withdrawal. Then the system calculates the interest per second for ether deposited and then that value is multiplied with the total time of staking, which gives the value of interest earned by the user. After which the user's staked ether amount is sent back to their wallet along with ERC20 tokens that are minted depending on the interest amount accumulated by the user.

11.3.3   Creation of loan functionality

The service of borrowing also takes place inside the dbank.sol contract. When the user wishes to take a loan, the function lend ( ) is executed as shown in Figure 11.1. The system makes sure that the collateral amount deposited is greater than that of 0.01 ETH and checks if the current users issuing for a loan have any previous loan yet to be paid off in this system. Depending on the collateral amount being deposited by the user, the loan amount is calculated. The loan amount given to the user will be 50% of the collateral amount deposited into the system. Then the ERC20 tokens are minted and then these tokens are sent to the user as loan. The user's loan status is changed to true which makes the user only take a loan once. If the user wishes to take more loans, the user would have to pay off the current loan and then borrow again. When the user wishes to pay back the loan borrowed, the function giving ( ) will be executed. The system will charge a fee of 5% for the loan that has been taken by the user. Learning and intelligence make the user pays off all the token that was taken as

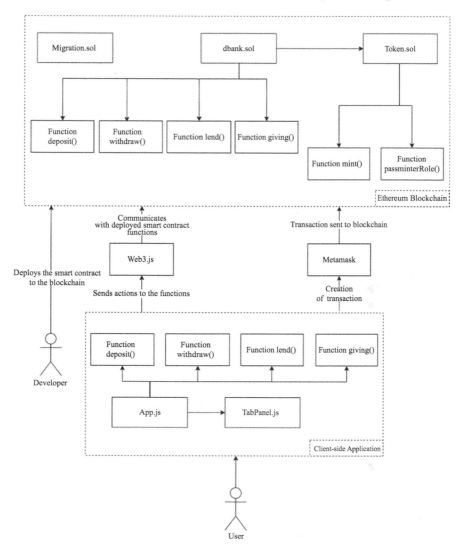

*Figure 11.1   High-level overview of how the system of the decentralized bank
application functions*

loan, the system will transfer the amount that was given as collateral by the user
minus the charged fees for using the service. After which, the system changes the
status of the loan to false which then allows the user to take another loan if needed.

11.3.4   Deploying smart contract to the blockchain

Then we create a migration file that will take care of the deployment and compi-
lation of the smart contracts in the proper order. Inside the deploy.js file, the async

0x90f4241cc2c88cd6549f02A49042ea00eA5d471f

Figure 11.2   Staking ether UI with connected wallet address and input field to enter amount of ether to be staked

function module.exports is where the order in which the smart contracts have to deploy is mentioned. While compiling, the Token.sol will be executed first after which we store the address of the Token.sol in a variable name token. Then the dbank.sol contract is deployed with the Token.sol address and then store the address of dbank.sol in a variable dbank as done earlier with Token.sol address. Then execute the function to pass to Token.sol address to the bank address by executing the function passMinter-Role ( ). Now all the contracts will be compiled using the truffle framework and then deployed to the ganache blockchain. Truffle finds the ganache blockchain by using the port number mentioned in the truffle-config.js file [13].

11.3.5   Interaction with client-side application

After the contracts are compiled and deployed to a local blockchain instance, then the truffle framework creates an Application Binary Interface (ABI) which is a .json file that describes the deployed smart contracts. This file allows us to call the functions that exist inside the smart contracts that were developed and deployed. This .json file is through which our client-side application will interact with the blockchain and to ease that process we use the web3.js library, which allows us to seamlessly interact with functions in the deployed smart contracts.

11.3.6   Applications

This section shows the various applications of blockchain technology as in Figures 11.2 and 11.13.

11.4   Security token application

This section focuses on the creation of the ERC1400 security token which enables the users the ability to trade and create these securities. Along with the creation and trading features of the token, the token must go through Know Your Customer (KYC) verification and Anti-Money Laundering (AML) verification.

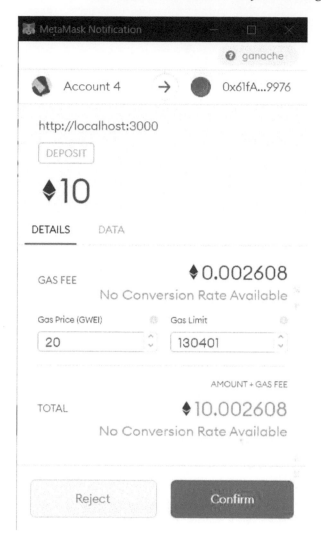

Figure 11.3 Meta Mask wallet confirmation of transaction UI before staking 10 ETH

The core smart contract of this system is the ERC1594.sol contract. The ERC1594 is a substandard of the ERC1400 standard. The ERC1400 standard is a highly detailed standard with many features and many substandards that may not be needed for this proposed system because the main objective of this proposed system is to create a template or a prototype that can be used to build various other applications which follow the different concepts that are mentioned in this proposed work. The Meta Mask Wallet UI before and after staking 10ETH is shown in Figure 11.4. Among all the substandard that exists under the ERC1400 standard,

ganache
Connected
Account 4
89.6879 ETH
Send
Swap
Assets
Activity
89.6879 ETH
0.0000362792602914...
ganache
Connected
Account 4
79.6862 ETH
Send
Swap
Assets
Activity
79.6862 ETH
0.0000362792602914...

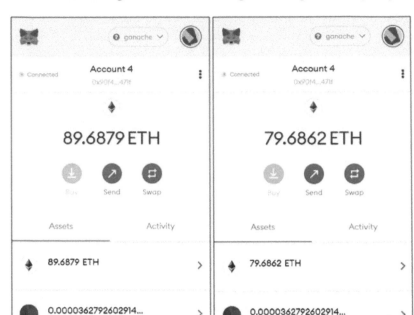

Figure 11.4 Meta Mask wallet UI left showing before staking 10 ETH and right showing after staking 10 ETH

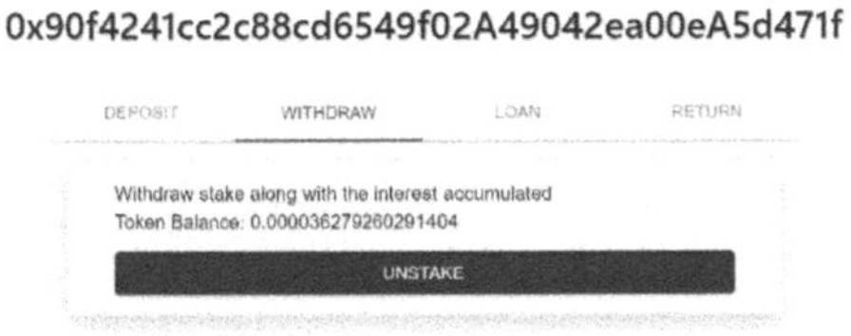

0x90f4241cc2c88cd6549f02A49042ea00eA5d471f
DEPOSIT
WITHDRAW
LOAN
RETURN
Withdraw stake along with the interest accumulated
Token Balance: 0.000036279260291404
UNSTAKE

Figure 11.5 High-level overview of how the system of the decentralized bank application functions

the ERC1594 substandard was selected and others were not because this substandard is the core of the security token standard. This substandard inherits from the general token standard ERC20 and incorporates error signaling or checker methods as a failure but more complex than the general ERC20 standard. The overview of the decentralized bank application functions is shown in Figure 11.5.

It provides support in terms of issuance, transfer, and redemption and provides the capability to check whether the transfer is valid. The Meta Mask Wallet confirmation of transaction UI before withdrawing staked ether is shown in

Figure 11.6. This substandard out of the other three substandard must be implemented to meet the minimum requirements of the ERC1400 standard. ERC1594 substandard also has the most essential functions that are needed for the creation and implementation of a security token.

The amount custom ERC20 token staying in the account after withdrawing staked ether is shown in Figure 11.7. After which borrowing custom ERC 20 tokens UI with input field to enter the amount of ether to be deposited as collateral is shown in Figure 11.8. The Meta Mask Wallet confirmation of transaction UI before

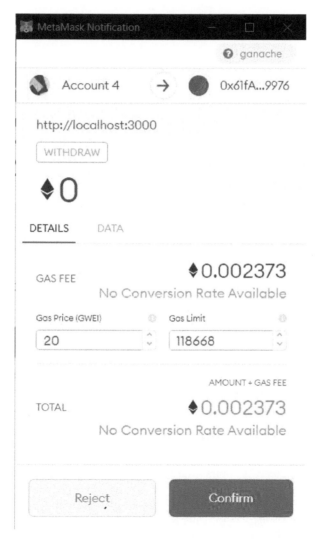

Figure 11.6   Meta Mask wallet confirmation of transaction UI before withdrawing staked ether

0x90f4241cc2c88cd6549f02A49042ea00eA5d471f

*Figure 11.7   Amount custom ERC20 token staying in the account after
withdrawing staked ether. Increased amount compared to Figure 3.6*

0x90f4241cc2c88cd6549f02A49042ea00eA5d471f

*Figure 11.8   Borrowing custom ERC20 tokens UI with input field to enter the
amount of ether to be deposited as collateral*

depositing 10ETH as collateral amount is shown in Figure 11.9. The Meta Mask
Wallet confirmation of transaction ERC20 tokens UI before and after depositing
10ETH as collateral amount is shown in Figure 11.10. UI returning the custom
ERC20 tokens taken as loan as shown in Figure 11.11.

11.4.1   Creation of security token

As mentioned earlier, the ERC1594.sol contract inherits from the general token
ERC20 standard, so there must be an ERC20.sol contract separately created. To do
this, the ERC20.sol contract from the OpenZeppelin library is used with few
changes done to the contract, so that it meets the requirements of the proposed
system. The changes done to the ERC20.sol contract is on the standard function
transfer ( ) because if not modified, then the function transfer ( ) can be accessed
without going through any error signaling or checker methods that exist in the
ERC1594.sol contract. So, now the function transfer ( ) is changed to function
transferWithData ( ) which is the same as the function transferWithData ( ) inside
the ERC1594.sol contract. Meta Mask Wallet Confirmation of transaction UI
before returning the custom ERC20 tokens as shown in Figure 11.12. The implementation of the ERC1594.sol contract is done using all the functions that are
defined by the substandard. ERC1594.sol contract has initialized variables queues
and controller that function as a reference to call the various methods that exist
inside the AMLQueues.sol and Controller.sol contracts, respectively. Any functions that are called in the ERC1594.sol contract goes through the general and KYC

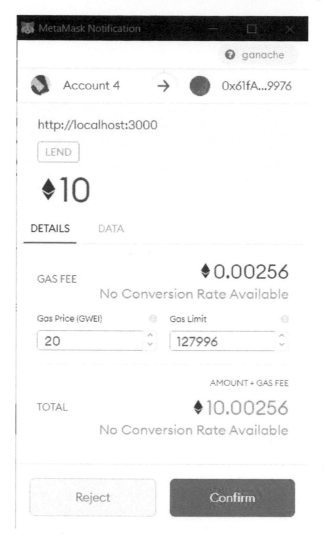

Figure 11.9   Meta Mask wallet confirmation of transaction UI before depositing 10 ETH as collateral amount

verification processes that are initialized inside the Controller.sol contract and goes through the AML verification process that is initialized inside the AMLQueues.sol contract. Meta Mask Wallet UI amount of custom ERC20 token in account after returning the custom ERC20 tokens as shown in Figure 11.13.

11.4.2   KYC and general verification process

The main aim of the Controller.sol contract is to call and check if the KYC verification and general verifications pass for a given function. The KYC verification

Figure 11.10   *Meta Mask wallet UI on left showing the amount of custom ERC20 tokens in account before depositing 10 ETH as collateral and right showing the amount custom ERC20 tokens after depositing 10 ETH as collateral*

0x90f4241cc2c88cd6549f02A49042ea00eA5d471f

| DEPOSIT | WITHDRAW | LOAN | RETURN |

Return the amount taken as Loan
You will be charged a fee of 5% of the deposited collateral

RETURN

Figure 11.11   *UI returning the custom ERC20 tokens taken as loan*

process in the blockchain space is simple and straightforward, as every user has a unique identity because of their wallet address, and they have their private key which makes sure that only the owner of the address can approve the transactions. So, to meet the smallest requirements of the KYC verification process, the system stores the addresses which are already KYC verified off-chain. The KYCChecker. sol contract will be responsible for managing and performing the verification process, this KYCChecker.sol contract has a map data structure that stores the address that are whitelisted i.e. stores the addresses that are already KYC verified off-chain

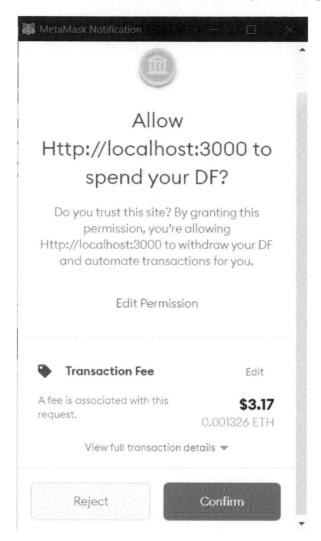

Figure 11.12   Meta Mask wallet confirmation of transaction UI before returning
the custom ERC20 tokens

as shown in Figure 11.14. The adding and removal of the authorized members to
the map data structure that stores the address of the already KYC verified users are
done only by the account which has the role called KYCRole which is defined in
the KYCRole.sol contract. This role-based access approach is commonly done
using the ownable pattern, in which a modifier is created which makes the deployer
of the contract the owner. Then only the owner will be able to perform certain
methods in the contract. So, to create a KYCRole for the system, a contract called
KYCRole.sol contract is created which inherits the Role.sol contract from the
OpenZeppelin library. Now in the KYCRole.sol contract, the KYCRole is

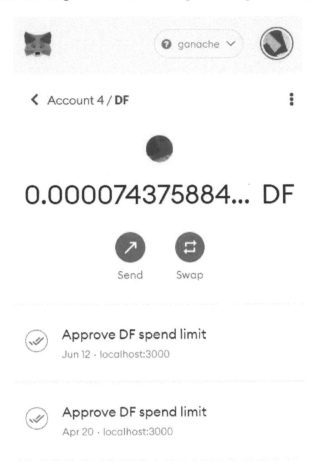

Figure 11.13   Meta Mask wallet UI amount of custom ERC20 token in account after returning the custom ERC20 tokens

initialized and has methods that allow to add and remove address that represents the KYCRole and also verify whether a user has the KYCRole or not. So, the Controller.sol contract will be the only contract that needs to be called by the ERC1594.sol contact as all the verifications for transfer, redeem, and issuance is done in this one contract alone as shown in Figure 11.15.

11.4.3   AML verification process

The other functionality that is added to this system is AML verification as mentioned earlier. The general AML procedure requires the deposit to remain in the account for a

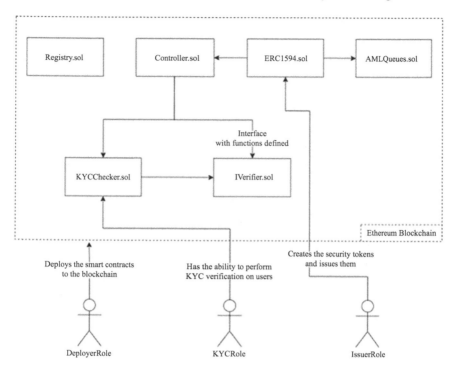

Figure 11.14   High-level overview of the major components in the smart contract system for the security token application

set time and checks if the total amount of money transferred crosses the limit amount that can be transferred in that set time. Using those same procedures, the system is designed to implement those functionalities automatically. So, AMLQueues.sol contract is created, whose main aim is to create a queue like data structure that stores the transactions that are done by an account. This structure AMLQueue is designed in such a way that there is a map data structure for the number of tokens being transferred and a map data structure that gives us the time when the transaction took place. The complete process of AML verification does not take place in the AMLQueues.sol contract but the functions like function enqueue ( ), function dequeue ( ), function peek ( ), function empty ( ), and function sumOfTransfers ( ) are defined and operated in this contract. However, the constants needed for the calculation like current time, limit number of token that can be transferred, deposit holding time and the function calculations ( ) exist inside the ERC1594.sol contract. The storage structure in the AMLQueues.sol contract is designed in such a way that the system does not waste space. The method through which the system does not waste space is by the following: every time the ERC1594.sol contract performs AML verifications, the start of the storage structure is checked by calling the function peek( ) in the AMLQueues.sol contract, after which all the transaction that have crossed the deposit holding time are

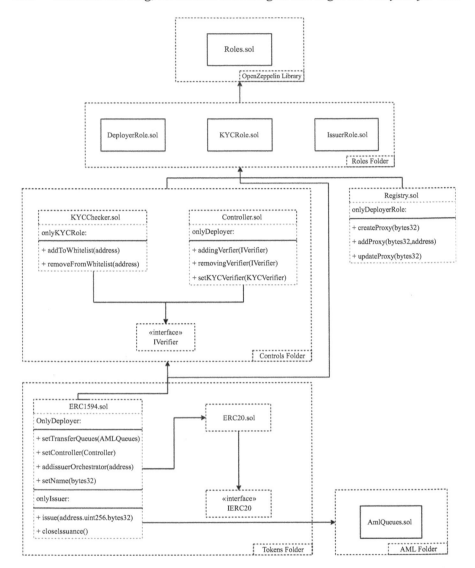

Figure 11.15   High-level overview of the role-based functions accessible in the smart contract system for the security token application

removed from the storage structure by calling the function dequeue() and then the new transactions are stored using the function enqueue().

11.4.4   Creation of required roles

As mentioned earlier about the role-based access approach done on the system to create a KYCRole, there are two more roles defined in this system and those are DeployerRole and Issuer Role. The Deployer Role is the account address through which the contracts are initially deployed to the blockchain system. This role's main aim is to connect all the contracts and initialize every other role existing in the system to an address. The Issuer Role is the account address through which the issuance of the security token takes place. This role issues as many tokens as it can within the set amount of token that can be transferred and till the issuance functionality allows it.

11.4.5 Upgradable smart contract

One of the functional technical requirements mentioned earlier was the ability to upgrade the smart contract system but the problem faced is that smart contracts after being-deployed are immutable and therefore not upgradable.

So, to achieve the upgradeable functionality, the system is designed using a proxy technique. The idea behind the proxy technique is to have a one storage contract, one registry contract which in the proposed model system is Unstructured. sol contract, Registry.sol contract and there must be a logic contract which can later be upgraded, which in the proposed system is all the other contracts mentioned earlier. Various proxy patterns solve the problem of shared storage but the three main are inherited storage, eternal storage, and unstructured storage. For the proposed system, the unstructured storage pattern is selected over the others as this storage pattern does not require the logic contracts to inherit state variables associated with upgradability. Also instead of storing the address in successive slots, the unstructured pattern stores the address in random slots. This pattern is easily executable as the upgraded versions of the logic contract must just inherit from the previous version.

11.5 Conclusion

The proposed system creates a platform that meets the requirements of creating ERC20 tokens that have financial services like yield farming, lending, and borrowing enabled on them. These all services are greatly supported by artificial intelligence. Due to this, the platform also meets the requirements of removing intermediaries as mentioned earlier and make the application automated by transferring the minting or issuance role of the custom ERC20 tokens to the smart contract that can be deployed onto the Ethereum blockchain network. The further extension of the proposed system allowed users and companies to issue their security tokens and allowing them to issue security tokens that follow one of the ERC1400 standards. The application with the use of intelligence makes sure that general verification, KYC verification, and AML verification process were performed when the security token was transferred, issued, created, and redeemed. The KYC verification process was done by allowed listing users that were already KYC verified off-chain and the AML verification process was imposed on the tokens by checking the deposit holding time and the number of tokens being transferred or issued in a set time. A simple user interface was created using react.js and web3.js library which allowed the users to stake ether that allowed them to earn custom ERC20 tokens of the platform. The user interface also provided the users with the ability to take loans of the custom ERC20 tokens by depositing ether as the collateral amount and also pay off the loan when wanted. All the transactions are confirmed before performing using the Meta Mask wallet. One of the main objectives of the proposed system which uses intelligence was to create a template or prototype that can be later used to build various application leveraging off this system, which the proposed system satisfies by implementing all the features and functionalities of creating ERC20 tokens that can be used with DeFi protocols like lending, borrowing, asset tokenization, and yield farming services.

11.6   Future work

This proposed system only achieves the adequate requirements of an application that can be implemented on a real-world basis. This system can be further upgraded in various aspects, like verification processes and financial services, which can be added to this system. Some of the extensions that can be added to this system are by: adding few more substandard to the security token like ERC1410, ERC1643, and ERC1644, which results in a token that has the capabilities of adding metadata, documents to the token, and makes the token controllable which gives the issuers the capability of forceful transfer of tokens. The KYC verification process can be improved by adding expiry date for the KYC users so that users will have to verify their account in set interval times and also by making the user register their account and verify the credential by filling a form with an OTP that is sent to their phone or e-mail that will create a much secure system. The AML verification process can be improved by creating an oracle that takes off-chain data and sends them to the blockchain. The data received from the oracle allows the system to calculate the actual amount of fiat currency that is being transferred in a set time. Also by the data that is gathered from the off-chain with help of oracles, the security tokens which act as equity can be measured as the company's corporate value. Financial services like Initial Coin Offering (ICO) and Security Token Offering (STO) can be introduced to the application that allows start-up companies and users to raise initial funds for their projects and ideas.

In near future, distinct network systems can be developed as per the different applications exists likely to be in Education, Sports, Healthcare, Agriculture, etc., specifically with respect to the different problems that prevail within the system.

References

[1]   Sanghvi HA, Pandya SB, Chattopadhyay P, Patel RH, and Pandya AS. Data science for E-healthcare, entertainment and finance. In 2021 Third International Conference on Inventive Research in Computing Applications (ICIRCA), IEEE; 2021, September, pp. 604–611.

[2]   Chod J, Trichakis N, and Yang SA. Platform Tokenization: Financing, Gover-Nance, and Moral Hazard, Governance, and Moral Hazard. Working Paper, Boston College; September 25, 2019.

[3]   Tyagi AK, Aswathy SU, Aghila G, and Sreenath N.AARIN: affordable, accurate, reliable and innovative mechanism to protect a medical cyber-physical system using blockchain technology. *IJIN* 2021;2:175–183.

[4]   Qin K, Zhou L, Afonin Y, *et al.* CeFi vs. DeFi — Comparing Centralized to Decentralized Finance, arXivLabs-Open access repository, Cornell University, June 2021.

[5]   Leonhard R. Decentralized finance on the ethereum blockchain. *SSRN Electronic Journal* 2019. Available at SSRN 3359732.

[6]   Zetzsche DA, Arner DW, and Buckley RP. Decentralized finance (defi). IIEL Issue Brief. 2020;2.

[7]   Sch a·r F. Decentralized finance: on blockchain-and smart contract-based financial markets. *FRB of St Louis Review*. 2021;103:153–174.

[8]   Bakaul M, Das NR, and Moni MA. The implementation of blockchain in banking system using Ethereum. *International Journal of Computer Applications* 202;975:8887.

[9]   OpenZeppelin. Access control-openZeppelin Docs. https://docs. open-zeppelin.com/contracts/4.x/access-control.

[10] OpenZeppelin. ERC20 – OpenZeppelin Docs. https://docs.openzeppelin. com/contracts/4.x/erc20.

[11] OpenZeppelin. Using with Upgrades, 2017–2021. https://docs.openzeppelin. com/contracts/4.x/upgradeable.

[12] ERC 1594: Core Security Token Standard; 2021.

[13] Bloo F. *Towards Updatable Smart Contracts*. Twente: University of Twente; 2018.

[14] Chen Y and Bellavitis C. Blockchain disruption and decentralized finance: the rise of decentralized business models. *Journal of Business Venturing Insights*. 2020;13:e00151.

Chapter 12

Vulnerabilities of smart contracts and solutions

Roshni Nawaz[1], Amit Kumar Tyagi[1,2] and M. Shamila[3]

Abstract

In recent decade, blockchain concept was proposed in cryptocurrency, completion of transition without any third party. Today, this concept is being used in all possible applications like e-healthcare, transportation, communication, etc. In general, blockchain technology uses the concept of smart contract to transfer any money to end user. Smart contracts provide efficient performance of credible transactions (trackable and irreversible functionality) without involving third parties. These contracts are self-executing contracts with the terms of the agreement between buyer and seller. Note that smart contracts have distributed, decentralized blockchain network. Some applications of smart contacts are the following: land records, cryptocurrencies like Bitcoin, Ethereum, etc. With this much popularity of smart contract, today we are facing many vulnerabilities on such contract, for example, today's potential vulnerabilities are nearly 30% on smart contracts (examined by national university of Singapore). It is a critical issue and legitimate (valid) cause for having concern in the blockchain technology and we should take care about such critical issue because people's money or information are being shared through such smart contracts. In general, security vulnerabilities in software can be fixed by patching, but patching security vulnerabilities of decentralized applications on the Ethereum blockchain is not so straightforward. Due to the immutable nature of smart contracts, it is very difficult to upgrade the already deployed contracts. But, having the availability of smart contract as public, chances of vulnerability are higher on stored smart contracts. Hence, this chapter provides several mitigated critical smart contract vulnerabilities (in the past decade), possible technique to detect vulnerabilities on smart contract, and possible suggestions including opportunity (and research gaps) for future toward protecting smart contract code or agreement.

Keywords: Smart contract; Vulnerability; Blockchain technology; Re-entrancy attack

[1]School of Computer Science and Engineering, Vellore Institute of Technology, Chennai Campus, India
[2]Centre for Advanced Data Science, Vellore Institute of Technology, Chennai, India
[3]Gokaraju Rangaraju Institute of Engineering and Technology, India

12.1   Introduction about blockchain and smart contract

The blockchain is a concept of sharing information/data in a distributed and decentralized manner. This concept was used previously in buying lands, but technically, it was sued in 2008 in a cryptocurrency called Bitcoin [1]. A lot of changes and a lot of people are using this technology in real-world applications that make things more distributed and more trustworthy. This technology has been around since 2008. There are different blocks that make up the blockchain concept, and each block makes up a chain. In which, each block has information about the blocks that came before and after it in a chain (future coming block in a chain). As a cryptographic hash, which can be used as a unique ID, this information is made up of the following items:

- The date and time of the last block.
- This is a list of everything that happened during the time.
- Another way to figure out which block is the last one.
- It is called nonce.

To set how hard cryptographic puzzles are, you can use "None" as a number. If you want to add a new block or find a new block in the blockchain network, you have to work for about 10 minutes. The value of this coin is automatically changed to make this happen. In a public blockchain, like Bitcoin, there are a lot of nodes that keep copies of the important content. In other words, there is a limit on how many transactions can be made in order to keep the system from becoming one big group of people. It is different when you use a private blockchain. Only nodes that have a stake in the transactions are adding or running them. Blockchain environments are not only very decentralized technologically but they are also very decentralized in how they make decisions, which makes them even more decentralized.

This is what most people think of when they talk about "blockchain". The Bitcoin blockchain is what most people think of when they talk about "blockchain". In terms of "permission-less" blockchains, Bitcoin is the first one to come along. Anyone can write data to it by running some free software and not even having to sign up for an account. Keep in mind that the Bitcoin blockchain file is a list of all the Bitcoin transactions that have been made since January 2009 until now. In simple terms, Bitcoin is a digital currency that uses blockchain technology [1]. In other words, a blockchain is a record of time-stamped transactions, each of which has a different number of output addresses (each address is a 160-bit number). A "header" is a piece of text that tells you what the block is about. It also tells you what is inside the block. Blockchain technologies are made up of six main parts.

- Decentralized: Blockchain does not need a single person or group to run it. The data can be recorded, stored, and updated all over the place (also in decentralized nature).
- When data is stored in a "blockchain", each node can see what other nodes are doing with it. This is why blockchain can be trusted because each node can see what other nodes are doing with the data.

- In most blockchain systems, everyone can see the records and make apps with them. People can also use blockchain technology to make any app they want.
- Consensus means that every node on the blockchain system can move or update data safely. The idea is to trust one person to the whole system, and no one can stop it.
- Unless someone can take control of more than 50% of the nodes at the same time, records will not be changed.
- There was a trust problem between nodes, so blockchain technologies solved that problem. This means that data can be sent or even sold anonymously, and you only need to know the person's Blockchain address.

So, here are some of the things that make blockchain technology different from the rest:

- When a deal is made, everyone who is in it must agree that the deal is legal.
- If people know where an asset came from and how its ownership has changed over time, that is important.
- A transaction cannot be changed after it has been added to the ledger, so no one can do that. In order to fix a transaction that was done in the wrong way, a new transaction must be made. As a result, both transactions can be seen.
- People can easily figure out who owns an asset or when a transaction is over if there is just one ledger that everyone can look at.
- It is important for a blockchain to be decentralized, accountable, and safe so that people can trust it. The following are some of the benefits of blockchain technology for business:
- It used to take days for complex, multi-party transactions like this to be done. Now, they are done in just a few minutes. People do not have to check a transaction with a central authority because it does not need to be done that way.
- There are a lot of ways blockchain networks save money, like by not having to pay for things.
- There is less oversight because the people who use the network keep it safe. All of the people on the network know each other, and they all know each other.
- People can trade things of value without the help of intermediaries.
- Because everyone has access to the same ledger, there is no need to do the same thing over and over again.

Tighter security and data validity are the two things that make the blockchain safer: this is because the blockchain's security features protect against tampering, fraud, and cybercrime, which are all bad things. The way the blockchain works makes it hard to change the data after it has been put in. It is possible to make member-only networks when a network has been approved. This lets people show that they are who they say they are and that their goods or assets are what they say they are. These are some of the ways blockchain is being used:

- Finance.
- Retail.

- Smart contracts and changes to the land can happen.
- There is going to be a new Internet in the future.
- Future computing environments, like a distributed cloud, will be used.

12.1.1   Smart contract

In the last few years, we have seen a great deal of both academic and practical interest in the topic of vulnerabilities in smart contracts, particularly those developed for the Ethereum Blockchain [2] (Blockchain 2.0: Ethereum Rise called smart contracts).

Smart contracts are just like the traditional pen–paper agreements in the real world but they are completely digitalized. Smart contracts are small software programs stored inside a blockchain (which is a distributed ledger that is corruption resistant and since it is not governed by any single authority, it is completely trustworthy. Only after the content is validated and verified by the miners to check if the data is accurate, it is added to the Blockchain with a timestamp). Smart contracts are self-executing and are also called blockchain contracts or crypto contracts [3].

12.1.2   Why do we need smart contracts?

Smart contracts are like icing on the blockchain cake. When dealing with valuable items, there is often lack of trust between parties and they require the oversight of reliable intermediaries. But this amazing piece of technology allows users to perform transactions, make transparent deals, automate processes, sell or exchange property, money or any other valuable assets without the interference or need of a third party. Everything agencies, banks or companies can do, can be pre-coded into a smart contract. Usually, when people make deals or exchange assets, a third person (like lawyers are involved), a legal written document takes a lot of time and costs too much. Here's where smart contract comes in handy as it is self-executing, it facilitates credible transaction without the involvement of a middleman and saves time and cost. Transactions using smart contracts are made according to specific conditions and time frames. The content signature is then verified, stored, and pushed into the blockchain. The data (written code) or information or contract stored in a blockchain is supervised by the computers in the network, so they are resistant to any modification and it is kept secure by sharing the information. Table 12.1 provides the difference between smart contracts with traditional contract.

There are some popular attacks or vulnerabilities [4] on smart contract (in current)/vulnerabilities and its preventions in smart contracts are

- Broken access controls
- Integer overflows and underflows
- Weak randomness
- Re-entrancy

Now each term is discussed in detail as:

- Broken access controls: In any website or company, there are different types of users that use an application for different purposes and can access only

Table 12.1   Comparison of smart contract and traditional contract

Smart contract	Traditional contract
Smart contracts are a self-executing computer program	Traditional contracts are bound by the legal terms
Smart contracts cannot be modified or changed according to people's requirement	Traditional contracts are flexible and can be modified at any time with the consent of both the parties
Smart contracts work on the distributed ledger technology	Traditional contracts work on the institutional factors and requirements of the two parties involved
Smart contracts limit human interaction and interference	Traditional contracts need human intervention

particular parts of an application. Like normal users just browse the page, administrators have the ability to make changes. The ability to restrict users to access the resources and data, keeping everyone else out of it is called access control. If a normal user gains access to administrator functions and features, a part they do not require access to, in such a case the access controls are broken. DAST and SAST (Dynamic And Static Application Security Testing Tools) identify if the access controls are present or absent but they cannot tell its efficiency and functionality. A lot of manual testing is required, Deny by default, build it once, and make sure the access controls are powerful, least privilege minimal amount of access and time required, web application firewalls.

- Integer overflows and underflows: Integer overflow occurs when a variable or number is incremented above its maximum capacity. When two numbers with different signs are added, it can never lead to integer overflow. If we consider an unsigned 4-bit number, the minimum value is 0000 and maximum value is 1111 i.e. from 0 to 15. If we have the number 1111 (15) and increment it by 1, we expect 16 but it is not possible to represent 16 in 4 bits so it reverts back to 0000. When an arithmetic operation is performed which gives a result too small to be represented in the given target integer size, it is called integer underflow. When two negative numbers are added to get a number smaller than -128 (which is the smallest number that can be represented by 2's complement 8-bit number) then integer underflow occurs. Integer underflow occurs more frequently that integer overflow as is not very easy to get the required amount for overflow. But both integer overflow and integer underflow are dangerous as the resulting value would mean a completely different number when interpreted in the target integer size. The places where integer overflow may occur is on YouTube when any video get a million views. Another huge problem caused by integer overflow was the y2k problem. Note that such problem can be fixed by increasing the memory space allocated to that particular data (32 bits replaced by 64 bits).
- Weak randomness: Computers are deterministic machines and so are smart contracts on the ethereum blockchain, they only appear to produce random

numbers but actually they are hard and complex algorithms. Higher the entropy means higher the randomness. But there is no source of entropy or randomness in ethereum.

- Re-entrancy attack [3]: Re-entrancy (one of the major dangers of calling external contracts is that they can take over the control flow, and make changes to our data by calling the same function repeatedly in a contract/that the calling function was not expecting). The attacker drains all the funds from the contracts due to this recursive loop. Re-entrancy guards can be used to wrap around functions and counter ensures that only one call (no other re-entrant calls) is made to the same wrapped function in a single transaction at a particular time.

Note that lack of randomness can affect the security of the system. Hashes, timestamps, blocknumber, or gas limit are unknown for future transaction blocks in smart contract. Hence, this section discusses several interested terms related to smart contracts. Now, the remaining part of this chapter is organized as: Section 12.2 discusses work related to smart contact, i.e., evolution of smart contract with blockchain technology's growth. Section 12.3 discusses motivation behind this work. Further, Section 12.4 discusses the scope of smart contract today and tomorrow. Section 12.5 will discuss necessity of finding vulnerabilities in smart contracts. Section 12.6 discusses several vulnerabilities of smart contracts. Section 12.7 discusses available techniques or mechanisms in secure smart contract. Section 12.8 discusses several problems raising during protecting smart contracts against any vulnerabilities. Further, several opportunities including future research directions toward smart contracts are discussed in Section 12.9. Finally, this chapter is concluded in Section 12.10 in brief.

12.2   Related work

Several improvements in technology have been received in the previous decade, for example, blockchain technology, cyber physical system, etc. Blockchain technology is used in cryptocurrency like Bitcoin [5] initially, then smart contract, etc., and moves to a different platform like Blockchain 1.0, Blockchain 2.0, Blockchain 3.0, and Blockchain 4.0 (DAaps) [6].

12.2.1   Y2K problem

By the late twentieth century, computers were used by almost everyone, from transaction of money to checking the date. Computers were not always the same, they have evolved with better efficiency and memory space. In the past, in old computers, there was very less memory space, so programmers want to save more space, the only way they found was to represent the year as a 2-digit number. Before the year was stored as 70 (in 2 digits instead of 4 digits as 1970) on a computer system to save memory space.

Expiry dates of credit and debit cards and goods or any testing system that requires the use of dates to satisfy or verify a condition became chaotic on

1 January 2000. The Y2K problem also known as Year 2000 problem or "Millennium Bug." Limited memory, lazy program saved 2 bytes of memory (every byte count). In the year 2000, there were many computers which still have very old data. These problems created havoc, people were afraid that the world would come to a standstill and the stock market would crash. On the 1st of January 2000, the digital dial of the computer reverted back to 1 January 1900. This might not sound like a huge problem because humans knew the correct date but, the data stored in computer machines would become invalid, any date corresponding equipment like missiles, plane navigation equipment would fail. The business and government depended on computers, if they failed, they would take the whole digital infrastructure down. The United States Navy Observatory (USNO) website showed the year 1900. The bus ticket system in Australia failed, banks were not able to transfer money and the transactions were frozen. Satellites in USA transmitted unreadable data for 3 days until it was fixed by patching. The Y2K problem was not very serious, just that the dates in cell-phones and computers were incorrect, but it made people realize how depended they are on computers.

12.2.2 Decentralized autonomous blockchain (DAO) hack

DAO [7] was built as smart contract on the ethereum blockchain which eliminated the need of single authority and any unfairness. It created a platform where people could give in practical and potential ideas and receive funding from DAO. People that have DAO tokens can vote for the plans and they are rewarded when it becomes successful. But, in June 2016, a hacker found a loophole in the code that he exploited and drained the funds from the platform of about ETH 3.6 million or 70 million dollars. Since then DAO has been folded but people still learn from DAO to establish secure blockchain platforms.

Hence, this section discusses work related to smart contract in detail (including some popular problem and its evolution). Now, next section will discuss about motivation behind this work, i.e., our main aim/intension to write this chapter related to this field.

12.3 Motivation

Securing essential items or documents in physical form is always a critical issue. Many problems like tearing or changing color of documents (after a certain period), etc. exist in saving documents in the physical form. To avoid such problem, we use the technology "Blockchain" with smart contracts. Smart contracts are a piece of code stored in a digital manner which can be accessed by the owner (anytime, and anywhere). But due to receiving higher attention toward smart contract, many industries or organizations/applications are facing much vulnerability on smart contract. As discussed in [8], a blockchain network can be corrupted through 51% attack. We feel to mitigate/identified some more attacks/vulnerabilities on smart contract since today's era, which provided some future opportunities to research communities to work on (carry on their research work). In near future, smart contracts will be used in every possible application to store their contract, agreement, or any documents digitally (in a secure manner). So having a lot of importance of smart contracts in near future, we need to provide (each and every) information related to smart contract at a single place. This chapter is an attempt to fulfill such requirement. Hence, this section discusses our main motivation behind write a chapter on "Smart Contract." Further, next section will discuss about the scope of smart contract in today' era and in near future.

12.4   Scope of smart contracts today and tomorrow

Blockchain and smart contracts encourage greater levels of trust in end-to-end transactions and bring us toward a true sharing economy. Smart contracts can support a fairer and transparent working relationship among cooperate and client. The essential purpose of smart contracts is to increase scalability and efficiency of the contracting and performance process but by the same time, it reduces the risk and cost by the application of automation. Smart contract is a software code that is used for transaction of currencies and exchange of assets. Some of the main features of blockchain technology help the smart contracts viable for a variety of uses. They are listed as below.

- Transactions on a blockchain are approved by a consensus among participants in the network, making fraud or corruption more difficult.
- The distributed nature of the platform gives same access privilege to records, which make data making data more resistant against attacks.
- Entire transaction history is easily traceable, which allow anyone in the network to monitor the records.
- The decentralized platform acts as a trust layer for the Internet as a result there is no requirement of any intermediary for performing transaction.

The use of smart contracting helps us to address some limitations in structural state of current contracts. It reduces the risk by combining real-time data with automated adjustments in the positions of the parties. Some use cases of smart contract are listed below:

- Auto insurance [9]: All the data of each policyholder is added to the blockchain and the smart policy monitor all the data in the blockchain. And automatically increase or decrease the monthly premium for the insurance policy and withdraws payment from the driver's account. In the case of an accident, the smart policy obtains data from vehicle sensors and performs automated initial assessment of damage and even file and process insurance claims.
- Stocktaking: Blockchain-based smart contract can be used in business-oriented areas like supply chains. Internet of Things (IoT) could be utilized all through the inventory network to record each stage an item takes. Smart contract supply chains could hypothetically basically dispose of in-house robbery as directors would have the option to follow a missing item back to the specific time and spot that it disappeared. The advancement of smart contracts helps to increase transaction times, reduce the costs, and even make processes much easier.

- Product development: Smart contracts can be used in product development in order to keep a record regarding the stages of development. Two parties would accept the contract and sign it. During the development process, the other necessary information also stored in the smart contract.
- Voting: Smart contract can also be used to verify the identity of individual voter rand record their voting related information. The recorded information could then be used further after the entire voting process has been completed. Since it is not possible to modify the blocks within a blockchain, manipulation of this record is impossible.
- Property ownership [10]: In the property market, the smart contract can be used in two ways. It can be used to store details of the property owner and also data-related property like location and address of the property, rental rates, capital values, tenant details, since from when the owner own the property, etc.
- Trade finance: The introduction of smart contracts benefits trade finance. Automated issuance of or substitution for letters of credit, guarantees, and trade finance instruments.
- Mortgage: In smart contract mortgages, prior to payment process two peers digitally agree to the sale. After this process, the modification of property ownership is made in the contract to reflect the change of ownership. In order to do this, unique key code authorization from original owner is required. This helps the entire process to be more secure and fraud free.
- Medical research: Highly sensitive data in health care records like genomic data [11] are encrypted using blockchain and are shared among different healthcare or research centers. Since many of the participants involved in medical research want to protect their sensitive medical information, they must keep secure from outsiders.

12.4.1 Advantages of smart contracts

- Smart contracts are completely digitalized, decentralized distributed ledger, no possibility that data can be lost because it is kept secure by sharing (every miner has access to it), eliminates the need of middlemen (banks, lawyers, etc.), code is the law.
- Sometimes we might wonder that the work lawyers and smart contracts do are similar, but lawyers can be bias as they are humans but in smart contracts, the code is the law.
- Smart contracts are accessible to everyone at any time 24/7, there is no limit in purchases and withdrawals, it is corruption resistant to a certain extent, there is little or no transaction cost at all. It gives freedom, i.e., anyone can access or enter into a contract, choose their counterparty and determine the reason and terms of the contract. For instance, if an organization needs funding, it tries to persuade people their cause and get supporters, if the mission becomes successful or reaches a targeted goal the funds are transferred to the organization else, they are reverted back to the people.
- Electronic storage, immutable, decentralized, transparency, security by sharing data in network.

Hence, this section discusses the scope of smart contract in today's era and in near future with providing several uses of smart contract in many possible applications. Now, the next section will discuss necessity of detecting vulnerabilities on smart contract in many applications.

12.5 Necessity of finding vulnerabilities in smart contract

As we have discussed in the previous section, the smart contract can be used to store different types of information based on the application. This information must be protected from outsiders (unknown/unauthorized users) to avoid misuse of data. In the Introduction section, we have mentioned some of the vulnerabilities to which smart contract is susceptible to. It is very essential to find a counter measure for this problem. Smart contract programing requires a different engineering mind set. So it is not enough to protect the system against existing vulnerabilities, but we must know the different development strategies as mentioned below:

(a) Ready to face the failure: We must code the contract in such a way that it must face the vulnerabilities gracefully with minimal damage. For example, use circuit breaker to pause the contract whenever something went wrong. It is better to identify the bugs prior to the complete product launch. In order to achieve this, we must test the contracts completely, whenever new attacks are found. We can also use bug bounties wherever required.

(b) Simple contract: If the complexity of the code is high, it is more prone to errors, it is always preferable to write contract in simple way. Modularization helps to keep the contract simple. And for the purpose of decentralization, we can use the blockchain. Whenever a new bug is identified, we can check the contract for error and this helps the system to keep up-to-date.

Security tools: The visualization tools such as

(i) Ethereum-graph-debugger: An Ethereum Virtual Machine (EVM) debugger displays the complete control flow of a program graphically.

(ii) Sūrya: It is a utility tool which provide different visual outputs and information about the structure of the contract. It also helps for function call graph querying.

(iii) Solgraph: The output of this tool is a DOT graph that gives information regarding flow of function control and major vulnerabilities.

The static and data analytic tools such as

(iv) Securify: It is an online static analyzer which is completely automated. It provides vulnerability pattern reports.

(v) SmartCheck: This is a static analyzer for the source code. It analyzes security vulnerabilities and best practices.

(vi) Octopus: With the support of EVM, this analytical tool examine the security of smart contracts.

(vii) Oyente: It is another smart contract analysis tool.
(viii) Hydra: It is a framework for crypto economic contract security, decentralized security bounties.

Hence, this section discusses necessity and process of detecting software vulnerabilities or any cyber-crime performed on smart contract/on a blockchain. It also discusses several tools to detect vulnerabilities on smart contracts. Now, next section will discuss available techniques or mechanisms for securing current smart contract (with every possible way/method).

12.6 Vulnerabilities in smart contract

The main smart contract vulnerabilities are given below:

(i)   Issues related with coding: It include problems related to implementation of smart contract.
(ii) Security-related issues: It is related to vulnerabilities that can cause different attacks to system.
(iii) Privacy-related issues: It consists of leakage of contract information to outsiders.
(iv) Performance-related issues: This issue is associated with the scaling factor of blockchain.

Table 12.2 represents a list of vulnerabilities and their proposed solutions.

To be effective, blockchain and smart contracts require certain standards, or more plainly, a set of common rules by which all participants operate, in order to ensure accuracy and trustworthiness. The decentralized model poses challenges when you need to change the rules because those changes need to be agreed upon

Table 12.2 Smart contract vulnerabilities

S. no.	Issue name	Issue category	Existing solution
1	Smart contract implementation issues [12]	Coding related	Semi-automated techniques, formal verification methods [13]
2	Smart contract modification or termination issues [14]	Coding related	Use of pre-defined protocols for modification or termination [15]
3	Programing language issues [15]	Coding related	Selection of appropriate logic-oriented programming language [16]
4	Transaction-oriented issues [16]	Security related	Use of built-in functions like "SendifReceived" [17], use of tool like "OYENTE" [17]
5	Mishandled exception and redundancy issue [18]	Security related	Use of tool like "OYENTE" [17]
6	Transaction privacy issue [18]	Privacy related	Use of "HAWK" tool [19] Encryption technique [19]
7	Order execution of blocks [20]	Performance related	Parallel smart contract execution [21]

and accepted by all participants to function consistently. A governance framework will be required to implement and operate blockchain as a legal application and needs to take into account oversight and monitoring functions, rule setting, and acceptance and change control management. Governance, in general, will be a requirement not only for legal but for all technologies that manage information. This transformation to some common rules for information governance is not only critical to blockchain but to other pursuits like e-discovery and cybersecurity. Governance standards around the blockchain will eventually contribute to market confidence in the technology and the legal and regulatory environment. This will accelerate the adoption and success of the smart contract. The practical implementation of smart contracts is also subject to several risks and challenges. These include:

- Interoperability: Making sure interoperability exists between different block-chain implementations is necessary so that they can communicate with one another.
- Performance: The performance potential and computer resources required to validate, process, and detect fraud will be a determining factor for applicability of smart contracts to various services such as banking, financial and payment services. In its current form, blockchain is not capable of handling thousands of transactions with the same level of efficiency that does not sacrifice on the security and decentralization aspects of it.
- Scalability: Each node in the particular blockchain network must know about every single transaction that occurs globally, which may create a significant drag on the network. The goal is to perform all transactions with higher efficiency, but in a way that does not sacrifice the decentralization and security that the network provides.

12.7 Available techniques/mechanism in secure smart contract

Generally, programmers can easily upgrade their software if there are any security bugs, patch bugs, fix exploit, and add missing features. Some of the best methods for the development of smart contract which support both security and accuracy are mentioned below.

Extra functionality: One of the main reasons which make the Ethereum and EOS popular is the functionality richness. Whenever dealing with complicated, multi-functionality contracts, if we are not using the best blockchain network practices, it will add vulnerabilities to the code. In few networks, for example, Zilliqa [21] and Cardano, the developers are adding more restrictions to the contract in order to improve the security of their code. Even though these restrictions reduce the functionality of the contract, it enhances the contract security. To achieve complete smart contract safety, we can use automatic validation tools.

Selection of programming language: The decision of language selection for the implementation of smart contract must be taken carefully. The choice of popular languages such as C++ and JavaScript, which provide many opportunities for developing complex, highly functional contracts, will cause major security issues. The main reason is that even experienced developer is making mistake in case of selection of popular languages. Because of these reasons, many blockchains use their own programming languages to develop contracts, which helps to reduce the chances of possible bugs and errors in the code. During language selection, we must take care of things such as problems with the interaction between the language, the compiler, and the blockchain. On the other side, the languages like Scilla (used to implement Zilliqa contract) are less complicated and the semantics of this language is very simple compared to other languages. This feature helps the developers to write the contract without much programming mistakes. Irrespective of the language selection, we must use the best practice to develop the blockchain contract. Currently, Ethereum smart contracts are recommended as the best practice for writing secure smart contracts for the EOS platform.

- Blockchain-oriented development strategies: Smart contract can be considered as a type of software, which needs some blockchain-specific development practices. If we compare the development cost, then the development cost of smart contract is much higher than other software solutions [22]. Otherwise, we can avoid many critical errors. For example, developers who are not much experienced may treat the mechanisms calling the code of a contract in an unexpected way as a vulnerable code.
- Testing and security audits: As we do with other software, the preliminary test is compulsory with smart contract. In the initial stage, we can make use of unit tests to check the basic contract functionalities. This helps to find critical errors in our code and can be fixed easily. Generally, we use network-oriented frameworks for separate blockchain, the reason behind this is the use of own languages for writing different smart contracts. For example, Truffle framework can be used in Ethereum and we can make use of EOSFactory or GTest in EOS. The other necessary measure for ensuring a high level of security for our smart contracts is security audits. A well-trained auditor not only detects possible errors in the code but also advise us about methods to fix the flaws. Since the testing team or auditors are not involved in the development part, they can identify the bugs easily, which make the process a bit faster.
- Usage of extra testing tools: We can also use additional testing tools which are more of network oriented. Some examples which are used in Ethereum are listed below.

These tools provide high-level security for individual contracts.

- Test coverage analyzers: Solidity coverage are initially called as SolCover. It can be used in Ethereum, for testing and code coverage of contracts which is written in Solidity.
- Linters: Specific tools can be used for running static and dynamic analysis of our contracts which help to identify suspicious code, bugs, etc. Mythril classic and Solidity linter solhint are two open-source security analyzer that can be used in Ethereum. These tools:

- Perform validation of both the style and security of the code.
- Formal verification: We can make use of K-Framework tool, to verify same smart contracts on several different platforms like Ethereum and Cardano.
- Symbolic execution: Manticore is a tool which can be used for checking the bugs present in the code logic.

The choice of tools for testing and security audits differs from blockchains to blockchains. Recent smart contract platforms could not find any particular security tools yet. Hence, this section discusses the several available tools and algorithms to secure smart contract (in current) in a public network. Now, next section will discuss problem raised during protecting smart contract in a worldwide, decentralized and distributed network.

12.8   Problem raised during protecting smart contract

A smart contract can define as protocol of a computerized transaction with the help of a contract. There is public blockchain/permissionless blockchain [23] that anyone can join and read but only few are authorized to write content and there are private blockchain/permissioned blockchain that only few people connected to it will have access, in this also few authorized people are allowed to write in data. Since the contract based on the blockchain is visible to all users of the particular blockchain, it leads to security issues. The main drawbacks of decentralized smart contracts are regulatory uncertainty and a lack of confidential execution. The legal issues related to decentralize smart contracts affect both improvement and clarity. Since the smart contract is just a preprogramed set of rules, we cannot capture all possible situations so as be able to universally remove the need for lawyers, legal hearings, or formal dispute resolution. Even though smart contracts might generally be more effective and efficient than traditional contracts, they cannot automatically resolve every dispute.

The two biggest legal problems of smart contracts lie in their blockchain provenance. The first one is the enforceability of smart contracts. Blockchain came into mainstream prominence as a decentralized and permission-less system that can be used to speedily conduct business transactions between multiple geographies. Current dispute resolution of contracts differs between countries and is settled in courts. But blockchain works in the opposite manner. Consensus for a transaction is a function of agreement between multiple nodes in a network that, in a complex system, may reside in multiple geographies. How will a decentralized system arrive at a consensus regarding disputes among stakeholders? Permissioned blockchains have a line of authority that helps resolve disputes. But they typically operate within private enterprises. For permission-less blockchains, which operate within the public realm, the problem is still there. There is also the problem of jurisdiction. How will disputes involving smart contracts for international transactions that span multiple geographies be resolved? More specifically, will the different jurisdictions involved have to work in concert with each other to piece together a judgment or resolution to disputes? The problem becomes further complicated when you consider the legal status of blockchain. Some states have taken the lead in recognizing smart contracts while others are still arriving at an understanding of the technology and its application to their society. The varying interpretations of contract laws with respect to blockchain could also present their own set of problems. In general, smart contract risk considerations include

1. Business and regulatory risk
2. Contract enforcement
3. Legal liability
4. Information security issues

Most smart contracts are not completely confidential. For example, there is already uncertainty exist whether blockchains violate the global data protections requirement (GDPR) of the European Union or not. The main reason for this is smart contract is immutable. Most of the regulation will not accept this contract. The patterns can be identified and information can be inferred by monitoring the input and the output of a smart contract. The public smart contracts are insufficient to replace traditional contract because of this confidentiality issue. Note that insufficient access controls on critical functions such as Ether transfers and self-destructs are a classic vulnerability. Integer arithmetic bugs are another common security flaw. It is possible for anyone to kill the contract.

In particular, difficulties in Ethereum mental treaties include ambiguities and non-serious, but dangerous systems in its contractual language. Solidity compiler errors, Ethereum virtual machine misses attacks on the chain of chains, invariability of misses and inaccessibility of central documenting of popular vulnerabilities, attacks, and problematic systems. One issue, yet to consider by the courts, is to what extent these smart contracts are valid and enforceable under contract law. Analysis of nearly one million smart contracts flags 34,200 (2365 distinct) contracts as vulnerable [24]. Another study found that upwards of 45% of smart contracts written in Solidity had some form of vulnerability [25]. Parties to a smart contract effectively gain control over the performance of a contractual obligation to a digitized process, which cannot be reasoned with or influenced. Another issue will be determining how rights and entitlements recorded "on the chain" accommodate rights and entitlements that arise "off the chain."

For example, what happens if share ownership is recorded on a blockchain as vesting in one entity, but surrounding circumstances place equitable ownership in another? or if a transfer of ownership of property is recorded on a blockchain but is sought to be set aside under the Corporations Act as a voidable transaction? The immutability of a blockchain system raises some interesting questions in this regard. The nature of the blockchain system means that the players involved will most likely be "distributed" around the globe. Parties intending to implement or utilize a blockchain system should therefore give advanced thought to which laws should apply and what type of forum is most appropriate to resolve disputes. It might be beneficial to have an arbitration dispute resolution clause rather than relying on the enforcement of a court award from a local court system. The governance position of public blockchain systems also poses an interesting challenge from a litigation perspective. While terms of use can be communicated to users of a public blockchain, such terms may be difficult to enforce as no single entity controls the system. The question also remains as to who will bear the liability for any faults in the technical code and who has the right to enforce against them.

12.8.1   Disadvantages of smart contracts

- Since smarts contracts are utilized for transactions of large amounts of money and property dealings, it is vital that it is absolutely corruption resistant and the data stored is accurate for the justice of mankind.
- In smart contracts, the software code acts as law and the participants (anonymous nodes) of the decentralized network verifies it.
- One of the major reasons for smart contracts to become vulnerable to attacks is poor coding that contains bugs which cannot be corrected once deployed into the blockchain. Some smart contracts vulnerable to hacks are contracts that lock fund indefinitely, leak them carelessly to arbitrary users and the ones that can be killed by any user.

Smart contracts and decentralized virtual machines are an almost unfathomably incredible innovation, but will be ever overshadowed if exploits continue to occur. Hence, this section discusses about several serious concerns/issues or problems which have raised during protecting smart contract on a non-private network. Now, next section will discuss several opportunities for future communities' toward creating and protecting smart contract.

12.9   Opportunities for future research communities toward smart contract

In near future, we can use smart contracts in Ethereum blockchain. Also, we can solve the bug issue raised due to immutable systems. Bitcoin is a digital or cryptocurrency that verifies the number of digital currencies a person has whereas, Ethereum blockchain mainly supports smart contracts. The programming language used in Ethereum blockchain is complete during high-level language called solidity. Ethereum blockchain is not restricted only to currencies, Ethereum protocol is not only visible to the parties involved in the smart contracts but also hundreds of people are witness and they validate the transactions. In near future, some possibilities of using smart contract in many applications are listed as:

- IoT networks [26]: The smart contract can be used with some other technologies like the IoT. Smart contracts and IoT can enable significant changes in industries, which help to develop new distributed applications.
- Agriculture: In agriculture, IoT sensors can be used which automatically initiate activities like irrigation or deployment of insecticide, this is being done with the help of programmed trigger values.
- Real estate: Internet-enabled lock can be used for automatic locking of a house whenever the tenant is not paying the rent and then can unlock immediately after the completion of payment.

- Health care [27]: Smart contract can be used to store sensitive personal health records, insurance related data. This also support supervising drugs and other supplies, and also enable secure sharing of patient data for clinical trials and research.
- Banking [28]: Smart contract can be used significantly in banking sector which is an alternative to the traditional way of transactions. Smart contracts help to perform make payments, loans, and other transactions automatically.
- Supply chain: In this area, smart contract can provide real-time visibility. Smart contracts guarantee inventory tracking which benefit supply chain financing and reduce the theft and fraud risks.
- Legal issues: Smart contract can replace the traditional model of legal issues solving and document certification. If we use smart contracts, it removes the requirement of notarization, offering automated, and cost-efficient solution.

We can protect smart contract from vulnerabilities by constructing smart contract using decentralized Blockchain 4.0 applications.

Hence, researchers are suggested to refer articles [29–36] to know more about blockchain and its importance in several other sectors like Governance, Transportation, Healthcare, finance (based on its evolution), etc. This section discusses several possible applications for which smart contracts can be created and also discusses several opportunities to protect smart contract for the same/similar applications. Now, next section will conclude this work in brief.

12.10   Conclusion

In the recent decade/century, people were using papers to make some agreements or any legal documents. But, with receiving attention toward smart contracts (due to having maximum security), many industries/applications are interested to use smart contract in their process/work (or securing documents digitally, related to respective applications). Smart contracts came to existence to make secure transactions and to provide superior security of legal documents (digitalized) in a corruption resistant blockchain and to make transactions at minimal or no cost at all. The transfer of assets between parties, i.e., without any third party, after defining the terms in a self-executing contract, smart contract does the other job for us (i.e., security, accessibility, etc.). Once smart contracts are deployed into a blockchain, it can never be altered again (except via 51% attacks, etc.), it becomes immutable. To make smart contracts secure, we need to provide some basic security guidelines to smart contract, and such digital contract should be tested thoroughly (at a regular interval), also the code should be as simple as possible and error-free before being deployed (on blockchain and cloud). In this chapter, we find some basic features of smart contract which are included here as: electronic storage, immutable, decentralized transparency, and higher security. Also, we discussed few disadvantages of blockchain is that it could harbor black hackers because the government is completely powerless over blockchain, government cannot interfere and freeze transactions on a crypto-currency-based monetary system. Hence, as future work (as an example), smart contracts (with an efficient algorithm) work can be used in vending machines for providing higher efficiency (in terms of improving productivity), also can be used for storing information on cloud securely. Also in future, researchers can work on "Decentralized Autonomous Blockchain (DAB)" and "Decentralized Web (DB)." Hence, we are still in the growing phase of smart contracts technology and they are proving to be the best alternative (with respect to concerning several features like security, storage, etc.), if we can solve a few minor issues maybe one day we will wake up in a world free of middlemen and commission. Hence, all researchers and readers are kindly invited to do their research work in listed issues/challenges/research gaps in smart contracts.

Glossary

Blockchain: It is distributed ledger which consists of blocks. This block store cryptographic data which can be used for transactions.
Bitcoin: It is a form of digital currency which operates without the intervention of bank or clearinghouse. It is also called as cryptocurrency.
Smart contract: It is a computer program, which support efficient, secure, and faster transactions between the entities. It is also called as crypto-contract.

References

[1]   Nakamoto S., "Bitcoin: A Peer-To-Peer Electronic Cash System," 2008. [Online]. Available: https://bitcoin.org/bitcoin.pdf
[2]   Bogner A., Chanson M., and Meeuw A., "A decentralised sharing app running a smart contract on the ethereum blockchain." In Proceedings of the 6th International Conference on the Internet of Things – IoT'16, 2016.
[3]   Neal K. and Alfred J. M., Cryptocash, Cryptocurrencies, and Cryptocontracts, Springer, New York, NY, 2016.
[4]   Kalra S., Goel S., Dhawan M., and Sharma S. "ZEUS: analyzing safety of smart contracts." In *Network and Distributed Systems Security (NDSS) Symposium*, 2018.
[5]   Andreas M. A., *Mastering Bitcoin: Unlocking Digital Cryptocurrencies*, O'Reilly, 2015.
[6]   Lin C., He D., Huang X., Choo K.-K.R., and Vasilakos A.V., "BSeIn: a blockchain-based secure mutual authentication with fine-grained access control system for industry 4.0." *Journal of Network and Computer Applications*, 2018.
[7]   Quinn D. "A history and ethnography of 'The DAO' a failed decentralized autonomous organization." In *Bitcoin and Beyond*, Taylor & Francis, 2017.
[8]   Sawal N., Yadav A., Tyagi A.K., Sreenath N., and Rekha G., "Necessity of Blockchain for Building Trust in Today's Applications: A Useful Explanation from User's Perspective." (May 15, 2019). Available at SSRN: https://ssrn.com/abstract=3388558 or http://dx.doi.org/10.2139/ssrn.3388558.

[9] Bader L., Burger J.C., Matzutt R., and Wehrle K., "Smart contract-based car insurance policies." In *IEEE Globecom Workshops*, 2018.

[10] O'Brien B. and Massey R., "Blockchain and smart contracts could transform property transactions." *CFO Journal, Deloitte*, 2017.

[11] Shamila, M., Vinuthna, K., and Tyagi, A., "A review on several critical issues and challenges in IoT based e-healthcare system." *IEEE*, 2019.

[12] Delmolino K., Arnett M., Kosba A., Miller A., and Shi E., "Step by step towards creating a safe smart contract: Lessons and insights from a crypto-currency lab." In International Conference on Financial Cryptography and Data Security, Springer, New York, NY, 2016, pp. 79–94.

[13] Bhargavan K., Delignat-Lavaud A., Fournet C., *et al.*, "Formal verification of smart contracts: short paper." In Proceedings of the 2016 ACM Workshop on Programming Languages and Analysis for Security, ACM, London, 2016, pp. 91–96.

[14] Marino B. and Juels A., "Setting standards for altering and undoing smart contracts." In International Symposium on Rules and Rule Markup Languages for the Semantic Web, Springer, New York, NY, 2016, pp. 151–166.

[15] Idelberger F., Governatori G., Riveret R., and Sartor G., "Evaluation of logic-based smart contracts for blockchain systems." In International Symposium on Rules and Rule Markup Languages for the Semantic Web, Springer, New York, NY, 2016, pp. 167–183

[16] Natoli C. and Gramoli V., "The blockchain anomaly." In 15th International Symposium on Network Computing and Applications (NCA), *IEEE*, 2016, pp. 310–317.

[17] Luu L., Chu D., Olickel H., Saxena P., and Hobor A., "Making smart contracts smarter." In Proceedings of the 2016 ACM SIGSAC Conference on Computer and Communications Security, CCS'16, ACM, 2016, pp. 254–269.

[18] Kosba A., Miller A., Shi E., Wen Z., and Papamanthou C., "Hawk: the blockchain model of cryptography and privacy-preserving smart contracts." In 2016 IEEE Symposium on Security and Privacy (SP), *IEEE*, 2016, pp. 839–858.

[19] Watanabe H., Fujimura S., Nakadaira A., Miyazaki Y., Akutsu A., and Kishigami J., "Blockchain contract: a complete consensus using block-chain." In 2015 IEEE 4th Global Conference on Consumer Electronics (GCCE), *IEEE*, 2015, pp. 577–578.

[20] Vukolić M., "Rethinking permissioned blockchains." In Proceedings of the ACM Workshop on Blockchain, Cryptocurrencies and Contracts, BCC'17, *ACM*, 2017, pp. 3–7.

[21] Mechkaroska D., Dimitrova V., and Popovska-Mitrovikj A., "Analysis of the possibilities for improvement of blockchain technology." *IEEE*, 2018.

[22] https://www.apriorit.com/dev-blog/581-security-tips-for-smart-contracts

[23] Gilcrest J. and Carvalho A., "Smart contracts: legal considerations." *IEEE*, 2018.

[24] https://arxiv.org/abs/1802.06038

[25] https://medium.com/hackernoon/smart-contracts-part-1-the-state-of-security-4c37988c770

[26] Dorri, A., Kanhere, S.S., Jurdak, R., and Gauravaram, P., "Blockchain for IoT security and privacy: the case study of a smart home." *IEEE*, 2017.

[27] Mettler M., "Blockchain technology in healthcare: the revolution starts here." *IEEE*, 2016.

[28] Gareth W. and Peters E.P., "Understanding modern banking ledgers through blockchain technologies: future of transaction processing and smart contracts on the internet of money." In *Banking Beyond Banks and Money*, Springer, New York, NY, 2016.

[29] Tyagi A.K., Gupta M., Aswathy S.U., and Chetanya V., "Healthcare solutions for smart era: a useful explanation from user's perspective." In *Recent Trends in Blockchain for Information Systems Security and Privacy*, CRC Press, London, 2021.

[30] Varsha R., Nair M.M., Nair, S.M., and Tyagi A.K., "Deep learning based blockchain solution for preserving privacy in future vehicles." *International Journal of Hybrid Intelligent System*, 16(4), 223–236, 2020.

[31] Tyagi A.K., "Analysis of security and privacy aspects of blockchain technologies from smart era' perspective: the challenges and a way forward." In *Recent Trends in Blockchain for Information Systems Security and Privacy*, CRC Press, London, 2021.

[32] Tyagi A.K., Rekha G., and Shabnam K., "Applications of blockchain technologies in digital forensic and threat hunting." In *Recent Trends in Blockchain for Information Systems Security and Privacy*, CRC Press, London, 2021.

[33] Shabnam K., Tyagi A.K., and Aswathy S.U., "The future of edge computing with blockchain technology: possibility of threats, opportunities and challenges." In *Recent Trends in Blockchain for Information Systems Security and Privacy*, CRC Press, London, 2021.

[34] Tibrewal I., Srivastava M., and Tyagi A.K. "Blockchain technology for securing cyber-infrastructure and internet of things networks." In Tyagi A. K., Abraham A., Kaklauskas A. (eds), *Intelligent Interactive Multimedia Systems for e-Healthcare Applications*, Springer, Singapore, 2022. https://doi.org/10.1007/978-981-16-6542-4_1

[35] Tyagi A.K., Fernandez T.F., and Aswathy S.U., "Blockchain and Aadhaar based electronic voting system." In 2020 4th International Conference on Electronics, Communication and Aerospace Technology (ICECA), Coimbatore, 2020, pp. 498–504, doi: 10.1109/ICECA49313.2020.9297655.

[36] Tyagi A.K., Aswathy S.U., Aghila G., and Sreenath N., "AARIN: affordable, accurate, reliable and innovative mechanism to protect a medical cyber-physical system using blockchain technology." *IJIN*, 2, 175–183, 2021.

Chapter 13

Data analytics for socio-economic factors affecting crime rates

Maheswari Raja[1], Pattabiraman Venkatasubbu[1] and Basim Alhadidi[2]

Abstract

Crime has always been a major issue in the society. The places having high crime rate affect social harmony, tourism, and several factors related to economy. This study tries to understand the socio-economic factors that affect the crime rate. In all countries, the blunder complication happens due to the fact that the crime occurrence signifies that there is a social phenomenon which reflects all the evidence that lead crime in the same way with minor changes in those areas. Thus, the proposed work demonstrates the analytics over a standard dataset of crime covering all the factors. And also due to the wider availability of the event/incidence of crime rate reported in the crime dataset of India. This work targeted to consider the socio-economic factors affecting crime rates in India. The post-independence data of 13 most populous states according to the 2011 survey has been collected. This study compares the socio-economic and criminal data of different states using the data visualization method and tries to understand factors that are highly responsible for increased rate of reporting of crime in these states. The factors such as Gender Ratio, Human Development Index (HDI), Anti-Corruption Efforts, Literacy Rate, Per Capita Income, Unemployment Rate, and Poverty Index were taken into account. This work also attempts to apply regression model on the dataset to predict the crime rate. The result of this study is that these factors affect the reporting of crime in India and, by working on these factors, will increase the beneficiaries of government policies.

Keywords: Data analytics; Crime rate analysis; Machine learning; Behavior analytics

13.1 Introduction

It is very difficult to understand that how much a particular factor is affecting the crime rate independently because socio-economic factors are correlated with each

[1]School of Computer Science and Engineering, Vellore Institute of Technology, Chennai, India
[2]Department of Computer Information Systems, Al-Balqa Applied University, Jordan

other [1]. Crime rate also depends on many unpredicted factors such as political stability, cultural harmony, and sudden changes in the political and the cultural environment. The study here compares the general trend that different states have followed and the effect of these factors on reporting of crime rate with the help of different types of graphs and regression model. The data collected for this study has been acquired only from the Government of India websites [2–6].

13.1.1   Polynomial regression

Polynomial regression is used to fit a non-linear equation by taking polynomial function of any degree [7]. General equation of polynomial regression is given in equation (13.1):

$$y = a + b1\, x + b2\, x2 + b3\, x3 + \cdots + bn\, xn \tag{13.1}$$

The attributes that were taken into model were Human Development Index (HDI), literacy rate, Poverty Index, and life expectancy. Polynomial feature of degree three was used to fit the data into the regression model [8]. Root mean square error (RMSE) is a standard way to measure the error of a model in predicting the quantitative data. R-square is a statistical measure of fit that indicates how much variation a dependent variable has is explained by the independent variable(s) in a regression model.

13.1.2   Data visualization and analysis tool

The data visualization tool used in this study is Tableau. Tableau is a software used for data visualization and analysis. The graphs and regression models can be applied on the dataset with the help of this tool [9]. Various analyses pertaining to crime dataset of the various states of India have been carried out using this tool. The datasets were converted into .csv format before any operation was performed on it. The language used for applying regression model is Python. Crime rate data is taken as per lakh population. It is implemented using algorithms such as support vector machine (SVM), Naïve Bayes, decision tree, random forest, log regression, and K-nearest neighbor (KNN). It was concluded that random forest algorithm provided the greatest accuracy of 76% compared to the other ML algorithms. It was verified that the classification using random forest was faster and took an upper hand over the rest in terms of computational time and efficient performance. This is done using advanced deep learning technique with artificial neural network (ANN) model and machine learning algorithms like logistic regression. The dataset comprises various factors of crime such as literacy rate, murder, and child marriage. The output variable will be binary and the model is trained using regression technique to predict the occurrence of crime rate. A comparative study of the results is done based on the accuracy of results procured from logistic regression algorithm and neural network models. This significantly helps in drawing a conclusion of which model gives accurate results. The proposed technique is also implemented using neural networks because they have the ability to procure non-linear relationship between the several input features and the modeling strength. The result of the neural network model will also be hierarchical in nature. From the conclusion of this research work, one can self-introspect the factors affecting and lead to the occurrence of crime at several parts of the nation. The prediction may help to prevent the crime at that location in future.

13.1.3   Literature survey

Understanding a mind setup of a human is one of the most difficult tasks. Several researches have shown that socio-economic factors play an important role in maintaining social, cultural, and political harmonies in the region [7]. These factors are co-integrated in some way or the other. Crime rate can be predicted using the previous criminal history of that region using various data mining techniques. Sharma *et al.* projected a perception which portrays nullified rate of crime in the society. For sensing the distrustful illegal happenings, the author focused on the significance of data mining technology and deliberated an active application for the same. In this work, he recommended a tool which spread over an enhanced decision tree algorithm to sense the distrustful e-mails about the criminal activities [8]. Hamdy *et al.* defined a method built on the people's communication with social media and mobile usage such as position indicators and call logs. They introduced a prototype for identifying suspicious activities in social media threads and to help crime examination with quicker and accurate decisions [10]. The next section of this chapter composed of proposed system which encapsulates crime rate analysis, crime rate model implementation, literacy rate analysis, Poverty Index, unemployment rate, per capital income, prohibition of child marriage, and crime against children. The subsequent section holds the various models and analyses such as prediction model, linear regression model, Lasso regression, decision tree model, and root mean square. Finally, the chapter ends with data visualization analysis and conclusion.

13.2   Proposed system

13.2.1   Crime rate analysis

After analyzing the various country datasets over the factor of crime, the study concludes that the crime factor variable across the countries looks more or less similar but the quantity of crime event occurs may vary based on their needs/geographical area. The crime dataset of regions such as Atlanta, Baltimore, and major regions of USA holds many common crime factors like crime against children, unemployment rate, per capital income, etc. Thus, in most/all countries, the blunder complication happens due to the fact that the crime occurrence signifies that there is a social phenomenon which reflects all the evidence that lead crime in the same way with minor change in those areas. The proposed work demonstrates the analytics over a standard dataset of crime covering all the factors. And also due to the wider availability of the event/incidence of crime rate reported in the crime dataset of India. This work targeted to consider the socio-economic factors affecting crime rates in India. The complete data flow of the proposed system is depicted in Figure 13.1 as a block diagram of crime rate analysis. The first stage of the proposed system is data collection pertaining to crime and socio-economic factors. The collected data is formatted in .csv format, which is then subjected into the second stage of data visualization. Using Tableau, the data visualization process is carried out. The output generated from Tableau is processed in the third stage such as polynomial regression model applied using Python. The result analysis has been carried out and classified based on virtualization and prediction of crime rate.

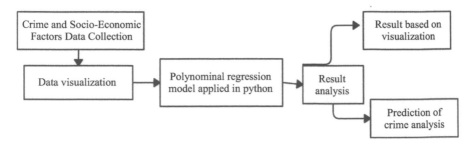

Figure 13.1   Block diagram of crime rate analysis

Table 13.1   Populous States for crime data

Populous states for crime data in India	
1. Uttar Pradesh	8. Rajasthan
2. Maharashtra	9. Karnataka
3. Bihar	10. Gujarat
4. West Bengal	11. Orissa
5. Andhra Pradesh	12. Kerala
6. Madhya Pradesh	13. Punjab
7. Tamil Nadu	

Table 13.2   Attributes of generalized dataset

Attributes in dataset	Meaning
Sex_Ratio	Sex ratio of states (number of male per female)
HDI	Human Development Index
Anti_Corruption_Effort	Anti-corruption effort in states
Literacy_Rate	Literacy rate of states percentage of literate population from total population)
Per_Capita_Income	Per capita income in Indian rupees (state income/population)
Poverty_Index	Poverty Index in states [4,5] (unemployed/total labor force)
Life Expectancy	Life expectancy in states [2,4]

The 13 various most populous states whose data was collected are listed in Table 13.1, holding the crime data.

This work tries to predict the value of crime rate in India using only socio-economic factors using the polynomial regression technique.

13.2.2   Socio-economic attributes of generalized dataset

The various attributes of generalized dataset are tabulated in Table 13.2. A generalized data taken from different states in different years were assembled and a dataset was formed. The generalized dataset based on socio-economic factors and different states in India holding the varying values for the specified attributes is structured in Table 13.3.

Table 13.3 Generalized dataset based on socio-economic factors-different states in India

Sex_Ratio	HDI	Anti_Corruption_effort	Literacy_rate	Per_Capita_Income	Poverty_Index	Life_Expectancy	Crime_rate
1.11	0.462	0.16	56.27	9,125	40.88	59.2	107.3
1.109	0.47	0.16	57.42	9,623	40.88	59.4	85.5
1.108	0.478	0.16	58.57	10,780	40.89	59.6	113.2
1.107	0.486	0.16	59.72	11,478	40.9	59.9	73.2
1.106	0.496	0.16	60.87	12,950	38.99	60.1	67.3
1.105	0.502	0.21	62.02	14,221	37.08	60.3	79.7
1.104	0.509	0.21	63.17	16,013	35.17	60.5	79.7
1.103	0.515	0.21	64.32	17,785	33.26	60.9	88
1.102	0.522	0.21	65.83	20,422	31.35	61.3	88.4
1.1	0.529	0.21	67.34	23,671	29.44	61.9	87.5
1.08	0.561	0.27	76.88	24,904	37.79	66.2	177
1.08	0.57	0.27	77.42	26,810	37.92	66.3	167.4
1.08	0.579	0.27	77.96	30,807	38.06	66.6	143.1
1.08	0.593	0.27	78.5	34,781	38.2	67.7	173.3
1.08	0.607	0.27	79.04	36,077	34.72	68	181.3

13.3   Crime rate model implementation

Crime data analysis helps to categorize the various crimes that is happening in various places/location, thereby enables to prevent or protect the occurrence of crime in those areas thereby targeting to reduce the crime rate. The proposed work ensures the reduction of the crime rate using appropriate machine learning algorithm such as classifications, clustering, and prediction. Crime density area has been identified based on its historical data of every state of India. Figure 13.2 represents the crime rate in India state wise holding the markable years such as 1956, 1963, 1971, 1981, 1991, 1999, 2005, and 2016. The analysis graph of crime rate contains year for each state in the *X*-axis and crime rate per lakh population in the *Y*-axis

The crime rate is analyzed considering several factors as tabulated in Table 13.4 and factors influencing crime rate. The prediction is done using machine learning

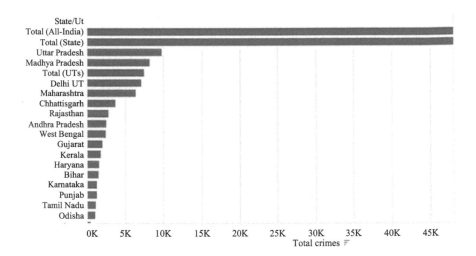

Figure 13.2   Crime rate in India state wise

Table 13.4   Factors influencing crime rate

Factors
Literacy rate
Poverty Index
Unemployment rate
Child Marriage Act
Crime against children
Sex ratio
Murder analysis

algorithms, "Linear regression model", "Logistic regression", and "Decision Tree", which help to precisely know the consequences of these factors over crime rate.

13.3.1 Literacy rate

Literacy rate of any age group is calculated by taking percentage of literate person to the population in that age group. According to the literacy data collected [11], there is a substantial increase in the literacy rate in all the states since 1971. In 2011, Kerala was having the highest literacy rate. But the crime rate in Kerala has also been increased significantly. Whereas, in other states, crime rate is also increased but does not seem to follow a particular pattern as shown in Figure 13.3 representing *X*-axis: year (for each state) and *Y*-axis: literacy rate.

State wise literacy rate analysis is shown in Figure 13.4, which infers that low literacy rate in Jammu and Kashmir may lead to higher occurrence of crime. This becomes an evident that any educated citizen may avoid himself exploring in crime-related activities when compared to an illiterate/uneducated individual. But this inference may not be true for all cases, there might be some exceptions which become evident in contradicting the conclusion.

13.3.2 State wise improvement in literacy rate

Figure 13.5 indicates the state wise improvement in the literacy rate since the year 1971 representing *X*-axis as states of India, and *Y*-axis as the literacy rate difference. The maximum literacy rate of 93.91% is observed in Kerala and the

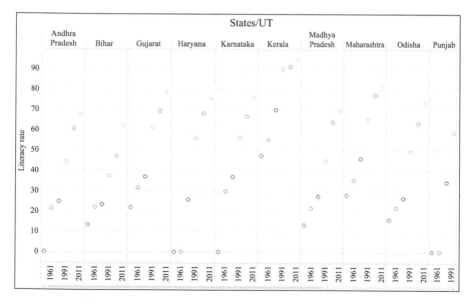

Figure 13.3   State wise literacy rate since independence

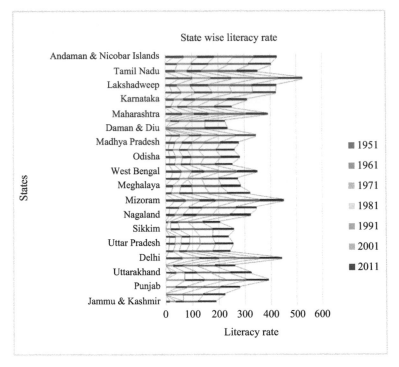

Figure 13.4   Literacy rate analysis state wise

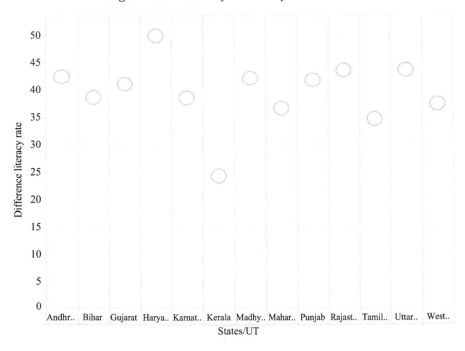

Figure 13.5   State wise improvement in literacy rate since 1971

minimum literacy rate of 63.82% is witnessed in Bihar. Every decade, there is a gradual increase in the literacy rate of all the states of India. Though there is a steady increase in literacy rate occurred in every state, the crime rate does not reciprocate toward the increased literacy rate. Since independence, many states observe very negligible imprint of literate people like Himachal Pradesh, Punjab, Haryana, Sikkim, etc. Since 1951, Kerala stands high in literacy rate with a pro-mising value of 47.81%. The understanding is there will be a wide range of job opportunities for the literate individual rather than illiterate. The living standard of the literate seems to be high which may reduce their involvement in crime activities like robbery, burglary, theft, etc. Even this might be one of the reasons where the illiterate may involve themselves in criminal activities. This is the one of the prime reasons for considering literate rate for the analysis of crime rate [12].

13.3.3   Poverty Index

According to the Poverty Index data collected, there was a significant increase in poverty rate [13,14] of states like Gujarat, Madhya Pradesh, Maharashtra, Orissa, and Uttar Pradesh in between 1993 and 2004. The poverty rate of Karnataka was stable between the years 1993 and 2004. The poverty rate of Karnataka and Tamil Nadu decreased during 1993–2004. But the crime rate in states Gujarat, Madhya Pradesh, Maharashtra, Orissa, and Uttar Pradesh fell down during 1993–2004, while the crime rate in Karnataka and Tamil Nadu showed an increase. Moreover, the poverty rate of Kerala fell from 25.43 to 19.60 in 1993–2004 but the crime rate increased from 254.6 to 313.0. Therefore, Figure 13.6 shows that on increasing poverty rate in any state, crime rate is decreasing and vice versa where X-axis: year (for each state) and Y-axis: Poverty Index. This could be because of an increase in the poverty rate also means that people are reporting less about the crime due to lack of awareness, police infrastructure, and proper education.

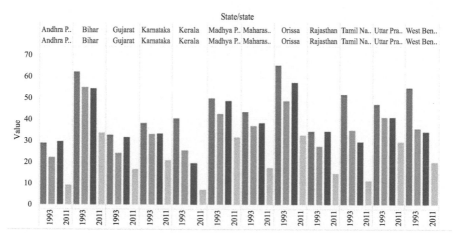

Figure 13.6   Poverty Index state wise (1983, 1993, 2004, 2011)

13.3.4   Unemployment rate

It is the percentage of jobless labor force in any state. It is the percentage of the unemployed labor to the total labor force in any state [15,16]. Unemployment rate has decreased in all the above-mentioned states from 2011 to 2017 which in turn has decreased poverty rate but the crime rate has increased significantly during 2004–2016 as given in Figure 13.7 representing *X*-axis—year and state, *Y*-axis—unemployment rate.

13.3.5   Per capita income

Per capita income is an average income per-person in any state in India. Per capita income for a state or region is calculated by dividing state's income by its population [17,18]. Per capita income has increased significantly (at least 250%) in all the states mentioned above from 2004 to 2012 but the crime rate has increased during 2005–2013 is given in Figure 13.8, where *X*-axis represents the year for each state and *Y*-axis represents the value in Indian Rupee.

HDI takes three factors into account such as (1) health-life expectancy at birth; (2) education-measured by adult literacy and the combined primary, secondary, and tertiary enrolment ratio; (3) income measured by GDP per capita. The data of HDI during 1995–2017 shows an increase in every above-mentioned state [19–21]. Although the states like Kerala, Karnataka, and Punjab have very high HDI when

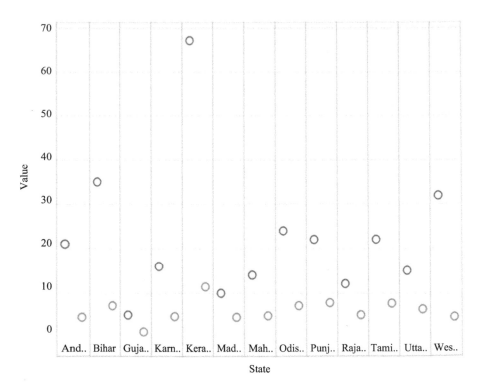

Figure 13.7   State wise unemployment rate change 2011–2017

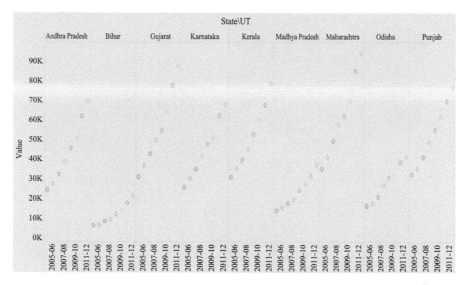

Figure 13.8 Per capita income state wise from 2004 to 2012 HDI

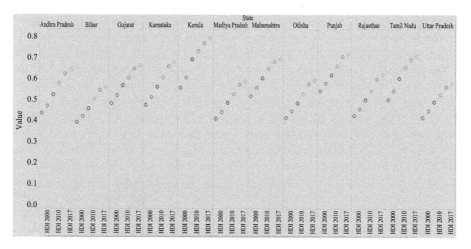

Figure 13.9 HDI state wise (1995–2017)

compared to other states. But there is also a significant increase in the crime rate in all the states between the years 2004 and 2017 and is depicted in Figure 13.9 with *X*-axis—year (for each state) and *Y*-axis—HDI.

13.3.6 Prohibition of child marriage

All citizens below the age of 18 are considered children or minors so a marriage proposal made for the minor individuals is always considered to be a child marriage.

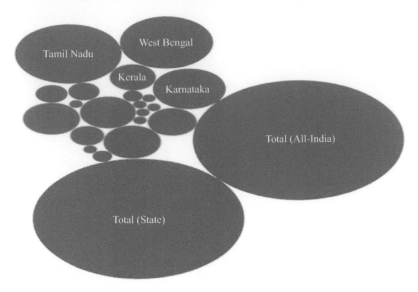

Figure 13.10   State wise prohibition of the Child Marriage Act

Conferring UNICEF, child marriage is constantly considered to be an act against human rights which directly leads to exploitation of minor girls and involve them in sexual abuse. The Prohibition of the Child Marriage Act is proposed by Central Government of India to nullify or declare void if marriage is solemnized for all the minor cases. So an activity which seems to be against Government protocol is always considered to be a crime [22]. The amendment says that whoever such as parents, guardian, or any member directly gets connected with child marriage activities shall be punishable with imprisonment along with a huge fine amount expediting in lakhs.

Figure 13.10 shows the pictorial representation of the existence of Prohibition of the Child Marriage Act in the various states of India along with its total rate of occurrence. This analysis ensures that this Child Marriage Act is more prevalent in rural part of the country and consistently happens in most backward, poor families, economically weaker section to overrule their burden of their daughter's marriage. The greater inference from this child marriage prohibition analysis is that many states in India had a sharp decline in child marriage over the decades.

13.3.7   Crime against children

Both physical and emotional (mental) abuse and exploitation happening to the minors are considered to be the crime against the children. Various preventive and protective measures have been carried out for those minor victims. Figure 13.11 depicts the total crime against children and the list of offences that may considered as part of crime against the children is tabulated in Table 13.5.

In Uttar Pradesh, Madhya Pradesh, and Delhi, the crime rate happening to minors clustered into crime against the children seems to be high. As Goa is the smallest state

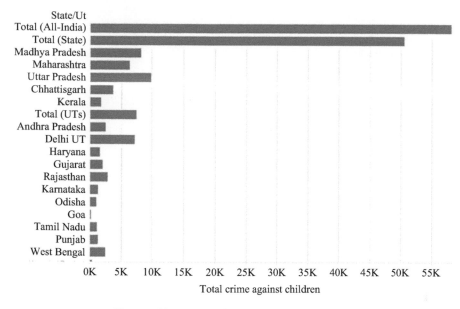

Figure 13.11   Total crime against children

Table 13.5   Factors influencing crime rate against children

Crime against children offence list
• Unnatural offences
• Infanticide
• Murder
• Rape
• Attempt to commit murder
• Sexual harassment
• Voyeurism
• Procuration of minor girls
• Selling of minors for prostitution
• Importing minor girls to foreign countries
• Buying of minors for prostitution
• Kidnapping and abduction
• Child labor

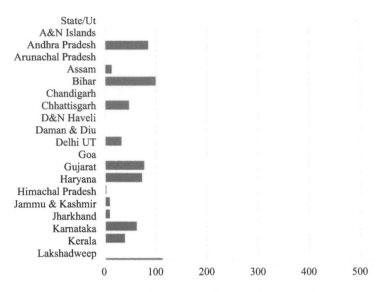

Figure 13.12   State wise murder analysis

in India, it seems to hold negligible crime rate against children. Figure 13.12 picturizes the state-wise murder analysis representing Bihar as higher murder rate.

13.4   Result analysis

This section concludes the result analysis that inferenced on both data visualization process and prediction model as well.

13.4.1   Methodology

A series of scripts comprising of Bash script along with a group of Python scripts that makes use of the source code of an application is observed to give accurate results. The user-defined classes were found using a recursive approach. The dataset is split into training and testing with test size as 50%. The next process is carried on with the training of model using Gini Index and entropy functions. The confusion matrix is then displayed with the correct and falsely predicted values by the decision tree model. This confusion matrix is further used to calculate and display the values for each of the two categories, i.e., "0" and "1." The values displayed for each category are precision score, *f*-score, recall score, and support. The resultant scores are obtained from the confusion matrix. The accuracy of the predicted decision tree model is also printed. The scores obtained suggest the extent to which the actual values are predicted correctly and the values which are incorrectly predicted. The decision tree algorithm would give the accuracy of the predicted decision tree model with the confusion matrix and Gini Index is also displayed which gives a clear perspective of how often the chosen value may be incorrectly predicted.

13.4.2   Using Jupyter (Python)

  (i)   Load the dataset in the environment.
 (ii)   Select the columns which are of interest in the data frame, i.e. the dependent and target variables.
(iii)   Initialize the linear regression and Lasso regression models.
(iv)   Determine the y_predicted value for each of the models.
 (v)   Evaluate the predicted model. In this case, RMSE is used for linear regression and mean absolute error for Lasso regression is computed.
(vi)   Print the error values after the evaluation of the models and the *y*-intercept.
(vii)   Plot the obtained linear regression in the form of a graph.

13.4.3   Prediction model analysis

- The following results are deduced with the help of prediction model.
- The reporting of case related to crime is dependent on socio-economic factors.
- Polynomial regression can be used to predict approximate crime rate in India while taking socio-economic factors into account.
- Polynomial regression was most fit for calculating crime rate while using HDI and Poverty Index independently.

13.4.4   Algorithm for linear regression model

Input: Crime Dataset containing various factors like Literacy Rate, Child Marriage Act, Poverty Index, Crime against Children, Unemployment Rate, Sex Ratio.
    Output: Graphical plot with predicted values using ML, using Tabulae programming

---

Algorithm 1: bestfit_slope_intercept(xs, ys)

---

   1. m = (((np.mean(xs)*np.mean(ys)) - np.mean (xs*ys))/
   2. ((np.mean(xs)2)-np.mean(xs2)))
   3. b = np.mean(ys) - m*np.mean(xs)
   4. m,b = best_fit_slope_intercept(xs,ys)
   5. y_predicted = m*xs + b
   6. Plot xs, ys and y_predicted using plot
   7. for i in range 0 to len(xs[0]):
   8. m1,b1 = best_fit_slope_intercept(xs[:,i],ys)
   9. Append m1 with a
  10. Append b1 with b
  11. Give legend to the graph for better understanding during analysis using plt. legend(loc = 'best')
  12. Save the graph in the notebook folder as png file using plt.savefig()
  13. plt.show() to display the graph
  14. Print m and b

13.4.5   *Algorithm for logistic regression model*

Input: The dataset comprising of features of crime factors and year is read as a csv file. Here,

input variable x = dataset.iloc[:, [1,4]].values

and target variable: y = dataset.iloc[:, 3].values

Output: Graph with the version number along the ordinate and the accuracy of prediction is displayed.

Algorithm 2: logistics_function()

---

1. xtrain, xtest, ytrain, ytest = train_test_split (x, y, test_size = 0.25, random_state = 0) where xtrain, xtest, ytrain , ytest are the input variable(x) used for training and testing, the target variable (y) used for training and testing, respectively.
2. classifier = LogisticRegression (random_state = 0) Initialise Logistic regression
3. Fit the logistic regression classifier.fit (xtrain, ytrain)
4. Predict using y_pred = classifier.predict (xtest)
5. cm = confusion_matrix(ytest, y_pred) to get the confusion matrix
6. Print cm (confusion matrix) and accuracy
7. Plot the predicted values with x and y labels. "0": no threats for the particular factor and "1": availability of threats for the factor considered.

13.4.6   *Lasso regression*

Algorithm

---

1. Determine the dependent and target variables in the Data frame
2. model = Lasso(alpha=1.0)
3. model evaluation method:
4. cv = RepeatedKFold(n_splits=10, n_repeats=3, random_state=1)
5. evaluate model:
6. scores = cross_val_score(model, x,y, scoring='neg_mean_absolute_error', cv=cv, n_jobs= (−1))
7. force scores to be positive:
8. scores = absolute(scores)
9. print 'Mean Absolute Error (MAE):' (mean(scores), std(scores)

13.4.7   *Decision tree model*

Decision tree model is a powerful algorithm to predict the target variable with great accuracy. The structure of the decision tree model is such that every internal node clearly depicts the test on a specific variable, i.e. the target variable. In the algorithms used, the process is divided into building phase, training phase, testing phase, and prediction phase. The leaf node is considered to depict a class label, i.e., after initializing the decision tree classifier and computing the target variables and the tree branches depicts concurrences of variable or features that result in class labels. Gini Index function and entropy functions are invoked. The Gini Index and entropy functions using (3.4) are used to precisely find out which values are predicted as true variables and the falsely predicted values.

13.4.7.1 Algorithm for decision tree model

Input: Crime dataset.

Output: Accuracy, confusion matrix and the classification report with precision core, f1 score, recall score and support value.

Algorithm 3: decision_tree_function()

---

1. Import the dataset.
2. Separate input and target variable, X = data_set.iloc[:,1].values.reshape (-1,1)
3. Y = data_set.iloc[:, 3].values
4. X_train, X_test, y_train, y_test = train_test_split(X, Y, test_size = 0.5, random_state = 100) Separate training and test dataset where test size is 50% and random_state is 100
5. clf_gini = DecisionTreeClassifier(criterion = "gini", random_state = 100, max_depth=3, min_samples_leaf=5) for training the dataset using Gini Index.
6. $H(x) = -\sum_{i=1}^{N} p(xi)\log 2 \, p(xi)$ where x can take N different values from 1 and p(xi) is the probability value and H(x) is the entropy value.
7. clf_gini.fit(X_train, y_train), fit the decision tree model.
8. clf_entropy = DecisionTreeClassifier (criterion = "entropy", random_state = 100, max_depth = 3, min_samples_leaf = 5) for training the dataset using entropy.
9. clf_entropy.fit(X_train, y_train), fit the decision tree model.
10. y_pred = clf_object.predict(X_test) Predict the values using Decision tree model.
11. Print accuracy, confusion matrix and the classification report with precision core, f1 score, recall score and support value.

The decision tree classifier is initialized and the test size during dataset split up is given as 50%. The values are predicted. Confusion matrix, precision, recall, f1-score, and support values are displayed. The accuracy of the predicted model is also found by using the calc_accuracy function.

- *m = (((np.mean(xs)*np.mean(ys)) - np.mean (xs*ys))/*
- *((np.mean(xs) 2)-np.mean(xs2)))* where xs and ys are the x and y coordinates and np here denotes the numpy library respectively.

- $b = np.mean(ys) - m*np.mean(xs)$
- $y = mx + b$ where m is the slope and b is considered as the y intercept.

$H(x) = - \sum_{i=1}^{N} p(xi)\log 2\, p(xi)$ where x can take N different values from 1

and p(xi) is the probability value and H(x) is the entropy value.

13.4.8   Root mean square

Root square value of both test and train datasets was calculated and Table 13.6 gives a clear perspective about the RMSE obtained after prediction of the model using linear regression [23].

Figure 13.13 shows the output displaying the results obtained from evaluation of linear regression model. Figure 13.14 shows the output displaying the results obtained from Lasso regression.

13.4.9   Data visualization analysis

The following results can be deduced with the help of data visualization charts.

- High literacy rate in any state leads to an increase in the reporting of crimes analyzed from Figures 13.3 and 13.4.
- The states which have consistently improved in Poverty Index such as Kerala and Tamil Nadu have shown an increase in the reporting of criminal case. On

Table 13.6   Square value of test and train dataset

Train dataset	Test dataset
RMSE: 30.71	RMSE: 12.84
R-square: 0.873	R-square: 0.975

```
Slope: [[2.44442117e-05]]
Intercept: [0.42952059]
Root mean squared error:  0.195354690909777944
R2 score:  0.2106881175362446
```

Figure 13.13   Output displaying the results obtained from evaluation of linear regression model

```
-----------------LASSO REGRESSION RESULTS-------------
Mean Absolute Error (MAE): 0.478 (0.108)
```

Figure 13.14   Results obtained from Lasso regression

another side, States such as Gujarat, Madhya Pradesh, Maharashtra, Orissa and Uttar Pradesh.

• Having an increase in the poverty rate, the reporting of criminal cases decreased is shown in Figure 13.5.
• Decrease in unemployment rate in any state lead to a decrease in Poverty Index, which in turn lead to an increase in the reporting of crime rate as inferenced in Figure 13.6.
• Per capita income has also increased in every state during 2005–2012 and the crime rate also increased during that period of time which is shown in Figure 13.7.
• Since calculation of HDI takes health, education, and income into account, the states have shown a significant increase in HDI after independence as shown in Figure 13.8.
• The states such as Kerala, Karnataka, and Punjab are having very high HDI when compared to other states. Kerala is having the highest HDI and is also having the highest crime rate as shown in Figure 13.8.
• The states such as Kerala, Gujarat, Madhya Pradesh, and West Bengal improved more than 15.0 which worked more on literacy after the independence till 1971. They showed a significant decrease in the Poverty Index in 1983–1993.

13.5 Conclusion

The reporting of criminal cases is mostly related to the Poverty Index of the state among all other factors. The states having high Poverty Index were reporting less cases of crime when compared to the states having low Poverty Index and high HDI. The above results show that improvement in Poverty Index in any state leads to high reporting of cases. States having high HDI, high literacy, low Poverty Index, and low unemployment rate reported highest cases that does not possibly mean that the state is most dangerous, but it shows that government and authorities of that state are more reachable to its citizens. People in these states are more aware about their rights and are more likely to reach the authorities for complaint. The state shall work on improving employment rate and literacy rate, which will lead to an increase in per capita income, lowering Poverty Index, lowering unemployment rate, and increasing HDI to increase its reach among the citizens and it will make people more aware about their rights. The various output graphs and pictorial representation depicted in various figures give a clear perspective of the statistical results like mean, median values, and the predicted values. Using the highly accurate results obtained from decision tree, Lasso, and linear regression models, concludes the data analysis with outcome of 88% accuracy with respect to test dataset and retaining 70% accuracy in training dataset. Similar analytics could be extended to the crime dataset across the globe, which may help the concern authority of the country to take appropriate action to bring down the crime rate occurrence.

References

[1]   T. Wang, C. Rudin, D. Wagner, and R. Sevieri, "Learning to Detect Patterns of Crime," In: H. Blockeel, K. Kersting, S. Nijssen, F. Železný (eds), *Machine Learning and Knowledge Discovery in Databases. ECML PKDD 2013. Lecture Notes in Computer Science*, vol. 8190, 2013. Springer, Berlin, Heidelberg. https://doi.org/10.1007/978-3-642-40994-3_33.

[2]   National Crime Record Bureau Website, https://ncrb.gov.in/.

[3]   Ministry of Statistics and Programme Implementation, http://www.mospi.gov.in/.

[4]   B. Sivanagaleela and S. Rajesh, "Crime Analysis and Prediction Using Fuzzy C-Means Algorithm", Proceedings of the Third International Conference on Trends in Electronics and Informatics (ICOEI 2019) IEEE Xplore Part Number: CFP19J32-ART, pp. 595–599; ISBN: 978-1-5386-9439-8.

[5]   Office of the Registrar General & Census Commissioner, Ministry of Home Affairs, India, http://censusindia.gov.in/.

[6]   M. Biswas, Crime and Socio-Economic Factors of India: Cointegration and Causality Analysis (E-ISSN 2348-1269, P-ISSN 2349-5138), www.ijrar.org.

[7]   H. Datta, Determinants of Crime Rate Crime, Deterrence and Growth in Post liberalized India, https://www.researchgate.net/publication/228545855_Determinants_of_crime_rates_Crime_Deterrence_and_Growth_in_post-liberalized_India.

[8]   M. Sharma, "Z-Crime: A Data Mining Tool for the Detection of Suspicious Criminal Activities based on the Decision Tree", International Conference on Data Mining and Intelligent Computing, 2014, pp. 1–6.

[9]   Open Government Data Platform India, https://data.gov.in/.

[10]   E. Hamdy, A. Adl, A. E. Hassanien, O. Hegazy, and T.-H. Kim, "Criminal Act Detection and Identification Model", Proceedings of 7th International Conference on Advanced Communication and Networking, 2015, pp. 79–83.

[11]   S. Yadav, M. Timbadia, A. Yadav, R. Vishwakarma, and N. Yadav, Crime Pattern Detection and Analysis Research Paper, 18 December 2017, IEEE, DOI: 10.1109/ICECA.2017.8203676.

[12]   J. Saini and V. Srivastava, "Impact of Population Density and Literacy Levels on Crime in India", 10th International Conference ICCCNT, 2019 July 6–8, 2019, IIT, Kanpur.

[13]   D. Benjamin and Suruliandi, Survey on Crime Analysis and Prediction Using Data Mining Techniques, 10.21917/ijsc.2017.0202.

[14]   O. Obamuyi, "Corruption and Economic Growth in India and Nigeria", *Journal of Economics and Management*, 2019;35(1):80–105, ISSN 1732-1948.

[15]   K. Sheehy, T. Rehberger, A. O'Shea, *et al.*, "Evidence-based analysis of mentally 111 individuals in the criminal justice system," 2016 IEEE Systems and Information Engineering Design Symposium (SIEDS), 2016, pp. 250–254. doi: 10.1109/SIEDS.2016.7489308.

[16] A. S. Kumar and R. K. Gopal, "Data Mining based Crime Investigation Systems: Taxonomy and Relevance", Proceedings of Global Conference on IEEE Communication Technologies, 2015, pp. 850–853.

[17] K. Bogahawatte and S. Adikari, "Intelligent Criminal Identification System", Proceedings of 8th IEEE International Conference on Computer Science and Education, 2013, pp. 633–638.

[18] R. Kiani, S. Mahdavi and A. Keshavarzi, "Analysis and Prediction of Crimes by Clustering and Classification", *International Journal of Advanced Research in Artificial Intelligence*, 2015;4(8):11–17.

[19] C.-H. Yu, M. W. Ward, M. Morabito and W. Ding, "Crime Forecasting using Data Mining Techniques", Proceedings of 11th IEEE International Conference on Data Mining Workshops, 2011, pp. 779–786.

[20] S. Sathyadevan, M. S. Devan and S. Surya Gangadharan, "Crime Analysis and Prediction using Data Mining", Proceedings of IEEE 1st International Conference on Networks and Soft Computing, 2014, pp. 406–412.

[21] P. Thongtae and S. Srisuk, "An Analysis of Data Mining Applications in Crime Domain", Proceedings of IEEE 8th International Conference on Computer and Information Technology Workshops, 2008, pp. 122–126.

[22] P. Arunachalam and K. Roja, "A Critical Analysis on Offences Against Child Marriage," *International Journal of Pure and Applied Mathematics*, 2018;120(5):687–698.

[23] Tableau https://www.tableau.com/.

Chapter 14

Deployment of automated teller machinery for e-polling

G. Vivek[1], Adarsh Bisi[1], Aswani Kumar Cherukuri[1], Terrance Frederick Fernandez[2] and Firuz Kamalov[3]

Abstract

Voting plays a significant role in electing a suitable person by the public to rule the country. In this modern age of digitalization, we still use electronic voting machine (EVM), which is not entirely automated and has got many limitations. This machine replaces the traditional way of collecting votes through boxes consisting of voting papers. This method is called as the paper ballot. This system has slowly changed or altered into a new technical and mechanical system that uses EVMs to avoid misconceptions. Even though this voting machine is fast and accurate, this system needs more work-force and also it is not much more reliable. Most of the eligible voters cannot cast their vote due to immigration for a job, education, etc. Also, the government spends a lot of money arranging the vote booths and maintaining the decorum of the election.

This chapter proposes a framework that changes the automated teller machine (ATM) framework to function as EVM. One of the fundamental advantages of utilizing ATMs as EVM is encouraging the political decision process for everybody and letting immigrants vote for their constituency. One of the main benefits of using ATMs as EVM is to facilitate the election process for everyone. Also, using ATMs as EVM will save time for all voters and eliminate the waste of your time in the long queue for the regular election process. Any voter needs just to hit for the closest ATM in his\her area and afterward utilizing electronic virtual card (EVC) embeddings it into the ATM picks the choice political decision.

Keywords: Automated teller machine (ATM); Blockchain; Electronic voting card (EVC); Electronic voting machine (EVM); One time password (OTP)

[1]School of Information Technology & Engineering, Vellore Institute of Technology, India
[2]Department of Computer Science & Engineering, Saveetha School of Engineering, Saveetha Institute of Medical & Technical Sciences (SIMATS), India
[3]Department of Electrical Engineering, Canadian University Dubai, UAE

14.1   Introduction

India is a country with a population of 1.25 billion, out of which the youth are around 600 million. Indian voters from Kashmir to Kanyakumari select their agents to frame their parliament by going to surveys. India's political decision is one of the most extensive vote-based exercises on the planet history. Around 850 million qualified voters figure out which ideological group or partnership will structure the administration and this way, will fill in as executive. In a wide range of elections (Presidential\Parliamentary) races, electronic voting machines (EVM) are considered. However, EVM is not totally mechanized and has numerous confinements.

As people are getting relocated due to their jobs, studies, etc., they are unable to cast their vote. This has become another major concern. Voting is a tiring and time-consuming process. It takes a lot of time to set up the arena for the voting. It all starts before a month of the commencement of the election. The election process is expensive which the world's biggest democracy will soon hold what's likely to be one of the world's costliest elections. India's six-week-long vote will span the Himalayan range in the north, the Indian Ocean in the south, the Thar Desert in the west, and the Sundarbans' mangroves in the east. A lot of money is invested in conducting the election in a hassle-free manner. The proposed model of our work provides an opportunity to mitigate these problems by allowing the voters to cast their votes wherever they are, by using their automated teller machine (ATM) cards.

This chapter is structured as follows. The next section describes the background, flashing lights upon the concept of blockchain and related works. In Section 14.3, the proposed model and its work is described. Detailed analysis of the proposed model and voting system is presented in Section 14.4. Finally, conclusion and a sneak-peak onto the future work are presented to the readers in Section 14.5.

14.2   Background

14.2.1   Blockchain

A blockchain is a sequence of time-stamped transactions, where each transaction includes a variable number of output addresses (each address is a 160-bit number). In a blockchain, each block contains contents of the block and a "header" which contains the data about the block. Blockchain technology is composed of six key elements.

- Decentralized: Blockchain never counts on a central node/framework for logging the data, recording it, or for upgrading purposes.
- Transparent: Every gathered or collected data, which is stored and maintained in the blockchain is highly transparent and flexible with respect to one other as well as for updating of data
- Open source: Predominantly, blockchain is a system which is accessible to quite a lot of people due to which records are easily accessible and visible. Even more, people can exploit blockchain techniques to create any application of their choice.

- Autonomy: Since the nodes have their foundation based on consensus, each and every individual node can assure the safe transmission of data with the core idea or perspective of making the entire system trustworthy without any malicious interventions.
- Immutable: Entire data will be recorded and saved for good and they cannot be modified unless an individual takes charge of more than 51% of the same simultaneously.
- Anonymity: Blockchain methodologies solve and eradicate trust issues between nodes, such that the data transfer or transactions are highly anonymous and calls are for the individual Blockchain addresses alone.

Figure 14.1 shows the structural block diagram of a blockchain and the technology is widely employed by researchers in [1–3].

Decentralization, accountability, and security (with building trust) are some core properties of a blockchain technology. Apart from characteristics of blockchain, for business, blockchain technology has the following benefits to users/organizations:

- Time savings: Transaction times for complex, multi-party interactions are slashed from days to minutes. Transaction settlement is faster, because it does not require verification by a central authority.

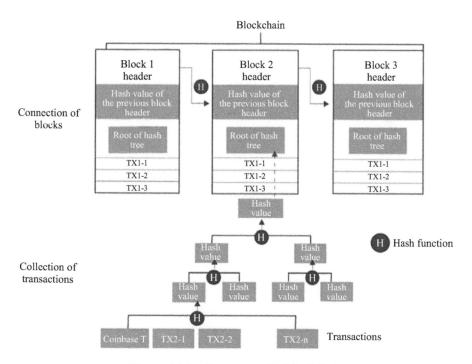

Figure 14.1 Structure of a blockchain

- Cost savings: Blockchain takes the edge off expenses in several ways:
  - Marginal oversight is needed because the network is self-policed by network participants, all of whom are known on the network.
  - Intermediaries are reduced because participants can exchange items of value directly.
  - Duplication of effort is eliminated because all participants have access to the shared ledger.
- Data validity and tighter security: Blockchain's security features protect against tampering, fraud, and cybercrime. Once you are in, the data is hard to tamper due to blockchain's nature. If a network is granted permission, it enables creation of members-only network with proof that members are who they say they are and that goods or assets traded are exactly as represented.

Bear in mind that blockchain can be used in any application to store data securely and with anonymity. Then it does not mean that similar blockchain can be used/ built for business. As discussed above, blockchain technology can be as publicly or privately (permission to specific person only). Some are granted permission while others are not. A permission network is critical for a blockchain for business, especially within a regulated industry. It enhances privacy, improves audit-ability and increases operational efficiency. Blockchain technology builds trust through the following five attributes in business/individual applications:

- Distributed and sustainable: The ledger is commonly shared, updated and upgraded every time a processing happens and is easily duplicated or replicated within the users in real-time. Since it is not under the ownership of any particular establishment, the blockchain offers a framework which is immaculately independent of individual instances.
- Secured, private, and indelible: Authorizations and encryption aid to keep away data flowing into malicious hands thus assures and verifies the validity and identity of the participants. Privacy is easily imposed through cryptography complemented by data partitioning methods to ensure participants are succumbed to selective access/visibility into the ledger. As per the agreement of the conditions, users will not be allowed to modify/harm the record filled with processed transactions.
- Transparent and auditable: Since the users participating in a particular process can access the same records, they are capable of validating the transaction procedures and authorizing ownership identities for the third-party middlemen.
- Consensus-based and transactional: All the active users of the network are obliged to agree toward the validity of a process and this is moderated with consensus algorithms. Each of these networks is efficient enough to develop the situations under which a process can take place.
- Orchestrated and flexible: Since business rules and smart contracts can be easily incorporated into this framework, blockchain networks evolve to be mature enough to complement end-to-end business techniques and a plethora of other activities.

In general, blockchain builds trust through the following five attributes in business/individual applications:

- Distributed and sustainable: The ledger is shared, updated with every transaction, and selectively replicated among participants in near real time. Because it is not owned or controlled by any single organization, the blockchain platform's continued existence is not dependent on any individual entity.
- Secure, private, and indelible: Permissions and cryptography prevent unauthorized access to the network and ensure that participants are who they claim them to be. Privacy is maintained through cryptographic techniques and/or data partitioning techniques to give participants selective visibility into the ledger; both transactions and the identity of transacting parties can be masked. Post conditions are agreed to, participants cannot tamper with a record of the transaction; errors can be reversed only with new transactions.
- Transparent and auditable: Because participants in a transaction have access to the same records, they can validate transactions and verify identities or ownership without the need for third-party intermediaries. Transactions are time-stamped and can be verified in near real time.
- Consensus-based and transactional: All relevant network participants must agree that a transaction is valid. This is achieved through the use of consensus algorithms. Each blockchain network can establish the conditions under which a transaction or asset exchange can occur.
- Orchestrated and flexible: Business rules and smart contracts (that execute based on one or more conditions) can be built into the platform, blockchain business networks can evolve as they mature to support end-to-end business processes and a wide range of activities.

14.2.2   ATM machine

The term ATM stands for automated teller machine. It is an electronic device that is used by only bank customers to process account transactions. The users access their accounts through a special type of plastic card that is encoded with user information on a magnetic strip. The strip contains an identification code that is transmitted to the bank's central computer by modem.

The users insert the card into ATMs to access the account and process their account transactions. The ATM was invented by John Shepherd-Barron in the year 1960. This chapter discusses an overview of the ATM. By using an automated teller machine or ATM, we can perform different financial transactions such as cash deposits, withdrawals, transfer funds, information of account, ATM personal identification number (PIN) change, and also linking the Aadhaar number to the bank account so that the interaction between the bank staff and the customer can be reduced.

The ATM is an automatic banking machine (ABM) that allows the customer to complete basic transactions without any help from bank representatives.

There are two types of ATMs. The basic one allows the customer to only draw cash and receive a report of the account balance. Another one is a more complex machine that accepts the deposit, provides credit card payment facilities, and reports account information.

The block diagram of the ATM consists of mainly two input devices and four output devices. The input devices are card reader and keypad whereas output devices are speaker, display screen, receipt printer, and cash depositor.

The input devices like card reader and keypad. The card reader is an input device that reads data from a card. The card reader is part of the identification of your particular account number and the magnetic strip on the backside of the ATM card is used for connection with the card reader. The card is swiped or pressed on the card reader which captures your account information i.e. the data from the card is passed on to the host processor (server). The host processor thus uses this data to get the information from the cardholders.

The card is recognized after the machine asks for further details like your identification number, withdrawal, and your balance inquiry. Each card has a unique PIN so that there is little chance for some else to withdraw money from your account.

There are separate laws to protect the PIN code while sending it to the host processor. The PIN is mostly sent in encrypted form. The keyboard contains 48 keys and is interfaced to the processor.

An ATM or cash machine (in British English) is an electronic tele-communications device that enables customers of financial institutions to perform financial transactions, such as cash withdrawals, deposits, funds transfers, balance inquiries, or account information inquiries, at any time and without the need for direct interaction with bank staff.

ATMs are known by a variety of names, including ATM in the United States [4–6] (sometimes redundantly as "ATM machine"). In Canada, the term ABM is also used [7,8], although ATM is also very commonly used in Canada, with many Canadian organizations using ATM over ABM [9–11]. In British English, the terms cashpoint, cash machine, and hole in the wall are most widely used [12]. Other terms include any time money, cashline, time machine, cash dispenser, cash corner, bankomat, or bancomat. ATMs that are not operated by a financial institution are known as "white-label" ATMs.

Using an ATM, customers can access their bank deposit or credit accounts in order to make a variety of financial transactions, most notably cash withdrawals and balance checking, as well as transferring credit to and from mobile phones. ATMs can also be used to withdraw cash in a foreign country. If the currency being withdrawn from the ATM is different from that in which the bank account is denominated, the money will be converted at the financial institution's exchange rate [13]. Customers are typically identified by inserting a plastic ATM card (or some other acceptable payment card) into the ATM, with authentication being by the customer entering a PIN, which must match the PIN stored in the chip on the card (if the card is so equipped), or in the issuing financial institution's database.

Due to heavier computing demands and the falling price of personal computer-like architectures, ATMs have moved away from custom hardware architectures using microcontrollers or application-specific integrated circuits and have adopted

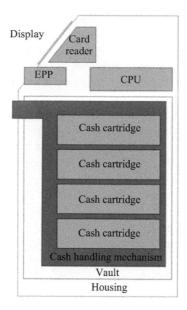

Figure 14.2   Block diagram of ATM [13, 28–37]

the hardware architecture of a personal computer, such as USB connections for peripherals, Ethernet and IP communications, and use personal computer operating systems.

Business owners often lease ATMs from service providers. However, based on the economies of scale, the price of equipment has dropped to the point where many business owners are simply paying for ATMs using a credit card.

New ADA voice and text-to-speech guidelines imposed in 2010, but required by March 2012, have forced many ATM owners to either upgrade non-compliant machines or dispose them if they are not upgradable, and purchase new compliant equipment. This has created an avenue for hackers and thieves to obtain ATM hardware at junkyards from improperly disposed decommissioned machines.

14.2.3   Literature survey

ATM is acting as EVM [4]. EVM is used during elections to collect and count the votes cast by the common, even though this voting machine not rapid and accurate enough. Hence, using ATMs would be beneficial.

This system uses a database to authenticate user and store votes and later on used for publishing results. We propose an improved method using blockchain as a service to store votes and maintain a decentralized network.

There are efforts in the literature in implementing new technologies for voting applications. Smart voting [5] the conventional voting mechanisms follows the issue of voter id and other details. However, during communication, votes can be manipulated. This system is a fingerprint-based application that enhances with a better voting system to ensure 100% voting.

Multi-part ballot-based name and vote separated E-voting system (M-NOTE) [6] utilizes a multi-part ballot to reduce the risk of identity leakage during the ballot distribution and vote counting phases. Voting online voters can be forced to vote for particular party.

The E-voting system based on multiple ballot casting the paper presents an electronic voting system based on blind intermediaries using multiple ballots. The basic requirements for systems are described: eligibility, fairness, individual verifiability, universal verifiability etc. Voting credentials can be shared, which make system very vulnerable.

Two-step authentication in ATM machine to transfer money and for voting application [8] the paper is to perform two operations such as transaction of money and for voting application through ATM machine, by providing the authentication like biometric – fingerprint and face recognition through the comparison with the Aadhar car for more security and privacy. Voting friendly model was proposed in [9].

Authentication and voting procedures will be performed with the help of the authentication server (AS) of Kerberos and the database of voting card issuing authority. Voters can participate in voting without relying on their respective voting areas. This model is also useful for handicapped voters who are not able to vote. In this model, all the ATMs are connected through an ATM network with different AVC issuing authorities to vote irrespective of the geographic location.

In this chapter, we propose a system where voters will be verified before entering ATM and authenticated using face and fingerprint.

14.2.4   Problem definition

We create a secure E-voting system using blockchain, which will enable voters to vote through ATMs. People from remote places can also vote without visiting their constituency. Digitalize the complete voting process and prevent manipulation of votes and prevent people from casting multiple votes. The solution should be usable to people who are not comfortable with English or have physical challenges such as blindness.

The objective of this work is to create a system which will make voting convenient and transparent. Make a secure portal for advanced login methods like face recognition and OTP.

14.2.5   Existing voting equipment

A voting machine is a machine used to record votes without paper. The first voting machines were mechanical but it is increasingly more common to use EVMs. Traditionally, a voting machine has been defined by its mechanism, and whether the system tallies votes at each voting location, or centrally. Voting machines should not be confused with tabulating machines, which counts votes done by paper ballot.

Voting machines differ in usability, security, cost, speed, accuracy, and ability of the public to oversee elections. Machines may be more or less accessible to voters with different disabilities.

Tallies are the simplest in parliamentary systems where just one choice is on the ballot, and these are often tallied manually. In other political systems where many choices are on the same ballot, tallies are often done by machines to give quick results.

14.2.5.1   Paper-based voting

The voter gets a blank ballot and uses a marker to indicate which candidate he wants to vote for. However, this process can take a long time to get the hand count under the current system. Reviewing paper ballot counts and making infinite arguments about whether the marker crosses the square of the square/circle.

14.2.5.2   Lever voting machine

Lever machine is peculiar equipment, and each lever is assigned to the corresponding candidate. The voter pulls the lever to vote for his preferred candidate. This kind of voting machine can automatically count votes. As its interface is not user friendly enough, it is necessary to provide some training to voters. However, these machines are causing hundreds of votes to go unnoticed.

14.2.5.3   Punch card

Voter uses metal hole-punch to insert a hole into an empty ballot. It may count votes automatically, but if the casting is incomplete, the result may be incorrectly determined.

14.2.5.4   Optical voting machine

After each voter completes a circle corresponding to the person, he or she loves in the blank ballot; the machine selects the darkest mark on each ballot ball and produces the complete result. This type of machine quickly calculates voting. However, if the voting fills the circle, it will result in an error of the optical scan.

14.2.5.5   Direct recording electronic (DRE) voting machine:

DRE meets keyboard; touch screen, or buttons for a polling publisher. Counting of votes is done very quickly. But DREs are too expensive and fail to produce evidence that the vote stored on the machine is actually what the voter saw and confirmed on screen.

14.2.6   Review of e-voting schemes

e-Voting systems were initially developed as a panacea for the problems inherent in the paper-based voting system as discussed in [14]. Several solutions have been proposed, and these solutions are examined in this section. A historical trend of voting systems in Nigeria was highlighted by [15] after which a secured voting system that was not prone to manipulation, rigging, and complaints from citizens and political parties was designed. However, it was able to achieve only authentication but was not able to achieve confidentiality, integrity, transparency, convenience and auditability of functional and security requirements; hence, it was impracticable to use. Ref. [16] provided a solution to the security issues of online voting systems with user biometric and password features for authentication. It was achieved by using the voter's fingerprint and password to achieve authentication while the least significant bit (LSB) was used to hide the results and Message-Digest algorithm 5 to achieve integrity.

The research achieved the authentication and confidentiality requirement of e-voting systems but could not solve the problem of convenience and auditability. In order to solve the problem of time wastage when it comes to counting ballot paper and wastage of resources and manpower, Ref. [17] proposed an advanced microcontroller-based biometric authentication voting machine.

The downside of this work was that it also could not achieve confidentiality, integrity, secrecy, transparency, convenience and auditability of e-voting functional and security requirements. Due to the problems of impersonation that eventually lead to false results, Ref. [18] developed a secure e-voting system where a KY-M 16 fingerprint sensor was used to capture the voter's fingerprints and WINCE 6 environment was leveraged on to interface the ARM processor.

Formulation of a fingerprint pattern technique to achieve authentication in fulfilling the security requirements of the electronic voting system was achieved. However, the solution failed to achieve confidentiality, integrity, transparency and convenience and audibility. Ref. [19] also addressed the problem of rigging and impersonation with another biometric fingerprint solution using the FIM 3030N scanner for extracting, processing, and storing the ridges of the prints in a database. The work was able to achieve a reasonable level of authentication; however, it also failed in the areas of confidentiality, integrity, convenience, and auditability.

To prevent impersonation in a situation of a stolen voter's ID card, Ref. [20] proposed an iris recognition-based voting system where voters' iris patterns are matched with pre-deposited images in the database. This work was also very good at achieving authentication but failed on the confidentiality, integrity, convenience, and auditability front.

An Internet-of-Things-based solution was proposed by [21] to curb the problem of impersonation and delay in result announcement resulting from slow process of collation. The ridge and valley features extraction techniques were used for authentication and the election data was transferred to the main database. A ridge extraction technique was presented and used to achieve authentication as a measure toward the attainment of e-voting requirements.

The challenges of confidentiality, integrity, secrecy, transparency, convenience, and auditability of e-voting functional and security requirements were not tackled. Another solution to impersonation and falsification of election results was proposed by [22] with the design, development, and evaluation of a secure electronic voting system using fingerprint and crypto-watermarking approach. This system worked by leveraging fingerprint biometrics, Advanced Encryption Standard and wavelet watermarking techniques. As voters registered their fingerprints, personal identification numbers were serially allotted for the purpose of authentication. The voting system could be accessed via a PC and it addressed the issue of authentication, integrity, and confidentiality. The problems of secrecy, transparency convenience, and auditability of e-voting functional and security requirements were not handled.

A smart voting machine was developed by [23] for the purpose of addressing the problem of manual checking of voters' details for identification, ineffective voting procedure and counting. A unique key and fingerprint biometrics were used for authentication and results were transmitted to the mobile phone of the election commissioner. The fingerprint biometrics and unique key were used to achieve verification. The problems of confidentiality, integrity, secrecy, transparency, convenience, and auditability of e-voting functional and security requirements were not addressed as the results communicated through the unprotected network could be intercepted by imposters.

Another IoT-based solution was developed by [24] to solve the same problem of impersonation as a result of the paper-based technique of voters' identification with the use of the PIC16F874A/877A microcontroller, fingerprint scanner, ZigBee (CC2500), liquid crystal display (LCD), buzzer, and power supply. The major setback of this work is the challenges of confidentiality, integrity, convenience, and auditability of the functional and security requirements.

This review of literature corroborates the extensive review done by [25] and it is clear that there are fundamental issues with e-voting systems that range from impersonation to authentication, to confidentiality, to integrity, to convenience, and to auditability. While some of the systems proposed by [20,22,23] solved the problem of authentication, the issue of confidentiality, integrity, convenience, and auditability were not addressed.

14.2.7   Contribution of the work

This system has revised the conventional voting system, which we have been following from years. It performs far better than any other systems developed for voting regarding security, reliability, flexibility, availability. Using blockchain checks the idea of hacking the system to manipulate the votes. Using voice assistance checks any kind of human intervention. Voice assistance guides the voter on how to vote and help them while voting. Implementing voice assistance in the system also let the visually impaired voters to vote. Text translation helps the locals by translating the text from English (by default) to their local language if voter not familiar with English. Implementing the 2-factor authentication using the voter's Aadhar card details confirms that the system does not any kind of forgery like multiple voting during the voting process. Full surveillance of the voting process makes it impossible to force and get someone to vote. It ensures that one-person castes only one vote. Every voter has the right to vote and elect its government. This system allows the immigrants to vote from their currently residing location without going to their constituency. Making the ATMs as a voting booth during election saves a lot of money invested in the infrastructure.

14.3   Proposed model

In this chapter, a voting system based on ATM and blockchain is proposed. The most important part of voting is authenticating the user and making sure no person can vote again. Hence, voting procedure is performed in three phases: authentication stage, voting stage, and completion stage. Public sector banks ATMs will be revised to incorporate the new voting facility. Necessary software updates will be done to support the voting system in ATMs.

Existing installations of the camera will be used to authenticate the person using his/her Aadhar data. We will ensure that a single person can cast his/her vote only once by using ATM card and sessions. To prevent any kind of human intervention, voice assistance will be provided, which voters can use if they need any help, making the voting more authentic. These three stages of the proposed model are described in this section one by one.

Vast numbers of hours, experts, and resources have been devoted to the implementation of the EMV standard for credit and debit cards in the United States. As the smoke begins to clear, however, a new EMV effort is beginning with a discussion of how to best implement EMV at the ATM.

EMV agreements struck between the major card brands and regional PIN networks will affect financial institutions and ATM-driving independent service organizations. As with nearly every aspect of business, the devil is in the details. It will be critically important for FIs and ISOs to uncover these details so they can plan for the financial and other ramifications of EMV in the future.

This list is merely a start. Notably, many of the same questions can be asked for any POS terminal vendors and processors, acquirers and others you work with to enable the routing of card holder transactions down the rails you chose.

Although there is no shortage of opinions on EMV transaction routing, mostly everyone agrees that all ATMs and POS terminals must support the common AIDs.

14.3.1   General constraints for the system

Before highlighting the proposed work, it is significant that we need to address the general constraints of the system. The country faces some very real problems with its election system. These problems can be classified into two types.

14.3.1.1   Problems related to the voter (citizen)

A lot of people do not go to the elections because of the far distances (geographical problem) between the places where they live and their place of election. Also another voter does not go because they do not really care and make the elections seem very difficult, even if not so difficult. There are employees and business owners who do not have the time to go to the polls and see that they are losing their time because overcrowding in the polling commissions. They believe that giving staff leave for all elections is detrimental to the business.

Employees also insist on this leave even if they are not interested in the elections but take it as a day of rest. Another issue which is the personal protection:

because sometimes in some polling commissions, some violence occurs because of overcrowding, unrest (stress) or because of some supporters of some candidates. It is possible to reducing in the privacy of the citizen. Voter problems can be summarized as: the geographical problem, crowdedness, lack of interest, occupational (lack of free time), and personal safety [28–37].

14.3.1.2 Problems related to the society and governmental economy

One of the most highlighted issues that will be solved by implementing the suggested system is reducing the cost of the election process. The country suffers from paralysis in many government jobs or at least less production in public and private businesses, especially those that have a primary role in elections such as educational and judicial institutions.

Education also stops because the government uses schools as polling stations and supervisors are teachers. Now the country only can use the ATM machines for elections and proceed in the daily work life. In Figure 14.3, the functional and non-functional requirements are given and it is based on the works described in [26,27].

Vast numbers of hours, experts, and resources have been devoted to the implementation of the EMV standard for credit and debit cards in the United States. As the smoke begins to clear, however, a new EMV effort is beginning with a discussion of how to best implement EMV at the ATM.

EMV agreements struck between the major card brands and regional PIN networks will affect financial institutions and ATM-driving independent service organizations.

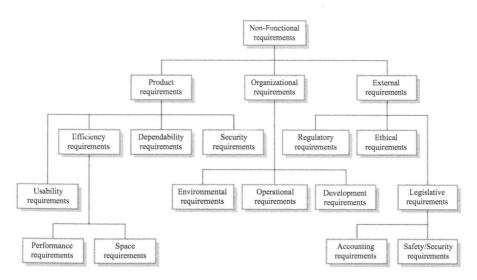

Figure 14.3   Non-functional requirements for ATM to EVM system

As with nearly every aspect of business, the devil is in the details. It will be critically important for FIs and ISOs to uncover these details so they can plan for the financial and other ramifications of EMV in the future.

Here are a few important questions for ISOs and card-issuing FIs to ask their vendor partners:

Without access to the common AID, all transactions will be limited to a single route eliminating an issuer's ability to benefit from the cost-savings and other benefits of its regional PIN network relationships. If a terminal has not been certified for the common AIDs, or if certain models only support out-of-the-box EMV implementations, then that flexibility and choice is eliminated.

The EMV Migration Forum has released guidance on the common AID at the ATM. However, the specifics of implementation will be somewhat unique to each terminal vendor or software provider. As your FI upgrades its ATM fleet for EMV, make certain that you are asking about those details to ensure maximum flexibility and choice with your investment.

ATM is a device used by bank customers to process account transactions. Typically, a user inserts into the ATM a special plastic card that is encoded with information on a magnetic strip or computer chip. The strip contains an identification code that is transmitted to the bank's central computer by modem.

To prevent unauthorized transactions, a PIN must also be entered by the user using a keypad. For additional security, transactions made with a computer chip also create a unique code for each transaction; this helps prevent information stolen during the transaction from being reused.

Once the transaction is authorized, the computer permits the ATM to complete the transaction; most machines can dispense cash, accept deposits, transfer funds, and provide information on account balances. Transactions at ATMs may also now be done using smartphones and a number of different methods, or using palm- or fingerprints for personal identification.

Banks have formed cooperative, nationwide networks so that a customer of one bank can use an ATM of another for cash access; by 2010, there were more than 420,000 ATMs across the United States.

The internationalization of banking networks also permits ATM cards to be used to make transactions abroad. Some ATMs will also accept credit cards for cash advances. The first ATM was installed in 1969 by Chemical Bank at its branch in Rockville Centre, NY. A customer using a coded card was dispensed a package containing a set sum of money.

Independent ATM owner or operator customers present varying levels of money laundering (ML) / terrorist financing (TF) and other illicit financial activity risks, and the potential risk to a bank depends on the presence or absence of numerous factors. It is said that not all independent ATM owner or operator customers pose the same risk, and not all independent ATM owner or operator customers are automatically higher risk.

The potential risk to a bank depends on the facts and circumstances specific to the customer relationship, such as transaction volume, locations of the ATMs, and the source of funds to replenish the ATMs. Because of the cash-intensive nature of an ATM, the source of funds used to replenish the ATM is a key risk factor.

Independent ATM owners or operators that fund their ATM replenishment solely with cash withdrawn from their account at a bank pose a relatively lower ML/TF risk because the bank knows the source of funds and can compare the volume of cash usage to EFT settlements to identify suspicious activity. Conversely, independent ATM owners or operators that replenish ATMs from other or unknown cash sources may present pot.

- The ATM and EVM are in the idle state when there is no operation.
- ATM card reader determines the account number from the entered card.
- The user is prompted to enter a PIN after a card is entered.
- A menu is displayed to the user with the three options: bank system, voting system, and exit.
- EVM system turns on in voting case.
- A menu is displayed to the user with the candidates' names.
- The user is prompted to choose.
- The system counts the vote for chosen candidates.
- The EVM back to the idle state.
- The transactions can be cancelled at any prompt by pressing the cancel button.
- ATM deletes EVM system from the menu of this user.
- The ATM can withhold a bank card.

14.3.2   Detailed architecture

In the proposed model, we will be using an E-voting card containing Aadhar card numbers and the voter's constituency details. Once the voter inserts the E-voting card, he/she would not be able to use the banking services. A token will be active during the voting period. AS will use the Aadhar database to verify the user data, and the OTP sent to his/her registered mobile number.

The voting process should be secured by multiple layers of encryption and authentication (more like a financial transaction). A closed blockchain is used in which only the authorities who are needed to access the smart contracts will be permitted. An incomplete transaction may cause the token to get deducted and the vote not to be cast. Although credits can be reverted to the voter id through manual verification (like in online money transfer), the scale of the operation makes it an unrealistic task to perform. Applying a smart contract in a blockchain ledger would only complete when the transaction has been completed and vote is cast. When deploying a smart contract, a regular transaction is created.

Additionally, some byte-code is added as input data. This byte-code acts as a constructor, which is needed to write initial variables to storage before copying the runtime to the contract's code. This architecture shows that the votes are converted into smart contracts and stored in blockchain.

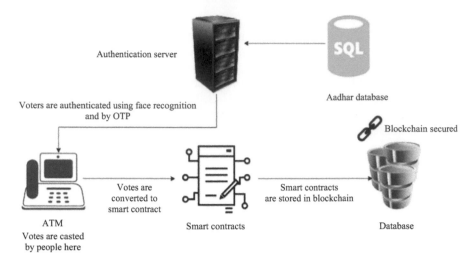

Figure 14.4   Solution architecture

14.3.3   Authentication stage

To conduct a transaction, a customer typically inserts a bank card into the appropriate slot in the ATM and inputs a PIN that verifies that the user is an authorized user for the bank account associated with the bank card. The account data is read from the card using the reader in the ATM and the PIN associated with the card.

The network communicator transmits the read data and PIN to a remote computer at the financial institution, which then transmits instructions back to the ATM regarding authorization to carry out the requested transaction

In the proposed system, we have incorporated two-factor authentication, which includes face detection and OTP verification. As soon as the voter reaches the ATM, he has to enter the E-voting card with a magnetic strip. The card contains the voter's information. The magnetic card reader of the ATM will read the card and will redirect to the landing page as voter to verify himself. Now, the voter has to carry out his authentication process.

The first step of authentication is face detection. Front camera of the ATM will be used to detect the face of the voter, and captured data will be verified by AS using Aadhar data. The next step of the authentication is the OTPs verification. The voter will receive OTP to his registered mobile phone the user has to enter the OTPs in the desired section and has to click continue. OTPs verification will be done. If verified, then a splash screen for voting will pop up otherwise, the error will be displayed and the voter will be redirected to the landing page of authentication.

14.3.4   Voting stage

After the authentication stage, the voting process begins. If the token in EVC is in an active state, then the voter will be able to vote. Each district's voting webpage is

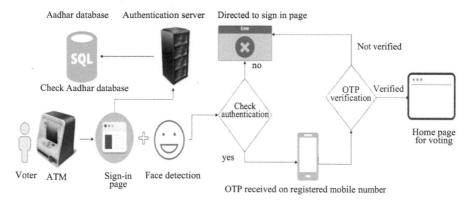

Figure 14.5   Authentication stage

associated with a port number. The server will process the request and display the required details about the constituency to which the person belongs to. The names of the candidates who have been elected and their party symbols will be displayed. Once the voter gets the green signal, he will be redirected to its constituency's voting page.

The voter has to select the party symbol they want to cast their vote and then tap on "Vote." A pop-up window will appear to ask for their confirmation to cast a vote. If they click on "Confirm," then their vote will be recorded and if they tap on "Cancel," he/they can choose the party symbol again and continue to vote. So, this enables immigrants to cast vote from their respective places where they are presently staying.

14.3.5   Completion stage

Manipulation of votes will be prevented as once vote is stored on the blockchain, it cannot be manipulated or altered. It is immutable. This is because of the architectural nature of blockchain constructions, where every block has a thorough summary of the preceding block in the kind of a secure hash value.

Ethereum smart contracts reside in electronic voting machines (EVMs), which isolates them from the blockchain network to prevent the code running inside from interfering with other processes. Once deployed, the smart contract obtains a unique address linked to a balance, similar to an externally controlled account (EOA) owned by a voter.

A smart contract can send transactions to an EOA or another contract. Smart contract for voting in a high-level language (Solidity). This smart contract is compiled into machine-level byte code where each byte represents an operation and then uploaded to the blockchain in the form of a transaction by EVM. A miner picks it up and confirms it in Block #i+1.

Once a voter has submitted his vote via the web interface, the queries the data from the web and embeds it into Transaction tx and deploy it to the blockchain. The state of the voting contract is updated in Block #i+2 with the confirmation of

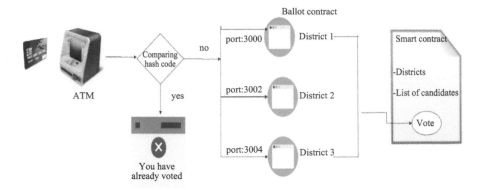

Figure 14.6   Voting stage

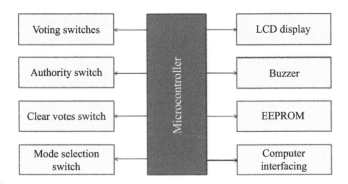

Figure 14.7   EVM block

transaction tx. If the coordinator later wants to check the states stored in the agreement, they have to synchronize up to at least Block #i+2 to see the changes caused by the transaction.

14.4   Analysis

We proposed a system using blockchain to store votes and maintain a decentralized network. In the proposed system, voter will be verified before entering ATM and also authenticated using biometric and OTP. Votes are stored in the blockchain which make them immutable and also does a two factor authentication. Usage of a simple voter database challenges the security of critical data, whereas we propose usage of Aadhar data which is highly secure and reliable. This proposed system scalable and also more secure. Since the system is using underlying ATM network, multiple users can access the network through ATM machines at any time. Hence, at any given point of time, multiple users can cast their vote.

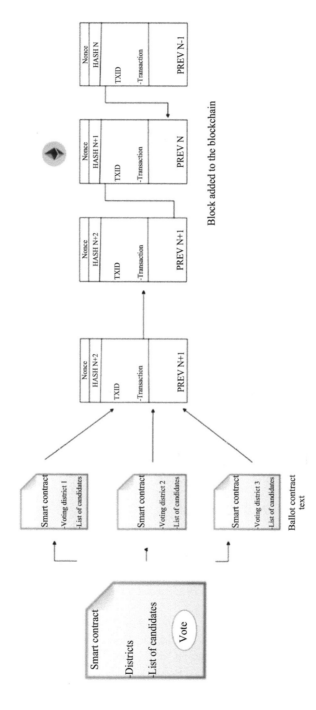

Figure 14.8 Storage of votes in blockchain

14.5 Conclusion and future work

In this chapter, a framework of voting with ATM using blockchain is proposed that can handle all earlier issues of conventional voting systems. This system has digitalized the process of voting completely. This system authenticates the user by performing face recognition and OTP verification. It has majorly solved the voting issues of immigrants. This system ensures high security to restrict the manipulation of votes and this has been done by storing votes as smart contracts in a closed blockchain node. Only authorized persons will be allowed to access the blockchain node. With the help of voice assistance, visually impaired people can also vote. Voters have also right to change the default language to their local language if needed. This model will increase the proportion of voting as the voters have to visit their nearby ATMs to vote. It provides accuracy in vote counts as everything is automated and there is no human intervention.

In future, two significant issues that should have been resolved are scalability and accessibility. Many numbers of security firms are attempting to improve validation in ATMs by using face recognition procedures so scalability is certainly not a major issue. Numerous banks have announced that they are going to expand number of ATMs in various districts like towns. As the proposed model is using ATM network as backbone, it is scalable.

References

[1]   A. A. Pandey, T. F. Fernandez, and A. K. Tyagi (2021) Maintaining Scalability in blockchain. In: Springer Proceeding of 21st International Conference Intelligent Systems Design and Applications (ISDA 2021), 13–15 December 2021.

[2]   D. Agarwal, A. K. Tyagi, and T. F. Fernandez (2021) Blockchain integrated machine learning for training autonomous cars. In: Springer Proceeding of 21st International Conference on Hybrid Intelligent Systems (HIS 2021), December 2021.

[3]   S. U. Aswathy, A. K. Tyagi, and T. F. Fernandez (2020) Blockchain and Aadhaar based electronic voting system. In: IEEE Proceeding of 4th International Conference on Electronics, Communication and Aerospace Technology (ICECA2020), 2020, ISBN: 978-1-7281-6387-1.

[4]   H. Elbehiery (2019) Automated Teller Machine (ATM) acting as Electronic Voting Machine (EVM). *IOSR Journal of Computer Engineering (IOSR-JCE)*, 21, 37–48.

[5]   R. Bhuvanapriya, V.K.G. Kalaiselvi, S. Rozil Banu, and P. Sivapriya (2017) Smart voting. In: 2nd International Conference on Computing and Communications Technologies (ICCCT), pp. 143–147.

[6]   H. Pan, E. Hou, and N. Ansari (2015) M-NOTE: a multi-part ballot-based E-voting system with clash attack protection. In: *2015 IEEE International Conference on Communications (ICC)*, London, pp. 7433–7437.

[7]   L. Babenko and I. Pisarev (2020) E-Voting system based on multiple ballot casting. In: Yang X. S., Sherratt S., Dey N., and Joshi A. (eds), *Fourth International Congress on Information and Communication Technology. Advances in Intelligent Systems and Computing*, Springer, Singapore, p. 1027.

[8]   K. Sudharsan, V. D. Ambeth Kumar, R Venkatesan, V. Sathyapreiya, and G. Saranya (2019) Two three step authentication in ATM machine to transfer money and for voting application. In: 2nd International Conference on Recent Trends in Advanced Computing ICRTAC-DISRUP–TIV INNOVATION 165, pp. 300–306.

[9]   Y. S. Patel and N. K. Singh (2013) Kerberos based ATM voting system: voting friendly model. In: IJCA Proceedings on International Conference on Distributed Computing and Internet Technology 2014 (ICDCIT-2014), pp. 1–7.

[10] H. Pan, E. Hou and N. Ansari (2015) M-NOTE: A Multi-part ballot-based E-voting system with clash attack protection, 2015 IEEE International Conference on Communications (ICC), London, pp. 7433–7437.

[11] H. Agarwal and G. N. Pandey (2013) Online voting system for India based on AADHAAR ID. In: Eleventh International Conference on ICT and Knowledge Engineering, Bangkok, pp. 1–4.

[12] J. Levine, H. Owen and J. Grizzard (2006) Detecting and categorising kernel-level rootkits to aid future detection. *IEEE Security & Privacy*, 2, 24–32.

[13] S. Kumar and E. Walia (2011) Analysis of electronic voting system in various countries. *International Journal on Computer Science and Engineering*, 3.

[14] A. A. Omotunde, M. Ejenobor, E. E. Onuiri, I. Aaron, A. Wumi, and A. Olubukola (2020) Automated teller machine-based voting system. *Technology,* 4(2), 31–41.

[15] L. B. Ajayi (2004) *A Secure Electronic Voting System*. Federal University of Technology, Department of Computer Science. Akure: Unpublished.

[16] G. Neha (2014) Study on security of online voting system using biometrics and stenography. *International Journal of Computer Science and Communications*, 5(1), 29–32.

[17] B. A. Farhath, M. Deepa, and C. N. Kalaivani (2014) Advanced micro-controller based biometric authentication voting machine. *International Organization of Scientific Research Journal of Engineering*, 4(5), 29–40.

[18] M. Sudhakar and B. S. Divya (2015) Biometric system-based electronic voting machine using ARM9 microcontroller. *Journal of Electronics and Communication Engineering*, 10(1), 57–65.

[19] S. Panja and S. Mondeddu (2015) Biometric finger print based electronic voting system for rigging free governance. *International Journal and Magazine of Engineering, Technology, Management and Research*, 2(12), 526–529.

[20] M. J. Nithya, G. Abinaya, B. S., and M. L. Saravana (2015) Iris recognition system. In: International Conference on Science, *Technology, Engineering and Management*, vol. 10, pp. 44–51.

[21] S. Nithya, C. Ashwin, C. Karthikeyan, and K. M. Ajith (2016) Advanced secure voting system with IoT. *International Journal of Engineering and Computer Science*, 5(3), 16033–16037.

[22] M. O. Olayemi, A. F. Taliha, A. Aliyu, and J. Olugbenga (2016) Design of secure electronic voting system using fingerprint biometrics and crypto-watermarking approach. *International Journal of Information Engineering and Electronic Business*, 8(5), 9–17, doi: 10.5815/ijieeb.2016.05.02.

[23] S. T. Trupti, S. Palak, D. P. Rashmi, K. Samit, and K. Saurabh (2017) Smart voting machine. *International Journal of Science Technology and Engineering*, 3(12), 143–147.

[24] S. Snega, S. Saundarya, and R. Balraj (2018). Highly secured electronic voting machine using aadhaar in IOT platform. *International Journal of Electrical and Electronics Research*, 6(2), 41–47.

[25] O. Adewale, O. Boyinbode, and A. Salako (2020) A review of electronic voting systems: strategy for a novel. *International Journal of Information Engineering and Electronic Business*, 1, 19–29. doi:10.5815/ijieeb.2020.01.03

[26] H. Elbehiery (2019) Automated Teller Machine (ATM) acting as Electronic Voting Machine (EVM). *IOSR Journal of Computer Engineering* (IOSR-JCE), 21(4), 37–48 (Ser. I), e-ISSN: 2278-0661, p-ISSN: 2278-8727.

[27] A. Devi, A. Sangeerani, D. Chinnasamy Kavitha, and A. Shali (2021) Any where vote: ATM as EVM. *Journal of Physics: Conference Series*, 1724(1), 012021 (IOP Publishing).

[28] F. Þ. Hjálmarsson, G. K. Hreiðarsson, M. Hamdaqa, and G. Hjálmtýsson (2018) Blockchain-based E-voting system. In: IEEE 11th International Conference on Cloud Computing (CLOUD), pp. 983–986.

[29] D. A. Gritzalis (2002) Principles and requirements for a secure e-voting system. *Science Direct* 21, 539–556.

[30] R. Hemavathi and A. E. Roopa (2018) Automated biometric-EVM implemented using lab-view. *International Journal of Trend in Scientific Research and Development* 2, 1065–1071.

[31] M. M. Karim, N. S. Khan, A. Zavin, S. Kundu, A. Islam, and B. Nayak (2017) A proposed framework for biometrie electronic voting system. In: 2017 IEEE International Conference on Telecommunications and Photonics (ICTP), pp. 52–56, doi: 10.1109/ICTP.2017.8285916.

[32] Z. Wei, C. Chuah, and C. Wen (2018) Blockchain-based electronic voting protocol JOIV. *International Journal on Informatics Visualization* 2.

[33] S. Kumar, N. Darshini, S. Saxena, P. Hemavathi, and Ananya (2019) Voteeth: an e-voting system using blockchain. *International Research Journal of Computer Science* 6, JNCS10081.

[34] S. P. Everett, K. K. Greene, M. D. Byrne, *et al.* (2008) Electronic voting machines versus traditional methods: improved preference, similar performance. In: Proceedings of the SIGCHI Conference on Human Factors in Computing Systems (CHI '08). Association for Computing Machinery, New York, NY, USA, pp. 883–892, https://doi.org/10.1145/1357054.1357195.

[35] E. Amankona and E. Paatey (2009) Online voting systems. *International Research Journal of Engineering and Technology* 6, 347–349.

[36] I. E. Eteng, U. D. Ahunanya, and P. U. Umoren (2018) An online voting system for colleges and universities: a case study of National Association of Science Students (NASS), University of Calabar. *Computing and Information Systems Journal* 22, 9–28.

[37] K. Malladi, S. Sridharan, and L. T. JayPrakash (2014) Architecting a large-scale ubiquitous e-voting solution for conducting government elections. In: 2014 International Conference on Advances in Electronics Computers and Communications. IEEE, pp. 1–6.

Chapter 15

Machine learning-based blockchain technology for protection and privacy against intrusion attacks in intelligent transportation systems

Yakub Kayode Saheed[1,2]

Abstract

Intelligent transportation system (ITS) is a rapidly growing field of technology that combines network connectivity, modern sensors, control system, and data processing technologies to improve our daily life. With the growing popularity of ITS, concerns about its security have garnered considerable attention. SQL injection, denial of service, and ransomware assaults are all prevalent types of threats in an ITS. In automation/transportation systems, privacy and trust are also significant challenges. Today, everyone requires a vehicle to move around. Together with this, data security is crucial in a computerization system since the vehicle's user data is transferred to the extra operator via the web through wireless devices and routes such as radio channels, optical fiber, and so on. Certainly, every device is linked to the internet and one another, constituting the Internet of Things (IoT). Even as the network transitions to wireless devices, numerous risks to autonomous cars/vehicles have developed into a serious issue for service providers and car owners. The bulk of these attacks is detectable and preventable using a variety of intrusion detection methods. The blockchain and, more broadly, peer-to-peer techniques may be critical in the development of decentralized and data-intensive applications that run on billions of devices while maintaining user privacy. To solve these problems, this chapter proposes a machine learning (ML)-based blockchain intrusion detection for protection and privacy against intrusion attacks in ITS. The blockchain was used for aiding information exchange in ITS. As a result of the immutable and decentralized nature of blockchain-enabled ITS systems, a variety of desirable qualities such as security, decentralization, transparency, automation, and immutability are expected to exist. The experimental analysis was performed on the UNSWB-NB15 dataset. The results obtained reached an accuracy that is more than

[1]Department of Computer Science, School of Information Technology & Computing, American University of Nigeria, Nigeria
[2]Department of Computer Science, Unicaf University, Zambia

99%. The AUC, recall, Mathew Correlation Coefficient (MCC), and training time metrics were also used to evaluate the performance of the models.

Keywords: Intelligent transportation system; Machine learning; Blockchain; Intrusion detection; Internet of Things; Internet of Vehicles; Smart vehicle; vehicular ad-hoc networks

15.1   Introduction

Developed nations worldwide (for instance, the United States of America, European Union associate countries, China, and Japan) are vigorously pursuing the digital transformation of the economic growth, particularly the transportation sector, which will inevitably result in the integration of communication devices built into vehicles, and the infrastructure objects [1]. Wireless connectivity technology for intelligent transportation system (ITS) applications has advanced significantly over the last decade in motor transport; these sophisticated information communication technologies are referred to as vehicular ad hoc networks (VANET). It is anticipated that message with infrastructure, between vehicles, and with susceptible members in traffic will provide critical benefits in terms of comfort and safety; these methodologies may also promote improved and much more qualified road traffic, as well as provide the best method for preventing or reducing traffic jams [2]. The term "vehicle to everything" (V2X) encompasses these kinds of communication. The ITS, especially particularly, notifies and alerts vehicles about potential roadblocks (speed limits, maintenance work, etc.) and offers options for coordinating coordinated actions (priority way on junctions, change of lanes, etc.).

The ITS connects people, roadways, vehicles, and urban networks wirelessly [3]. It processes, determines, shares, and safely publishes data collected from a variety of sources on the communications system platform, which greatly simplifies people's lives [4,5]. The management and control system is responsible for the scheduling, management, and maintenance of the whole ground transportation system in an ITS [6]. We can achieve real-time, dynamic, and efficient traffic management by sharing, collecting, and evaluating information about road conditions, cars, and people's movement. Now, management and control systems frequently give services to users through websites [7]. It is critical to the intelligent transport system, and its security concerns are becoming increasingly severe [8,9].

As a result, any failure of its operation has a direct impact on the protection of people and automobile engineering on the highway, making issues of ITS cyber resilience critical. Several researchers defined cyber resilience as a VANET's ability to offer and sustain an adequate level of service by ITS standards for V2X of real concern information under adverse situations (e.g., cyber-attacks). In Ref. [10], the writers advanced alike argument. The growing number of publications on different facets of ITS cyber resilience, combined with the rapid development of exposed cyber-attacks (as well as zero-day attacks) to immature (that is, lacking in "best practice"), almost innovative cyber systems, creates the same counterintuitive situation that requires a scientific decision. Identification of cyber dangers is the initial step in this strategy and classification of ITS telecommunication components' cyber resilience. Therefore, intrusion detection has been identified as the technology that can fill this gap.

A persistent intrusion can steal or destroy data from a computer or network system in a short period. As a result, infiltration is one of the most serious problems in network security. System hardware is also harmed as a result of intrusions. Various intrusion detection systems are used; however, accuracy is one of the key issues. The accuracy analysis relies heavily on the detection rate and false alarm rate. To reduce false alarms and maximize detection rates, intrusion detection must be enhanced [11]. We have produced a list of the top important cyber dangers facing ITS nodes founded on our examination of multiple bases unfolding critical aspects of information security in ITS networks: denial of service [12–14], broadcast tampering [15], routing [16,17], traffic analysis, Sybil attack [18,19] Jamming, [20,21], man-in-the-middle attack [22,23], Timing attack [23,24], message tampering/fabrication/suppression [25–27], brute-force-attack [28,29], and malware spamming [30,31]. Blockchain functions as a distributed system that saves similar blocks of data all over its network (meaning the system has no point of failure and cannot be controlled by a single node, user, or entity) [32].

In the sense that participants are permitted to trade transactions and communicate information, blockchain has been used in a variety of industries to ease data privacy and trust [33], while retaining a high level of trust, honesty, and openness [34]. Particularly, blockchain technology is useful for purposes other than digital currency and financial services [35], and some examples of applications include the power sector [36], online voting [37], IoT [38,39], manufacturing and supply chain [40,41], healthcare and pharmaceutical [42], cyber security [43], government services [44,45], and big data. The past of data exchange is preserved in immutable logs that may be viewed only by organizations or cloud providers with appropriate permissions and trust requirements. The following is a list of the different advantages of blockchain's architecture in ITS:

- Due to the lack of a centralized authority, all participants enjoy equal rights.
- It is based on a decentralized ledger of transactions, where there is either no controlling entity or a single network failure point.
- Counterfeiting and fraud may be avoided because of the blockchain system's high level of security and trust.
- There is no risk of collusion because everyone has the same copy of the ledger.

There has been a lot written (by numerous authors) regarding self-driving cars recently (e.g., from 2025 to 2030). Self-driving cars will, in many circumstances, traverse the streets, picking up commuters on demand. Nevertheless, there are several significant obstacles to overcome. Before this can happen, several issues must be addressed with efficient solutions, including secure identity, safe authentication, safety from vehicle cyber-attacks, genuine autonomous vehicles, and large bias-free datasets, as well as ensuring the privacy of commuters and users always.

As a reliable solution, these limitations can be solved by integrating blockchain technology (ultra-security, immutability, smart contract, and decentralization), unbiased big data, self-sovereign identification, machine learning (ML), and artificial intelligence. Blockchain technology, artificial intelligence, and cyber security will be the focus of the next decade to solve real-world challenges. Using blockchain technology, it is possible to ensure that automobiles are not remotely hijacked, that the correct riders are picked up and charged for rides, that identifications are not taken, that human preferences are valued, and that networks improve over time. Each vehicle, as well as everyone, will most likely have a bot assistant with whom they may engage for payment, scheduling, routing, and automobile preferences. These components will communicate via smart contracts and learn from one another to better design future rides depending on both systems (e.g., cost, efficiency, vehicle utilization) and human feedback (i.e., dislikes, likes, preferences).

IDS and blockchain can be used together to detect cyber-attacks and protect personal information [46]. Host-based IDS (HIDS) monitors and inspects operating system audit data as memory and process audit on a virtual machine. To avoid user-to-root threats via VM hopping and getting access to the next VM, the source IP is designated as admittance to the entire system if the host IDS spots malevolent behavior from a single host. At the infrastructure layer, a NIDS system monitors network traffic of all linked schemes within such a subnet [34,47]. Smart contracts and blockchain solutions are two prevalent types of privacy preservation that provide cloud elements with authentication and integrity. With cryptography and consensus procedures, blockchain overcomes the absence of accountability, security, and trust [34]. Bitcoin is widely regarded as one of the early success stories of a dispersed cryptocurrency, in which all transactions are completed without the use of third parties. This helps to ensure the integrity and validity of data. Crypto-currency system architecture is secured by substantial peer-reviewed cryptographic hash methods [48]. Ethereum is a decentralized computer technology that enables developers to create virtual environments that function as smart contracts on a blockchain network [49]. Unfortunately, there is currently a lack of a viable concept of trust for electronic smart contracts executed systematically in blockchains [43]. Users should be able to view the position of their migrated data within the blockchain ledger and trace audit files between clouds, thanks to the smart contract's flexibility and transparency. Several security issues and assaults in blockchain and related technologies such as Ethereum and bitcoins have been revealed in recent papers [43,50]. As indicated in this chapter, developing a ML IDS-based blockchain system is critical for detecting cyber-attacks and ensuring data privacy of IDS engines installed at various ITS nodes. The following are the chapter main contributions:

(a) A cooperative IDS system based on ML blockchain framework for achieving privacy and data security in ITS.
(b) A privacy-preserving technique is proposed that utilizes blockchain technology and smart contracts to allow irreversible movement and data sharing between ITS and to provide data protection and consensus to ITS nodes.
(c) An ID approach based on five ML algorithms for detecting cyber-attacks originating from network traffic movement in ITS nodes is proposed.

(d)   The suggested system and its methodologies are evaluated using the UNSW-BN15 network datasets, and the system's performance is compared to determine its efficacy when deployed on ITS nodes.

The remainder of this chapter is structured in the following manner. Section 15.2 discusses the background and related work. Section 15.3 presents the proposed approach. In Section 15.4, we explain the experimental results and discussion. Finally, in Section 15.5, we finish the chapter and explore its future direction.

15.1.1   Background

15.1.2   Internet of Vehicles (IoV) and Intelligent Transportation System (ITS)

With developments in communications, sensors, and electrical systems, traditional embedded systems and controllers are being phased out in favor of a more advanced sort of system known as a cyber-physical system (CPS). Typically, this CPS is coupled to Internet technology to create a link between the online and physical worlds. CPS has recently gained popularity and has been extensively used across many facets of our industries and lives. ITS, which is a term that refers to future modes of transportation, is one of the examples of CPS. ITS aims to provide more pleasant, dynamic, safer, and efficient modes of transportation and urban infrastructure [32]. Simultaneously, the automobile industry is creating the technologies that will enable smart vehicles, and as a result, the vehicles are transforming the travel experience and way of life. Figure 15.1 shows the communication of vehicles in a smart city.

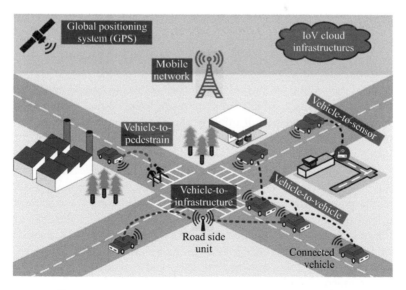

Figure 15.1   IoV communication in a smart-city [51]

15.1.3   Security and privacy

Incorporating blockchain into the IoV provides security and prevents data tampering due to the blockchain's capacity to ensure the immutability of data. However, because blockchain is built on several methodologies, it cannot ensure security and privacy directly. IDS is used in this research to raise any form of suspicious threats in the system. To solve the issues, several initiatives have been launched to secure the security and privacy of blockchain-enabled IoT. For example, the work in [52] offered to address the issue of protecting the propagation of fraudulent messages while also ensuring the privacy of vehicles. To accomplish these objectives, an anonymous reputational system is built. Contributes to the establishment of a privacy-preserving trust management protocol for automotive networks. In another relevant literature, Ref. [53] proposes a blockchain-assisted security framework for heterogeneous ITS networks. Blockchain technology is used in this case to accelerate the distributed key management process in heterogeneous networks and hence improve efficiency. The intelligent vehicles are often equipped with embedded compute and storage units, control units, EDR, such as OBUs and ECUs software and firmware systems, a broad array of sensors, and various wireless devices. In this setting, to take appropriate actions, the control units rely on data produced first from cameras and sensors, and the connections amongst these elements are built on several forms of wired (local interconnect network (LIN) bus and controller area network (CAN) bus) and wireless technologies [54]. Figure 15.2 illustrates the integration of IoV and blockchain technology. These innovative technologies may soon be integrated into conventional automobiles. Additionally, automobiles are more secure with these advanced systems. Vehicles are also becoming increasingly autonomous and semi-autonomous, as well as the potential to reshape the ITS.

15.1.4   Current ITS trends

As a result of the significant increase in various travel demands, including as automobile traffic, public transit, freight, and even pedestrian traffic, congestion, accidents, and pollution problems related to transportation are getting increasingly serious. ITSs, which may combine a wide range of technologies, including sensing, communications, dissemination of information, and traffic control, have been created to address these difficulties. Data collection, data analysis, and data/information transfer are three fundamental components for any ITS to perform its function (s). For further analysis of current traffic conditions, data-collection components collect all observable information from the transportation system (e.g., traffic flow at a specific point on the road network, average travel time for a specific road section, total passengers boarding a transit line, etc.). Traditionally, basic traffic information such as traffic volume and spot speed has been collected using inductive loop detectors [55], which indicate the presence of vehicles based on the induced current in the loop with passing cars, and pneumatic tubes [56], which detect the presence of vehicles based on pressure changes in the tube. These solutions, however, have become less common, especially in congested locations, due

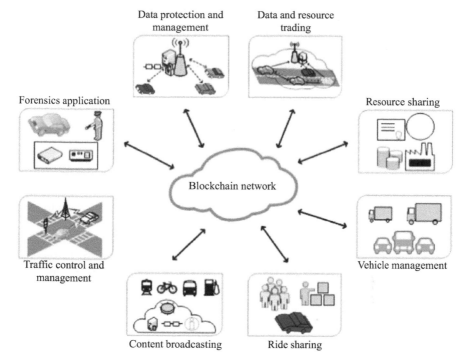

Figure 15.2 IoV and blockchain integration

to their high implementation costs and impact on traffic during deployment. Video cameras and RFID readers are increasingly being evaluated for use in traffic data collection as a result of developments in sensing and imaging technology. To capture traffic videos, cameras can be placed at various points around the network. The recordings are then processed using editing software (e.g., Autoscope) to extract data such as traffic flow, speed, and vehicle types [57]. Automatic license plate recognition is a critical area of research in this context, since it can provide extra information such as recommended paths and trip times by recognizing and matching license plates. Radio-frequency identification (RFID) data, on the other hand, is routinely gathered at locations that accept contactless payment for freight transportation. Different traffic-related information, such as path choice and journey time, can be recovered by matching unique RFID tags. Global positioning system (GPS) data, media access control (MAC) addresses from Wi-Fi and Bluetooth components [58], and mobile phone data have recently become available for the analysis of traffic conditions or even travel behavior, thanks to the increasing popularity of mobile and advanced communication technologies. These new sorts of data are more at the individual level than the data sources listed above, as gadgets are frequently individualized and able of actively looking (e.g., GPS and mobile phone data). More extensive and/or behavioral-related analysis could be undertaken with such features.

15.2 Related works

Bissmeyer *et al.* [59] proposed a signature-based approach based on a plausible scenario. Each vehicle is represented by a layered rectangle of varying sizes, with overlapping rectangles from various vehicles representing false position data. Due to the inadequacies of location tracking like GPS, the likelihood of an accident is increased. Each vehicle's incursion certainty and trust values are associated with an actual intersection. Intrusion certainty value is derived based on the number of detected intersections. Unless the attack exceeds a predefined threshold, it is not detected.

Bouali *et al.* [60] built the intrusion prevention and detection system (IPDS), a predictive system capable of detecting various misbehaviors before their occurrence by forecasting future vehicle behaviors. The vehicles are organized into one-hop clusters, each of which has three responsibilities.

Zaidi *et al.* [61] proposed a method for detecting multiple misbehaviors that relies on statistical approaches. It employs a model known as Greenshield's model to forecast and evaluate patterns in real-time traffic flows. Intrusion detection, as demonstrated by Robert Mitchell [62], is a popular issue with a wide range of applications.

The study in [63] presents a configuration for the smart vehicle ecosystem's security and privacy. This design is composed of three distinct types of entities: smart vehicles, manufacturers of equipment, and providers of service. Additionally, these entities in the integration node are split into clusters, with each cluster containing a cluster head charged with managing the blockchain network beneath it, broadcasting transactions, and verifying new blocks. As a result, cluster heads are referred to as overlay block managers (OBMs). In this approach, blockchain technology eliminates the architecture's need for centralized control. To provide privacy, each vehicle is equipped with an in-vehicle storage compartment to retain data that is sensitive to privacy, such as location traces. The design includes an access control feature that enables the vehicle's authority to specify which data will be shared with others and which will be stored in the vehicle's in-vehicle storage. The architectural design with other security and privacy attributes are mostly derived via blockchain technology.

A blockchain-assisted security structure for heterogeneous networks of ITS is proposed in [64] another related paper. Blockchain technology is used in this case to improve the efficiency of decentralized key management in heterogeneous networks. Ref. [65] introduces another study on message authentication mechanisms with blockchain-based connected vehicles. It assures that the broadcasting messages exchanged by connected vehicles are anonymous and decentralized.

PDS, a unique and lightweight policy-driven signature scheme for blockchain-assisted transportation systems, is introduced in [66] to control access. Finally, Ref. [67] presents a technique for protecting the location privacy of vehicles that employ location-based services in blockchain-assisted ITSs. The goal of this suggested system is to address some of the drawbacks of a widely used privacy protection technique known as distributed k-anonymity, such as the inability to detect malevolent cars and sensitive location privacy leaks. Apart from the foregoing statements and conversations, there are several open problematic topics as well as new study directions that could be regarded as future research prospects. In this section, we will go through these opportunities in detail, highlighting how blockchain, along with other cutting-edge technology, can improve things, even more, the IoV's ability to construct the future transportation infrastructure. Table 15.1 highlights the current studies on IoV and blockchain integration.

Table 15.1   A review of the literature on current IoV and blockchain integration issues

Authors	Center issues	Methodologies	Results
[52]	• Internal cars are sending out forged messages. • Vehicle identity security is threatened by tracking threats	• Instead of real identities, pseudonymous addresses are used. • Using previous encounters as well as views to determine the reputation	• The proposed approach may be used to create a trust model while simultaneously meeting transparency, robustness, and conditional anonymity requirements
[64]	• Modern authentication techniques lack a decentralization component	• Mutual authentication using elliptic curve cryptography (ECC)	• Anonymity, Lightweight, decentralization, and Scalability are all features of this authentication and key-exchange technique
[68]	• Problems with centralized privacy solutions	• Security approach for remote attestation	• The proposed paradigm can meet decentralization, traceability, and user anonymity
[69]	• There are not any decentralized, effective keyword search systems	• Encryption that can be searched. • Smart Contracts	• By incorporating forward and backward privacy, the suggested approach can significantly enhance privacy protection. • The centrally controlled search technique is phased out in favor of smart contracts
[53]	• Key management that is insecure	• Secure group broadcasting	• The suggested system enables more efficient distributed key

(Continues)

Table 15.1 (*Continued*)

Authors	Center issues	Methodologies	Results
		• A novel network topology is proposed	management while minimizing key travel times
[66]	• In comparison to public blockchains, users of permission blockchains have some limits	• Cryptography without certificates. • Signature-based on attributes. • Authorization by the specified policy	The suggested signature technique is characterized by a small signature size and a minimal computational overhead
[65]	• Problems with secure authentication and privacy protection	• Code for message authentication	• The suggested authentication technique is secure against a variety of typical threats

15.3 Proposed system

An MLBTID-ITS is developed to predict and safeguard data in the ITS system from cyber-attacks. The suggested framework's systematic architecture is composed of three major components: as mentioned below and depicted in Figure 15.3, the privacy-preserving smart contract and blockchain, the centralized coordination component (CCU), and IDS. Because it integrates a consortium blockchain, the privacy-preserving blockchain and smart contract layer are distinct from a regular network. More precisely, a disseminated digital ledger that records all ITS nodes transactions. This entity is duplicated and maintained across the network's nodes, including the data centers, CCU, and individual hosts. MLBTID-ITS has been designed in a manner like that of Bitcoin. The act of adding a new transaction to the chain must be suitably rewarded. The CCU functions as a SIEM, storing audit logs, and alarms from IDS. By utilizing the CCU's abilities, inbound data from various sources, namely cloud data centers, is analyzed and connected to differentiate among normal and anomalous events. These will enable network managers to quickly neutralize risks and raise security awareness among blockchain cloud network participants.

The CIDS entity coordinates the validation of frames operating on the cloud including that and ensures that they comply with stated regulations. The CIDS entity coordinates the validation of frames operating on the cloud including that and ensures that they comply with stated regulations.

They are composed of several IDSs deployed on big distributed networks or on individual hosts that interact with one another to identify synchronized cyber-attacks and to avert possible criminal actions. CIDS' principal objective is to improve the prediction performance of a single IDS node by comparing attack data across many sub-networks [70]. Thus, the CIDS encourages collaboration among

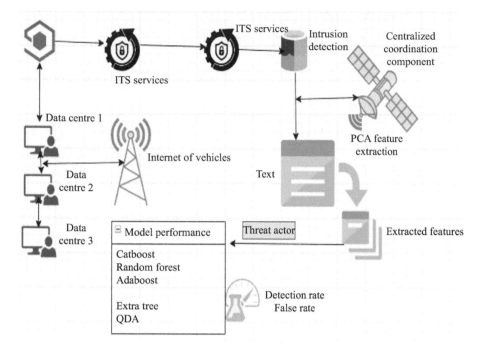

Figure 15.3 Architecture of the proposed MLBTID-ITS

nodes and enhances the capability to detect complex intrusions such as distributed denial of service (DDoS), malicious insiders, and DDoS [71].

15.3.1 Maintaining privacy with the use of blockchain technology and smart contracts

Blockchain-based privacy safeguarding in the ITS nodes expands on the concept of a blockchain agreement, which utilizes peer-to-peer technology to transmit encrypted information transactions in a distinct manner [72]. These encrypted communications establish a sequence of records or blocks that are saved on each contributing cloud node, ensuring the ledger's integrity, and preventing data from being removed or faked. Additionally, blockchain enables the construction of smart contracts, which are rule-based technologies that sit on multiple of the blockchain network and enforce data usage policy negotiation amongst cloud nodes involved [73]. These policy-based guidelines characterize each IDS node's raw data alerts as blockchain data transactions. Participating IDS node can leverage the blockchain consensus process to ensure the legitimacy and privacy of recorded warnings, thereby establishing persistent and tamper-resistant records of data utilization. While blockchain and smart contract technology eliminate any need for middlemen to secure data, they are insufficient to provide data privacy due to the public nature of all activities, especially in public network applications. Figure 15.4 shows a

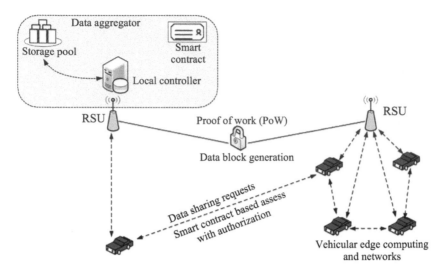

Figure 15.4   The study [74] proposes a blockchain-assisted data exchange strategy for automotive edge computing networks

blockchain-assisted data exchange strategy for automotive edge computing networks.

15.3.2   Collaborative IDS based on Machine Learning

As a result of its diverse approach and virtualization technology, the suggested collaborative intrusion detection system (CIDS) is designed and implemented on cloud computing infrastructure. Various cloud vendors may share log files and share alarm data on harmful software activity. Nevertheless, if these IDS systems are not recognized and integrated properly, the actual use of data sharing gets constrained.

When creating a cloud-based CIDS, the unique properties of cloud computing provide various obstacles. These added values include the ability to detect insider and outsider threats efficiently while minimizing false positives (FP) and false negatives (FN). The capacity to flexibly grow across several data center networks across the whole cloud. Additionally, the architecture would offer optimum security by mitigating zero-day flaws and ensuring authentication, integrity, and data confidentiality throughout all CIDS nodes [73]. Based on implicit trust, multiple IDSs in the same cloud domain cooperate to exchange data and notify intrusion occurrences.

Conversely, rogue nodes can offer misleading data and avoid aggregation's efficiency, like in the instance of colluding and treachery attacks [75]. One emerging concern in CIDS is to maintain data privacy and avoid assaults modifying data, monitoring, or communications during live data movement across multi-cloud operators. The raw alarm data gathered by the IDS sensors are exchanged between participants' entire network via a blockchain transaction.

15.3.3 IoV based on blockchain

Safe navigation and greater service quality are achieved in an IoV network by data exchange among vehicles in a lane. In the Internet of Things (IoT), the typical centralized management structure necessitates a lot of data and information storage. This demand presents numerous obstacles including real-time answers that are incompatible with the current design. Furthermore, data tampering of personal information submitted to the infrastructure could stymie IoV's future growth. As a result, blockchain technology improves the security, scalability, and fault tolerance of the system. The roadside units (RSU) is installed in the VANET environment with blockchain as the administrator. RSU contributes to the blockchain by recording information about passing cars. Because RSUs, gas pumps, and toll gates are all stationary, they operate as blockchain miner nodes. As shown in Figure 15.5, each car in the blockchain network is connected to neighboring peer vehicles. Vehicles employ data held in toll gates, petrol pumps, and RSU for quicker contact

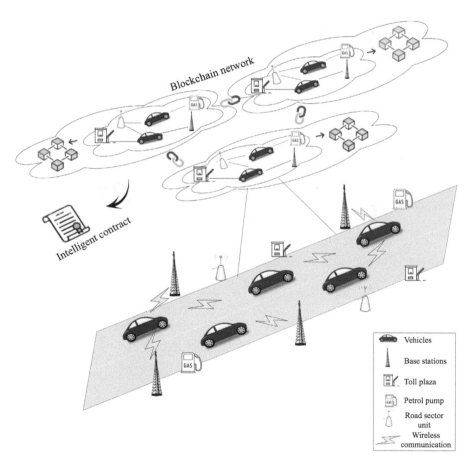

Figure 15.5   Blockchain-enabled IoV [76]

with infrastructure. In the blockchain network, each car is registered separately. Ethereum blockchain transactions take place when automobiles register with the help of RSU.

15.3.4   CatBoost

Yandex created CatBoost, a novel supervised learning algorithm, in 2017 [75]. Another gradient boosting version, CatBoost [77], contains a stage that uses permutation methods and target-based metrics to handle category information [78]. CatBoost effectively handles category characteristics during training and avoids the requirement for them to be converted before training [79]. It enhances decision trees using gradient boosting [75]. It requires less training time than other gradient boosting methods. Additionally, this approach is unique in that it instantly converts categorical attributes to numerical attributes. When determining the tree structure, the algorithm employs a novel schema for calculating leaf values, which reduces overfitting.

15.3.5   Random forest (RF)

RFs are ensemble learners that are used to analyze intrusion detection data for regression and classification [80]. The RF architecture is based on many decision trees, each one of which functions as a classifier [81]. Rather than that, some features are chosen at random from all the other features. Then, from the randomly chosen features, the optimal attributes are chosen [81,82]. In the training period, RF generates a variety of decision trees and outputs the target class for those with the majority vote [83]. RF achieves a high degree of classification accuracy and can deal with outliers and noise in the data. The RF algorithm is utilized in this study because it is less prone to overfitting and has previously demonstrated strong classification results [80].

15.3.6   AdaBoost classifier

AdaBoost is an adaptation boosting algorithm invented by Freund and Schapire [84,85]. AdaBoost, short for "Adaptive Boosting," is a way of boosting that creates a very accurate method by merging several simple ones [86]. AdaBoost is a well-known learning technique that can significantly improve the ability to characterize by several cycles [87,88]. AdaBoost proposed using weighted variations of the same training data rather than randomly selecting a portion of the training samples [89,90].

15.3.7   Extra tree (ET)

ET is a similar algorithm to the RF approach in that it fits multiple decision tree (DT) [91] to accomplish regression or classification [92,93]. ET is a supervised ML strategy that is similar to RF [94]. Additional tree classification [95] is nothing more than a completely random tree categorization. Additionally, because the entire sample is used in tree measurements, decision bounds should be viewed as random. This approach enables the use of bootstrap replicas of sample training and the determination of the optimum cut-off position for each randomized feature at a node. It alleviates the mathematical burden on typical trees and forests to calculate optimal ripped [95].

15.3.8   *Quadratic discriminant analysis*

linear discriminant analysis (LDA)Quadratic discriminant algorithms are fast and mathematically robust [96], and they frequently result in classifications with a precision of as much as effective as more complicated ones [97]. The quadratic discriminant analysis (QDA) is a generalized variant of the linear discriminant analysis (LDA) and can distinguish between only two types of points [98]. A quadratic core implies the independent variables have a quadratic relationship [99]. The discriminant function for quadratic functions presupposes that f(x) is a Gaussian with distinct variances and mean values [100].

15.4   Results and discussion

To assess the proposed MLB's efficiency, a secluded blockchain was established using Ethereum [49], an open-source blockchain system that enables users to create and operate private blockchains within organizational datasets, as well as a pre-processing module for evaluation. The Ethereum platform creates a digital engine runtime environment in which smart contracts can be launched and executed. The machine learning based technology intrusion detection system for intelligent transportation system (MLBTID-ITS) used the classifiers; CatBoost, RF, AdaBoost, ET, and QDA. The suggested MLBTID-ITS for intrusion detection in ITS was evaluated using the UNSW-NB15 network datasets. The accuracy, area under curve (AUC), recall, Mathew correlation coefficient (MCC), and training time were used to evaluate the performance of MLBTID-ITS. The suggested approach outperforms existing approaches in terms of maintaining privacy and recognizing attack activities, which can be ascribed to the IDS model's layered abstract of the data. By authenticating data transactions and collecting attributes from the source training data and verification of the IDS model, the blockchain and smart contracts' dual privacy model can accomplish perfect protection. Its first stage of the privacy-based blockchain verifies data security and checks records for potential poisoning by the attached hash chain, rendering malicious record change impossible. The data is then stored in the second phase using anomalous behavior identification as an instance of performance and efficiency measurement.

15.4.1   *Performance of the models with 25% training data of*
       UNSW-NB15

As can be seen in Table 15.2, the AdaBoost outperformed all the other models with 100% accuracy, 100% of the AUC, 100% recall, 100 MCC, and 0.13 seconds training time. The ET also gave competitive results with 100% accuracy, 100% of the AUC, 100% recall, 100 MCC, and 0. 1404 seconds training time. The cat boost

Table 15.2   Experimental analysis results with 25% training data of the models on UNSW-NB 15 dataset

Model	Accuracy	AUC	Recall	MCC	Training time (sec)
CatBoost	100	100	100	100	18.18
RF	99.99	100	100	99.97	0.1394
AdaBoost	100	100	100	100	0.13
ET	100	100	100	100	0.1404
Quadratic discriminant analysis	57.20	68.56	37.11	100	0.7847

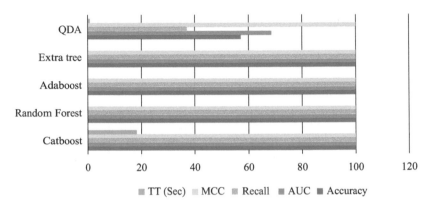

Figure 15.6   Performance of the proposed models with 25% training data on UNSW-NB15 dataset

classifier gave 100% accuracy, 100% of the AUC, 100% recall, 100 MCC, and 18.18 seconds training time. The RF revealed a 99.99% accuracy, 100% of the AUC, 100% recall, 99.97% MCC, and 0.1394 seconds training time. The QDA gave 57.2% accuracy, 68.56% of the AUC, 37.11% recall, 39.02% MCC, and 0.7847 seconds training time.

As illustrated in Figure 15.6, the AdaBoost algorithm performed better than other models in terms of accuracy, AUC, recall, MCC, and training time. AdaBoost has the lowest training time out of all the classification algorithms employed. The ET came second with training time lower than the RF, CatBoost, and QDA.

15.4.2   Performance of the models with 30% training data of UNSW-NB 15

As can be seen in Table 15.3, the AdaBoost outperformed all the other models with 100% accuracy, 100% of the AUC, 100% recall, 100 MCC, and 0.1475 seconds training time. The ET also gave competitive results with 100% accuracy, 100% of the AUC, 100% recall, 100 MCC, and 0.1538 seconds training time. The cat boost classifier gave 100% accuracy, 100% of the AUC, 100% recall, 100 MCC, and 18.18 seconds training time. The RF revealed a 99.97% accuracy, 100% of the

Table 15.3   *Experimental analysis results with 25% training data of the models on UNSW-NB 15 dataset*

Model	Accuracy	AUC	Recall	MCC	Training time (sec)
CatBoost	100	100	100	100	18.78
RF	99.97	100	99.99	99.93	0.19
AdaBoost	100	100	100	100	0.14
ET	100	100	100	100	0.15
Quadratic discriminant analysis	83.83	88.12	76.24	76.01	0.86

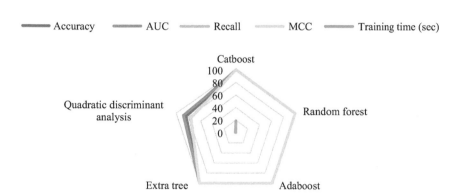

Figure 15.7   *Performance of the proposed models with 30% training data on UNSWNB-15 dataset*

AUC, 99.9% recall, 99.93% MCC, and 0.1956 seconds training time. The QDA gave 83.83% accuracy, 88.12% of the AUC, 76.24% recall, 76.01% MCC, and 0.868 seconds training time.

As shown in Figure 15.7, the AdaBoost model gave competitive performance than other proposed models. This showed that the AdaBoost model performed excellently on the two hold-out strategies employed in this research.

15.4.3   Comparison of attacks in existing methods and attacks considered in this research

For the past two decades, automobiles have piqued the curiosity of not just mechanical engineers but also computer engineers. Next-generation automobiles will be outfitted with onboard units (OBU) technology that lets them interact with other vehicles as well as roadside units, forming a communication network known as a VANET. The primary goal of VANET is to make roadways safer and more efficient by delivering timely information to other drivers and relevant authorities; this is known as ITS. The development of such networks has resulted in several security challenges concerning mobile and wireless communication as well as user privacy. VANETs are subject to numerous forms of attacks because of their open nature [19]. Inside attackers and outside attackers are two types of attackers. Table 15.4 lists some of the assaults that have been suggested in previous publications as well as the attacks that our article reviewed.

Table 15.4   Existing attacks in ITS reported in previous studies and attacks covered in this chapter

Existing attacks in ITS from the previous studies	Attacks considered in this chapter
Denial of service: This form of attack can be carried out by either an insider or an outsider to the network. An attacker can employ this technique to disrupt the network for legitimate users by flooding or jamming the signal	*Analysis*: It includes port scan, spam, and html file penetration assaults
Spamming: If there are spam messages in the VANET, they may increase the chance of transmission latency. Because VANET lacks some essential infrastructure and centralized administration, spamming is extremely difficult to control	*Fuzzers*: Attempting to stop a program or network by feeding it randomly generated data
Blackhole attack: When a node loses all messages sent to it for routing purposes, this is referred to as a black hole attack, or when a node refuses to participate in the network, this is referred to as a black hole attack	*Denial of service*: A malicious attempt to render a server or a network resource unavailable to users, typically by temporarily halting or suspending the services of an Internet-connected host
Replay attack: In a replay attack, an attacker continuously introduces data into the network to decrease network performance	*Generic*: Without regard for the structure of the block-cipher, a strategy works against all block ciphers (with a particular block and key size)
Message tempering: It jeopardizes genuineness. If an unauthorized user can alter the messages sent during vehicle-to-vehicle or vehicle-to-infrastructure connection, he or she may introduce false information into the network, endangering numerous lives	*Worms*: To propagate to additional systems, the attacker copies itself. It frequently spreads itself over a computer network, relying on security flaws on the target computer to get access to it
Position faking: Unsecure communication on a VANET can allow an attacker to change the vehicle's current position and send it on to other cars. In this manner, he broadcasts its false viewpoint, which may endanger countless lives	*Shellcode*: A short bit of code that is used as the payload in the exploit of a software vulnerability
Sybil attack: It is a sort of attack in which a malicious driver generates many phony identities to give the impression that there is significant traffic nearby so that traffic following him will select an alternate route and the attacker would receive an empty path	*Reconnaissance*: This contains all strikes that can replicate information-gathering attacks

15.5　Conclusion and future work

To identify cyber-attacks, we designed an MLBTID-ITS cooperative intrusion detection based on ML with blockchain technology for ITS. It is also intended to maintain privacy in its node. To be more precise, the privacy-preserving solution employs a hybrid approach that combines blockchain technology with a trusted execution environment to ensure the privacy of smart contracts while retaining their availability and integrity. Following that, the networking information is encrypted using ML models. Due to its resistance to data poisoning attacks and inference, the hybrid privacy-preserving technique provides superior performance. The identification approach is based on ML models: CatBoost, AdaBoost, RF, ET, and QDA that were assessed on the UNSW-NB15 data for categorizing attacks that leverage ITS. The suggested ID method outperformed existing techniques in terms of accuracy, recall, AUC, MCC, and training time. Additionally, it will serve as a decision-making tool, assisting consumers and ITS service providers in securely migrating their data. This study will be extended in the future by evaluating the framework's scalability and utility on a variety of real-world datasets.

References

[1]　M. Buinevich and A. Vladyko, "Forecasting Issues of Wireless Communication Networks' Cyber Resilience for An Intelligent Transportation System: An Overview of Cyber Attacks," *Information*, vol. 10, no. 1, p. 27, 2019, doi: 10.3390/info10010027.

[2]　A. Zubedi, Z. Jianqiu, Q. A. Arain, *et al.*, "Sustaining Low-Carbon Emission Development: An Energy Efficient Transportation Plan for CPEC," *J. Inf. Process. Syst.*, vol. 14, no. 2, pp. 322–345, 2018, doi: 10.3745/JIPS.04.0067.

[3]　Q. Li, F. Wang, J. Wang, and W. Li, "LSTM-Based SQL Injection Detection Method for Intelligent Transportation System," *IEEE Trans. Veh. Technol.*, vol. 68, no. 5, pp. 4182–4191, 2019, doi: 10.1109/TVT.2019.2893675.

[4]　L. F. Herrera-Quintero, J. C. Vega-Alfonso, K. B. A. Banse, and E. Carrillo Zambrano, "Smart ITS Sensor for the Transportation Planning Based on IoT Approaches Using Serverless and Microservices Architecture," *IEEE Intell. Transp. Syst. Mag.*, vol. 10, no. 2, pp. 17–27, 2018, doi: 10.1109/MITS.2018.2806620.

[5]　L. Li, J. Liu, L. Cheng, *et al.*, "CreditCoin: A Privacy-Preserving Blockchain-Based Incentive Announcement Network for Communications of Smart Vehicles," *IEEE Trans. Intell. Transp. Syst.*, vol. 19, no. 7, pp. 2204–2220, 2018, doi: 10.1109/TITS.2017.2777990.

[6]　M. Chaturvedi and S. Srivastava, "Multi-Modal Design of an Intelligent," *IEEE Trans. Intell. Transp. Syst.*, vol. 18, no. 8, pp. 1–11, 2016.

[7]　G. Xiong, D. Shen, X. Dong, B. Hu, D. Fan, and F. Zhu, "Parallel Transportation Management and Control System for Subways," *IEEE Trans.*

Intell. Transp. Syst., vol. 18, no. 7, pp. 1974–1979, 2017, doi: 10.1109/TITS.2016.2622282.

[8] D. Fernandez-Llorca, R. Q. Minguez, I. P. Alonso, *et al.*, "Assistive Intelligent Transportation Systems: The Need for User Localization and Anonymous Disability Identification," *IEEE Intell. Transp. Syst. Mag.*, vol. 9, no. 2, pp. 25–40, 2017, doi: 10.1109/MITS.2017.2666579.

[9] P. Sui, X. Li, and Y. Bai, "A Study of Enhancing Privacy for Intelligent Transportation Systems: K-Correlation Privacy Model Against Moving Preference Attacks for Location Trajectory Data," *IEEE Access*, vol. 5, pp. 24555–24567, 2017, doi: 10.1109/ACCESS.2017.2767641.

[10] F. Ahmad, A. Adnane, and V. N. L. Franqueira, "A Systematic Approach for Cyber Security in Vehicular Networks," *J. Comput. Commun.*, vol. 04, no. 16, pp. 38–62, 2016, doi: 10.4236/jcc.2016.416004.

[11] Y. K. Saheed, "Performance Improvement of Intrusion Detection System for Detecting Attacks on Internet of Things and Edge of Things," in S. Misra, K. A. Tyagi, V. Piuri, and L. Garg, Eds., *Artificial Intelligence for Cloud and Edge Computing. Internet of Things (Technology, Communications and Computing)*, Springer, Cham, 2022.

[12] G. Karagiannis, O. Altintas, E. Ekici, *et al.*, "Vehicular Networking: A Survey and Tutorial on Requirements, Architectures, Challenges, Standards and Solutions," *IEEE Commun. Surv. Tutorials*, vol. 13, no. 4, pp. 584–616, 2011, doi: 10.1109/SURV.2011.061411.00019.

[13] R. Shringar Raw, M. Kumar, and N. Singh, "Security Challenges, Issues and Their Solutions for Vanet," *Int. J. Netw. Secur. Its Appl.*, vol. 5, no. 5, pp. 95–105, 2013, doi: 10.5121/ijnsa.2013.5508.

[14] L. He and W. T. Zhu, "Mitigating DoS Attacks Against Signature-Based Authentication in VANETs," *CSAE 2012 – Proceedings, 2012 IEEE International Conference on Computer Science and Automation Engineering*, vol. 3, pp. 261–265, 2012, doi: 10.1109/CSAE.2012.6272951.

[15] H. Hasrouny, A. E. Samhat, C. Bassil, and A. Laouiti, "VANet Security Challenges and Solutions: A Survey," *Veh. Commun.*, vol. 7, no. January, pp. 7–20, 2017, doi: 10.1016/j.vehcom.2017.01.002.

[16] R. Rawat, S. Sharma, and R. Sushil, "Vanet: Security Attacks and Its Possible Solutions," *J. Inf. Oper. Manag.*, vol. 3, no. 1, pp. 301–304, 2014.

[17] J. T. Isaac, S. Zeadally, and J. S. Cámara, "Security Attacks and Solutions for Vehicular Ad Hoc Networks," *IET Commun.*, vol. 4, no. 7, pp. 894–903, 2010, doi: 10.1049/iet-com.2009.0191.

[18] G. Samara, W. A. H. Al-Salihy, and R. Sures, "Security analysis of Vehicular Ad Hoc Networks (VANET)," *Proc. – 2nd Int. Conf. Netw. Appl. Protoc. Serv. NETAPPS* 2010, pp. 55–60, 2010, doi: 10.1109/NETAPPS.2010.17.

[19] D. Kushwaha, P. Kumar Shukla, and R. Baraskar, "A Survey on Sybil Attack in Vehicular Ad-hoc Network," *Int. J. Comput. Appl.*, vol. 98, no. 15, pp. 31–36, 2014, doi: 10.5120/17262-7614.

[20]   A. M. Malla and R. K. Sahu, "Security Attacks with an Effective Solution for DOS Attacks in VANET," *Int. J. of Comput. Appl.*, vol. 66, no. 22, pp. 45–49, 2013.

[21]   A. Mpitziopoulos, D. Gavalas, C. Konstantopoulos, and G. Pantziou, "A Survey on Jamming Attacks and Countermeasures in WSNs," *IEEE Commun. Surv. Tutorials*, vol. 11, no. 4, pp. 42–56, 2009, doi: 10.1109/SURV.2009.090404.

[22]   L. Song, Q. Han, and J. Liu, "Investigate key management and authentication models in VANETs," *2011 Int. Conf. Electron. Commun. Control. ICECC 2011 – Proc.*, pp. 1516–1519, 2011, doi: 10.1109/ICECC.2011.6067807.

[23]   M. C. Chuang and J. F. Lee, "TEAM: Trust-Extended Authentication Mechanism for Vehicular Ad Hoc Networks," *IEEE Syst. J.*, vol. 8, no. 3, pp. 749–758, 2014, doi: 10.1109/JSYST.2012.2231792.

[24]   M. Raya and J. P. Hubaux, "The Security of Vehicular Ad Hoc Networks," *SASN'05 – Proc. 2005 ACM Work. Secur. Ad Hoc Sens. Networks*, vol. 2005, pp. 11–21, 2005, doi: 10.1145/1102219.1102223.

[25]   J. Guo, J. P. Baugh, and S. Wang, "A Group Signature Based Secure and Privacy-Preserving Vehicular Communication Framework," *2007 Mob. Netw. Veh. Environ. MOVE*, pp. 103–108, 2007, doi: 10.1109/MOVE.2007.4300813.

[26]   R. Rajadurai and N. Jayalakshmi, "Vehicular Network: Properties, Structure, Challenges, Attacks, Solutions for Improving Scalability and Security," *Int. J. Adv. Res.*, vol. 1, no. 3, pp. 41–50, 2013.

[27]   I. Memon, Q. Ali, A. Zubedi, and F. A. Mangi, "DPMM: Dynamic Pseudonym-Based Multiple Mix-Zones Generation for Mobile Traveler," *Multimed. Tools Appl.*, vol. 76, no. 22, pp. 24359–24388, 2017, doi: 10.1007/s11042-016-4154-z.

[28]   N. J. Patel and R. H. Jhaveri, "Trust Based Approaches for Secure Routing in VANET: A Survey," *Procedia Comput. Sci.*, vol. 45, no. C, pp. 592 601, 2015, doi: 10.1016/j.procs.2015.03.112.

[29]   S. Zeadally, R. Hunt, Y. S. Chen, A. Irwin, and A. Hassan, "Vehicular Ad Hoc Networks (VANETS): Status, Results, and Challenges," *Telecommun. Syst.*, vol. 50, no. 4, pp. 217–241, 2012, doi: 10.1007/s11235-010-9400-5.

[30]   J. C. Park and S. K. Kasera, "Securing Ad Hoc Wireless Networks Against Data Injection Attacks Using Firewalls," *IEEE Wirel. Commun. Netw. Conf. WCNC*, pp. 2843–2848, 2007, doi: 10.1109/WCNC.2007.527.

[31]   D. Singelee and B. Preneel, "Location Verification Using Secure Distance Bounding Protocols," *2nd IEEE Int. Conf. Mob. Ad-hoc Sens. Syst. MASS 2005*, vol. 2005, pp. 834–840, 2005, doi: 10.1109/MAHSS.2005.1542879.

[32]   A. M. Krishna and A. K. Tyagi, "Intrusion Detection in Intelligent Transportation System and its Applications using Blockchain Technology," *Int. Conf. Emerg. Trends Inf. Technol. Eng. ic-ETITE 2020*, pp. 1–8, 2020, doi: 10.1109/ic-ETITE47903.2020.332.

[33]   O. B. L. Y. K. Saheed, R. D. Magaji, and A. Tosho, "Adopting Machine Learning Blockchain Intrusion Detection for Protecting Attacks on Internet of Things," *Proceeding of the 27th iSTEAMS multidisciplinary Innovations*

&*Technology Transfer (MINTT) Conference, Academic City University College, Accra, Ghana*, 2021, pp. 343–354.

[34] O. Alkadi, N. Moustafa, B. Turnbull, and K.-K. R. Choo, "A Deep Blockchain Framework-enabled Collaborative Intrusion Detection for Protecting IoT and Cloud Networks," *IEEE Internet Things J.*, vol. 4662, no. c, pp. 1–1, 2020, doi: 10.1109/jiot.2020.2996590.

[35] G. W. Peters and E. Panayi, "Understanding Modern Banking Ledgers Through Blockchain Technologies: Future of Transaction Processing and Smart Contracts on the Internet of Money," *Banking Beyond Banks and Money*, 2016.

[36] M. Keshk, B. Turnbull, N. Moustafa, D. Vatsalan, and K. K. R. Choo, "A Privacy-Preserving-Framework-Based Blockchain and Deep Learning for Protecting Smart Power Networks," *IEEE Trans. Ind. Informatics*, vol. 16, no. 8, pp. 5110–5118, 2020, doi: 10.1109/TII.2019.2957140.

[37] F. S. Hardwick, A. Gioulis, R. N. Akram, and K. Markantonakis, "E-Voting with Blockchain: An E-Voting Protocol with Decentralisation and Voter Privacy," *Proc. – IEEE 2018 Int. Congr. Cybermatics 2018 IEEE Conf. Internet Things, Green Comput. Commun. Cyber, Phys. Soc. Comput. Smart Data, Blockchain, Comput. Inf. Technol. iThings/Gree*, pp. 1561–1567, 2018, doi: 10.1109/Cybermatics_2018.2018.00262.

[38] M. A. Khan and K. Salah, "IoT Security: Review, Blockchain Solutions, and Open Challenges," *Futur. Gener. Comput. Syst.*, vol. 82, pp. 395–411, 2018, doi: 10.1016/j.future.2017.11.022.

[39] T. M. Fernández-Caramés and P. Fraga-Lamas, "A Review on the Use of Blockchain for the Internet of Things," *IEEE Access*, vol. 6, no. c, pp. 32979–33001, 2018, doi: 10.1109/ACCESS.2018.2842685.

[40] C. K. Oh, M. Neurath, J. J. Cho, T. Semere, and D. D. Metcalfe, "A Supply Chain Traceability System for Food Safety Based on HACCP, Blockchain & Internet of Things," *Biochem. J.*, vol. 323, no. 2, pp. 511–519, 1997, doi: 10.1042/bj3230511.

[41] S. A. Abeyratne and R. P. Monfared, "Blockchain Ready Manufacturing Supply Chain Using Distributed Ledger," *Int. J. Res. Eng. Technol.*, vol. 05, no. 09, pp. 1–10, 2016, doi: 10.15623/ijret.2016.0509001.

[42] X. Yue, H. Wang, D. Jin, M. Li, and W. Jiang, "Healthcare Data Gateways: Found Healthcare Intelligence on Blockchain with Novel Privacy Risk Control," *J. Med. Syst.*, vol. 40, no. 10, 2016, doi: 10.1007/s10916-016-0574-6.

[43] W. Meng, E. W. Tischhauser, Q. Wang, Y. Wang, and J. Han, "When Intrusion Detection Meets Blockchain Technology: A Review," *IEEE Access*, vol. 6, no. c, pp. 10179–10188, 2018, doi: 10.1109/ACCESS.2018.2799854.

[44] S. Ølnes, J. Ubacht, and M. Janssen, "Blockchain in Government: Benefits and Implications of Distributed Ledger Technology for Information Sharing," *Gov. Inf. Q.*, vol. 34, no. 3, pp. 355–364, 2017, doi: 10.1016/j.giq.2017.09.007.

[45] A. Alketbi, Q. Nasir, and M. A. Talib, "Blockchain for Government Services – Use Cases, Security Benefits and Challenges," *2018 15th Learn. Technol. Conf. L T 2018*, pp. 112–119, 2018, doi: 10.1109/LT.2018.8368494.

[46] S. Mishra and A. K. Tyagi, "Intrusion Detection in Internet of Things (IoTs) Based Applications using Blockchain Technolgy," 2019 Third International conference on I-SMAC (IoT in Social, Mobile, Analytics and Cloud) (I-SMAC), 2019, pp. 123–128, doi: 10.1109/I-SMAC47947.2019.9032557.

[47] Y. K. Saheed and F. E. Hamza-Usman, "Feature Selection with IG-R for Improving Performance of Intrusion Detection System," *Int. J. Commun. Networks Inf. Secur.*, vol. 12, no. 3, pp. 338–344, 2020.

[48] F. Tschorsch and B. Scheuermann, "Bitcoin and Beyond: A Technical Survey on Decentralized Digital Currencies," *IEEE Commun. Surv. Tutorials*, vol. 18, no. 3, pp. 2084–2123, 2016, doi: 10.1109/COMST.2016.2535718.

[49] G. Wood, "Ethereum: A Secure Decentralised Generalised Transaction Ledger," *Ethereum Proj. yellow Pap.*, vol. 151, pp. 1–32, 2014.

[50] X. Liang, S. Shetty, D. Tosh, C. Kamhoua, K. Kwiat, and L. Njilla, "ProvChain: A Blockchain-Based Data Provenance Architecture in Cloud Environment with Enhanced Privacy and Availability," *Proc. – 2017 17th IEEE/ACM Int. Symp. Clust. Cloud Grid Comput. CCGRID 2017*, pp. 468–477, 2017, doi: 10.1109/CCGRID.2017.8.

[51] M. A. Javed, E. Ben Hamida, and W. Znaidi, "Security in Intelligent Transport Systems for Smart Cities: From Theory to Practice," *Sensors*, vol. 16, p. 879, 2016, doi: 10.3390/s16060879.

[52] Z. Lu, W. Liu, Q. Wang, G. Qu, and Z. Liu, "A Privacy-Preserving Trust Model based on Blockchain for VANETs," *IEEE Access*, vol. PP, no. c, p. 1, 2018, doi: 10.1109/ACCESS.2018.2864189.

[53] A. Lei, H. Cruickshank, Y. Cao, P. Asuquo, C. P. A. Ogah, and Z. Sun, "Blockchain-Based Dynamic Key Management for Heterogeneous Intelligent Transportation Systems," *IEEE Internet Things J.*, vol. 4, no. 6, pp. 1832–1843, 2017, doi: 10.1109/JIOT.2017.2740569.

[54] M. B. Mollah, J. Zhao, D. Niyato, *et al.*, "Blockchain for the Internet of Vehicles towards Intelligent Transportation Systems: A Survey," *IEEE Internet Things J.*, vol. 8, no. 6, pp. 4157–4185, 2021, doi: 10.1109/JIOT.2020.3028368.

[55] H. X. Liu, X. He, and W. Recker, "Estimation of the Time-Dependency of Values of Travel Time and Its Reliability from Loop Detector Data," *Transp. Res. Part B Methodol.*, vol. 41, no. 4, pp. 448–461, 2007, doi: 10.1016/j.trb.2006.07.002.

[56] K. Nordback, S. Kothuri, T. Phillips, C. Gorecki, and M. Figliozzi, "Accuracy of Bicycle Counting with Pneumatic Tubes in Oregon," *Transp. Res. Rec.*, vol. 2593, no. 2593, pp. 8–17, 2016, doi: 10.3141/2593-02.

[57] A. Sumalee and H. W. Ho, "Smarter and More Connected: Future Intelligent Transportation System," *IATSS Res.*, vol. 42, no. 2, pp. 67–71, 2018, doi: 10.1016/j.iatssr.2018.05.005.

[58]   A. Danalet, B. Farooq, and M. Bierlaire, "A Bayesian Approach to Detect Pedestrian Destination-Sequences from WiFi Signatures," *Transp. Res. Part C Emerg. Technol.*, vol. 44, pp. 146–170, 2014, doi: 10.1016/j. trc.2014.03.015.

[59]   N. Bißmeyer, C. Stresing, and K. M. Bayarou, "Intrusion Detection in VANETs Through Verification of Vehicle Movement Data, 2010 IEEE Vehicular Networking Conference, VNC 2010," IEEE, Jersey City, New Jersey, USA, pp. 166–173, 2010.

[60]   S.-M. Senouci and H. S. Tarek Bouali, "A Distributed Detection and Prevention Scheme from Malicious Nodes in Vehicular Networks," *Int. J. Commun. Syst.*, vol. 23, no. 5, pp. 633–652, 2016, doi: 10.1002/dac.

[61]   K. Zaidi, M. B. Milojevic, V. Rakocevic, A. Nallanathan, and M. Rajarajan, "Host-Based Intrusion Detection for VANETs: A Statistical Approach to Rogue Node Detection," *IEEE Trans. Veh. Technol.*, vol. 65, no. 8, pp. 6703–6714, 2016, doi: 10.1109/TVT.2015.2480244.

[62]   R. Mitchell and I. R. Chen, "A Survey of Intrusion Detection in Wireless Network Applications," *Comput. Commun.*, vol. 42, pp. 1–23, 2014, doi: 10.1016/j.comcom.2014.01.012.

[63]   A. Dorri, M. Steger, S. S. Kanhere, and R. Jurdak, "A Blockchain-Based Solution to Automotive Security and Privacy," *Blockchain Distrib. Syst. Secur.*, December, pp. 95–115, 2019, doi: 10.1002/9781119519621.ch5.

[64]   K. Kaur, S. Garg, G. Kaddoum, F. Gagnon, and S. H. Ahmed, "Blockchain-Based Lightweight Authentication Mechanism for Vehicular Fog Infrastructure," *2019 IEEE Int. Conf. Commun. Work. ICC Work. 2019 – Proc.*, pp. 1–6, 2019, doi: 10.1109/ICCW.2019.8757184.

[65]   J. Noh, S. Jeon, and S. Cho, "Distributed Blockchain-Based Message Authentication Scheme for Connected Vehicles," *Electronics*, vol. 9, no. 1, 2020, doi: 10.3390/electronics9010074.

[66]   Y. Mu, F. Rezaeibagha, and K. Huang, "Policy-Driven Blockchain and Its Applications for Transport Systems," *IEEE Trans. Serv. Comput.*, vol. 13, no. 2, pp. 230–240, 2020, doi: 10.1109/TSC.2019.2947892.

[67]   B. Luo, X. Li, J. Weng, J. Guo, and J. Ma, "Blockchain Enabled Trust-Based Location Privacy Protection Scheme in VANET," *IEEE Trans. Veh. Technol.*, vol. 69, no. 2, pp. 2034–2048, 2020, doi: 10.1109/ TVT.2019.2957744.

[68]   C. Xu, H. Liu, P. Li, and P. Wang, "A Remote Attestation Security Model Based on Privacy-Preserving Blockchain for V2X," *IEEE Access*, vol. 6, no. c, pp. 67809–67818, 2018, doi: 10.1109/ACCESS.2018.2878995.

[69]   B. Chen, L. Wu, H. Wang, L. Zhou, and D. He, "A Blockchain-Based Searchable Public-Key Encryption with Forward and Backward Privacy for Cloud-Assisted Vehicular Social Networks," *IEEE Trans. Veh. Technol.*, vol. PP, no. 1, p. 1, 2020, doi: 10.1109/TVT.2019.2959383.

[70]   A. Patel, M. Taghavi, K. Bakhtiyari, and J. Celestino Júnior, "An Intrusion Detection and Prevention System in Cloud Computing: A Systematic

Review," *J. Netw. Comput. Appl.*, vol. 36, no. 1, pp. 25–41, 2013, doi: 10.1016/j.jnca.2012.08.007.

[71] M. Ahmed, A. Naser Mahmood, and J. Hu, "A Survey of Network Anomaly Detection Techniques," *J. Netw. Comput. Appl.*, vol. 60, pp. 19–31, 2016, doi: 10.1016/j.jnca.2015.11.016.

[72] G. Liang, S. R. Weller, F. Luo, J. Zhao, and Z. Y. Dong, "Distributed Blockchain-Based Data Protection Framework for Modern Power Systems Against Cyber Attacks," *IEEE Trans. Smart Grid*, vol. 10, no. 3, pp. 3162–3173, 2019, doi: 10.1109/TSG.2018.2819663.

[73] G. Creech, J. Slay, and N. Moustafa, *Anomaly Detection System Using Beta Mixture Models and Outlier Detection*, vol. 710, Springer, Singapore, 2018.

[74] J. Kang, R. Yu, X. Huang, M. Wu, and S. Maharjan, "Blockchain for Secure and Efficient Data Sharing in Vehicular Edge Computing and Networks," *IEEE Internet of Things J.*, vol. 6, no. 3, pp. 4660–4670, 2019.

[75] W. Li, W. Meng, L. Kwok, and H. H. S. Ip, "Enhancing Collaborative Intrusion Detection Networks Against Insider Attacks Using Supervised Intrusion Sensitivity-Based Trust Management Model," *J. Netw. Comput. Appl.*, vol. 77, pp. 135–145, 2016, doi: 10.1016/j.jnca.2016.09.014.

[76] Y. Manaswini, G. D. Vivekanandan, H. Sampath, K. Dev, and A. K. Bashir, "AI-Powered Blockchain – A Decentralized Secure Multiparty Computation Protocol for IoV," *Sustainability*, vol. 13, pp. 865–870, 2021.

[77] A. V. Dorogush, V. Ershov, and A. Gulin, "CatBoost: Gradient boosting with categorical features support," *arXiv*, pp. 1–7, 2018.

[78] S. Bhandari, A. K. Kukreja, A. Lazar, A. Sim, and K. Wu, "Feature Selection Improves Tree-based Classification for Wireless Intrusion Detection," *SNTA 2020 – Proc. 3rd Int. Work. Syst. Netw. Telem. Anal.*, pp. 19–26, 2020, doi: 10.1145/3391812.3396274.

[79] A. Lazar, A. Sim, and K. Wu, "GPU-based Classification for Wireless Intrusion Detection," SNTA'21: Proceedings of the 2021 on Systems and Network Telemetry and Analytics, pp. 27–31, 2020, doi: 10.1145/3452411.3464445.

[80] I. Ahmad, M. Basheri, M. J. Iqbal, and A. Rahim, "Performance Comparison of Support Vector Machine, Random Forest, and Extreme Learning Machine for Intrusion Detection," *IEEE Access*, vol. 6, no. c, pp. 33789–33795, 2018, doi: 10.1109/ACCESS.2018.2841987.

[81] X. K. Li, W. Chen, Q. Zhang, and L. Wu, "Building Auto-Encoder Intrusion Detection System Based on Random Forest Feature Selection," *Comput. Secur.*, vol. 95, p. 101851, 2020, doi: 10.1016/j.cose.2020.101851.

[82] A. Verma and V. Ranga, "Machine Learning Based Intrusion Detection Systems for IoT Applications," *Wirel. Pers. Commun.*, vol. 111, no. 4, pp. 2287–2310, 2020, doi: 10.1007/s11277-019-06986-8.

[83] Y. K. Saheed and M. O. Arowolo, "Efficient Cyber Attack Detection on the Internet of Medical Things-Smart Environment Based on Deep Recurrent Neural Network and Machine Learning Algorithms," *IEEE Access*, vol. 9, pp. 161546–161554, 2021, doi: 10.1109/ACCESS.2021.3128837.

[84]   Y. Freund and R. E. Schapire, "A Decision-Theoretic Generalization of On-Line Learning and an Application to Boosting," *J. Comput. Syst. Sci.*, vol. 55, pp. 119–139, 1997, doi: 10.1145/2818346.2823306.

[85]   Z.-H. Zhou, *Ensemble Methods, Foundations and Algorithms*, CRC Press Taylor & Francis Group, London, 2012.

[86]   Y. Yuan, L. Huo, Y. Yuan, and Z. Wang, "Semi-supervised Tri-Adaboost Algorithm for Network Intrusion Detection," *Int. J. Distrib. Sens. Networks*, vol. 15, no. 6, 2019, doi: 10.1177/1550147719846052.

[87]   A. Yulianto, P. Sukarno, and N. A. Suwastika, "Improving AdaBoost-Based Intrusion Detection System (IDS) Performance on CIC IDS 2017 Dataset," *J. Phys. Conf. Ser.*, vol. 1192, no. 1, 2019, doi: 10.1088/1742-6596/1192/1/012018.

[88]   Y. Zhou, T. A. Mazzuchi, and S. Sarkani, "M-AdaBoost–A Based Ensemble System for Network Intrusion Detection," *Expert Syst. Appl.*, vol. 162, no. April, p. 113864, 2020, doi: 10.1016/j.eswa.2020.113864.

[89]   A. Shahraki, M. Abbasi, and Ø. Haugen, "Boosting Algorithms for Network Intrusion Detection: A Comparative Evaluation of Real AdaBoost, Gentle AdaBoost and Modest AdaBoost," *Eng. Appl. Artif. Intell.*, vol. 94, no. February, p. 103770, 2020, doi: 10.1016/j.engappai.2020.103770.

[90]   M. A. Hambali, Y. K. Saheed, T. O. Oladele, and M. D. Gbolagade, "Adaboost Ensemble Algorithms for Breast Cancer Classification," *J. Adv. Comput. Res. Q.*, vol. 10, no. 2, pp. 1–10, 2019.

[91]   N. B. Olaniyi, A. Sulaiman, S. Yakub Kayode, H. Moshood Abiola and T. T. Salau-Ibrahim, "Student's Performance Analysis Using Decision Tree Algorithms," *Ann. Comput. Sci. Ser.*, vol. XV, pp. 55–62, 2017.

[92]   S. M. Kasongo and Y. Sun, "Deep Learning Method with Wrapper Based Feature Extraction for Wireless Intrusion Detection System," *Comput. Secur.*, vol. 92, 2020, doi: 10.1016/j.cose.2020.101752.

[93]   Y. K. Saheed, T. O. Oladele, A. O. Akanni, and W. M. Ibrahim, "Student Performance Prediction Based on Data Mining Classification Techniques," *Niger. J. Technol.*, vol. 37, no. 4, p. 1087, 2018, doi: 10.4314/njt.v37i4.31.

[94]   R. Patgiri, U. Varshney, T. Akutota, and R. Kunde, "An Investigation on Intrusion Detection System Using Machine Learning," *Proc. 2018 IEEE Symp. Ser. Comput. Intell. SSCI 2018*, pp. 1684–1691, 2019, doi: 10.1109/SSCI.2018.8628676.

[95]   B. A. Ashwini and S. S. Manivannan, "Supervised Machine Learning Classification Algorithmic Approach for Finding Anomaly Type of Intrusion Detection in Wireless Sensor Network," *Opt. Mem. Neural Networks (Inf. Opt.)*, vol. 29, no. 3, pp. 244–256, 2020, doi: 10.3103/S1060992X20030029.

[96]   K. M. A. Alheeti, A. Gruebler, and K. McDonald-Maier, "Using Discriminant Analysis to Detect Intrusions in External Communication for Self-Driving Vehicles," *Digit. Commun. Networks*, vol. 3, no. 3, pp. 180–187, 2017, doi: 10.1016/j.dcan.2017.03.001.

[97]   T. Rasymas and V. Rudžionis, "Evaluation of Methods to Combine Different Speech Recognizers," *Proc. 2015 Fed. Conf. Comput. Sci. Inf. Syst. FedCSIS 2015*, vol. 5, pp. 1043–1047, 2015, doi: 10.15439/2015F62.

[98]   S. Bhattacharyya, A. Khasnobish, S. Chatterjee, A. Konar, and D. N. Tibarewala, "Performance analysis of LDA, QDA and KNN Algorithms in Left-Right Limb Movement Classification from EEG Data," *Int. Conf. Syst. Med. Biol. ICSMB 2010 Proc.*, pp. 126–131, 2010, doi: 10.1109/ICSMB.2010.5735358.

[99]   F. Salo, M. N. Injadat, A. Moubayed, A. B. Nassif, and A. Essex, "Clustering Enabled Classification using Ensemble Feature Selection for Intrusion Detection," *2019 Int. Conf. Comput. Netw. Commun. ICNC 2019*, pp. 276–281, 2019.

[100]   X. Shi, Y. Cai, and Y. Yang, "Extreme Trees Network Intrusion Detection Framework Based on Ensemble Learning," *Proc. 2020 IEEE Int. Conf. Adv. Electr. Eng. Comput. Appl. AEECA 2020*, pp. 91–95, 2020, doi: 10.1109/AEECA49918.2020.9213695.

Chapter 16

Blockchain-enabled Internet of Things (IoTs) platforms for vehicle sensing and transportation monitoring

Ömer Melih Gül[1]

Abstract

Technical evolution of Internet of Things (IoTs) shifts its power, storage, and computational capabilities away from centralized cloud platforms to a decentralized IoT edge. Traditional security policies may not be effective against modification attacks, eavesdropping, distributed denial-of-service (DDoS) because of large attack surface area in IoT where devices cannot have their own ID and cannot keep their privacy and resiliency to the cyber-attacks. Blockchain can support secure, transparent, immutable data and computation-intensive applications such as services for factory automation, assisted living and automotive driving, transportation monitoring and vehicular networks. In addition, for facilitating blockchain applications at low-power mobile IoT systems, mobile edge computing (MEC) can be a convenient alternative for solving consensus protocols for mobile IoT users (offloading to MEC providers).

In this chapter, blockchain-enabled IoT platforms and solutions for vehicle sensing and transportation monitoring from various aspects are investigated. After providing a more general background, we consider vehicular networks and blockchain applications. In a typical vehicular network, a large number of vehicles need ultra-reliable, low-latency communications and secure, transparent, immutable data sharing to avoid multiple-vehicle collisions. Therefore, we consider blockchain applications in vehicular networks for more scalable, transparent, and secure Internet of Vehicles (IoV). In addition, we consider cybersecurity issues in Internet of Drones (IoD) and unmanned traffic monitoring (UTM) systems and then provide the existing blockchain-based solutions/platforms for these problems.

With 5G of mobile broadband systems, blockchain needs to deal with scalability problems due to a very large number of users in IoV. Artificial intelligence (AI) techniques can be applied with blockchain in connected vehicles in this manner. Implementing AI techniques can provide more scalable, transparent, and secure blockchain applications in vehicular networks. AI techniques also help blockchain achieve privacy and personalization for the users in IoV at the same

[1]Department of Electrical and Electronics Engineering, Middle East Technical University, Turkey

time. In the sequel, we consider more lightweight protocols for more scalable blockchains. Moreover, we consider the solutions of game-theoretic models to jointly maximize the profit of the MEC service provider and the individual utilities of the miners. Then, we can consider resource–provision problems under different pricing schemes offered by MEC service providers. Finally, we conclude the chapter.

Keywords: Blockchain; Internet of Things; Vehicle sensing; Transportation

16.1 Introduction

Internet of Things (IoT) not only brings lots of opportunities but also helps emergence of many other crucial paradigm like Industry 4.0, smart cities, etc. As a typical IoT network has the new devices other than computers/laptops, it is more susceptible to cyber-attacks. Most of IoT infrastructure has centralized structure that hinders scalability and its wide adoption in addition to its challenges in security and privacy manner [1]. For bringing a solution for these issues, IoT devices require more distributed and lightweight protocols than the existing solutions for a typical network of computers.

Especially in the last decade, blockchain emerged a very promising security and privacy-preserving solution for IoT networks including IoV [2]. In last dozens of years, lots of papers on blockchain was published in various subtopics [3]. Blockchains provide security, privacy, transparency, decentralization for the system, and data-tamper proofness. However, they depend energy highly and their implementations are hard due to synchronization.

In a centralized system, each user communicates with others via middlemen because of no trust between them. In a decentralized system, each user communicates with others via blockchain because of no trust between them [4].

The remainder of this chapter is organized as follows. Section 16.2 investigates security issues and challenges where we consider the disadvantages of centralized security and simple replication protocols in IoV. Section 16.3 studies security threats and countermeasures in IoV where we investigate the differences between the former IoT systems & blockchain and then its data immutability against malicious attack. Section 16.4 presents blockchain mechanisms and algorithms in IoV. Section 16.5 presents security issues in IoD and UTM systems. Section 16.6 presents innovative blockchain solutions for IoV. Section 16.7 presents innovative blockchain solutions for IoD. Section 16.8 presents blockchain applications in Industrial IoV. Section 16.9 presents future possible research directions. Section 16.10 concludes this chapter.

16.2 The security issues and challenges in IoV

In this section, we investigate security issues and challenges in IoV. First, we consider the security issues including malicious attacks in IoV such as majority attacks, Finey attacks, MitM attacks, DDoS attacks, DoS attacks, or Sybil attacks. Then, we consider challenges/disadvantages of some of the existing solutions which are based on centralized security protocols or simple replication protocols in IoV.

16.2.1   Disadvantages of centralized security & simple replication protocols in IoV

Blockchain can be a promising security solution for IoV. Despite promising future of the blockchain, the following questions need to be asked by considering the current examples of blockchain and their drawbacks/requirements or implementation difficulties.

1.   In the IoV, do we need blockchains?
2.   Is that a necessity or a high-cost option?

Nevertheless, disadvantages of centralized security protocols for IoV are shortly provided as:

- Availability is very crucial issue for centralized security protocols [5]. While centralized systems are under malicious attack, users face service problem.
- Extensive amount of delay and energy are required for the data communication between centralized security and each vehicle in IoV so the centralized security is an inefficient option particularly for large vehicular networks.
- We need to consider the complex topologies of vehicles and wireless medium between each vehicle-pair in IoV. In large vehicular networks, centralized security might lose communication opportunities with a portion of vehicles because of security/other problems whereas neighbor vehicles keep their communication with those vehicles. As centralized security is not able to communicate with them because of wireless channel conditions, it might be render helpless to vehicle clusters where some of the vehicles suffers from other problems. Consequently, depending on wireless medium conditions, the delay with centralized security may be much greater than any simple or complex distributed security protocols particularly in large-sized vehicular networks.
- The scalability issues of centralized security protocols prevent them from enabling security of wide-sized vehicular networks. By the advances in IoT technology, a network capacity in 2022 is expected to be 1000 times than the capacity in 2016 [6]. Moreover, this exponential growth is expected to continue within forthcoming years.
- Single point of failures is quite common type of security problems for centralized protocols. See the following example.

Example 1 (Snowden): In the sequel of leaks by Snowden, technological partners cannot be trusted as they give access & control to authorities for collecting & analyzing the data risking users' anonymity and privacy. They should adapt open-source approaches to improve trust and transparency [7].

Hence, central security is an inappropriate solution for Industrial IoT. As a result, distributed protocols can be utilized in robot clusters for reducing amount of consumed energy, solving scalability & single-point-of-failure problems and also meeting latency constraint. As a result, simple replication algorithms are candidate solutions for smart factories if each robot trusts others and no malicious attack exists.

However, simple replication algorithms have following drawbacks:

- If any distributed security protocol does not exist, then all IoT nodes in smart factory are vulnerable to malicious attack like DoS attack. This is the most fundamental security problem of IoT compared to Internet of Computers (see the following example).* Blockchain may bring some cost of latency compared with simple replication protocols. However, unless blockchain is used in IoT networks, there arise numerous potential threats which include proxy/replay attack and man-in-the-middle (MitM) attack [6]. To eliminate those potential threats, an IoT network equipped with blockchain signs those records cryptographically and verify signatures to ensure that they originate from each of related devices.
- Consumer and industrial IoT devices are susceptible of malicious attacks [8].
- Security in smart grid is another significant concern for Industrial IoTs. Although a smart factory including only machines/robots needs no energy for illumination, it may still need extensive energy in some manufacturing stages in Industrial IoT era. As a common type of security problems, hacker may perform malicious attacks to a very critical factory in another country because of various reasons.
- Due to the lack of their IDs, IoT devices cannot maintain resiliency and their privacy to malicious attack.

Example 2 (Dyn): As an example, in October 2016 [6], Dyn, a DNS provider, dealt with cyber-attacks caused by "millions of IP addresses" and intensive traffic from IoT devices. Those devices were infected with Mirai malware. It uses those devices for launching DDoS attacks, which shows vulnerability level of security of the IoT devices.

Consequently, strong security precautions should be taken especially for preventing vehicles to be broken down or crash each other. The vehicles need more efficient security protocols (totally/partially) for keeping their resiliency and privacy against malicious attacks and keep the transparency of the vehicular network in case of (communication) failed vehicles.

16.3   The security threats and countermeasures in IoV

In this section, we investigate counter measures against security issues and challenges in IoV. First, we consider main differences of blockchain systems from the existing systems based on centralized security or simple replication protocols in IoV. Then, we consider the tamper-proofness of blockchain against malicious attacks in IoV such as majority attacks, Finey attacks, MitM attacks, DDoS attacks, DoS attacks, or Sybil attacks.

---

*For the details of the example in October 2016 about Dyn, a DNS provider, see [6].

16.3.1 Main differences of blockchain systems from past systems in IoV

What is the fundamental new thing we can do with blockchain that is different from past systems and how can we evaluate that well? Although blockchain is a promising security technology for IoT, the place hosting blockchain still stays as a debatable topic. As IoT nodes generally have low-power and resource constraint, clouds and fogs (edges) can be considered as the host places for blockchain. Although cloud has much larger resource capacity than the fogs, it has a centralized architecture compared with the fog (edge) and suffers from the higher consumed energy for the IoT node-cloud communications and the latency than fog [9]. Especially for the security in the latency-sensitive applications in the resource-constrained IoT nodes, fog computing can be preferred with lightweight blockchain protocols (for the consensus, PoS-based protocol may be used instead of PoW-based protocols). Based on the constraints, characteristics, and challenges of IoT devices, various models are suggested for IoT and blockchain combination in literature. There are three main approaches: IoT–IoT, IoT–blockchain, and hybrid approach [10].

- IoT–IoT approach is used for the communications between fully trusted IoT nodes. IoT data will be partly kept at blockchains while IoT interaction takes place without blockchains. It can be applied for the scenario with reliable IoT interactions with low latency requirements. In Industry 4.0, this approach (or simple replication protocols) can be used for fully trusted robots which worked at the fault tolerant stages of the manufacture.
- IoT–blockchain approach is used for the communications between trustless IoT nodes. This approach is quite applicable for trading (smart contract) & quality control scenario in order to obtain reliability & security; however, to record each interaction increases bandwidth & data resource consumption.
- In hybrid approach, interaction/s places partly at blockchains and IoT devices share remainder directly.

16.3.2 Tamper-proofness of blockchain against malicious attacks in IoV

Blockchain utilizes numerous methods to achieve highest level security in transaction. Blockchain utilizes public keys for encrypting data and private keys for decrypting data in a secure manner. Blockchain deals with numerous security problems like 51% majority attack by malicious attacks. First, blockchain eliminate forking problem and 51% majority attacks by deciding longest chain as authentic block [11]. When one of the participants in the blockchain dominates majority of the mining power, majority attack emerges and that participant can control consensus of the network. Advances in mining pools increase probability of majority attacks that can close with integrity of blockchain [12].

Under double-spend attacks, although the victim has already delivered the service, the victim cannot receive a validated payment. Bitcoin users avoid this problem by waiting for confirmations during the payments. There exist multiple variants of these attacks. The race attacks work only for fast payment scenarios. The users send unconfirmed transactions directly to that merchant accepting the transaction without blockchain confirmations. Meanwhile, they broadcast conflicting transactions toward blockchain. Since the merchant saw their own transaction first, they seem to get paid, whereas the rest saw the double-spend first and thus that merchant seems not to get paid. Second, one of the transactions will probably be confirmed, and that merchant is cheated. Moreover, Finey attacks, MitM, DoS, or Sybil can prevent network operation [13].

As other solution for majority attacks, private blockchains are more efficient solution candidates than public blockchains [14]. Known validators save the private blockchain against majority attacks. That group provides high-level of privacy to read restricted permissions (permissioned blockchains). The transactions in the private blockchains are cheaper as fewer validators use less processing power. In addition, each validator can alter rules of private blockchain, return transactions, and set the balance.

A security company Gladius proposes solution for security issues by DDoS attacks for achieving majority [15]. That firm allows people to pool their available bandwidth which can be used for either mitigating against DDoS attacks or hosting static files. As hackers need to simultaneously subvert multiple nodes to mount attacks in decentralized networks, the result of this strategy will be revolutionary. Moreover, developers and consumers can communicate directly with each other by allowing for tailor made solution (cutting out the middleman). This can be considered as great development over centralized platforms which massive DDoS attacks can target easily. In addition, massive bandwidth pools created by Gladius will easily be able to handle information flood caused by DDoS attacks. Furthermore, as many users will oversee Gladius simultaneously, malicious activities are spotted quickly. It also creates revenue streams.

16.4   Blockchain mechanisms or algorithms in IoV

We can begin this brief background with very popular definition for blockchain [16].

Definition 1 (Blockchain): The blockchain is an incorruptible digital ledger of economic transaction that can be programmed to record no just financial transactions but virtually everything of value.

From [17,18], the basic operation/mechanisms of blockchain can be briefly explained as follows.

Blockchain participant A wants to transfer digital coins to another participant B. By using user's wallet, A's device requires for making a transaction. They generally use mobile devices like computers with low-processing capability, laptop, and smartphone in order to make transactions. A's private key sign the transactions digitally and B's public key encrypt the contents of these transactions if required. In the sequel, A's device sends those transactions through the peer-to-peer network system including nodes which are high-processing devices. Blockchain protocols and algorithms are implemented on the networking system. Then, network nodes of the blockchain replicate transactions, they broadcast it through the network. They store a number of transactions in a block.

All participants only bind the block to the current chain of already verified blocks when a miner node produces the new block 's target hash code using Proof of Work method also known as computational puzzle. Its verification process is called consensus mechanism varying with respect to turn-around time and computational cost. Finally, B's device can access that transaction by using its private key from the confirmed block.

In 2009, "Bitcoin" [19] which is the first cryptocurrency introduces blockchain. It is considered as Blockchain 1.0. In the sequel, a whitepaper [20] considered Bitcoin as weak version of "smart contracts" and proposed its more advanced versions by introducing another cryptocurrency "Ethereum" [20]. It is considered as Blockchain 2.0. The smart contracts solve double-spend problems without requiring a third-party as centralized authority. This is so promising that it increases applicability of blockchain. In [21], the author has proposed Hyperledger Fabric for tackling both flexibility & privacy issues. It is considered as Blockchain 3.0. With the support of its channels, it is a distributed database only for one choosing group of parties. Consequently, its channels can be compared with channels on typical Internet message services where a particular group holds each access permission.

From [22], Table 16.1 provides a classification with respect to accessibility to blockchain data.

After considering accessibility-based classification, let us investigate consensus protocols. There exist two main approaches for the consensus protocols: Proof-of-Work (PoW) and Proof-of-Stake (PoS). Although PoS consumes less energy, it encourages to hoard and discourage to store private wallet keys securely and offline.

However, PoW consumes much more energy and does not produce any useful information except a few results. A continuing research challenge for PoW is to find such a class of difficult scientific computing problems that it is easy to verify by reproducing used steps of the solution. As a result, another challenge is assuring to be able to compute a valid solution with no need for a computation-intensive solution.

Table 16.1   Classification based on access to blockchain data [22]

Name of the class	Definitions
Public blockchain	Has no limits on block-reading & on submitting of transactions for inclusion into blockchain
Private blockchain	Has limited to a predefined list of users of direct access to the blocks & submitting transactions
Permissioned blockchain	Has no restrictions for the users which are eligible to create blocks of transactions
Permissionless blockchain	Has list of the predefined users which are eligible to performed to process the transactions

Table 16.2   Classification of common consensus protocols for blockchains [23]

Consensus protocols	Highlights	Advantages	Disadvantages
Proof of Work	Selects next block miner, uses complex math problem for easy verification	Very complex to solve	Huge power and computation needs
Practical Byzantine Fault Tolerance	Fault tolerance among nodes in consensus, uses default votes for faulty nodes	Energy efficient, handling faulty nodes	Improper for large networks
Proof of Burn	Nodes burn coins irrevocably, nodes with more burned coins becomes miner	No energy or hardware wastage	No burned coin usage, unfair advantage to nodes with more coins
Proof of Stake	Node with higher bet (on coin) becomes the miner, incentive-based algorithm	No expensive resource usage	Some node can dominate as miners they have higher invested coins
Proof of Elapsed Time	Each node waits for a while, after then, that node becomes the miner	Fair miner selection, equal opportunity for each node	Waiting time
Proof of Capacity	Nodes share hard drive space, node with maximum space becomes the miner	No coin wastage, energy efficient	Disk space wastage
Proof of Authentication	Nodes using ElGamal encryption scheme	No resource wastage, energy efficient	Not Applicable
Proof of Authority	Nodes use identity as trust	No resource wastage	Not Applicable

For the last decade, there has emerged new types of consensus protocols. From [23], we classify common consensus protocols in Table 16.2.

After this brief background on blockchain, its uses are investigated in the remainder of this chapter. In the next chapter, we will consider disadvantages of centralized security and simple replication protocols in IoV which can be considered as a more advanced large-scale vehicular network in the IoT era.

16.5   Security issues in Internet of Drones (IoD) and unmanned traffic management (UTM) systems

We investigate the cybersecurity threats of IoD systems comprehensively. Unmanned traffic management (UTM) system is a drone (commercial UAV) traffic management system, automated and located in the cloud with the mission of organizing the flight of drones. The future UTMs will depend on the advances of

Table 16.3   Classification of common cyber-attack types of UTM and affected security parameters

Types of cyber attacks	Considered threats	Confidentiality	Integrity	Availability	Authentication	Privacy
UAV and its components	Hijacking	X		X		
	GPS spoofing	X	X		X	
	GPS jamming			X		
GCS	Software-related threats	X	X	X	X	
Communication links	Man in the Middle	X	X			
	Denial of Service			X		
	Traffic Analysis	X				X
	GCS Control Signals spoofing	X	X		X	
	Eavesdropping	X			X	X
	Identity spoofing	X			X	
	False location update	X				
Cyber systems	Malware Injection	X	X	X		
	Insecure APIs	X	X		X	
	SQL injection	X	X	X		
	NoSQL injection	X	X	X		

interconnected systems based on novel technologies like IoD. However, security is a major challenge for the adoption of UTM system, particularly if a drone operates for providing nearly real-time data toward ground control systems (GCS) in order to give timely decision. As a result, we address security issues in the UTM systems with their affected security parameters comprehensively.

The cyber security threats of UTMs are classified as in Table 16.3.

16.5.1   Cyber attacks on Unmanned Aerial Vehicle (UAV)

1. **Hijacking**: is an important cybersecurity threat for UAVs. Unauthorized commands can be sent for controlling drones under proper protection or with insecure communications. This may result in failed mission.
2. **GPS spoofing attack:** Drones using GPS signals for navigation are susceptible of spoofing attack because of lack of encryption. GPS spoofing attacks can transmit stronger amplitude fake GPS signals into a UAV for misleading its

path. GPS-spoofed signals provide the drone incorrect data. These attacks may cause accurate positional information to be lost, which threatens safety of drones and other UTM units.

3. **GPS jamming attack:** UAVs use GPS signals for navigation. A jammer may aim to jam GPS signals used by UAVs for their navigation. In this case, UAVs cannot determine their location and so not plan their trajectories. Attackers mainly use vulnerabilities of UAV for threatening UTM by changing flight plans of drones, which can increase probability of collisions with other flying objects/drones.

16.5.2 Attacks on GCS

Software-related threats can cause attacks on GCS. They can be listed as virus, Trojan, malware, keylogger. They may cause to lose important data of UAV.

16.5.3 Attacks on data communication links

UTM units communicate with each other via wireless channels. Communication links between GCS and UAVs are unencrypted, which makes these links susceptible to several attacks. Those on data links are briefly listed as follows:

1. **Man in the middle (MitM) attacks:** They can be successfully established on telemetry and Command-and-Control data links. Attackers may intercept messages exchanged between GCS and UAVs. Especially, attackers can capture those exchanged packets in the sequel, by relaying those packets with modified data, they can obtain important information. This makes both believe that they have successful communications with each other with no interceptions.

2. **Denial of Service (DoS/DDoS):** Those attacks compromise availability of UTM, especially by flooding its network via fake request, which interrupts that system by causing UTM to appear unavailable and prevents it from sending another legitimate packet. As a result, the UAV can get no authorized control messages and data and so it fails its mission. DDoS attacks send lots of unauthorized packets via communication links by adversaries to GCS or UAVs which causes improper communications between them. At these attacks, the adversary aims to disrupt data links between UAVs and GCS via collision or interference before reception. Especially, the jammer close to UAVs generates interference within radio channels at their frequencies. Consequently, receivers of an UAV or GCS can receive improper signals sent by unauthorized senders, which may result in unavailable services.

3. **Traffic analysis attacks:** They are kind of passive attacks, which is performed by a third parties for examining UTM's traffics in order to obtain useful information from UTM units. Their traffics includes sensitive data exchanged among UTM units.

4. **GCS control signals spoofing**: Unless the system protects data links between GCS and UAV, unauthorized parties can send spoof Micro Air Vehicle Link (MAVLink) commands for taking over the UAV illegitimately.

5. **Eavesdropping**: In case of insecure communications between GCS and UAVs, attackers can eavesdrop on exchanged messages between them. Thus, they may

obtain important information from their exchanged messages such as control and command data, their positions, and flying speeds. Although it is some kind of passive attacks, active attacks like hijacking can use extracted information via eavesdropping for controlling UAVs which affects their missions significantly.

6. **Identity spoofing**: In case of unencrypted MAVLinks, the third party can capture authentication credentials of GCS or UAVs. Then, it can use them for sending messages to receivers.

7. **False location update:** If GCS communicates with UAVs insecurely, communication links can be used for sending incorrect position data of UAV to GCS, which may result in incorrect path planning and failed missions of UAVs.

16.5.4   *Attacks on cyber systems*

UTM uses cyber-systems like cloud and Internet for coordinating flight and access of UAVs. For offloading heavy computations, cloud computing resources are used. Moreover, they are also useful for supporting processing and storage of data streams produced by the UAVs. It can generally use regular relational databases like distributed file system or SQL for information and data storage. With a compromised database, UTM is affected considerably in security manner.

1. **Insecure APIs**: Cloud infrastructures generally offer APIs data manipulation and access. Nonetheless, APIs can have vulnerabilities which attackers can exploit [24]. Especially, API developers may use open-source codes for accelerating development processes. Nevertheless, open-sources may be insecure and they may also own several codes unknowingly tainted with cryptocurrency mining codes. APIs need to support secure protocols for guaranteeing high-level security in terms of confidentiality/privacy, encryption, error handling, authentication, access control, privileges, and data segregation.

2. **Malware injections**: In a commonly used way of malware injections Cross-Site Scripting [24], an attacker can inject malicious scripts including JavaScript, HTML, ActiveX, and VBScript into a vulnerable webpage in order to execute malicious script on web browser. As a result, they can steal session cookies or trick into that victim via a malicious link.

3. **SQL and NoSQL injection attacks**: A database may have some vulnerabilities if it works improperly and insecurely. In this case, hackers send malicious SQL codes for gaining and controlling access to backend databases. With successful access, the attackers can control that webserver or manipulate contents in its databases [24].

16.6   Innovative blockchain solutions in IoV

Recent advances in computing device, sophisticated sensing and information technology enables smart transportation services to grow significantly. This has important effects on our lives in various aspects. Integrating with edge, cloud and IoT, blockchain can enables secure, resilient, decentralized intelligent transport ecosystems. Integrating blockchain with high-security features, fog computing with processing capabilities and cloud with virtually limitless storage enables service quality and security of smart transportation. Smart transportation applications can be divided in two classes: secure vehicle operation and vehicle communication management.

Jiang *et al.* [25] propose a blockchain-based IoV architecture where a vehicle sends its data blocks to other nodes via dynamic neighbor nodes (charging stations, wash stations, toll stations, neighbor vehicles, road side units), or via 4G network in case road side system does not exists. This blockchain-based network architecture consists of five types of blockchains which can be defined with respect to block generation and diffusion as follows:

1. *Blockchain 1:* Road side nodes generate data and distribute it to their neighbors.
2. *Blockchain 2:* Vehicles generate data and send it to roadside nodes which forward further.
3. *Blockchain 3:* Road side nodes generate data and distribute it to neighbor roadside nodes.
4. *Blockchain 4:* After collecting data, road side units transmit them to toll station nodes, which forward to others.
5. *Blockchain 5:* Vehicles, charging station, wash station, gas station generates, and keep those data.

Blockchain incorporated with Cloud/Edge computing enables secure, efficient communications in autonomous vehicular networks. Yin *et al.* [26] propose blockchain-enabled vehicular cloud communication network for implementation of an established framework. Private cloud of vehicles which are manufactured by different companies enable a vehicle-to-vehicle connected infrastructure via blockchains. Hence, this system enables various car services which can be listed as sharing of ownership, asset management, collaboration, and co-operation among private Cloud.

Liu *et al.* [27] implement multi-layer architectures which comprise Cloud/Edge network and electric vehicles. The system creates shared-resource pool by enabling collaboration of electric vehicles for providing seamless communication among heterogeneous entities. Blockchains can provide its users security by sharing information & energy. Novel blockchain cryptocurrencies are introduced for vehicular applications where two coins are introduced energy and data coin. Each of the transactions generated in information-exchange is added to consortium blockchain after encryption.

Nadeem *et al.* [28] propose blockchain on cloud-based vehicular ad hoc network for keeping privacy in vehicle drivers' lives via low-cost & on-demand access. Three interconnected components, roadside Cloud, vehicle Cloud, and central Cloud form a hierarchical cloud architecture for tackling issues emerging with the broadband bandwidth constraints, computation and storage of vehicular ad hoc networks. The joint Cloud network connects service providers, cars securely via a blockchain-based peer-to-peer network which can become resilient malicious attacks and handle bottleneck problems in vehicles.

Xie *et al*. [29] design blockchain-based system for integrity management in SDN-enabled vehicular network in 5G era. Each of the vehicles shares a road-information-contained tag with the others. Its neighbor vehicles recommend that vehicle scores by considering veracity of shared information, which prevents inaccurate knowledge from impacting destination vehicles. A vehicle which provides score decides a trust value regarding its distance from that vehicle which shares its road information, then inserts this value in blocks. PoW and PoS are utilized as consensus mechanism for confirming blocks on this blockchain. Its simulations are hold with OMNET++.

Michelin *et al*. [14] propose SpeedyChain which separates block header from block content. It processes block header on-chain. In this system, an expiration time is set in block forming duration for decreasing its size. Moreover, key updates of the algorithms are recommended for minimizing traceability of the transactions. Furthermore, access level is incorporated for controlling the permission of vehicles. For assessing the performance of SpeedyChain, the experiments were hold by using Common Open Research Emulator.

Baza *et al*. [30] suggest blockchains for providing autonomous vehicles firmware updates regularly. By using attribute-based encryption mechanisms, manufacturers of autonomous vehicles insert proofs into on-board units of their autonomous vehicles. Smart contracts contain the algorithms about who has the right to download and use the firmware update. Zero-Knowledge Proof is proposed in the work where each distributor provides their autonomous vehicles encrypted firmware updates. Smart contracts provide decryption keys if each autonomous vehicle is able to exhibit the proofs provided by distributors.

Future transport systems will accommodate autonomous vehicles carrying people. Autonomous electric charge stations will take place of human-driven gas stations. For this scenario, current credit-based systems are insufficient for enabling machine-to-machine transactions in those autonomous intelligent transport systems. From [31], blockchain facilitates machine-to-machine transactions in more flexible and scalable manner by considering its usage for driverless vehicles while being charged in electric stations. Nonetheless, the paper does not investigate feasibility of the proposal.

Li *et al*. [32] propose blockchain-enabled vehicular edge computing for carpooling services whereby one or many passengers share the same car to travel in same direction. A driver or a malicious user may report its locations falsely in that system. Destination matching, one-to-many proximity matching, applied conditional privacy, and audibility of data are applied for carpooling scenarios to keep passenger's security and privacy. Blockchain is proposed for roadside unit deployed in edge layers. User's queries generate hash of data transactions and they are stored at blockchains while data is stored at cloud server. Road side unit blockchain transmits the route plan, queries, and reports regarding positions of cars to cloud server so that a malicious user is not able to change information. Its experiments are performed on private blockchain.

Yao *et al.* [33] suggest blockchain-enabled authentication approach in distributed vehicular edge networks. Authentication process consists of four stages: (1) registration stage when on-board units at vehicles ask the audit department the partial public keys; (2) authentication stage, when the authentication phase includes communication among service manager, vehicular edge services and on-board unit for providing on-board unit access to resources; (3) consensus stage when a consensus protocol is run by service manager and witness peers for putting transactions of authentication process in blockchain; (4) service delivery stage when blockchain removes the need of on-board unit for initiating any authentication process if it moves to other edge services or data center.

Gao *et al.* [34] combine blockchain, edge computing, and SDN in a vehicular network. Base stations, roadside unit, and vehicles with on-board units operate instead of SDN data planes such as selecting channels, updating counters, receiving packets, and taking action on the packet. Nonetheless, roadside unit is deployed in edge layer acting as SDN controller and determines network flows. Roadside unit hub connects interzonal vehicular networks each other via blockchain. The proposed blockchain provides a trust model by using information collated from peers to decide on messages to be sent from source vehicle to destination vehicle. NS3 is used for simulating the network parameter to analyze performance with respect to time and packet delivery ratio. The proposed blockchain is developed for 5G vehicular network by using Hyperledger Fabric.

Recently, vehicular ad-hoc network has been suggested for allotting dynamic car parking. In this network, each vehicle serves as a hop for information exchange by considering saturation status of parking lots [35]. It deals with several issues such as security, sustainability since no incentive mechanism exists for exchanging information with others and no consensus mechanisms exists for increasing the user trust levels. Ref. [36] proposes a DTL and DAG-based system for allocating parking lots where DTL forms a protected peer-to-peer network with free spaces, garages, user, and owners of parking lots. The time-stamped consensus system in a DAG network processes transactions regarding parking reservation requests for providing each user the possible services cost-optimally. Adaptive pricing models are developed for park requests regarding multiple parameters for providing most available slots to users in less expense and time.

Many promising blockchain protocols use PoW-based consensus mechanisms for overcoming the generic constraints of blockchains. Proof-of-Stack (PoS), Proof of Burn (PoB), and Proof of Elapsed Time (PoET) work like Proof-of-Work (PoW) principally. Furthermore, applying PoS is challenging for applying in blockchain since the network nodes own no stake or cryptocurrency for burning initially. For that, Hassija *et al.* [37] propose a DAG-enabled energy trade platform for grid to vehicle and vehicles to grid. Furthermore, buyers and sellers can add new transactions to ledger by using a tip selection algorithm with no need for miners. buyers and sellers use a game-theoretic optimization algorithm for best deals in energy trading.

Bera *et al.* [38] propose blockchain-enabled secure frameworks in order to manage IoDs. The work presents applicability and importance of blockchain in 5G IoD, then develops blockchain-enabled data collection protocols for secure communications between control centers, geographic stations, and drones. Comparative analysis of security & privacy exhibits those suggested policies can be resilient against numerous malicious attacks in IoD.

Traffic jam prediction models help vehicles avoid traffic congestion. They require users' locations, real-time traffic data, participants' private details such as the phone numbers and names. Google maps use crowdsourcing for data pertaining to live traffic congestion. However, not all users might be motivated to share their sensitive information about routes and locations with crowdsourcing without sufficient incentives. For this, Hassija *et al.* [39] suggest blockchain-based system for traffic jam estimation where Ethereum smart contracts were used for verifying/storing information from participants. Peer-to-peer network of blockchain guarantees to share confidential data of live traffic jam securely. LSTM-based neural network is applied for estimating traffic jam probabilities in specific positions. An incentive model provides a user token provided that each of users shares real-time traffic data with others willingly. This token will be used to access same services in the future.

16.7   Blockchain solutions for IoD

This section presents several blockchain solutions proposed for multirobot systems and Internet of Drones.

Ferrer [40] proposes the first study which details blockchain interests for multirobot systems. It considers integrating blockchains with multirobot swarm systems. The paper presents its advantages with regard to security, consensus, and transparency whereas implementation difficulties and increase in overall system complexity.

Kapitonov *et al.* [41] propose a protocol based on Ethereum-based smart contracts and any agents compatible with communication framework by Robot Operating System (ROS). The paper also discusses the applicability of the protocol in an infrastructure operator system for regulatory, navigation, and economical activities by UAVs.

Afanasyev *et al.* [42,43] present blockchain-based robotics applications, where financial use of the blockchain is identified for implementing the rewards with market-based coordination strategies. Blockchain smart contracts are used for task allocation to the robots unambiguously.

Strobel *et al.* [44,45] provide a robot-to-robot communication analysis. It evaluates the security performance of a collective decision-making scenario, connected by an Ethereum-based protocol. It is apparently shown that blockchain solutions are much more resistant than classical consensus protocols in the presence of Byzantine robots.

Tran *et al.* [46] tackle a problem arising from partitions of swarms. To obtain stable partitions, the SwarmDAG protocol was proposed for managing the splits and merges of the network correctly during the partitions.

Falcone *et al.* [47] design a new kind of blockchain protocol aiming for the devices with very low computation power by also studying its performance aspects. The authors implement that blockchain successfully on an ARM Cortex M0 processor clocked at 48 MHz.

As a more recent work, Santos De Campos [48] proposes a blockchain-enabled multi-UAV surveillance framework enabling financial exchange between the users and UAV coordination. It aims to allow a set of Points-Of-Interest (POI) to be surveyed by a set of autonomous UAVs that cooperate to minimize the time between successive visits while exhibiting unpredictable behavior to prevent external agents from learning their movements.

We can consider that system as a marketplace where POIs and UAVs are service seekers and service providers, respectively. This concept focus on embedding blockchain on some nodes on the ground and the UAVs. It provides two main functionalities. First, the route of each UAV is planned through a robust smart contract-based game-theoretic decision algorithm. Second, financial transactions is allowed between the system and its users, where POIs buy tokens for subscribing to surveillance services. On the other hand, that system pays tokens to the UAVs for each service. The experiments exhibit that IOTA blockchain has a potential as a blockchain solution and the chosen decentralized coordination strategy is lightweight and efficient enough for filling the mission requirements.

16.8   Blockchain applications in IoV

From Gartner investigation [49], IoT industries in 2025 will face five problems which will be faced in IoV as an important sector among the IoT industries.

Those problems can be solved by blockchain as given below:

1. *Connecting 50-billion devices by 2025:* Blockchains are capable of storing 2160 address that provides IoT devices addressability. Furthermore, blockchains create direct connections among the devices for each of them to send their information instead of look through a database of billions of records to find that device.

2. *Creating control for lots of decentralized devices:* Blockchains send cryptographical signed messages between devices which any hackers cannot make MitM attacks. A central user is able to send control signal to other decentralized devices.

3. *Enabling peer-to-peer communications among global-distributed nodes:* Blockchains enable connectivity for intra-device communications naturally. As a result, it is so simple to communicate directly in the network.

4. *Providing compliance & governance to autonomous systems:* As blockchain is immutable, stored data cannot be edited or deleted whereby compliance and governance of autonomous systems becomes feasible.

5. *Addressing security complexities of IoT landscapes:* With its dozen-year history, Bitcoin has demonstrated that powerful protection method of blockchains can provide the strongest communication security for all IoT devices.

Blockchain provides enough opportunities to the IoT infrastructure encouraging firms to enhance network-based IoT to blockchain-based IoT. Blockchains can be regarded as promising solutions for reliability, privacy, scalability issues in IoT.

Hence, in 2025 IoT industries, the blockchain is a necessity to provide the distributed security in the Industrial IoTs [49]. Various blockchain technology can be utilized for security problems of Industrial IoT depending on the (throughput, latency, security, consumption resources) requirements (expectations) in that IoT networks. For medium expectations in the Industrial IoT, it may be better to use hybrid approach instead of pure IoT–IoT or IoT–blockchain approaches.

16.9 Future possible directions

Considering the 5G user-centric communications trends, MEC has become more crucial than ever especially considering its applications in some IoT areas including IoV. Therefore, as the first possible research direction, we can consider MEC for IoV with blockchain.

Blockchain applications are generally not suitable for the low-powered, geographically distributed, and possibly mobile IoT devices since the consensus protocols requires to consume too much power. This is the major barrier for applying blockchain to many other mobile systems. On the other hand, *MEC* allows service providers to deploy cloud computing services at edge. By supplying local computing power, MEC enables blockchain deployment in IoT networks to support encryption algorithms, hashing, solving PoW puzzles, and possibly consensus. MEC provides the mobile IoT networks available computing power which they need for mobile tasks, e.g., IoT sensed data analytics and data processing. Edge computing service providers deploy servers and local data centers at edge. Offloading computing tasks from mobile IoT users to MEC services decreases the latency and backhaul bandwidth usage considerably, compared with going to data center and remote cloud. Thus, MEC becomes promising for mobile blockchains. [50]

While the blockchain users can offload tasks required by consensus protocols to the MEC services to maximize their reward, the MEC service provider targets to maximize its own benefits. Accordingly, if MEC service provider adopts the pricing, each of blockchain user needs optimizing its demands for MEC service for consensus protocols such that their payoff is maximized. Thus, *the trade-off between the used computing power and the reward from successful mining turns into the trade-off between the payoff of the mobile user and the reward from successful mining.* MEC service provider can consider uniform pricing where the price is same for each miner, and discriminatory pricing where different miners are offered different unit prices.

Some other research problems in IoT with blockchain are listed as follows.

1. *Security problems in MEC for IoV with blockchains:* Even though blockchains provide good security properties for storage and distributed data processing, some security problems arise if blockchains are applied to IoT systems using MEC. As IoT devices have less protection and rely on wireless communication, they are vulnerable to DDoS and jamming attacks. More secure networks are required for private users.
2. *Resource allocation and utilization*: Since mobile IoT nodes cannot efficiently afford consensus protocols of blockchain, they use MEC service to

perform the mining. On the other hand, the prices of these resources are determined by MEC service providers. Resource utilization–allocation problems can be handled via game theory.

3. *Type of economic pricing models:* The economic pricing models are currently considered as on-demand pricing with uniform variable cost for all users and different variable costs for different users. However, spot pricing can be used for the services.

4. *Micro-credit systems for low-income people:* Many women farmers or workers have no bank account. By receiving money from various investors, blockchain enabled microcredit systems can provide the required microcredits to these women securely.

5. *Supply chain:* Supply chain has two important challenges which are to provide trust and transparency among stakeholders & participants and to ensure an efficient operation. Their difficulties come from the alterability of the records of supply chains by participants. Blockchain technology has been identified as a promising solution to resolve these issues, blockchain can be considered as promising [51]. Moreover, people need to make payments via smart contracts in supply chain and the smart factories need ultra-reliable, low-latency communications to give a better faster service to their customers. Hence, secure, and scalable blockchain protocols are needed.

6. *AI-enabled vehicular networks:* In autonomous vehicles, people need to make payments via smart contracts and the vehicles need ultra-reliable, low-latency communications to avoid multiple-vehicle collisions. Therefore, secure, fast and scalable blockchain protocols are required.

   With 5G of mobile broadband systems, blockchain needs to deal with scalability problems due to a very large number of users in IoV. Artificial intelligence (AI) techniques can be applied with blockchain in connected vehicles in this manner. Implementing AI techniques can provide more scalable, transparent, and secure blockchain applications in vehicular networks. AI techniques also help blockchain achieve privacy and personalization for the users in IoV at the same time.

7. *Simulation software for blockchain-based UAV systems:* Implementing blockchains for UAVs bring out a very hard system integration problem. Before it is rolled out commercially, it needs rigorous testing. Some research studies use agent-based simulation softwares for testing. We need more dedicated platforms which incorporate features of UAVs and blockchain.

8. *Protecting private/permissioned blockchain systems against intelligent attacks:* Many blockchain applications in UAVs need private/permissioned blockchains. It should also be noticed that more susceptible to attacks than public blockchains which host quite many participants and executing majority attacks on them is really difficult. In addition, with more developed kinds of attacks such as quantum attacks, ML and game-theory-based attacks, blockchain security is required more than ever. As an important research direction, private blockchains are needed to be considered more in order to make them safer and more immutable.

9. *Optimizing UAV power consumption and increasing their fly-time:* The fly-times of UAVs are very little because of their limited-capacity batteries. Consequently, UAV operations need to be optimized for increasing their fly-times blockchains and its applications generally need processing power. One of the crucial bottlenecks for flytimes of UAVs is the excessive power consumption by many blockchain applications. Therefore, more robust solutions are required for tackling this problem.

10. *Using machine learning (ML) with blockchain in UAVs*: ML can be used for improving performance of blockchain in UAVs. ML can optimize scalability, energy and resource efficiency. ML can improve security& privacy. ML can also make smart contracts smarter. Using ML with blockchain applications is quite a promising research direction.

16.10 Conclusions

In this chapter, we investigate the security issues and challenges in IoV. The existing centralized security systems for IoV bring up many security problems like single point of failures, middleman problem, malicious attack.

Blockchain have produced promising results to tackle security threats at IoT network for one dozen of years. However, numerous blockchains have no low transaction latency, since its consensus protocol has to synchronize that block chain. Therefore, it should first be questioned when the users/customers need blockchain or not instead of simple replications, key graphs local caching, for IoV.

Therefore, we mainly tackle when we should use blockchain. In the sequel, we consider security threats and countermeasures in IoV. Then, we consider fundamental mechanisms and algorithms in blockchain. Finally, we investigate innovative blockchain solutions for vehicle sensing and transport monitoring in IoV.

References

[1] M. S. Ali, M. Vecchio, M. Pincheira, K. Dolui, F. Antonelli, and M. H. Rehmani, "Applications of Blockchains in the Internet of Things: A Comprehensive Survey", *IEEE Communications& Surveys Tutorials*, vol. 21, no. 2, 2019, pp. 1676–1717.

[2] M. A. Uddin, A. Stranieri, I. Gondal, and V. Balasubramanian, "A Survey on the Adoption of Blockchain in IoT: Challenges and Solutions", *Blockchain: Research and Applications*, Early access at https://doi.org/10.1016/j.bcra.2021.100006.

[3] S. Zeadally and J. B. Abdo, "Blockchain: Trends and Future Opportunities", *Internet Technology Letters,* vol. 2, 2019, p. e130.

[4] T. Dursun, "Blockchain Technology", Available at https://medium.com/@tdursun/blokzinciri-teknolojisi-ffc5e9faf7b5

[5] E. Karaarslan and E. Adiguzel, "Blockchain Based DNS and PKI Solutions", *IEEE Communications Standards Magazine*, vol. 2, no. 3, 2018, pp. 52–57.

[6]   N. Kshetri, "Can Blockchain Strengthen the Internet of Things", *IT Professional*, vol. 19, no. 4, 2017, pp. 68–72.

[7]   T. M. Fernandez-Carames and P. Fraga-Lamas, "A Review on the Use of Blockchain for the Internet of Things", *IEEE Access*, vol. 6, 2018, pp. 32979–33001.

[8]   J. Wurm, K. Hoang, O. Arias, A. R. Sadeghi, and Y. Jin, "Security Analysis on Consumer and Industrial IoT Devices", In *Design Automation Conference (ASP-DAC), 2016 21st Asia and South Pacific*, IEEE, 2016, pp. 519–524.

[9]   H. F. Atlam, A. Alenezi, A. Alharthi, R. J. Walters, and G. B. Wills, "Integration of Cloud Computing with Internet of Things: Challenges and Open Issues", In *2017 IEEE International Conference on IoT (iThings)/ IEEE Green Computing &Communications (GreenCom)/IEEE Cyber, Physical and Social Computing (CPSCom)/IEEE Smart Data (SmartData)*, pp. 670–675.

[10] A. Reyna, C. Martin, J. Chen, E. Soler, and M. Diaz, "On Blockchain and its Integration with IoT Challenges and Opportunities", *Future Generation Computer Systems*, 2018.

[11] A. P. Joshi, M. Han, and Y. Wang, "A Survey on Security and Privacy Issues of Blockchain Technology", *Mathematical Foundations of Computing*, vol. 1, no. 2, 2018, pp. 121–147.

[12] I. Eyal and E. G. Sirer, "Majority is not Enough: Bitcoin Mining is Vulnerable", *Communications of the ACM*, vol. 61, no. 7, 2018, pp. 95–102.

[13] G. O. Karame, E. Androulaki, and S. Capkun, "Double-Spending Fast Payments in Bitcoin", In *Proceedings of the 2012 ACM conference on Computer and communications security*. ACM, 2012, pp. 906–917.

[14] R. A. Michelin, A. Dorri, M. Steger, *et al.*, "Speedychain: A Framework for Decoupling Data from Blockchain for Smart Cities", In *Proceedings of the 15th EAI International Conference on Mobile and Ubiquitous Systems: Computing, Networking and Services*, 2018, pp. 145–154.

[15] Could Blockchain Wipe Out DDoS Attacks? – BestVPN.com", BestVPN. com, 2017. [Online]. Available: https://www.bestvpn.com/blockchain-gladius-ddos/.

[16] A. Bahga and V. Madisetti, "Blockchain Platform for Industrial Internet of Things", *Journal of Software Engineering and Applications*, vol. 9, 2016, pp. 533–546.

[17] M. A. Uddin, A. Stranieri, I. Gondal, and V. Balasubramanian, "Rapid Health Data Repository Allocation Using Predictive Machine Learning", *Health Informatics Journal*, vol. 26, no. 4, 2020, pp. 3009–3036.

[18] M. A. Uddin, A. Stranieri, I. Gondal, and V. Balasubramanian, "A Survey on the Adoption of Blockchain in IoT: Challenges and Solutions", *Blockchain: Research and Applications*, vol. 2, 2021, 100006.

[19] S. Nakamoto, "Bitcoin: A Peer-to-Peer Electronic Cash System", March 2009, available at https://bitcoin.org/bitcoin.pdf.

[20] "Ethereum Project", Originally Jan. 2014, available at ethereum.org/ whitepaper/

[21] E Androulaki, A Barger, V Bortnikov, *et al.*, "Hyperledger Fabric: A Distributed Operating System for Permissioned Blockchains", In *EuroSys '18*, New York, NY: ACM; 2018, pp. 30:1–30:15.

[22] J. Garzik and BitFury Group, "Public versus Private Blockchains. Part 1: Permissioned Blockchains. White Paper", Oct. 2015.

[23] N. Pathak, A. Mukherjee, and S. Misra, "AerialBlocks: Blockchain-Enabled UAV Virtualization for Industrial IoT", *IEEE Internet of Things Magazine*, vol. 4, no. 1, 2021, pp. 72–77.

[24] O. B. Fredj, O. Cheikhrouhou, M. Krichen, H. Hamam, and A. Derhab, "An OWASP Top Ten Driven Survey on Web Application Protection Methods", In Garcia-Alfaro, J., Leneutre, J., Cuppens, N., Yaich, R. (Eds), *Risks and Security of Internet and Systems*, Cham, Switzerland: Springer International Publishing, 2021, pp. 235–252.

[25] T. Jiang, H. Fang, and H. Wang, "Blockchain-Based Internet of Vehicles: Distributed Network Architecture and Performance Analysis", *IEEE Internet of Things Journal*, vol. 6, no. 3, 2016, pp. 4640–4649.

[26] B. Yin, L. Mei, Z. Jiang, and K. Wang, "Joint Cloud Collaboration Mechanism Between Vehicle Clouds Based on Blockchain", In *2019 IEEE International Conference on Service-Oriented System Engineering (SOSE)*, 2019, pp. 227–2275.

[27] H. Liu, Y. Zhang, and T. Yang, "Blockchain-Enabled Security in Electric Vehicles Cloud and Edge Computing", *IEEE Network*, vol. 32, no. 3, 2018, pp. 78–83,.

[28] S. Nadeem, M. Rizwan, F. Ahmad, and J. Manzoor, "Securing Cognitive Radio Vehicular Ad Hoc Network with Fog Node Based Distributed Blockchain Cloud Architecture", *International Journal of Advanced Computer Science and Applications*, vol. 10, no. 1, 2019, pp. 288–295.

[29] L. Xie, Y. Ding, H. Yang, and X. Wang, "Blockchain-Based Secure and Trustworthy Internet of Things in SDN-Enabled 5G-Vanets", *IEEE Access*, vol. 7, 2019, pp. 56656–56666.

[30] M. Baza, M. Nabil, N. Lasla, K. Fidan, M. Mahmoud, and M. Abdallah, "Blockchain-Based Firmware Update Scheme Tailored for Autonomous Vehicles", In *2019 IEEE Wireless Communications and Networking Conference (WCNC)*, 2019, pp. 1–7.

[31] A. R. Pedrosa and G. Pau, "Chargeltup: On Blockchain-Based Technologies for Autonomous Vehicles", In *Proceedings of the 1st Workshop on Cryptocurrencies and Blockchains for Distributed Systems*, 2018, pp. 87–92.

[32] M. Li, L. Zhu, and X. Lin, "Efficient and Privacy-Preserving Carpooling Using Blockchain-Assisted Vehicular Fog Computing", *IEEE Internet of Things Journal*, vol. 6, no. 3, 2018, pp. 4573–4584.

[33] Y. Yao, X. Chang, J. Mišić, V. B. Mišić, and L. Li, "BLA: Blockchain-Assisted Lightweight Anonymous Authentication for Distributed Vehicular Fog Services", *IEEE Internet of Things Journal*, vol. 6, no. 2, 2019, pp. 3775–3784.

[34] J. Gao, K. O.-B. O. Agyekum, E. B. Sifah, *et al.*, "A Blockchain-SDN-Enabled Internet of Vehicles Environment for Fog Computing and 5G

Networks", *IEEE Internet of Things Journal*, vol. 7, no. 5, 2019, pp. 4278–4291.

[35]   R. Hussain, F. Hussain, and S. Zeadally. "Integration of Vanet and 5g Security: A Review of Design and Implementation Issues", *Future Generation Computer Systems*, vol. 101, 2019, pp. 843–864.

[36]   V. Hassija, V. Saxena, V. Chamola, and R. Yu. "A Parking Slot Allocation Framework Based on Virtual Voting and Adaptive Pricing Algorithm", *IEEE Transactions on Vehicular Technology*, 2020.

[37]   V. Hassija, V. Chamola, S. Garg, N. G. K. Dara, G. Kaddoum, and D. N. K. Jayakody, "A Blockchain-Based Framework for Lightweight Data Sharing and Energy Trading in V2G Network", *IEEE Transactions on Vehicular Technology*, 2020.

[38]   B. Bera, S. Saha, A. K. Das, N. Kumar, P. Lorenz, and M. Alazab, "Blockchain-Envisioned Secure Data Delivery and Collection Scheme for 5G Based IoT-Enabled Internet of Drones Environment", *IEEE Transactions on Vehicular Technology*, vol. 69, no. 8, 2020, pp. 9097–9111.

[39]   V. Hassija, V. Gupta, S. Garg, and V. Chamola, "Traffic Jam Probability Estimation Based on Blockchain and Deep Neural Networks", *IEEE Transactions on Intelligent Transportation Systems*, 2020.

[40]   E. C. Ferrer, The Blockchain: A New Framework for Robotic Swarm Systems, 2016. *arXiv preprint arXiv:1608.00695.* doi:10.1007/978-3-030-0268 3-7_77

[41]   A. Kapitonov, S. Lonshakov, A. Krupenkin, and I. Berman, "Blockchain Based Protocol of Autonomous Business Activity for Multi-Agent Systems Consisting of UAVs," In *2017 Workshop on Research, Education and Development of Unmanned Aerial Systems (RED-UAS) (Linköping)*, 2017, pp. 84–89.

[42]   I. Afanasyev, A. Kolotov, R. Rezin, K. Danilov, A. Kashevnik, and V. Jotsov, "Blockchain Solutions for Multi-Agent Robotic Systems: Related Work and Open Questions," In *Proceedings of the 24th Conference of Open Innovations Association FRUCT, FRUCT'24 (Moscow; Helsinki: FRUCT Oy)*, 76, 2019, pp. 551–555.

[43]   I. Afanasyev, A. Kolotov, R. Rezin, *et al.*, Towards Blockchain-Based Multi-Agent Robotic Systems: Analysis, Classification and Applications, 2019. Available online at: https://arxiv.org/abs/1907.07433

[44]   V. Strobel, E. Castelló Ferrer, and M. Dorigo, "Managing Byzantine Robots via Blockchain Technology in a Swarm Robotics Collective Decision-Making Scenario," In *Proceedings of the 17th International Conference on Autonomous Agents and MultiAgent Systems, AAMAS '18 (Stockholm)*, 2018, pp. 541–549.

[45]   V. Strobel, E. Castelló Ferrer, and M. Dorigo, "Blockchain Technology Secures Robot Swarms: A Comparison of Consensus Protocols and Their Resilience to Byzantine Robots," *Frontiers in Robotics*, vol. AI7, 2020, p. 54. doi:10.3389/frobt.2020.00054

[46]   J. Tran, G. Ramachandran, P. Shah, C. Danilov, R. Santiago, and B. Krishnamachari, "Swarmdag: a20. Partition Tolerant Distributed Ledger

Protocol for Swarm Robotics", *Ledger*, vol. 4, 2019, pp. 25–31. doi: 10.5195/ledger.2019.174

[47]   S. Falcone, J. Zhang, A. Cameron, and A. Abdel-Rahman, "Blockchain Design for an Embedded System", *Ledger*, vol. 4, 2019, pp. 7–16. doi:10.5195/ledger.2019.172

[48]   M. G. Santos De Campos, P. C. Chanel Caroline, C. Chauffaut, and J. Lacan, "Towards a Blockchain-Based Multi-UAV Surveillance System", *Frontiers in Robotics and AI*, vol. 8, 2021, pp. 90.

[49]   L.-O. W. M. Walker and N. Jones, *How to Address the Top Five IoT Challenges with Enterprise Architecture*, Gartner. Inc, November 2016.

[50]   Z. Xiong, Y. Zhang, D. Niyato, P. Wang, and Z. Han, "When Mobile Blockchain Meets Edge Computing", *IEEE Communications Magazine*, vol. 56, no. 8, 2018, pp. 33–39.

[51]   D. Shakhbulatov, I. Medina, Z. Dong, and R. Rojas-Cessa, "How Blockchain Enhances Supply Chain Management: A Survey", *IEEE Open Journal of the Computer Society*, vol. 1, 2020, pp. 230–249.

Chapter 17

Blockchain-enabled Internet of Things (IoTs) platforms for the healthcare sector

G. Devika[1] and Asha Gowda Karegowda[1]

Abstract

In the last decade, world has changed gradually from mechanical to smart digital world. Defense, supply chain, industries, finance, healthcare, education, automation, and more applications are automated by the use of sensors. The world is built like a small village with inclusion of smart devices. Also, the latest developments in information technology and blockchain technology have enhanced market of the electronic healthcare sector. In healthcare, Internet of Things (IoT) provides real-time sensory data from patients to process and analyze, which requires either centralized or decentralized computation, processing or storage. For various sectors including finance, defense, healthcare, and many more, the security concerns during transmission or processing needs are very important. Security concerns include single points of failure, distrust, data tampering, and privacy evasion of IoT platforms. For healthcare systems in particular, maintaining the privacy of data is most important. Hence, security problems require resolution without relying on trusted third parties. Blockchain provides security by exchanging digital tokens and transparency of data among health sector members in a peer-to-peer network, avoiding the requisite of trusting centralized third-party entity. In this chapter, we will survey solutions to security related issues of healthcare data in IoT platforms. Future context of IoT platforms analysis for sensor data scenarios consider different healthcare applications with Blockchain. Finally, we discuss future scope and challenges in the health sector.

Keywords: Blockchain-based Internet of Things; Smart healthcare; Security and privacy issues in healthcare; Smart era

17.1 Introduction

Due to the lack of medical professionals, remote monitoring services supported by IoT and wearable devices are being developed to take care of a larger number of

[1]Government Engineering College, K R Pet & Siddaganga Institute of Technology, Tumkur, India

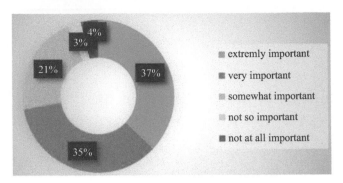

Figure 17.1   Current usage of blockchain

patients. The availability of advanced software technology & the decreased cost of data storage have paved the way to store huge amount of medical data, but this brings major security concerns [1–4]. Blockchain is a boon in this direction to efficiently exchange information in a secured way in healthcare networks [5,6]. Blockchain not only ensures security in the sharing and storage of electronic medical records, insurance records, and clinical trial data, but it also supports the development of secured mobile health applications and monitoring healthcare devices. Figure 17.1 illustrates the relevance of blockchain in terms of its usage for handling transactions in the healthcare sector (mostly medical records, IoT, payment, identity proof, currency, and supply chain).

Many firms have stated that blockchain is a rapidly evolving and accelerating technology. Blockchain technology improves distributed ledger technology to change aspects of digital transactions to some bigger to aspects as in Internet [5]. Blockchain will provide three major benefits according to IBM: building trust, cost reduction, and the acceleration of transactions. It builds trust between parties and devices, reduces risk collusion, and tampering. It removes overhead associated with middlemen and intermediaries to reduce cost. It increases transactions and reduces settlement time from days to instants [6–9]. The blockchain domain is expanding its market and also gaining immense popularity. The report of global blockchain development proves this statement stating that there will be approximately a $34.47 million growth in 2024 to $1415.59 million; the CAGR increase will be around 70.45% between years 2018 and 2024. Blockchain saves cost by automation and paper less work as listed in Table 17.1.

17.1.1   Why blockchain for healthcare?

A large amount of critical data often remain scattered and unorganized in the health sector due to the lack of adequate infrastructure, resulting in not only a poor management of data but also cumbersome to access vital information. In addition, medical data is liable to fissure and exploitation [11–13]. In this perspective, IoT and blockchain technologies can be embraced in the healthcare sector to provide proper means for apt storage and secured retrieval of data by authorized people.

Table 17.1   Cost saving by automation

Cost saving in paper	Unified electronics health record/exchange E-prescribing Intra-hospital staff communication Clinicians' virtual assistants
Cost saving in automation	Nurse mobile connectivity Barcoding medication administration radio-frequency identification (RFID) tracking Vital parameter tracking Hospital logistics robotics Process automation through robots E-referrals

17.1.2   Why IoT for healthcare?

Healthcare professionals and patients benefit from using IoT, to connect with each other actively. IoT devices enable the automatic collection of health metrics such as blood pressure, heart rate, temperature, and other information which can be sent to family members and doctors. This can also be used for research purposes as it enables the collection of a massive amount of patient data [21–31].

17.1.3   Innovative projects of IoT and blockchain in 2019

- Filament networks: long radio range self-forming wireless end-to-end networks
- Atonomi: provides secure interoperability between millions of connected devices.
- Chain of things: deliver security solutions for IoT through Blockchain solutions.
- IOTA: a peer-to-peer new consensus based on Tangle.
- IoTeX: privacy centric distributed blockchain network.
- IoT chain: an operating system to protect and transfer data allowing layers network structures.
- Integrated Watson IoT and blockchain: provides better solution using the existing Watson IoT through private IoT.
- Ambrosus: to manage records for the pharmaceutical and food industries.
- Waltionchain: a trustworthy chain for e-commerce.
- OriginTrail: a distributed decentralized knowledge graphs.
- Steamr: a single site for data delivery and payment.
- Helium: simplifies interconnection issues.
- Moeco: a machine to machine simplified protocol.
- FOAM: provides secure location services based on radio beacons.
- Fysical: easy means for transparent data exchanges through traffic sensor in commute routes.

17.1.4   Workflow

Several research works have been carried to address the use of IoT and blockchain technologies in different applications but their full potential has not yet been exploited. This chapter investigates the use of IoT and blockchain in the healthcare sector. The major contributions of this chapter are the following:

- Current status of blockchain and IoT in the healthcare sector
- Benefits of the integration of blockchain and IoT
- Applications of blockchain and IOT for disease identification, treatment and preventions
- A layered architecture of blockchain and IOT for the healthcare sector
- Challenges and future perspectives of blockchain and IOT

17.2   Theoretical foundations

In this section, we present what impacts have been made by IoT and blockchain in the healthcare sector.

17.2.1   Blockchain

In today's digital era, blockchain appears to be a highly suitable means to monitor, develop, and generate efficient digital applications and platforms. Blockchain ensures security, auditability, and transparency in the exchange of information without the support of any intermediaries and immutability. Currently, small-to-large companies provide a number of opportunities to accumulate physical component or objects called tokenized assets. The evolution is shown in Figure 17.2 and shows how blockchain has evolved.

17.2.2   Advantages of blockchain

Blockchain also supports third parties, when an application requires it through digital distributed ledgers. This allows to share and exchange information among digital twins whenever required. Software network functions in distributed network as a digital ledger. It enables to secure assets without any intermediaries. It facilitates the exchange of digital data units. Currencies and any item can be stored, tokenized, and exchanged in a blockchain network. Entities interact with the presence of central trusted third party with blockchain. Maintains a continuous set of data entries bundle as block of data. The blockchain is linked upon acceptance to previous and future blocks with cryptographic protocols [17]. Its origin form of data records or blocks readable to all can be written by all and secure proof with all access to all. It allows the decentralized management of data and data transactions. It is easy to assemble into any kind of application. It permits for smart contracts, self-execution contracts with central authority. As of date, the largest facilitator of smart contracts on blockchain is blockchain Ethereum.

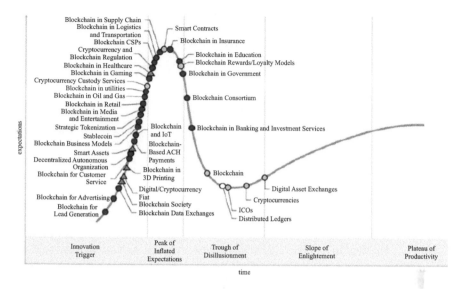

Figure 17.2   Blockchain evolution

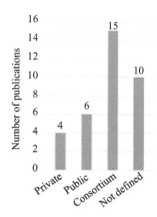

Figure 17.3   Type of blockchain

17.2.3   Blockchain types

A blockchain definition and the categorization of different types of blockchains are still being deliberated. Consensus broad category of distributing qualities does not exist. Consensus mechanisms are required to label a technology as "blockchain" [8]. Blockchains are categorized as: public (permissionless), consortium (public permissioned), and private [18]. It is depicted in Figures 17.3 and 17.4 with its features. They possess different characteristics regarding who can access, write, and read the data on the blockchain [31–34].

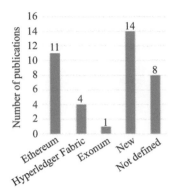

Figure 17.4   Platform/framework

- Public: The data in a public chain can be viewed by all, and anyone can join and contribute to both consensus (in theory) and make changes to the core software [18]. Public blockchain prominently used in crypto currencies. Bitcoin [19] and Ethereum [20] are categorized as public permissionless chains.
- A consortium blockchain: It can be considered partially centralized, with only a limited number of selected groups of entities having access to view and participate in the consensus protocol.
- A private blockchain: The network is distributed and also centralized. Only selected nodes can participate in the network, and they are often managed by one central authority [18].

Type	Consensus determination	Read permission	Immutability	Efficiency	Centralized	Consensus process
Private	One organization	Public or restricted	Could be tampered with	High	Yes	Permissioned
Consortium	Selected set of nodes	Public or restricted	Could be tampered with	High	Partial	Permissioned
Public	All miners	Public	Nearly impossible	Low	No	Permission less

17.2.4   Real time

Digitalization crafts new opportunities and openings to reshape health-care organizations and deliver services. Efficient techniques provide satisfactory services to patients, outcome to increase, and provide cost benefit. It evolves IoT and blockchain technologies to understand and update to continue for essential requirement. Assess to executive advancement for real technologies provide many application use-cases to expand if required.

Blockchain is the preferred type of consortium to include by 38% for publication approach. Blockchain uses publication for different types of approach currently 10% use private blockchain, 15% is of public blockchain, and nearly 26% research papers do not define technique employed. The results are pictorially represented in Figures 17.3 and 17.4. Commonly used platforms or frameworks are Ethereum, Hyperledger Fabric, and Exonum. In publication nearly provided with new techniques are 36% which shows more research is ongoing in field of blockchain and 21% are not defined one.

Blockchain is a promising application prominently benefit to the confined area to benefit future of health stakeholders in support for their professional requirement now and ahead. It benefits a supply chain to develop future secure technologies against WannaCry attacks to teach in the healthcare industry. Combined with IoT, blockchain provides double edged knife support to optimize and to provide convenience, increasing risks on the other. It is vulnerable to risks and can be hacked. Embrace job prevention, enhance security risk, and gain access to vital technology.

17.2.5   Key characteristics of blockchain

- Decentralized: Control is not by central authority. Entries are passed on to the blockchain or agreed on a peer-to-peer network with a various consensus protocols.
- Persistency: Once created, it is not possible to delete entries once accepted by the distributed ledger and stored in multiple nodes.
- Anonymity/pseudonymity: It makes audit and traceability possible by linking a block to the previous one by including a hash.
- Enhanced security: No one is allowed to set or change characteristics of the network.
- Distributed ledgers: Maintains full information on each and every transaction and participant.
- Consensus: The architecture is clearly and intelligently carved so as to support network decisions.
- Faster settlement: Transactions will be finalized at a faster rate in comparison to traditional banking systems.
- Transparency: Each transaction will be recorded and verified publicly.
- Immutability: Data once stored cannot be modified by anyone. Only a genuine user can alter it.
- Security: The data stored in all systems which increase its hack proof.
- Reduced transaction cost: Eliminates third party or banks reduces transaction costs.
- Innovation: Provides innovation platform for conventional business model.

The basic structure is shown in Figure 17.5, it includes a tree structure to verify data by storing in the root of the tree on the blockchain [35–41].

17.2.6   Blockchain in the healthcare sector

Activities in the healthcare sector are problem driven, and data and personnel intensive. It has ability to modify, access, and implement evolving problems in this

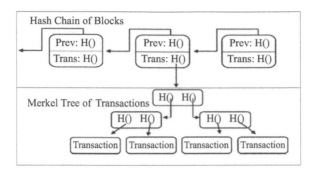

Figure 17.5   Structure of blockchain

area. Care operations can be divided into triage, problem solving, decision making, comprehensive, and assessment. The outcomes hinge therefore also into multi-disciplinary problems. Healthcare personnel can apply the obtained knowledge, and acquired skills and technologies to solve problems with patients. The medical decision taking and patient treatments, and skills can be exchanged with educational institutes where students can be trained. Students can experiment with new technologies by combining or improving existing technologies [42–56].

Blockchain has identified numerous technological platforms. The most prominent ones are compared in Table 17.2.

17.3   Internet of Things (IoTs)

IoT is not a new term. It was initially propounded in 1999 by Kevin Ashton. Its use started with the growth of the RFID market in 2005. Even then go proficiency in 2014. IoT is also known as machine-to-machine communication technology, smart systems, Web of Things, Industrial Internet (of Things), Industry 4.0, intelligent systems and pervasive computing. It is interconnection of physical components or objects with common objectives by identifying with embedded computing systems capable to exchange data and commands utilizing available infrastructure. Market analysis estimated that IoT would increase to over 20 billion by 2020 to support useful data streams called digital twins, they will get its opportunities more only when used in large scale as Internet. Researchers have estimated that IoT would become a major pillar in digitalization. IoT can be grouped as Consumer IoTs (CIoTs) and Industrial IoTs (IIoTs). The most focused ones so far seem to be IIOTs. Standardized infrastructure, open application programming interfaces, and collaborations are still required in IoT to increase occupancy in life areas [51–66].

17.3.1   IoT for healthcare

Healthcare issues are increasing gradually due to the ignorance of health. It can perform on regular basis which can now be looked after by the fast-growing

Table 17.2 Comparison of blockchain technological platforms

Name of platform	Token	Language	Consensus	Time units	Transaction/sec	DApps	Smart contract	SDK	Atomic swaps	sidechains
QTUm	PoS	Solidity	120	70	Y	Y	Y	Y	Y	Y
ETH	PoW/PoS	Solidity	15	15	Y	Y	Y	Y	Y	y
NEO	dBFT	C#, Java, Python	15	1,000	Y	Y	Y	Y	N	Y
Wanchain	WAN	Solidity	PoS	Not found	5	Y	Y	In progress	N	Y
Lisk	LSK	Javascript	DPoS	10	5	Y	In progress	In progress	N	In progress
Ark	ARK	Javascript	DPoS	8	25	Y	In progress	In progress	In progress	Y
Eos	SOS	C, C++	DPoS	0.5	100j	Y	Y	Y	N	N
Stratis	STRAT	C#, .NET	PoS	60	20k	Y	Y	Y	N	Y
Waves	LPoS	100	33	Scale	Y	In progress	Y	In progress		In progress

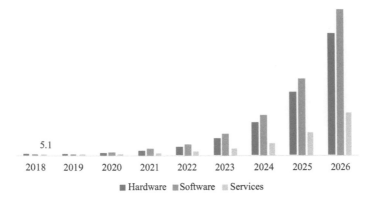

5.1

2018　2019　2020　2021　2022　2023　2024　2025　2026

■ Hardware ■ Software ■ Services

Figure 17.6　Projection of blockchain sales

communication technologies and smart devices. According to the World Health Organization (WHO), 4.9 million people die every year from lung cancer due to the consumption of tobacco, overweight causes 2.6 million deaths, 4.4 million deaths are caused by elevated cholesterol, and 7.1 million people die from high blood pressure. It is said that in the next 10 years, deaths from chronic diseases will increase by 17%, which means about 64 million people. These chronic diseases are highly variable in their symptoms, evaluation and treatments. This requires continuous monitoring. Here are several examples of monitoring technologies which have been recently developed:

- A robust healthcare model was developed for continuous monitoring of the patients even when traveling. Sensitive data was collected from the IoT sensors connected to the patient's body and sent to a server through the patient smart phone (Selvi, 2018).
- New microwave ovens like the GE Brillion Microwave oven and, MAID microwave oven are already connected to the Internet and can share data to smart phones.
- New IoT devices are now being integrated in connected kitchens. New products such as smart food scales allow users to place a food item on a scale. Smart sensors send a full nutritional profile to the user's smart phone within seconds. The scale currently recognizes over 300,000 food items and 80,000 restaurant dishes. This Wi-Fi and Bluetooth compatible Food Scale is great for nutrition and dieting (Figure 17.6).

17.4　Blockchain, IoT and healthcare systems

In this subsection, we discuss IoT and healthcare systems.

17.4.1　Why both blockchain and IoT?

According to market analysis from source of research dive analysis, blockchain and IoT software segments witnessed an account of US$15.4 million in 2018 and estimated to increase at a 91.1–93.6% CAGR even with the impact of COVID-19. As shown in Figure 4.1, sales are projected to markup to $1459.8 million by end of 2026 with an average growth of 94.8%. It is possible to identify avenue offered for both in hardware, software and service domains. Applications such as smart contracts, data security, data sharing, and asset tracking and management segments usage of both technologies are promising today [56–62].

17.4.2 Shortfall in existing systems

Current IoTs are designed on server–client models in which all objects are to be authenticated and connected. For processing and storage high-capacity, cloud servers are required. The device communicated through Internet even if they are connected nearby which is not practical (in small IoTs/local IoTs). System requires connecting links, cloud storage, networking equipment's, network establishment all requires large cost. IoTs are currently more exposed to single point failure is data being stored at single location in cloud. Blockchain for IoT looks like promising for e-healthcare paradigms as it is a peer-to-peer network. It reduces single point failures. It addresses privacy concerns for IoT with cryptographic methods using tamper-resistant ledgers.

Blockchain and IOT technologies are providing favorable environments for the healthcare sector. Data transactions have become distributed with the incorporation of these skills. Any authorized person can analyze and track from staying in their place. By doing so, the transparency of data is maintained. Challenges of combining the blockchain and IoT are:

(a) Privacy or anonymity benefits: Privacy hides the real identity of IoT applications with sensitive data.
(b) Trustworthiness: In IoTs, data will get exchanged between organizations under different infrastructures. This requires application monitoring to improve trust.
(c) Smart contracts: Improve efficiency and security through contracts.
(d) Notifications and mitigations: Most applications in distributed systems provide solutions based on smart solutions to resolve through combine technological efforts.
(e) Resource limitations: IOT devices are capable of performing only limited computation because of their low storage, but a blockchain operation demands excessive computations which require higher.
(f) Bandwidth limits: The information exchange in blockchain involves the validation of transactions at intermediate nodes but IoTs operate basically on end-to-end layer with limited bandwidth.
(g) Connectivity limits: The blockchain protocol supports access and modifications by all nodes parallel. With the inclusion of IoTs, the connected may be susceptible to security attacks.
(h) Memory limits: Healthcare records can be very large in size and include analysis at different levels to reward involved blocks.

17.4.2.1 Current status of blockchain in healthcare

Blockchain has been adopted in healthcare project applications with a goal to design quality services. Blockchain provides major advantage in terms of the transfer of health services in a secure manner with the adoption of recent innovative technologies in core infrastructures.

Figure 17.7 depicts a traditional representation of a patient's visit to a medical doctor, and the manual analysis and recording of data by a medical expert. There is no interconnection from one system to another, all are independent and operate separately. When a patient visits a doctor, doctor performs a checkup to identify symptoms and possible disease. Then, accordingly suitable medicine prescribed. The patient will collect the recommended medicine from a pharmacy. Patient's data is often stored online but with little security. The devices could be compromised by intruders. The traditional patient health record system in hospitals or medical institutions is not well protected. This can lead to information loss and the misuse of data. The problems can be avoided with the inclusion of blockchain into the healthcare ecosystem to achieve the following:

- Access control: It defines polices to control and manage health record data by establishing trust between the owner of the data and the staff performing and managing patient data entries.
- Interoperability: It gives the ability to connect systems and to share and use data in an interoperable manner across the organization
- Data provenance: The systems can provide data origins and details of data records. The storage of historical data is useful for training students and to take further decisions and keeping reference. It is also helpful in designing software systems to assist in the management of medical record.
- Data integrity: This refers to the quality of data. The degree to expected quality of data is meeting or exceed. Its expectancy is estimated to provide data integrity.

Some effective and successful practical applications of Blockchain are listed below:

(i) Doc.AI:
Doc.AI (https://doc.ai/) is a Palo Alto-based start-up. They combine computer vision and natural language processing technologies to secure

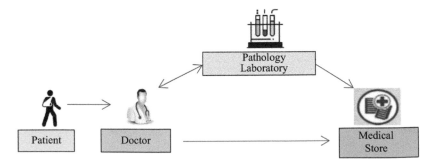

Figure 17.7 Traditional way of representation of medical system

medical data and extract meaningful insights. It was initially structured in 2016 by Walter and Sam De Brouwer Doc.AI. Users can access medical data in this system to launch a data trial. It is a collection of all kinds' medical data. Once the data is retrieved, it will be forwarded for data analysis by data scientists. All predictions will be done by connecting dots of all data. The collected and sequenced data can then be sent for training to medical professionals to get more evidence on data.

(ii)   FarmaTrust

FarmaTrust (https://www.farmatrust.com/) is a drug-based medical supply chain company. Its main objective is to distribute drugs in a trustworthy manner using the blockchain concept. It allows the tracking, monitoring and supply of drugs and related activities from pharmaceutical companies through a digital supply chain. FarmaTrust helps the industry to monitor at each and every level of the supply chain, from manufacturing to delivery in person. This reduces the possible propagation of fake or non-genie drugs. These operations are performed by connecting pharmaceutical industries, suppliers, manufacturers, pharmacies, companies, and logistics companies. Single-integrated network to ensure limpidity within the supply chain.

(iii)   Chronicled

Chronicled (https://www.chronicled.com/) is combination of both IoT and blockchain technologies. They aim to improve accountability and traceability for the drugs' supply chain. The key features are speed and delivery time of drugs products, in certain instances in a time sensitive manner. The end-to-end chain solution is provided with blockchain and IoT driven with artificial intelligence. A tracing and tracking feature was incorporated in Chronicled with the launch of MediLedger in 2017 in partnership with LinkLab. It also seeks to reduce non-generous or phony drugs supply into the delivery chain.

(iv)   Patientory

Patientory (https://patientory.com/) provides an end-to-end medical data encryption based on blockchain technology. It maintains HIPAA compliance requirements. Data is effectively stored, retrieved, and exchanged in a safer manner between staff and involved in processing health information. It allows users to connect with the Patientory community to discuss issues thereby supporting information exchange between medical experts who are involved in resolving the problems. This provision is made on a restricted basis for the interconnected staff such as correlated doctors on a particular set of medical data of a patient.

17.5   SimplyVitalHealth

SimplyVitalHealth (https://www.f6s.com/simplyvitalhealth) was started in 2017 by Katherine Kuzmeskas with the aim to stop and eliminate surrounding value-based care. It connects on tables different healthcare staff members from various clinical institutions. It is driven by blockchain technology allows healthcare workers to optimize and streamline the healthcare process by reducing cost as well as the duration of care for patients. SimplyVitalHealth also helps in reducing cost required care patients. It also supports financial and clinical healthcare solutions for patients.

Currently blockchain-based application projects are striving more in secure delivery of services to required patients are data analyzers. Blockchain helps support longitudinal records of disease registries, lab test results, and any major or minor health related patient information. It also helps maintain medical data such as lab reports or server details in a systematic manner. The duplication of data, misuse or the sharing of unintended data will be avoided through the incorporation of blockchain. The complete ledger registrar of medical data pertaining to a patient stored in using primary and secondary keys in exchange of information secure manner.

17.5.1 Blockchain and IoT-based architecture

IoT is the collection of devices physically connected and capable of extension which are capable of communicating with each other via the Internet with embedded electronics. Blockchain can secure a network and stored data. Blockchain also provides a secure platform to all connected IoT devices to communicate with each other in a secure manner as shown in Figure 17.8.

17.5.2 Comparison of existing approaches for layer-oriented use cases

Blockchain and IoT-layered systems

IoT supports two ways of applicational usage in healthcare services clinical and operation support. It is patient centric, and activities are carried on remotely.

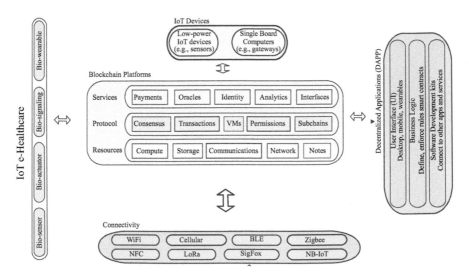

Figure 17.8   IoT and blockchain architecture

Aids in clinical trials, track signs, and indicators to study on blood sugar levels and other data collected about patient through sensors remotely. Blockchain securely collects the generated data and distribute permanent, unalterable records of transactions. The transaction in blockchain includes blocks and records on an ongoing chain of events to share among members of a network. The processing of sensing to transactions can be grouped into three layers as (i) process, (ii) endpoint, and (ii) application. The three-layered structure is shown in Figure 17.6. The first is IoT healthcare network, an interconnection of hospitals and patients. In the next layer exchange of information remotely in secure distributed way to intended through blockchain. The top layer is a record maintenance layer. Here patient medical records are kept for further use.

A detailed comparison of the approaches is discussed in Table 17.3.

17.5.3   Combined efforts of blockchain and IoT: benefits

Both blockchain and IoT technologies complement each other to explore ways to implement new increased services in the healthcare sector. Strive to get deeper insights, efficacy, accountability, and responsibility. A few benefits for the healthcare sector are:

- Enhance security: Blockchain enhances encryption to secure data. It is a good solution to store sensitive data of patients or medical notes. IoT helps in fast transactions and apps building.

Table 17.3   A detailed comparison of the approaches is discussed

Author	Year	Technique	Merits	Demerits
Wsim *et al.*	2017	Service architecture to monitor issues of injunctions	Results provided with explanation and discussed thoroughly	No optimum resource allocation
Kim	2018	Blockchain based edge computing	Execute complex program	Results are not amenable
Luong *et al.*	2018	Used for application mining	Well-documented results	Optimal allocation of resources
Aly *et al.*	2019	Blockchain-based IoT	Explanation of design and architecture is informative	No resource allocation and data analysis model
Yumna *et al.*	2019	Three-layer architecture mode for data exchange	Better program identification	Results are not detailed
Abdellatif *et al.*	2020	Blockchain and IoT	Good education model can be extendable to other fields	Security exchange information is not detailed

- Healthcare solutions at affordable rates: blockchain supports distributed secure data access, provides handy transaction storage and the possibility to retrieve information from large pools of data. IoT transmits the data over the Internet. Using these methods, remote patients can access healthcare solutions at low cost.
- Optimize energy consumption: IoT and blockchain have proven that they are energy concern as applied in Google. Additionally, data mining can lower energy consumption in maintaining health records.

Potential applications of blockchain and IoT are the following.

17.5.3.1 Supply chain management

Healthcare supply chains currently insecure and convoluted. The drugs manufactured in companies have to pass through different stakeholders before reaching customers. Verification, identification, and authentication are required at every stage of the supply chain. Blockchain and IoT are suitable solutions to check many issues including ingredients detection in medicines and the traceability of counterfeiting sources.

17.5.3.2 Medical records integrity

Blockchain and IoT provide absolute proof protection. Health records and files stored using blockchain cannot be thereby supporting the records' integrity.

17.5.3.3 Schedule and plan treatment

Provide solution for medical research purposes. Intended patient's data can be effectively studied and impacted for any specific treatment over a patient population. Improvements can be found in adoption of such treatment in patient population based on blockchain and IoT.

17.5.3.4 Identification of a single patient

The mismatch and duplication of patient's record is common in the healthcare sector. The different schema in EHRs make the task more difficult. Manipulation is not easy in simple data problem can be resolved with blockchain as data is hashed. IoT devices provide information of individual patients as and when, and from anywhere when required.

17.5.3.5 Entitlements

Payer and provider contract terms and conditions to settle claims require more time. These could be resolved more easily with the incorporation of blockchain and IoT. The processing of claims from providers is effectively submitted through a proper IoT deployment.

17.5.3.6 Operational change

Create change in business models of healthcare sector is possible through blockchain. IoT and blockchain have potential benefits to revolutionize pharmacy companies or healthcare professionals. Companies can collect real-time data and professional such as doctors and nurses can access patients' real-time data safely and remotely.

17.5.3.7   Medical equipment manufacturing automation

Traditional methodologies do not provide enough flexibility from manufacture design to use. Progressively, product testing, and quality control have become automated. The automation of manufacturing can bring transparency, amenability checks, production, and security (Table 17.4).

17.6   Future research and challenges

Many researchers are looking at combining these blockchain and IoT technologies to but, some obstacles remain [63].

17.6.1   Healthcare sector: challenges

Percentage of people agreeing for changes to existing healthcare sector is more than vice versa. Blockchain technology has gained importance since 2014. One pioneer of blockchain, Frank Gens has explained the importance of third generation security technologies. The blockchain incorporated IoT platform clear the bigger technologies urges for artificial intelligence with new deep learning algorithms, next-generation security encryption principles, edge, and fog computing. Incorporate high-performance chips, machine vision and computer, and others pretty endless. The five challenging use cases for the deployment of both are: the supply chain, share networks, network management, smart contracts, and authentication.

Both supports cluster in healthcare to benefit applications. Implement emerging technology in applications like healthcare on a large scale is not easy.

- Uncertainty: Blockchain is still a new technology which requires more application-level habituation. It has found applications as cryptocurrencies but has yet seem many other successful applications. Not yet initiatives taken for blockchain in healthcare as of IoT.
- Ownership of data: Healthcare records ownership cannot be established with grants of permission for sharing with both blockchain and IoT.
- Cost: The cost for building blockchain technology in healthcare is not predictable as there is no clear idea to find cost for its establishment. Hence, it is difficult to consider for any sectors. That is not case of IoT.
- Rules & regulations: No standard rules and privacy regulations act in place for both IoT and blockchain.
- Storage capability: Healthcare records consist of medical records, images, lab reports, and documents. The files can exceed storage capacity in blockchain which is challenging. It is same with IoT devices which come with small storage capacities.
- Technical barriers: Blockchain requires a decent infrastructure and interconnectivity to be implemented.

Table 17.4 Comparison Internet of medical things mechanisms for healthcare in the blockchain

	Blockchain techniques	Data	Merits	Demerits
42	Community blockchain	IoT data	Localization security of network	More malicious attacks and small network attack
43	Hyperledger platform Reserved Blockchain	IoT data	Dyslexia diagnosis record for medical practitioners	Preprocessing and processing time is more
44	Undefined	EMR, EHR, and PHR	Reduced overhead of mining and storage	Open to secure and privacy issues
45	Information proof and reserved blockchain	Medical records	Health prediction mode for privacy	Attacks can happen
46	Fabric platform Hyperledger	IoT data and EHR	Node down against fault in network is distributed	Attacks can happen
47	Community blockchain	IoT data	Ensures anonymity and immutability	High risk of computational time
48	Reserved, Ethereum platform blockchain	IoT data	Data security, storage and transparency use PoW mechanism	Real-time monitoring is longer
49	Community blockchain and proof-of-concept	IoT data	Automation of secure smart integration of wireless body area network (WBAN)	Data ingestion inefficiency
50	Community blockchain.	IoT data	Validation time reduced with cluster	Transparency and trustworthiness
51	Stake proof and reserved blockchain	Medical records	Artificial healthcare systems	Treatment scenarios are limited
52	Ethereum-based smart contracts with monetary-based mining	Remote sensed data	Access control	Integrity and scalability can be minimum
53	Key management with private blockchain	Medical data	Accountability and rescission	Privacy leakage possible
54	Distributed private blockchain	IoT data	Secure search and access control	Intrusion attacks not considered
55	Public blockchain with permission	PHR and IoI data	Time controlled rescission	Privacy issues still exists
56	Index blockchain with public blockchain	IoT data	Manages blockchain and privacy issues	Confidentiality not defined
57	Notary-based blockchain	Medical records	Fair analysis and traceability	Malicious operation not addressed
58	Private blockchain	IoT data	Data sharing and QOS	Data versioning can be a hurdle for large scale datasets
59	Public two-layer blockchain	IoT data	Tamper resistance	Anonymous information sharing issues
60	Public blockchain	IoT data	Immutability, identity management	Efficient delivery of message may block sometimes

- Knowledge gap: Many people are not knowledgeable enough to implement blockchain in healthcare.
- Legal and compliance: Law is very different in the connecting countries which is an issue.
- Dispensation power: It is algorithm for CPU intensive and IoT with consensus of encryption. The computational capabilities of different systems are different [18]. They are not able to run computational steps at the required speed.
- Scalability: The adoption of new distributed ledgers creates new security challenges for decentralization which have to be managed.

17.6.2   Healthcare sector: future research

1. Health professionals, doctors, therapists, medical specialists, researchers, and insurers engaged in the medical sector are provided full accessibility to electronic medical reports for the efficient treatment of patients.
2. Increased institutional interoperability.
3. More empowerment of patients for long and active lives.
4. Interoperability will increase at the institutional level.
5. Medical prescriptions and treatments are better controlled.
6. Provision for remote distribution of doctors' certificates.
7. In pace identity management, digital ID card, patients' centric view, personalized use cases.
8. Data storage and security transparency.
9. Better IT-based knowledge transfer with GDPR.
10. Efficiency, cost reduction, payment solution on smart contracts between hospitals, to insure company, client, process and bureaucracy.
11. High-cost effectiveness and value improvement with better healthcare model.
12. Improvement in the quality of treatments.
13. Easy tracking of drug authenticity, pharmaccutical companies, medical equipment, in the supply chain management.

17.7   Conclusions

This chapter has identified existing problems in the healthcare sector and how blockchain and IoT can help minimizes these issues. We have presented innovations and advances and architecture. We have also introduced a proposed model and layered architecture for healthcare systems. We also covered existing and remaining challenges as well as future perspectives. Blockchain will boost the healthcare sector as it. Allow the sharing of information among stakeholders without compromising on data security and integrity.

References

[1]   D. Gunasekaran Manogaran, C. Lopez, K.M. Thota, S.P. Abbas, and S. Revathi, "Big data analytics in healthcare Internet of Things", *In: Innovative*

Healthcare Systems for the 21st Century, Springer, Cham, pp. 263–284, 2017, DOI: 10.1007/978-3-319-55774-8_10

[2]   A.K.M. Jahangir, Alam Majumder, Y.A. ElSaadany, R. Young and D.R. Ucci. "An energy efficient wearable smart IoT system to predict cardiac arrest", *Advances in Human–Computer Interaction*, 2019, pp. 1–21, 2019, Article ID 1507465.

[3]   A. Ud Din, M. Almogren Guizani, and M. Zuair, "A decade of Internet of Things: analysis in the light of healthcare applications," *IEEE Access*, vol. 7, pp. 89967–89979, 2019. doi: 10.1109/ACCESS.2019.2927082

[4]   R. Giuliano, F. Mazzenga, A. Neri, and A.M. Vegni, "Security access protocols in IoT capillary networks," *IEEE Internet of Things Journal*, vol. 4, pp. 645–657, 2016.

[5]   A. Kulkarni and S. Sathe, "Healthcare applications of the Internet of Things: a review," *International Journal of Computer Science and Information Technology*, vol. 5, pp. 6229–6232, 2014.

[6]   M. Samaniego and R. Deters, "Blockchain as a service for IoT," In: Proceedings of the 2016 IEEE International Conference on Internet of Things (iThings) and IEEE Green Computing and Communications (GreenCom) and IEEE Cyber, Physical and Social Computing (CPSCom) and IEEE Smart Data (SmartData), Berlin, Germany, 4–8 April 2016, pp. 433–436.

[7]   X. Liang, S. Shetty, D. Tosh, C. Kamhoua, K. Kwiat, and L. Njilla, "Provchain: a blockchain-based data proven an architecture in cloud environment with enhanced privacy and availability," In: 2017 17th IEEE/ACM International Symposiumon Cluster, Cloud and Grid Computing (CCGRID), IEEE, 2017, pp.468–477.

[8]   R.O. Jr., "The Machinery Behind Health Care Reform," https://www.washingtonpost.com/wpdyn/content/article/2009/05/15/AR2009051503667.html, 27-May-2020](2020).

[9]   M.A. Khan and K. Salah, "IoT security: review, blockchain solutions, and open challenges," *Future Generation Computer Systems*. vol. 82, pp. 395–411, 2018.

[10]   U. Khalid, M. Asim, T. Baker, P.C. Hung, M.A. Tariq, and L. Rafferty, "A decentralized light weight block chain-based authentication mechanism for IoT systems," *Cluster Computing*, pp. 1–21, 2020.

[11]   L. Linn and M. Koo, "Block chain for health data and its potential use in health IT and health care related research," In: ONC/NIST Use of Block Chain for Health Care and Research Workshop, Gaithersburg, MD, USA, 2016.

[12]   T. Hardin and D. Kotz, "Blockchain in health data systems: a survey," In: 2019 Sixth International Conference on Internet of Things: Systems, Management and Security (IOTSMS), IEEE, 2019, pp. 490–497.

[13]   Z. Zheng, S. Xie, H.N. Dai, X. Chen, and H. Wang, "Blockchain challenges and opportunities: a survey," *International Journal of Web and Grid Services*. vol. 14, p. 352, 2018.

[14]   D. Minoli and B. Occhiogrosso, "Blockchain mechanisms for IoT security," *Internet of Things*, vol. 1, pp. 1–13, 2018.

[15]   O. Novo, "Blockchain meets IoT: an architecture for scalable access management in IoT," *IEEE Internet of Things Journal*, vol. 5, pp. 1184–1195, 2018.

[16]   N. Scarpato, A. Pieroni, L. Di Nunzio, and F. Fallucchi, "E-health-IoT universe: a review," *Management*, vol. 21, p. 46, 2017. *Applied Science.* 2020, 10, 6749 19 of 23

[17]   A. K. Tyagi, S. Chandrasekaran, and N. Sreenath, "Blockchain technology: a new technology for creating distributed and trusted computing environment," In: 2022 International Conference on Applied Artificial Intelligence and Computing (ICAAIC), 2022, pp. 1348–1354, doi: 10.1109/ICAAIC53929.2022.9792702.

[18]   N. Team, NEO White Paper: A Distributed Network for the Smart Economy. Available online: https: //docs.neo.org/docs/en-us/basic/whitepaper.html (accessed on 10 August 2020).

[19]   Z. Zheng, S. Xie, H. Dai, X. Chen, and H. Wang (Eds.), "An overview of blockchain technology: architecture, consensus, and future trends," In: 2017 IEEE International Congress on Big Data (BigData Congress), IEEE, 2017.

[20]   A.K. Tyagi and A. Abraham (eds.), *Recent Trends in Blockchain for Information Systems Security and Privacy*, 1st edn., CRC Press, New York; 2021. https://doi.org/10.1201/9781003139737.

[21]   A. Buterin, *Next-generation Smart Contract and Decentralized Application Platform*, vol. 3(37), 2014.

[22]   A.R. Liaqat Ali, A. Khan, M. Zhou, A. Javeed, and J.A. Khan, "An automated diagnostic system for heart disease prediction based on χ^2 statistical model and optimally configured deep neural network," *IEEE Access*, vol. 7, pp. 34938–34945, 2019, doi: 10.1109/ACCESS.2019.2904800

[23]   A.U. Haq, J.P. Li, M.H. Memon, S. Nazir, and R. Sun, "A hybrid intelligent system framework for the prediction of heart disease using machine learning algorithms," *Mobile Information Systems*, 2018.

[24]   P.K. Gupta, B.T. Maharaj, and R. Malekian, "A novel and secure IoT based cloud centric architecture to perform predictive analysis of users activities in sustainable health centres," *Multimedia Tools and Applications*, vol. 76, no. 18, pp. 18489–18512, 2017, DOI: 10.1007/s11042-016-4050-6

[25]   Blockchain Council, "How Blockchain Can Solve Major challenges of COVID-19 Faced by Healthcare Sectors?" Available: https://www.blockchain-council.org/blockchain/how-blockchain-can-solve-major-challenges-of-covid-19-faced-by-healthcare-sectors/.

[26]   P.M. Kumar, S. Lokesh, R. Varatharajan, G.C. Babu, and P. Parthasarathy, "Cloud and IoT based disease prediction and diagnosis system for healthcare using Fuzzy neural classifier," *Future Generation Computer Systems*, vol. 86, pp. 527–534, 2018, doi: 10.1016/j.future.2018.04.036

[27]   M. Abdel-Basset, A. Gamal, G. Manogaran, and H. Viet Long, "A novel group decision making model based on neutrosophic sets for heart disease diagnosis," *Multimedia Tools and Applications*, pp. 1–26, 2019, doi: 10.1007/s11042-019-07742-7.

[28]   P.M. Kumar and U.D. Gandhi, "A novel three-tier Internet of Things architecture with machine learning algorithm for early detection of heart diseases," *Computers & Electrical Engineering*, vol. 65, pp. 222–235, 2018, doi: 10.1016/j.compeleceng.2017.09.001

[29]   J. Vijayashree and H. Parveen Sultana, "A machine learning framework for feature selection in heart disease classification using improved particle swarm optimization with support vector machine classifier," *Programming and Computer Software*, vol. 44, no. 6, pp. 388–397, 2018.

[30]   S. Mohan, C. Thirumalai, and G. Srivastava, "Effective heart disease prediction using hybrid machine learning techniques," *IEEE Access*, vol. 7, pp. 81542–81554, 2019, doi: 10.1109/ACCESS.2019.2923707

[31]   A. Panesar, *Machine Learning and AI for Healthcare: Big Data for Improved Health Outcomes*, Springer, Emeryville, CA, USA, 2019.

[32]   H. Peter and A. Moser, "Blockchain – applications in banking & payment transactions: results of a survey," In: Proceedings of the 14th International Scientific Conference Pt, European Financial Systems, Brno, Czech Republic, 26–27 June 2017, vol. 2, pp. 141–149.

[33]   S. Pirbhulal, W. Wu, and G. Li, "A biometric security model for wearable healthcare," In: Proceedings of the 2018 IEEE International Conference on Data Mining Workshops (ICDMW), Singapore, 17–20 November 2018, pp. 136–143.

[34]   A. Hudaya, M. Amin, N.M. Ahmad, and S. Kannan, "Integrating distributed pattern recognition technique for event monitoring within the iot-blockchain network," In: Proceedings of International Conference on Intelligent and Advanced System (ICIAS), August 2018, pp. 1–6.

[35]   S. Velankar, S. Valecha, and S. Maji, "Bitcoin price prediction using machine learning," In: Proceedings of 20th International Conference on Advanced Communications Technology (ICACT), February 2018, pp. 144–147.

[36]   Y. Zhao, Y. Yu, Y. Li, G. Han, and X. Du, "Machine learning based privacy-preserving fair data trading in big data market," *Information Science*, vol. 478, pp. 449–460, 2019.

[37]   W. Meng, E.W. Tischhauser, Q. Wang, Y. Wang, and J. Han, "When intrusion detection meets blockchain technology: a review," *IEEE Access*, vol. 6, pp. 10179–10188, 2018.

[38]   M. Saad and A. Mohaisen, "Towards characterizing blockchain-based cryptocurrencies for highly-accurate predictions," In: Proceedings of the IEEE Conference on Computer Communications Workshops (INFOCOM WKSHPS), April 2018, pp. 704–709.

[39]   N.C. Luong, Z. Xiong, P.Wang, and D. Niyato, "Optimal auction for edge computing resource management in mobile blockchain networks: a deep learning approach," in Proceedings of the IEEE International Conference on Communication (ICC), May 2018, pp. 1–6.

[40]   J. Vora, P. DevMurari, S. Tanwar, S. Tyagi, N. Kumar, and M.S. Obaidat, "Blind signatures based secured e-healthcare system," In: Proceedings of the

International Conference on Computer, Information, and Telecommunication Systems (CITS), July 2018, pp. 1–5.

[41] P. Sarda, M.J.M. Chowdhury, A. Colman, M.A. Kabir, and J. Han, "Blockchain for fraud prevention: a work-history fraud prevention system," In: Proceeding of the 17th IEEE International Conference on Trust, Security and Privacy in Computing and Communications/12th IEEE International Conference on Big Data Science and Engineering (TrustCom/BigDataSE), August 2018, pp. 1858–1863.

[42] K. Sgantzos and I. Grigg, "Artificial intelligence implementations on the blockchain, use cases and future applications," *Future Internet*, vol. 11, no. 8, p. 170, 2019.

[43] K.N. Griggs, O. Ossipova, C.P. Kohlios, A.N. Baccarini, E.A. Howson, and T. Hayajneh, "Healthcare blockchain system using smart contracts for secure automated remote patient monitoring," *Journal of Medical Systems*, vol. 42, p. 130, 2018.

[44] M.A. Rahman, E. Hassanain, M.M. Rashid, S.J. Barnes, and M.S. Hossain, "Spatial blockchain-based secure mass screening framework for children with dyslexia," *IEEE Access*, vol. 6, pp. 61876–61885, 2018.

[45] C. Esposito, A. De Santis, G. Tortora, H. Chang, and K.K.R. Choo, "Blockchain: a panacea for healthcare cloud-based data security and privacy?" *IEEE Cloud Computing*, vol. 5, pp. 31–37, 2018.

[46] T.T. Kuo and L. Ohno-Machado, Model Chain: Decentralized Privacy-Preserving Healthcare Predictive Modeling Framework on Private Blockchain Networks. arXiv 2018, arXiv:1802.01746

[47] D. Ichikawa, M. Kashiyama, and T. Ueno, "Tamper-resistant mobile health using blockchain technology," *JMIR mHealth uHealth*, vol. 5, p. e111, 2017.

[48] R. Saia, Internet of Entities (IoE): A Blockchain-based Distributed Paradigm to Security. arXiv 2018, arXiv:1808.08809.

[49] B. Jo, R. Khan, and Y.S. Lee, "Hybrid blockchain and Internet-of-Things network for underground structure health monitoring," *Sensors*, vol. 18, p. 4268, 2018.

[50] D.V. Dimitrov, "Medical Internet of Things and big data in healthcare," *Healthcare Informatics Research,* vol. 22, pp. 156–163, 2016; A. Dorri, S.S. Kanhere, and R. Jurdak, "Towards an optimized blockchain for IoT," In: Proceedings of the ACM Second International Conference on Internet-of-Things Design and Implementation, Pittsburgh, PA, USA, 18–21 April 2017; pp. 173–178.

[51] J. Qiu, X. Liang, S. Shetty, and D. Bowden, "Towards secure and smart healthcare in smart cities using blockchain," In: Proceedings of the 2018 IEEE International Smart Cities Conference (ISC2), Kansas City, MO, USA, 16–19 September 2018, pp. 1–4.

[52] G.G. Dagher, J. Mohler, M. Milojkovic, and P.B. Marella, "Ancile: privacy-preserving framework for access control nd interoperability of elec-tronic health records using blockchain technology," *Sustainable Cities and Society*, vol. 39, pp. 283–297, 2018.

[53]   A. Al Omar, M.S. Rahman, A. Basu, and S. Kiyomoto, "Medibchain: a blockchain based privacy preserving platform for healthcare data," In: International Conference on Security, Privacy and Anonymity in Computation, Communication and Storage, Springer, Cham, 2017, pp. 534–543.

[54]   J. Xu, K. Xue, S. Li, *et al.*, "Healthchain: a blockchain-based privacy preserving scheme for large-scale health data," *IEEE Internet of Things Journal*, vol. 6(5), pp. 8770–8781, 2019.

[55]   A. Zhang and X. Lin, "Towards secure and privacy-preserving data sharing in e-health systems via consortium blockchain," *Journal of Medical Systems*, vol. 42(8), p. 140, 2018.

[56]   M. Du, Q. Chen, J. Chen, and X. Ma, "An optimized consortium blockchain for medical information sharing," *IEEE Transactions on Engineering Management*, 2020.

[57]   A.-S. Kleinaki, P. Mytis-Gkometh, G. Drosatos, P. S. Efraimidis, and E. Kaldoudi, "A blockchain-based notarization service for biomedical knowledge retrieval," *Computational and Structural Biotechnology Journal*, vol. 16, pp. 288–297, 2018.

[58]   K.N. Griggs, O. Ossipova, C.P. Kohlios, A.N. Baccarini, E.A. Howson, and T. Hayajneh, "Healthcare blockchain system using smart contracts for secure automated remote patient monitoring," *Journal of Medical Systems*, vol. 42 (7), p. 130, 2018.

[59]   A.A. Abdellatif, A.Z. Al-Marridi, A. Mohamed, A. Erbad, C.F. Chiasserini, and A. Refaey, "ssHealth: toward secure, blockchain-enabled healthcare systems," *IEEE Network*, 2020.

[60]   L. Chen, W.-K. Lee, C.-C. Chang, K.-K.R. Choo, and N. Zhang, "Blockchain based searchable encryption for electronic health record sharing," *Future Generation Computer Systems*, vol. 95, pp. 420–429, 2019.

[61]   M. Aly, F. Khomh, M. Haoues, A. Quintero, and S. Yacout, "Enforcing security in Internet of Things frameworks: a systematic literature review," *Internet of Things*, p. 100050, 2019.

[62]   H. Yumna, M.M. Khan, M. Ikram, and S. Ilyas, "Use of blockchain in education: a systematic literature review," In: Asian Conference on Intelligent.

[63]   S.K. Singh, S. Rathore, and J.H. Park, "Block IoT intelligence: a blockchain-enabled intelligent IoT architecture with artificial intelligence," *Future Generation Computer Systems*, to be published, doi: 10.1016/j. future.2019.09.002.

Chapter 18

An integrated dimensionality reduction model for classifying IoT-enabled smart healthcare genomic data

Micheal Olaolu Arowolo[1], Moses Kazeem Abiodun[1], Samuel Olawepo[1], Bukola Fatimah Balogun[2] and Amit Kumar Tyagi[3]

Abstract

Machine Learning (ML) is now a powerful factor in everyday life, and in most fields that we desire to improve. ML is a field for creating systems that can learn from data, whether labeled or unlabeled, or from the ambient. ML is employed in various of disciplines, but it is incredibly useful in the healthcare sector since it leads to improved decision-making and prediction approaches. Since ML in healthcare services is scientific research, we need to save, obtain, and properly utilize data, knowledge, and provide expertise to the issues that face the healthcare industry, as well as learning for proper decision-making. Owing to most of these innovations there is indeed a big development in health care sectors over the decades. Healthcare analysis of data has become one of the greatest favorable research fields. Healthcare includes data from diverse kinds with medical data, functional genomic data, in addition sensor data, obtained through involvement of various wearable and wireless sensor devices. Manually processing this relevant data is really challenging. ML has developed as a crucial data analysis technique. Health professionals employ these tools and techniques to analyze healthcare data to identify hazards as well as provide effective diagnosis and management. In this study, a dimensionality reduction model is suggested for classifying IoT enabled healthcare data analysis, using a COVID-19 dataset with partial least square (PLS), linear discriminant analysis (LDA) on support vector machine (SVM) and Kth nearest neighbor (KNN) classifiers. This study uses COVID-19 dataset, ML approach such as PLS, LDA, SVM, and KNN on a MATLAB tool for the analysis.

[1]Department of Computer Science, Landmark University Omu-Aran, Nigeria
[2]Department of Computer Science, Kwara State University, Nigeria
[3]School of Computer Science and Engineering, Vellore Institute of Technology, Chennai, India

The result obtained shows that PLS–LDA–SVM outperformed PLS–LDA–KNN with 90% accuracy. The review of this study has proven that this study is efficient for decision making by practitioners to adopt for efficient analysis of healthcare data analysis.

Keywords: Machine learning; Dimensionality reduction; HealthCare; Classification

18.1 Introduction

The advent of Internet-connected sensing products enabling annotations and data capacities from the physical environment has been aided through rapid advances in hardware, software, and internet technology. The overall number of Internet-connected strategies being utilized in the world is expected to reach around 50 billion. As the rise in figures and knowledges improves, the amount of information exposed rises as well. The Internet of Things (IoT) technology, which connects Internet-connected strategies, remains extended with the contemporary Internet by allowing intercommunication across the related to cyber worlds. The IoT creates big data that is categorized by its swiftness in relationships of period and place interdependence, with diversity of various modes and fluctuating data value, in due to enhanced volumes [1].

Present trend toward "smart technology," information are created in vast symmetrical quantities, with increase to the idea of big data. The "Five High-V's" are used to define big data: velocity, value, variety, volume, then veracity. Understanding entirely the value of big data, an intelligent, value, and inventive methodology for gathering and dealing out raw data is required. This will lead to increased understanding, procedure automating, and problem-solving. The IoT takes potentials in producing new datasets. A machine can interact with another machine, transmit crucial information codes, and make rapid judgments with little human aid just by emulating several human sensory qualities like as vision, hearing, and thinking [2].

Context-awareness, which incorporates environmental sensing, network connectivity, and data analysis approaches, will bridge the connections among the physical and computer-generated computation units in the years to come for IoT. Several progressive IoT applications, for instance, smart transportation systems, intelligent health care systems, smart energy classifications, and smart structures, are enabled by advancement. The underlying IoT sensor networks and smart IoT-based application services are both part of the unified architecture of IoT networks. The prominent part of sensors and Internet in the current period of the IoT gives resolution to diversity of factual challenges. Smart cities, smart healthcare, smart buildings, smart transportation, also smart location are examples of such applications. However, there are significant issues with real-time IoT sensor data, including a surfeit of impure sensor data in addition a high consumption cost of resource [2].

Machine learning (ML) models will aid in the development of symmetrical IoT systems as a major source of potential knowledge. As a result, networking devices are capable of receiving a huge spectrum of innovative symmetrical information from a multitude of connected devices, analyzing data, acquiring knowledge, and making intelligent judgments particular dataset available. To properly evaluate this information to develop the related smart and automation solutions, artificial intelligence (AI) technologies, specifically ML, are necessary. In this area, supervised, unsupervised, semi-supervised, and reinforcement learning are all forms of data mining algorithms. Deep learning, that is part of a huge spectrum of ML and AI, can examine large volumes of data efficiently [3].

AI, namely ML, has expanded rapidly mostly regarding data analytics and analysis, allowing applications to function effectively [4]. ML is widely termed to as a prominent recent knowledge in the fourth manufacturing revolt since it allows systemic learning and developments from knowledge lacking explicit programming. In the field of learning algorithms, there are four main categories: supervised, unsupervised, semi-supervised, and also reinforcement learning [5]. The nature and qualities of information, along with the efficiency of the learning procedures, govern the efficacy and proficiency of a ML results. To efficiently develop data-driven systems, ML procedures such as classification, regression, clustering, dimensionality reduction, association rule, or reinforcement learning are in existence [6]. As a result, selecting a good learning algorithm for a specific domain's goal application is difficult. This is because various learning procedures provide different aims, and even similar learning algorithms might perform differently based on input properties [7].

It is critical to comprehend the perceptions of diverse ML systems and their relevance in a variation of everyday applications, with IoT systems, services in cybersecurity, economic and management analytics, smart cities, and health are just a few examples [8,9]. Healthcare is one of the many fields that has benefited from the widespread adoption of IoT technologies to assist healthcare facilities' fundamental tasks. Ancient medical facilities are all being turned into next-generation digitalized workplaces leveraging interrelated sensor systems also Big Data approaches. Smart healthcare is an ongoing ecosphere of smart cities (i.e., intensive care houses, ambulance services, drug stores), aided by an effective technology layer (i.e., edge devices and sensor systems, wireless application protocol infrastructures, Cloud services, and so on) and propelled by new business opportunities and legislative changes that facilitate Healthcare Sector 4.0 [10,11].

Premised on the usefulness and significance of "Machine Learning" analyzing smart health information, this research demonstrates dimensionality reduction-based ML models that may be used to increase the aptitude and capacities of an operation in the healthcare sector using partial least square (PLS) with linear discriminant analysis (LDA) feature extraction to fetch latent components, support vector machine (SVM), and *K*th nearest neighbor (KNN) classifiers are then used in evaluating the performance of the experiments with the results compared.

18.2   Related works

A review of numerous articles on ML algorithms and dimensionality reduction approaches is offered in this part. Because the IoT is a novel idea for the Internet and smart data, researchers have examined several elements of ML. It is a tough subject in the aspect of computer science. Preparing and processing data are two major obstacles for investigators working with IoT. Numerous IoT suggestions have been proposed for smart health monitoring, as well as several findings have already been evaluated to determine the relevant evolution of IoT-based healthcare services, ranging from initial monitoring systems that use edge nodes for cognitive activities to more ideal target that use ML algorithms.

Several ML models that interact with the suggestion made by IoT data were recommended by presenting an arrangement of ML processes elucidating how dissimilar procedures are useful to the information in order to fetch developed knowledge, with smart cities as the key use case [1]. The ML's benefits and problems for analyzing IoT data were explored. For a more in-depth look, a use case of using a SVM on Aarhus smart city location information is described. It is discussed how data properties and application specifics can influence the selection of appropriate data analytic algorithms. Current questions and the impending route to explore in smart data analytics advancements are covered.

The smart healthcare field and data transformation concerns in IoT networks have been recognized by presenting a dispersed modular data fusion framework, whereby a separate data inputs are integrated for each step of the IoT classification to generate highly accurate results [12]. As a solution, operation decisions are taken with the least possible latency, as exemplified by the smart healthcare instance, as quickly as the required data is generated and retrieved. The recommended method was employed utilizing contemporary complex event processing platforms, which intrinsically support the multilayered computing paradigm and manage streaming information "on the fly," which is a prerequisite for IoT nodes with limited capacity and time-sensitive key technologies. According on preliminary research, the proposed strategy entails perfectly alright strategic thinking at different information fusion levels, enhancing overall results and response speed of health services, and hence increasing the implementation of IoT technologies in Healthcare Industry 4.0.

Using a public databases Cardiotocography dataset, two most common features extraction methodologies, LDA in addition principal component analysis (PCA), had been evaluated on multiple commonly used algorithms, decision tree induction, SVMs, Naive Bayes, and random forests. PCA surpasses LDA throughout the field, according to the findings of the studies. However, PCA and LDA had less impact on the success of classifiers, decision trees, and random forest. Further the determine the suitability of PCA and LDA, experiments are conducted using datasets from Diabetic Retinopathy and the Intrusion Detection System. Work demonstrated that existing methods with PCA generate superior results when its complexity of the data is high. When a dataset has a low dimension, it has been discovered that ML do not diminish computational complexity to yield better results [13].

The growth of several research areas such as IoT, ML, Big Data among others has transform cities and metropolis into a generally known word—Smart City [14]. The rise of smart cities, a wealth of data sources for a wide range of applications, has become available. Data fusion is a common strategy for dealing with many data sources that advances data output excellence or pulls knowledge from original data. Smart city studies must use data from numerous causes and assess their performance grounded on various criteria in order to adapt to ever-growing highly complex applications. To this purpose, they provided a novel data fusion classification for evaluating smart city applications. Furthermore, we evaluated selected apps in respective domain of the smart city using the suggested multi-perspectives classification. The study concludes with a discussion of data fusion integration's probable future directions and problems.

Physical activity recognition and measure (PARM) has been ubiquitously accepted as an important approach for an adoption of interest sensor networks due to its major improvements to health and wellbeing with significant correlation with various treatment programs [15]. In order to recognize distinct types of physical involvement and reduce its contradictions, typical PARM systems require designing and implementing knowledge integration or ML algorithms in the assessment of ubiquitous and external sensor data. They do, therefore, prefer to focus on controlled scenarios in increase the number of different sorts of identified activity subjects, improve identification accuracy, and determine persistence. The IoT innovative tool is transforming PARM studies to an open and flexible uncontrolled environment by merging diverse premium wearable gadgets and smartphone devices, as well as different groupings. Few people know if traditional data fusion methodologies can manage the new problems of IoT settings, or how to use and develop these technologies successfully right now. In order to comprehend the potential usage and advantages of Information fusion approaches in IoT-empowered PARM implementations, this work may give a complete analysis analyzing PARM researches from the aspect of an innovative 3D interactive IoT-based physical activity collecting and validation model. It covered typical state-of-the-art information fusion methodologies from major planar contexts: device, humans, and chronology in the 3D dynamic IoT model. The report then goes on to discuss various key enabling tactics for tackling some new research challenges and data fusion characteristics in IoT-empowered PARM researches.

ML approaches will help symmetric IoT solutions become one of the utmost imperative sources of new data in the future [16]. In this sense, network systems are capable of receiving a diverse variety of quantitative unidirectional information from a number of computer systems, analyzing the data, gaining knowledge, and providing knowledge given dataset. This study is limited to supervised and unsupervised ML approach, that is the cornerstones of IoT smart predictive analytics. This study reviews and analyzes significant subjects using computational intelligence methodologies, emphasizing the strengths and downsides of every approach, and new breakthroughs and related literature. Surge have been witnessed in the deployment of advanced sensing devices and Industrial IoTs in recent years, that are radically affecting the way healthcare is given around the globe. A grouping of

Cloud and IoT technologies is widely utilized to construct smart healthcare services ready to help quick set plans when evaluating and implementing Machine Intelligence on the large volumes of data collected by pervasive IoT devices. Notwithstanding, catalyst concentration and system administration accessible, and even some privacy concerns, be many obstacles that prevent IoMT systems and infrastructures from it being a reliable and efficient alternative to the purpose. Increasingly, there seems to be a surge in research in infrastructures and approaches that employ Edge and Clouds ML to reimburse for the inadequacies of the cloud. In this study, investigators provide a comprehensive analysis of the general utilization IoT solutions in healthcare, preliminary with experimental smart structural health monitoring and moving to a survey of the recent technologies in cloud cover computation for personalized medicine [17].

In the existing advent of the IoT, the important component of sensing and the Internet offers a method to a varied range of development difficulties. Relevant concepts include sustainable development, intelligent health care, intelligent cities, industrial automation, and intelligent transportation. Despite this, there have been substantial problems using meaningful IoT data sources, such as a flood of con-taminated sensor data and an increasing system consumption number [2]. As a solution, this issue goes over where to investigate IoT sensor data, unification with these other information sources, and investigation to acquire a greater compre-hension of implicit training datasets and make important conclusions. This chapter describes the approaches of removal of noise, information outlier detection, data packet replacement, and aggregating. It also goes through the relevance of data fusion and various data fusion methodologies, such as explicit unification, corre-lated feature extraction, and identifying declarations intelligent systems. In further, in order to effectively manage various challenges in IoT communication system and sensor predictive analytics, this investigation seeks to solve predictive analytics integration with evolving technologies such as the Internet, edge devices, and cloud technologies. Finally, this is the very first article of its sort to include a thorough examination of IoT sensor software development, synthesis, or analysis techniques.

Wireless networks of the future must be dependable and self-contained. The IoT is altering individual technology adaption in everyday life. IoTs are many, ranging from vital applications such as smart cities and health-related businesses to commercial IoT [18]. IoT incorporates ML approaches to make the network more efficient and self-contained. Deep learning is a sort of ML that is computationally complicated and costly. Combining deep learning technologies with IoT to enhance the work performance of sensor networks is among the problems. For next-generation IoT networks, combining various strategies while maintaining a balance between computational cost and efficiency is critical. In order to meet the needs of ML and the IoT, the information transmission infrastructure must be overhauled from the physical layer to the application layer. As a result, software built on top of the improved architecture will gain greatly, and the network will be faster and more reliable broadly.

To properly analyze this information and construct the necessary smart and autonomous applications, understanding in AI, notably deep learning, is important

[3]. In this discipline, there are many multiple approaches for computer systems, includes supervised, unsupervised, semi-supervised, and reinforcement learning. AI, which again is capable of ML and AI, can indeed analyze large datasets successfully. They deliver a powerful strategic of ML methods that can still be developed to assess the intelligence and skills of a service in this post. As a consequence, the current study significant element is to show the principles of numerous ML approaches and their relevance in a variety of novel research areas, such as cyberattacks, new technologies, healthcare, e-commerce, farming, as well as others. We also emphasize the limitations and potential future research avenues based on the findings. Overall, this research is intended to serve as a user profile for academic and business specialists, along with decision-makers in a number of alternative scenarios and implementations.

Flooding in rivers is a natural event that would result in patient deaths as well as lost revenue. Although several ways for studying storm surges are being utilized, the growth of flood treatment and prevention tactics has been impacted by a lack of understanding about flood situations [19]. The ensemble model is used in this research to develop a new strategy for predicting water level in relation to flood severity. Their analysis incorporates advantage of recent advances in the IoT and ML to simplify flood data analysis that could be valuable in preventing environmental hazards. Ensemble learning appears to be a more reasonable method for predicting flood severity levels, according to scientific studies. Ensemble learning utilizing the Long–Short Term Memory model and random forest beat classifiers with sensitivity, specificity, and accuracy of 71.4%, 85.9%, and 81.13%, accordingly, in the experiments.

Unsupervised learning, which uses fragmented incoming packet data to improve network demands and ensure services like computational modeling, anomaly-based, Internet usage classification, and development of integrated enhancement, has greatly increased in recent years [20]. The prominence of unsupervised classification algorithms in several other fields like as image processing, natural language, voice control, and optimization algorithms (e.g., in the construction of unmanned self-driving cars) has prompted interest in using them in networking. Unsupervised ML is desirable because it does away with the necessity for test training and manual dimensionality reduction, permitting for more customizable, accessible, and autonomous algorithms. The aim of the research study should provide an understanding of networking-related unsupervised enabling technologies. They offered a thorough examination of current breakthroughs in unsupervised learning approaches, as well as their applicability in the framework of connectivity for a wide range of learning tasks. They also look into the research's future directions and outstanding goals, and gently sloped hurdles. While several customer address on ML techniques in infrastructure are being released earlier, we can see the need for an investigation of equal depth and breadth in the research. They increase the scientific understanding in this work by meticulously combining the lessons from all these review chapters and giving healthcare plans of latest innovations.

The multitude of sensors used in IoT environments generates massive amounts of data, resulting in a data flood. Data collected from these sensors can be utilized to better understand, analyze, and regulate the complex environments we live in, allowing us to have more intelligence, make better decisions, and outperform [21]. The main issue here is figuring out how to extract useful information from such vast amounts of data. Many methods for generating meaningful extrapolations and understandings have been offered; however, these resolutions are still in the early phases of development. Traditional methodologies are also insufficient to tackle the expanding analytical challenges of IoT systems. This study analyzes the essential enablers for doing desired data analytics in IoT applications to overcome this challenge. A thorough examination of the main enablers discovered is presented, including their importance in IoT data analytics, use-cases in which they have been deployed, and the performance results of the use-cases. In addition, open issues and research limits are addressed. This chapter can be used as a starting point for more IoT data analytics study.

IoT technologies could be combined with ML approaches to map real-world problems into the AI arena. ML methods have been utilized in data analysis, wireless communication, healthcare systems, industrial systems, and security, to name a few IoT applications [22]. Despite this, the growing usage of ML-based approaches on the IoT has caused a slew of problems for systems, including a scarcity of valid datasets, data integrity difficulties, and restricted resources. This research examines current ML-based methodologies for IoT systems, as well as a number of common opportunities and challenges. Their investigation may reveal new research options for academics and enterprises interested in ML techniques on the IoT.

The problem is exacerbated by the vast number of IoT devices that can be connected, as well as the unplanned nature of such networks. Security and privacy have emerged as significant roadblocks to IoT administration [23]. Deep learning algorithms have recently been found to be very effective for assessing the security of IoT devices, with a number of advantages over traditional methods. The purpose of this research is to demonstrate a comprehensive role for deep learning applications in IoT security and privacy concerns. Their main focus is on using deep learning to improve IoT security. They begin by examining deep learning applications in IoT security from the perspective of system design and methodology. Second, they looked at whether deep learning is a good way to improve security in IoT systems from a security standpoint. Finally, we evaluate the performance of deep learning in terms of IoT system security.

Intelligent sensor systems have presented a variety of advanced ML techniques with advanced computing devices to focus of the analysis "smart" methods specifically tailored for wearable electronics, combining spatial multiplexing to achieve an even more interventional understanding of how it works under extrapolation [24]. This chapter provides a survey of contemporary application areas that leverage ML-enabled smart communication systems. This chapter discusses the first extensively used ML techniques for practical sensing applications. Following that, descriptions of how sensor advances are linked with ML "smart" models and how these systems accomplish genuine advantages are given for two main classes of useful optical devices: physical and chemical sensing and visual image sensing.

Finally, the current trajectory and challenges that future smart sensing systems would then encounter, as well as the possibilities that may have been unlocked, are discussed.

Healthcare has adopted IoT and ML so that automated equipment can create medical records, detect diseases, and, very crucially, treat conditions in real time [25]. On various data, different ML algorithms behave better. Because the prediction outcomes differ, this may have an impact on the total results. In the clinical decision-making procedure, the variability in prediction findings is a major factor. As a result, understanding the various ML methods used to handle IoT data in the healthcare sector is critical. This chapter addresses well-known ML algorithms for classification and prediction, and also how they have been used to healthcare. The goal of this study is to give a detailed overview of existing ML algorithms and how they might be applied to IoT medical data. Following a thorough examination, they discovered that various classification prediction algorithms have numerous flaws. We must select the best strategy for predicting crucial healthcare data based on the type of IoT dataset. The report also shows how IoT and ML can be used to forecast future healthcare system trends.

18.3   Methodology

As of July 21, 2020, more than 15 million established cases of COVID-19 had been described in 185 nations since its detection in late December 2019, with a daily increase of about 2%. More than 95 thousand people have died as a result of these incidents, representing a 4.2% mortality rate. The World Health Organization declared this new coronavirus a pandemic on March 11, 2020. Inopportunely, there is no effective behavior or vaccine available at this time. The creation of an operative vaccine is projected to take more than a year, specifically since the virus's wildlife has not yet been fully described. At the moment, the nation's only choice for managing with this coronavirus is to use interpersonal separation, personal hygiene, and surgical shields to limit its development (i.e., "deform the curvature"). By permitting for rapid recognition (or prognosis) and observation of new instances, technologies, but in the other extreme, may also be ready to assist slow overall spread of infectious infection. Cloud computing, online, and cloud technologies, through the use of data obtained from remote access, including mHealth and tele-health, as well as medical professional situation accept, are characteristics of such innovations.

Through mixing transmission and sensory techniques with ubiquitous computing technology, the IoT converts physical goods into physical sensors. People were able to obtain communication technology that will benefit the world as a consequence of this. Physical, network, and application layers make up the majority of IoT architectures. Sensors are built into physical items to collect a variety of data. These sensors have a finite amount of computing power and a finite lifespan. They will indeed be able to draw any conclusions if they gain more information. Simplicity in processing data, but in the other hand,

Figure 18.1   Design framework

causes a delay. Networking will be used to substitute also for restricted storage capacity of the detectors. Among the technological developments employed are 6LoWPAN, Wireless, IEEE 802.15.4, RFID, and near-field communication (NFC). Health insurance, new technologies, smart cities, farming, and communications systems are really just a several of the areas where if the IoT could be useful. In healthcare, IoT also was recognized as the Internet of Medical Things (IoMT). Telemedicine and telemedicine, two well-known information and communication technology approaches, have mostly been phased out. The enhanced functionality of IoMT is lacking in these ancient approaches. Traditional approaches, for example, can connect patients with medical doctors over the Internet, but IoMT also allows for machine–human and machine–machine interactions, as well as AI assessments. ML allows technology to dynamically improve personal experiences rather than aiming to construct inflexible application routines. By creating a strong correlation between input sample points and output actions, ML methods can conduct forecasting and choice in IoT applications. Learning methods are divided into three categories: supervised, unsupervised, and reinforced. Supervised learning approaches construct links and connections between intended relative distribution and input qualities based on the dataset's associations, allowing outcomes for prospective sample points to be anticipated.

The created model, as well as the two most often utilized dimensional reduction methodologies, PLSs and LDA with SVM and Kth nearest neighbor (KNN) classifiers, are thoroughly described in this study. When it comes to analyzing IoT-enabled healthcare data, a variety of ML algorithms are frequently used. The purpose of classifying data acquired from healthcare IoT sensors includes pre-processing, feature subspace data representation, classification model design, and training utilizing processed information, and a proposed way to employ an unexpected testing dataset. Figure 18.1 depicts the experimental framework.

18.4   Dataset

The COVID-19 Open Research Dataset (CORD-19) repository included a dataset of 14251 confirmed COVID-19 cases. Each case's data contains a variety of various types of information. Symptoms, travel history to suspect places, and communication antiquity with possibly infected people were the focus of our investigation. However, for many of the cases listed in the database, part of this information was missing [26].

18.5   Algorithms

18.5.1   PLS

PLS is a popular method for constructing predictive analytics with genomics input and denotes the number of regression model (metabolites) approaches the amount of data (samples). PLS uses the projecting to latent building data to model the logistic valves between two matrices (X and Y). A PLS model will search the X space for a multidimensional direction that explains the maximum simultaneous variability in the Y space. If another X sequence is assumed of it as a collection of N pieces of data in M-dimensional low orbit (in which N is the number of iterations and minimizes the number of receptors), and Y is a dichotomous variable of size N referencing set point (e.g., case = 1 & control = 0), then PLS spins and initiatives those sets of data into a subspace (generally 2 or 3 components) so that segregation can be attained [27]. Classification PLS also is a term for PLS discriminant analysis (PLS-DA). As its completed modeling approach can also be significantly decreased to the linear probability context $y=0+1\times1+1\times2+...+n\times N$, where $0....N$ is a variable of partial least squares (PLS) variables and y is the method hypothesis (commonly, a beneficial category is characterized as $y>0.5$ and a negative categorization is described as $y<0.5$), PLS-DA is a linear regression method. For this experiment, the SIMPLS [33] approach was employed to enhance each PLS model. In PLS models, the number of latent variables is the single tuning hyperparameter (i.e., the number discriminant dimensions the X matrix is projected).

In general, the PLS algorithm operates as follows:

This component's variance (information) is converted into a digital X-data, a process known as deflation. The dependent variable that maximizes the correlation between X and y is determined as a PLS component. Only the intrinsic dimensionality of the remaining matrix that has the same columns and row lengths as the X-data, has been reduced by one.

The next PLS element is generated from the buffering effect matrix, and it creates the biggest correlations between X $(1..., j)$ and y, provided that it would be jointly significant to the previous one, as in step 1. This is repeated until another representation of y cannot be improved any further or X has become a null matrix.

18.5.2   Linear discriminant analysis (LDA)

As a pre-processing step is based on ML applications, LDA is another popular dimensionality reduction technique. LDA's main purpose is to condense a huge dataset with many features into a smaller space with satisfactory class separation. The expenditure of computation will be reduced as a result of this. In the purpose of this study, LDA tries to discover a prediction equation of the newest features, T, obtained by the prior PCA or PLS data reduction procedure. A key problem in LDA's implementation is its inability to deal large np datasets. As a result, employing PCA or PLS preceding classifications decreases the dimensions of the actualize data, allowing the formal model produced by LDA to handle it better. This is done by transferring the observations into the new coordinate system and then sending them to the classifier. After that, a model is built to anticipate the subclass of an unidentified observation, Li, using prior probabilities derived from a learning set. These priors should really be maintained for group membership in order to achieve the right separability. The complete set is calculated to increase the percentage of multi variability to between deviation *d*, which is really the optimal direction for distinguishing differences between classes in the smaller dimensional space generated by PLS or PCA. It is worth remembering that Li is referring to the observations from the learning set. For LDA to work, the data has to be long-term profitability distribution with equivalent variability vectors [28].

18.5.3   Support vector machine (SVM)

SVM is a procedure that requires supervision. SVM learns the hyperplane that many times positions the instances in each class and reduces the distance between data instances and the hyperplane itself given a collection of labeled training examples (i.e., each instance in the training set either belongs to the positive or negative class). Any new test item is subsequently assigned (or predicted) a class label using the obtained hyperplane.

SVMs are supervised learning algorithms that can be applied to classification and regression problems. SVM is based on soft margin classification, which is consistent with descriptive statistics theory notions. SVM addresses the optimal control issue with a training sample consisting of example case pairs $(x1, y1)$ ..., (xN, yN), where $xi \, R \, d$ and $yi \, 1, +1)$.

SVM produces the distinct mark that optimizes the data margin to distinguish two classes. I and C are slack variables that specify the extent of computational complexity, whereas I allows for the misclassification of complicated or noisy patterns. By solving an optimization problem, the separation hyperplane can be identified, allowing support vectors to be chosen that optimize the maximum margin (e.g., normal vs. abnormal water level in this case). In the design of a generalizable model, the penalty correlation matrix is an important tuning factor. A number of learning algorithms are also available to aid in the transition of data supplied into a larger space with exponential distinction [19].

18.5.4   KNN

KNN is a supervised instance-based learning approach. The learning process moves at a snail's pace. It does not produce a model. Specific a collection of labeled training examples, KNN calculates distances between a given test instance and all of the training instances (each instance belongs to either the positive or negative class). These distances are then used to assign (or predict) the test instance's class label. The learning styles of the K training instances closest to the test instance are combined to achieve this.

The KNN classifier is a passive supervised learning algorithm used in statistical analysis, data analysis, and pattern identification. To categorize data, the nearest training examples in subspace are employed. The purpose is to use a specified number of their nearest neighbors to classify new (unseen) input patterns. KNN is the best solution when there is no background knowledge of the statistical analysis. It works well for both training and testing. The technique is divided into four steps. To begin, training set and their labels are retained in feature space. The number of "k" nearest neighbors is then determined, and the appropriate distance metric. KNN receives unseen data and locates the closest 'k' instances. Each new piece of data is assigned a label that matches the prevailing label of its neighbors [19].

18.5.5   Evaluation

We require a set of performance measures to evaluate the performance of ML-based approaches such as accuracy, sensitivity, specificity, precision, recall, and F-measure, as well as a benchmark dataset to verify the ML framework [29,30].

Performance measurements such as accuracy, sensitivity, specificity, precision, recall, F-measure, and receiver operating characteristic curve (ROC) area were employed to evaluate the learning algorithms' performance. A confusion matrix and cross validation methods can be used to calculate these measures.

The confusion matrix is a 2-by-2 matrix that is used to visualize the performance of a binary (2-class) supervised learning issue. The anticipated (or computed) class is represented by each row in the matrix, whereas the actual class is represented by each column.

The number of cases that were labeled as positive (using the prediction model) and are truly positive is known as true positive (TP). False positive (FP): the number of events that were labeled as positive but were actually negative using the prediction model. False negative (FN): this is the number of events that were labeled as negative by the prediction model but are actually positive. True negative (TN): This is the number of cases that were identified as negative (using the predictive model) and are in fact negative [31].

18.6   Potential healthcare domains

This study implores the recent COVID-19 dataset to show the potentials of ML techniques in healthcare sector. As it is known, ML has helped diverse works and sectors. It has been employed in diverse health factors like cancer diagnostics, malaria infections among others, this work is not limited to COVID-19 as it can be explored on other healthcare domains. Learning collaboratives have undertaken quality improvement efforts all around the globe, based on a well-known continuous improvement idea with little scientific support. Our results may be utilized by healthcare organizations to build effective infrastructure to support improvement and to create the circumstances for everyone's work to include quality and safety improvement. Despite the increasing availability of computerized decision support systems in a variety of healthcare settings, there is still a lack of data on their adoption and efficacy. The majority of barrier studies concentrate on a small number of decision points in small-scale academic contexts. The target group's lack of understanding of the system is a significant obstacle, highlighting the necessity of a thorough introduction to the system. Furthermore, obstacles linked to a lack of integration into everyday practice seem to be a top priority, implying that improving the system's flexibility and learning capacity in order to adjust decision assistance to suit changing requirements is a priority [32].

18.7   Results and discussions

The research was carried out on the COVID-19 Open Research Dataset (CORD-19) repository, which contains a dataset of 14,251 confirmed COVID-19 instances that was obtained using MATLAB from a publicly available ML repository. This study was performed on a personal laptop with Windows 10 installed and 8 GB of RAM.

Feature extraction is a crucial stage in the classification process, especially when dealing with high-dimensional data and a small number of training examples. Traditional feature extraction approaches, such as PLS and LDA, necessitate the calculation of scatter matrices. Within-class and between-class scatter matrices are employed to establish the class separability criterion in these methods. The precise estimation of these matrices is not possible due to the large quantity of training samples. As a result, while working with a limited sample size, these approaches' classification accuracy suffers. A hybridized feature extraction method combining PLS and LDA is presented to address this issue. As a result, it performs effectively with small training data. This chapter combines the PLS and LDA schemes to take benefit of this technique and LDA. PLS extracted 33 latent features with LDA.

In a limited sample size condition, the experimental findings indicate the performance evaluation of the suggested hybrid technique in comparison to other state-of-the-art techniques using SVM and KNN classifiers. The confusion matrix of the experiments is shown in Figures 18.2 and 18.3, and Table 18.1 shows the performance evaluation.

Feature extraction algorithms were used to perform an integrated dimensionality reduction in this work. The feature extraction techniques were PLS and LDA,

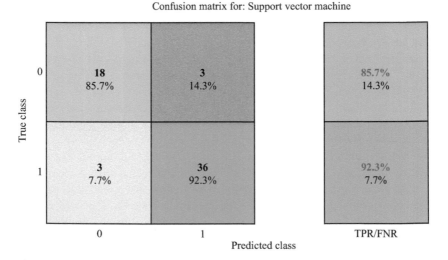

Confusion matrix for: Support vector machine

Figure 18.2   Confusion matrix for PLS+LDA+SVM; TP = 18; TN = 36; FP = 3; FN = 3

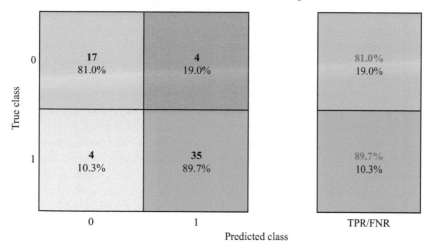

Confusion matrix for: K-Nearest neighbor

Figure 18.3 Confusion matrix for PLS+LDA+KNN; TP = 17; TN = 35; FP = 4; FN = 4

Table 18.1 Performance metrics table for the PLS+LDA+SVM and PLS+LDA+KNN classification

Performance metrics (%)	PLS+LDA+SVM	PLS+LDA+KNN
Accuracy	90	86.44
Sensitivity	85.71	80
Specificity	92.31	89.74
Precision	85.71	80
Recall	85.71	80
F-score	85.71	80

while the classification algorithms were SVM and KNN, with a 10-fold cross-validation parameter.

As may be seen in Table 18.1, the outcome was improved. In contrast to the state-of-the-art, the accuracies improved. Several academics have investigated the topic of pandemic classification using data mining techniques in attempt to develop a reliable COVID detection and prediction method. By adopting this approach for creating a professionally generated dataset for training classifiably, the results acquired in this investigation can be used for training needed preponderance of COVID infection by physicians. Thousands of genes have been studied to provide deep insight into malaria categorizing issues, as well as a wealth of information for drug development, COVID therapeutic prognosis and detection, and identifying genomic information and interconnections in normal and aberrant circumstances. The approach in this study enhances classification performance and decrease dependency on the training set.

18.8 Conclusion

In this study, an IoT-based COVID-19 health monitoring system is suggested, which uses smart care technologies to assess vital signs and detect biological and behavioral changes in patients. An IoT-based method for decreasing the impact of communicable diseases is presented in this study. Using possible COVID-19 case information and patient data from confirmed COVID-19 cases, the proposed framework was used to build a machine-learning-based prediction models for disease as well as examine therapy response. The findings are also shared with doctors, who can promptly respond to probable cases identified by the predictive model by completing any extra clinical studies required to confirm the diagnosis. This allows for the identification and treatment of validated cases. In an experiment employing authentic COVID-19 datasets, PLS and LDA with SVM, as well as KNN, are utilized to test ML algorithms (KNN). According to the findings, SVM achieved accuracies of more than 90%. This approach will enable for the quick and accurate detection of COVID-19 patients. The suggested linear model could potentially reduce the epidemic and mortality rates by detecting cases early. This method would also make it possible to track recovered cases and gain a better knowledge of the condition. The connection between health care quality and measure is one of the most basic health policy issues. To improve health-care system actions targeted at information provision, a deeper understanding of these connections is required. Future research will focus on further developing and validating performance assessment tools and theoretical models in dynamic medical domains that include data from a variety of illnesses. This will assist in the improvement of efforts and the development of clinical work systems that promote successful patient care. In conclusion, this work is of enormous contribution to healthcare and medical practitioners, the future direction of this study suggests that classifiers such as deep learning approach can be suggested to compare the classification result for further enhancement and decision making.

References

[1] Mahdavinejad, M. S., Rezvan, M., Barekatain, M., Adibi, P., Barnaghi, P., and Sheth, A. P. (2018). Machine learning for internet of things data analysis: a survey. *Digital Communications and Networks*, 4(3), 161–175. https://doi.org/10.1016/j.dcan.2017.10.002

[2] Krishnamurthi, R., Kumar, A., Gopinathan, D., Nayyar, A., and Qureshi, B. (2020). An overview of IoT sensor data processing, fusion, and analysis techniques. *Sensors*, 20(21), 6076. https://doi.org/10.3390/s20216076

[3] Sarker, I. H. (2021). Machine learning: algorithms, real-world applications and research directions. *SN Computer Science*, 2(3), 160. https://doi.org/10.1007/s42979-021-00592-x

[4] Catania, L. J. (2021). Current AI applications in medical therapies and services. In *Foundations of Artificial Intelligence in Healthcare and Bioscience*

(pp. 199–291). New York, NY: Elsevier. https://doi.org/10.1016/B978-0-12-824477-7.00013-4

[5] Das, S., Dey, A., Pal, A., and Roy, N. (2015). Applications of artificial intelligence in machine learning: review and prospect. *International Journal of Computer Applications*, 115(9), 31–41. https://doi.org/10.5120/20182-2402

[6] Beuzen, T., and Splinter, K. (2020). Machine learning and coastal processes. In *Sandy Beach Morphodynamics* (pp. 689–710). New York, NY: Elsevier. https://doi.org/10.1016/B978-0-08-102927-5.00028-X

[7] Basha, S. M., and Rajput, D. S. (2019). Survey on evaluating the performance of machine learning algorithms: past contributions and future roadmap. In *Deep Learning and Parallel Computing Environment for Bioengineering Systems* (pp. 153–164). New York, NY: Elsevier. https://doi.org/10.1016/B978-0-12-816718-2.00016-6

[8] Hashem, I. A. T., Chang, V., Anuar, N. B., *et al.* (2016). The role of big data in smart city. *International Journal of Information Management*, 36(5), 748–758. https://doi.org/10.1016/j.ijinfomgt.2016.05.002

[9] Lim, C., Kim, K.-J., and Maglio, P. P. (2018). Smart cities with big data: reference models, challenges, and considerations. *Cities*, 82, 86–99. https://doi.org/10.1016/j.cities.2018.04.011

[10] Zeadally, S., Siddiqui, F., Baig, Z., and Ibrahim, A. (2019). Smart healthcare. *PSU Research Review*, 4(2), 149–168. https://doi.org/10.1108/PRR-08-2019-0027

[11] Khan, S. U., Zomaya, A. Y., and Abbas, A. (Eds.). (2017). Handbook of Large-Scale Distributed Computing in Smart *Healthcare*. Berlin: Springer International Publishing. https://doi.org/10.1007/978-3-319-58280-1

[12] Dautov, R., Distefano, S., and Buyya, R. (2019). Hierarchical data fusion for smart healthcare. *Journal of Big Data*, 6(1), 19. https://doi.org/10.1186/s40537-019-0183-6

[13] Reddy, G. T., Reddy, M. P. K., Lakshmanna, K., *et al.* (2020). Analysis of dimensionality reduction techniques on Big Data. *IEEE Access*, 8, 54776–54788. https://doi.org/10.1109/ACCESS.2020.2980942

[14] Lau, B. P. L., Marakkalage, S. H., Zhou, Y., *et al.* (2019). A survey of data fusion in smart city applications. *Information Fusion*, 52, 357–374. https://doi.org/10.1016/j.inffus.2019.05.004

[15] Qi, J., Yang, P., Newcombe, L., *et al.* (2020). An overview of data fusion techniques for Internet of Things enabled physical activity recognition and measure. *Information Fusion*, 55, 269–280. https://doi.org/10.1016/j.inffus.2019.09.002

[16] Alsharif, M. H., Kelechi, A. H., Yahya, K., and Chaudhry, S. A. (2020). Machine learning algorithms for smart data analysis in Internet of Things environment: taxonomies and research trends. *Symmetry*, 12(1), 88. https://doi.org/10.3390/sym12010088

[17] Greco, L., Percannella, G., Ritrovato, P., Tortorella, F., and Vento, M. (2020). Trends in IoT based solutions for health care: moving AI to the edge.

Pattern Recognition Letters, 135, 346–353. https://doi.org/10.1016/j.patrec. 2020.05.016

[18] Zikria, Y. Bin, Afzal, M. K., Kim, S. W., Marin, A., and Guizani, M. (2020). Deep learning for intelligent IoT: opportunities, challenges and solutions. *Computer Communications*, 164, 50–53. https://doi.org/10.1016/j.comcom. 2020.08.017

[19] Khalaf, M., Alaskar, H., Hussain, A. J., *et al.* (2020). IoT-enabled flood severity prediction via ensemble machine learning models. *IEEE Access*, 8, 70375–70386. https://doi.org/10.1109/ACCESS.2020.2986090

[20] Usama, M., Qadir, J., Raza, A., *et al.* (2017). Unsupervised machine learning for networking: techniques, applications and research challenges. *IEEE Access*, 7, 65579–65615. https://doi.org/10.1709.06599v1

[21] Saleem, T. J., and Chishti, M. A. (2019). Data analytics in the Internet of Things: a survey. *Scalable Computing: Practice and Experience*, 20(4), 607–630. https://doi.org/10.12694/scpe.v20i4.1562

[22] Yousefi, S., Derakhshan, F., and Karimipour, H. (2020). Applications of big data analytics and machine learning in the Internet of Things. In *Handbook of Big Data Privacy* (pp. 77–108). New York, NY: Springer International Publishing. https://doi.org/10.1007/978-3-030-38557-6_5

[23] Yue, Y., Li, S., Legg, P., and Li, F. (2021). Deep learning-based security behaviour analysis in IoT Environments: a survey. *Security and Communication Networks*, 2021, 1–13. https://doi.org/10.1155/2021/ 8873195

[24] Ha, N., Xu, K., Ren, G., Mitchell, A., and Ou, J. Z. (2020). Machine learning-enabled smart sensor systems. *Advanced Intelligent Systems*, 2(9), 2000063. https://doi.org/10.1002/aisy.202000063

[25] Aldahiri, A., Alrashed, B., and Hussain, W. (2021). Trends in using IoT with machine learning in health prediction system. *Forecasting*, 3(1), 181–206. https://doi.org/10.3390/forecast3010012

[26] Otoom, M., Otoum, N., Alzubaidi, M. A., Etoom, Y., and Banihani, R. (2020). An IoT-based framework for early identification and monitoring of COVID-19 cases. *Biomedical Signal Processing and Control*, 62, 102149. https://doi.org/10.1016/j.bspc.2020.102149

[27] Mendez, K. M., Reinke, S. N., and Broadhurst, D. I. (2019). A comparative evaluation of the generalised predictive ability of eight machine learning algorithms across ten clinical metabolomics data sets for binary classification. *Metabolomics*, 15(12), 150. https://doi.org/10.1007/s11306-019-1612-4

[28] Sampson, D. L., Parker, T. J., Upton, Z., and Hurst, C. P. (2011). A comparison of methods for classifying clinical samples based on proteomics data: a case study for statistical and machine learning approaches. *PLoS ONE*, 6(9), e24973. https://doi.org/10.1371/journal.pone.0024973

[29] Arowolo, M. O., Adebiyi, M. O., Aremu, C., and Adebiyi, A. A. (2021). A survey of dimension reduction and classification methods for RNA-Seq data on malaria vector. *Journal of Big Data*, 8(1), 50. https://doi.org/10.1186/ s40537-021-00441-x

[30] Arowolo, M. O., Adebiyi, M. O., Ariyo, A. A., and Okesola, O. J. (2021). A genetic algorithm approach for predicting ribonucleic acid sequencing data classification using KNN and decision tree. *TELKOMNIKA (Telecommunication Computing Electronics and Control)*, 19(1), 310. https://doi.org/10.12928/telkomnika.v19i1.16381

[31] Arowolo, M. O., Adebiyi, M. O., Adebiyi, A. A., and Olugbara, O. (2021). Optimized hybrid investigative based dimensionality reduction methods for malaria vector using KNN classifier. *Journal of Big Data*, 8(1), 29. https://doi.org/10.1186/s40537-021-00415-z

[32] Mahdavi, M., Choubdar, H., Zabeh, E., *et al.* (2021). A machine learning based exploration of COVID-19 mortality risk. *PLoS ONE*, 16(7), e0252384. https://doi.org/10.1371/journal.pone.0252384

[33] Jong, S. (1993). SIMPLS: an alternative approach to partial least squares regression. *Chemometrics and Intelligent Laboratory Systems*, 18(3), 251–263. https://doi.org/10.1016/0169-7439(93)85002-X.

Chapter 19

Blockchain-based learning automated analytics platform in telemedicine

Akbar Ali Khan[1], Prakriti Dwivedi[1], Sareeta Mugde[1] and Garima Sharma[1]

Abstract

Telemedicine – a field having immense potential to improve the landscape of healthcare domain with its innovative and interactive concept of e-cure. Having created its niche in the healthcare ecosystem, it has now become an integral part of it after the genesis of COVID-19. The world has witnessed the rapid growth of telemedicine according to their literacy and technological maturity but the rate of adopting varies between countries. Telemedicine is becoming the boom in India's healthcare industry where 65% of the population resides in rural and remote areas. It delivered essential healthcare at a critical time where traditional medicine is perceived to be at risk as a result of the nature of the infectious disease like COVID-19. This communicable infection has shifted the paradigm of telemedicine to necessity with providing solutions and forming a cushion at the demand–supply shock and also has a potential to take care of the skewed doctor and patient allocation which exist in India, where for every 10 lakh patients, there are six doctors. With its increasing demand in this new normal and across all ages, genres and geographies, had made the organizations and many new age start-ups not only strive toward improved services in this area but also for the storage and security of its digital assets through a variety of technology tools and keeping this in mind the aim of this chapter is to design a framework to deploy Blockchain technology to protect the most important element of telemedicine that is data. Deployment of blockchain in telemedicine, still in its infancy, will be a boon for the confidentiality and data security while automated analytics can be instrumental not only to improving the service quality, but also to make it quick and personalized [33]. This chapter is an attempt to bring to light all these vital aspects of telemedicine domain in healthcare.

Keywords: Blockchain-based e-healthcare; Automated analytics; Telemedicine Sector; Security; and Privacy

[1]Prin. L.N. Welingkar Institute of Management Development & Research, Mumbai University, India

19.1   Introduction

The rapid technological advancement in every domain and its use for social good has been responsible for emergence of "Society 5.0" which aims not only to leverage the advanced and emerging technologies in domain where it can serve human for their betterment but also work toward increasing its pace for early adoption of these technologies. Its requirement in the healthcare domain has given rise to e-healthcare which includes telemedicine and telecare. Telemedicine, also referred to as telehealth, is the provision of healthcare and the sharing of information at a distance whereas telecare is an umbrella term which covers all the e-care services – being provided using telecommunication or IT technology – falling under the medical domain. The key objective of e-healthcare is to provide easily accessible health services through maximum patient engagement.

Telemedicine has given a paradigm shift to the entire healthcare sector. After the onset of COVID-19, the trend of digital health has gained immense popularity as telehealth services are being preferred by the non-COVID patients over in-person consultation. Maybe the buzz about telemedicine is high nowadays but it had been there around us from a very long time with just the difference of approach and acceptance rate among various countries. The term telemedicine was coined by Thomas Bird in 1970s which was derived from the combination of Latin term "medicus" and Greek term "tele" which in English means "healing at a distance." Although the term telemedicine was coined in 1970s but the actual work related to it is considered to be done in 1906 when a Dutch physiologist named Willem Einthoven developed the first electrocardiograph in his laboratory in Leiden. With this experiment, he was able to record the cardiac signals of patients in a hospital 1.5 km away.

Willem [1], after his successful experiment, stated "Where there is a link, actual and figurative, between laboratory and hospital, and collaboration between physiologist and clinician, each remaining master in his territory, there one may fruitfully utilize these new electrical methods of research." After this, a similar attempt of healing with distance has been made like those in 1920s where the Norwegian doctors provided medical consultation for sick ship crew members at sea via radio link. In 1967, Bird and his colleagues established a link between Logan Airport and nearby hospital which had the potential to evaluate over 1,000 airport staff and travelers who were ill. After this, several researches and studies were done related to telehealth services before the official coining of the term in 1970s. With time, telemedicine improved and broadened its horizon by proving its potential to provide services related to any medical specialty.

Barriers [2] in the progress of any technological advancement is like that edge of its lifecycle which can either construct or destruct its progress completely. The same is the case with telemedicine which has its own unique set of barriers in its maturity journey which differs from country to country and region to region [2] of which the primitive one is infrastructure barrier which varies across geographies like for North American region have a robust and suitable infrastructure which soothingly leverages the service of telemedicine among its population, whereas

Canada has still not accepted telemedicine completely even after having all the infrastructure needed for it. Within a continent like Europe itself, the infrastructure facility differs. On the one side, there are countries like Spain, The Netherlands, and some of the Nordic countries which are digitally highly advanced and are easily embracing emerging technologies like Artificial Intelligence (AI) and healthcare analytics in its healthcare sector and, on the other side, there is country like Germany which is highly advanced and have the required digital health infrastructure but are still reluctance when it comes to the use of telemedicine.

Similarly, in the APAC region, on the one side, there are countries like Japan, China, and Australia which are highly investing in the digital infrastructure to improve their healthcare system and, on the other side, there is country like India, with 65% of its population residing in rural areas and still have a long way to go as far as adequacy of digital infrastructure is concerned to be able to execute telemedicine throughout the nation. Country [3] like India is not only trying to overcome the infrastructure barriers but is also fighting hard to overcome geographical, cultural, technological, linguistic, or even demographical barrier due to its vast geographical spread, presence of various cultural diversity, poor technological maturity rate, presence of 1,652 languages, and dialects and unbalanced demographical diversity, respectively. But the dynamics have changed after the onset of COVID-19 as it has increased the acceptance rate and pace of telemedicine in countries like India overcoming various barriers and this has shown to the world that the time for telemedicine has come and its penetration in the healthcare sector is faster than ever.

Technology is always considered to be the backbone of healthcare industry whose growth is directly proportional to pace at which technological advancement and maturity takes place in that particular nation. It has not only enabled a faster interaction between its stakeholders but had also improved the healthcare services through various technological advancements in the medical equipment's too. These developments not only help in getting accurate medical result but also in automatically collecting and sharing medical data of the patient with the doctor. Various technology enablers are information and communication technology (ICT), AI, analytics, blockchain and cloud computing. These are the major technologies which run the healthcare industry and also led to the rise of telemedicine services. But the level of establishment of this telehealth services varies from country to country depending on the level of their maturity and the readiness of their population to accept this new addition in the healthcare domain. Technology has always been the major requirement to infuse telemedicine into the healthcare system of any nation.

The most vital and the basic technology needed for telemedicine services to work is the ICT technology which ensures the basic connectivity between the doctors and the patients through Wi-Fi, laptop, computer hardware, software, modem, satellite link, etc. With various collaborations between public and private sector and also NGOs, the supply deficiency of public healthcare facilities can be minimized with the use of telemedicine services. Even developing country like India with its fast penetration of internet, smartphone and other basic ICT technology had been able to overcome its various barriers to telemedicine and accept its benefits. One major thing to look after in telemedicine is its high volume of digital assets being generated every moment. With the growing pace of the use of telemedicine services, daily trillions of bytes of data are being generated and data being the biggest digital asset of current time its safe and secured storage has become a must for organizations. This had led to the adoption and integration of various other technologies in telemedicine sector like cloud computing for the storage of data and block chain for the maintenance of transparency and security of data. If ICT technology has been the blood of telemedicine, then cloud computing and blockchain had been the veins for them. With data becoming the new currency and heath being a very private affair for any individual the primitive motive of any telemedicine service provider is to have a safe, systematic and centralized storage of data being generated from e-health services. Apart from this, technology like AI, machine learning (ML), automated advanced analytics have also found its importance in the telemedicine sector. AI is helping the telemedicine service providers to come up with various automated platform where health data of the patient is recorded periodically and a proper analysis is performed on them to gain various trends in their health pattern thus eventually helping them managing the health in an effective manner.

19.2   Literature review

As per the World Health Organization (WHO) [4], the provision of health services, in which distance is a critical factor by all health professionals by applying communication and information in order to validate the examination, treatment and prevention of injuries and disease, research and assessment, as well as the ongoing training of healthcare workers, all of this is aimed at benefitting and advancing the health of people and their communities. Anthony and Kadir [5,6] in their research have talked about how the healthcare centers are rapidly adopting telemedicine and telehealth during COVID-19 using digital technologies and tools. It is expected that telemedicine would reduce the risk of health practitioners, workers, and patients being exposed to the pandemic world. Telemedicine is not only providing its services in urban areas but rural areas are benefitting from it. Nichani, Pistowala, and others [7] have proposed a device with biomedical sensors which can be distributed among the rural population to collect their indispensable information and store it in a database whose data can be retrieved by a city hospital to analyze and build insights from it. This would help the health practitioners provide customized and better diagnosis as well as treatment to that set of population. On the similar grounds, Gros, Albert, and other authors [8] have put forward an infrastructure of telematics which can offer its services to remote patients with its mobility and flexibility.

Similarly, Hamid and Mohamad [9] have talked about patient monitoring system in their work which has a capability of providing an integrated web service assisted by multiple sensors and is under control of Arduino Uno. Healthcare industry is one of the most sensitive and key areas which requires greater efficiency and effectiveness in the works. Worldwide nations are researching and spending more on the extensive use of telemedicine services. Hau *et al.* [10] refer telemedicine as a "remote medical care" and have talked about the advantage of enhanced telecommunication applications on the physical and mental wellbeing of the gray population. It is undeniable to say that these online consultations are boon to those who are suffering from problems like HIV and are hesitant to be open about it. Rogers *et al.* [11] have highlighted the same in their work that how the online consultations can improve care and medication for HIV patients. Ohannessian *et al.* and Calton [12,13] have addressed the challenges COVID-19 has put forward to all the stakeholders and the way they should adopt the telemedicine – a critical technology to provide safe and secure services. Telemedicine is a diversified, fast-growing, and changing medical field. Raskas *et al.* [14] stated the edge which telecare provides to pediatrics urgency by expanding its reach. It includes models like "hub and spoke," satellite models, load-balancing, kiosk, D2C (directly to consumer) benefits, consultations from specialists and their mentorship. American Hospital Association [15] in 2016 have talked about the benefits derived from telehealth makes sure that patients receive the right care, where and when they need it. All of this can be done by increasing access to medical practitioners and experts. Dash, Aarthy, and Mohan [16] emphasize that the guidelines by MoHFW in India need to broadened to take into account ethical concerns regarding the use of privacy use, patient data, and their storage. Improvement in infrastructure and Internet facility synchronously would make telemedicine in India equitable. Over the past few years, the application of Blockchain technology for a variety of applications has been the subject of much debate in the research industry. Yaqoob *et al.*, Farouk *et al.*, and Li and Liu [17–19] have stated the threat of privacy, security, and trust faced by the healthcare data management systems. They have discussed the benefits of adding blockchain to boost innovations and make major enhancements. Whereas, Ray, Dash, Salah, and Kumar [20] have proposed an ABE technique – blockchain-based IoT system where information on the channel only be accessed by the new members and cannot be assessed by recalled members. On the other hand, Griggs *et al.* [21] have developed a smart device based on ethereum (ETH) protocol. As organizations prepare for the Industry 4.0 revolution, the use and operation of new digital platforms become more important than ever. Shahnaz, Qamar, and Khalid [22] outline a framework which could be a blockchain-based solution with appropriate scalability, effectiveness, and security in the electronic health records. McGhin, Choo, and Liu [23] have addressed the unique requirements of healthcare applications which remain generally ignored. Lee *et al.* and Peterson *et al.* [24,25] have combined technologies like mobile computing and wireless communications to authorize the data by the admissible users. The system proposed by them not only improves IT performance but also ensure the safety of earlier approaches. Chen *et al.* [26], in their paper, have characterized the medical blockchain and analyzed by comparing it with the conventional system. Figure 19.1 provides country wise forecasted CAGR for 2020–2030 in detail.

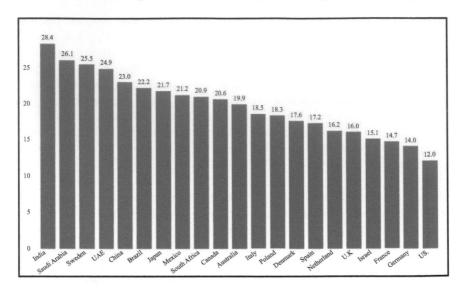

Figure 19.1   Country wise forecasted CAGR for 2020–2030 (in %)

19.3   Telemedicine market segmentation

The telemedicine market had proven to be a high revenue generator for the healthcare sector in a very short span of time. The four main contributors to this are telemedicine service providers, technology software providers, infrastructure and connectivity providers, and remote patient monitoring (RPM) service providers who are generating revenues in billions toward the contribution of telemedicine sector. It can be easily concluded that apart from the telemedicine service providers the other three can be put under the umbrella of hardware providers. The telemedicine market is a multi-billion-dollar market which can be best understood from the below graph showing the CAGR and the market share of telemedicine industry:

19.3.1   Market segmentation based on components

The main purpose of telemedicine service has always been to serve the patients by connecting them with the doctor virtually. But even to reach at this point and make it this achievable a set of hardware components are needed to make the service receivable and deliverable to both patient and doctors, respectively. On the basis of components, telemedicine market can be the following.

19.3.1.1   Hardware-based segmentation

Some of the major hardware components required in the telemedicine programs are:

1.   Digital camera which can either be in-built in the laptop or the smartphone or can also be available as a standalone device.

2. Telemedicine kit which consists of portable devices like stethoscope, pulse oximeter, etc.
3. Mobile medical devices such as ultrasound probes, vital sign monitor, and digital ECG.
4. Home care kit which consists of devices which are extremely light weight, easy to carry, and can be integrated with smartphones. These can comprise of blood pressure cuff, dermatoscope, etc.
5. Telemedicine Kiosk which enables the healthcare providers to make it possible for remote or rural areas and is an extremely important telemedicine service for country like India.

19.3.1.2 Software-based segmentation

The software-based telemedicine services enable the patient to interact with the doctor in a virtual manner, have a consultation with them, share and receive test reports, etc. Software-based telemedicine services include the services of remote patient monitoring which is the virtual tracking of patient's health through mobile medical devices. It is very beneficial where continuous health monitoring of patient's health is required. These types of software-based telemedicine services are very effective in the case of chronic diseases. Other such software-based services are store and forward telemedicine services where sharing old medical data such as lab result takes place virtually with the doctor, at any different location, through a software. This speeds up the treatment process and it saves time by sharing the medical data virtually through secured and safe software platform. Figure 19.2 depicts the information of Expected market share (of tele-medicine) by 2030.

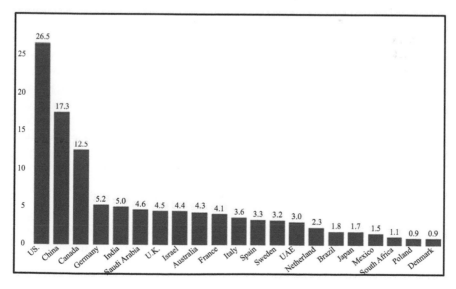

Figure 19.2   Expected market share by 2030 (in billion USD)

19.3.1.3   Service-based segmentation

In service-based segmentation of telemedicine industry, it includes teleconsulting which usually make use of basic ICT to make the virtual consultation possible which usually takes via an audio or video call and tele-monitoring which basically deals with the remote monitoring task of patient health under the supervision of a medical expert. Teleconsultation also includes the sharing of reports with doctor and get consultation based on the health report of the patient.

19.3.2   Technology-based segmentation

Technology-based segmentation telemedicine leverages the proper use of ICT which allows the patient and doctors to connect virtually and take share information among them. This type of segmentation basically involves the categorization of telemedicine into four which are the following.

19.3.2.1   Real-time video

The use of real-time video in telemedicine services involves solution consisting of virtual and live face-to-face interaction between the doctors and the patients. To make it happen, display devices like smartphone, laptop, tablets, etc. and video devices like digital camera, software program, and a proper Internet connection is required. Some of the leading telemedicine software leveraging real-time video solution are AMD Global, Doxy Me, Mend, Practo, etc. Major benefit of real-time video-based telemedicine services is that it reduces the overall cost, makes it more convenience for both the doctors and patients, provides better accessibility, etc.

19.3.2.2   Remote patient monitoring (RPM)

RPM also called synchronous telemedicine includes the tracking of patient's health through mobile medical devices like pulse oximeter, etc. and the corresponding result is then shared with the doctor. It also deploys wearable devices such as Fitbit to track the basic health of patient by recording their heart rate, pulse rate, cholesterol level, etc. [30]. Some major pros of using RPM in telemedicine are that it can provide the amount of care based of the intensity of illness of the patient thus saving time, it makes thing easy for hospitals and reduce the overall consultation time per patient as the data is already recorded and kept ready, if not serious patient can be treated virtually itself, etc. This benefit of treating the patient completely at home gained a major momentum after the onset of COVID-19 as this minimized the physical interaction, reduced kiosk at the hospital and clinics, and also maintained social distance.

19.3.2.3   Store and forward

These are also known as asynchronous telemedicine which involves sharing of medical data by the healthcare providers with the physician or the specialist located at a different place. Reports can be lab reports, videos, images, etc. In short, it can be concluded that this type of telemedicine services involves a high amount of sensitive data transfer and hence a proper facility to store and secure the data becomes the most vital task here. Some of the major benefits of this service is that this saves a lot of time by reducing the waiting time for receiving the necessary treatment, easy accessibility of doctors even if located at any place and it helps in overcoming the linguistic and cultural barrier occurring in the delivery of tele-medicine service. These are more widely used to treat illness pertaining to the respective specialty like radiology, pathology, dermatology, etc. Even for this type of telemedicine services, COVID-19 had been a boon as it had made more and more people accept such services to maintain social distance to avoid the spread of the virus. Some major players offering services such telemedicine services are Mouth Watch, Athena Health, etc.

19.3.2.4   Others

All other technology-based services not falling under the above three can be put into this segment which usually refers to the mobile health or mHealth services. The increasing popularity and usage of smartphone aided with the increased penetration of Internet has surged the demand for mHealth services exponentially [28]. Also other digital platform like e-Sanjeevani, an initiative by Ministry of Health and Family Welfare (MoHFW) also helped in catalyzing in the digital initiative in the healthcare sector. This is mostly used in case where a quick diagnosis is possible and involves a prescriptive method of tele-consultation where suggestions like health diet, lifestyle tips, food habits can be easily asked from the doctor. This has gained more popularity among the dieticians where not much of the health criticality is involved. With the onset of COVID-19, may telemedicine service providers have launched their mobile app to attend the less critical illness completely virtually and at a go to avoid physical contact and also to maintain COVID protocols. Some players who have done so are Med Life, Practo, etc. Some other benefits of using mobile health services are that it provides a faster access to healthcare, automated alert, and suggestive guidelines against various epidemics and pandemic too, enables increased interaction between doctors and patients, etc. One major example of this is Aarogya Setu App developed by the Indian Government to deal with the outbreak of CVOID-19 by applying a real-time tracking technique which can help in tracing the COVID-19 patients.

19.3.3   Specialty-based segmentation

Telemedicine services are not just limited to consultation with general physician to deal with the cure of basic illness but it has proved its mettle by resolving medical issues and illness related to diverse medical fields. This has been possible due to the shortage of care provider, lack of accessibility in rural areas, remote location of patients, etc. as it has bolstered the demand of telemedicine services in various spe-cialties. Some specialty had been early adopter of these services like tele radiology while other has been taking their own sweet time to let telemedicine resolve their issue like podiatry, orthopaedic, etc. To cover a few, some of them are listed below.

19.3.3.1   Telepsychiatry

It is a medical specialty that makes use of electronic device to offer services related to psychiatry thus expanding access to behavioral health services. Psychiatry itself is a broad domain which includes services like individual therapy, client education, medi-cation management, relationship therapy, and psychiatric evaluation. The demand of psychiatry has always been high which has got speeded up due to the COVID-19 as isolation and quarantine as it has caused a mental stress to people. This surging demand of psychiatrist has popularized telepsychiatry among people and it has come as a boon for country like India as due to its cultural and societal barrier people, there are reluctant in approaching psychiatrist physically. Telepsychiatry had also been proven effective in treating post-traumatic stress disorders and depression. Telepsychiatry is convenient, affordable, and also readily available which has also helped in integrating behavioral health care and primary care leading to improved mental health services.

19.3.3.2   Teledermatology

It is one of the branches of telemedicine which is growing at a very fast pace due to its easy fitting into the model of telemedicine services. After teleradiology, it is considered to be the fastest developed application area among all the medical specialty mainly due to rapid increase of cases of melanoma across the world which is one of the most aggressive forms of cancer [29]. The biggest survivor of melanoma is the United States and hence causing a rapid gain in the application of teledermatology among the American. Apart from the United States, cases of melanoma are also increasing significantly in the tropical nations like India which is making them demandable and immensely popular among them. Teledermatology allows easy communication between doctor and patient as transfer of data is also easy in it. Patient can easily send the photo of a rash, mole, acne, or any other skin disease availing the quick diagnosis through remote consultation or real-time video consultation. The reason for growth of teledermatology is also due to the rapid technological advancement in this domain like ML and deep learning (DL) technology which has the potential to detect skin disease accurately with just a click of a photo. Also, it has been observed that globally there has always been a shortage of dermatology especially in the rural and the under-developed areas. Hence, it has been like a boon for dermatology. Some major players in this domain are Meta Optima, Ksyos, 3Gen, etc.

19.3.3.3   Telegynecology

It is another fast-emerging specialty where an easy guidance and consultation can be provided virtually to women by reviewing their test results, monitoring their medication and symptoms, and also managing their entire post-delivery care through remote technology. It is currently being used to track and manage the conditions like postpartum depression, hypertension, etc. but slowly it had started assisting every aspect of a woman's health [27]. Some of the examples of the above include fetal heart rate (FHR) monitoring, bladder diary tracking with smartphone apps, postpartum blood pressure monitoring with Wi-Fi connected devices, fertility tracking with patient generated data, etc. Although it is gaining pace but still telegynecology is still considered to be in a nascent stage and has a lot of room for improvement and areas to cover in the domain of gynecology itself.

19.3.3.4   Tele-ICU

It is a domain of telemedicine which enables off-site clinicians to interact with bedside staff to consult on patient care. It has the potential to reduce the ICU mortality rate controlling on the increasing rise of inter-hospital ICU transfer of critically ill patients. Although the adoption of tele-ICU has increased over time but still it is in its nascent stage as people are reluctant in taking the tele services when comes to ICU. On an average, the ICU beds at any hospital accounts for 10% of the total hospital beds but still generating 30% of their revenue. Hence, due to this mismatch proportion and high cost and demand for the ICU will make the growth trajectory of tele-ICU steeper in the coming years. Some existing barriers associated to ICU are the high capital cost of constructing a new ICU unit and training the staff, lack of well-trained staff who can settle easily with the use of technologically advanced equipment's, etc. which can easily be overcome with the use of tele ICU services. Some major companies working in this domain are GE Healthcare, Omni cure, etc.

19.3.3.5 Telecardiology

It is one of the fast-growing areas of telemedicine as it is proving to be beneficial in treating and proper monitoring of hypertension, CT scans, acute ST-elevation myocardial infarction, heart failure and arrthymias. Here, patient data can be remotely monitored by health professional via a secured connection enabling better interaction between patient and doctor. Telecardiology has the potential to reduce the rate of hospitalization of patients and lower the mortality rate caused due to myocardial infarction by attending such issues virtually and helping in de-stressing on the health infrastructure of a nation. It also helps in strengthening of the health chain among the practitioner and cardiologists.

19.3.4 *Region-based segmentation*

The market share of telemedicine sector also varies from region to region. Like North America is currently ahead of others in this sector due to its early adoption and acceptance by both its public and the medical fraternity. Telemedicine has gained a rapid pace due to COVID-19 as enables the people to interact with doctors virtually and get diagnosed without making a crowd or kiosk at the hospital and hence allowing everyone to follow the COIVD-19 protocols. Some major countries and the maturity level of telemedicine in these countries are discussed below.

19.3.4.1 United States of America (USA)

US spends around 20% of its GDP on healthcare and that is one of the major reason they have invested well on telemedicine services and also have been successful in adopting it at a very early stage. Along with telemedicine, US have also invested heavily on blockchain technology due to its potential to make the storage and transfer of data transparent and safe in every manner. This attitude of US toward telemedicine has also helped them deal with COVID-19 efficiently as basic medication, consultation, treatment of chronic disease, etc. were easily taken care by telemedicine thus helping in containing the spread of virus without compromise on the health services. Currently more than three-fourth of the US hospitals provide telehealth services while others are in the process of doing so. Some challenges which they still need to overcome are unequal access to broadband services, lack of consistent access to the services, slow acceptance of telemedicine services among the older generation, etc.

19.3.4.2   India

India being the second most populous country in the world and highly distorted doctor to patient ratio poses a major challenge of providing a quality healthcare for all and to make a quality healthcare services available for all. With 65% of its population thriving in the rural areas even accessibility of telemedicine becomes an issue as it requires some basic digital infrastructure and connectivity which generally lacks among the rural population and also its varied cultural and linguistic diversity add on to this issue. But with time, the scenario has been changing rapidly toward a positive growth and it had been paced up due to COVID-19. With the fast paced infrastructural and technological development like rapid penetration of Internet at the world's cheapest rate and also increased use of mobile phones have kept its rural population just a step away from availing the telemedicine services.

Telemedicine was first launched in India when ISRO launched a Telemedicine Pilot Project in 2001 which aimed to create a telemedicine network between the Apollo Hospital of Chennai and other hospitals of rural areas of Tamil Nadu to facilitate the health services with ease. The Ministry of Health and family Welfare of India also took steps toward creating an ecosystem for e-healthcare which can reduce the increasing strain of its healthcare system. For this, they created a National e-Health Authority in 2013 to keep an EHR of tis population and also launched Natural Rural AYUSH telemedicine network to promote the use of telemedicine services across the nation.

After the onset of COVID-19 in India, the awareness and the acceptance rate of telemedicine services among the population have witnessed a surge. Mobile application like Aarogya Setu has been released by the government to digitally track the COVID-19 patients. Some major players in India related to telemedicine are mFine, Practo, Doc Prime, etc.

19.3.4.3   China

China is one of the leading countries in adopting digital health services where majority of the health professionals use some kind of digital health technology but with only two physicians available per 1,000 patients as per World Bank report of 2017, China faces a major crisis of having adequate medical professionals. The best remedy to overcome this situation is telemedicine services like virtual diagnosis, teleconsultation, and Internet-based hospital service which can attend more patients in less time. Hence, reducing the burden from its healthcare sector and reducing the congestion at the hospitals and clinics. With telemedicine platform like Ali Health and JD Health, China launched virtual COVID-19 clinics to deal with the increasing COVID-19 cases and curb the pandemic. Apart from this they also partnered with Huawei to connect various hospitals under a single system to diagnose and consult patients suffering from COVID-19.

19.4 Automated analytics

19.4.1 All about analytics

Analytics refers to the extraction of insights from data through various systematic computation applied on it using various statistical and mathematical tools and techniques. Analytics have been around from last 70 years which has evolved with time due to advancement of various technologies and its proper amalgamation with analytics. The entire transformation journey of analytics can be termed from Analytics 1.0 to 4.0.

1. Analytics 1.0: It refers to the era which began in the early 1950s and continued till almost the end of the last millennium. This era marked the beginning of the Data Analytics where not much of technological advancement were taking place but still were abundant enough for companies to collect the information for analyzing and making better business decisions. Here, the data collection was mostly done online and was manually analyzed which made the entire phase a slow one due to lack of proper tool and technique to process and analyze data.

2. Analytics 2.0: This was the era was which began in the early 2000s and was there till the end of it. It was during this phase where the term "Big Data" was coined due to the enormous increase in the amount of incoming data across the globe and also saw a huge increase in the adoption of analytics related work by various start-ups and mid-range organizations. With the improving digital infrastructure and the increasing demand and popularity of Internet, a lot of data mining and online analytics tools came up which took the advancement of analytics to a new height. Even technologies were maturing at a faster pace which leveraged the automation of task related to managing and processing data and give precise and accurate suggestions and recommendations to organizations to make better business decisions. A problem that erupted during this phase was the lack of infrastructure for the storage of data as the pace at which data were coming was much higher than the pace at which it was getting processed and this speed of incoming data was catalyzed due to the formation of companies like Google, PayPal, Amazon, etc. during this phase.

3. Analytics 3.0: This was the era which began in the late 2000s and continued till early 2010s which also saw the coming up of various social interaction sites like twitter and Facebook which had a huge contribution in generating trillions of data on a daily basis. This phase also witnessed an increased use of smartphones and various other devices which were digitally connected through Internet of Things (IoT) and generated a huge volume of data every moment. With the availability of data all around them, various organizations came up with better search algorithms which when applied through analytics helped in generating accurate suggestions and recommendations which eventually helped in making better business decisions in an ethical manner. Here, many organizations came up with "Online Analytical Processing" platforms which made the best use of analytics in different verticals of business. It also made

them capable of managing unstructured data which led to the faster processing of data through various ML models and other advanced analytics tools.

4. Analytics 4.0: This phase is still in its early days but has mastered itself in getting data from hundreds of sources at an ease. This phase also witnessed the pro-activeness of the organization which went a step ahead in implementing various automated analytics platform ensuring proper storage of data using cloud computing and full security of this stored data with the help of block chain technology.

Along with its evolution with time, analytics had always been categorized on the basis of their applications. On a broader perspective, analytics can be termed into four levels which are the following (refer Figure 19.3).

- Descriptive analytics – This is the first stage of analytical processing of data, often historical, which answers the fundamental question of "what happened"? It is about looking at the past data and get a trend out of it which can be utilized to decide the further course of action in any business. This is the basic level of analytics which forms the base for the other three types.
- Diagnostic analytics – It is the next step of analytical processing of data which answers the fundamental question of "why did it happen"? It basically involves various levels of drill down into the data to understand the relation between various elements of it and if any relation exists between them. This can be done with the use of various data mining techniques.
- Predictive analytics – Once the "what" and "why" of the data are answered, the predictive analytics comes into picture which based on past trend of data tries to answer the fundamental question of "what is likely to happen"? This analytic makes use of complex statistical techniques like regression, multivariate statistics, predictive modeling, etc. Predictive analytics demands a high

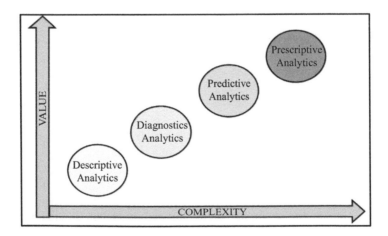

Figure 19.3   Types of analytics based on their complexity

quantity of data and a deep understanding of statistical tools and programming languages like R and python.

- Prescriptive analytics – This is the most advanced and the final level of analytics which answers the fundamental question of "what should be done further"? This type of analytics involves the use of various complex techniques like simulation, heuristics, recommendation engines, ML, and DL. The efficiency and the efficacy of this level of analytics depend on the level of accuracy achieved in the previous three levels of analytics.

19.4.2 Growth of automation in analytics

Analytics process automation or APA is the technology that makes it easy for everyone in your organization to share data, automate time-consuming and complex processes, and transform data into results. With APA, anyone can decipher the predictive and prescriptive information that allows for fast gains and quick returns on investment. The rapid technological advancements in digitalization and data & analytics have reshaped the business landscape, boosted performance, and made it possible for new commercial innovations and new forms of competitiveness to emerge. Meanwhile, the technology itself is still evolving, bringing new stream of progress in analytics, AI, robotics automation, and specifically ML. Together all these represent radical shift in technical capabilities that could have deeper impact on businesses, the economy and, more generally, society. The concept of AI is not novel, but the pace of recent advances is. There are three reasons that account for the acceleration of this concept:

- ML algorithms have progressed over the past few years, including the development of DL and reinforcement techniques based on neural networks.
- Computational ability has become easily available for training large and highly complex faster. The graphics processing units (GPUs), which were initially developed to make computer graphics into video games, have now been reallocated to perform the calculation of the data and algorithms required for ML with much faster speeds than conventional CPU chips. This IT capacity has been aggregated into highly scalable data centers and is available to the users through the cloud.
- Large quantities of data today can be used for training the ML models that are produced daily let's say for example the daily creation of billions of images, web-based click-through, mobile locations, websites, voices, videos, and sensors are built into and integrated with the IoTs.

19.4.3 Why automated analytics in telemedicine?

Virtual is the new physical – apart from the advancements in medicine and medicinal equipment or accessories another technological breakthrough is the evolution of healthcare through automation. Everyone wants to see greater efficacy and efficiency when it comes to healthcare. Not only efficiency and efficacy but we all also want to use most of the state-of-the-art strategies and systems out there to see the continued success. Talking about automation in healthcare sector, automation may resemble a daily batch of text communications reminding the patients about their appointments the following day. Or to be more precise, automation could include a database that detects and warns clinicians about known contraindications and drug interactions. Citing the following few examples would help to easily understand the role of automation in reducing the workload – in emergency room, results of the CT scan are texted to the referring physician moments after he struck the EHR. Here, the automated scheduling system had enabled staff to quickly identify and alert the respective employees: dermatologists and oral surgeons. Patients can learn about skin cancers at an early stage when they are treatable and before they pose a serious risk to the patient's PPC health and referring physicians can be informed when their patients pass through various hospital departments and functions. Fetal health can be classified using CTG data, a manual procedure that can take a significant amount of time. Automation of CTG data can help the physician know the state of fetal health beforehand and may assist in making appropriate and timely decisions in the event of a suspect or pathological.

19.4.4   Leveraging the potential of Machine Learning in automated analytics

In order to provide effective and efficient services to the patients, the healthcare companies should find a solution to reduce hospitalization and its associated hospitality costs. Not only this, they should focus more on treating a greater chunk of population in lesser time keeping in mind the safety, security, and privacy of the patient's data. Automation and blockchain have provided a one stop solution to this problem. Leveraging predictive analytics has help in detecting the disease, a person is suffering from – due to a huge amount of data storage across thousands of people suffering from the similar disease in the cloud, it is more reliable. This will make medical professional not to rely on a single source for prediction and the algorithmic pattern will provide him direction to proceed further. The use of natural language processing to record voice notes for patient's visit has reduced the burden of telehealth providers by automatically transferring it to EHRs. COVID-19 havoc has pushed people to adapt themselves to the digital world and hence we can say that teleconsultations will be preferred more in coming years.

19.5   Blockchain in telemedicine

19.5.1   All about blockchain

Blockchain is a data logging system in a way that makes it hard or impossible to alter, cheat, or hack the system. It is basically a large digital commercial book that is duplicated and distributed across the entire network of computer systems on the blockchain [32]. In other words, we can say that blockchain is the decentralization of data storage may not be possessed, controlled, or manipulated by a core player. This technology has the potential to change the design of one's privacy, ownership, collaboration, and uncertainty in the digitalized environment with disrupting sectors and practices as diverse as financial markets, distributing content, managing of supply chain, dispersing humanitarian assistance and even voting in general elections.

There are different types of blockchain as discussed in brief below.

19.5.1.1   Public blockchain

These are open and decentralized computer networks which are accessible to anyone who wishing to request or validate a transaction thereby verifying accuracy. It uses the consensual mechanisms of proof-of-work or proof-of-interest. Two most common examples cited here include the Bitcoin, ETH, and Dogecoin blockchain.

Hence, Figure 19.4 provides information about annual growth rate (%) blockchain technology, whereas Figure 19.5 provides market size of blockchain technology and Figure 19.6 provides information about impact of blockchain technology around the world by 2030.

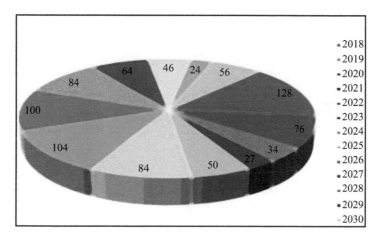

Figure 19.4   Annual growth rate (%) blockchain technology

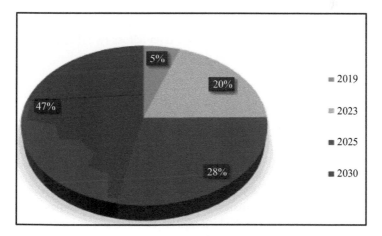

Figure 19.5   Market size (USD in Billion) of blockchain technology

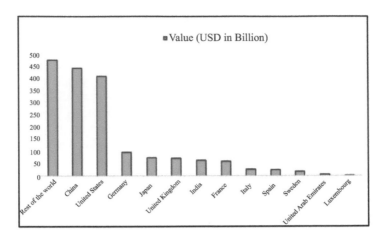

Figure 19.6   Blockchain global impact in 2030

19.5.1.2   Private blockchain

Unlike public blockchain, private blockchains are centralized inaccessible for everyone but to a selected group of people or organizations. Its architecture decodes the smart contract layer from the primary blockchain protocol.

19.5.1.3   Hybrid blockchains or consortiums

Consortiums are more alike public blockchain architecture where anyone willing to view may view but with the permission of the existing participants. For example, Energy Web Foundation, R3, and dragonchain. All of this is aimed at enhancing the confidence of costumers, consumers, or societal confidence.

19.5.1.4   Sidechains

As its name implies, it is another type of blockchain that works alongside the primary content. It enables its users to move data across two different blockchains thereby increasing its effectiveness and scalability.

19.5.2   Architectural design

The outer layer of telemedicine seems like just an involvement of phone or laptop will the needful but there is a lot beyond this which can be best understood with its architectural structure which is shown in Figure 19.7 which reflects the basic architecture of blockchain technology and Figure 19.8 which gives the complete and detailed architecture of the same.

It can be witnessed that even from the above image that even a basic architecture of telemedicine is an amalgamation of various technologies of which the most vital and primitive one is ICT which in itself is a combination of various hardware and software devices placed in a very synchronized manner to enable the service of telemedicine [31]. It begins with the data collection though various home

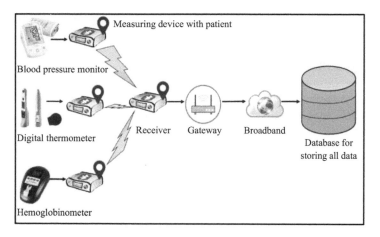

Figure 19.7 Basic architecture

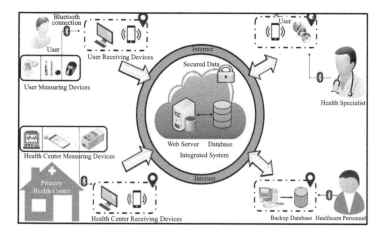

Figure 19.8 Complete architecture

devices like blood pressure monitor, pulse oximeter, digital thermometer, etc. and wearable devices like Fitbit which though Bluetooth transferred into the related telemedicine app available in the phone and, from there through gateway and broadband, the entire data is passed on to cloud and stored in a secured manner with the help of blockchain technology.

Different users like patients, doctors, healthcare workers, etc. have different access to a particular mobile application capturing health data and providing telemedicine services. Data collected through different users of the application are stored in the enterprise resource planning (ERP) of the organization which when required are given to the concerned authority. For example, say a basic health report of a patient is stored on the cloud of the telemedicine service provider organization and then are passed to the healthcare worker for their review and if required it is further passed to the doctor enabling smooth and easy interaction between all the stakeholders. Beyond this, the most crucial aspect of the telemedicine industry that is data is kept securely and in a safe manner. To make it happen various other technologies like blockchain is used which not only provides safety to the data but also make it immutable and its movement transparent. Blockchain is coming out like a boon for the telemedicine industry as it is taking care of the most important of this entire ecosystem that is data.

19.5.3   Data security and its cloud storage with the aid of blockchain

The most vulnerable part of this entire ecosystem of telemedicine is its digital asset that is data. With health being a private affair for any individual, its data too becomes private and sensitive too to manage its safe and secured storage and also sharing it with complete security and control. With the benefits of blockchain to store the data securely, there lies a strong future for healthcare when telemedicine services are amalgamated with it. Telemedicine data are generated through various available telemedicine-based apps who collects the data and stores it on remote servers accessible via the Internet. The physical environment of these data storage is owned by various organizations who build the data warehouse either on premise or on a remote location keeping data and their application running in addition to the data security and availability. These organizations store the data on cloud through various cloud delivery models which are:

(a)   Software-as-a-Service (SaaS) – It is basically a software that is owned and also delivered by a particular provider on a pay-per-use manner.
(b)   Platform-as-a-Service (PaaS) – Here, the deployment environment is provided as a service where consumer can use the equipment to develop their own program and deliver it to the users.
(c)   Infrastructure-as-a-Service (IaaS) – It provides a virtual platform service which are generally outsourced. Here the entire resources are bought by the consumer as an operating system.

Irrespective of cloud delivery model used by any telemedicine service provider, data storage is not the only concern but also its safety and security are of equal importance which can be attained with the help of blockchain. Apart from just providing security to the health data with its distributed ledger working principle, it also provides many other benefits like auditability, anonymity, transparency and immutability of data. There are various blockchain enabled opportunities provided to the telemedicine data which can be best explained in Figure 19.9.

19.5.4   Democratization of blockchain in telemedicine and beyond

Time and again, blockchain is proving out to be one of the most promising and revolutionizing emerging technologies which can structure the entire working model for most of the industries wherever applied. Blockchain being in its nascent stage, its

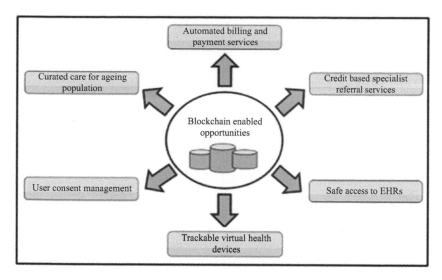

Figure 19.9   Blockchain-enabled opportunities

full potential and capability is yet to be mined out but wherever applied till date, it has proven to be beneficial for that domain. As per the report by Inside Pro of 2019, the five most anticipated industries to be disrupted by Blockchain are Banking, Financial Services & Insurance (BFSI), government, healthcare, energy, and logistics. It not only democratizes the application of that service but also ensures a secured data storage which cannot be hacked by a single source. Telemedicine sector fits best into the motive of blockchain technology which has the potential to remove the barriers that prevents people from accessing healthcare services. Beyond this, it also democratizes the access of telemedicine services breaking the basic barriers of cost, time, and location to make it reach to the maximum population. In developing countries like India and China, telemedicine with the help of blockchain is democratizing the access of its service to their rural population and helping them to connect with the best of the doctors and the hospitals with the help of telemedicine.

19.5.5   Pros and cons of blockchain in telemedicine

Blockchain has been like an icing on the cake for telemedicine industry. It has been boon for it as it takes care of the most important asset of this domain that is data. It has the potential to securely store any kind of healthcare data across platforms. Blockchain has been applicable in telemedicine industry in different ways. Some of the pros of using telemedicine are the following:

(a)   Interoperability – It makes the system able to store all the data in a single format which can be easily shared with the hospitals creating a data sharing eco-system based on trust and structured manner.

(b)   User access – It gives the privilege to the patient to choose which data to share and whom to share as health has always been a private affair for any individual.

(c)   Data security – Blockchain ensures the storage of data in a very secure manner without any possibility of tampering the data or the risk of losing them.

(d)   Low cost fast transaction – Here, the blocks are processed at the interval of every few minutes and at a very low cost.

(e)   Transparency – Since the data are entered with the help of the token assigned to their respective block and with the consensus of 51% of the stakeholder of that data. Thus providing a high degree of transparency for the data owners.

Along with its benefits, blockchain comes with its own set of disadvantages which are as follows:

(a)   Emerging technology – Blockchain as a technology is still in its nascent stage and will take its own sweet time to mature. Even many corporations are having a hard time to integrate this technology with their core system.

(b)   High set-up cost – The initial cost of providing it with the proper infrastructure and processing power can be a costly affair and thus making it reluctant at time to adopt it with ease.

19.5.6   Use cases in telemedicine from India and overseas

Use Case: Control of Counterfeit or Spurious Drugs

"Niti Aayog working on Blockchain Technology for Drug Industry" August 3, 2018, Economic Times

"Niti Aayog is working with Apollo Hospitals and Information Technology Major Oracle on applying blockchain (decentralized) technology in pharmaceutical supply chain management to detect spurious drugs," CEO of Niti Aayog, Mr Amitabh Kant as quoted in Economic Times of August 3, 2018.

This initiative has been rolled out by Niti Aayog to counter spurious drugs menace and provide complete end-to-end tracking and tracing of drugs from manufacturer to consumer.

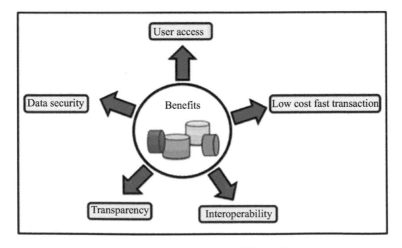

Figure 19.10   Benefits of blockchain

That India faces a huge challenge of spurious drugs in life-saving drugs as well as other categories has been adequately reported and covered in newspapers and other media channels (cf. https://timesofindia.indiatimes.com/city/thane/thane-kalyan-woman-arrested-for-illegal-stocking-sale-of-duplicate-cancer-medicines/articleshow/86687561.cms Retrieved on October 1, 2021).

Analyticsindiamag.com (February 14, 2020) informed that Indian Government's policy think tank, Niti Aayog, has come out with a strategy document recognizing many crucial areas blockchain technology can significantly benefit the country and healthcare figures in the list prominently.

Use Case – Healthcare Data Management

Healthcare data sharing services provided by OpenLedger using Blockchain.

Issues which best healthcare Industry have been listed by OpenLedger (https://openledger.info/) as – "Drug traceability, Poor healthcare data management, Data security in clinical trials, Medical device tracking, Patient records, Micropayments, High cost of new innovations, Lack of access to advanced treatments, Errors in prognosis and Overdiagnosis."

The reason for the use of blockchain technology is as it affords safeguarding of the integrity of data exchanges between various stakeholders of the healthcare ecosystem namely healthcare service providers, users or patients and third parties like insurance service providers. Further, the fact that blockchain empowers individuals to be accountable for their own healthcare helps in bringing down costs and making the healthcare industry more efficient.

Use case – genomics

LeewayHertz (https://www.leewayhertz.com/about-us/) a digital solutions provider in USA provides an exhaustive list of use cases four domains of healthcare – genomics being one of them.

EncrypGen owns a DNA data marketplace based on blockchain and branded as Gene-Chain. This platform is deployed for searching, storing, sharing, and selling of genetic data. Genetic data is purchased-for advanced healthcare research- on the platform using "secure and traceable DNA tokens."

Nebula Genomics uses "Distributed Ledger Technology" for eliminating intermediaries and the associated costs from the genetic study processes thereby helping biotechnology and pharma firms.

Use cases – miscellaneous

Indian IT bellwether, Infosys classifies "Healthcare Blockchain Use Cases" under four heads namely, constituent management (namely, Health Risk Assessment, Billing and Payment Management), benefits management (claim to payment tracking and other tracking systems), business administration (medical services fraud detection, etc.), and health & wellness management (referral management, clinical trial, etc.).

19.6 Telemedicine and the law: worldwide perspectives

Within a short span of time, telemedicine field has become a multi-billion-dollar industry with most hospitals, clinics, private practitioner, etc. are using some sort of telemedicine services to reach to their patients. Looking from the consumer's perspective, telemedicine had been proven as the best alternative to the time consuming in person availing of medical services making them readily accept it readily due to its easy availability but if seen from doctor's perspective, they are still not free to avail the services of telemedicine. They can only utilize it under certain laws and regulations set by the rule maker of that particular nation. Like in US, some of the basic rules that doctors need to abide by are:

(a) Having a proper license before they start providing the health services to patients.
(b) Establishing a valid physician patient relationship and accepted modality by both the parties.
(c) Conduct of an appropriate assessment to be given by the doctor before continuing the telemedicine services.
(d) Doctors should follow the accepted practice standards.
(e) The services provided through telemedicine must be listed among the eligible CPT/HCPCS codes.

In country like India, telemedicine services were regulated only after the onset of COVID-19 when it became the need of the hour to regulate it and promote it as the alternative for in person consultation to avoid the congestion at clinics and hospitals. Keeping the need and benefit of telemedicine in mind, especially during COVID-19, Ministry of Health and Family Welfare, Government of India in association with NITI Aayog formulated the Telemedicine Practice Guidelines on March 25, 2020. Some of the guidelines were the following:

(a) Only a registered medical practitioner (RMP), enrolled under State Medical Register or the Indian Medical Register under the Indian Medical Council Act 1956, can practice telemedicine services.
(b) A registered medical practitioner is can provide telemedicine service anywhere in India.
(c) It classifies telemedicine application four categories that is the mode of interaction, the timing of information transmittal, reason for consulting the doctor, and the interaction between the doctor and the patient.
(d) To provide the telemedicine services, only three modes can be used which are video like various telemedicine facility app, Skype etc., audio like phone, voice over internet protocol (VOIP) etc. and text based communication.
(e) Taking the consent of the patient before delivering the telemedicine service is a must
(f) A specified framework should be followed by the RMP for providing the telemedicine services which can be generalized into four step and it is shown through the flowchart as in Figure 19.11.

In a similar manner, a basic rules and regulation have been framed by all the telemedicine provider countries so that no malpractices can be attempted and also some strict guidelines have been made so that proper storage of health data can be done without leading to any such data phishing incidents.

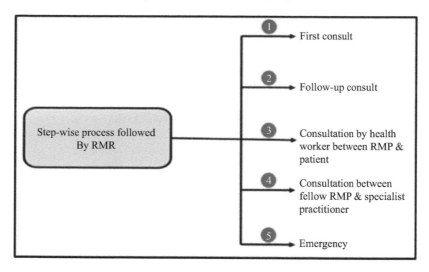

Figure 19.11   Step-wise framework to be followed by RMP

19.7   Future of telemedicine: disruptive technologies

Like any chemical reaction fastens after adding a catalyst to it, in a similar manner a disruptive technological innovation in healthcare domain needs a catalyst to reach its maturity. Telemedicine industry is estimated to grow at a paced up rate of 18% till 2027 due to the onset of COVID-19. It can be a convincing option to chronic, acute and preventative care and can lead to better clinical outcomes. In developing countries like India, after industrialization telemedicine will be a bridge between patients and telehealth hospitals. The hospitals will be providing their remote services using predictive analytics on the data stored in their cloud whereas patient will render services based on the referrals and credits. It is assumed that telemedicine will be a standardized service available to every patient at the root level. When a patient will realize the level of comfort telemedicine provides to him sitting at home, consulting the doctor, uploading his records, and receiving his reports online – no one would choose to move out for the doctor's appointment unless found necessary. With the integration of sensors, nanotechnology, analytics, telecommunication, and big data, telemedicine is the future of healthcare system to be adopted not only by top 1% society but also the rural population. The future of telemedicine can also be amalgamated with technologies like virtual reality and augmented reality for better visuals and clear images for diagnosis by the doctor in cases like mammography, CT scan, chest X-ray, ultrasound images, ECG, echocardiogram, eye problems, etc.

19.8   Conclusion

In conclusion, telecare has provided a positive impact in the lives of millions of patients by providing services as per their demands, comfortability, economic status, and schedule. Not only it has saved the time and money but it has also provided a facility to communicate with the best doctor sitting anywhere nationally or internationally which was not possible earlier. Along with providing effective services, blockchain in telemedicine has been the savior by offering an extra layer of security to the data being stored. This huge amount of data is then used for analysis by the healthcare practitioners, healthcare organizations, government entities, etc. to come up with a solution to a disease which is predicted to be spread among larger populations in any specific area. This integrated service will help a lot to take steps in prior before any disease starts reaching its maturity and become fatal.

References

[1]   Strehle E.M. and Shabde N. (2006). One hundred years of telemedicine: does this new technology have a place in paediatrics? *Arch Dis Childhood* 91 (12):956–959. https://doi.org/10.1136/adc.2006.099622

[2]   Rispoli M. and Machalicek W. Advances in telehealth and behavioral assessment and intervention in education: introduction to the special issue. *J Behav Educ* 2020;29:189–194.

[3]   Kasthuri A. Challenges to healthcare in India—the five A's. *Indian J Commun Med* 2018;43(3):141–143. https://doi.org/10.4103/ijcm.IJCM_194_18.

[4]   WHO Global Observatory for eHealth. Telemedicine: opportunities and developments in Member States: report on the second global survey on eHealth. World Health Organization; 2010. https://apps.who.int/iris/handle/10665/44497. Accessed 20 April 2020.

[5]   Bokolo A. Jr. Use of telemedicine and virtual care for remote treatment in response to COVID-19 pandemic. *J Med Syst* 2020;44:132.

[6]   Kadir M.A. Role of telemedicine in healthcare during COVID-19 pandemic in developing countries. Telehealth and Medicine Today; 2020.

[7]   Nichani A.V., Pistolwala S.T., Deshmukh A.A., and Godse M.J. Telemedicine: making health care accessible. In: Vasudevan H., Deshmukh A., Ray K. (eds), *Proceedings of International Conference on Wireless Communication. Lecture Notes on Data Engineering and Communications Technologies*, vol. 19. Springer, Singapore; 2018.

[8]   Görs M., Albert M., Schwedhelm K., Herrmann C., and Schilling K. Design of an advanced telemedicine system for remote supervision. *IEEE Syst J* 2016;10(3):1089–1097.

[9]   Hameed R., Mohamad O., and Hamid O. Patient monitoring system based on e-health sensors and web services. In: 8th International Conference on Electronics, Computers and Artificial Intelligence, pp. 17–22.

[10]   Hau Y.S., Kim J.K., Hur J., *et al.* How about actively using telemedicine during the COVID-19 pandemic? *J Med Syst* 2020;44:108.

[11]   Rogers B.G., Coats C.S., Adams E., *et al.* Development of telemedicine Infrastructure at an LGBTQ+ clinic to support HIV prevention and care in response to COVID-19, Providence, RI. *AIDS Behav* 2020;24:2743–2747.

[12] Ohannessian R., Duong T., and Odone A. Global telemedicine implementation and integration within health systems to fight the COVID-19 pandemic: a call to action. *JMIR Public Health Surveill* 2020;6(2):e18810.

[13] Calton B., Abedini N., and Fratkin M. Telemedicine in the time of coronavirus. *J Pain Sympt Manag* 2020;60(1):e12–e14, ISSN 0885-3924, https://doi.org/10.1016/j.jpainsymman.2020.03.019.

[14] Raskas M.D., Gali K., Schinasi D.A., and Vyas S. Telemedicine and pediatric urgent care: a vision into the future. In: Edmunds M., Hass C., and Holve E. (eds), *Consumer Informatics and Digital Health*, Springer, Cham; 2017, https://doi.org/10.1007/978-3-319-96906-0_11

[15] American Hospital Association. Issue Brief: Telehealth: Helping hospitals deliver cost-effective care; 2016. Retrieved from http://www.aha.org/content/16/16telehealthissuebrief.pdf. Accessed December 20, 2016.

[16] Dash S., Aarthy R., and Mohan V. Telemedicine during COVID-19 in India—a new policy and its challenges. *J Public Health Pol* 2021;42(3):501–509, https://doi.org/10.1057/s41271-021-00287-w

[17] Yaqoob I., Salah K., Jayaraman R., *et al.* Blockchain for healthcare data management: opportunities, challenges, and future recommendations. *Neural Comput Appl* 2021;2:130–139, https://doi.org/10.1007/s00521-020-05519-w

[18] Farouk A., Alahmadi A., Ghose S., and Mashatan A. Blockchain platform for industrial healthcare: vision and future opportunities. *Comput Commun* 2020;154:223–235.

[19] Yu Y., Li Y., Tian J., and Liu J. Blockchain-based solutions to security and privacy issues in the internet of things. *IEEE Wirel Commun* 2018;25(6):12–18.

[20] Ray P.P., Dash D., Salah K., and Kumar N. Blockchain for IoT-based healthcare: background, consensus, platforms, and use cases. *IEEE Syst J* 2020;99:1–10, https://doi.org/10.1109/JSYST.2020.2963840

[21] Griggs K.N., Ossipova O., Kohlios C.P., Baccarini A.N., Howson E.A., and Hayajneh T. Healthcare blockchain system using smart contracts for secure automated remote patient monitoring. *J Med Syst* 2018;42(7):130.

[22] Shahnaz A., Qamar U., and Khalid A. Using blockchain for electronic health records. *IEEE Access* 2019;7:147782–147795.

[23] McGhin T, Choo K.-K.R, Liu C.Z., and He D. Blockchain in healthcare applications: research challenges and opportunities. *J Netw Comput Appl* 2019;135:62–75.

[24] Lee T.F., Li H.Z., and Hsieh Y.P. A blockchain-based medical data preservation scheme for telecare medical information systems. *Int J Inf Secur* 2020;20:589–601.

[25] Peterson K., Deeduvanu R., Kanjamala P., and Boles K. A blockchain-based approach to health information exchange networks. In: Proceedings of the NIST Workshop Blockchain Healthcare, vol. 1, pp. 1–10 (Mayo Clinic).

[26] Chen Y., Ding S., Xu Z. *et al.* Blockchain-based medical records secure storage and medical service framework. *J Med Syst* 2019;43:5, https://doi.org/10.1007/s10916-018-1121-4

[27] Nair U., Armfield N.R., Chatfield M.D., and Edirippulige S. The effectiveness of telemedicine interventions to address maternal depression: a systematic review and meta-analysis. *J Telemed Telecare* 2018;24(10):639–650, https://doi.org/10.1177/1357633X18794332

[28] Press Information Bureau, New Delhi. A big win for Digital India: Health Ministry's 'eSanjeevani' telemedicine service records 2 lakh tele-consultations; 2020. https://pib.gov.in/PressReleasePage.aspx?PRID=1646913. Accessed 06 December 2020.

[29] Massone C. and Mendes Schettini A.P. Teledermatology. In: Nunzi E., Massone C. (eds), *Leprosy*, Springer, Milano, 2012, https://doi.org/10.1007/978-88-470-2376-5_37

[30] Ali F., El-Sappagh S., Islam S.R., *et al.* An intelligent healthcare monitoring framework using wearable sensors and social networking data. *Futur Gener Comput Syst* 2021;114:23–43.

[31] Syed T.A., Alzahrani A., Jan S., Siddiqui M.S., Nadeem A., and Alghamdi T. A comparative analysis of blockchain architecture and its applications: problems and recommendations. *IEEE Access* 2019;7:176838–176869.

[32] The Global Blockchain in Healthcare Report: The 2020 Ultimate Guide for Every Executive, https://healthcareweekly.com/blockchain-in-healthcare-guide/. Accessed 22 May 2020.

[33] Deloitte Consulting LLP. Blockchain: Opportunities for Health Care, 2016, https://www2.deloitte.com/us/en/pages/public-sector/articles/blockchain-opportunities-for-health-care.html. Accessed 15 September 2018.

Chapter 20

A sensor-based architecture for telemedical and environmental air pollution monitoring system using 5G and blockchain

M. Leeban Moses[1], T. Perarasi[1], L. Lino[1] and M. Ramkumar Raja[2]

Abstract

Within the recent advancements in technology, there is a tremendous growth in digital healthcare technologies for refining and transmuting healthcare which takes the account of plummeting human miscalculations, enlightening clinical consequences, facilitating care coordination, and humanizing practice efficiencies, with the help of integrated approaches. To create a more effective and safer health care environment in the places where there is no medical health care facility, Internet of Medical Things (IoMT) can provide a Tele medical room with a 5G infrastructure. The Tele medical room contains a smart chair facility, wherein the data of patient denotes heart rate of the patient, electrocardiography, blood pressure of the patient, and body temperature of the patients that can be monitored remotely and the assistance can be provided by the doctors through remote conferencing. The 5G-enabled communication environment is created to withstand higher data transmission in the remote correspondence interface.

During the recent decade, we have seen an incredible improvement concerning miniaturized electronic devices, in order to facilitate their integration in handheld equipment. This invention demonstrates the estimation of blood glucose level by designing a substrate-based flexible antenna. The change in the concentration of raw material provides moderate dielectric constant that is attained in the flexible antenna. Synthesized nickel particle-based flexible nickel aluminate ($NiAl_2O_4$) is utilized as a substrate material for microwave applications. The substrate was made with 42% of nickel, with a dielectric constant of 4.979 and a thickness of 1 mm. Design and performance analyses were investigated based on the reflection coefficient in normal and bent conditions. Dielectric properties of human blood over a broad frequency range were measured with and without adding the glucose content

[1]Department of ECE, Bannari Amman Institute of Technology, India
[2]King Khalid University, Saudi Arabia

for different types of blood groups. These results were manipulated as a data set required for machine learning approaches.

The optimized Ensemble algorithm which provides feature reduction, hyper parameter optimization, along with asymmetrical cost assignment can be used to segregate the normal and abnormal heart beat signal. The receiver unit comprises a headphone jack which can be inbuilt with a Wi-Fi modem in order to clearly hear the pulmonary, cardiac, or digestive noises being monitored. The Internet of Things (IoT) sensor information is created from different heterogeneous gadgets, correspondence conventions, and information organizes that are gigantic in nature. This gigantic measure of information is not incorporated and examined physically. This is a huge issue for IoT application designers to make the mix of IoT sensor information. Semantic explanation of IoT information is the establishment of IoT semantics. Bunching is one way of settling the combination and investigation of IoT sensor information. Semantics and learning approaches are the keys to resolve the issue of sensor information combination and investigation in IoT.

Keywords: Internet of Healthcare Things; Internet of Medical Things; Tele medical room; Heart rate; ECG; Blood pressure; remote correspondence interfaces

20.1 Introduction

The development in Internet of Things (IoT) allows medical devices for remote monitoring in the healthcare, to wrinkle necessary information and transference to physicians in real time which can endow doctors to deliver superlative care. The efficiency of healthcare devices in IoT is made by gathering all sensor information's from the connected devices, storing and analyzing the data information obtained by all devices, predicting the diseases by using machine learning algorithm which contains a predefined data set for identification, information exchange through reliable communication, early diagnosis of diseases, and to monitor them remotely by providing assistance. The IoT has unlocked a world of openings in medicine: wearable devices like biosensors and smart watches which monitor pulse and oxygen levels when connected to the Internet can collect valuable data and map those data with the previously available data sets and give extra insight into symptoms and trends, empower remote caring of individuals, and usually give patients a better treatment. By collecting information from medical devices, the individual statistics of the patients can be viewed and diagnosed in real time by improving the entire system of individual patient.

The healthcare administrations would have been instigated IoT technology by now, but today many healthcare devices are operated in silence and one-third of the healthcare administrations do not deploy information from associated devices other processes. This is due to the deficiency of data transfer and errors in identification. The efficiency of healthcare hangs on rapidity and diagnosis of data and we have seen more quantity of campaigns associated in IoT platform. Over 50% of the medical devices on healthcare linkages will be of IoT devices because the industry is taking on the biosphere with associated things. The normal language and a solitary stage for the gadgets to work the potential for IoT are boundless. The capacity to handily screen and oversee patient can help and save valuable moment consistently. Without having a visit to every persistent, the master specialists can offer guidance and track clinical resources. This can give and deal with the medical care office effectively. From patient heart screen to temperature measures, this continuous checking information as of now exist in medical care and now it tends to be utilized to establish a more secure and more viable climate. Through a solitary application on a cell phone, the patient and staff can sequentially oversee IoT information.

20.1.1 Architecture—IoT

Monitoring the patients remotely can be done by using body area network which can monitor the different sensor that is placed on the body surface and does not information will be collected by a variable receiver and transmitter the information by using any wireless gateway. As we require high bandwidth and high quality of service for transmitting the information, 5G technology provides personal trusted gateway for healthcare professional and the central server for patient monitoring system.

Figure 20.1 represents the 5G architecture for IoT healthcare devices by the implementation of body area networks. The body area network mentioned in the architecture consists of many different IoT devices enabled with different types of sensors. Patient-trusted gateway provides short-range communication to the centralized server from the body area network. The short-range communication which is provided by the patient-trusted gateway can actors wireless link and provides trusted communication. The centralized trusted server can provide communication to long range by using the spectrum allocation that is provided in the 5G network.

Generally monitoring of biological signals continuously can provide the changes in the health information that occur in a human body due to any diseases, infections, or stress. For example, the blood pressure signals are measured in order to prevent the heart getting over work and arteries become damaged. The measurement of biological signals using different types of sensors can be done in two different ways. The first the sensor type can be of variable by using different metal plates attached into the body. Even though systems provide reliable performance and provide accurate measurements, the comfort provided to the patient will be low. The second type of sensor I can be designed by clothing type and can be affixed in any chairs or beds in order to monitor the patient status. This system can provide less comfort to the patients. To monitor ECG, two electrodes are used in a clothing surface and the measured data can be processed using some signal processing techniques and then transmitted. The signals can provide the information about the pumping action of heart. In order to monitor photo plethysmogram (PPG) signal optically obtained plethysmogram can be used to send the rate of flow of

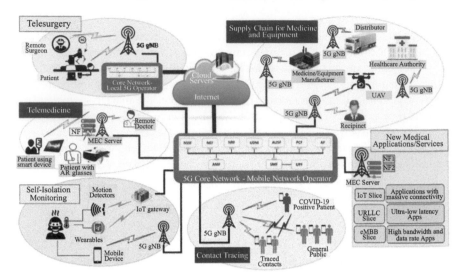

Figure 20.1   5G architecture for IoT healthcare devices

blood which is controlled by heart pumping action. The Bacille Calmette-Guerin (BCG) indications characterize the engagements of the physique in reaction to the cardiac ejection of blood. The three different types of signals can be used to monitor the different heart activities of a human body.

20.2   Background

Jaiee Sitaram Adivarekar *et al*. [1] as indicated by the creator in this fast contest of life, it is hard to continually screen the affected human's physique considerations, for example, level of sucrose content in blood, pulse rating, illness related to physique variations, etc. cannot be monitored continuously by other persons of the family when the affected person's illness varies suddenly. In order to eliminate this problem, a heart rate sensor has been integrated with Global System for Mobile (GSM) module by using a controller, which can sense the heart rate and transmit through text message if the person's illness gets varied to abnormal conditions. This illness of humans checking framework histories corporeal potentials either by standard interims of time or by ceaselessly.

Wanqing *et al*. [2] exploration intended to create adaptable material anodes. In particular, four cathodes with various inside developments for estimating continuous ECG signals. The exhibition terminals are assessed depending on the comfort level, SNR, skin–cathode impedance, and electrical attributes of ECG signal. The other bio-signals such as PPG and breath signals gathered by utilizing proposed material anodes can give a harmony between signal qualities and ease (SQC).

Heye Zhang *et al*. [3] explore the wearable gadget with biofeedback work that has been the one rise looking into the application, which can incorporate current biofeedback speculations into the best in class detecting and body sensor arrange (BSN) innovations. The wearable gadget created is nonexclusive with low cost and multifaceted nature, which tends to be extended increasingly wearable gadgets. This study utilized wearable preparing examples and to practice biofeedback capacities.

Mukhopadhyay *et al.* [4] explore the screen physiological parameters, for example, skin temperature, pulse, and body sway. A model was effectively evolved and tried to set up the evidence of idea. The calculations were tried and seen as precise and solid at this created/advancement stage. The tale part of the structure is its ease and identification of clinical misery which does not require squeezing any signal for an emergency response. This is a colossal improvement over existing business item. A signal for an emergency response has likewise been given in the created framework which can be utilized under a crisis circumstance.

A. N. Reddy *et al.* [5] framework gives persistent observing of patient after release from medical clinic. In the framework actualized principally two parameters internal heat level and heartbeat are estimated. The parameters like pulse, ECG of the patient can be incorporated as the circuit. Additionally, the entire framework can be incorporated as a wearable gadget which expands adaptability of the framework.

M. Ahmid *et al.* [6] introduced a novel secure and smart engineering for the IoT depending on the agent. In view of experimentation, it was discovered that ECC-ElG beats to RSA and ElGamal in regard to operational productivity and security with lesser key size. An ECC-ElGamal is especially generally appropriate for IoT gadgets. With experimentation, the upsides of our framework have developed, and are the following: the client can change or get the gadget state whenever and anyplace with just a single collaboration. Our design guarantees the privacy of information detecting, validation, and approval.

C. Chokphukhiao *et al.* [7] present the genuine instance of IoT-based emergency vehicle activity center and its comparing Virtuoso Wellbeing Rescue vehicle and keen wristband. The entire framework expects to build personal satisfaction of Thai individuals when if there should arise an occurrence of crisis. K. Vijayakumar *et al.* [8] introduced a conventional structure for IoT medicinal services application. A point to point by IoT communication advancements, sensors are organized exhaustively. The system talked about will provide food the requirement for uses of medicinal services to screen and track patients. We have likewise talked about the difficulties and confinement of the IoT for human services application.

J. G. Ramani *et al.* [9] observe the framework which foresee breakdowns in the indispensable signs that include continuous accumulations and values, and furthermore have a precise emergency revelation which will be related to a nursing organization. It likewise advises medical clinics in case of crisis. In the event that notice not reacted, the framework will send accurate GPS co-ordinates of the casualty to the clinic, so the worker can be given the emergency vehicle administrations. During typical days, the wellbeing parameters will be observed at the control room or by the administrator through a portable application which had been created so as to take note of the parameters that had been put away in the cloud which can assist us with having a documentation of those wellbeing records for later reference [10].

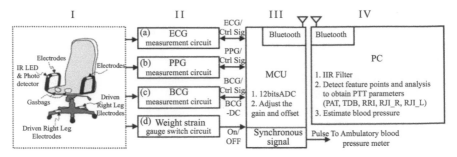

Figure 20.2   Proposed tele medical room—a smart chair with ECG, BCG, PPG measurements

20.3   Research methodology—measurement of biological signals

This chapter aims to provide remote patient monitoring system in a rural environment using the existing mobile architecture. A tele medical room was proposed as shown in Figure 20.2 in order to monitor the status of a patient and provides remote assistance to the patient. To make the tele medical room in a smart mode, new chair is modeled in which the electrodes and sensors are inbuilt to measure the ECG, BCG, PPG signals and also body temperature.

By measuring all these biological signals, we can determine the basic test measurements in which the doctor can learn about the status of a patient. All this obtained information will be processed by using some signal processing techniques and the obtained information's will be transmitted instantly to the doctor by the establishment of 5G architecture provided. The doctor can also give the patient directly buy video conferencing and diagnosis the patience status remotely and can guide him with proper medical assistance.

20.3.1   Measurement of ECG signals through cloth material provided

The ordinary ECG estimation technique must be actualized in a medical clinic condition. Extraordinary hardware and a few wired direct-skin-contact Ag/AgCl anodes are required, and it is not reasonable for long haul day by day life ECG checking in view of the skin bothering it causes, event of movement ancient rarities, and unsettling influence of day-by-day life exercises brought about by the wired anodes.

ECG is a non-intrusive technique to screen heart action and can uncover essential data on cardiovascular clutters, including heart musicality irregularities, aggregately known as arrhythmias or dysrhythmias. Two cathodes E1 and E2 were set on chest near heart and third reference anode E3 actualized in sock was put on right leg. This arrangement empowers to acquire great nature of QRS top sign. ECG anodes are associated with differential speaker of extremely low

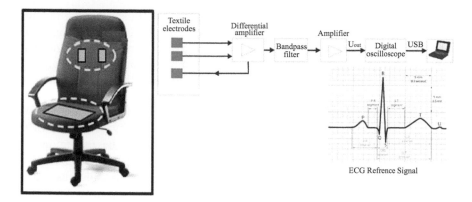

Figure 20.3   Measurement and analysis of ECG signals through capacitive coupling

counterbalance voltage and high increase. Plentifulness of ECG signal is around 1 mV and recurrence range is from 0.05 Hz to 100 Hz [2]. Band pass channel cuts off unneeded recurrence behind this band. Extra speaker with gain coefficient $K = 5.5$ V/V builds signal from channel. Yield voltage of this intensifier UOUT is estimated by advanced oscilloscope. Information from oscilloscope is sent to scratch pad by USB interface was ECG signals is examinations. Every electronic component and journal were provided from battery to keep away from power line impedances.

Impedance between skin and sensor will be relatively high because of the insulating effect produced by the clothing. In each of the cathode section, we need to convert the displacement current into a voltage and this can be achieved using the high input impedance amplifier. The placement of the sensors is shown in Figure 20.3 and will be shielded with them in the case of aluminum. Output signals from each of the electrode placed will be amplified, filtered, and transmitted. When the signals are measured from two of the electrodes placed at the back of chair, the noise will be very high due to the large impedance created between skin and the sensor. To avoid the common mode noise cancellation, we require additional third electrode which has been installed in the base of the cushion and associated with base by using a cable. Therefore, the noise reduction has been increased by creating a negative feedback with the gain of thousand.

20.3.2   Measurement of BCG signals through cloth material provided

Ballistocardiography is a non-invasive technique which depends on the capacity of the body gesticulation engendered by the expulsion of the blood at collectively cardiac cycle. The BCG signals were estimated progressively utilizing the poly-vinylidene fluoride (PVDF) films connected to the trial mechanical assembly. To affirm that the BCG signals were estimated precisely, the PPG signals were all the while estimated as a source of perspective by utilizing a PPG sensor. The crude

BCG signals were sent to a PC framework by means of Bluetooth. The product created in this examination gives highlights, for example, commotion handling extraction, just as demonstrating and elements of circulatory strain estimation. The product was created on a MATLAB base. After the preparation stage, it can assess circulatory strain at time frames through the signs estimated by means of the seat. The idea of the framework is delineated in Figure 20.4.

The main objective of measuring BCG signal is to determine the heart rate. As the heart rate signals are measured in the bank with of very few Hertz, the BCG signal should be obtained without any noises and this can be passed into a Butterworth third-order band pass filter with the same cutoff frequency obtained in the heart rate signal. The noise signal present in BCG signal is called as cardio respiratory signal and these signals cannot be removed by using normal filtering process. Empirical mode decomposition technique has been adopted to remove the distortion in the BCG signal. To uptime empirical mode decomposition first, the maximum and minimum of the signal is to be identified and interpolation technique is used to estimate the envelope of the maximum and minimum signals and cal-culating the average mean obtained by the lower and upper envelope and new time series signal has been extracted by subtracting the mean of the envelope. The obtained new time series signal will contain the higher peak and due to the absence of higher peak from the obtained signal, the blood pressure cannot be estimated properly. Therefore, to obtain the blood pressure, the instantaneous phase was obtained from the above signal by using the Hilbert transform and inpatient department care (IPD) was determined. The blood pressure value will be estimated by taking the median of the IPD values of two to BCD signals and artificial neural

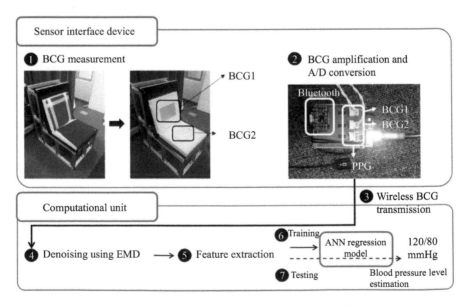

Figure 20.4   Measurement and analysis of BCG signals

network is used for regression analysis and finally the blood pressure value will be estimated from the BCG signal transmitted.

20.3.3 Measurement of PPG signals through cloth material provided

In order to obtain the PPG signal, we can place a three series of LED at the back of chair and three series of photo detector to collect the reflected light back. Three series of LED have been placed in order to increase the intensity of the light for transmission and to produce circular emission pattern as in Figure 20.5. In order to obtain the PPG signal through clothing, we are showing that the cloth behaves as an additional tissue layer and it observes a few amounts of light. Therefore, when a PPG sensor is placed at their back of chair, we need to consider that there are three tissues present at the front of LED light. The first tissue is considered as the material off the chair and the second issue is considered as the cloth that is wearied by a human and the third tissue is considered as be normal human body tissue. The variation in intensity of light should be done. The intensity variations of the LED can be provided by the different output voltages produced by digital to analogue converter.

20.3.4 HR monitoring and BP estimation

ECG PPG and BCG signals help to calculate the heart rate and blood pressure. By measuring the correlation factor and mean of the ECG and BCG signal, the cardiac cycle can be calculated. Using regression algorithms and calculating the interludes among neighboring R crests of ECG and J crests of BCG, the hundred can be estimated and compared with the derivative of PPG signals. When a patient enters into this tele medical room and sit in the smart chair, the biological signal of the patient will be estimated and displayed on the screen and also will be transmitted to the doctor through a 5G communication environment. The smart chair will be able to obtain ECG BCG and PPG signal and also estimate the temperature of the patient

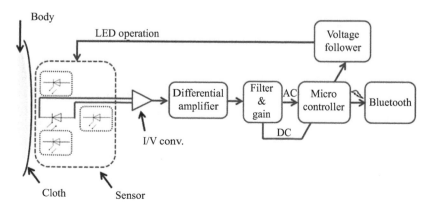

Figure 20.5   Measurement and analysis of PPG signals

and transmitted directly to the doctor and the measurement with temperature of patient can be estimated from the above signals and displayed on the screen which helps the patient to know the detail about his body condition.

20.4 Research methodologies—non-invasive blood glucose monitoring device

During the new decade, we have seen an amazing improvement concerning scaled down electronic gadgets, to work with their combination in handheld equipment's. This development shows the assessment of blood glucose level by planning a substrate-based adaptable receiving wire at 2.4 GHz mechanical, logical, and clinical radio groups. An adaptable radio wire is a huge piece of the new age of remote correspondence frameworks wherein the base material suggests restrained dielectric esteems by altering the centralization of the crude constituents. Integrated nickel molecule based adaptable nickel aluminate ($NiAl_2O_4$) adapted as a base material to ensure a powerful receiving wire for multiple high-frequency needs. Plan and execution examinations of the receiving wire were performed and the radio wire exhibitions were researched dependent. Dielectric properties of human blood over a wide recurrence range were estimated with and without adding the glucose content for various sorts of blood gatherings. The acquired outcomes show a critical variety between the dielectric properties of blood with and without glucose specialists and the distinction are bigger in conductivity than in relative permittivity. The variation with the conductivity of signals received by the antenna can predict the level of glucose content present in the blood.

20.4.1 Ultra-thin compact flexible antenna

Due to the technological advancements in electromagnetic fields, it can be widely used in medical applications to detect various diseases. In this work, we present a novel idea to detect the glucose content of blood by designing a planar inverted F antenna (PIFA) which is more commonly available in mobile devices. Our basic idea is to design PIFA antenna using computer simulation technology (CST) software and thereby fabricating the antenna with one port and identifying its reflection parameters and VSWR ratio. Different groups of blood samples (A, B, AB, and O) were collected and their dielectric parameters such as conductivity dielectric constant and dielectric loss were strong minded. Antenna is excited by a source and radiated towards the finger of the human body. The permittivity, conductivity, permeability, and absorption power by the skin tissues and bloods are identified and compared with the standard values determined by the blood samples. Results showed that the energy received from the normal blood sample and affected blood with increased glucose content gets varied and from this simulation results we can be able to conclude the amount of glucose content present in the blood.

20.4.2 CPW-PIFA antenna design

Trademark impedance is controlled by the proportion a/b, subsequently a size decrease is conceivable without restrictions, hypothetically. The subsequent CPW-PIFA is made out, taking care of strip, cross over emanating patch with a double-band activity. The component of coplanar waveguide (CPW) feed is determined by

$$Zo = \frac{30\pi 0\left(k_t'\right)}{\sqrt{\varepsilon_{\text{eff}}}K\left(k_t\right)} \tag{20.1}$$

$$K_t = \frac{a_t}{b_t}, K = \frac{a}{b} \tag{20.2}$$

where f determines the thickness of the substrate, t determines the thickness of the metal plate, ε_{eff} denotes the presence of effective permittivity in the material, $K(\cdot)$ determines the values, k' and k'_t which harmonizing components of k and k_t, and t determines relation between thickness of metal.

This antenna is premeditated on a material with the ratio of 0.42 nickel, 0.58 aluminum nitrate and with the base substrate material of flexible nickel aluminate (NiAl$_2$O$_4$). This substrate material has permittivity of 4.97, 0.007 loss tangent, and 0.5 mm as thickness as in Figure 20.6.

The recital of CPW-PIFA beneath bending conditions and the reflection coefficient is experimentally determined as in Figure 20.7.

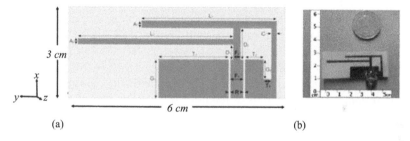

(a)   (b)

Figure 20.6   CPW-PIFA internal dimensions of the designed and structured antenna

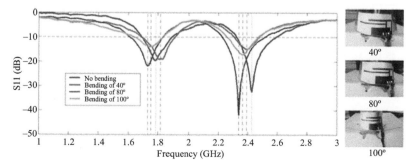

Figure 20.7   Reflection coefficient analysis of CPW-PIFA

20.4.3   Dielectric properties of fresh human blood

Blood is a profoundly utilitarian complex body liquid that fills in as the chief vehicle mechanism of the body. It conveys oxygen, supplements, nutrients, and metabolites to crucial pieces of the body and as such is an essential piece of the invulnerable framework.

The dielectric properties of blood are critical for different clinical applications, for example, microwave imaging, hyperthermia and removal. These properties uncover different powerful cycles. Besides, dependable estimation and assurance of safe cutoff points for electromagnetic energy assimilation by human body are beyond the realm of imagination without exact information on dielectric properties of blood. By covering a recurrence scope of 2.4 GHz, data on all the average scattering locales of organic matter is gotten. By and large, both the dielectric consistent and the conductivity of the glucose fluid arrangements decline as the focus increments. This is clearly not quite the same as the outcomes at high frequencies. At high frequencies, the dielectric steady reductions with expanding glucose fixation, yet the conductivity increments with expanding glucose focus.

A proto typical structure of the stratums of human body was made by reenactment of the radio wire which can furnish outcomes predictable with those that would be discovered when utilized related to genuine s of humanoid soft tissue. The prototypical structure enumerated in the diagram comprises of a film of protection layer, a 0.009 mm film of desiccated skin, a 0.29 mm thickness film of pouring skin, a 0.19 mm film thickness of muscular fat, a 0.48 mm thickness of blood, and 2 mm film thickness of muscular tissue.

A customary conductivity cell structure was carefully chosen for different dielectric readings of blood and its different elements. The identified cell structure encompasses two parallel plates, in which the leads are plugged unswervingly into the sentient terminuses of capacitance evaluating bridge. The components of the dielectric medium can be evaluated by the relationship given below:

$$\text{Dielectric constant, } \epsilon' = C_s/C_a = (C_s' - C_L)/(C_a' - C_L)$$

where,

C_s is the authentic model capacitance
C_1 is the authentic principal capacitance
C_a is the tangible airborne capacitance
C_s' is the restrained capacitance of identified cell structure through liquescent
C_a' is the restrained capacitance of identified cell structure without liquescent, at 20 kHz

$$\text{Dielectric loss, } \epsilon'' = (1.8 \times 10^{12}k)/\nu$$

where ν is the frequency; k is the electrical conductivity

$$\text{Conductivity, } k = GL/A$$

where

G is the conductance; A is the area of the plates; D is the distance between the plates of the cell.

Therefore, we accomplish that the occurrence of erythrocyte sheath causes noteworthy dissimilarities in the dielectric parameters of human blood, apart from proteins and salt solutions, the comparison values are listed in Table 20.2. When a signal from a source is transmitted at 2.4 GHz, antenna radiates and electro-magnetic signal is passed into the fingers of human.

As mentioned in the Table 20.1, the signals pass through a wet or dry skin, fat, muscle, and blood with different groups in which the dielectric properties are known. When there is a change in glucose content of the blood, the dielectric property of the blood gets varied which results in the variation in scattering para-meters, reflection parameters, and absorption power. These changes made can be calculated and the processor estimates the content of blood glucose level in a binary value. The Node MCU module connected with the processor transmits the value obtained to the cloud platform and the values can be viewed continuously in the mobile application.

20.5 Wireless stethoscope using Wi-Fi technology for remote access of patients

Stethoscopes are utilized routinely by clinical work force to pay attention. In spite of the fact that stethoscopes assume a vital part in the analysis interaction, the chest piece and the relationship can be determined to work with transmission of micro-organisms by one infected person to another and from the infected person to the punter. Succeeding the connecting link with a remote background may decrease the expected danger and further permit broadcasting of the signs to multi-clients for assessment. The computerized stethoscope was planned by changing a simple stethoscope and accumulation of a simple forward-facing end and scaled down controllers by providing Wi-Fi for converting data into digital format and communication.

A continuous heart sound sign procurement, intensification, sifting is culti-vated using sensor sub-framework. Multi-strung python script was composed to obtain, cradle, ongoing pre-measure, and group the heart sound information in the host PC. The optimized Ensemble algorithm which provides feature reduction, hyper parameter optimization, along with asymmetrical cost assignment can be used to segregate the normal and abnormal heart beat signal. The receiver unit comprises a headphone jack which can be inbuilt with a Wi-Fi modem in order to clearly hear the pulmonary, cardiac, or digestive noises being monitored.

A stethoscope is an investigative tool used by numerous health care specialists to pay attention to the reverberations of patient's heart, lungs, abdomen, etc. It is an important tool for initial non-invasive examination of the patient. Careful listening of the sounds is imperative for detecting subtle manifestations of cardiac

Table 20.1 Conductivity cell structure

Category of tissue	$\varepsilon\infty$	Change in permittivity, 1	$\tau1(ps)$	Change in permittivity	$\tau2$ (ns)	$\Delta\varepsilon3$	$\tau3$ (µs)
Pure blood with all concentrations	3.9	54	8.52	4911	126.86	0	0
Fat deposition near the blood vessels	1.96	8.86	7.924	38.65	12.89	2.9×10^4	129.34
Muscular tissues below the skin	3.85	49	7.645	6986	298.46	3.4×10^6	246.86
Upper lay of wet skin	3.65	35.49	7.865	1124	45.23	0	0
Upper lay of dry skin	3.75	39.96	7.865	198	82.18	9.0×10^4	2.21

Table 20.2   Parameter comparison of blood samples

Blood group	Parameter	Whole blood	Plasma
Group A	Dielectric constant, ε'	73.55×10^3	138.04×10^3
	Dielectric loss, ε''	222.70×10^7	322×10^7
	Conductivity, K (mho cm^{-1})	1.230	1.81
Group B	Dielectric constant, ε'	76.12×10^3	138.31×10^3
	Dielectric loss, ε''	21.6×10^7	318×10^7
	Conductivity, K (mho-cm^{-1})	1.12	1.77
Group AB	Dielectric constant, ε'	51.74×10^3	137.81×10^3
	Dielectric loss, ε''	186.6×10^7	324×10^7
	Conductivity, K (mho cm^{-1})	1.04	1.81
Group O	Dielectric constant, ε'	70.65×10^3	148.16×10^3
	Dielectric loss, ε''	216×10^7	322.2×10^7
	Conductivity, K (mho cm^{-1})	1.2	1.8

Figure 20.8   Overall system block diagram

abnormalities. The designed unit serves as a communication link between the two main components. The chest-piece embodies the microelectronic instrument which imprisonments the analog indications or reverberations from the body and communicates the information in the form of voltage signals over the communication link to the head-piece.

The proposed electronic remote stethoscope permits medical services experts to record, interaction, and offers the auscultation rapidly and effectively briefly assessment or the therapy follow-up. The entire block diagram is projected in Figure 20.8. This is the cycle by which specialists can pay attention to patients' souls and lungs from a protected distance with the utilization of outside speakers, or earbuds or earphones that fit over or under close to home defensive gear. This gadget has been designed to improve the effectiveness, both for analysis and follow-up of the patient's development. It does likewise improve the medical services staff proficiency since it takes out superfluous goes by permitting the auscultation to be sent, and hence reserve funds for the medical care framework.

The utilization instance of the remote stethoscopes is

(i)   Pediatricians: Recording, envisioning, and sharing the auscultation empower pediatricians a substantially more exact development of the patient's advancement.

(ii)   Essential medical services and home consideration units: A more exact determination will be accomplished with the canny electronic remote stethoscope since it tends to be checked rapidly with an expert specialist.

(iii)   Experts with hearing debilitations: By setting the advanced remote stethoscope volume they can have again an auscultation as per their necessities.

(iv)   Cardiologists and nervous system specialists: They empower the quantity of clinical discussions to be diminished.

(v)   Colleges: Recording and looking at a few clinical cases through a shrewd stethoscope builds the presentation by understudies and improves their arrangement.

The remote stethoscope comprises of a Wi-Fi based coordinated chest-piece component for capturing wide-ranging audio signals in order to enable transmission, a controller-based head-piece collector component for understanding the facts and a presentation gadget to appraise the disparities in heartbeat.

20.5.1   Chest-piece

The pumping and subsequent progression of blood produces heart sound. The heart sounds D1 and D2 are shrill. Typical heart sounds D1 and D2 have recurrence scopes of 45–55 Hz and 88–98 Hz, individually. D3 can be observed during the surge of blood section to the ventricle from chamber and is ordinarily a pre-diastolic low-pitched sound and has a transmission capacity of 20–30 Hz. D4 occurs toward finish of diastole and has a recurrence range under 20 Hz. Notwithstanding being discernible, S1 and S2 have their sufficiency shift and now and then become powerless and couldnot be heard because of irregularities.

Radio frequency controller utilizes Arduino IDE as UI package that enhances the testing. Radio frequency controller has 10-cycle in ADC module, which is equipped for procuring acoustic sign near 500 Hz with 3.08 mV. In the framework, radio frequency controller connected to sensor module started the solicitation to transfer information. This controller in the PC-side was functioning as host was answerable for getting the information parcel. To guarantee solid information to host without losing any information bundle. Also, to build a inspecting recurrence of the radio frequency controller to 1800 Hz in information obtaining, heart sound information were cushioned in the radio frequency controller before transmission and after each 15 ms supported casing, 35 PCG tests were shipped off have.

20.5.2   Analysis—display unit

For the continuous execution, 10 s were used to transfer heart sound and afterward pattern float to be adjusted, that are sectioned to pulsate. There are a few pre-preparing ladders that are functional to the AI calculation. Division of the signs into heart cycles or stamping beginning occasions is vital for creating the age of revenue in preparing and the AI calculation are done at the receiver side as in Figure 20.10.

20.5.3   Ear piece

The receiver unit is capable of receiving a wireless signal from one or more wire-less sensors. The receiver unit comprises a headphone jack which can be inbuilt with a Wi-Fi modem, so that the practitioner can more clearly hear the pulmonary, cardiac, or digestive noises being monitored. The strategy is illustrated in Figure 20.9. The signal processor which is a microcontroller (MSP430) performs filtering operation on the received wireless signal. Three operational modes were developed to conform to the stethoscope applications: bell mode (20–190 Hz), diaphragm mode (40–600 Hz), and protracted mode (30–2000 Hz). These frequency bands define the characteristic frequency spectra that apply to the various applications. For example, heart sounds are usually of low frequency and therefore,

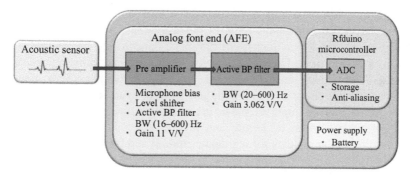

Figure 20.9   Block representation of processing the captured acoustic signal

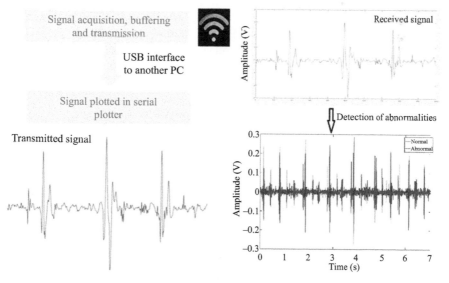

Figure 20.10   Extraction of signals at the receiver end

fall within the Bell mode band. To facilitate the selection process, three buttons to change the operational modes and three LEDs were provided, one for each mode to provide feedback to the user.

The order model choice is shown in Figure 20.11 with process outline for pre-handling AI calculation. The HS information from the dataset was sectioned to preparing and testing datasets. Signal pre-handling and programmed division were refined utilizing the sign preparing tool compartment, and preparing and order of HS were achieved by the insights and AI tool compartment. The pre-handling steps of the HS are summed up in the investigation segment. A few time (*t*)- space, recurrence (*f*)- area, what's more, Mel recurrence cepstral coefficients highlights were removed from the portioned HS information. The preparation dataset went through pre-handling ventures before it was taken care of into the AI calculations for preparing. The subtleties of the pre-preparing steps and recognition calculation will be examined in the examination segment.

The web of clinical things requires quick availability, the board, and high information abilities which 5G system can make conceivable like imaging, deter-mination, and treatment. The gadgets which incorporate wearable's gadgets, sen-sors, and those that transmit clinical information which gives treatment, determination administrations, and high-goals video, every one of these adminis-trations would be given improved the nature of administration at sensible rates. The patient information must be secure and private and this information ought to approach different specialists for legitimate finding and treatment and it will like-wise help in dynamic. The data will be shared electronically to improve pro-ductivity of cost all through the clinical consideration.

There are a few applications where clinical needs high information unwavering quality and accessibility of association with low inertness implies down for hardly any milliseconds. The 5G will make these things workable for the client to improve the clinical human services. In Figure 20.12, it is outlined how future system 5G will functions. The patient should take a gander at their advanced cell to check the wellbeing results. As an individual, late release from the emergency clinic is con-nected to cloud by which specialists can get to them for additional drugs.

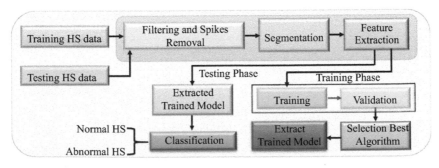

Figure 20.11   Machine learning-based abnormality detection algorithms at the receiver end

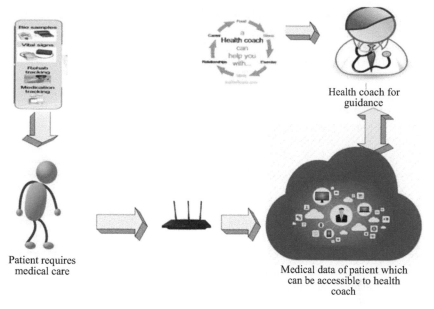

Figure 20.12   IoMT system for healthcare

The spine for IoMT is 5G which interfaces diverse versatile and clinical gadgets together. Presently a-days their numerous applications that will give scope of advantages to enterprises that requires solid availability and high data transmission. These sorts of things are one of the parts of the up-and-coming 5G innovation.

20.6   IoT-enabled environmental air pollution monitoring and rerouting system using supervised learning algorithm

The main objective is to provide cost effective and reliable method of detecting the air pollution in the environment and updating in maps for the benefit of user to travel in a pollution free route. The narrow band IoT network has been deployed for collecting the data from different type of sensors which is deployed in the field to calculate the air pollution. The information obtained through the narrow band IoT network is processed and the air quality index value is estimated and transmitted through any mobile broadband network.

The air pollution in a roadside environment is increasing day by day and it causes inconvenience of the passengers during their travel with few health issues according to their body conditions. In order to avoid their travel through a polluted environment, a low-cost wireless air pollution monitoring system was developed in this work as mentioned in Table 20.3 to measure the levels of polluted gases and update the information in Google maps which can help the passengers to reroute

Table 20.3   AQI category, pollutant level and health break points

AQI category (range)	PM$_{10}$ (24 h)	PM$_{2.5}$ (24 h)	NO$_2$ (24 h)	O$_3$ (8 h)	CO (8 h)	SO$_2$ (24 h)
Good (0–50)	0–50	0–30	0–40	0–50	0–1.0	0–40
Satisfactory (51–100)	51–100	31–60	41–80	51–100	1.1–2.0	41–80
Moderately polluted (101–200)	101–250	61–90	81–180	101–168	2.1–10	81–380
Poor (201–300)	251–350	91–120	181–280	169–208	10–17	381–800
Very poor (301–400)	351–430	121–250	281–400	209–748	17–34	801–1600
Severe (401–500)	430+	250+	400+	748+	34+	1600+

their journey based on low polluted area. The work has three parts in which the first part deals with the hardware components, the second part deals with the software component that is updating in Google maps, and third part deals with the rerouting system which can able to reroute travel based on least polluted area.

To decide air quality in a zone, contamination fixations are truly estimated and detailed. The air quality index (AQI) is determined dependent on the normal centralization of a specific toxin estimated over a standard time span (24 h for most poisons and 8 h for carbon monoxide and ozone). For instance, the AQI for PM2.5 depends on 24-h normal fixation and processed.

The air is polluted by different mixture of small particles with a diameter less than 10 μm and this refers to a term called particulate matter. This is of most concern because the particles with a diameter of less than 10 μm can be inhaled by a human being and enters into the lungs which cause serious health effects. This can be measured by an optical dust sensor module which transcends the dust particles in air by the transmission of light. In this sensor, light is transmitted in air and this light gets reflected, refracted, and scattered bite the dust particles present in the air. Depending upon the measure of scattering property, reflective index, and absorption of light, the particle count can be measured and the size of particles can be estimated. Ozone is a colorless and highly irritating gas and this considered as a secondary pollutant that is formed when the pollutant emitted by car, power plant, industrial boilers, and other resources reacts chemically in the presence of sunlight. MQ131 ozone sensor detects and measures ozone (03) concentration from 10 ppb to 2 ppm which is ideal for monitoring air quality or for use in environment and research experiments.

Oxides of nitrogen are mixed in the air from the emissions of car trucks, buses, power plants, and due to the burning of fuels. Breathing and with the high concentration of nitrous oxide can cause some respiratory diseases which leads to wheezing and asthma problems. Carbon monoxide is a poisonous gas which is produced due to burning of gasoline, wood, propane, charcoal, and other fuels. Breathing carbon monoxide regularly can cause many uncomfortness in human body and death may occur if the humans are exposed to higher levels. MQ7 is low-cost sensor which can be able to measure the concentration of carbon monoxide in air. Due to the burning of coal and oil in power plants, sulfur dioxide is released in the air. This can also be emitted from trains, large ships, and some diesel equipment's that burn high sulfur fuel. When humans are exposed in such air pollution, the respiratory system may be affected and causes irritation to the eyes. 110-602 Sulfur dioxide electrochemical sensors can be used to send the amount of gas mixed with air and it provides easy integration into wireless solution.

20.6.1 NB-IoT transmission module

Most of the air pollution is man-made and derived from the poor combustion of fossil or biomass is experienced by the population living in and around urban areas. Narrowband IoT (NB-IoT) is a suitable technology that is based on 4G LTE networks and uses the same infrastructure to connect to the network. The information obtained through the different types of sensors is transmitted to the network by using the narrow band device. NB-IoT is low-power wide area networking technology that is developed to enable efficient communication by providing much wider coverage with long battery life and lower cost.

Processing of data

The data from narrow band IoT devices is transmitted via an LTE network along with orthogonal frequency division multiple access (OFDMA) and single carrier frequency division multiple access (SCFDMA) signal waveforms in downlink and uplink, respectively. The data received from NB-IoT is highly unstructured and it is very difficult to analyze the obtained data. WISE-4000 wireless sensor node supports MQTT open communication protocol in which users can transmit data to specific public cloud services or existing private cloud platforms. By pre-integration with MQTT protocol, NB-IoT nodes can integrate with cloud services automatically, reducing setup complexity for rapidly implementation. Figure 20.2 explains the process of environmental air pollution monitoring and rerouting system. The information transmitted through a NB-IoT device is transmitted to some specific public cloud service. The air quality index value should be estimated from the data obtained from particulate matter sensor, nitrous oxide sensor, carbon monoxide sensor, ozone sensor, and sulfur dioxide sensor. The air quality index value depends on the amount of gas that is mixed in the atmosphere.

In numbers, AQI is represented between 0 and 500 with 0 representing good air and 500 representing hazardous air. The AQI is calculated based on the average concentration of a particular pollutant measured over a standard time interval (24 h for most pollutants and 8 h for carbon monoxide and ozone). For example, the AQI for PM2.5 is based on 24-h average concentration and computed. The goal of an AQI is to rapidly scatter air quality data (nearly progressive) that involves the framework to represent contamination's which have momentary effects. It is similarly significant that the majority of these toxins are estimated persistently through a web-based observing system. An example of AQI calculation and description for Coimbatore (online air quality monitoring network) is presented here. The sub-index (Ip) for a given pollutant concentration (Cp), as based on "linear segmented principle," is calculated as:

$$Ip = [\{(IHI - ILO)/(BHI - BLO)\} * (Cp-BLO)] + ILO$$
BHI = break point concentration greater or equal to given conc.

BLO = break point concentration smaller or equal to given conc.
IHI = AQI value corresponding to BHI
ILO = AQI value corresponding to BLO

The AQI framework ought to have web-based AQI spread which ought to be intended for online count. The website should deliver a snappy, straightforward and an exquisite looking reaction to an AQI inquiry. The other features of the website should include reporting of pollutant responsible for index, pollutants exceeding the standards and health effects.

20.6.2   Updation in Google maps and rerouting

The estimated air quality index from each area is updated in Google maps using an API from Google map. To suggest an alternative route for the passengers, the location of the particular point and the distance of the routes were considered. For example, if a person has to travel different place which has a moderate air quality index, then the optimal distance for the moderate AQI and good AQI will be estimated and depending upon the passengers convenience, the routes can be selected with moderate AQI or good AQI. If the current route is moderate, then it will check the optimal distance based on data[i].dist< maxDistance and data[i].dist - minDistance < C, where C is the constant.

When a passenger has to plan a travel with pollution-free environment, he can also view the prediction status of air pollution level of the particular location at any time. The air quality index has been estimated by time series prediction analysis using neural network and support vector machine regression algorithms. In order to predict the AQI value, it is necessary to estimate the activation function using multilayer perceptron which was chosen as an approximate sigmoid for learning. Here the time Index was set automatically and the time interval was set on a daily basis. Support vector machine regression algorithm is used to minimize the error tolerated by individualizing the hyperplane which maximizes the margin. To perform the mapping implicitly, the kernel function maps the data into higher dimensional space kernel function.

This chapter deliberates the implementation of cloud-based IoT system for air quality monitoring in which the sensors are used to calculate CO, PM2.5 and PM10, O_3, SO_2, and NOx pollution level with environmental condition like temperature and humidity. The estimated sensor values are transmitted into the network by using NB IoT devices and this information is processed at cloud environment. The AQI value is estimated and, using these values, the pollution conditions are updated in maps. By using these updated values, a passenger can select a route without pollution. The passenger can also plan a travel in prior by predicting the AQI value using machine learning algorithm.

20.7   Results and discussion

The higher hear rate people of different age groups were considered with equal male and female ratio. This test was done with the help of electric cardio version, a method used for reset the vibrations of heart. The exclusion of few patients with other medical issues was omitted in the whole result.

Some of them possessing sinus rhythm before the electro cardio version is included in the results. Also some of the patient showed premature ventricular beats. Many of the other patient's details are added to the AF group. As a whole, we gathered details of about 60 patients. In the examination of the participants, we found the heart rate before cardio version with the corresponding AR and SR values ((AF 83± 19 & SR 66± 17) beats in a minute. In Table 20.3, the observations made with the participants were summarized.

The AF to SR conversation increased the length significantly by 300 ms. In contrast, the length of BCG increased about 220 ms. During the electro cardio version, the BCG signal increase significantly with low deviation and exhibits consistent heart rate refer the SR table. In Figures 20.13–20.15, the BCG signal

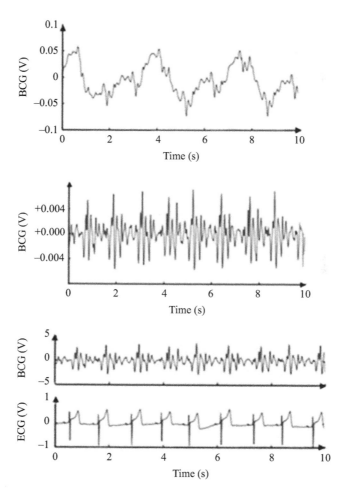

Figure 20.13   BCG raw signal and filtered version and comparison of ECG with BCG signal

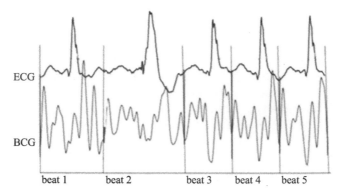

Figure 20.14   Estimation of heart rate by comparing ECG and BCG signals

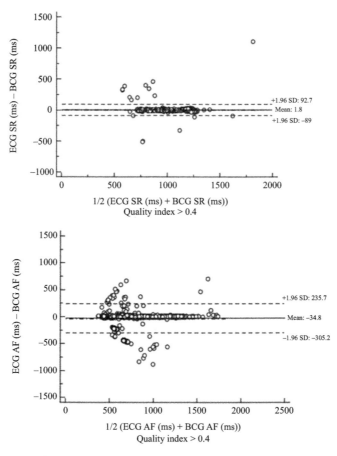

Figure 20.15   SR data filter by Q-Index >0.4

measurement was shown to indicate the highest and lowest inhalation and exhalation, followed by its filtered version of the BCG obtained by the band pass filtering and then differencing in time domain eliminates the breathing components further illustrate the repeating oscillations from the contraction is clearly verified.

By extending the integral of BCG complex amplitude beat to beat, we estimate the synchronization to ECG signal. In reference to the above, we conclude, the BCG recorded vibrations of the body due to cardiac activity benefits for the closer observations of body heart rate yields detection of abnormalities so as to reduce the morbidity as in Figure 20.14. The function of estimating the heart cycle length includes the analysis of repeated observation of specific window of amplitude patterns. In addition to this idea is to calculate the length in two consecutive heartbeats from the recorded patterns.

The black ECG signal synchronized with the blue heartbeat count gives the required ECG average cycle length. In addition to it estimated BCG cycle length and quality index are simultaneously illustrated in Figure 20.14 and Table 20.4. The second beat displayed exposes the contraction of ventricle results minor change in ECG and BCG cycle variance, as the third beat showed the effect of contraction of ventricular in advance with the high-quality index.

Table 20.4   ECG and BCG interval characteristics before and after cardioversion

	Atrial fibrillation Mean (±SD)	Sinus rhythm Mean (±SD)	*P* value
ECG interval [ms]	719 (±226)	991(± 160)	< 1%
BCG interval [ms]	764 (± 256)	964(± 170)	< 1%
Quality index [AU]	0.39 (± 0.16)	0.52(± 0.19)	< 1%
BCG amplitude [AU]	0.079(± 0.034)	0.048(± 0.03)	< 1%
Integral BCG complex [AU]	0.016(± 0.015)	0.009(± 0.004)	< 1%

Table 20.5   Filtering of the BCG during AF and SR from the Q-Index and correlation coefficient

Q-Index	Atrial fibrillation				Sinus rhythm			
	n	%	*R*	94% CI	*n*	%	*r*	94% CI
> 0.1	4217	94	0.67	0.67 to 0.72	4356	88	0.65	0.67–0.76
>0.15	4401	97	0.75	0.63 to 0.74	4323	91	0.87	0.63–0.79
>0.2	4009	92	0.73	0.67 to 0.76	4122	72	0.79	0.67–0.88
>0.25	3523	76	074	0.79 to 0.84	3444	76	093	0.79–0.88
>0.3	2343	65	0.83	0.77 to 0.78	2455	67	0.76	0.77–0.87
>0.35	2088	56	0.87	0.88 to 0.99	2771	69	0.87	0.88–0.91

20.8   Conclusion

Tele medical room in urban area which does not have any medical facility and need assistance for a doctor remotely is explained. First the proposed and medical chair in the Tele medical room in which the basic necessity of biological signals can be measured and transmitted to the respective doctor who gives medical assistance to the patient. The medical chair calculates the temperature, ECG signal, BCG signal, PPG signal from a patient and using signal processing techniques the body temperature the heart rate and the blood pressure level is estimated and displayed on to the screen present in front of the patient and also transmitter to the doctor through a 5G communication environment. This Delhi medical room also provides video conferencing architecture in which the doctor can view the patient remotely and give some medical assistance by looking into the biological signals which has been transmitted. The doctors can also prescribe some medicines regarding their treatments and can assist them to get proper treatments from the nearby hospitals depending upon their body conditions. The internet of medical things architecture plays a vital role in transmitting all the medical data of a patient remotely and the communication is maintained securely and the speed of transmission as large because of using 5G architecture for communication.

References

[1]   J. S. Adivarekar, A. D. Chordia, H. H. Baviskar, P. V. Aher and S. Gupta, "Patient Monitoring System Using GSM Technology," *International Journal of Mathematics and Computer Research*, vol. 1, no. 2, pp. 73–78, 2017, ISSN 2320-7167.

[2]   W. Wu, S. Pirbhulal, A. K. Sangaiah and S. C. Mukhopadhyay, "Optimization of Signal Quality over Comfortability of Textile Electrodes for ECG Monitoring in Fog Computing Based Medical Applications," *Future Generation Computer Systems*, vol. 86, pp. 1–19, 2018.

[3]   W. Wu, H. Zhang and S. Pirbhulal, "Assessment of Biofeedback Training for Emotion Management Through Wearable Textile Physiological Monitoring System," *IEEE Sensors Journal*, vol. 15, no. 12, pp. 7087–7095, 2015.

[4]   K. Malhi, S. C. Mukhopadhyay, J. Schnepper, M. Haefke and H. Ewald, "A Zigbee-Based Wearable Physiological Parameters Monitoring System," *IEEE Sensors Journal*, vol. 12, no. 3, pp. 423–430, 2012, doi:10.1109/JSEN.2010.2091719.

[5]   N. Reddy, A. M. Marks, S. R. S. Prabaharan and S. Muthulakshmi, "IoT Augmented Health Monitoring System," *2017 International Conference on Nextgen Electronic Technologies: Silicon to Software* (*ICNETS2*), Chennai, 2017, pp. 251–254, doi: 10.1109/ICNETS2.2017.8067942.

[6]   M. Ahmid, O. Kazar, S. Benharzallah, L. Kahloul and A. Merizig, "An Intelligent and Secure Health Monitoring System Based on Agent," *2020*

IEEE International Conference on Informatics, IoT, and Enabling Technologies (ICIoT), Doha, Qatar, 2020, pp. 291–296, doi: 10.1109/ICIoT48696.2020.9089602.

[7] C. Chokphukhiao, R. Patramanon, K. Maitree and S. Kasemvilas, "Health Monitoring Platform for Emergency Medicine: User Perspective and Implementation," *2020 Joint International Conference on Digital Arts, Media and Technology with ECTI Northern Section Conference on Electrical, Electronics, Computer and Telecommunications Engineering (ECTI DAMT & NCON)*, Pattaya, Thailand, 2020, pp. 133–136, doi: 10.1109/ECTIDAMTNCON48261.2020.9090731.

[8] K. Vijayakumar and V. Bhuvaneswari, "A Ubiquitous first look of IoT Framework for Healthcare Applications," *2020 International Conference on Emerging Trends in Information Technology and Engineering (ic-ETITE)*, Vellore, India, 2020, pp. 1–7, doi: 10.1109/ic-ETITE47903.2020.146.

[9] J. G. Ramani, M. S, N. A L, P. A and M. S, "IOT Based Employee Health Monitoring System," *2020 6th International Conference on Advanced Computing and Communication Systems (ICACCS)*, Coimbatore, India, 2020, pp. 298–301, doi: 10.1109/ICACCS48705.2020.9074168.

[10] M. L. Moses and B. Kaarthick, "Multiobjective Cooperative Swarm Intelligence Algorithm for Uplink Resource Allocation in LTE-A Networks," *Transactions on Emerging Telecommunications Technologies*, vol. 30, p. e3748, 2019. https://doi.org/10.1002/ett.3748

Chapter 21

Blockchain-enabled Internet of Things (IoT) platforms for financial services

Sapna Jain[1], M. Afshar Alam[1], Neveine Makram Labib[2] and Eiad Yafi[3]

Abstract

Blockchain technology is considered a breakthrough since the advent of Internet. This technology can be used financially for the Internet of Things (IoT)-based commerce platform building and marketing platform is a new business model based on the management of private transactions on IoT devices technologies that can manage a shared network using current blockchain solutions, most of which are digital currencies. The emerging popularity of digital currency makes them acceptable as one of the payment sources. The use of IoT-based blockchain technology such as social procurement, e-commerce blockchain applications and use cases describes various aspects of finance, including payments, security, supply chains, automation of work with smart contracts, and ethical practices for financial transaction transparency. With the rapid development of cryptography and the proliferation of computers systems, blockchain technology is widely expected to transform many industries with better clarity, higher security, and lower purchase costs. This chapter shall provide IoT-based blockchain technology use in ecommerce applications such as social shopping. The chapter shall provide the number of impacts of learning bodies, platform operators, and developers of blockchain technology in the finance field. The chapter discusses the use of IoT and blockchain technology in the finance industry. Blockchain applications and use cases are discussed for various aspects of finance like payment, security, supply chain, work automation with smart contract, ethical practices for transparency in financial transactions.

Keywords: Blockchain; Digital currency; Internet of Things; Platform; Artificial Intelligence

[1]Department of Computer Science, Jamia Hamdard University, New Delhi, India
[2]Department of Computer and Information Systems, Sadat Academy for Management Sciences, Egypt
[3]Malaysian Institute of Information Technology, University Kuala Lumpur, Malaysia

21.1   Blockchain era

Blockchain era is an economic era (FinTech) that changed into the first advanced as allotted ledgers for Bitcoin. The blockchain era has been overshadowed through the Bitcoin phenomenon for a few times, however, in current years, it has commenced drawing interest on its personal and is turning into a center era withinside the FinTech family [1,2]. Many professionals and educational researchers have found out that the effect of blockchain extends past Bitcoin or even past the economic enterprise to pressure alternate in lots of company areas [3]. Blockchain is quite possibly the most extraordinary promising overwhelming advancement inside the absolute FinTech space that connects past bitcoin. A blockchain is fixed squares of records, with each square made to document the exchange. Each square incorporates cryptographic hashes, timestamps, and exchange data of the past square [2] with huge capacities inside the field of money. Value techniques and expense structures are dynamic because of new turns of events. Computerized cash utilizes a redistributed network which uses cryptography. The public and private key establishment is used in which general society and private key pair now do not guard the trading of data [4]. An extra utility for the blockchain period is a free, free, and self-actuating framework to advance decentralized independence manager [5–8]. For encouraging elective arrangements, the information and work should not be prepared through the basic power needed by the methods for the elective framework. As an outcome, the switch is irreversible and charges are decreased.

21.2   Blockchain in finance

Established in 2008, blockchain technology represents the potential changes that can be made in various business environments. But in the early stages, this technology has confused industry and various sectors. Stability, as well as transparency, is the banking and financial industries. At present, there are some obstacles, but it can be said that the blockchain is very effective. To maintain the widespread impact of technology, companies are constantly exploring ways to use blockchain in many areas and a large number of dollars are moved to start with one district of the world then onto the next consistently, particularly with regard to the banking and monetary areas. The Global Fintech Report 2017 predicts that 77% of fintech institutions will receive a blockchain as a feature of a creation plan or cycle by 2020 [9].

21.2.1   *Banks and insurance agencies augment the capability of smart agreements*

The savvy contracts are intended to consequently empower exchanges and permit gatherings to concur with the result of an occasion without the requirement of a focal position. The principal highlights of brilliant agreements are requesting, multi-site confirmation, and Oracle establishment: shrewd agreements work consequently based on programming. World of information may have to handle exchanges, and Oracle services encourage you to enter astute agreements in a secured way [10]. Banks and insurance agencies can implement smart contract in their services. For a model, one of the activities we have is Talking-Process, that had worked with an insurance agency with regard to network safety protection. By progressively computing your items and administrations, you can rapidly play out the underlying testing itself and the fast testing, testing, and emphasis measure. As well as can be expected to be accomplished through different savvy contract activities, as shown in Figure 21.1. The countries like London, Berlin, and Silicon use establishments which are protected with the financial gathering R3 to keep looking for more data on conveyed record technology.

21.2.2   Computerized monetary standards

In this monetary world in the advancing terms of electronic installment techniques, national banks do not print advanced monetary standards, and advanced monetary standards are currently viewed as rules of the game as shown in Figure 21.1, that does not cause the monetary emergency. The considered banks can use and print more cash to cover state obligations which can be used in their monetary standards and bitcoin does not work that way. Advanced monetary standards or digital forms of money utilizing cryptography for security purposes, which made it extremely hard for digital forms of money to be falsified, were incomprehensible a couple of years prior. Their fundamental job is to help online web-based business and

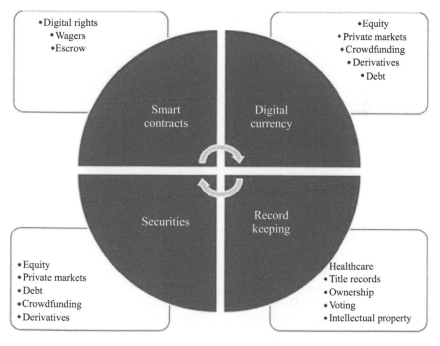

Figure 21.1   Application areas of finance

encourage exchanges, and the second purpose behind the development of electronic cash is the data transformation, described by a decrease in lessening geographic contrasts through the combination of correspondence advancements and electronic data preparing. Data can be moved far and wide. The data upheaval is changing the monetary area, making installments more secure and more effective, and giving extra motivation to the development of new money advancements. Theoretical cutting edge empowers the advancement of installments and worldwide rivalry. The vagueness encompassing advanced monetary standards is yet adequate.

The organization gives an open acknowledgment with the rules and assumptions which help in the expansion of the organization which is possible only because of basic new exchange of responsibility for hidden innovation of these digital currencies over the long haul. It should be deliberately considered as a technique. This section gives an examination of digital currency utilization. All in all, the target mentality of utilizing Bitcoin, particularly as a reception of innovation with network externalities, is that the fate of advanced monetary standards today is an open inquiry. Furthermore, this part examines monetary protection. The utilization of advanced monetary standards and individual decisions and political principles uncover that the development of e-cash achievement could prompt the eventual fate of digital currencies if some institutional and formal conditions are met. Cash requires building secure installments through three models: normalization, similarity, and advancement. Web exchanging has expanded its utilization with the spread of innovations, the interest for new electronic installment techniques is expanding. Indeed, the new electronic installment is in the deal and utilization of the Internet is another monetary market. Unquestionably, the reason for such an apparatus is to improve the exhibition of the customary installment framework. It brings up numerous issues about the utilization of advantages and dangers of insufficient investigation of unhindered acknowledgment, trust, and assumptions, which is a significant factor in organization circulation. Therefore, the target is that the fate of the current computerized account stays uncertain because of the presence of "basic weight." There are numerous before you begin utilizing it successfully.

21.2.3   Identifying security holders inside blockchain

Under government security law, the go-between responsible for different protections should advance a delegate's assertion to the recipient under the security law [11,12]. Luckily, the blockchain does not need to be mysterious nor does it need to be an alias. It empowers the total straightforwardness of blockchain members, at any rate for guarantors, moves specialists, and agent sellers. If it is a genuine issue for the bitcoin blockchain backer, the blockchain that enrolls the security possesses the blockchain security guarantor, moves specialist, and other such blockchain protections. Cornerstone [13] can be utilized for overloaded blockchain protections whose exchanges depend on dealers, and every client is wishing to exchange blockchain protections. At keystone, you need to open a record, just as in a roundabout way procure or mastermind. ATS is equivalent to accusing an online security client of realizing that the client has failed. R Requirements apply while tolerating clients for the business, reasonableness, and security.

21.2.4   Blockchain use for file retaining

Identity facts, including delivery certificates, passports, driving force's licenses, and marriage certificates, are a few of the most popular facts dispatched via a regular Canadian for the duration of his lifetime. As another occurrence, the Bit country control 2.0 stage is fuelled by the blockchain time whose objective is to offer a distributed independent administration gadget by utilizing.

International relations have applied a screening answer that comprises of blockchain and this property, specifically land and scholarly bequest, has arisen as an essential concentration for blockchain time advancement. Bination mining association Bitcoin works with the countrywide organization of Public Registry Georgia's Justice office (Battery), Georgia's working environment of Justice, to build a worldwide title deeds framework utilizing the blockchain [14]. Human beings and groups use blockchain to provide dependable registration and certification offerings for highbrow assets. Ubiquity registration of intellectual belongings in blockchain and technology is used in an equal way as copyrighted. Blockchain presence and testaments may be essentially two models among numerous that utilize this blockchain membership programming [15], quite possibly the most extraordinary cases of the usage methods of British craftsman, artist associations Heap who makes music on his new blockchain assortment, and license costs getting ready portions [16]. Virtual imprints empower the checking of records, through online arrangements. Virtual imprints using similar PKI rely on government verifications, as an untrusted third-birthday celebration party, public key confirms that public key is utilized in automated imprints.

21.3   Blockchain in commercial banking

Blockchain technology allows investment in banks to create encrypted decentralized ledgers among the numerous stakeholders concerned in an investment bank to validate transactions. Transactions are made from very popular information, constantly developing facts and transactions which are greener than, tightening regulatory controls and brokers. It can be applied to customer Know Your Customers (KYC), data sharing anti-money laundering (AML), collateral control, transaction and transaction agreement exchange cloud settlement. Blockchain innovation empowers banks to decrease foundation costs as an organization. Of PC, frameworks keep up exchanges on web stages without the endorsement of focal specialists. It additionally enables reducing running fees totally based on back workplace tactics which include securities clearing, transaction support, compliance, and settlement. This lets in to dispose of the adjustment. E-transactions are decentralized and correctly tampered with proof. The database can lessen banking costs via integrated database control with investment banks because it invests a massive sum of money in preserving the database. The database presents statistics about customers and monetary transactions. Created for storage, validation, and conversion, blockchain era afford a centralized platform for databases, allowing access to information between counterparties in conjunction with a fairly covered get right of entry to gadget [18,19] because of anti-money laundering regulations.

It also helps in verifying the authenticity of client identities which is frequent and important mission for banks [19,20]. Given the ever-growing terrorist difficulty, KYC is a critical aspect in terms of stopping crook use, banking money, and offerings within the shape of cash laundering and terrorism [21]. But, KYC charges a sizable quantity of banks at Thomson Reuters [22] which estimates that economic institutions spend 60–500 million bucks a year to capture up, indicating consequently that the contemporary KYC procedure is not always the most effective highly priced, however, additionally inefficient and offers a bad purchaser enjoy for banks [23]. The Directive calls for ordinary tracking and updating of patron information [24] while the general records protection law (GDPR) calls for strict inner controls relating to customer protection [23]. As is, blockchain generation, if applied efficaciously, KYC can be extraordinarily useful, that is due to the fact, the usage of blockchain generation can get rid of the want for finishing countless KYC polls when opening a bank account [25]. An illustration of a blockchain-based absolutely KYC banking framework is delineated through parent [26] blockchain that can permit banks to share buyer insights across their association safely and consequently streamlines the administration cycle by utilizing lessening duplication of records and demands (refer Figure 21.2). The modern-day FB facts scandal raised the case for information privateness, and the blockchain can help this way as it can be only percentage or percentage information [27]. Business endeavor class record "Corda" allows banks to limit who sees realities and specifically share information with pertinent events as an approach to lessen misrepresentation peril, in any event, for tech goliaths like Microsoft. The money-related instrument will for the most part play a persuasive capacity in the appropriation of the innovation and what is not the same as the blockchain period. The financial organization will

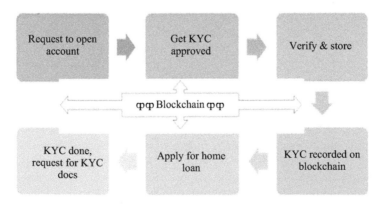

Figure 21.2   KYC transaction

consider an advantage appraisal to choose the ability of blockchain execution. It covers all immediate and angled costs and endeavors in light of the question of providing security using exchange fantastic judgment depicted in code shape [28].

21.3.1 Blockchain strengthens threat control

A couple of various areas that have made parkways to battle against money laundering (aml) is the utilization of blockchain age to better objective dubious exchanges through following customer exchanges and ongoing exchanges [29]. The aml alludes to sports pointed inside the course of halting medication-related violations, wrongdoing, illegal intimidation, dealing seasons of debasement, defilement and pay off, and hostile to money laundering wrongdoing. If the mistaken withdrawal takes the region, it is going to drastically pork up the security of the worldwide financial tool. Offering effective and inexperienced offerings to clients can be expensive. The motive also states that clients need to take extra time to gadget files and facts. He says, "there isn't always one or blockchain skills that provide this era and trap the attention of people". Of its clients and assume the ability risks of legitimate organization participants of the family competencies [30]. Third, the Financial Accounting and Controlling (FICO) assessment data and conventional normal execution records of all people are put away in an acclaimed blockchain record and imparted to every hub. On the off chance that the KFC technique is approved, all new purchaser realities might be get faster, save time, and embellish productivity. Blockchain period can safeguard difficult work costs and innovation for aml and KYC costs.

21.4 Blockchain platforms

The blockchain platform allows you to create packages that put into effect the blockchain idea. Each person or each company has no sources or time to extend their private blockchain from scratch. The blockchain stage is arising like Samsung phones, with new structures with new highlights and the equivalent idea at the backend dispatched every month. Data of those assorted structures can be extremely basic even on the off chance that you are not included as of now. Eventually, your business undertaking will require you, may in no way, buy wireless without checking its particulars and contrasting it with other moving cell phones inside the market [31].

21.4.1 Existing blockchain platforms

21.4.1.1 Bitcoin

Bitcoin is digital money that works on a distributed (blockchain) network. Dislike banking strategies and popular charge procedures, bitcoin depends absolutely on shared accept power; there is no tenable head authority inside the bitcoin contraption as it is based on the cooperation of assorted supporters inside the environmental factors. It is using various perspectives on the bitcoin gadget with its running guidelines in the sidebar on-site in specialized and non-specialized way.

The individual with pockets using the wallet keeps up the customer's key pair. The excavators rivaling each other to highlight new squares to the shared record as a relied upon supply for all transactions. Spots in which clients should purchase BTC in substitute for different monetary forms. A large portion of these principles have been perceived sooner than bitcoin, however, the mixes a blockchain changed into new and made advances with exciting houses. A large portion of those ideas likewise is utilized by other blockchain structures and decentralized record time. Inquisitively, it is not, at this point simply a specialized thought. Not, at this point just does it make the public blockchain artworks, anyway, it moreover presents financial and social impetuses. For instance, the organization individuals who contributed the most (computational) power for the most compensations from the bitcoin framework, and venture may achieve the best punishment for concurring with inside the organization.

Popular functions of bitcoin are the following:

- Community and digital foreign exchange: bitcoin and virtual information bitcoin are a medium-sized community and digital forex that makes use of a peer-to-peer gadget to verify and execute the transaction way. Managing online transactions often requires a third birthday celebration as a relied on the hyperlink to confirm the transaction, brit, and c as an instance, while Alice desires to send $10 to bob, she can use a third-birthday celebration service which incorporates a credit card community or PayPal. Alice has a switch and the recipient, bob, has successfully secured price variety. This is feasible due to the truth that those mediators assist to keep a file, or ledger, of stability of their account holders. Here, while Alice sends bob $10, a hyperlink like PayPal will withdraw the amount from his account, and 4050 will deposit it into bob's account, with the charge of the transaction rate. So, bitcoin is itself virtual foreign cash, which means that exists "digitally" and meets the financial definition of coins for max intents and purposes. In other phrases, it is far a medium of exchange, a unit of account, and a way of storing fee. Uppercase "bitcoin" stands for community and technology, and lowercase "bitcoin" stands for foreign cash unit, a few exchanges use "bt," but the foreign money is normally abbreviated to "BTC," Forex code compatible with ISO 4217 [33].
- Starting spot and decentralized deal with the main bitcoin was mined or made in 2009 after the web guide of a paper through Satoshi Nakamoto, in which the evidence of thought has got depicted for money that utilizes encryption instead of depending on the valuable position (Nakamoto, 2008). Left the endeavor in 2010 and his personality is obscure. Due to the Nakamoto idea of the bitcoin programming program convention, explicit developers have suffered to artistic creations on it nowadays, and the bitcoin network is flourishing nowadays. Open-source stays anonymous, clients do not have to expect that he or somebody is furtively in complete control of bitcoin. Nakamoto's temperament of bitcoin way that they convey code is genuinely revealed. This exposure lets any of them to take a gander at the log and make their non-public forms of the product program for endeavoring out or moreover improvement, and no pink

banner has been lifted for the presence of Nakamoto or each other birthday festivity with secret oversee. Likewise, bitcoin is intended to work on art top-notch with the entire agreement of all organization clients. Open convey guarantees that product engineers who manage the bitcoin convey code of their variants of the product program extends a detestable trade inside the bitcoin convention without bargaining similarity with the unwinding of the network. This possibility to exchange the bitcoin convention calls for complete assent among bitcoin clients and builders [39].

- The opportunity of value bitcoin is intended for moment exchanges at a low charge (Nakamoto, 2008). Installments can be prepared for a small charge or not, at this point charged in any regard, with the sender having the occasion to enter the exchange for moment assertion. The buyer has whole control of their bitcoins and the freedom to send and get hold of bitcoins on each event, all over the place, and to one and all. The diminished cost of settlements can be immense on the off chance that they are given the utilization of bitcoins. It plots one of the other advanced accuse systems that are not abnormal of the guide of companies. Tolerating FICO assessment playing a card game is rich for vendors, clients as often as possible compensation for a specialist co-op account and several costs for exchanges, alongside yet now not controlled to exchange expenses, trade charges which epitomize the expense of tolerating FICO rating card installments. The financial specialists who postpone FICO assessment cards and charge cards can likewise lose business undertaking to customers who have been utilized to take care of FICO rating scorecard. Card installments, that can utilize unprotected attractive strips and marks, dislike FICO rating card charges, which may be feasible for deceitful discounts. Low exchange costs moreover grant financial specialists to acknowledge the installments making ready for bitcoin to be notable at a lower exchange charge.
- Internal trade and volatility as a network-led undertaking, bitcoin keeps exchanging as software program developers decorate and alter their software primarily based on the consensus of community clients. At some time, bitcoin costs are currently at events keep ranging as they have an impact on costs. A few big rate modifications are stated to resemble traditional speculative bubbles that could arise when optimistic media insurance attracts buyers

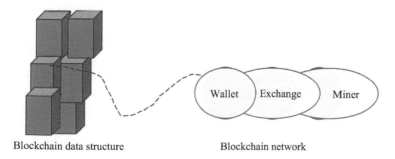

Blockchain data structure   Blockchain network

Figure 21.3   Bitcoin structure

(Salmon, 2013). You could moreover be acquainted with bitcoin, so the value of bitcoin can be a whole lot less volatile. Cash will increase over the years.

Figure 21.3 shows the Bitcoin structure in brief.

21.4.1.2 Ethereum

The most extreme basic commitment is fulfillment, which implies that Ethereum permits a wide range of calculations, which incorporate circles. The domain of exchanges, notwithstanding various upgrades to the blockchain shape. Ethereum speaks to a blockchain with a fused Turing-complete programming language. It bears the cost of a rundown layer that allows everybody to make their special approaches on belonging, exchange codecs, and the realm change abilities. That is done through shrewd agreements, a set generation of cryptographic arrangements that can be most obviously done if certain circumstances are met [34]. It is difficult to decide whether the circumstances made certain to be met specifically depends entirely on the changed phantom convention (most getting a handle on critiqued subtree) [35]. It is transformed and made to cure the issues of antique squares inside the network. Antique squares can tolerate the rise on the off chance that one mining business venture blended in a mining pool has higher computational strength than different squares, which means blocks from the principal pool will make a commitment further to the organization, for thought processes there is a developing difficulty of consideration. The apparition convention comprises of old squares for ascertaining the longest chain. Concentrated unpredictability is disposed of utilizing passing square prizes to blocks, wherein the vintage block gets 87.5% of the acclaim and the grandson of that old square gets the absolute last 12%. Around 5% of the recognition. This way, diggers are as yet remunerated even though their square turns out not to be important for the essential blockchain (blocks are known as notes). Ethereum utilizes a change of the apparition convention which consolidates notes of all things considered in the seven ages.

Cash Ethereum owed the Ethereum country, which comprises obligation money, wherein each record has a 20-byte exchange and state change. The domain of the area is planning among addresses and record country. Ethereum helps in the following obligation types: remotely claimed (oversaw through non-public keys) and arranged value range understanding (oversaw using their settlement code) [36]. An Ethereum account is made of 4 fields: nonce, ether steadiness, understanding hash, and capacity root [35,37]. Nonce speaks to the assortment of exchanges that are dispatched from an extraordinary arrangement with or the scope of arrangement creatives made by methods for an account and is utilized as a confirmation that each best exchange might be handled once. Another soundness is the scope of web possessed for the term of this adapt to Wei speaks to the smallest part of the ether. Ether is utilized for the charge of exchange expenses. The Keccak-256 hash code of the record's Ethereum computerized machine (EVM) hash code is refined if an arrangement with it gets a name. The capacity root is Merkle's 256-cycle hash hub Patricia's tree that speaks to the substance material of the record [17]. Markle Patricia tree (endeavor) is utilized to keep all requirements (key, cost) in the

Ethereum air. The square header contains three stubs from three takes: a stab at speaking to notoriety, exchange, and receipt [38] exchange. Ethereum and message exchange is a specific marked direction. There are two types of exchanges depending on their items (exchanges that achieve text calls and individuals that bring about new record presentation).

Dispatched from a remotely possessed record, each exchange comprises of the beneficiary of the mail, the mark recognizing the sender, the amount of ether to be dispatched, the discretionary field, and the qualities start fuel and impulse [39,40]. The field is vital in battles. Digital aggressors are similar to "a central unit." Of calculation, the exchange requires a positive measure of calculations, and the area shows the greatest wide assortment of PC exchanges that are as considered enormous exchanges and is depicted inside the beginning gas subject [36]. As excavators are considerably compensated while contemplating gas-40ice then again, the sender needs to choose with the guide of dealing with the cost of caprice if they need their exchange to. It takes away this sum from the senders account equilibrium and builds its nonce. If that is exact, the cost is charged per byte in the exchange, and the asked sum of ether is moved to the beneficiary. The account is made on the off chance that it does not as of now exist, and if it is far an arrangement, an understanding code is made. Releases are much the same as exchanges, anyway are produced by methods for a settlement. Similarly, as with exchanges, the message proposes the beneficiary's record strolling its code. The square amount, issue, nonce, thus on. However, likewise posting of exchanges and most current status. For each exchange inside the posting of exchange, a fresh out of the plastic new state is made via applying the previous state.

21.4.1.3 Hyperledger fabric

Hyperledger material is an open-supply venture grade apportioned record (DLT) innovation stage, intended for use in manager settings, that presents some key differential abilities over other popular conveyance or blockchain frameworks. One key separation factor is that Hyperledger was established under the Linux establishment, which has an all-encompassing and a triumph tune record of encouraging open-source projects under open administration that creates durable web facilitating networks and flourishing environments. Hyperledger is administered by utilizing various specialized controlling councils, and the Hyperledger material endeavors by methods for various arrangements of hosts from various groups. It has an advanced network that has developed to more than 35 organizations and almost 200 designers because of the way that its soonest responsibilities. Texture has been phenomenally measured and the design is configurable, empowering development, performing various tasks, and improvement for a gigantic assortment of industry use occasions that are incorporated in banking, account, inclusion, medical services, HR, conveying chain, and even advanced track transport. The texture is the essential allocated record stage to help smart agreements written when all is said in one reason programming dialects like Java, cross, and Node.js, in inclination to banishing space exact dialects (DSL). This implies that most organizations as of now have the range of abilities needed to create astute agreements, and no extra tutoring is needed to gain proficiency with another dialect or DSL. The material stage is moreover permitted, which implies that, in contrast to an unapproved public organization, people are known to one another, rather than anonymous and in this manner inconsistent. This implies that simultaneously as members may not be believed (they can, for instance, be rivals in the indistinguishable venture), a network can be worked under an administration model dependent on the trust that exists between members, along with a legitimate understanding or a system for taking care of debates. One of the greatest basic differentiators of the stage is its guide for pluggable agreement conventions that allow in the stage to be all the more effectively modified for exact use cases and accept models (e.g. conveyed inside a solitary organization or worked with the guide of relied upon foundations all things considered). Notwithstanding, full byzantine shortcoming open-minded (BFT) agreement conventions might be reasonable in such conditions, while complete byzantine adaptation to internal failure (bft) agreement conventions might be fitting in these conditions, which is not reasonable and can be viewed as an unreasonable imperative on generally speaking execution and throughput. The texture can use an agreement convention that does not need nearby digital money to support costly mining or to encourage savvy arrangement execution. Avoiding digital forms of money considerably lessens your opportunity/attack. The deficiency of vector and crypto mining tasks may be that it is sent as operational worth practically or as the same to various dispensed frameworks. The total of these separated design capacities makes material one of the higher acting structures that we have today with regard to exchange preparing and exchange certification dormancy and might be utilized for exchanges and smart agreements (texture calls it "chain code"). Hyperledger texture is uniquely intended to have a secluded engineering. In pluggable agreement, pluggable distinguishing proof control conventions including LDAP or OpenID join, key administration conventions or cryptographic libraries, the stage is planned at the center to be arranged to satisfy the necessities of an assortment of organization use cases [38]. At a more significant level, texture is that that it comprises of particular added substances. The pluggable requesting supplier builds up an agreement at the request of exchanges and afterward articulates a square. A pluggable membership transporter supplier is responsible for partner substances at the network with cryptographic personalities. The non-required P2P tattle supplier engenders the square yield employing requesting contributions to different companions. Shrewd agreements ("chain code") run inside a field climate (e.g. Docker) for disengagement. They might be written in vogue programming dialects, anyway presently do not have direct get passage to record nation. Records might be designed to help a choice of database management system (DBMS). There might be a reasonable settlement from the business that there is no "block-chain." Hyperledger material can be designed in a determination of approaches to satisfy exceptional answer necessities for unique business use instances [38].

21.4.2   Future blockchain platforms

The blockchain stage permits you to make programs that have an impact on the blockchain thought. One and all or each organization has no sources or time to grow its own blockchain without any preparation. In this manner, these offices will take advantage of the blockchain stage created through tech goliaths quicker. The blockchain stage is arising like Samsung cell phones, a spic and span stage with new abilities, and a similar idea is delivered month to month at the backend. Data of those various frameworks could be significant regardless of whether you are not stressed in them.

1. Algorand: It is a public open-source blockchain dependent on a genuine guaranteed agreement methodology that underpins the energy and by and large execution of an exchange. Job principally based resource control in stupendous permits us to apply this blockchain stage for parcels purposes, for example, resource switch.

2. BigChainDB: It is anything but a blockchain stage anyway as a substitute to a blockchain advertiser that permits us to apply blockchains with an information-tion base that comprises of coordinated resource help and rich inquiries and progressed input, helping various enterprises and utilization occasions.

3. Credits: It is an open-supply, totally dispensed blockchain programming pro-gram convention. It is most appropriate to be utilized conditions along with microtransaction, mass bills, and extraction for tokens.

4. Chain Core: This application allows you to control monetary resources with an allowed blockchain gadget. For programs specifically in the monetary endeavor, chain focus can control any amount of impartial blockchains through safeguarding their books or can go about as a blockchain shopper for various authorized blockchains.

5. Coco: It is an improved dispersion by utilizing conferring 1000 exchange control very much coordinated with the unwinding of the blockchain stage along with Hyperledger sawtooth, Ethereum, Corda, and majority. Intended for public and individual use occurrences, and also provides trusted execution environments.

6. EOS: It gives a decentralized organization that licenses fair blockchains with particular administration to change with each extraordinary without inter-cession. Unmistakably positioned, it licenses move-US installments through blockchain unprejudiced of fiats.

7. Iota: It is an IoT blockchain that has been given another definition in this particular blockchain platform. Iota grants exchanges among machines and IoT gadgets. It is called miota to depict exchanges inside the community. Iota's knot is a gadget of hubs used to check exchanges and is the zenith of particle.

8. Lisk: It makes a forte of the spotless improvement of blockchain applications and, in this way, the Lisk software development kit (SDK) accompanies engineer hardware, a functioning network, and a strength-proficient block-chain network.

9. Multichain: This multichain blockchain helps groups for undertaking of developing and conveying blockchain applications at a quick fee. It is broadly utilized which incorporate assignments along with sap for drug, prebudget, tag cash KYC, and its blockchain.

10. Nem: It is a legitimate individual blockchain that can give industry apex exchange rates to inward records and its progressive agreement component and super node application ensure that once Nem's open, open blockchain can develop continuously influencing throughput or strength.

11. Openchain: It is an open chain that records time and the open-source decentralization is reasonable for associations that need to distribute and oversee advanced resources in a strong, secure, and adaptable way. It offers a solitary advantage for exchange validation. Each organization has handiest one illustration of a record that conveys exchanges that can connect with as wished.

12. Quorum: Ethereum rules the universe of a public blockchain, and it is far appropriate to outfit offices with a believed stage utilizing Ethereum's thoughts, versatility, encryption, and specialized perspectives in an approved manner. It is an open stockpile and has exact organization help from the Ethereum network.

13. Smilo: It is developed at the possibility of a mixture of blockchain. One might say, public blockchain versatility and straightforwardness are needed without trading off the wellbeing and privateness of the whole endeavor that made the possibility of half and half blockchain. Smilo presents a blockchain stage that underpins a mix of mixture exchanges, crossbreed savvy agreements, and crossover dispensed bundles.

14. Stellar: It acquaints a route with blend fiat cash in with computerized unfamiliar cash. It is a decentralized stage that permits you to shop, boat, and substitute advanced varieties of regular monetary forms. You could make fast go-outskirt exchanges between any unfamiliar cash pair, the use of heavenly through its neighborhood resource, and an advanced forex alluded to as lumens (xlm).

15. Straitis: This network foundation that calls for more noteworthy exertion and time in this manner is the genuine advancement of the blockchain and accordingly a stage like Straitis becomes an integral factor. Basic necessity is agreement and distributed network setups, anyway it is evident that we are fulfilled that we do not have to widen them if we need to fuse blockchain into our business venture, so tender mint has developed a motor that functions as a motor for a car. You need to format the design and reason for the vehicle with the universe and tender mint will power it with its motor.

16. Tezos: It is an innovation for providing a blockchain that is equipped for its own rules with negligible disturbance to the network from a one substitute chain administration form. It utilizes a proof-of-stake-based agreement model.

17. Universa: Universa is a protocol that allows the use of reducing area technological advances along with IoT, BIM, and believe finance, which allows more transparent, straightforward, and faster transactions and, for that reason, an opportunity to attach all members within the metropolis's digitization system. Universa Mainnet is a global decentralized network that offers extraordinarily speedy and comfy blockchain and statistics storage at the organization degree.

18. Xinfin: It is a blockchain stage with its wallet that is a half and half blockchain stage that centers around real-time go-fringe exchange and money.

XDC token is the basic programming badge of Xinfin cross-breed blockchain and goes about as an arrangement component for dApps built at the Xinfin half and half blockchain.

19. Zilliqa: It is a contract settlement language scilla and being the essential public blockchain to place its impact on sharing in its test network, Zilliqa is an extreme speed blockchain stage that plays more than 2828 exchanges for each second. The versatile throughput guarantees that Zilliqa's capacity can keep on developing with the developing number of nodes [39].

21.5   Blockchain-based IoT platforms

During the latest decade, IoT has tremendously wandered and forwarded to accomplish, and a significant measure of devices is interconnected over the web, permitting them to pass on and secure experiences. In any case, there are different particular impediments to prevail upon for a victory blockchain and IoT compromise these days, more than five billion IoT devices across the field are creating huge measures of geographic and fragment real factors and changing them at the web. Data might be abused and abused if appropriate security highlights are not performed to safeguard the privacy, honesty, and legitimacy of realities further, slanted and connected devices along with reconnaissance cameras can likewise be utilized by aggressors to encourage noxious games. Utilizing the blockchain to control access insights on IoT contraptions can add a layer of insurance to your IoT network. It could beat the single purpose of disappointment bother, anyway because of the deficiency of enough registering and dispatch abilities, it is an enormous mission for IoT gadgets to quickly partake inside the blockchain network, the blockchain is depicted as a capacity lacking connection. Numerous specialists state that among security and IoT, this time is as agreeable as a cryptographic component. Human errors in joining those two rising innovations can bring about security weaknesses. Regardless of the number of specialized obstacles and execution factors, the blockchain and IoT intermingling is an opportunity for mass programs comprised of supply chains and coordination's. Positions among themselves in the inventory network without human oversight, terrible exercises or activities/picks might be perceived at the stock and moment remedial movement can be produced to decrease the results. Inside the course of this intention, various analysts have investigated the reasonableness of coordinating IoT and blockchain networks in different programming spaces [42–45].

1. Walton chain

   Walton chain is fresh out of the plastic new blockchain stage for the IoT undertaking. Developing on these inspirations, Walton affixes objectives to upset the current IoT industry through utilizing and coordinating the straightforwardness, duty, and starting region credits of the blockchain with radio-frequency identification (RFID) principally based IoT equipment. The center stage is another guarantor known as cost IoT fitting for different IoT as RFID equipment (both

RFID labels and per users), the applications such open blockchain stage and the production stage interface equipment and blockchain. Walton chain is a public blockchain that in reality, every individual can participate inside the agreement instrument, while the baby chain is public. Or on the other hand, it is very well may be private. Walton chain can be the same number of baby ties as imperative to execute business office, not unordinary experience for a specific industry or there, and another newborn child chain can be made utilizing a totally interesting exchange recorded in the parent blockchain. The Walton chain stage has added a half and half agreement set of approaches known as Walton chain proof of contribution (WPC). WPC is an aggregate of three understanding estimations: evidence of work (PoW), stake (PoS), and affirmation of extraordinary canvases (PoL). Pow is a lot of equivalents to that utilized in bitcoin. PoS is a stake-on a very basic level-based arrangement set of rules, while pol has been portrayed as another understanding figuring for stream chain information switch and token substitute [46]. Unfortunately, there are no experiences about this plan of rules and bundles which express a decentralized public blockchain-engaged estimation sharing stage for multi-progressive conditions [46].

2. Origin trail

Origin trail stage incorporates a blockchain period with a virtual vehicle chain to this chain that grants realities with unchanging nature and uprightness. Conveying this thought is item guidelines and the buyer's security, executing the system of the virtual item code insights transporter to encourage the layered, extensible, and secluded plan across the total shape. Genuine epic as the biological system might be contemplated the-level device. On the highest point of the blockchain layer, there are structure layers which can be the network and information layers that put the impact on an off-bind decentralized shared organization called genuine decentralized network (ODN). On the apex of the organization layer, there is a decentralized arrangement layer that interfaces among clients and the framework to offer measurements to enter offices. The front-line model of a four works verification of work (authentic) that sudden spikes in demand for the zenith of the particular blockchain. Pow expects that the rendition absolute last could incorporate the Ethereum blockchain with stand-out agreement calculations.

3. Block.it

Block.it is an IoT stage on the most noteworthy purpose of the Ethereum blockchain [33]. It is the vision to set up a genuinely decentralized splitting financial gadget with the objective to allow direct association between producer/proprietor and customer of IoT gadgets. 4040 the resolution of sharing monetary structure is to allow individuals to share their unused or considerably less used genuine or virtual assets rooms or homes, vehicles, strength, or maybe time, for cash-related inspirations. The customary methodology calls for stores of human mediation with a giant issue of agreeing with and straightforwardness. The contemporary-day activities of not sharing money-related machine-like Uber and Airbnb are decentralized. They depend on their monumental plan of action of huge carriers who charge an unbelievable cost, regardless, the security, trust, and straightforwardness burdens are supported in such applications. It centers to adjust to these issues by giving a phase that involves IoT things, a clock programming program stage, and a sharp plan maintained through the Ethereum blockchain [41] delivering totally electronic devices-to-device, gadget-to-human, and human-to-human affiliations. Each iot thing can have joint effort with every exceptional the usage of a sharp transitory specialist (or an undaunted of canny arrangements) embedded in the Ethereum blockchain. Besides, slock does not have its blockchain. Taking everything into account, it utilizes Ethereum as its concealed blockchain stage. Thusly, it depends on the current day Ethereum section settlement, a beneficial strategy, and different frameworks.

4. Moeco

It is a blockchain stage that foresees utilizing the conviction that DNS is everything. The stage coordinates a portion of the systems administration prerequisites and presents network to billions of devices internationally through partaking passages. It makes use of a community useful resource approach to integrating current networks. There is a proprietor port one after the other in its infrastructure. Moe co with a conversation connection can emerge as a gateway service company. Every person someone with a Wi-Fi router at home or a cell phone can be part of a gateway company and start serving vendors, joint companies. Enterprise is owned sensor system, to facilitate that their Internet connections are searching for connection, cellular networks or different kinds of networks, works as if the sensor gadgets of the relationship. Consumers use the fast connection from available ports 40a4 infrastructure that is the advantages of each event. eBay vendors can avoid the huge price of established order even as portal owners earn money with the aid of providing their unused bandwidth. This gadget makes use of blockchains namely shipping blockchain and invoice blockchain.

5. IOTA

It is an extraordinary kind of digital money and is a disseminated record intended for the web of things (IoT). With its versatility, free and quick exchanges, and the capacity to simultaneously approve a limitless scope of exchanges, IOTA is fitting for use occasions along with IoT. Rather than the utilization of verification of work and developing squares, IOTA uses Tangle, an experience's structure made out of directed non-cyclic graph (DAG) The Tangle is an arrangement building machine that discards the prerequisite for diggers and real factors that block on the stage. Agreement building network part (framework) wishing to conduct an exchange should affirm the past two exchanges, effectively taking an interest in the organization agreement. Each way, every exchange interfaces these exchanges it evaluations, and during that time it associates with the predetermination transaction to every approval, the validator plays a little artistic creation connecting the exchange to the total Tangle. The estimation of the utilization of a network is equivalent to the energy that ate up through, because of the reality each new contraption on the network invigorates figuring the organization when sending exchanges. A device for validating the two required transactions, a modern addition to IOTA, is a convention that indicates IOTA's response for majority-based calculations, revaluated calculations, and sharp agreements. It runs an independent arrangement that comprises of speaking IoT gadgets, allowing machine-to-machine (M2M) report.

6. IBM Watson

IBM Watson is an included period that blends the Watson IoT stage and blockchain. Cubic utilizes surface. Structure supervises blockchain carrier. You will be able to clutch records in Watson by the utilization of IoT contraptions. It is other than gives clients records assessment and discernment commitments. The Hyperledger assignment could be a planned exertion among IBM and the Linux Establishment to shape a business attempt grade opensource dissipated record structure and codebase. The inspiration driving this assignment is to offer an open standard blockchain stage so that any endeavor who can work here have diverse exceptional activities in headway under the umbrella endeavor of Hyperledger, unequivocally Burrow, Texture, Sawtooth, Iroha, and Indy. The surface is the head fitting stage for this current gather. It is far an approved blockchain framework with appropriately planned structures, for clever interchanges (called "chain code" in the material) and enrolment administrations provided using the endorsements of authority, to control authentication used, to confirm club and jobs. An underwriter is a unique kind of companion that ensures exchanges by utilizing and ensuring that their endeavor is vital and wonderful circumstances are met. The arranged hub offers a correspondence channel to clients and companions that can communicate messages containing exchanges. As it is an approved blockchain, broad assistance is doable. Notwithstanding, the reach relies upon your utilization case and how you set up it. It utilizes a measured building configuration to help unique agreement components. At present, the material just backings agreement instruments, SOLO and Kafka more noteworthy agreement instruments will be included in what's to come.

7. NetObjex platform

NetObjex utilizes IoT and blockchain to serve four basic market portions: convey chain and coordination's, creation industry, shrewd city, and vehicle association. It is miles a decentralized virtual resource at the executive's stage. The stage utilizes it for realities arrangement. It permits a broad scope of correspondence conventions, for example, cell, mid-range conventions (Lora, Sigfox, NB-IoT), Wi-Fi, Ethernet, link, exceptional conventions (SRC), and licenses foundations to rate records safely through the blockchain. Set into impact business endeavor hints through keen agreements. To cause certain legitimate to get appropriate of section to touchy measurements, NetObjex utilizes blockchain innovation to hold it in a cryptographic record. The NetObjex stage offers an adaptable fitting and play encompassing that lets clients to develop and set up their own special shrewd items. A mechanical manufacture through the token. The system likewise bears the cost of help for the symbolic local digital money for exchanges among gadgets. Furthermore, skip discussion among brilliant parts. An innovative manufacture through the token. The system it likewise manages the cost of help for the symbolic local cryptographic money for exchanges among gadgets [41,47] and [48].

21.6   Blockchain-based artificial intelligence platforms in finance

WOTNOT is used to automate the whole thing from engaging potentialities to teaching them during the lifecycle. Help your purchasers get to the proper banking and monetary products, assist in hazard profiling, and provide tailor-made services based totally on their character. Be it a current patron, or a prospect looking for information—your monetary services chatbot can deal with any and all banking queries, and initiate all requests concerning monetary transactions. With seamless integrations to terminals, payment processors, and external structures, the provision of round-the-clock assistance through an intuitive conversational enjoy offers an unprecedented client revel in. A massive part of aid calls involves personnel, contractors, providers, and clients asking an equal set of questions over and over. A banking and financial services chatbot, embedded with a knowledge base of FAQs, can be used to answer these questions, and create miles more study as well as exceptional revel in for now not simply the clients, but additionally inner employees. A huge part of aid calls contains employees, contractors, providers, and clients asking the same set of questions over and over. A banking and monetary offerings chatbot, embedded with an understanding base of frequently asked questions, may be used to reply to these questions, and create a far extra robust as well as the best experience for no longer simply the customers, but also inner employees.

21.7   Conclusion

IoT and blockchain are rising technology that is anticipated to have a prime impact on the global community. The type of technology has its own set of utilization and some considerable shortcomings. Is this combination opens the door to opportunities for applications with greater benefits. This bankruptcy goals to check this technique. One at a time, this key motivation for this bankruptcy is to create a take look at a framework that can be utilized by programs. The chapter provides the overview of how the blockchain, IoT, and artificial intelligence platforms that are significantly playing an important role in the day-to-day operations of the financial services.

References

[1]   O. Ali, M. Ally, Clutterbuck, and Y. Dwivedi (2020). The state of play of blockchain technology in the financial services sector: A systematic

literature review. *International Journal of Information Management*, 54, 102199. doi:10.1016/j.ijinfomgt.2020

[2] W. Du, S. L. Pan, E. Dorothy, D. E. Leidner, and W. Yinga. (2019). Affordances, experimentation, and actualization of FinTech: A blockchain implementation study. *The Journal of Strategic Information Systems*, 28, 50–65.

[3] S. Ølnes, J. Ubacht, and M. Janssen. (2017). Blockchain in government: Benefits and implications of distributed ledger technology for information sharing. *Government Information Quarterly*, 34(4), 355–364.

[4] S. Abramova and R. Böhme. (2016). Perceived benefit and risk as multi-dimensional determinants of bitcoin use: A quantitative exploratory study. *The 37th International Conference on Information Systems,* pp. 1–20.

[5] R. Beck, C. Müller-Bloch, and J. L. King. (2018). Governance in the blockchain economy: A framework and research agenda. *Journal of the Association for Information Systems*, 19(10), 1020–1034. https://doi.org/10.17705/1jais.00518

[6] G. Chapron. (2017). The environment needs crypt-governance. *Nature*, 545, 403–405. China International Capital Corporation (2016). *Changing the infrastructure of the financial sector*.

[7] G. W. Peters and E. Panayi. (2016). Understanding modern banking ledgers through blockchain technologies: Future of transaction processing and smart contracts on the internet of money. In: P. Tasca, T. Aste, L. Pelizzon, N. Perony, (eds) Banking Beyond Banks and Money. New Economic Windows. Springer, Cham. https://doi.org/10.1007/978-3-319-42448-4_13

[8] D. Wörner, T. von Bomhard, Y. P. Schreier, and D. Bilgeri. (2016). The bitcoin ecosystem: Disruption beyond financial services? *The Twenty-Fourth European Conference on Information Systems,* pp. 1–16.

[9] A. A. Pandey, T. F. Fernandez, R. Bansal, and A. K. Tyagi. (2022). Maintaining scalability in blockchain. In: Abraham, A., Gandhi, N., Hanne, T., Hong, T. P., Nogueira Rios, T., and Ding, W. (eds), *Intelligent Systems Design and Applications. ISDA 2021*. Lecture Notes in Networks and Systems, vol 418. Springer, Cham. https://doi.org/10.1007/978-3-030-96308-8_4.

[10] A. K. Tyagi and A. Abraham (eds.). (2021). *Recent Trends in Blockchain for Information Systems Security and Privacy*, 1st ed. CRC Press. https://doi.org/10.1201/9781003139737.

[11] R. Ryan and M. Donohue. Securities on blockchain. *The Business Lawyer, 73*, Winter 2017–2018.

[12] SEC Rules 14b-1, 14b-2, 17 C.F.R. §§ 240.14b-1, 240.14b-2 (2017).

[13] A. K. Tyagi, G. Rekha, and N. Sreenath (eds.). (2021). *Opportunities and Challenges for Blockchain Technology in Autonomous Vehicles*. Hershey, PA: IGI Global. http://doi:10.4018/978-1-7998-3295-9.

[14] S. Higgins. (2016, April 22). "The Republic of Georgia to Develop Blockchain Land Registry," Coindesk. Retrieved from http://www.coindesk.com/bitfury-working-with-georgian-government-on-blockchain-land-registry/

[15] The LTB Network, YouTube. Retrieved from https://www.youtube.com/user/LetsTalkBitcoinChan

[16] L. Kuo. (2016, February 19). "Imogen Heap wants to use blockchain technology to revolutionize the music industry." Retrieved from http://qz.com/620454/imogen-heap-wants-to-use-blockchain-technology-to-revolutionize-the-music-industry/

[17] M. Rouse (2014). "Digital signature," SearchSecurity. TechTarget. Retrieved from http://searchsecurity.techtarget.com/definition/digital-signature

[18] A. K. Tyagi, S. Chandrasekaran, and N. Sreenath. (2022). Blockchain technology: a new technology for creating distributed and trusted computing environment. *International Conference on Applied Artificial Intelligence and Computing (ICAAIC)*, pp. 1348–1354. doi: 10.1109/ICAAIC53929.2022.9792702.

[19] Are you exploring Blockchain technology for your investment bank? (2019). Retrieved from https://www.accenture.com/in-en/insight-perspectives-capital-markets-blockchain

[20] H. Hassani, X. Huang, and E. Silva. (2018). Banking with blockchain-ed big data. *Journal of Management Analytics*, 5(4), 256–275. https://doi.org/10.1080/23270012.2018.1528900.Taylor & Francis group

[21] B. Marr. (2017). Practical Examples of How Blockchains Are Used in Banking and the Financial Services Sector. Retrieved from https://www.forbes.com/sites/bernardmarr/2017/08/10/practical-examples-of-how-blockchains-are-used-in-banking-and-the-financial-services sector/#f1b33831a116

[22] A. K. Tyagi, M. M. Nair, S. Niladhuri, and A. Abraham. (2020). Security, privacy research issues in various computing platforms: a survey and the road ahead. *Journal of Information Assurance & Security*, 15(1), 1–16.

[23] G. Walker. (2018). Is KYC Using Blockchain the Answer for Banks? Retrieved from https://blogs. thomsonreuters.com/financial-risk/financial-crime/kyc-using-blockchain-answer-banks/

[24] S. Wolos. (2017). Are You Ready for the 4th EU Money Laundering Directive? Retrieved from https://blogs. thomsonreuters.com/financial-risk/risk-management-and-compliance/are-you-ready-for-the4th-eu-money-laundering-directive/

[25] A. Sarnitz and R. Maier. (2017). Blockchain in Retail Banking. Retrieved from https://www. banking hub.EU/innovation-digital/blockchain-retail-banking

[26] J. Lang. (2017a). Three Uses for Blockchain in Banking. Retrieved from https://www.ibm.com/ blogs/blockchain/2017/10/three-uses-for-blockchain-in-banking

[27] A. Garcia. (2018b). IBM's Blockchain App Store Wants to Help Banks Cut Costs. Retrieved from https://money.cnn.com/2018/07/30/technology/ibm-blockchain-app-store/index.html

[28] R. Beck. (2018). Beyond bitcoin: The rise of the blockchain world. *Computer*, 51(2), 54–58.

[29]   K. Lai. (2018). Blockchain as AML tool: A work in progress. *International Financial Law Review.* [Online], Retrieved from https://www.iflr.com/ Article/3804315/Blockchain-as-AML-tool-awork-in-progress.html (Accessed: April 5th, 2020)

[30]   T. Dhanabalan and A. Sathish. (2018). Transforming Indian industries through artificial intelligence and robotics in industry 4.0. *International Journal of Mechanical Engineering and Technology,* 9(10), 835–845.

[31]   A. K. Tyagi, D. Agarwal, and N. Sreenath. (2022). SecVT: securing the vehicles of tomorrow using blockchain technology. *2022 International Conference on Computer Communication and Informatics (ICCCI),* pp. 1–6. doi: 10.1109/ICCCI54379.2022.9740965.

[32]   L. P. Nian and D. L. K. Chuen. (2015). *Introduction to Bitcoin. Handbook of Digital Currency,* pp. 5–30. doi:10.1016/b978-0-12-802117-0.00001-1

[33]   J. Matonis. (2013). Bitcoin Gaining Market-Based Legitimacy as XBT. Retrieved from CoinDesk: http:// www.coindesk.com/bitcoin-gaining-market-based-legitimacy-xbt/

[34]   V. Buterin. (2013). Ethereum White Paper: A Next Generation Smart Contract & Decentralized Application Platform. Retrieved from http://www. theblockchain.com/docs/Ethereum_white_papera_next_generation_smart_ contract_and_decentralized_application_platform-vitalik-buterin.pdf

[35]   Y. Sompolinsky and A. Zohar. (2015). Secure high-rate transaction processing in bitcoin. *Financial Cryptography,* 8975, 507–527.

[36]   Ethereum Community. "A next-generation smart contract and decentralized application platform," White Paper, Retrieved from https://github.com/ ethereum/wiki/wiki/White-Paper

[37]   G. Wood. (2018). Ethereum: A Secure Decentralised Generalised Transaction Ledger, Byzantium Version. Retrieved from https://ethereum. github.io/yellowpaper/paper.pdf

[38]   Retrieved from https://hyperledger-fabric.readthedocs.io/en/release-2.2/ whatis.html

[39]   V. Akshay Kumaran, A. K. Tyagi, and S. P. Kumar. (2022). Blockchain technology for securing internet of vehicle: issues and challenges. *2022 International Conference on Computer Communication and Informatics (ICCCI),* pp. 1–6. doi: 10.1109/ICCCI54379.2022.9740856.

[40]   M. S. Ferdous, K. Biswas, M. J. M. Chowdhury, N. Chowdhury, and V. Muthukkumarasamy. (2019). Integrated platforms for blockchain enablement. *Advances in Computers.,* 115, 41–72

[41]   Slock.it, Decentralizing the Emerging Sharing Economy. Retrieved from https://blog.slock.it/slock-itdecentralizing-the-emerging-sharing-economy-cf19ce09b957, 2015. [Online: accessed on November 5, 2018].

[42]   A. Panarello, N. Tapas, G. Merlino, F. Longo, and A. Puliafito. (2018). Blockchain and iot integration: A systematic survey. *Sensors,* 18(8), 704–709. https://doi.org/10.3390/s18082575 URL. Retrieved from http://www. mdpi.com/1424-8220/18/8/2575

[43] M. Chowdhury, M. Ferdous, K. Biswas, N. Chowdhury, and V. Muthuk kumarasamy. (2020). A survey on blockchain-based platforms for IoT use-cases. *The Knowledge Engineering Review*, 35, E19. doi:10.1017/S0269888920000284.

[44] M. Ferdous, M. Chowdhury, K. Biswas, N. Chowdhury, and V. Muthuk kumarasamy. (2020). Immutable autobiography of smart cars leveraging blockchain technology. *The Knowledge Engineering Review*, 35, E3. doi:10.1017/S0269888920000028.

[45] A. Azaria, A. Ekblaw, T. Vieira, and A. Lippman. (2016). Medrec: Using blockchain for medical data access and permission management. In: *International Conference on Open and Big Data (OBD), IEEE*, pp. 25–30.

[46] Waltonchain Waltonchain White Paper, V2.0.Retrieved from https://waltonchain.org/templets/ default/doc/Waltonchain-whitepaper_EN_20180525. pdf, [Online]. Accessed 1 November 2018.

[47] QuantumMechanic, Proof of Stake Instead of Proof of Work, https://bitcointalk.org/index.php?topic=27787.0, 2011. [Online: accessed on 5 November, 2018].

[48] Qubic IOTA. Retrieved from https://qubic.iota.org/ [Online: accessed on 30 November 2018].

Chapter 22

Blockchain and machine learning: an approach for predicting the commodity prices

J.S. Shyam Mohan[1], Vanam Venkata Chakradhar[1], Vedantham Hanumath Sreeman[1], Narasimha Krishna Amruth Vemuganti[1], Naga Venkata Kuladeep[1] and Charishma Chinthakayala[2]

Abstract

In today's environment, visualizing data is getting attraction from various organizations and sectors. Visualization of the commodities data on individual countries are correlated with GDP and the development of their individuals. Machine learning (ML) deals with the data to perform the Mathematical and Statistical operations to find exciting patterns present in the data. ML models rely on different algorithms and techniques used to make predictions on the collected datasets that are used for prediction and try to provide stakeholders an overview of growth and development. Moreover, prediction of commodity prices will significantly determine the economic status of the Country. This chapter presents a forecast of commodity prices, especially crude oil, gold, and wheat, by ML techniques. We have built a neural ML model to predict the respective commodity prices. Results presented in this work are helpful for the students, researchers, etc., working in the area of ML and their applications to understand the overall working process, steps in determining or building effective ML models for any datasets in real-time.

Keywords: Blockchain; Machine learning; Analysis of commodity prices; Advanced analytics

22.1 Introduction

The stock market plays a key role in a country's economic and social organization. Stock market forecasting models are considered more important and effective. Stock

[1]Department of CSE, SCSVMV University, India
[2]Data Science, Technische Universität Dortmund, Germany

market forecasting is a very difficult and challenging task for investors, professional analysts, and financial market researchers due to the highly noisy, non-parametric, volatile, complex, non-linear, dynamic, and chaotic nature of stock price time series. Consequently, stock prices will lead to profitable gains from making wise decisions. With stagnation and noisy data, stock market forecasts pose a big challenge for investors. Stock market forecasting uses mathematical strategies and educational tools. Therefore, predicting the stock market is a big problem for investors who want to use their money to get more profit. Predicting the stock market is an important task and an important research area in the financial field, as investing in the stock market carries higher risks. However, advances in computing intelligence can mitigate many risks [1]. Selected studies showed that machine learning (ML) methods along with their dataset for predicting the stock market proved to be successful. The artificial neural network (ANN) and neural network (NN) methods are most commonly used to obtain accurate stock forecasts. Many relevant works have been done on stock market forecasting before. The latest stock market forecasting methodology has many limitations [2].

A commodity is a mining item that can be handled and exchanged. A few instances of such products are soya beans, wheat, unrefined oil, and gold. Huge volumes of commodities are purchased and sold around the globe every day. Buyers and sellers need to sell their items, and producers need to buy crude items. This should be possible on the global market, where products are purchased and sold "on the spot." The spot market is a term that indicates many decentralized areas at which the great might be bought or sold. Mineral products have been fundamental to human development and countries' economy and misused for over 7000 years [3]. The export of essential commodities is a significant wellspring of foreign trade for some countries, particularly non-industrialized nations. Commodity prices, developments and volatilities are related to financial and investment activities [4]. Trade analysts focus on the past information, like a commodity contracts, to foresee its future to check or verify the financial transactions involved in commodity markets across the globe on a daily basis. This information is useful for the researchers to find out the gaps in the commodity markets and provide an effective solution using latest technologies say like ML. There are stock brokers working on stock markets, trade owners, producers or firms, etc. involved in commodity markets [5]. Trade analysts use various techniques for prediction of commodity prices in a global market scenario. For example, Box–Jenkins's method determines the relationship among the variables in the commodity markets.

In fact, many researchers have found out the relationship among the variables that either directly or indirectly affects the prices of commodities in a global market. There are other ways too for predicting the commodity prices, like ML-based techniques deployed or implemented on a blockchain network. ML considers all the dependent and independent variables for prediction. The values or results obtained when implemented on a blockchain will make it even easier for quick and effective, transparent, decision making, or prediction in real-time [6].

The formation and merging blockchain technology (BCT) with emerging economies presents the potential opportunity for rapid advancement, and benefits for numerous fields. According to the United Nations Conference on Trade and Development (UNCTAD), the usage of blockchain in commodity trading is growing rapidly. So merging this into economics gives a potential impact and transparent logs. Blockchain is ledger of records in which transactions are carried out that are cryptographically secure [7]. Each block in a blockchain consists of transaction squares that record all the transactions that happen in a blockchain network. The decentralized database managed by various individuals is known as Distributed Ledger Technology (DLT) [8]. It offers a tough, solid, straightforward, and a decentralized method of recording and controlling information over all the nodes of a system. This interface ensures that all blocks are connected on the blockchain network. Everyone in the organization can access a copy of the blockchain; therefore, different clients can span any process. These copies of the blockchain are updated as another block expands. BCT uses the services of a cryptographic secure hash algorithm like Secure Hash Algorithm (SHA), SHA-256, and SHA-512 to secure the information and does not have a chance to tamper the existing data in blocks. Each block has secure hash keys. For instance, Ethereum uses the services of Keccak-256 and Keccak-512, whereas Bitcoin uses twofold SHA-256. SHA is a secure computation of tamper-proof impact, where two different pieces of information cannot produce the same return (hash value).This chapter is organized into the following sections:

Section 22.2 discusses about state-of-the-art works on ML and BC. Section 22.3 states about leverages of ML on blockchain (BC). Section 22.4 explores the methodology. Section 22.5 highlights the discussion and experimental setup. Section 22.6 discusses simulation results of our proposed work. Section 22.7 provides results followed by conclusion.

22.2   State-of-the-art works

The techniques for abusing financial news, online media information, and analytical findings, as well as the offices that have been established, are discussed in the recent years. A prediction model or ML model has been developed that uses information collected from web, online, social media, etc. To intermittently predict stock exchange patterns. The model shows that sentiment analysis supplemented with social information exhibits specialized research techniques such as regression analysis. It shows that the instability of the business sector and the framework of future exposure are affected by financial and political news from online media. Despite digital information, misuse of web-based media information builds the nature of the information and provides improved predictions [9]. When the information in the information is standardized to a typical type of information using fast-changing metrics, the results of regression strategies can be improved. The use of sequential information types to make predictions that depend on the positioning frame provides an alternative measure of the prediction results.

22.3   Leveraging Machine Learning on BCT

Blockchain innovation has been moving as of late. This innovation permits a protected way for people to manage each other through an exceptionally solid and decentralized framework, without a mediator. Notwithstanding its own abilities, ML can help in dealing with numerous restrictions that blockchain-based frameworks have. The blend of these two innovations can give high-performing and helpful outcomes. Blockchain can be profoundly practical in wiping out the requirement for a centralized authority to administer and check collaborations and exchanges among all users. In blockchain, each exchange is cryptographically marked and confirmed by all mining nodes which hold a copy of the whole record which contains chained blocks for all transactions. This makes synchronized, safe, and time-stamped records that cannot be tampered [10]. On the other hand ML allows to learn and adapt some functions based on data. In other terms, ML model is mainly depended on data. The model which can be used and created for healthy prediction and classification is decided with the help of data. The enormous creation of data is occurring from transactions, smart devices, and some web applications in this new digital world. The generated, historical data can be used by ML and deep learning techniques to create a model that forecasts the future information. However, the centralized idea of these techniques might prompt the chance of data altering, as information can be liable to hacking and control as it is overseen and put away in unified way. Additionally, the information provenance and validness of the sources producing the information are not ensured. This might prompt Artificial Intelligence (AI) choice results that can be profoundly incorrect, unsafe, and risky [11,12]. The idea of decentralized AI has been arising. Decentralized AI is fundamentally a blend of AI and blockchain. The decentralized AI empowers to process and perform investigation or decision making on trusted, carefully marked, and secure shared information that has been executed and put away on the blockchain, in a disseminated and decentralized design, without trusted third parties or middle people. AI is known to work with gigantic volumes of information, and blockchain has now been predicted as a confided in stage to store such information. The element of blockchain smart contracts enables to program the blockchain to oversee exchanges among members engaged with direction or producing and getting to the information. Smart contracts-based independent frameworks and machines can learn and adjust to changes over the long haul and settle on trusted and exact choice results that are checked and approved by all mining nodes of the blockchain. Such choices cannot be discredited, and can be followed, followed, and confirmed by every single taking part element. Computer-based intelligence procedures that use blockchain can offer decentralized figuring out how to work with a trust and secure sharing of information and choice results across countless independent specialists, which can contribute, direction, and decision on additional choices [13]. The ML calculations work better when information are gathered from a repository or a stage that is dependable, secure, trusted, and valid. Blockchain fills in as a distributed ledger on which information can be put away and executed in a manner that is cryptographically approved, and settled on by all mining nodes. Blockchain information is put away with high trustworthiness and strength and cannot be altered. At the point when smart contracts are utilized for AI calculations to simply decide and perform investigation, the result of these choices can be trusted and undisputed. The combination of AI and blockchain can make secure, permanent, decentralized framework for the profoundly sensitive data that AI-driven frameworks should gather, store, and use. This idea brings about huge enhancements to get the information and data in different fields, including clinical, individual, banking, and monetary, exchanging, and legitimate information [14]. Innovations in blockchain and ML are, of course, gaining energy and forcing it all over the planet. The problematic innovation is that blockchain has sprinkled a lot of digital form of money development and exchange. It will be repeated, but ML is to combine existing information with clear-cut calculations with foresight to recognize patterns and gain some knowledge with a ripple effect. ML connects to high-functioning models and BCT makes the system more efficient and graffiti by integrating ML and blockchain in all applications to enhance the security of applications. It has the ability to decentralize the blockchain network. Including this distribution of the various components of a neural network, be it algorithms or computational power, enables greater innovation. The operation and design of the blockchain is purely based on various parameters such as security and decentralization. With the help of artificial intelligence, the decision-making process for these parameters is simple and provides optimal results. The combination of these two technologies helps improve the productivity and performance of your application. Rather than the benefits through security and freedom, the significant advantage of the innovation is an uncommon decrease of the time expected to give proprietorship. Accentuating the reality that this is additionally the time during which the freight must be financed. As an outcome, the utilization of the innovation shows a possibility to significantly diminish expenses of money. This combination can help increase the time it takes to build a smart contract. Blockchain data cannot be modulated, but can be used in general. In this case, AI plays an important role in providing privacy and confidentiality. Also, this leads to a window to create a better distributed structure. The AI strategies installed inside the decentralized framework help to foresee and react to basics that might happen in a unique transportation climate and give an optimal solution.

The problems faced in during the pre-processing need to be sorted out first, this can be done by the machine learners or researchers those who have sound knowledge in the same domain. Machine learners have experience and good understanding of the problem such that they can request data or manipulate the same according to the need. New techniques must be introduced to validate the data before making arriving at a final decision. The use of statistical models for validation must be incorporated using the correct statistical principles [15]. The ML approach in blockchain-based smart contract is shown in Figure 22.1.

Data collected from the date resources are pre-processed. The updated data is used for smart applications. It can now be applied to data loaded into ML applications to improve analytics and predictions. Data sets are stored in a decentralized network of blockchains.

Therefore, they are at the forefront of reducing data-induced errors (such as duplication of data and noise present in the data) when used in model building and prediction. Since blockchain is purely data-based, errors made in the ML process have the potential to be abolished.

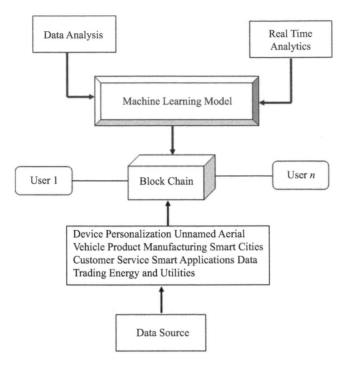

Figure 22.1   Block diagram of ML approach in blockchain-based smart contracts

Both concepts and application integrations for many organizations will continue to develop new innovations. Entire data in a blockchain network is securely encrypted with cryptographic hash keys. BCT is safe and layers added to it cannot be easily attacked. Thus, automatic learning techniques predict every possible point in the system and help eliminate and implement these types of attacks. Blockchain is commonly used to combine learning models in smart contracts that helps to keep track of data stored by individuals. For practical implementation of BCT and ML for stock market prediction, we have adopted some of the techniques used in [16].

BCT makes transactions easier without any third party and thereby making the transaction process transparent. This information can help improve the implementation of ML models to update the blockchain environment at low cost. Smart contracts can be implemented on multiple machines and the ML model helps out in obtaining accurate results. Today, many organizations rely on blockchain smart contracts because they can allow production, safety and excellent transparency directors while transporting products. Enterprises relying on traditional methods have started adopting BCT for automating the entire transaction process transparent.

22.4   Steps/process of proposed methodology

We relied upon convolutional neural networks, bi-directional long short-term memory (CNN-BiLSTM), ensemble ML model named support vector regression

(SVR) and ensemble adaptive neuro fuzzy inference system (ENANFIS) for stock price prediction by combining features for predicting the stock closing price of the next day proposed [17,18]. Stock market prediction can be done using sentiment analysis where stock comments and sentiment forecasting is applied using deep neural networks. Moreover, empirical results obtained using deep sentiment analysis showed 9% improvement compared with logistic regression algorithm [14]. We tried combining all the methods of artificial neural network like linear regression, k-nearest neighbors algorithm (k-NN), Naïve, moving average (MA), autoregression (AR), autoregressive-moving-average (ARMA), autoregressive integrated moving average (ARIMA), and autoARIMA for forecasting the stock markets [19]. We have used some of the ML models as mentioned in [20]. The steps involved in the proposed model are shown in Figure 22.2. The first step in the process is collection of raw data. After collecting raw data, pre-processing is done to remove null values. Classification of data is done using the data pre-processing techniques. The pre-processed data can be trained by keeping a standard data kept as reference and comparing it alongside done using ML techniques.

The steps of the proposed ML model as shown in Figure 22.2 are given below:

1. *Data pre-processing* operations are performed from the data scraped from the source using Python Pandas.
2. *Analyze* the pre-processed data to find the patterns.
3. *Visualization techniques* are performed on the data for clear understanding using inbuilt python libraries.
4. Data is split into the ratio 8:2, where 8 is for training and 2 is for testing.
5. For prediction, we rely upon Scikit.

Data pre-processing is done from the raw data. This raw data needs to be changed depending on our analysis. No operations can be done on the raw data; therefore, data pre-processing has to be done based on the assumptions. Therefore, data evaluation has to be executed in the pre-processed records to apprehend each element in the records and in fact, this leads to an interesting aspect for making investment in the business. Data for commodity prices are scraped from web and it is organized according to our perspectives possibly it is in excel form. From the excel file, we assign the dataset in our workspace keeping in view our necessities and dropping the undesirable columns from the table. Knowledge and data are represented graphically in data visualization. Data visualization techniques are used for obtaining the desired results. Data visualization tools are useful for Big Data analytics and testing [21–23]. The code snippet below shows the pre-processed table of crude oil.

Figure 22.2   Proposed model—steps

```
In [4]:crudeoil_data.isnull().sum()
Out [4]: Date 0
Open 1135
High1135
Low 1135
Close 1135
Adj Close 1135
Volume1135
dtype: int64
In [5]:crudeoil_data.dropna(axis = 0, how = 'any' , inplace = True)
crudeoil_data.isnull().sum()
Out [5]: Date 0
Open 1135
High1135
Low 1135
Close 1135
Adj Close 1135
Volume1135
dtype: int64
```

The datasets of crude oil, gold, and wheat that are taken from external sources are organized and loaded in the software. In the pre-processing process, null values and unwanted columns from the table are removed.

The Code Snippet of Pre-processed table for crude oil is shown below:

```
In [7]:crudeoil_data. Drop(crudeoil_data[['Adj close']], axis=1,inplace=True)
In [7]:crudeoil_data
Out [8]:DateOpenHighLowCloseVolume

02000-03-2227.65000028.25000027.250000 27.45000092202.0
1 2000-03-2227.65000027.25000027.160000 27.30000079373.0
2 2000-03-24 27.85000028.15000027.540000 27.98000055693.0
4 2000-03-27 27.65000028.02000027.410000 27.73000059199.0
5 2000-03-28 27.60000027.87000027.000000 27.08000039487.0
5099 rows X 6 columns
```

Figure 22.3 illustrates the price of crude oil from the year 2000 to 2020. The price of crude increased in the year 2008. In the year 2020, the cost of oil decreased drastically.

The Code Snippet Pre-processed table for gold is given below:

```
In [24]:gold_data.drop(gold_data[[ '% Deli.Qty to Traded Qty', 'Spread H-L',
'Spread C-O' ,'WAP', 'No.of Shares', 'No.of Trades' ]]
In [25]:gold_data
Out [25]: DateOpen High LowCloseTotalturnoverDeliverable Quantity

0 2017-02-06 0.79 0.79 0.76 0.76 5848.07430.0
1 2017-02-03 0.79 0.79 0.79 0.79 244.0 310.0
2 2017-02-02 0.83 0.83 0.83 0.8362.075.0
```

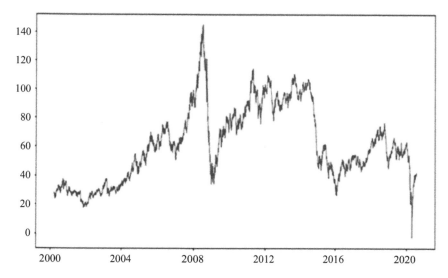

Figure 22.3   Price graph for crude oil—visualization in blockchain

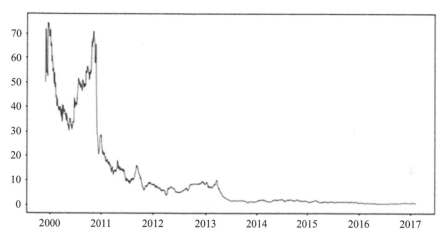

Figure 22.4   Price graph for gold—visualization in blockchain

3 2017-01-31 0.87 0.87 0.87 0.87913.0 1050.0
4 2017-01-25 0.91 0.91 0.91 0.91364.0 400.0
1660 rows X 7 columns

For gold data, we did not find any null values to remove unwanted columns from the table. Therefore, the graph is shown in Figure 22.4.

Figure 22.4 illustrates the price of gold from the year 2010 to 2017. The cost of gold was high during 2010 and 2011 and maintained the constant price from 2014 to 2017.

Figure 22.5 shows the analysis of wheat price from the year 2010 to 2018. For wheat data, data pre-processing is ignored or it is not performed.

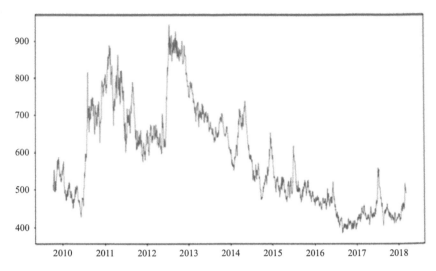

Figure 22.5   Price graph for wheat—visualization in blockchain

22.5   Discussion and experimental setup

For performing the data analysis, we relied on Jupyter Notebook as a software environment. It is a free, open-source platform for python. There are in-built libraries that are useful for Python for importing the project. Some of the libraries that were used are Pandas, Numpy, Matplotlib, and Scikit-Learn. The system setup for performing ML implementation on BC is of the following configuration: Intel I3 with hard disk capacity 1 TB of RAM 4 GB.

22.5.1   Model 1—linear regression

Linear regression is a direct model that expects a direct connection between the dependent factors (x) and the single independent variable (y) more explicitly, that y can be determined from a direct mix of the dependent factors (x). Learning a linear regression model means assessing the upsides of the coefficients utilized in the portrayal with the information that we have accessible. To appraise the coefficients, need to compute factual properties from the information like means, standard deviations, relationships, and covariance. Each of the information should be accessible to cross and ascertain insights. The ordinary mean squares method tries to limit the amount of the squared residuals. This implies that given a relapse line through the information we work out the separation from every information highlight the regression line, square it, and aggregate each of the squared errors together. This is the amount that common mean squares try to limit. This methodology regards the information as a lattice and utilizations direct variable-based math activities to assess the ideal qualities for the coefficients. It implies that every one of the information should be accessible and you should have sufficient memory to fit the information and perform grid tasks. It is uncommon to execute the ordinary mean squares system yourself except if as an activity in direct variable based math. Almost certainly, you will call a methodology in a direct polynomial math library. This method is extremely quick to ascertain. Hence, Figure 22.6 shows regression line, and Figure 22.7 shows multiple hypothesis functions for a regression.

Simple linear regression is a regression investigation where the quantity of independent variables is one, and there is a linear connection between the independent (*x*) and dependent (*y*) variables.

In the regression problem, we have trained to predict values within a continuous output, i.e., we have tried mapping input variables to some continuous function. We have to find the hypothesis for an obtained training set with the help of some learning algorithms there by *h(x)* is a good predictor for the corresponding value of *Y* [26,27].

Here, *h(x)* is a hypothesis function.

$$h(x) = a + b\,x \#\#\text{Linear Equation}$$

The cost function helps us sort out the ideal qualities for *a* and *b*, this helps to get the optimal prediction line. $pred_i - y_i$ is the difference between the predicted

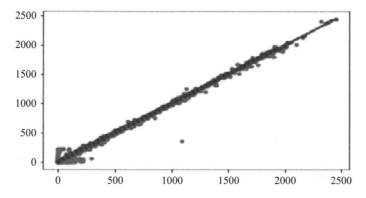

Figure 22.6   Regression line

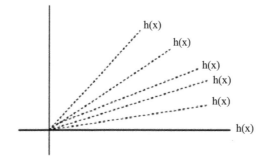

Figure 22.7   Multiple hypothesis functions for a regression

value and the actual value. For the obtained dataset, we can find a greater number of hypothesis functions, whereas we have to find the best fit $h(x)$. Hence, we can use cost function J to find the optimal prediction line:

$$\text{minimize} \frac{1}{n} \sum_{i=1}^{n} (pred_i - y_i)^2$$

$$J = \frac{1}{n} \sum_{i=1}^{n} (pred_i - y_i)^2$$

When there are at least one input sources, you can utilize a course of advancing the upsides of the coefficients by iteratively limiting the mistake of the model on training data. Gradient descent works by beginning with irregular qualities for every coefficient. The amount of the squared errors is determined for each pair of info and output esteems. A learning rate is utilized as a scale factor and the coefficients are refreshed toward the path towards limiting the blunder. The cycle is rehashed until a base total squared mistake is accomplished or no further improvement is conceivable. When utilizing this strategy, you should choose a learning rate (alpha) boundary that decides the size of the improvement step to take on every cycle of the methodology:

$$\Theta_J = \Theta_J - \frac{\alpha}{n} \sum_{i=1}^{n} [(pred_i - y_i)x_i]$$

We can use a counter plot graph to find the best fit line with the help of cost functions. A counter line of two variable functions which has a constant value at all points of the same line. We will find the specific hypothesis which is best fit to the training model with the help of counter plot graph. We pick the above function to minimize. The different $h(x)$ in the below graph represents the different linear regression lines for the data plotted. These lines spotted with different alpha values.

The distinction between the anticipated qualities and real truth estimates the error contrast. We square the error distinction and sum over all the data points and partition that esteem by the absolute number of data points. This gives the average squared error over all the data points. Along these lines, this cost function is otherwise called the mean squared error (MSE) work. Using MSE, the estimation values of a_0 and a_1 are changed to such an extent that the MSE value has low minima [28].

22.5.2 *Debugging gradient descent*

If the event that we decide α to be extremely enormous, gradient descent can overshoot the base. If the event that we decide α to be tiny, gradient descent will find little ways to arrive at neighborhood minima and will invest in some opportunity to reach minima. So, the learning rate value is crucial to work with gradient descent. Debugging the result with alpha results the good learning rate and it indicates the good flow of learning model. Gather and plot the cost esteems determined by the calculation every emphasis. The assumption for a well performing slope drop run is a reduction in cost every cycle. Assuming that it does not diminish; have a go at lessening your learning rate. The learning rate esteem is a little genuine worth, for example, 0.1, 0.001, or 0.0001. Attempt various qualities for your concern and see which works best. The calculation will arrive at the base expense quicker assuming the state of the expense work is not slanted and mutilated. You can accomplish this by rescaling the information factors as a whole (X) to a similar reach, for example, [0, 1] or [−1, 1]. Stochastic gradient descent regularly need not bother with more than 1 to 10 goes through the preparation dataset to meet on great or sufficient coefficients. The updates for each preparation dataset occasion can bring about a boisterous plot of cost over the long haul when utilizing stochastic angle plunge. Taking the normal more than 10, 100, or 1000 updates can provide you with a superior thought of the learning pattern for the calculation.grapg cost function as a component of boundary gauges for example boundary scope of our speculation work and the expense coming about because of choosing a specific arrangement of boundaries. We move descending towards pits in the diagram, to track down the base worth. The method for doing this is accepting subsidiary of cost work as clarified in the above figure. Inclination descent step-downs the expense work toward the steepest drop. The size of each progression is dictated by learning rate.

22.5.3 Model 1—SVM

SVMs or support vector machines are one of the most well-known and broadly involved methods for managing categorization problems in ML. In any case, the utilization of SVMs in relapse is not all around reported. This calculation recognizes the presence of non-linearity in the information and gives a capable expectation model. SVMs are directed learning models with related learning calculations that dissect information utilized for classification and regression analysis. In SVR, the line that is needed to fit the information is alluded to as hyperplane.

The goal of a SVM is to find a hyperplane in a n-layered space that particularly orders the relevant elements. The relevant informative items on one or the other side of the hyperplane that are nearest to the hyperplane are called support vectors. These impact the position and direction of the hyperplane and in this way assist with building the SVM. Hyperplanes are decision limits that are utilized to anticipate the consistent result. The informative elements on one or the other side of the hyperplane that are nearest to the hyperplane are called support vectors. These are utilized to plot the necessary line that shows the anticipated result of the calculation.

SVR is a managed learning calculation that is utilized to anticipate discrete qualities. SVR involves a similar rule as the SVMs. The fundamental thought behind SVR is to track down the best fit line. In SVR, the best fit line is the hyperplane that has the most extreme number of focuses. Not at all like other regression models that attempt to limit the blunder between the genuine and anticipated worth, has the SVR attempted to fit the best line inside edge esteem. The edge esteem is the distance between the hyperplane and the limit line. The fit time intricacy of SVR is more than quadratic with the quantity of tests which makes it difficult to scale to datasets within excess of two or three 10,000 examples. Straight SVR gives a quicker execution than SVR yet just thinks about the direct portion. The model created by SVR relies just upon a subset of the preparation information, on the grounds that the expense work overlooks tests whose forecast is near their objective.

From the Sklearn library containing SVM, import the class SVR, make an occasion of it, and allocate it to a variable. We set the boundary part to rbf, which represents revolutionary premise work portion and is predominantly utilized in SMV. The .fit() work permits us to prepare the model, changing loads as indicated by the information esteems to accomplish better precision. Subsequent to preparing, our model is prepared to make forecasts, which is called by the .foresee () technique. Assuming factors are normalized, need to change. so to get them in their unique structure, should apply the inverse_transform function on the standard scale for y.

R^2 score lets us know how well our model is fitted to the information by contrasting it with the normal line of the reliant variable. Assuming the score is more like 1, then, at that point, it demonstrates that our model performs well versus on the off chance that the score is farther from 1, then, at that point, it shows that our model does not perform so well. From sklearn.metrics need to import the r2_score method. By passing the test values and predicted values, we can obtain the score. This score is used to evaluate the model which is predicting the prices.

22.6   Results

In the results section, we explore the mean squared error (MSE), r2 score and the results obtained from the project. After creating the model, we trained the data and tested the data for predictions. When we finally acquired the predictions, we stored them in table with separate column [24].

MSE is the normal of the squared error that is utilized as the loss function for least-squares regression:

$$\sum_{i=1}^{n} \frac{\left(w^T x(i) - y(i)\right)^2}{n}$$

The total over all the data points, of the square of the contrast between the predicted and actual target variables, is isolated by the number of data points. r2 score is the proportion of the variance in the dependent variable that is predictable from the independent variable(s) [25,29]:

$$R^2 = 1 - \frac{SS_{res}}{SS_{tot}}$$

where SS_{res} is the residual sum of squares and SS_{tot} is the total sum of squares. Following is the Code Snippet Predicted values table of Crude Oil.

DateOpenClosePredicted_Close

2000-03-2227.65000027.450000 27.701961
2000-03-2227.65000027.300000 27.701961
2000-03-2427.85000027.980000 27.901672
2000-03-2727.65000027.730000 27.701961
2000-03-2827.60000027.080000 27.652033
5099 rows X 6 columns

The Code Snippet Predicted values table of Gold mentioned below
DateOpen Close Predicted_Close

2017-02-06 0.79 0.76 0.875146
2017-02-03 0.79 0.79 0.875146
2017-02-02 0.83 0.83 0.914256
2017-01-31 0.87 0.87 0.953367
2017-01-25 0.91 0.91 0.992477
1660 rows X 7 columns

Following is the Code Snippet Predicted values for wheat
DateOpen Close Predicted_Close

2018-03-12488.50 490.00 488.559449
2018-03-09499.25 490.25 499.262207
2018-03-08497.50 499.25 497.519898
2018-03-07506.00 497.50 505.982544
2272 rows X 3 columns

Figures 22.8, 22.9, and 22.10 represent the regression plots of the commodities. The regression plot contains the predicted close and actual close values; the regression line represents our ML model.

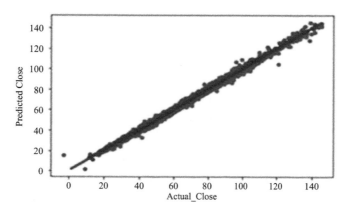

Figure 22.8   Regression plot of crude oil

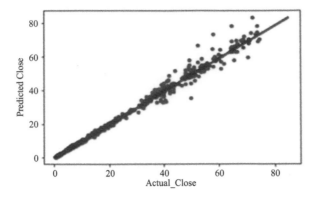

Figure 22.9   Regression plot of gold

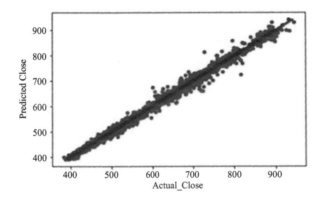

Figure 22.10   Regression plot of wheat

22.7   Conclusion

Innovations in ML and BCT have made enterprises to invest in the same. Researches in BC and ML provide enterprises to reduce their overall cost and obtain optimal results and thereby making prediction easier. In this chapter, we presented a ML model to predict product prices using blockchain in which data obtained is secured in a transparent way. The proposed system has undergone three major breakthroughs. The first step consists of updating the model boundaries of training the extension model of information. The next step was the approval part. We took advantage of this and modified the hyper-parameters to get the ideal model settings. This chapter is useful for students and researchers to learn and understand the basic concepts of ML and their implications for leveraging the same on BC.

References

[1] D. Kumar, P. K. Sarangi, and R. Verma, "A systematic review of stock market prediction using machine learning and statistical techniques," *Materials Today: Proceedings*, ISSN 2214–7853, 2021, https://doi.org/10.1016/j.matpr.2020.11.399.

[2] G. Kumar, S. Jain, and U. P. Singh, "Stock market forecasting using computational intelligence: a survey." *Archives of Computational Methods in Engineering*, vol. 28, pp. 1069–1101, 2021. https://doi.org/10.1007/s11831-020-09413-5

[3] C. A. Tapia Cortez, S. Saydam, J. Coulton, and C. Sammut, "Alternative techniques for forecasting mineral commodity prices," *International Journal of Mining Science and Technology*, vol. 28, pp. 302–322, 2018.

[4] Q. H. Do and T. T. H. Yen., "Predicting primary commodity prices in the international market: an application of group method of data handling neural network," *Journal of Management Information and Decision Sciences*, vol. 22, pp. 471–482, 2019.

[5] M. C. Roberts, "Technical analysis in commodity markets: risk, returns, and value," in Proceedings of the NCR-134 Conference on Applied Commodity Price Analysis, Forecasting, and Market Risk Management.

[6] A. Ray, "Commodity market price analysis and prediction using machine learning framework." *International Journal of Innovative Technology and Exploring Engineering*, vol. 8, 2019.

[7] Z. Zheng, S. Xie, H. Dai, X. Chen, and H. Wang, "An overview of blockchain technology: architecture, consensus, and future trends," in Proceedings of IEEE International Congress on Big Data, Big Data Congress, Jun 2017, pp. 557–564.

[8] G. B. Mermer, E. Zeydan, S. Suayb Arslan, *et al.*, "An overview of blockchain technologies: principles, opportunities and challenges," in Proceedings of 26th Signal Processing and Communications Applications Conference (SIU), May 2018, pp. 1–4.

[9] M. Prokopczuk, "Robust estimation of conditional risk measures using machine learning algorithm for commodity futures prices in the presence of outliers," *Journal of Commodity Markets*, vol. 24, 2021.

[10] K. Salah, M. H. U. Rehman, N. Nizamuddin, and A. A.-Fuqaha, "Blockchain for AI: review and open research challenges," *IEEE Access*, vol. 7, pp. 127–149, 2018.

[11] T. N. Dinh and M. T. Thai, "Ai and blockchain: a disruptive integration," *Computer*, vol. 51, no. 9, pp. 48–53, 2018.

[12] Nebula Ai (NBAI)—Decentralized ai Blockchain Whitepaper, Nebula AI Team, 2018.

[13] S. Wang, Y. Yuan, X. Wang, *et al.*, "An overview of smart contract: architecture, applications, and future trends," In 2018 IEEE Intelligent Vehicles Symposium (IV). IEEE Press, 108–113, 2018. https://doi.org/10.1109/IVS.2018.8500488

[14] A. K. Tyagi and A. Abraham (eds.), *Recent Trends in Blockchain for Information Systems Security and Privacy*, 1st edn. CRC Press, New York; 2021. https://doi.org/10.1201/9781003139737.

[15] I. Kyriakou, P. Mousavi, J. P. Nielsen, *et al.*, "Forecasting benchmarks of long-term stock returns via machine learning," *Annals of Operations Research*, vol. 297, pp. 221–240, 2021. https://doi.org/10.1007/s10479-019-03338-4

[16]   H. Sebastião and P. Godinho, "Forecasting and trading cryptocurrencies with machine learning under changing market conditions," *FinancInnov*, vol. 7, no. 3, 2021. https://doi.org/10.1186/s40854-020-00217-x

[17]   W. Lu, J. Li, J. Wang, *et al.*, "A CNN-BiLSTM-AM method for stock price prediction," *Neural Computing and Applications*, vol. 33, pp. 4741–4753, 2021. https://doi.org/10.1007/s00521-020-05532-z

[18]   J. Zhang, L. Li, and W. Chen, "Predicting stock price using two-stage machine learning techniques," *Computational Economics*, vol. 57, pp. 1227–1261, 2021. https://doi.org/10.1007/s10614-020-10013-5

[19]   N. Passalis, S. Seficha, A. Tsantekidis, and A. Tefas, "Learning sentiment-aware trading strategies for bitcoin leveraging deep learning-based financial news analysis," In: I. Maglogiannis, J. Macintyre, L. Iliadis (eds), Artificial Intelligence Applications and Innovations. AIAI 2021. IFIP Advances in Information and Communication Technology, vol. 627. Springer, Cham, 2021. https://doi.org/10.1007/978-3-030-79150-6_59

[20]   M. Iyer and R. Mehra, "Forecasting price of Indian Stock Market using supervised machine learning technique," In: C. R. Panigrahi, B. Pati, B. K. Pattanayak, S. Amic, K. C. Li (eds), *Progress in Advanced Computing and Intelligent Engineering. Advances in Intelligent Systems and Computing*, vol. 1299. Springer, Singapore. https://doi.org/10.1007/978-981-33-4299-6_1

[21]   S. Mokhtari, K. Yen, and J. Liu, "Effectiveness of artificial intelligence in stock market prediction based on machine learning," 2021. arXiv:2107. 01031. Available at: https://doi.org/10.5120/ijca2021921347

[22]   S. P. Patil, V. M. Vasava and G. M. Poddar, "Gold market analyzer using selection based algorithm," *International Journal of Advanced Engineering Research and Science*, vol. 3, no. 4, pp. 55–102, 2016.

[23]   Y. C. Hossein Mombeini, "Modelling gold price via artificial neural network," *Journal of Economics, Business and Management*, vol. 3, no. 7, pp. 699–703, 2015.

[24]   Fetty FitriyantiLubis, "Gradient descent and normal equations on cost function minimization for online predictive using linear regression with multiple variables." in International Conference on ICT For Smart Society (ICISS), 2015.

[25]   M. Torabi, "Estimation of mean squared error of model-based estimators of small area means under a nested error linear regression model." *Journal of Multivariate Analysis*, vol. 117, pp. 76–87, 2013.

[26]   D. G. Navin, "Big data analytics for gold price forecasting based on decision tree algorithm and support vector," *International Journal of Science and Research*, pp. 2026–2030, 2015.

[27]   I. Sharma, "Linear regression model to identify the factors associated with carbon stock in Chure Forest of Nepal," *Scientifica*, vol. 2018, p. 8, 2018, Article ID 1383482.

[28]   K. Kumari and S. Yadav, "Linear regression analysis study." *Journal of the Practice of Cardiovascular Sciences*, 2018.

[29]   D. F. Hamilton, M. Ghert, and A. H. R. W. Simpson, "Interpreting regression models in clinical outcome studies," *Bone Joint Research*, vol. 4, pp. 152–153, 2015.

Chapter 23

Knowledge extraction from abnormal stock returns: evidence from Indian stock market

Molla Ramizur Rahman[1], Anirudh Bharadwaj[2] and Pabitra Mitra[3,4]

Abstract

In perceptive, the stock market seems to be enigmatic, with days in which the stock values burgeon unparallel to the initial stocks and days it shrivels to plummet like a falling knife nobody wants to catch. In contrast, companies put their best foot forward to boost investors' morale and keep their company aloft in the ever dynamically changing market by declaring dividends. In its vital sense, data analytics aims to scrutinize and model this dynamic scenario to assist with future prediction and overall decision making. This chapter thus fixates upon one of the applications of big data in finance. This chapter mainly examines abnormality in stock returns pre and post-dividend declaration using data analytics. Our sample includes dividend-paying companies featuring in Nifty Mid-Cap, for the financial year 2018–2019. Statistical validation of actual and predicted returns obtained by regression coefficients through a series of regression runs can help one converge to an inference of abnormality on the dividend declaration. The study reveals an abnormality between actual and predicted stock returns on the first-day post-declaration of dividend. The study provides valuable knowledge extraction to understand the behavior of stock market participants over abnormality in returns using big data.

Keywords: Big Data; Data analytics; Knowledge extraction; Abnormal returns; Dividend declaration

23.1 Introduction

The financial market's captivating presence has repeatedly proven to have a remarkable footprint in various societal sectors, thus impacting the economy. These

[1]Amrut Mody School of Management, Ahmedabad University, India
[2]Department of Information Science and Engineering, B.M.S. College of Engineering, India
[3]Centre for Computational and Data Sciences, Indian Institute of Technology Kharagpur, India
[4]Computer Science and Engineering, Indian Institute of Technology Kharagpur, India

markets empower industries to augment capital and trade publicly. Metaphorically speaking, the performance of a country's stock market serves as a barometer of how well the economy is doing. The cycle of the economy puts forth a picture that may be influenced by liquidity and speculations. With a vivid knowledge of the rise or fall of stocks in a country, one can promote investment. The stock market in all its glory is a boon for potential investors who are seeking to earn a share in companies and industries. In the course of time, investors and data scientists have shown a keen interest in the development and testing models of stock price behaviors. Speaking of which, inspecting the movement of the stock market and its price is extremely exigent because of the market dynamics, nonparametric, non-stationary, chaotic, and nonlinear nature. It is also observed that stock markets are contrived by many interrelated factors like economic, psychological, political, and company-specific variables [1]. One of the experimental studies of financial markets is to test how institutional changes affect the market outcome [2]. The stock market was studied to predict its growth through the years by considering stock scores of particular firms and forecasted using ARIMA time series analysis models [3]. Stock markets being extremely volatile is susceptible to hard changes in their arena. The structure to establish the price balance is extremely difficult in financial markets. The dooming reason for such an imbalance is the repercussion of many imperfections in the market, which does not allow the establishment of total market equilibrium according to conventional traditional models. One of the many reasons is undeniably the heterogeneity of the investor's expectations regarding risk and return [4]. Developing and assembling new multi-factor models are a desideratum and ultimatum to inch closer to the root complication of describing the balance of markets that are underdeveloped.

Stock prices are extremely volatile and are often inflated and deflated for an array of reasons. Among the many causes of this instability, specific news about the industry's revenue and change in the mindset of huge investors and potential investors happen to be the most general factor in this abatement in prices of stocks. A company's performance can have a sharp impact on the prices of the stock [5]. Any news regarding profits or future investments to any positive remarks and talks about the minimum viable product (MVP) to blooming interests and sell-outs of new product release to acquiring a huge contract to layoffs or even mergers or expected takeovers. All seem to significantly impact how stock prices can shape up in the market.

As discussed above, investors' sentiments can flip the market demand of stocks either by making it a "Bull Market" where stock prices are soaring sky high and boosting confidence to invest in one. On the contrary, flip it around to make it a "Bear Market" where there is inevitable plummeting of stock prices and confidence of investors. This shift relies entirely on the sensitivity of perceived sentiments and expectations bolted by the underlying plausible growth rate in the future against present market conditions [6]. Yet, this is one of several factors which prove to be made or break points in stock prices.

Swing in market stock prices can also be triggered by economic factors predominantly inflation or deflation, unprecedented political and economic shocks (case in point – COVID-19 pandemic), change in dollar value/interest rates, or abrupt changes in market policies as regulated by the government. Givoly and Palmon [7] seconded Akerlof's [8] work that pointed out that a market character-ized and influenced by unconstrained and unrestricted opportunities in the presence of information asymmetry can completely ruin the market leading to market failure and crisis. Givoly and Palmon [7] further asserted that information symmetry does not undermine the confidence in investors, but rather it can be seen as "Market-Makers," nourishing and boosting confidence in certain securities that which is already known prior disclosure.

Fluctuation in market stock prices can also be triggered by economic factors predominantly inflation or deflation, unprecedented political and economic shocks (case in point – COVID-19 pandemic), change in dollar value/interest rates, or abrupt changes in market policies as regulated by the government.

Akerlof [8] thinks that if the information is adequately asymmetric, then the market can vanish completely. This paper aims to identify the information asymmetry present in the dividend declaration. This asymmetrical information, also called "information failure," manifests when one seems to have much greater material knowledge in economic transactions than the other. The service provider or the seller seems to have more substantial knowledge than the investor, and vice versa. Information Asymmetry seems to be involved in all economic transactions. This results in the financial strata's negative impact, leading to an unhealthy market economy.

Key delineation from a healthy market policy due to asymmetrical information is that it can promote the growth of adverse selection, moral hazard, or both. The market breakdown will be an eventuality. A small quantity of adverse selection in the financial market can cause drastic up-pricing, and if coincided by flight-to-liquidity, erroneous assessment of symmetric risks or uncertainty about market values will favor the breakdown of the whole market [9]. By using regression and statistical analysis, this paper aims to check on the asymmetric information presence.

The stock market runs because investors invest in different sectors. Any investment roots to profit in the making, and this profit is what investors seek upon their investment. Many researchers believe that dividend announcements portray positive information about the company and make a healthy impact on stock prices. Thus, dividends are the rate of return obtained by the investors upon their invest-ment in the company. The investors can utilize this rate of return to reinvest in the company or for their personal requirements. Companies pay out dividends in mainly two key ways – stock dividends and cash dividends. Stock dividends offer additional shares up to the value of the return on investment obtained by dividend amount issued in the name of all shareholders, while cash dividends disbursal simply issue out monetary funds to all the accounts of shareholders. Dividends often depict the insight performance of the company. As in dividends often gain the confidence of the investors, for it conveys that business performance is up to the mark and well-doing and companies opting to retain their annual business earnings fail to kindle investors owing to a mindset that the company has incurred a loss on that annual year. Erratic dividend pay-outs also succumb to the same reputation as an extremely risky investment.

The effect of dividend rolls out is more farfetched than just the performance of the company. It is often attributed to an increase in the company's stock prices so as I bolster the profits. The increase in share prices unconditionally adjusts itself upon dividend declaration. Be it to drop in its value if the demand falls immediately prior to the previous dividend date, as investors not obtaining the stock benefits on or after the ex-dividend date. Technically speaking, companies that roll out dividends periodically for all their shareholders implicitly indicate the long-term performance of share prices to be on the high verge, indicating the company's high annual profits and performance. Investors try hard and fast tactics to make money in the financial markets. While a few hold onto their shares for years, there are others who just hold their shares for short terms to make quick cash. One of the many ways dividends affect the prices of the stock is the Dividend Rally, wherein investors buy shares before months on the announcement of dividends as to concord to the increase in share prices. Upon announcement of the dividends, they sell out the shares earning hefty profits.

Thus, any imperfections in the marketing system like asymmetrical information spread can profoundly hamper the company's share distribution and profits. Issue of debt over equity indicates that management is confident enough in making a profit from the investment and is a characteristic of information asymmetry, thereby highlighting undervalue of the current stock price. Such an equity issue would imply a lack of confidence in the board fixated over the dilemma of the overvalued share price. In addition, an issue of equity tremendously would endorse to drop-in share value. High-tech companies are an exception to this claim where the issue of equity is superior due to the high cost of debt issue as assets are imperceptible.

However, when dividends are announced, it gets reflected in the share price, and hence there is an abnormality in returns in the stock price. The abnormality in the returns disappears sooner or later. In an efficient market, the abnormality due to any event gets absorbed in very little time. It is in a less efficient market, where more time is required for abnormality in returns to disappear. In this context, we select dividend-paying mid-cap companies featuring in the NIFTY mid-cap index to examine whether abnormality exists before and after dividend declaration in the Indian stock market. Further, it examines the time required for the abnormality to absorb.

The remaining chapter is organized as follows. Section 23.2 covers literature surveyed on various analytical techniques used in the stock market. Section 23.3 designs methodology to examine abnormality in stock returns using big data analytics. Section 23.4 discusses the results over the existence of abnormality between actual and predicted returns. Section 23.5 concludes by highlighting the future scope of the study.

23.2 Literature survey

As the stock market involves processing a large amount of data, studies in the stock market using big data analytics have grown in significant importance. Studies are carried out on stock market parameters like price prediction, volatility, liquidity, etc. There are various macro-economic and company events affecting stock market parameters. Dividend declaration is one such event that affects stock prices, resulting in abnormality in stock returns. Suwanna [10] has calculated the effect of stock price surrounding forty days of the announcement by dividend signaling theory and has statistically observed that stock prices move up significantly after dividends are announced. Further, studies also reveal that dividend declarations also impact trading volume and liquidity. Naik *et al.* [11] observed that there is a short-term fall in trading volume with the declaration of dividends, resulting in a lowering of liquidity post-announcement period.

With the development in analytics and use of the big data stock market, Jaiswal and Bagale [12] have affirmed that Big Data has completely transformed the overall business functioning by finding applications in enterprise operations and processes. Further, they have highlighted its challenges and applications in the banking sector. Data analytics is gaining importance in the financial sector, especially in the stock market. Tiwari *et al.* [13] have used data analytics strategies in order to assist investors in making the right financial decision, by using the two platforms for operation – Python and R. R. are used to predict opening index prices using several forecasting techniques like Arima, Holt winters, neural networks, linear regression, and time series. On similar lines, multi-layer perceptron and support vector regression are employed in Python to forecast Nifty 50 stock price. The authors also carried out sentiment analysis for a period of 9 years. The accuracy was calculated using 2–3 years of forecast results in R and 2 months of forecast results in Python. Mean squared error and other error parameters for every prediction system were calculated. It is found that the feed-forward network only produces a 1.82% error when the stock's opening price is forecasted using it. Shah *et al.* [1] provide classifications of various techniques to predict stock prices. Further, they give us an insight into technical, fundamental, short, and long-term approaches used for stock analysis and opens up research opportunities in this field.

As Big Data uses high-frequency stock market data, modern analytical techniques drastically reduce information asymmetry in the market. Yassin *et al.* [14] have examined the effect of information asymmetry on stock returns, considering accounting conservatism. The study was carried out for companies listed in Amman Stock Exchange (ASE) for the period from 2006 to 2012. It was found that investor with private information gains outstanding returns, thereby indicating information asymmetry positively influence stock returns. But this effect got faded with the consideration of conservative accounting policies.

Various analytical techniques are deployed to extract knowledge-based information on various stock market parameters like stock price, returns, volatility, trading volume, etc. Floros [15] has made use of various models to calculate the volatility based on high, open, closing, and low prices. By making use of S&P indices especially S&P 100, S&P 400, S&P 500, and S&P Small-Cap 600, it is observed that a basic measure of volatility overrates the other measures. Parkinson [16] described the general random walk problem to depict how diffusion constant is estimated and followed by a traditional and extreme method to calculate the same. Furthermore, they concluded the extreme estimation method is roughly 2.5–5 times better than the traditional method of calculation. Finally, the paper concludes by estimating the variance of the rate of stock returns. Mallikarjunappa and Afsal [17] studied the volatility on stock markets upon introducing derivatives by using the S&P CNX Nifty Index. The GARCH model is fitted with option dummy variables and futures to account for non-constant error variance in the return series. It was observed that the persistence of volatility and clustering pre and post-derivatives while listing seemed to be independent of any stabilization and destabilization effects on volatility. It was seen that in the post derivatives period, index returns sensitivity to market returns and with any given day of the week seemed to have disappeared, indicating the character of volatility pattern has changed in post derivation timeline. Bollen [18] measured the impact of option introductions of underlying stocks on the return variance. The author concluded that option introductions have a minor effect on stock return variance. This effect was studied by observing the fluctuations in the return variance of optioned stocks and a control group.

Barclay and Warner [19] examined the proportion of changes in the cumulative stock prices in the trade size category for a sample of NYSE firms by using transactions data. The observations from the study found that stock price fluctuations and movements are majorly due to informed stealth traders' insider and private information. This was on par with the hypothesis that informed trades are mainly clustered around the medium-sized trade category.

While insider trading is active even today, the major focus is centered on sensitive information on the stock price. This move eliminates the risk of forecast errors and rationalizes when dealing with "expert" market makers. This maneuver will incur costs for search and data processing, which counterweights the gains as expected [20]. This is evident as pointed out by Grossman and Stiglitz [20], Shleifer and Vishny [21], and Glosten and Milgrom [22] from their studies that confirmatory information as provided by the market investors will be made use in transactional activities. Thus, this attained information is reflected naturally in market stock price, and any fluctuations in market price can provide information regarding the forthcoming prospects of the industry.

Dow and Rahi [23] claim that information regarding companies many individual investors keeping managers in the dark know profits. However, this information is restricted and has little to no influence on the strategy of decisions in the firm. Yet, if all this information from individual investors is collected and analyzed, it could shake up the market and influence every decision strategy of the firm. Hence, the pivotal role of stock prices is to centralize and limit the scattering and dispersion of sensitive information, influencing the firm's decision stratagem.

Furthermore, studies focus on information asymmetry, which is centered between stakeholders and managers (principal-agent relationship) and investment. Wang and Zhang [24] have illustrated the principal-agent relation in a model that factors and impacts firm investment. Cui and Deng [25] back this study in their theoretical paper on information asymmetry, which proposes a model on principal-agent relation and organization process assets, and governance, which concludes to prove that information asymmetry does affect and influence stock prices.

Ahmad, Muhammad, and their team investigated the impact of information asymmetry on the under-investment and over-investment in firms. By using system generalized effects of moments and fixed effect model for the selected sample DataStream of 280 non-financial firms under Pakistan Stock Exchange. The observation from the study concluded that information asymmetry negatively influences the decision-making leading to under-investment in firms, which, therefore, can lead to the adverse effect of advantageous leverage in firms. Furthermore, the obtained information can swing the market stock prices in either direction.

Peng *et al.* [26] observed that any positive news resolves the uncertainty of investors, and any unfavorable news can worsen the uncertainty to invest in firms. Conversely, Dwijayani *et al.* [27] reported that information asymmetry could have no adverse effect on investment as well-established proven investment policies could diminish any unfavorable effects.

Alti [28] observed that the ratio of sensitivity of investment to cash flow is greater for an investment firm with a lower growth to dividend ratio. Fazzari *et al.* (1998) again observed the impact of asymmetry of information on investment and reported that investment is more dependent on internal firms in relation to the nexus of cash flow. Zhao [29] reported that the empirical study indicated cash flows with greater inconsistencies might put firms from hedging even when they are under tremendous financial distress.

Huei-Hwa, Szu (2020) delineated the relation between stock momentum and information asymmetry. Using winner and loser methodology, it is observed that winners with an extreme forecast of revenue per share seem to have profits against popular opinions in the consequent holding period. While winners in lower-middle grounds of information asymmetry tend to clutch their returns for future holding periods and losers tend to attain the highest profits against popular opinions having middle grounds in information asymmetry, termed as "white lie effects."

Moore [30] subtly implied that information asymmetry within an organization could make the market risker and vulnerable for ordinary investors as they would regulate by demanding a discount in stock price. Givoly and Palmon [7] seconded Akerlof's [8] work that pointed out that a market characterized and influenced by unconstrained and unrestricted opportunities in the presence of information asymmetry can completely ruin the market leading to market failure and crisis. Givoly and Palmon [7] further asserted that information symmetry does not undermine the confidence in investors but rather can be seen as "Market-Makers," nourishing and boosting confidence in certain securities that are already known before disclosure.

Irvine [31] states that asymmetric information and insider trading do not hurt all investors as they give investors its full picture, and most investors are kept in the dark. Hogan [32] claims no evidence stands to support insiders' ability to excerpt reliable and consistent positive abnormal returns in investment. Barbaroux [33] claims that information asymmetry plays a dual role as it can lead to market failures and give rise to many market opportunities. Asymmetric information can indeed lead to a market crisis as it can impede the quality of services and goods produced in the market and effectively shake up the process of allocating resources in the market. It can also generate tremendous market opportunities, as not all individuals possess the same complete sets of information.

Sudipto Bhattacharya, Jay Ritter [34], in the article "Innovation and Communication: Signaling with Partial Disclosure," introduced a model called "feedback effect equilibrium," wherein an agent who possesses asymmetric information can send signals directly through channels to competing agents in the market. This model serves as an instance to real-world financial markets wherein the value of exhaustive and privately held information engenders from the communication from agents whose motive is to expand market opportunities in favor of them.

Stankevičienė and Akelaitis [35] have examined the relationship between the values of stock prices and their change with various categories of public announcements for companies listed in Vilnius Stock Exchange. The study was carried out using a Simplified version of the event study. Average absolute and abnormal returns were estimated, and negative correlation between stock price and its change with a public announcement. The authors gave a trade-based explanation by studying the association between actual prices to both the implied price and the trading activity of the two markets by using a bi-variate model. Chandrapala [36] examined the connection between stock returns and trading volume and concluded that these returns are dependent on the current changes in the trading volume, and stock returns are negatively related to past trading volume. This negative relation could be a manifestation as a repercussion of illiquidity of stocks of low volume or misspecification of future incomes by investors.

Econometric modeling is used widely as a tool for predicting stock-related parameters. Ariyo *et al.* [37] used the autoregressive integrated moving average (ARIMA) for building a stock price predictive model. Stock data from New York Stock Exchange (NYSE) and Nigeria Stock Exchange (NSE) indicated that the ARIMA model has the capability and potential to compete with other forecasting techniques to predict a short-term trend in stock price. The drawback was that the results obtained with the best ARIMA model indicated that it has satisfactory potential to forecast stock prices only on a short-term basis. Anderson [38] made use of various models and techniques to estimate the parameters of the lognormal stochastic volatility model, which assumes non-dependent fat-tailed asset return distributions over time.

Besides such econometric time series models like ARIMA, various other hybrid models have drawn significance. Wei [39] proposed a hybrid model to forecast trends in stock price by implementing an adaptive expectation genetic algorithm. Such an algorithm optimizes the adaptive network-based fuzzy inference system (ANFIS). The effectiveness is examined using performance evaluations, and root mean squared error (RMSE). The experiment is carried out on a dataset of 6 years from Taiwan Stock Exchange Capitalization Weighted Stock Index (TAIEX). The drawback was that the model could not withstand the fluctuations in the market due to some uncontrollable reasons. Mitra [40] highlighted that with varied profitability in trading rules, it is difficult to obtain a better risk-adjusted return of a portfolio from a single rule. Instead, it becomes more efficient with a combination of trading rules. Thus, artificial neural network (ANN) is used to combine signals generated from moving averages of varied window sizes. However, the drawback lies in the fact that the experiment was carried out by considering a low transaction cost of 0.05%, which is realistic in futures markets, where trade settlements are done without delivery. Atsalakis and Valavanis [41] used ANFIS controller and stock market process models inputs, chosen by comparing fifteen combinations of past models so that it has a minimum error in terms of root mean square in predicting the next day's stock trend. The fall of the method is due to the fact that it does not factor commission and tax liabilities, indicating actual returns are less than that reported. Lee *et al.* [42] investigated the performance by measuring the accuracy of the back-propagation neural network (BPNN) model and the seasonal autoregressive integrated moving average (SARIMA) model in predicting the Korea Composite Stock Price Index (KOSPI) and its return. The flaw was that the accuracy of forecasting values is dependent on the developing process of forecasting models, and therefore, the results of this study are also very sensitive to the developing process of the BPNN model and SARIMA model. Further, it is to be noted that it is applicable only to the local stock exchange. Merh *et al.* [43] attempted to predict future index value and Indian stock market trend by developing a three-layer feed-forward back-propagation ANN and autoregressive integrated moving average (ARIMA). The convergence and performance of models have been evaluated. It is noted that when error forecasting is done through ARIMA to ANN in a hybrid model, it encounters an over-fitting problem.

Rahman [44] examined the efficiency for Trend Following Strategy for Indian IT stocks as an application of data science in finance. Network theory is applied to assess banking competition [45]. The commonality in liquidity and examining interrelations between capital and liquidity is performed for banks [46,47]. Therefore, unexplored machine learning techniques can examine concepts of competition and commonality concerning the banking sector.

Extant literature has discussed various analytical techniques in the stock market domain for knowledge extraction. It has also examined the various impact of stock market-related parameters like liquidity, volatility, etc. However, it lacks in examining the abnormality in stock returns in the event of dividend declaration, especially in an emerging economy like India. In this context, our chapter has framed the following objectives:

1. Assessing abnormality in stock returns using mid-cap companies featuring in NIFTY mid-cap.
2. Examining the efficiency of the stock market, on the perspective of time required for abnormality of returns to disappear.

23.2.1 Data and period of study

We have considered dividend-paying stocks featuring in Mid Cap NIFTY 50 to examine the abnormality in returns before and after dividend declaration. The period of the study is between 2018 and 2019. There exist 50 companies in the NIFTY 50 mid-cap. We usually consider the final dividend declaration date for gathering each company's historical stock price data. If the company does not provide a final dividend, then we use the interim dividend date. However, it was observed that 10 companies did not declare a dividend in the financial year 2018–2019, and hence, such companies were eliminated from our sample. Therefore, our sample size consists of 40 mid-cap companies featuring in various sectors like automobile, cement & cement products, chemicals, construction, consumer goods, energy, financial services, healthcare services, industrial manufacturing, information technology, media & entertainment, metals, pharmaceuticals, and textiles.

23.3   Methodology

Dividend-paying mid-Cap Nifty fifty companies featuring various sectors are used to assess abnormal returns before and after dividend declarations. We gathered stock prices of companies sixty days pre and ten days post-dividend declaration and divided the time period into three parts (T1, T2, and T3). The time period T1 (early pre declaration period) describes early phases of dividend declaration, and it includes stock prices of the companies from 59 days to 10 days prior to dividend declaration. The time period T2 (pre declaration period) indicates the time just before the declaration of dividend, and it ranges from 10 days to 1 day before the declaration of dividend. The time period T3 (post declaration period) depicts the time covering the date of dividend declaration and 10 days post to the event. The corresponding NIFTY 50 index is also collected. The daily returns of companies and the market are estimated using the closing value, as depicted in the formula:

$$R_{i,t} = \ln\left(\frac{P_{i,t}}{P_{i,t-1}}\right) \ldots \tag{23.1}$$

where $R_{i,t}$ stock returns for stock i at time t, $P_{i,t}$ and $P_{i,t-1}$ are the stock price for company i at time t and t-1, respectively.

Returns of stock prices of individual companies are influenced by market returns, as shown by the regression equation (23.2). The returns during early periods of declaration of dividends (during T1) are used to estimate the regression coefficients, where slope (Beta) determines the strength with which the market affects stock returns.

$$R_{i,t} = \alpha + \beta R_{m,t} + \varepsilon_{i,t} \ldots \tag{23.2}$$

where t is time for the period T1.

The regression coefficients (α and β) obtain from (23.2) are used to predict the returns during the periods T2 (pre-declaration period) and T3 (post-declaration periods) as depicted in (23.3):

$$\widehat{R_{i,t}} = \alpha + \beta R_{m,t} \ldots \tag{23.3}$$

where t is time for the period T2 and T3.

The actual returns calculated with (23.1) and predicted returns estimated using (23.3), daily for all companies during the pre- and post-declaration period (T2 and

T3) is tested for mean as depicted in (23.4) with a hypothesis as there is no significant difference between actual and estimated returns for the particular day:

$$z_t = \frac{\overline{R_{o,t}} - \overline{R_{p,t}}}{\sqrt{\frac{\sigma_{o,t}^2}{n_{o,t}} - \frac{\sigma_{p,t}^2}{n_{p,t}}}}\ldots \qquad (23.4)$$

$\overline{R_{o,t}}, \overline{R_{p,t}}$, are mean of actual and predicted returns, respectively, $\sigma_{o,t}$, $\sigma_{p,t}$ are standard deviation of actual and predicted returns, respectively, $n_{o,t}$ and $n_{p,t}$ are the sample size for actual and predicted returns, respectively.

The above discussed empirical design provides a framework to extract knowledge to analyze behavior stock market participants using Big Data.

23.4   Results and discussions

Table 23.1 depicts the returns for three time periods, namely T1, T2, and T3. Average returns are maximum during period T1, followed by T2 and T3. This indicates as the dividend declaration date approaches, stock returns decrease. As the study was conducted during the bearish phase of the Indian stock market, all three time periods witnessed negative returns. However, the maximum stock return is positive for all three time periods, with Mind Tree possessing the highest return during T1, DHFL during T2, and SRF during T3. In our sample, 19, 14, and 10 companies exhibit positive returns during the periods T1, T2, and T3, respectively. The company-wise stock returns during all three periods, with corresponding NIFTY returns, are depicted in Appendix 1.

Appendix 2 depicts the strength of the market in determining stock returns. Among the sample companies, it is observed that stock returns for Adani Power is highly responsive to the market, followed by Reliance Infra, SRF Ltd., Dewan Housing Finance Corporation, and NBCC Ltd. Oil India Ltd shows a negative response to the stock market, indicating stock market and price for Oil India Ltd. moves in the opposite direction.

Table 23.2 depicts descriptive statistics of predicted stock returns for pre and post-dividend declaration periods. Similar to actual returns, it is found that predicted returns are negative for both the pre and post-dividend declaration period, with post dividend declaration phase yielding inferior results. Appendix 3 exhibits predicted

Table 23.1   Descriptive statistics of stock returns for time periods T1, T2, and T3

	Actual stock returns		
	Early pre-dividend declaration (T1)	**Pre-dividend declaration (T2)**	**Post-dividend declaration (T3)**
Average	−0.02%	−0.07%	−0.29%
Maximum	0.52%	1.50%	1.15%
Minimum	−1.02%	−0.75%	−2.30%

Table 23.2   Predicted returns for the period T2 and T3

	Predicted stock returns		
	Pre-dividend declaration (T2)	Post-dividend declaration (T3)	Pre- and post-dividend declaration (T2 and T3)
Average	−0.15%	−0.17%	−0.16%
Minimum	−1.83%	−1.85%	−1.39%
Maximum	0.64%	0.80%	0.50%

Table 23.3   Statistical differences in the mean between actual and predicted returns

Time phase	Trading day	F-Stat	P-value	Correlation
T2	−10	0.0234	0.9814	0.4491
	−9	−0.8407	0.4031	0.4573
	−8	1.7469	0.0846*	0.3314
	−7	−0.7910	0.4313	0.6541
	−6	−0.3001	0.7649	0.6216
	−5	0.0965	0.9234	0.4238
	−4	1.7210	0.0892*	0.5477
	−3	−0.5119	0.6102	0.3709
	−2	0.6309	0.5299	0.4349
	−1	0.6971	0.4878	0.3741
T3	0	1.2579	0.2122	0.4901
	1	−2.7330	0.0078***	0.1843
	2	−1.4555	0.1495	0.5878
	3	0.7584	0.4505	0.3573
	4	−0.5366	0.5931	0.3370
	5	−0.9943	0.3232	0.5693
	6	0.1975	0.8440	0.6278
	7	0.7351	0.4645	0.5886
	8	0.9362	0.3521	0.4427
	9	0.6949	0.4892	0.4558
	10	−0.9584	0.3408	0.4238

Note: ***, **, * indicates 1%, 5%, and 10% level of significance, respectively.

returns for the sample companies. Fourteen companies have expected positive returns, as against 26 companies having negative returns, for pre dividend declaration period. Thirteen companies are observed to have predicted positive returns, as against 27 companies in post dividend declaration phase. Cholamandalam Investment and Finance Company exhibits the highest predicted returns, followed by Mind Tree, Jubilant Foods, and Sun TV, during the pre-dividend declaration period T2. NBCC is estimated to have the least predicted returns during this period.

Table 23.3 depicts the results for differences in the mean between actual and predicted returns. The study revealed that there is an abnormality between predicted and actual returns at a 1% level of significance on the first day of declaration of dividend, indicating that stock returns behave differently than expected on the immediately following day of dividend declaration. On similar lines, the least correlation is observed between actual and predicted returns on the first-day post dividend declaration. However, the information of dividend declaration gets absorbed in the market quickly, as none of the trading days (after first day) shows an abnormality in returns.

23.5   Conclusions

Big Data has drawn significant attention with increased digitalization, finding applications in various research domains. With no exception, it is widely used in finance, especially in the stock market. With the advent of high-frequency trading, petabytes of data are generated in this field of the stock market. In this context, the study uses "big data" by using stock returns of NIFTY mid-cap companies to assess abnormality in returns before and after dividend declaration to perceive the behavior of traders and investors.

The research indicated that average stock returns are negative during the early, pre- and post-dividend declaration period, as the time period involved in our study was the bearish phase of the Indian stock market. However, some companies yielded positive returns. The study found that returns of Adani Power were most responsive to the stock market. In contrast, Oil India Ltd is the only company in our sample whose share price moves in the opposite direction to that of market movement. The study revealed no abnormality between actual and predicted stock returns except for the first-day post dividend declaration. The novelty of the chapter lies in the fact that analytical techniques can be used to examine the abnormality in stock returns by considering past stock prices. The research uses big data as strong evidence of knowledge extraction from an abnormality in stock returns. Though conducted for stocks in the Indian economy, the study applies to stocks in other emerging economies.

23.6   Future scope

While predicting stock returns, we assumed that stock returns are influenced only by the bench-mark index, but there could be many factors influencing stock returns. Future research could incorporate such factors while predicting stock returns. We have performed our analysis for mid-cap stocks in an emerging economy – India. Researchers can study large-cap or small-cap stocks to examine investors' behavior over such scripts. Besides, they can carry out research for a developed economy with different market conditions. In our study, we have considered dividend declaration as an event. However, there are many events in stock markets for which a replicated study with this methodology can be carried out to perceive the behavior of market participants towards such events. As this study was performed when India was passing toward the bearish face of the economy, researchers can carry out the study during the economic up-cycle having dissimilar market perceptions, thereby giving different outcomes.

Appendix 1

Stock returns along with corresponding NIFTY returns

	Stock returns			Corresponding Nifty Index		
	−59 days to −11 days	10 to −1 day	0 to 10 days	−59 days to −11 days	10 to −1 day	0 to 10 days
ADANI POWER	−0.49%	−0.28%	−2.30%	0.08%	−0.14%	−0.71%
AJANTAPHARMA	0.00%	0.00%	0.76%	−0.10%	−0.11%	0.55%
AMARAJA	0.14%	−0.30%	−0.78%	0.09%	−0.52%	−0.19%
APOLLOHOSP	−0.24%	−0.35%	−0.24%	−0.01%	−0.12%	−0.01%
APOLLOTYRES	0.16%	−0.06%	−0.44%	0.08%	−0.14%	−0.71%
BALKRISHNA	0.23%	−0.32%	−0.51%	0.10%	−0.51%	−0.14%
BERGER	0.28%	0.66%	−0.37%	−0.01%	−0.12%	−0.01%
BEL	−0.41%	−0.13%	−0.13%	0.00%	−0.15%	−0.05%
BHARATFORGE	−0.03%	−0.65%	−0.73%	0.11%	−0.79%	−0.13%
CASTROL	0.30%	−0.39%	−0.57%	0.05%	−0.52%	−0.33%
CHOLAFIN	0.33%	0.25%	0.59%	−0.09%	0.24%	−0.05%
CUMMINS	−0.10%	−0.49%	−0.74%	0.05%	−0.72%	0.13%
DHFL	−0.11%	1.50%	−0.18%	−0.02%	0.18%	−0.53%
EXIDEIND	0.37%	0.19%	−0.04%	0.13%	−0.21%	−0.62%
FEDERALBANK	0.09%	0.64%	−2.00%	0.14%	−0.08%	−0.73%
GLENMARK	−0.15%	0.70%	0.82%	0.00%	−0.15%	−0.05%
GODREJ	0.22%	−0.58%	0.60%	0.12%	−0.74%	−0.05%
HEXAWARE	0.21%	0.88%	−0.35%	0.02%	−0.02%	−0.45%
IDFCBANK	−0.33%	−0.37%	−0.59%	−0.10%	0.21%	−0.15%
IGL	−0.16%	−0.33%	0.15%	0.12%	−0.74%	−0.05%
JUBILANTFOODS	0.44%	0.64%	−0.31%	0.15%	−0.05%	−0.68%
LICHSGFIN	−0.02%	−0.40%	−0.50%	−0.09%	0.24%	−0.05%
M&MFIN	0.01%	0.46%	−0.16%	−0.08%	0.16%	−0.30%
MRPL	−0.19%	−0.24%	−0.95%	0.11%	−0.65%	−0.12%
NBCC	−1.02%	−0.70%	−0.70%	−0.01%	−0.59%	0.23%
NATIONAL ALUM	0.31%	−0.62%	−0.19%	0.02%	−0.41%	−0.02%
OIL	−0.60%	−0.75%	0.09%	0.02%	−0.41%	−0.02%
RBLBANK	−0.01%	0.41%	−0.08%	−0.05%	0.17%	−0.35%
RECLTD	−0.39%	−0.45%	0.22%	0.02%	−0.41%	−0.02%
RELINFRA	−0.23%	0.05%	−0.13%	−0.09%	0.24%	−0.05%
SRF	−0.67%	0.53%	1.15%	−0.16%	0.26%	0.17%
TVSMOTOR	−0.03%	−0.50%	0.31%	−0.10%	−0.04%	0.28%
TATACHEM	0.17%	−0.31%	−0.10%	0.09%	−0.36%	−0.26%
TATAGLOBAL	0.09%	−0.12%	−0.84%	0.08%	−0.29%	−0.31%
TATAPOWER	−0.02%	0.06%	−0.75%	0.02%	0.16%	−0.63%
RAMCO	0.33%	−0.51%	−0.51%	0.12%	−0.74%	−0.05%
TORNTPHARMA	0.03%	−0.01%	0.40%	−0.01%	−0.12%	−0.01%
VOLTAS	0.16%	−0.58%	−0.80%	0.10%	−0.51%	−0.14%
SUNTV	−0.17%	0.34%	−0.10%	−0.09%	0.42%	0.31%
MINDTREE	0.52%	−0.63%	−0.81%	0.09%	−0.94%	−0.31%

Appendix 2

Regression coefficients for sample companies

Company	α	β
Adani Power Ltd.	−0.0064	1.7168
Ajanta Pharmaceuticals Ltd.	0.0012	1.2315
Amara Raja Batteries Ltd.	0.0008	0.6871
Apollo Hospitals Enterprise Ltd.	−0.0023	0.6275
Apollo Tyres Ltd.	0.0006	1.1550
Balkrishna Industries Ltd.	0.0013	1.0160
Berger Paints India Ltd.	0.0028	0.5565
Bharat Electronics Ltd.	−0.0040	0.6677
Bharat Forge Ltd.	−0.0011	0.6818
Castrol India Ltd.	0.0025	0.8465
Cholamandalam Investment and Finance Company Ltd.	0.0041	0.9503
Cummins India Ltd.	−0.0013	0.4759
Dewan Housing Finance Corporation Ltd.	−0.0008	1.4538
Exide Industries Ltd.	0.0026	0.7905
Federal Bank Ltd.	−0.0003	0.8764
Glenmark Pharmaceuticals Ltd.	−0.0014	0.7258
Godrej Industries Ltd.	0.0016	0.4851
Hexaware Technologies Ltd.	0.0020	0.2967
IDFC First Bank Ltd.	−0.0023	0.9544
Indraprastha Gas Ltd.	−0.0022	0.5285
Jubilant Foodworks Ltd.	0.0039	0.3566
LIC Housing Finance Ltd.	0.0007	1.0482
Mahindra & Mahindra Financial Services Ltd.	0.0010	1.0634
Mangalore Refinery & Petrochemicals Ltd.	−0.0026	0.6420
MindTree Ltd.(30)	0.0052	0.0400
NBCC (India) Ltd.	−0.0100	1.4034
National Aluminium Co. Ltd.	0.0030	0.7558
Oil India Ltd.	−0.0058	−0.8364
RBL Bank Ltd.	0.0003	0.7882
REC Ltd.	−0.0040	0.7690
Reliance Infrastructure Ltd.	−0.0008	1.5812
SRF Ltd.	−0.0043	1.4948
Sun TV Network Ltd.(30)	−0.0007	1.0642
TVS Motor Company Ltd.	0.0003	0.5858
Tata Chemicals Ltd.	0.0010	0.7634
Tata Global Beverages Ltd.	0.0000	1.2146
Tata Power Co. Ltd.	−0.0003	0.7879
The Ramco Cements Ltd.	0.0026	0.5777
Torrent Pharmaceuticals Ltd.	0.0003	0.4643
Voltas Ltd.	0.0008	0.8659

Appendix 3

Predicted returns for sample companies

	Pre-declaration (T2)	Post-declaration (T3)	Pre- and post-declaration
ADANI POWER	−0.89%	−1.85%	−1.39%
AJANTAPHARMA	−0.02%	0.80%	0.41%
AMARAJA	−0.28%	−0.05%	−0.16%
APOLLOHOSP	−0.31%	−0.24%	−0.27%
APOLLOTYRES	−0.11%	−0.76%	−0.45%
BALKRISHNA	−0.39%	−0.01%	−0.19%
BERGER	0.22%	0.28%	0.25%
BEL	−0.50%	−0.44%	−0.47%
BHARATFORGE	−0.65%	−0.20%	−0.41%
CASTROL	−0.18%	−0.03%	−0.10%
CHOLAFIN	0.64%	0.37%	0.50%
CUMMINS	−0.47%	−0.06%	−0.26%
DHFL	0.18%	−0.86%	−0.36%
EXIDEIND	0.10%	−0.22%	−0.07%
FEDERALBANK	−0.10%	−0.67%	−0.40%
GLENMARK	−0.25%	−0.18%	−0.22%
GODREJ	−0.20%	0.13%	−0.03%
HEXAWARE	0.20%	0.07%	0.13%
IDFCBANK	−0.03%	−0.37%	−0.21%
IGL	−0.61%	−0.25%	−0.42%
JUBILANTFOODS	0.37%	0.15%	0.26%
LICHSGFIN	0.32%	0.02%	0.16%
M&MFIN	0.27%	−0.22%	0.01%
MRPL	−0.68%	−0.33%	−0.50%
NBCC	−1.83%	−0.68%	−1.23%
NATIONAL ALUM	−0.01%	0.29%	0.15%
OIL	−0.24%	−0.57%	−0.41%
RBLBANK	0.17%	−0.24%	−0.05%
RECLTD	−0.72%	−0.42%	−0.56%
RELINFRA	0.29%	−0.16%	0.05%
SRF	−0.04%	−0.18%	−0.11%
TVSMOTOR	0.01%	0.20%	0.11%
TATACHEM	−0.18%	−0.10%	−0.14%
TATAGLOBAL	−0.35%	−0.37%	−0.36%
TATAPOWER	0.10%	−0.52%	−0.23%
RAMCO	−0.17%	0.23%	0.04%
TORNTPHARMA	−0.02%	0.03%	0.00%
VOLTAS	−0.37%	−0.04%	−0.20%
SUNTV	0.37%	0.26%	0.31%
MINDTREE	0.48%	0.51%	0.50%

References

[1] Shah, D., Isah, H., and Zulkernine, F. (2019). Stock market analysis: A review and taxonomy of prediction techniques. *International Journal of Financial Studies*, 7(2), 26.

[2] Friedman, D. (1993). How trading institutions affect financial market performance: Some laboratory evidence. *Economic inquiry*, 31(3), 410–435.

[3] Umadevi, K. S., Gaonka, A., Kulkarni, R., and Kannan, R. J. (2018, September). Analysis of stock market using streaming data framework. In *2018 International Conference on Advances in Computing, Communications and Informatics (ICACCI)* (pp. 1388–1390). IEEE.

[4] Minović, J. (2016). Asymmetric information influence on efficiency of capital market. In: *Serbian road to the EU: Finance, Insurance and Monetary policy*, pp. 164–179.

[5] Milosevic-Avdalovic, S. and Milenković, I. (2017). Impact of company performances on the stock price: An empirical analysis on select companies in Serbia. *Ekonomika poljoprivrede*, 64. 561 Minović, J. (2016). Asymmetric information influence on efficiency of capital market. Economic analysis, 164–179570. 10.5937/ekoPolj1702561M.

[6] Barsky, R. and Long, J. (1989). Bull and bear markets in the twentieth century. *The Journal of Economic History*, 50, 265–281. 10.1017/S0022050700036421.

[7] Givoly, D. and Palmon, D. (1985). Insider trading and the exploitation of inside information: Some empirical evidence. *The Journal of Business*, 58.

[8] Akerlof, G. A. (1970). The market for "Lemons": Quality uncertainty and the market mechanism. *The Quarterly Journal of Economics*, 84(3), 488–500.

[9] Kirabaeva, K. (2010). *Adverse selection, liquidity, and market breakdown* (No. 2010, 32). Bank of Canada Working Paper.

[10] Suwanna, T. (2012). Impacts of dividend announcement on stock return. *Procedia-Social and Behavioral Sciences*, 40, 721–725.

[11] Naik, P. U., Parab, P. P., and Reddy, Y. V. (2018). Impact of dividend announcements on the stock prices and liquidity: Evidence from India. *Amity Journal of Finance*, 1(2), 51–63.

[12] Jaiswal, A. and Bagale, P. (2017, October). A survey on Big Data in financial sector. In *2017 International Conference on Networking and Network Applications (NaNA)* (pp. 337–340). IEEE.

[13] Tiwari, S., Bharadwaj, A., and Gupta, S. (2017, December). Stock price prediction using data analytics. In *2017 International Conference on Advances in Computing, Communication and Control (ICAC3)* (pp. 1–5). IEEE.

[14] Yassin, M. M., Ali, H. Y., and Hamdallah, M. E. (2015). The relationship between information asymmetry and stock return in the presence of accounting conservatism. *International Journal of Business and Management*, 10(5), 126.

[15] Floros, C. (2009). Modelling volatility using high, low, open and closing prices: Evidence from four S&P indices. *International Research Journal of Finance and Economics*, 28, 198–206.

[16] Parkinson, M. (1980). The extreme value method for estimating the variance of the rate of return. *Journal of Business*, 61–65.

[17] Mallikarjunappa, T. and Afsal, E. M. (2008). The impact of derivatives on stock market volatility: A study of the nifty index. *Asian Academy of Management Journal of Accounting & Finance*, 4(2).

[18] Bollen, N. P. (1998). A note on the impact of options on stock return volatility. *Journal of banking & Finance*, 22(9), 1181–1191.

[19] Barclay, J.M. and Warner J. B. (1993). Stealth trading and volatility: Which trades move prices? *Journal of Financial Economics*, 34.

[20] Grossman, S. J. and Stiglitz, J. E. (1980). On the impossibility of informationally efficient markets. *The American Economic Review,* 70(3), 393–408. http://www.jstor.org/stable/1805228.

[21] Shleifer, A. and Vishny, R. (1997). The limits of arbitrage. *Journal of Finance*, 52, 35–55.

[22] Glosten, L. R. and Milgrom, R. (1985). Bid, ask and transaction prices in a specialist market with heterogeneously informed traders. *Journal of Financial Economics*, 14, 71–100.

[23] Dow, J. and Rahi, R. (2003). Informed trading, investment, and welfare. *Journal of Business*, 76(3), 439–454.

[24] Wang, Z. and Zhang, Z. (1998). Asymmetric information and firms' investment. *Economic Science*, 2, 66–70 (in Chinese).

[25] Cui, P. and Deng, K. (2007). Asymmetric information, agent-principle, corporate governance, and firms' investment. *Studies of Economics and Management*, 10, 31–34 (in Chinese).

[26] Peng, Z., Johnstone, D., and Christodoulou, D. (2020). Asymmetric impact of earnings news on investor uncertainty. *Journal of Business Finance & Accounting*, 47. 10.1111/jbfa.12428.

[27] Dwijayani, H., Surachman, S., Sumiati, S., and Djawahir, A. H. (2017). The influence of the investment policy and information asymmetry. *International Journal of Economic Perspectives*, 11(3), 2036–2042.

[28] Alti, A. (2003). How sensitive is investment to cash flow when financing is frictionless? *Journal of Finance*, 58(2), 707–722. https://doi.org/10.1111/1540-6261.00542.

[29] Zhao, L. (2004). Corporate risk management and asymmetric information. *Quarterly Review of Economics and Finance*, 44(5), 727–750. https://doi.org/10.1016/j.qref.2004.04.00.

[30] Moore, J. (1990). What is really unethical about insider trading? *Journal of Business Ethics*, 9.

[31] Irvine, W. B. (1987). Insider trading: An ethical appraisal. *Business and Professional Ethics Journal,* 6(4), 3–33.

[32] Hogan, W. P. (1989). Insider trading: Implications and responses. *Abacus*, 25.

[33] Barbaroux, P. (2014). From market failures to market opportunities: Managing innovation under asymmetric information. *Journal of Innovation and Entrepreneurship*, 3, 5. https://doi.org/10.1186/2192-5372-3-5

[34] Bhattacharya, S. and Ritter, J. R. (1983). Innovation and communication: Signalling with partial disclosure. *The Review of Economic Studies*, 50(2), 331–346, https://doi.org/10.2307/2297419.

[35] Stankevičienė, J. and Akelaitis, S. (2014). Impact of public announcements on stock prices: Relation between values of stock prices and the price changes in Lithuanian stock market. *Procedia-Social and Behavioral Sciences*, 156, 538–542.

[36] Chandrapala, P. (2011). The relationship between trading volume and stock returns. *Journal of Competitiveness*, 2011, 3.

[37] Ariyo, A. A., Adewumi, A. O., and Ayo, C. K. (2014, March). Stock price prediction using the ARIMA model. In *2014 UKSim-AMSS 16th International Conference on Computer Modelling and Simulation* (pp. 106–112). IEEE.

[38] Anderson, T. (1994). Stochastic autoregressive volatility. *Mathematical Finance*, 4, 75–102.

[39] Wei, L. Y. (2013). A hybrid model based on ANFIS and adaptive expectation genetic algorithm to forecast TAIEX. *Economic Modelling*, 33, 893–899.

[40] Mitra, S. K. (2009). Optimal combination of trading rules using neural networks. *International Business Research*, 2(1), 86–99.

[41] Atsalakis, G. S. and Valavanis, K. P. (2009). Forecasting stock market short-term trends using a neuro-fuzzy based methodology. *Expert Systems with Applications*, 36(7), 10696–10707.

[42] Lee, K., Yoo, S., and Jin, J. J. (2007). Neural network model vs. SARIMA model in forecasting Korean Stock Price Index (KOSPI). *Issues in Information System*, 8(2), 372–378.

[43] Merh, N., Saxena, V. P., and Pardasani, K. R. (2010). A comparison between hybrid approaches of ANN and ARIMA for Indian stock trend forecasting. *Business Intelligence Journal*, 3(2), 23–43.

[44] Rahman, M. R. (2021). Algorithmic trading using trend following strategy: Evidence from Indian Information Technology Stocks. *Data Science and Data Analytics: Opportunities and Challenges*, 293.

[45] Rahman, M. R. and Misra, A. K. (2021). Bank competition using networks: A study on an emerging economy. *Journal of Risk and Financial Management*, 14(9), 402.

[46] Kumar, G., Misra, A. K., Pant, A., and Rahman, M. R. (2020). Assessing commonality in liquidity: Evidence from an Emerging Market's Index Stocks. *Global Business Review*, 0972150920942902.

[47] Roy, S., Misra, A. K., Padhan, P. C., and Rahman, M. R. (2019). Interrelationship among liquidity, regulatory capital and profitability – A study on Indian Banks. *Cogent Economics & Finance*, 7(1), 1664845.

Chapter 24

Impact of influence analysis of social media fake news—a machine learning perspective

V. Kakulapati[1] and S. Mahender Reddy[2]

Abstract

Nowadays, fake news and fake user profiles spread across online communities, such as social media. This fake news is becoming more popular and influencing people's opinions, emotions, and behaviors due to information diffusion among social media users. Social media influence analysis becomes more prevalent in the activities of billions of users on a day-to-day basis. Sometimes this fake news is spread by posts using some fake user profile. This work predicts fake news in social media and fake profiles using machine learning algorithms. We calculate the influence study of this fake news by predicting the online user behavior analysis. The experimental study evaluates the effects of such news propagation on online users and uses simple prediction techniques. We analyze the influence of fake news on public psychological analysis by using machine learning techniques. The proposed system analyses various possible real and fake news indicators and implementation that correctly represent the classifications. The outcomes show that the influence score seems to be more efficient in determining actual essential factors.

Keywords: Influence; Fake; Prediction; Social media; Post; Impact

24.1 Introduction

Nowadays, people spend their time online on social media like Facebook, Twitter, Linked In, etc. Social media is electronic communication through online websites for sharing ideologies, audio, video, and text messages. Social media platforms differ from conventional transmission in that people may distribute information, comments, and views, communicate with each other, and influence many other viewers' perspectives. Online users spend more time interacting with other users via social networks, such as sharing their views, messages, audio, video, and gaming. Some people

[1]Sreenidhi Institute of Science and Technology, India
[2]Otto-Friedrich University of Bamberg, IsoSySc, Germany

are inclined to search for news like stack market predictions, movie reviews from these networks instead of newspapers, and other traditional methods. This searching news online in spending attitude is intrinsic to the popularity of social media. The reasons for devouring information via online media are (i) more affordable than conservative news media, such as newspapers or television, and (ii) it is easier to post, comment, and talk with friends online. Gradually increasing the percentage of people reading the news on online media proves only 49% of people gather information in traditional methods in 2012, rising to 70% in 2017.

Additionally, discovered that online media beats TV as a significant news source. Even though online media has more benefits, news on these networks is underneath traditional methods. Though publishing online consumes less time and is transmitted quickly to publicize online media, much fake news is reported. That news information with purposefully counterfeit data is published on online media for an assortment of purposes, for instance, monetary and political advantage. Fake news related to COVID-19 is disseminating quickly. That is even before the first corona positive case reports on January 30. In contrast, online communities were prevalent with misinformation, rumors, developing fear in public regarding the pandemic, doctor videos about the pandemic origin, and many more. When positive cases are increasing in India, a flood of misinformation has commenced crowding through online communities.

Misinformation is a significant issue throughout the world, and significant advancements are on their way to cognitive hoaxes or phishing and harmful information emerging AI. For instance, FB (Facebook) utilized a diverse workforce to evaluate the present newsfeed, and they were also terminated after 2016 when they attempted to eliminate cautious content from news items. The analysis of societal influence becomes increasingly relevant in social media. It can serve as a conceptual framework for the public outcome. Consequently, social influence analysis in social media has significant social and practical relevance. Nevertheless, assessing social influence for a specific system has various complications. There are numerous obstacles in this scenario, and I'll name a few of them here [1].

Counterfeit media has been happening for several generations:

- Specific developing trends can be used to recognize counterfeit content online.
- Misinformation analysis is in its initial phases. Several challenging aspects require additional exploration.

Counterfeit statistics are endorsed on social websites to deceive the users for the intangible benefit [2]. Many articles demonstrate that these social network users familiarize themselves with the quest for information from other users who are more similarly interested or like-minded with their sentiments and mentalities [3]. Some researchers demonstrated that this counterfeit information could reinforce even it belongs to the personal user situation [4]. The ultimate strength lies with those particular people who are more prominent or vocal [5]. Social media users' requirements to support the content, or a message, can be decided by the user's perception of the messenger [6]. These messengers or "influencers" may be anyone, from celebrities to businesses.

Many investigations show that social networks like FB, Twitter, and other media platforms increase due to communication or info associated with convinced users or influencers. The exchange of information depends on the ratings given by the persuasive users related to the data. Online users' consequence with like-minded people develops the influence and amplifies the reach hugely because these social media influencers will quickly disseminate the knowledge to many social media users [7].

The intensification of misinformation features the attrition of established institutional fortifications compared to counterfeit in the digital age. This fake news issue is a primary challenging task throughout the world. However, considerable persists unfamiliar about users, organizations, and society's weaknesses to controls by malevolent entertainers. There is a need for new methodologies for securing social media users' personal information. This deliberate situation about the research states the belief in fake news and how the data can spread so virally and quickly. Though false information is a burning issue of present and past, try to solve some challenges associated with fake promotion by propagating recent news such as COVID-19, political issues, and other counterfeit information [8].

One of the social media platforms is FB, where both post creators and influencers share one similar interest. The traditional methodologies and culture's inception from growing up is gone, and online media platforms' spreading misinformation is out of control. Fake news [9] is not eased back by spreading rate and is disseminated through online media virally. It concludes an unfortunate circumstance where anyone can create any false information, influence, spread it virally, and be overwhelmed by customized "facts" intended to impact.

SNAM (Mining of Social Network Analysis) is a technique depending on the retrieval of fake users' profiles. The latter tends to create dubious links to other users in the networks. FB user personal profiles are developed based on their wish or interest. These profiles contain the five dimensions of different personal interests known as the Five-Factor Model [10]. The impact inclination for change in the behavior of social situations. Friendliness replicates how benevolent, reliable, and agreeable influenced communication with like-minded people. Thoroughness resonates with trustworthiness, society, and precise detection of goals. There is solid proof that a person's status on these measurements can be surmised from their online media impressions [11,12], suggesting that every one of these measurements impacts social media usage.

Using machine learning techniques, this work predicts the bogus accounts and misinformation regarding users' news on different online media networks. Machine learning approaches are used to the effectiveness of the proposed technique.

This chapter will remain to underpin the proposed work in Sections 24.2 and 24.3, discussing prior studies that serve as a platform for the work below. Sections 24.4 and 24.5 discuss the impact of misleading information, followed by Section 24.6 on the methodological approach. Sections 24.7 and 24.8 detail and evaluate the methods and findings implemented for misleading addition to its influence, respectively. Section 24.9 concluding remarks and Section 24.10 essential aspects of future perspectives work as crucial topics of a prospective analysis.

24.2 Background

With the Internet and social media, each consumer has become a consciousness, with no manipulation, no actuality, and absolutely no responsibility. The observations are supplied without validity, and for users worldwide, using them on the web browser validates the reliability of the content published to consumers. Mintz [13] discusses the risks of using Online services, such as malicious misrepresentation, disinformation, and half-truths used to mislead users' attention away from the facts being sought. As outlined in the document, everyone's use of technology to promote misinformation, misrepresentation, diversion, cheating, deflection manipulation, and rumors have materialized. Online community networks can be used for factors that were not originally intended. Analyzing online information is a complicated task, and both experienced and beginners frequently fall into traps.

Analyzing the insights of communication, misrepresentation, deception, and rumors is extremely important. The description of content is evident to consumers due to this inherent aspect. However, the many aspects it might accept must be described. Researchers tend to be highly knowledgeable through online communities to communicate certain content to influence people's beliefs or emotions [14]. In online communication, cognitive vulnerabilities refer to content deception to impact the conceptual collection of communication and how users infer it. Psychological incidents in online communities may happen due to disseminating data in various forms.

It might be misleading, deceptive, or rumors. It is essential to distinguish between fact, misleading information, and deception. Misleading information is defined as biased or imprecise news, particularly that which has been meant to confuse. A false report is represented as incorrect facts intended to deceive, mainly misinformation released by the word. Rumors are applied to data, particularly biased or inaccurate information, supporting the political objective or perspective.

Misinformation influences are every perspective of everyday life, including the interpersonal, political, and monetary spheres and the equity sector and disaster relief during catastrophic incidents and humanitarian emergencies. Its goal is to purposefully or accidentally deceive public perception, influence election campaigns, and damage community safety and societal resilience. Because of media networks such as FB, Twitter, and many other online communities, it has become easier to disseminate disinformation instantly.

While assessing socially concordant news, individuals are increasingly accurate, not less. Users generally think there is no difference between facts and opinions instead of being deceived by bias. Accessible interventions that direct attention to consistency enhance the effectiveness of information shared online. Efforts of such a type, such as offering online learning recommendations, are not restricted by specific intensity difficulties that plague evidence efforts.

In the 2016 United States Campaign and the UK Brexit Referendum, a modern type of hoaxes emerged: fraudulent or misleading contemporary "news" articles originated mainly on digital networking [15]. The factually inaccurate factors causing the news and biased reporting are consequences for negative information articles that contribute to turmoil [16]. So what is it about cognitive thinking that causes the inability to discriminate between correct and incorrect digital information?

False news spreads too far broader viewers once recognized news catches its sources either by direct repeat or inappropriate propagation. Investigations have also identified interconnections among social conservatives and deception beliefs. People who participated in the lower analysis were observed publishing stuff from relatively low news services on social networks [17].

The online social network methodology, which measures influence, provides an appropriate tool for studying large amounts of content spread on social networks. The level of influence by networks evaluated by the popularity and shared comments yielded disparate findings, without a relationship between them. When determining trustworthiness, consumers are inadequate observers of reality relying only on information and are impacted by the user, graphic, and communication theme [18].

Propaganda or rumors is contextually dependent; therefore, user reactions are significant. If multiple users consistently respect knowledge in a given origin as reliable, that origin is very likely legitimate. On the other hand, if there are differences in acceptance levels, the fundamental reason is the apparent lack of trustworthiness of the document's statements. Furthermore, if the highest number of respondents receiving input does not reproduce information from multiple sources, his reliability is inadequate.

Gossips gain popularity in a community when more connectivity peers believe things. To bridge observations against reality, a fascinating methodology has been developed. On the way to resolve this concern, algorithmic approaches are indeed being investigated, such as presenting a system that can effectively estimate connection knowledge based on the instances Links shown in a web of news sources.

24.3   Related work

Many researchers developed different techniques to perceive fake profiles and newscasts online. Several methods describe the fake accounts [19–22] based on browsing history similarity, the similarities between their associate networks, systematic analysis of their profile, and their network similarities. A scalable approach [23] demonstrated several fake accounts created by a social media user. The primary technique utilized in this machine learning classification technique is to categorize clusters from malevolent or authorized accounts. A framework-based detection of unauthorized accounts is analyzed by the social network percentage increases and collaborates with consistent online media users with their contacts. Map-reduction and pattern identification methods [24] identify fake accounts. They differentiate between real and fake profiles based on the number of followers and communicating contacts used for individual profiles per day.

Social networks are web resources that allow users to establish a communal or semi-public account by guaranteeing and linking partners, friends, and family members to share their thoughts, knowledge, and connections with other contacts [25]. The influence factors [26] demonstrate the association among their contacts' data and privacy of their actions on social media and analyzed the standard connection between protection commitment with revelation observation. Social media platforms generate and maintain many user profiles and their personal information. Likewise, these networks are possible for illegitimate information accumulators and profilers, such as socbots, which usually use fake profiles that endeavor online media to crop user information. Automated data collection techniques [27–29] described that socbots could send data on social networks effectively. These are mainly identified on public platforms; for example, FB successfully harvests data on social media platforms. It was particularly vulnerable to significant invasions of open social networks, including FB.

The widespread distribution of online social media sites like FB and Twitter led, for example, to alerts about eminence and interaction between users of user information [30]. Twitter claimed that political advertisements were exempt, appealing that online advertising campaigns had adverse effects on power and impacts [31]. In this situation, there was a wide range of scientific literature on the influence and impact of information and automation (socbots) on political elections [32].

The influence of fake news on the recent US constitutional elections shows that a sensitive user connects to his political inclination. The phony news consumption [33] is confined to a few well-defined users, such as the elderly, conservative, and politically active. Spreading Twitter news [34] found that false information applies more quickly and broadly than actual news. As an alternative, [35] focused on the persistent role of socbots in disseminating misinformation for business conversations, while 71% of consumers talking about hot US stocks considered themselves bots. The outcomes of other significant events in the world are affected by false news objects. For example, the development of the Facebook Brexit debate was discussed [36], where the evidence pointed out the effect on news consumption and the clustering of echo chambers. However, the consequences of these and other investigations, as discussed in [37], are somewhat inconsistent. This dispute may stem from discrepancies in the meanings of false news or misinformation adopted by different writers, which, as previously noted, have slightly changed the emphasis from fake to description. The medicine described disinformation spilling out three bogus profiles [38]. The first would be the trolls or tweets of the tangible general population behind them. These trolls use the hashtag #VaccinateUs to disseminate encouraging yet hostile immunization communications, sometimes in individuals' exact degree of urgency to separate the clinical network.

A further type is known as "sophisticated bots," an artificial intelligence method that automatically transmits the tweet message content through Twitter, matching unbiased of making users accept as accurate that the medical community partitioned. The last one contains content contaminators, using anti-immunization messages to draw users to click on links to give users more income behind the site every click. Some research indicated the need, with presumptions or past unchecked experiences, to improve media awareness, methodology, and instruments to track impact, reliability, and demonstrations [39].

Many techniques are available in data mining [40], which helps to perceive bogus accounts. Exceptional features retrieved from current user actions, such as how frequently users send friend requests and accept invitations, by utilizing these features for machine learning classification methods [41]. In one more study [42], the authors provided a China-based social network data set containing a click-stream and developed cluster online user profiles based on their behavior analysis of browsing genuine and counterfeit profiles.

24.4   About influence analytics

Social media platforms are also being recognized to rely on the actions of influencers and associated members. However, specific influencers were considered to express beliefs that share personal beliefs, particularly influential beliefs on social and international issues. Interactions with the dissemination of news have revealed that such influential individuals contribute to influencing opinions in a specific way via false news and misrepresentation in terms of getting particular benefits or implementing such a perspective of the group.

Although misinformation is not a new issue [43], concerns, including why it has arisen as a popular topic worldwide and why it is receiving a growing number of societal awareness, are especially pertinent this time. The primary reason is that incorrect information can be generated and published online more quickly and cheaply than conventional news sources such as newspapers, radio, and television. Social media's growth and attractiveness have also contributed to this explosion of attention. Social-psychological [44] aspects play vital roles in false news, obtaining public credibility, and spreading faster.

Individuals are consuming an incredible amount of time communicating on social media since the proliferation of mobile devices allows them to use it practically at any time and from any location. That is not the situation with conventional media. Furthermore, commenting lines enable connection with colleagues, relatives, and even total outsiders, whether by posts, debates, or like and dislike options. As a result, social media has become a primary route for content transmission. In 2020, most of the US people claim they get their information via social media "usually" or "frequently," Twitter users and Facebook users getting their news from the network continuously [45]. Social networking serves as a place for interpersonal opinions to play a more significant part in assimilation and purchasing choices. Profiling critical consumers might aid organizations in improving the popularity of company commodities, activities, and public perception.

A contact developed among two persons for a particular event is social influence. Anxiety plays a role in social influence. The degree of community influence can be characterized by a continuous numerical value, known as the social influence value, if the influencers feel that the impact would do the activity without hesitation. The term "social influence" [46] is generally described as "the ability to affect others positively." In a social media platform with two members, a and b, and a imposes control over b. The former person is generally the influencer, while the latter is the influencer.

Most online users are influenced by checking review rates, likes, dislikes, and comment other social network users [47]. Users observe that many likes and reviews around a communicative problem motivate the users to trust without any agitation. For example, some movie trails give more hype before releasing, and people are influenced to see that movie. Once the movie reviews, people start how much fake information they believe in a specific film. The main idea behind this impact is that individuals who do not utilize online media platforms are indirectly affected when communicating with others who are not directly affected by this misinformation. This type of communication is spreading fake information in society quickly. The site administrator has been delaying in acting on these issues. A fundamental factor is that this fake information along fake profiles boosts consumption, which means an upsurge in advertisement income and a significant revenue source for most online platforms.

Three issues about false news and online media [48]:

1. Will fake social media messages be detected?
2. In 2017, when the study was carried out, the Facebook flag intended to help people recognize false news was released. Did the cynical flag people about articles?
3. What happens when people get false news, and this alarm flag is also presented?

The consequences reported in November showed ineffective at finding fake Facebook news. Moravec says 75% of research participants have the right headlines, fewer than half of them.

24.4.1   The influence of counterfeit news

Mainly advertisement [49] powers the Internet. Sensational websites with headlines are widespread, resulting in the high traffic capitalizing of advertising companies on this platform. Fake website developers and information subsequently found money from automated advertising that charged high traffic to their websites. The question remains how this misinformation would impact the public. The spread of misinformation can lead to insecurity and unnecessary stress for the public [50]. Digital misinformation is known as false news, intentionally generated to deceive and harm the public [51]. Propaganda can cause millions of people to corrupt electoral systems in minutes, provoking uncertainty, conflict, and public hatred.

Fake news is utilized to describe facts of various flavors, in general, and interchanged: deception, misrepresentation, counterfeit knowledge, publicity, sarcasm, gossip, click bites, and junk news.

Many investigators describe false news as information that might mislead the readers because it is verifiable and purposely misleading [52]. They can represent information generated that is not intended or structured to imitate conventional news content in the form [53]. It emphasizes how neologism's fake news is commonly used with the more traditional false statement in political terms [54]. Misinformation is described as inexact or misleading information. It could be unintended [55] spread because of honest reporting errors or wrong interpretations. However, deception is incorrect information that is intentionally distributed to mislead or encourage the biased agenda [56]. Likewise, to discover misinformation, hoaxes are intended to confuse readers; they are hilarious and repulsive [57]. Satirical news is writing to amuse or ridicule readers, but it can be dangerous if published in a sense like a hoax [58]. They are well-known for satire, irony, and exaggeration and can imitate true stories. Marketing describes the information that attempts through upsetting, selectively omitted, and wrong messages to manipulate target people's feelings, opinions, and behavior. Political, social, or religious motives can be used. Click-bait is described as low-quality journalism that attracts and monetizes traffic through advertisements. The term fake news is more general and includes different information sources, from propaganda to hyper-partisan and conspiracy news. It typically applies not to a particular article but rather to the overall content of an author.

A rumor can briefly describe a story not derived from news events and was not confirmed as it spreads between people. Owing to the complexity of detecting counterfeit content online, it is evident that a viable solution should include numerous components to resolve the challenge correctly. The proposed model is a hybrid of the Naive Bayes classifier, support vector machines (SVMs), and semantic analysis. The learning algorithms are essential to classify the genuine and the fake accurately as each one of these methods may be utilized independently to categorize and recognize false news.

24.4.2   Main factors that affect fake news

- *Deception spread unintentionally*: some misinformation is unintended to discourage the beneficiaries. Benign, frequent users may contribute only to disseminating knowledge because they trust information sources such as friends, relatives, colleagues, or prominent social network users. You typically aim to warn your social network friends about any problem or circumstance instead of trying to mislead them. The prevalent misinformation about Ebola is an example [59].
- *Disseminate misinformation purposefully*: some deception is purposely circulating to mislead its beneficiaries, which recently prompted intense debate on falsehoods and fabricated stories. In general, there are writers and organized groups of spreaders behind the popularity with a specific aim and a clear purpose to gather and encourage misinformation. Speculation and false news circulating throughout the 2016 President's Election are typical instances of deliberately distributed disinformation. For example, a fake news blogger [60] claimed credit for some fake news articles, which came virally in 2017.
- The Urban legend is an intentional myth related to myths about local events, and enjoyment can also be the goal.
- *Fake news*: these are disinformation, which is knowingly circulated and in the news format. These are misinformation that can be used and disseminated in the press and social media [61], according to a recent incident

- *Unconfirmed information*: in our description, unverified information is also included, while it can be valid and reliable at times. A piece of information may contain classification before verification as unverified information, and those verified as incorrect or inaccurate are misinformed. The effects of other kinds of misinformation, such as terror, hate, and wonder, may be similar.
- *Speculation*: the truth is uncontrolled data. One example of true rumors is the deaths caused by avian influenza by several ducks in Guangxi, China [62]. It was a mere rumor before the government announced that it was real. A typical example of avian flu was that some were infected with well-cooked chick [63] and turned out wrong.
- *Crowd surfing*: it is an astroturfing phenomenon that disguises its backers and promoters such that it appears to be initiated by popular contributors. Crowd surfing is astroturfing "crowdsourced," where supporters mostly get grassroots internet participants. Similarly, the information spread by crowd surfing may also be accurate as unchecked information or gossip, but the success of crowdsourcing workers is false and unjust. Some misinformation events cause crowdsurfing because of adverse effects. There are many online platforms where people can quickly recruit. Crowdsourcing has been alleged to threaten some politicians [64]. There were reports related to Crowd surfing claiming to threaten some politicians.
- *Spam*: unrequested knowledge overwhelms the recipients unfairly. It is noticed on different networks such as SMS, e-mail, and social networks.
- *Troll*: a troll is one more fabrication that the user concentrates on. It seeks to annoy a specific group of people and complain about that. Unlike those trying to persuade their heirs, fishing aims to raise the conflict among impressions and eventually intensify the animosity and enlarge the gulf. For instance, a middle voter is likely to vote for a specific candidate after being trolled. In 2016, the troll military, which the Russian government claimed to monitor, explored key election moments [65].
- Hate speech applies to offensive social media material that affects people and communicates hatred and threats. Between the presidential elections of 2016 and hate speeches against some protected groups, a complex interplay was created, reaching the highest level of hate speech during election days [66].
- *Cyber bullying*: bullying online can be misinformation, such as gossip and hate speech, typically in social media.

24.5 Methodology

We proposed combining current ensemble methodologies to increase overall efficiency when determining if the news is valid or invalid. Ensemble learners have improved precision since more than one classifier is developed using such a specific approach to minimize the total noticeable error rate and increase the algorithm's effectiveness. Various methods can be learned on distinct variables to provide different decision thresholds on selected randomly training samples.

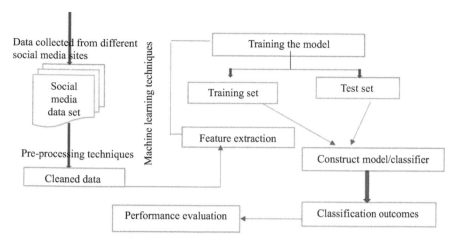

Figure 24.1 The workflow of the proposed system

Ensemble learners have improved precision since more than one classifier is developed using such a specific approach to minimize the total noticeable error rate and increase the algorithm's effectiveness (Figure 24.1).

Consequently, utilizing ensembles training methods, various issues may be handled and alleviated by learning numerous algorithms [67] and combining their findings for a near-optimal conclusion. This work is analyses fake news using different classification techniques such as bagging, boosting, and random forest algorithms and compares their scores. One of the most common and efficiently utilized in machine learning is Random Forest (RF). An ensemble learning machine is an algorithm called the Bootstrap Aggregation or Bagging form. Here the Bagging community algorithm for predictive models is used and the RF algorithm.

- The form of Bootstrap is for estimating a sample of statistical numbers.
- The Bootstrap Aggregation algorithm develops numerous models from a single dataset for training.

Bagging is a slight tweak that contributes to a comprehensive classification. Bagging: Bagging is short for adding a bootstrap. Bootstrap is a replication method when the learning set is small. Several different stages of learning are produced in bagging. When the number of examples is n, each new study set will randomly choose a sample from the original learning set (replication). There may be multiple examples, and specific examples may not happen in a new collection (36.8% of samples on average). Every new learning set uses the learning algorithm as its input. Therefore, get various probably different assumptions utilized to forecast a dependent variable's cost by combining all generated hypotheses.

Bagging is brilliant if unpredictable-based algorithms, such as a decision or regression trees, are used with high variance. Bagging is robust since increasing the number of hypotheses produced does not overpower.

Boosting: It is an integrated system of education that is technically well-founded. The fundamental idea is to learn how difficult it is to weight examples. It assumes that the base learning algorithm can manage a weighted learning example. If not, the weighted models of learning are simulated by sampling the learning collection in a baggage manner. The only deviation is that the definition is not arbitrary but relatively proportionate to its weight.

Reinforcing the learning process involves multiple iterations. The first iteration of the research algorithm introduces a hypothesis based on equivalent study examples (the weight of any model is 1). A belief forecasts a dependent variable (the class label). Both values are subsequently modified. Weights decrease for instances with the proper predictions, and consequences increase for samples with wrong predictions.

RF: It is a classifier with many tree predictors where each tree depends on a random vector's values independently. Also, all forest trees are distributed equally. Suppose n is the number of training observations, and p is the number of tree-building variables (features). With other tree algorithms, we select $k <$, trees are generated and not cut. In a dataset, random forests can handle several variables. Also, an internal unbiased evaluation of the generalization error created during the forest building process.

Moreover, the missing data can be well calculated. The lack of reproducibility as the forest building method is random is a significant downside of random forests. Furthermore, it is not easy to analyze the final and subsequent effects since many autonomous decision-makers are found here.

24.6   Implementation results

Online news gathers from various outlets, including homepage newsagents, search engines, and blogs for social media. However, manually evaluating knowledge integrity is not easy, typically requiring domain expert annotators to carefully examine statements and other facts from authoritative sources, backgrounds, and records. News data may typically be viewed with annotations: journalists' experts, fact-check blogs, detectors from the industry, and Crowdsourced staff. But for the fake news detection problem, no accepted benchmark data sets.

24.6.1   Data pre-processing

When the two datasets are merged, the final composite dataset only has two columns. The course comprises 5405 news items and 1352 news items in the test set—the US political news stories. The sample data is shown in Table 24.1, and Table 24.2 represents the sample of unique values.

Evaluation metrics: Test the efficiency of algorithms for problems in identifying false news. We study the most frequently used indicators for fake news identification in this subparagraph. The faulty news issue is viewed as a problem in most current methods which predicts whether or not a news item is fake:

- Real Positive (TP): when false news annotated as fake news has been anticipated.

Table 24.1   First five lines of train data

Id	Title	Author	Text	Label
0	House Dem Aide: We Didn't Even See Comey's Let...	Darrell Lucus	House Dem Aide: We Didn't Even See Comey's Let...	1
1	FLYNN: Hillary Clinton, Big Woman on Campus - ...	Daniel J. Flynn	Ever get the feeling your life circles the rou...	0
2	Why the Truth Might Get You Fired	Consortiumnews.com	Why the Truth Might Get You Fired Oct 29, ...	1
3	15 Civilians Killed In Single US Airstrike Hav...	Jessica Purkiss	Videos 15 Civilians Killed In Single US Airstr...	1
4	Iranian woman jailed for fictional unpublished...	Howard Portnoy	Print \nAn Iranian woman has been sentenced to...	1

Table 24.2   Sample of unique values of train data

Id	Title	Author	Text
0	House Dem Aide: We Didn't Even See Comey's Let...	Darrell Lucus	House Dem Aide: We Didn't Even See Comey's Let...
1	FLYNN: Hillary Clinton, Big Woman on Campus - ...	Daniel J. Flynn	Ever get the feeling your life circles the rou...
2	Why the Truth Might Get You Fired	Consortiumnews.com	Why the Truth Might Get You Fired Oct 29, ...
3	15 Civilians Killed In Single US Airstrike Hav...	Jessica Purkiss	Videos 15 Civilians Killed In Single US Airstr...
4	Iranian woman jailed for fictional unpublished...	Howard Portnoy	Print \nAn Iranian woman has been sentenced to...

- True Negative (TN): news items annotated as accurate news, when expected.
- False Negative (FN): if accurate news articles are forecast to be annotated as incorrect information.

- False Positive (FP): When anticipated, false news articles are annotated as current news.

Confusion matrix: The matrix is a normally utilized programming model for learning algorithms analysis. Every category of the model shows an example

Table 24.3 Removing Nan values from train data

Index	Id	Title	Author	Text	Label
0	0	House Dem Aide: We Didn't Even See Comey's Let...	Darrell Lucus	House Dem Aide: We Didn't Even See Comey's Let...	1
1	1	FLYNN: Hillary Clinton, Big Woman on Campus - ...	Daniel J. Flynn	Ever get the feeling your life circles the rou...	0
2	2	Why the Truth Might Get You Fired	Consortiumnews.com	Why the Truth Might Get You Fired Oct 29, ...	1
3	3	15 Civilians Killed In Single US Airstrike Hav...	Jessica Purkiss	Videos 15 Civilians Killed In Single US Airstr...	1
4	4	Iranian woman jailed for fictional unpublished...	Howard Portnoy	Print \nAn Iranian woman has been sentenced to...	1
5	5	Jackie Mason: Hollywood Would Love Trump if He...	Daniel Nussbaum	In these trying times, Jackie Mason is the Voi...	0
7	7	Benoît Hamon Wins French Socialist Party's Pre...	Alissa J. Rubin	PARIS France chose an idealistic, traditi...	0
9	9	A Back-Channel Plan for Ukraine and Russia, Co...	Megan Twohey and Scott Shane	A week before Michael T. Flynn resigned as nat...	0
10	10	Obama's Organizing for Action Partners with So...	Aaron Klein	Organizing for Action, the activist group that...	0
11	11	BBC Comedy Sketch "Real Housewives of ISIS" Ca...	Chris Tomlinson	The BBC produced spoof on the "Real Housewives...	0

forecast of a classification, whereas each known as the theory a precise abstract class, allowing us is to see if the system is misinterpreting two distinct categories.

After removing non values, the train data is shown in Table 24.3.

Accuracy: The efficiency observation measures the percentage of accurately predicted instances concerning the provided dataset. Many learning algorithms do better when the correctness is improved. The total portion of real news (TP + TN) is equivalent to the frequency of false news data sets (P + N):

$$Accuracy = \frac{(TP + TN)}{(TP + TN + FN + FP)}$$

Precision: It is a measure the accurateness. This one is calculated by dividing the proportion of forecasted positives by the percent of influential predictions that were actual positives.

$$Precision = \frac{TP}{(TP + FP)}$$

F1-score: It is obtained by measuring performance in terms of accuracy, which is essential for a validation set with an imbalance category:

$$F - measure = 2 \ \frac{Precision * Recall}{(Precision \ + \ Recall)}$$

Recall: The correctness is evaluated as the proportion of predicted positive accurately detected divided by the total of correctly predicted:

$$Recall = \frac{TP}{TP + FN}$$

24.6.2 Bagging classifier

Bagging chooses a few variations randomly from the substitute training set. The newly created training set would have similar trends with the initial training set with various inconsistencies and variations. The valuable training set is considered a copy of Bootstrap. Bootstrap observations are selected from the data in bagging, and each sample is qualified in the classification. Bagging weakens the classification variance through several data sets from random data samples, with rearrangement of the feature space.

Train result:

- Accuracy score: 98.4%
- Classification report:
- Precision: 99%
- Recall score: 99%
- F1 score: 99.3%
- Confusion matrix:
- [[9257 68]
- [21 7110]]
- Test result: accuracy score: 86.6%
- Classification report:
- Precision: 79.9%
- Recall score: 92.1%
- F1 score: 85.6%
- Confusion matrix:
- [[853 183]
- [62 731]]

24.6.3 Random forest classifier

The random wild forest produces the random sampling of a group of decision trees. With many random samples, it repeats the process. This algorithm handles missed values successfully but is vulnerable to overfitting. Suitable modifications of parameters are used to prevent overfitting.

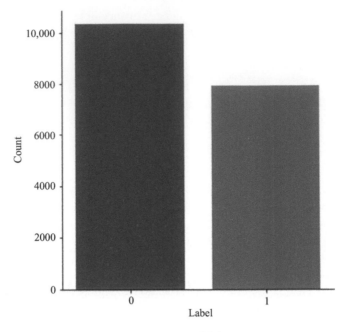

Figure 24.2   Histogram of fake news or not

The initial dataset is partitioned into separate subsets in boosting. The classifier learns to generate a range of moderate output models with a subset. The components which are not appropriately defined in the previous model are dependent on new subsets, and Figures 24.2 and 24.4 represents the random forest classification of fake news.

Train result: accuracy score: 99.9%
Classification report:

- Precision: 1.0
- Recall score: 1.0
- F1 score: 1.0
- Confusion matrix:
- [[9325 0]
- [0 7131]]
- Test result: accuracy score: 88.3%
- Classification report:
- Precision: 79.2%
- Recall score: 99%
- F1 score: 88%
- Confusion matrix:
- [[830 206]
- [7 786]]

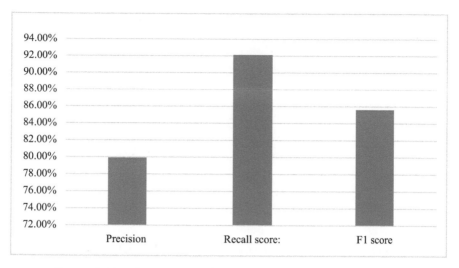

Figure 24.3   Comparison of measures of bagging classification

24.6.4   Boosting algorithms: Ada boosting, gradient boosting

AdaBoost is a meta-algorithm used by the computer that integrates individual hypotheses sequentially to increase their precision. Boosting algorithms transform weak learners into efficient learners.

Gradient boosting is a strategy for gradually, significantly, and sequentially learning classifiers. It employs a stochastic gradient approach to minimize the prediction error by incorporating training examples: including simple methods, a mean multi-model learning process, or the most likely utilized category. Regarding the expected estimated value and actual value, examine the variance.

We used three ensemble methods to compute the roots medium square error classification values: boosting, AdaBoost, and gradient boosting. RMSE displays the degree to which the expected values are similar to the actual values and that a lower RMSE value means better model output.

Train result: accuracy score: 90%

- Classification report:
- Precision: 81.6%
- Recall score: 99%
- F1 score: 89.5%
- Confusion matrix:
- [[7729 1596]
- [57 7074]]
- Test result: accuracy score: 88.4%
- Classification report:

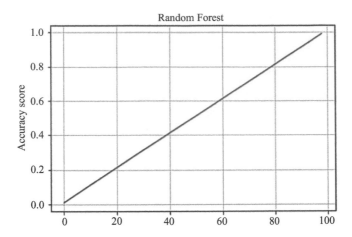

Figure 24.4   RF classification of fake news and fake profiles

- Precision: 79.3%
- Recall score: 99%
- F1 score: 88 %
- Confusion matrix:
- [[831 205]
- [7 786]]

24.6.4.1   Stochastic gradient boosting (SGD)

The gradient is a random variable that indicates the weighted' direction. It informs us to adjust the weighting factors such that the reduction varies the quickest. This method is also known as gradient descent, as it employs the gradient to reduce the loss function to its most negligible significance. As smaller samples are significantly distinct, labeled SGD, training is random. The method predicted the gradient of the stochastic gradient descent using one observation at a time. The model's training percentage drops for each repetition. Because the sample learning algorithm includes all samples to be corrected, the learning algorithm becomes increasingly inefficient as the number of observations grows. SGD is presented as a solution to this disadvantage.

When the dataset sample is extensive, significant examples can be utilized to repeat to the optimum instead of batch gradient descent, which takes more training data once per training phase and is not even optimal once per generation. Nevertheless, one of several issues with SGD is that this is noisier than BGD, causing SGD not optimize each iteration's position continuously. The downside is that owing to the noise generated by various samples, not each algorithm seems to be at the global optimum. Benefits include: relatively quick learning; drawbacks: lower precision, not optimum; difficult to execute concurrently

Train result: accuracy score: 90.2%

- Classification report:
- Precision: 0.8175543540779938

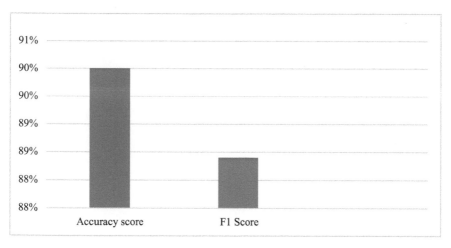

Figure 24.5   Comparison of measures of boosting classification

- Recall score: 0.9966344131257888
- F1 score: 0.8982558139534884
- Confusion matrix:
- [[7739 1586]
- [24 7107]]
- Test result: accuracy score: 88.5%
- Classification report:
- Precision: 79.4%
- Recall score: 99%
- F1 score: 88%
- Confusion matrix:
- [[832 204]
- [5 788]]

24.7   Discussion

In this work, we have carried on classification algorithms RF and the second with a feature selection process three ensemble methods Bagging, AdaBoost, and Gradients Boosting. The data set obtained from various social media blogs is analyzed for experimental purposes. The results shown by ensemble techniques for fake news prediction lie in choosing the input variable and classification method. The Bagging classifier provides 98.4% and 86.4% accuracy for false news content, respectively, for training and test results. The random forestry algorithm produces 99.9% and 88.3% for training and testing results, as seen in Figure 24.3. Boosting algorithms give testing and training data at 90% and 88.4%, while stochastic gradients' boosting

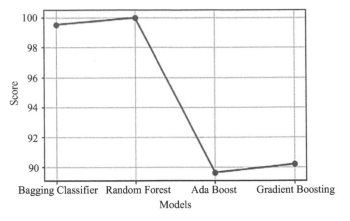

Figure 24.6   The classification techniques comparative analysis of fake profiles and news and scores

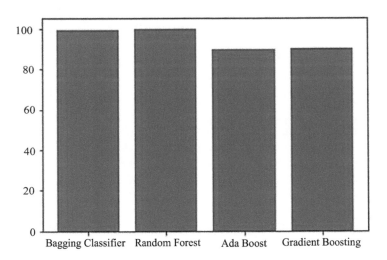

Figure 24.7   The classification techniques comparative analysis of fake profiles and news bar graph representation

offers 90.2% and 88.5%. The RF provides greater precision than other classifiers, seen in Figures 24.2 and 24.3, across all classification algorithms.

24.8   Conclusion

Because of the rapidly shifting social media landscape, it has been originating that the dissemination of false news on social media platforms has a significant social impact. Enforcement and peer impacts, social comparison and mockery, and humorous counterfeits significantly influence false information sharing. We looked at the similarities between several accounts from different public figures. A broad view of these phenomena and a range of misunderstandings are getting from profiles that do not show social behavior. A wide variety of friends is frequently perceived as false rather than social habits and relationships. To predict the effect of fake news, we used bagging and boosting algorithms and random forest classification. In conclusion, it addressed the connection between registered accounts, user data quality, and public influences. We also illustrated the comparison shown in Figure 24.7 of proposed fake accounts and news classification strategies and ratings.

24.9   Future enhancement

In the future, studies will further examine current behaviors as the outcome of impacts on third parties, such as interaction frequency and ratings. In this work, we discuss fake news using various classification techniques. Develop user privacy strategies, clustering approaches based on user background, and different factors affecting fake news indicators. Further research focuses on creating a human-centered computational model using user browsing history similarity and contact frequency with other users for counterfeit news detection.

References

[1]   S. Peng, G. Wang, and D. Xie. Social influence analysis in social networking big data: Opportunities and challenges. *IEEE Network.* 2017;31(1):11–17.

[2]   S.M. Jang and J.K. Kim. Third-person effects of fake news: Fake news regulation and media literacy interventions. *Computers in Human Behavior.* 2018;80:295–302.

[3]   J. Buschman. Good news, bad news, and fake news: Going beyond political literacy to democracy and libraries. *Journal of Documentation.* 2019;75 (1):213–228.

[4]   Q. Wang, X. Yang, and W. Xi. Effects of group arguments on rumor belief and transmission in online communities: An information cascade and group polarization perspective. *Information and Management.* 2018;55(4):441–449.

[5]   S. Lewandowsky, U.K.H. Ecker, and J. Cook. Beyond misinformation: Understanding and coping with the 'Post-Truth' era. *Journal of Applied Research in Memory and Cognition.* 2017;6(4):353–369.

[6]   S. Vijaykumar, G. Nowak, I. Himelboim, and Y. Jin. Virtual Zika transmission after the first US case: Who said what and how it spread on Twitter. *American Journal of Infection Control.* 2018;46(5):549–557.

[7]   B. Jang, S. Jeong, and C.-k. Kim. Distance-based customer detection in fake follower markets. *Information Systems.* 2019;81:104–116.

[8]   https://journalistsresource.org/studies/society/internet/fake-news-conspiracy-theories-journalism-research.

[9]   https://www.mediaheroes.com.au/insights/impact-of-fake-news-on-social-media-marketing-and-small-businesses.

[10] P.T. Costa and R.R. McCrae. Revised NEO Personality Inventory (NEO PI-R) and NEO Five-Factor Inventory (NEO FFI): Professional manual. Psychological Assessment Resources. 1992.

[11] D. Azucar, D. Marengo, and M. Settanni. Predicting the Big 5 personality traits from digital footprints on social media: A meta-analysis. *Personality and Individual Differences*. 2018;124:150–159.

[12] J. Hinds and A. Joinson. Human and computer personality prediction from digital footprints. *Current Directions in Psychological Science*. 2019;28:204–211.

[13] A.P. Mintz. *Web of Deception: Misinformation on the Internet*. Information Today, Inc., New Jersey, USA, 2002.

[14] K.P.K. Kumar and G. Geethakumari. Detecting misinformation in online social networks using cognitive psychology. *Human-Centric Computing and Information Sciences*. 2014;4:14.

[15] R.L. Kaplan. Yellow journalism. In W. Donsbach (Ed.), *The International Encyclopedia of Communication*, New York, NY: John Wiley & Sons; 2008.

[16] S. Lewandowsky, L. Smillie, D. Garcia, *et al. Technology and Democracy Understanding the Influence of Online Technologies on Political Behaviour and Decision-Making*, EU Science Hub; 2020.

[17] M. Mosleh, G. Pennycook, A.A. Arechar, and D.G. Rand. Cognitive reflection correlates with behavior on Twitter. *Nature Communications*. 2021;12:1–10.

[18] M.R. Morris, S. Counts, A. Roseway, A. Hoff, and J. Schwarz. Tweeting is believing? Understanding microblog credibility perceptions. In: *Proceedings of the ACM 2012 Conference on Computer Supported Cooperative Work*, 2012, 441–450, ACM, Raleigh, NC, USA. 10.1145/2145204.2145274

[19] L. Bilge, T. Strufe, D. Balzarotti, and E. Kirda. All your contacts belong to us: Automated identity thief attacks on social networks. In: *Proceedings of the 18th International Conference on World Wide Web*, 2009, Madrid, Spain, pp. 551–560.

[20] L. Jin, H. Takabi, and J.B.D. Joshi. Towards active detection of identity clone attacks on online social networks. In: *Proceedings of the First ACM Conference*, 2011.

[21] M. Conti, R. Poovendran, and M. Secchiero. FakeBook: Detecting fake profiles in online social networks. In: *Proceedings of the 2012 IEEE/ACM International Conference on Advances in Social Networks Analysis and Mining, ASONAM*, 2012, Turkey, pp. 1071–1078.

[22] Z.H. Shan, H. Cao, J. Lv, C. Yan, and A. Liu. Enhancing and identifying cloning attacks in online social networks. In: *Proceedings of the 7th International Conference*, 2013, Kota Kinabalu, Malaysia, pp. 1–6.

[23] G. Kontaxis, I. Polakis, S. Ioannidis, and E.P. Markatos. Detecting social network profile cloning. In: *Proceedings of the 3rd International Workshop on Security and Social Networking*, 2011, USA.

[24] S. Gurajala, J.S. White, B. Hudson, B.R. Voter, and J.N. Matthews. Fake Twitter accounts: Profile characteristics obtained using an activity-based pattern detection approach. In: *Proceedings of International Conference on Social Media & Society*, 2015, Toronto, Ontario, Canada.

[25] D. Boyd and N.B. Ellison. Social network sites: Definition, history, and scholarship. *Journal of Computer-Mediated Communication*. 2007;13(1).

[26] F. Stutzman and J.K. Duffield. Friends only: Examining a privacy-enhancing behavior in Facebook. In: *Proceedings of the 28th International Conference on Human Factors in Computing Systems*, 2010, New York, NY: ACM.

[27] H. Gao, J. Hu, C. Wilson, Z. Li, Y. Chen, and B.Y. Zhao. Detecting and characterizing social spam campaigns. In: *Proceedings of the 17th ACM Conference on Computer and Communications Security*, 2010, New York, NY: ACM.

[28] L. Bilge, T. Strufe, D. Balzarotti, and E. Kirda. All your contacts belong to us: Automated identity theft attacks on social networks. In: *Proceedings of the 18th International Conference on World Wide Web*, 2009, New York, NY: ACM.

[29] Y. Boshmaf, I. Muslukhov, K. Beznosov, and M. Ripeanu. The social bot network: When bots socialize for fame and money. In: *Proceedings of the 27th Annual Computer Security Applications Conference*, 2011, New York, NY: ACM.

[30] M. Del Vicario, A. Bessi, F. Zollo, and W. Quattrociocchi. The spreading of misinformation online. *Proceedings of the National Academy of Sciences*. 2016;113(3):554–559.

[31] Twitter Stops All Political Advertising; https://twitter.com/jack/status/1189634360472829952.

[32] A. Bovet and H.A. Makse. Influence of fake news in Twitter during the 2016 US presidential election. *Nature Communications*. 2019;10(1):7.

[33] N. Grinberg, K. Joseph, L. Friedland, B.S. Thompson, and D. Lazer. Fake news on Twitter during the 2016 US presidential election. *Science*. 2019;363 (6425):374–378.

[34] S. Vosoughi, D. Roy, and S. Aral. The spread of true and false news online. *Science*. 2018;359(6380):1146–1151.

[35] A. Bessi and E. Ferrara. Social bots distort the 2016 US Presidential election online discussion. *First Monday*. 2016;21(11–7).

[36] R. Wald, T. Khoshgoftaar, and C. Sumner. Predicting susceptibility to social bots on Twitter. In: *2013 IEEE 14th International Conference on Information Reuse & Integration (IRI)*. IEEE, 2013, pp. 6–13.

[37] N. Mele, L. David, M. Baum *et al.* Combating fake news: An agenda for research and action. Di https://www.hks.harvard.edu/publications/combating-fake-news-agenda-research-and-action; 2017.

[38] A.M. Jamison, D.A. Broniatowski, and S.C. Quinn. Malicious actors on Twitter: A guide for public health researchers. *American Journal of Public Health*. 2019;109:688–692.

[39] S.M. Jones-Jang, T. Mortensen, and J. Liu. Does media literacy help identification of fake news? Information literacy helps, but other literacies don't. *American Behavioral Scientist*. 2019.

[40]   R. Kaur and S. Singh. A survey of data mining and social network analysis-based anomaly detection techniques. *Egyptian Informatics Journal*. 2016;17 (2):199–216.

[41]   Y. Boshmaf, D. Logothetis, G. Siganos, *et al.* Integro: Leveraging victim prediction for robust fake account detection in large scale, OSNs. *Computers & Security*. 2016;61:142–168.

[42]   A Social Network used in China. Internet draft. [Online] Available: http://www.renren-inc.com/en.

[43]   H. Allcort and M. Gentzkow. Social Media and Fake News in the 2016 Elections. National Bureau of Economic Research (NBER); 2017.

[44]   X. Zhou, R. Zafarani, K. Shu, and H. Liu. Fake news: Fundamental theories, detection strategies, and challenges. In: *The Twelfth ACM International Conference on Web Search and Data Mining (WSDM '19)*, February 11–15, 2019, Melbourne, VIC, Australia. New York, NY: ACM, 2 pages. https://doi.org/10.1145/3289600.3291382

[45]   A. P. Miguel, V. David, G. R. Carlos, *et al.* Sentiment analysis for fake news detection. Electronics. https://10.1348.10.3390/electronics10111348

[46]   D. Cercel and S.T. Matu. Opinion propagation in online social networks: A survey. In: *Proceedings of the 4th ACM International Conference on Web Intelligence, Mining and Semantics (WIMS 2014)*, 2014, Thessaloniki, Greece, pp. 5–8.

[47]   https://www.digitalinformationworld.com/2020/07/fake-accounts-influence-what-you-see-on-social-media.html.

[48]   https://www.kut.org/post/fake-news-study-finds-truth-has-very-little-influence-what-we-believe.

[49]   J.M. Burkhardt. History of fake news. *Library Technology Reports*. 2017;53 (8):5–9.

[50]   Á. Figueira and L. Oliveira. The current state of fake news: Challenges and opportunities. *Procedia Computer Science*. 2017;121:817–825.

[51]   IEC South Africa: Real411. Keeping it real in digital media. Disinformation Destroys Democracy; 2019.

[52]   H. Allcott and M. Gentzkow. Social media and fake news in the 2016 election. *Journal of Economic Perspectives*. 2017;31(2):211–236.

[53]   D.M.J. Lazer, M. Baum, Y. Benkler, and A.J. Berinsky. The science of fake news. *Science*, 2018;359(6380):1094–1096.

[54]   S. Vosoughi, D. Roy, and S. Aral. The spread of true and false news online. *Science*. 2018;359(6380):1146–1151.

[55]   M. Fernandez and H. Alani. Online misinformation: Challenges and future directions. In: *Companion of the Web Conference 2018 on The Web Conference 2018*. International World Wide Web Conferences Steering Committee, 2018, pp. 595–602.

[56]   S. Volkova, K. Shaffer, J.Y. Jang, and N. Hodas. Separating facts from fiction: Linguistic models to classify suspiciously and trusted news posts on Twitter. In: *Proceedings of the 55th Annual Meeting of the Association for Computational Linguistics*, 2017, vol. 2, pp. 647–653.

[57] S. Kumar, R. West, and J. Leskovec. Disinformation on the web: Impact, characteristics, and detection of Wikipedia hoaxes. In: *Proceedings of the 25th International Conference on the World Wide Web*, pp. 591–602. International World Wide Web Conferences Steering Committee, 2016.

[58] N.J. Conroy, V.L. Rubin, and Y. Chen. Automatic deception detection: Methods for finding fake news. In: *Proceedings of the 78th ASIS&T Annual Meeting: Information Science with Impact: Research in and for the Community*, American Society for Information Science, 2015.

[59] J. Bollen. Determining the public mood state by analysis of microblogging posts. *ALIFE*. 2010, pp. 667–668.

[60] C. Castillo, M. Mendoza, and B. Poblete. Information credibility on Twitter. In *Proceedings of the 20th International Conference on World Wide Web*, 2011, New York, NY: ACM, pp. 675–684.

[61] K. Sharma, F. Qian, H. Jiang, N. Ruchansky, M. Zhang, and Y. Liu. Combating fake news: A survey on identification and mitigation techniques. arXiv preprint arXiv:1901.06437, 2019.

[62] C. Castillo, M. Mendoza, and B. Poblete. Predicting information credibility in time-sensitive social media. *Internet Research*. 2013;23(5):560–588.

[63] A. Friggeri, L.A. Adamic, D. Eckles, and J. Cheng. Rumor cascades. In *ICWSM*, 2014.

[64] J. Gao, F. Liang, W. Fan, C. Wang, Y. Sun, and J. Han. On community outliers and their efficient detection in information networks. In *SIGKDD*, 2010, New York, NY: ACM, pp. 813–822.

[65] G.B. Guacho, S. Abdali, N. Shah, and E.E. Papalexakis. Semi-supervised content-based detection of misinformation via tensor embeddings. In *2018 IEEE/ACM International Conference on Advances in Social Networks Analysis and Mining (ASONAM)*, 2018, IEEE, pp. 322–325.

[66] A. Gupta and P. Kumaraguru. Credibility ranking of tweets during high impact events. In: *Proceedings of the 1st Workshop on Privacy and Security in Online Social Media*, 2012, New York, NY: ACM.

[67] D. Ruta and B. Gabrys. Classifier selection for majority voting. *Information Fusion* 2005;6(1):63–81.

Chapter 25

Application of machine learning techniques based on real-time images for site specific insect pest and disease management of crops

MD. Tausif Mallick[1], Amlan Chakrabarti[1] and Nilanjan Deb[2]

Abstract

This research work is concerned with the innovative methodology of the deep learning (DL) (convolutional neural network) techniques, where we implemented a novel approach to accurately recognize the *mung bean (Vigna radiata)* pests and diseases. Our methodology significantly increases the mean Average Precision (mAP) to 77.16% (approx.); in comparison with the existing models, the final result improved by 9.8% approximately. In this chapter, we sophisticatedly instill our designed model to the Android-based mobile platforms which are easy to operate for the farmers and experts. Our advanced application smoothly identifies real-time pests and diseases and deliver necessary measurements on pest and disease control. So, we have assembled a healthy and disease and pest infected *mung bean* crop imaging database with eleven typical *mung bean* varieties (WBU 109 (Sulata), IPU 02-43, NUL 7, LU 391, KUG 479, VBG 04-008, TU 40, LBG 787, VBN 8, SONALI, and PANNA). The acquired database was trained by five consecutive models, finally, single shot detector (SSD) with inception optimized the model. Furthermore, the data augmentation (DA) method with a dropout layer was employed for achieving high mAP value. We developed an Android application where we performed the experiment and the designed model application appropriately illustrate and recognized images after trial and testing. In our database, there are different types of images collected like a plenty of images are diseases and pests affected and the rest images are healthy samples. In a few images, we can properly identify the indistinct objects, which specifies when the pests or the disease affected portion is blurred in that particular image, our application accurately identified that portion from that image. Few images show the diverse postures of disease, and in many images, we have displayed that the variety of colors of each sample. So, our methodology indicated that our model efficiently operates for

[1]A.K. Choudhury School of Information Technology, University of Calcutta, India
[2]Department of Agronomy, University of Calcutta, India

different shapes and different colors of the several classes of the image data set. The two main elements in multi-object identification are feature extraction and occlusion processing, which have been included in our work. The experimental result shows that our methodology is very useful both for pest and disease control and performs superior to the many more advanced or existing models. This application is simple and requires low cost and is improved in terms of ecological compliance, turnaround time, and correctness by color and texture compared with earlier works. This makes the proposed method suitable for pest and disease monitoring tasks through drones and the Internet of Things (IoT). In this work, we have also given attention towards the commercial perspective, because the *pulse* is a high-priced commodity and the cultivation of *pulses* are restricted due to excessive insect pest and disease impedances, particularly in *mung bean* in India. Our approach based on machine learning interventions provides immense benefit to the farmers to tackle the disease and insect pests and to increase the productivity of *mung bean* in India.

Keywords: Mung bean; Computer vision, Deep learning; Convolutional neural network

25.1   Introduction

Our proposed crop *mung bean*, which is also known as green gram, is one of the major crops in India. Huge people in our country are entirely dependent on *mung bean* for their daily food habits. So, it plays a significant role to provide high protein on a daily basis to a large number of populations in our country. So, we require extremely high production efficiency for *mung bean*, which is not happened due to an excessive attack of insect pests and disease impedance on *mung bean* in India. For a better view of the present inferior scenario of pulse production, according to the data analyzed by the Agricultural and Processed Food Products Export Development Authority (APEDA), India imports a huge amount of pulses of 2.23 million tonnes for the period between April 2018 and February 2019. The over-all import of pulses in India is estimated at approx. 2.5 million tonnes in the year 2019, which is worth about 80 billion Indian currency [1]. There are many pest and disease control actions that have been taken by both different state and central government to protect *mung bean* from pests & diseases, and also try to raise the growth rate of production of *mung bean*. However, the farmers are used or straight to point misused the pesticides excessively to overcome the problem, which generally related to huge economic losses and serious environmental contamination in our country [2,3]. Look at the statistics, the annual worldwide crop production damages are about 20–45% due to diseases and pests attacks according to the final estimation of the Food and Agriculture Organization of the United Nations (FAO), in spite of the huge pesticides uses, which is near about two million tons of pesticides [4]. Therefore, precise and well-timed analysis & diagnosis of *mung bean* pests & disease is essential for high and healthy *mung bean* production. For a long time, only a few numbers of crop experts and experienced farmers properly identify the pest in *mung bean* but in a lengthy manner and others only dependent on pesticide and other insignificant procedures.

However, the earlier artificial identification methods for pest identification were subjective, inefficient, and also delay in the time of execution. Therefore, it is urgently essential for designing and developing an independent, effective & firm technique for accurately identifying diseases & pests in *mung bean*. We need a unique model because after the acquisition of a large number of images, for advance several types of processing, the pest & disease images must be enlarged, here the dataset which is used for processing is mainly images, we know very well that it is exciting job for the experts of computer vision (CV) domain for the recognition of objects in images [5]. The CV techniques are used for automatic feature extraction of image data, which illustrates the extensive exploration and perception of beneficial details from classified or section of image set [6]. There are different jobs of CV performed which include categorization, localization, object recognition, segmentation [7], etc. One of the key feature is object identification which is the procedure to discover real-world occurrence objects from imageries or videos [8]; more specifically, bounding boxes and class labels are generated in object identification for the localization & detection of several objects from each image data. Commonly, we follow three predictable phases for object identification, in the first step, the extraction of characteristics from target image, the second step selects the functional identification window, and lastly develop the classifier [9]. The conventional identification algorithms lack robustness and sensitivity to diversity variations as they are assembled on theory base structures and low accuracy training architectures. In addition, the section selection tactics are primarily established on a sliding window which is computationally very much costly and also takes a long time for execution, as a result, it usually produces redundant windows [10]. In most of all CV methods, the recent identification algorithm deployed on deep learning (DL) techniques with improved execution rate in each aspect than the conventional identification methods which are used in earlier [11]. High-dimensional, computational, sequential data, etc. are frequently and efficiently understood by the DL techniques and DL attained definite & truthful results in various areas of audio recognition, speech identification, social media purifying, instrument interpretation, bioinformatics, drug design, medical imagery study, an endorsement scheme and programmed driving, etc. [12,13]. The performance of deep neural networks are consistent and the adaptability is high for the several kinds of variety of image dataset, so usually, the networks do not need to design the features manually [14]. We notice that the instantaneous advancement of DL in object identification in recent years, there are many more deep and accurate identification models has been proposed but unfortunately, in many cases, they are not constructed. We learned and know about the usual identifiers, which contain faster region-based convolutional neural networks [15], region-based fully convolutional network [16], You Only Look Once [17], Single Shot Multi-Box Detector [18], and so on. Most of the shared evaluations for the two-stage identifiers are both used for précised identification but the drawback is that they are both require a big computational cost. In the case of one-stage identifiers, for example, YOLO and single shot detector (SSD), which have more speed in the time of execution but lower the accuracy level, which means they are suitable for mobile devices only. In this proposed work, we have chosen the SSD as the identification framework after the mean Average Precision (mAP) values, model size and detection time have been compared with previous working models. Recently, we observe the emerging interest to use the SSD identification frameworks in sustainable agriculture to determine plant infections and pest control [19]. Only a few DL-based research studies show that the pest and disease identification models are capable of pest and disease identification jobs in comparison with the conventional identification algorithms and have improved adaptability in different surroundings, however, they are not maintaining the 100% accuracy rate or not efficiently working in some cases. For this study, we face some difficulties, after studying them we categorized three major issues: initially, huge absence of accessible open pest and disease dataset, so in the maximum number of existing research works and the scientists employ insect and disease images assembled in perfect laboratory surroundings [20]. Second, the cultivation land background is very complicated in different climates and weather conditions, so the already existing pest and disease models unable to directly employed for pest and disease identification process, so the procedure requires additional training and testing phases to attain the finest and accurate performance. Third, the tools used for pest and disease identification system which are performed presently are too expensive and large and also provide uncertain and inefficient results. In this work, a variety of *mung bean* pest and disease identification models of deep convolutional neural networks have been engaged and examined on the *mung bean* pest and disease image dataset to build an automatic and efficient identification model for properly identify and diagnosis the pests and diseases of *mung bean* in the different climates and environments. Furthermore, we developed an Android-based application for pest and disease identification, which was designed and established using DL techniques. The complete work is organized as follows: literature survey and earlier research works are discussed in Unit two. In the next Unit, we analyzed the *mung bean* pest and disease dataset and methodologies. After that, in the following Unit, the final performance result of five models and two proposed methods are compared to increase the mAP. In the successive module, our team developed and analyzed a disease and pest identification system of *mung bean* entirely based on the Android platform. Eventually, our team provided a conclusion in the final part.

25.2   Literature survey and related works

Our team represents some significant object identification approaches briefly in the related and literature survey module. Generally, there are two sets of identifiers as one-stage and two-stage identifiers are used in advance object identification methods. These kinds of proposed developments of identification executions are established on regular data sets, like the MS COCO [21], PASCAL VOC [22], and ILSVRC [23]. The two-stage identifiers have used two types of networks as box proposal and classification network, for example the faster region-based convolutional neural network, the region-based fully convolutional network & feature pyramid network [24]. These methods extracts key characteristics from the data set and generate Region of Interests (RoIs). Region of Interests (RoIs) usually applied in case of object classification and bounding-box regression. The earlier method for Object Identification is one of the applications of faster region based convolutional neural network. Then, several sustainable and highly upgraded models have been proposed includes compound convolution layers, which want enormous computation volume. At that point, faster region-based convolutional neural network resolves a rapidity jam or block for both fast region-based convolutional neural network and region-based convolutional neural network, by means of, this one proposed an idea of implementing region proposal network (RPN) that initiates the region proposals. Henceforth, region-based fully convolutional network is suggested for additional improvement of overall capabilities. Currently, the object identification procedures require speediness and great effectiveness.

In one-stage identifiers like YOLO and SSD, the faster speed and high efficiency are definitely generated; this type of algorithms generally performs quicker, however achieves a lesser mAP in comparison with standard two-phase identifiers. In case of one-stage identifiers, the region proposals & classification are combined into single network. Without involving region proposals, the bounding boxes and classification are concurrently anticipated in several spots of image dataset. Although, the "You Only Look Once" performs instantly and processed the image on convolutional neural network on one occasion. SSD can identify multiple scales from a multi-scale feature map. Whereas those types of models may be employed for object identification, it is hard to discover a model which can achieve appropriate stability between speed and accuracy at the time of execution. For many years, the sliding window dominates in the arena of object identification. For example, we get that Ding and Taylor [25] have accumulated and arranged data set of the pictures of the coddling moth from the field, and then they have been successfully proposed a spontaneous moth identification application established on Sliding Window for correctly predict the calculation and identification of the pest. The desired results of their subsequent work demonstrated that the optimum model precision is 93.4%, and the minimal log-average error rate 9.16%. On the other hand, this method is undesirable because this approach is computationally very much expensive and only appropriate for a particular work. As soon as it runs in non-laboratory surroundings, the experimentation cannot touch satisfactory identification performance. At present, a large number of object identification approaches of DL have been employed in the field of agronomy, essentially for the accurate disease and pest identification of crops. In the domain of Object identification, there is a massive change that has occurred, and the region proposals successfully replaced the original sliding window approaches [26]. To achieve accurate and effective key parts of tomato identification, Zhou *et al.* [27] offered new classification network architecture established on visual geometry group network (VGGNet) and configured with transformer-based end-to-end network

(TD-Net) based on the technology of fast region-based convolutional neural network, then finally, a tomato plant parts identifier is developed. As a result, for fruits, flowers, and stem, the average precision (AP) of the identifier was 81.64%, 84.48%, and 53.94%; separately, performance and speed of the identifier have been much more enriched in comparison with region-based convolutional neural network and fast region-based convolutional neural network. Fu *et al.* [28] have accomplished a research experiment on kiwi-fruit, then designed and established a LeNet network based Kiwifruit detection model, which suitably calculated the intersection and blockage of multi-cluster on kiwi-fruit. The overall recognition rate achieved a considerably high rate of 89.29%, and the regular time to recognize each fruit is 0.27 second, so it is fast and decent and could be applied for the use of robotics in the field of agriculture. For the classification work, researchers' use various techniques for generating a prediction model mainly established on spectral features of imagery data set and the model produced satisfactory outcomes [29–32].

25.3   Resources and approaches

25.3.1   Image data-set

25.3.1.1   Image data assemble

At first, we designed a novel *mung bean* pest and disease dataset in two ways as the *mung bean* image dataset is not sufficiently available in the public domain. First, we collected pictures from different Internet sources. But at the advanced stage in that procedure, we faced a major problem, the resolution and brightness of the pictures which we collected from the Web sources are different and the desired pests & diseases are not in appropriate shape and different postures shown in the images. Second, we are capturing both the laboratory and field images to improve the quality and quantity of the dataset. In case of cultivation land, mobile device (Redmi Note 7 Pro, Samsung In.) and digital camera (Nikon, Sony) are provided for gathering living pests and disease infected imageries from different angle, positions from our University of Calcutta farm situated in Baruipur, West Bengal in India. The acquired images contain untidiness, and few image quality is poor [33], so our preferred pests and diseases are little and unclear. At the same time, the pests and diseases images were taken at the cultivation land using a digital camera in sufficient lighting conditions and other well-being conditions for appropriate capturing to ensure better quality and shapes. The image capturing device was designed and built to capture images from the hydroponic system which is displayed in Figure 25.1 [34]. We used a hydroponic system which contains a digi-cam and lights, for holding the digi-cam & light sources we have used tripods; the camera is directly connected with the desktop computer for better access; we also used Wi-Fi enabled smart mobile phone to transfer the captured images directly from the digi-cam. The *mung bean* pests and diseases surely outspread on the system uniformly apart from the healthy plants, so we can easily complete the image segmentation and identification process. A total of 2698 *mung bean* pests and disease; also healthy images were obtained under multi-angle shooting or

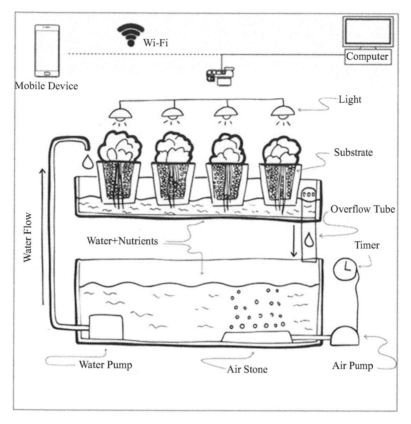

Figure 25.1 An image capturing hydroponic system

capturing by these ways using the digital camera. We combined the images into JPEG format, after-that named and labeled them in consecutive numbers [35].

25.3.1.2 Dataset arrangement

In the time to arrange the data, we filtered the dataset by hand to dodge the annotation faults and duplication of imageries affected by disease and pest inter-species similarities. To make our job more precise and clearer, the image annotation tool LabelImg (v1.3.0) was applied by us so we can generally spot the classifications and rectangular bounding boxes of the pest and disease imageries.

In Table 25.1, we demonstrate the total number of images that are collected and the number of objects for every sample. The dataset contains 11 typical *mung bean* verities. As shown in Table 25.1, our dataset has an unequal class of collected images and the quantity of several data differs significantly. Here, 240 images are collected for LBG 787 variety but we acquired only 40 images of WBU 109. VBN 8 has 410 annotated objects while WBU 109 only has 25 objects.

Moreover, SONALI has 600 images and has the highest number no. of objects of 710. Additionally, PANNA variety has both a sufficient number of images and objects. When the collected images are not sufficient in the dataset, so we essentially rise the number of images to illustrate that most of the images have a certain aspect ratio in comparison with the small number of images (Figure 25.2) [36].

Table 25.1   Details of the mung bean *species dataset*

Variety	Season	No. of images	No. of objects
WBU 109 (Sulata)	Spring	40	25
IPU 02-43	Kharif	150	264
NUL 7	Kharif	180	285
LU 391	Spring	200	320
KUG 479	Spring	180	380
VBG 04-008	Kharif	178	327
TU 40	Rabi	215	314
LBG 787	Rabi and Summer	240	384
VBN 8	Summer Irrigated	205	410
SONALI	Post-Kharif	600	710
PANNA	Post-Kharif	510	580
Total	–	2698	3589

Figure 25.2   A representation of damage and healthy leaves of mung bean. Imageries (a) collected from web; (b) captured at cultivation land; (c) captured in laboratory

25.3.1.3 Data augmentation (DA) methodology

DA is the procedure of modifying the training data-set to multiple the quantity of the training data-set irrespective of keeping the labels unchanged. DA is a regular approach that is used to rise the quantity of training data-set and the data-set has been chosen for definite jobs [36,37]. So, we artificially multiple the data and spontaneously the interventions are also increased, which helped us to overcome the difficulty such as inadequate data and extreme label distribution [38], and it also improved the generalization of the model. We can divide the DA method into two groups, one group is called regular DA and another is Complex DA. Regular DA calculation is easy to implement and a low-cost method [39]. Whereas the complex DA uses a domain-specific synthesis of complex DA, it artificially enlarges the dataset and generates additional training data however the cost of computation process is high for complex DA and the implementation of this method is also time-consuming. Thus, the regular DA method is a more applicable technique for small data sets and for the experimental environments set up in this work. Usually, the object identification procedure is extravagant by some intervention, for example occlusion, view-point, position and variation of brightness, etc.

In the DL process, the common DA is used which includes techniques like cropping, rotation, color jittering, and also mixing noise to produce multiple images and separately the images can duplicate a set in the physical world. The particular patterns of DA are shown in Figure 25.3(a–j). Our team employed several DA

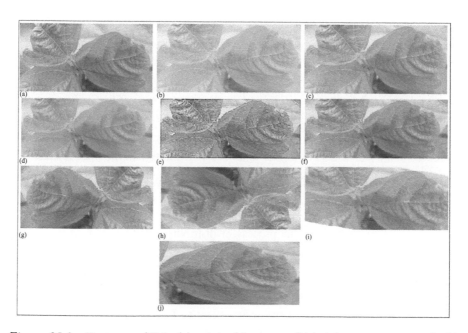

Figure 25.3   Patterns of DA: (a) original imagery; (b) brightness accustomed; (c) contrast accustomed; (d) saturation accustomed; (e) sharpness adjusted; (f) softness adjusted; (g) reversed horizontally; (h) flipped diagonally; (i) interchanged 45 degree; (j) random crop

procedures on the original image set which includes brightness, contrast, saturation, sharpness, softness, image flipping, rotation, random cropping, translation, and so on.

25.3.2 Methodologies

In our research work, our team generally concentrated on three main frameworks for object identification: (a) faster region-based convolutional neural network, (b) region-based fully convolutional network, and the third is SSD, also dropout methodology is applied for overcoming the overfitting obstacles.

25.3.2.1 Dropout

We know that due to the overfitting obstacle, it is extremely hard to train large neural networks for a dataset. In a shorter time, it is non-viable to execute a model incorporation to avoid overfitting. Thus, in neural networks, we implement the "Dropout" process, that is simultaneously drop out the entities to solve this difficulty. We acquired innovative fine networks, which are easier to practice smaller sub-models with improved execution after successfully removed the units. For every unit the dropout is random. For instance, static probability p is unable to function individually with each unit.

25.3.2.2 Faster region-based convolutional neural network (R-CNN)

Precisely, the faster region-based convolutional neural network process is originated to exchange the previous sluggish discerning search algorithm by way of the assistance of RPN. Just because of this, the RPN executes more quickly and accurately from earlier. Faster R-CNN procedures have 4 phases: Region Proposal Generation, Feature Extraction, Classification and Location Optimization. To record the imageries irrespective to their dimension, shape, etc., the RPN applies convolutional neural network and precisely generated a collection of region proposals which also includes refine candidate structures and categorizations. Faster R-CNN output will determine very fixed placed an object or background. So the inference speed and better accuracy increase significantly and have 10× more than previous results.

25.3.2.3 Region-based fully convolutional network (R-FCN)

A completely sectoral convolutional network is R-FCN that recommends the area-sensitive score maps. The advantage of this method is avoiding supernumerary calculation. This model follows the process of distributed computation on the whole area of the image to increases the overall speed. On the way for produce, the area-sensitive score maps the convolution layer is added. R-FCN can simply resolve the ambiguity between the object identification relocation-variance and the image classification relocation-invariance. In several kinds of research, we noticed in a shorter time R-FCN can obtain equivalent accurateness to faster R-CNN [16,40,41], that indicates R-FCN maintains a decent equilibrium among speediness & accurateness.

25.3.2.4 SSD

SSD runs quicker than faster region-based convolutional neural network like the region-based fully convolutional network, nevertheless, the functioning model is considerably not the same as region-based fully convolutional network. The classifications of bounding boxes with various aspect ratios are instantaneously anticipated in several spots on the target image. In different convolutional layers, the features are extracted which will support the multiple scales and also decrease the size. Using the appropriate kernel, the calculation is executing at every individual position and produces decent accuracy of every box. Several studies show for the low-resolution image the SSD performs better which indicates the model will succeed a superior score because of the small size of pest and disease posture and shape. We decided to select the meta-architecture SSD which is practically optimal identification model because it has multi-scale and features with extraordinary accuracy. In Figure 25.4, we have shown the complete implementation procedure of the SSD network.

Throughout the training phase, our team possess the input image initially. This shared convolution layer of inception will generate feature maps. And finally, for each and every object we obtained the location and label the information.

25.3.2.5 Evaluation indicators

As in the time of evaluation, in a modest exact metric, the significant result of the non-uniform distribution of the dataset cannot quantify the performance of the model properly. Thus, the typical metric for this research work is established on PASCAL VOC 2007 [19] to properly assess the simplification capability of this model. In Table 25.2, the evaluation notation is used [42]. In this work, precision & recall both are generally applied to calculate how smoothly the certain objects identified in comparison with the reference objects. The recall is explained as the fraction of properly identified items amid most of the objects which must be identified. Precision is the fraction of entire positive class samples beyond that class. Precision is correct proportion of identified items [43].

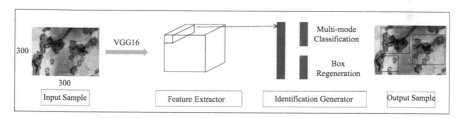

Figure 25.4   A figure of the SSD-based identification network

Table 25.2   Confusion matrix

	Definite positive	**Definite negative**
Predicted positive	True positives (TP)	False positives (FP)
Predicted negative	False negatives (FN)	True negatives (TN)

The precision and recall both calculated by way of

$$\text{Precision} = TP/(TP + FP')$$
$$\text{Recall} = TP/(TP + FN)$$

(25.1)

The overall representation of a specified class is defined by the computational value of AP. Generally, for object identification, we employed this type of common performance indicator in our model for the assessment of the performance of the collected dataset. As a whole, AP expresses its score as the mean precision of a set of equally positioned recalls standards (0, 0.1, 0.2, 0.3 . . . 1) and summarizes the outline of the precision/recall curve:

$$AP = 1/11 \sum_{r \in \{0, 0.1, \ldots, 1\}} Pinterp\,(r)$$

(25.2)

The *Pinterp (r̂)* is described as

$$Pinterp(\hat{r}) = \max_{\hat{r}\,:\,\hat{r} \geq r} P(\hat{r})$$

(25.3)

where $p\,(\hat{r})$ is the computed precision on the time of recall $(\hat{r})$.

The mAP is the mean value of entire AP values in multi-class identification. We applied both AP and mAP for analyzing the performance of each individual model on image-set. The both AP and mAP are the metrics which are selected for the models.

An evaluation metric, Intersection over Union (IoU) is used for location accurateness. IoU calculates the physical object borderline which is very beneficial and generates the pest and disease boundary by implementing the algorithm of an image.

TP: positively labeled the truthful samples. FP: negative samples wrongly considered as positive. FN: positive samples falsely considered as negative. TN: relate to negatives properly considered as negative.

The two conditions are followed by the IoU, first is, when the value of IoU is 1, it specifies that the two are absolutely equivalent.

Second, once the value of Intersection over Union is 0, it determines that the predicted bounding box and the true bounding box cannot intersection at each other.

At our experiment, the value of IoU was 0.6. We used a formulation to compute the IoU (given below):

$$IoU = \frac{\text{area (true bounding box} \cap \text{predicted bounding box)}}{\text{area (true bounding box} \cup \text{predicted bounding box)}} > 0.5$$

(25.4)

25.4   Experiments

The training and trail samples were executed on a computer equipped system. In Table 25.3, we presented the complete description of the system which is

Table 25.3   Experiment apparatus

Apparatus	Configuration
Processor	Intel Core i7 10700KF CPU
Memory	64 GB
Graphics	NVIDIA GeForce RTX 3070
Operating system	Linux Ubuntu 20.10 LTS "Focal Fossa"

employed. A processor of Intel Core i7 10700KF, 64 Gigabyte RAM and two NVIDIA GeForce RTX 3070 GPU are used to conduct the parallel-computing process.

At the time of experiments, we integrated the identification model deployed on a pre-trained model, which was processed on the COCO dataset to overcome the difficulty of the shortage of data. In that case, faster region-based convolutional neural network and region-based fully convolutional network models are the training models that performed accurately applying stochastic gradient descent (SGD) which has an impetus of 0.8–0.9 with a preliminary learning rate of 0.0001 and batch size of 1. The convergence rate of that network was affected by the initialization of the weight. The normal distribution process has randomly initialized the weight of all system-network layers with the mean of 0 and the standard deviation of 0.01. We observed that except for the batch size of 24, the hyper-parameters in SSD are the same as above and the typical deviance of the standard distribution was 0.03. Additionally, preliminary learning rate was 0.001 and decomposing all epoch individually with an exponential value of 0.955.

25.5   Outcomes

The outcome or result division has been distributed into some sub-sections, each of which delivers a brief and specific explanation of our exploratory outcomes.

25.5.1   Object identification network models

The ratio of data-set partition has an outstanding outcome on the performance of the model in a given dataset. First, we divided the dataset into three different subsets: training set, validation set, and test set on a ratio of 0.7:0.2:0.1. In case of training set, the image dataset was trained and evaluated, after that we have to select model parameters in a validation set and finally, we evaluate the model performance in the ultimate test set. The experiment used an open platform model, which has already successfully run on the COCO dataset in a consideration of conditions like calculations and the cost of training time.

We considered the conditions like the calculations and the total cost of training time, in this study, transfer learning was employed which can be used for a similar *mung bean* pest and disease image set for the training of several network models.

So, we can discover the optimal model by combining the meta-architectures of faster region-based convolutional neural network, region-based fully convolutional network and SSD through the characteristics extractors (ResNet, Inception, & MobileNet) & must consider conditions like mAP, memory usage, running speed, and loss.

From Table 25.4, we got the statistical results and Figure 25.5 expresses the training loss curves for differently used models, correspondingly, the model selection process is entirely based on different curves.

In Table 25.4, we observed that mAP of faster region-based convolutional neural network with ResNet-101, SSD with inception and region-based fully convolutional network with ResNet-101 are all superior to the value of 0.64. So, we have achieved satisfactory identification results. Unlike other earlier architectures, the execution times are almost three times quicker in case of applying SSD. We closely observed that, after executing 85,000 iterations, the loss of training on every individual network-model, each and every curvatures congregated swiftly and not shifted intensely. Finally, within a smaller range, the loss values are looks like in a stable stage. The system will be operated in transportable and handset devices in near future so the memory size should be minimum. When summarized in this section of the experiment, after trained the data, the SSD with Inception performed much better clearly. As a result, we successfully developed our model based decent Android-based mobile application to recognize the high-precision identification of *mung bean* pests and diseases in real-time and environment.

Table 25.4   Entire results of five differently used models

Meta-architecture	Faster R-CNN	R-FCN		SSD	
Feature extractor	ResNet101	Inception	ResNet101	Inception	Mobile Net
WBU 109 (Sulata)	0.8322	0.8394	0.7704	0.8219	0.8303
IPU 02-43	0.5744	0.5528	0.6084	0.5861	0.5952
NUL 7	0.8766	0.8247	0.9162	0.6177	0.6031
LU 391	0.6563	0.4163	0.4345	0.7556	0.4981
KUG 479	0.7564	0.7030	0.7107	0.7739	0.6248
VBG 04-008	0.2150	0.3004	0.3607	0.3773	0.3237
TU 40	0.9289	0.8446	0.9281	0.9671	0.8432
LBG 787	0.5376	0.2638	0.3557	0.2248	0.3477
VBN 8	0.7605	0.5198	0.6125	0.6276	0.6761
SONALI	0.8144	0.8041	0.8433	0.9112	0.6610
PANNA	0.8630	0.7891	0.7881	0.8768	0.7847
mAP at 0.6	0.6891	0.6065	0.6555	0.6745	0.6289
Time (second)	0.159	0.14	0.149	0.053	0.046
Memory (MB)	191.4	53.0	201.8	60.7	23.7

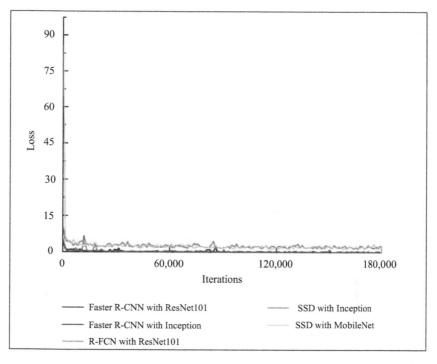

Figure 25.5   Graphical representation of model loss on the set of image data

25.5.2   DA processing

As we mentioned before, in this essential experiment, the insect *mung bean* pest and disease dataset, the number of images we collected or captured are lesser, which possibly will occur the overfitting difficulty but another obstacle we may face that accumulating countless images is a costly and time-consuming practice.

Therefore, we used the DA technique which has been convenient to develop and expand the data for training which was already stored. Finally, we select the DA process to simulate different capturing conditions because we need as much attention as possible in the cultivation field.

The nature of the captures are given below:

Color jittering: Here, in different lighting conditions, at first we have accustomed the contrast, brightness, sharpness, and softness of images of dataset for the identification of instances or objects in a random way.

Random flipping/translation: The random flipping or translation is applied to avoid the objects from emerging not just in a particular location but also in different angels and spots of the image.

Random rotate: By using this method, we make that the model could learn the objects across several viewpoints.

Random cropping: Random cropping is completely different from the random flipping and the stability can be enhanced and also minimize the influence of the background of the model.

During the training phase, we showed in Figure 25.6(a) and (b) that one or more joined DA procedures were employed to expand the pest and disease image dataset rapidly.

From Figure 25.6(a), we got that the maximum enhancement is achieved by using the random cropping method, followed by other methods of random rotation and random flipping. The finest three approaches are applied methods of cropping & flipping which is revealed in Figure 25.6. In this work, these dual techniques are appropriate to upgrade the performance of our set of images. Then, our team presents the results in Table 25.5 where we systematically compared the effect with DA (flip + crop) and without DA on individually disease & pest.

SSD with inception is used to perform these experiments. After practicing the DA method, we have a total of 2698 number of imagery data for the training phase. Table 25.5 clearly shows the change of effect of DA on the prototypes. From Table 25.5, we have taught that after applied the DA, the mAP value has been significantly enriched. Between them, the AP values of WBU 109 (Sulata), TU 40, SONALI, and PANNA decreased successfully, although the average precision values of other disease and pest samples improved considerably. When we closely observed our image dataset, TU 40, SONALI, LBG 787, VBN 8, and PANNA have the biggest amount of images, but the overfitting problem in the image set.

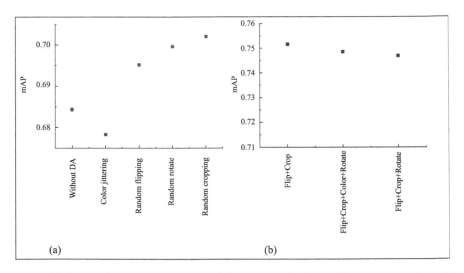

Figure 25.6   Exploratory outcomes of the DA applied on SSD with inception: (a) every experiment applies single DA methodology; (b) the best methodologies are displayed after testing of all combinations of DA methods

Table 25.5 *Validation set results of our developed model after applying the techniques of with and without DA*

Methodology	WBU 109 (Sulata)	IPU 02-43	NUL 7	LU 391	KUG 479	VBG 04-008	TU 40	LBG 787	VBN 8	SONALI	PANNA
Without DA	0.8219	0.5861	0.6177	0.7556	0.7739	0.3773	0.9671	0. 2248	0.6276	0.9112	0.8768
DA	0.7859	0.6107	0.8594	0.9168	0.8421	0.5915	0.9578	0.3011	0.7760	0.7729	0.8063

After increasing the images, the results show that they are much closer to the actual condition, which specifies the drop of average precision value of the diseases and pests in this portion. The remaining sample is small and also deficient. When the DA process applied, we have learned additional properties, also got greatly increased AP values, thereby the mAP value of our model is improving. Hence, our team discovered that if the number of images is increased properly, then it can be very beneficial for improving the performance of the model.

25.5.3   Impression of dropout on model evaluation

We observe the model, which may have face overfitting difficulty because of less number of training data. In deep neural network, a dropout is an effective approach for overfitting prevention. It randomly dropping out the neurons by applying the process of combining exponentially different neural network architectures in the network. The final inclusive averaging scheme can overlook overfitting difficulties whenever our data is used on several neural networks. As the probability q ($q = 1 - p$), used neurons were dropped out by their layers during the training phase. In Figure 25.7, we noticed that the different outcomes of dropout rates on disease and pest image datasets. Srivastava *et al.* [41] provided the distinctive values of p; usually for the hidden layer in their research work. For smooth calculation, we take the value of p from 0.5 to 0.8 of the neural network. We prepared the data by combining the value of p with several hidden units' n. The less value of

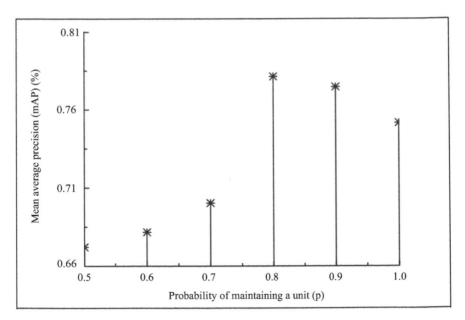

Figure 25.7   Outcome of variation of dropout rates on mAP, we fixed p = 0.5, 0.6, 0.7, 0.8 & 0.9, the mAP alterations consequently. When the value of p = 1.0, there is no dropout happens for our model

p requires a large unit of n to obtain better results. We can decide that our developed model acquires the optimum mAP, when the value p is 0.8 which is shown in Figure 25.7.

This is because when the value p is between 0.5 and 0.7, the produced model hides the unnecessary feature details, also the created model has the poor capability to suitably fix the data.

The value of mAP increases with the increase of the value of p, we get the peak value at $p = 0.8$. From the graph, we decided that that the identification performance of our model initiates to reduce if the value of p further increased, this happened because the small dataset cannot able to bound the model parameter size [44].

25.6   Design and execution of *mung bean* pest & disease identification system

We observed that a pest and disease identification model is accomplished the discussed tasks successfully in earlier works. So, our team established this *mung bean* pest and disease identification application to the Android-based mobile platform. The model perfectly operates the computing capabilities of standard smartphone devices which are provided the real-time identification not only for the healthy agricultural production but the pests and disease effects of the crop. In comparison with several earlier works, we have decent advantages using our developed model are follows:

(a)   In the same device, the capture and identification both are processed in the same period and the app illustrates the identify outcomes rapidly without delay.
(b)   The application can easily practice the images which are captured by various camera devices in a variety of resolutions, angles, and aspect ratio.
(c)   The adaptability of our desired system is highly satisfactory which accurately works in different conditions of illumination and has a composite background (both field and laboratory environment); the system functions effectively for different pests and diseases in various positions. The system is simple to operate and efficient to identify.

25.6.1   Software information

The proposed architecture is developed on operating system of Mac OS Mojave version 10.14.1 platform. The Android Studio 3.2 JDK 1.8 designed this aforesaid operating system.

25.6.2   Proposed Android-based application structural design

Our designed Android-based application of *mung bean* pest and disease identification system is presented in Figure 25.8. An integrated design idea will be implemented in the noble system, which will be divided into four sections of

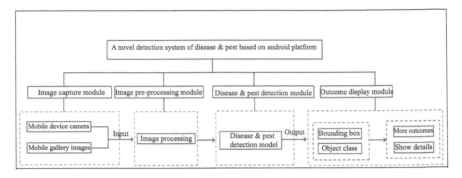

Figure 25.8 Proposed design of the disease & pest identification system

image acquisition module, where user can capture images randomly; image pre-processing module where the system automatically filters and process the features of image data; image identification module that correctly identifies whether the image data is affected or not and finally the display module where the user will get the result.

Now, we elaborately discuss the work function of the desired system. The image capturing section will capture an image with the help of a hand-set or mobile device image capturing system or from the mobile stored photo gallery and album; the image pre-processing unit appropriately changes the size of the input image into a fixed dimension, therefore the interference of the background is nullified so our system is able to identify objects efficiently with proper accurateness; the imagery identification unit is able to identify three regular *mung bean* pests and three common diseases; the ultimate display section will display the types and position of pest in that image (an example is shown in Figure 25.9). After learning the skills of artificially identifying healthy or unhealthy images using this application which will be called Dr. Disease & Pest, the customers can acquire truthful trial results and inclusive protection measurements according to the corresponding outcomes of any image set.

When different user will launch the application, at first the start-up or opening page appears where the application name also displayed with the icon of the application and the image select or image capturing switch. Then they will operate the identify button for disease or pest, etc.; the user can directly pick a photo from the hand-set stored photo gallery then assemble and arrange the imagery that is identified, after that the user can wait for a moment to get the outcome which is shown in the identification result display page. Different shapes and various color boxes were employed to characterize several pests and disease classifications from that image data set.

As we provided some the example of images with different objects, classes of pest and diseases, detection accuracy and diagnosis measurements also interrelated expressions of diseases and pests in our article. Furthermore, we are trying to create a detailed summary of the disease and pest control methods in a website, direct and open access for the users to a specific and relevant web page shortly.

Figure 25.9   Android-based mung bean. Leaf beetle pest identification application interface. (a) Application opening page interface. (b) Identification results representation interface. (c) Comprehensive overview interface

25.6.3   Software testing

As we have already installed the program package into the Android operating installation package file to test our novel system called Dr Disease & Pest, which is installed into the Redmi Note 8 Pro smart handset which has an Android version of Android 9 Pie. The complete mobile system specification is displayed in Table 25.6.

We have verified overall correctness and identification spell of the application using this Android-based mobile device.

Following our close observation, in Table 25.7, we determine that it takes around 1 second to determine the accurateness, missing rate and a false reject rate of substances of the image. Moreover, we will test other sets of image sets of data to prove our application is trustworthy and works efficiently.

25.6.4   Discussion

We discussed that the model correctly identifies the test images which are shown in Figure 25.10(a–f). Figure 25.10(a–c) is taken for the diseases, while the rest are mostly reflecting the pest effects in the images. Figure 25.10(e) identifies the indistinct object correctly, which establishes that when the captured pests are fuzzy, the model can also perfectly identify the object from that particular image. Figure 25.10(c) displays the different positions of the disease spread and the

Table 25.6   Specification of Android-based mobile system

Items frequency	Parameter measures
Mobile	Redmi Note 8 pro
ROM	64GB
Size of screen	1080 × 2340
Number of CPU cores	Octa-core (2×2.05 GHz Cortex-A76 & 6×2.0 GHz Cortex-A55)
RAM	6 GB
Pixels of camera	Primary camera: 64-megapixel with an f/1.79 aperture. Second camera: 8-megapixel with an f/2.2 aperture. Third camera: 2-megapixel and fourth camera: 2-megapixel with minimum aperture

Table 25.7   The experimental results of the Android-based mobile application

Methodology	Model accuracy	Missing rate	False reject rate
mung bean disease and pest identification model	0.6983	0.2075	0.0945

variation of color in that sample. Figure 25.10(a) is different in comparison with others, which indicates that our model efficiently detects the different shapes of affected areas of disease and, in Figure 25.10(b), the color differences of damaged portions within the same class. We focus on the feature extraction and occlusion processing conditions that are the important fundamentals in multi-object identification [45]. We have seen that the two pests have similarities in Figure 25.10(d), and some minor objects of the pest are out-of-focus in Figure 25.10(e); it shows that either of images is not captures to understand the intact pests, so it demonstrates that the system also has a definite generalization capability for misplaced features. In Figure 25.10(f), we can indicate that our model correctly and clearly detects the pest from the image. This kind of results validates the feasibility and efficiency of our decent identification system. Especially the designed model can precisely and efficiently identify each object in different circumstances when only one class of object remains in the image. We consider that there still have few possibilities for improvements for our pest and disease identification system. The identification capability of our developed model is deficient in a few cases, so we can focus on it for our next research work shortly.

For our experiment, when the data are captured from the side and back, in that case, it is impossible to accurately recognize most of the object. However, we used different Internet sources to collect and arrange the dataset for this experiment. The identification model which we developed has the limited capability to identify small objects from the images when the image size is small. By the way, the size, shapes, textures of pests, and diseases in the web images are decent and large and the image dataset acquired from the cultivation lands and laboratory contains only

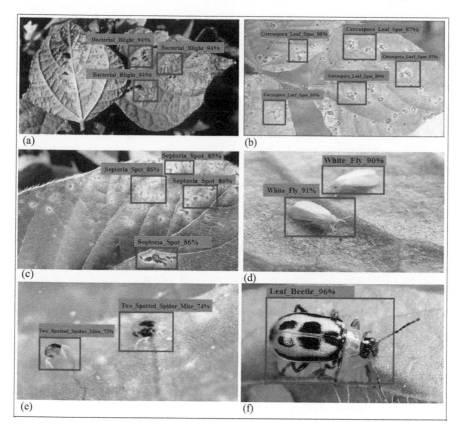

Figure 25.10   Examples of the trial images for accurate identification. Our model successfully performed which was displayed in six images: (a) bacterial blight. (b) Cercospora leaf spot. (c) Septoria spot. (d) Two spotted spider mite. (e) White spot. (f) Leaf beetle

limited minor objects, such the developed model performed better for the image set which was collected from various Internet sources.

25.7   Conclusion

This research work created 11 varieties of *mung bean* healthy, pest and disease dataset that covers the six typical *mung bean* pests and diseases from our dataset. The application of common object identification algorithms in *mung bean* pest and disease identification is compared and analyzed with our model. Among them, SSD with inception stabilities the performance indicators such as identification accurateness, memory usage, and time. The application is also operated on Android-based mobile devices. To make the model more effective, in the experimental dataset, we used the DA method to resolve the inconsistent class stability difficulty.

The operational outcomes evidenced that our new technique can significantly increase the identification accuracy by 0.8 percentage points. The dropout layer is added to avoid the data overfitting problem. When the value of $p = 0.8$, the mAP value of the model was as reach at 77.16%. Under different illuminations, backgrounds, and environment, the experiments are accomplished on the collected images. The model has a decent ability to identify *mung bean* pests and diseases under complex noise and circumstances. Eventually, we are trying to install the trained model into the Android platform to develop a *mung bean* pest and disease identification system (we have already finished some tests on different image datasets). The pest and disease identification of *mung bean* in the real-time and normal environment by the users from the field by operating the Android mobile phone has a spontaneous and simple interface for the identification. It can effectively improve the production of agricultural supplies.

As a drawback, the identification skill of our model is still deficient, which encourages the multi-object intersection, character obstruction, and minor object recognition tasks that shall be our future work objective to make the model more precise and efficient. In imminent work, we will certainly solve the aforesaid obstacles by increasing the *mung bean* disease and pest dataset and other major crops by modifying the model network structure. As we successfully reaching the initial goal of our work, the commercial perspective of *mung bean* cultivation is partially fulfilled, as because *mung bean* is a high priced commodity and the cultivation of *mung bean* (only cultivates in few states of India) are restricted due to excessive insect pest and disease impedances. By applying our approach which is exclusively based on machine learning interventions and the model also mounted in Android-based mobile application provides immense benefit to the farmers to humbly tackle the disease and insect pests in a very short time in a real-time environment and take the necessary measures immediately and increase the productivity of mung bean in India. Besides, the *mung bean* pest and disease diagnosis system has only accomplished the earliest development work but further research works are required for more enhancement in the coming stage for the massive change in Indian agriculture.

25.8   Tools used

LabelImg (v1.3.0): LabelImg is an annotation tool used for evaluating the graphical images. It is performed in Python and practices Qt for its graphical interface and we used this tool to spot the groups and rectangular bounding boxes of the disease and pest image set.

25.9   Acknowledgment

The Department of Science & Technology and Biotechnology, Government of West Bengal (Project Sanction Number: (memo no: 345(sanc)/ST/P/S&T/1-G/2018)) has funded this research work.

References

[1] https://www.business-standard.com/article/economy-policy/pulses-import-falls-to-2-5-mln-tonnes-from-6-6-mn-tonnes-two-years-ago-119042301471_1.html.

[2] D. J. Ecobichon, "Pesticide use in developing countries," *Toxicology*, vol. 160, no. 1–3, pp. 27–33, 2001.

[3] D. Pimentel, H. Acquay, M. Biltonen, *et al.*, "Environmental and economic costs of pesticide use," *Bioscience*, vol. 42, no. 10, pp. 750–760, 1992.

[4] A. King, "Technology: the future of agriculture," *Nature*, vol. 544, no. 7651, pp. S21–S23, 2017.

[5] A. Fuentes, D. H. Im, S. Yoon, and D. S. Park, "Spectral analysis of CNN for tomato disease identification," in *Proceedings of the International Conference on Artificial Intelligence and Soft Computing*, Cham, Switzerland, June 2017, pp. 40–51.

[6] A. V. S. Madhav and A. K. Tyagi, "The world with future technologies (post-COVID-19): open issues, challenges, and the road ahead," In: Tyagi A.K., Abraham A., Kaklauskas A. (eds.), *Intelligent Interactive Multimedia Systems for e-Healthcare Applications*. Springer, Singapore; 2022. https://doi.org/10.1007/978-981-16-6542-4_22.

[7] S. Hwang and H. E. Kim, "Self-transfer learning for weakly supervised lesion localization," in *International Conference on Medical Image Computing and Computer-Assisted Intervention*, Cham, Springer, 2016, pp. 239–246.

[8] S. Gossain and J. S. Gill, "A novel approach to enhance object identification using integrated identification algorithms," *International Journal of Computer Science and Mobile Computing*, vol. 3, pp. 1018–1023, 2014.

[9] S. Ding and K. Zhao, "Research on daily objects identification based on deep neural network," in *Proceedings of the International Symposium on Application of Materials Science and Energy Materials*, Shanghai, China, December 2017, pp. 28–29.

[10] Z. Q. Zhao, P. Zheng, S. T. Xu, and X. Wu, "Object detection with deep learning: a review," in *IEEE Transactions on Neural Networks and Learning Systems*, vol. 30, no. 11, pp. 3212–3232, 2019.

[11] A. Voulodimos, N. Doulamis, A. Doulamis, *et al.*, "Deep learning for computer vision: a brief review," *Computational Intelligence and Neuroscience*, vol. 2018, p. 13, 2018, Article ID 7068349.

[12] Y. Lecun, Y. Bengio, and G. Hinton, "Deep learning," *Nature*, vol. 521, no. 7553, pp. 436–444, 2015.

[13] C. Szegedy, W. Liu, Y. Jia, *et al.*, "Going deeper with convolutions," in Proceedings of the IEEE Conference on Computer Vision and Pattern Recognition, Boston, MA, June 2015, pp. 1–9.

[14] J. Ubbens, M. Cieslak, P. Prusinkiewicz, and I. Stavness, "The use of plant models in deep learning: an application to leaf counting in rosette plants," *Plant Methods*, vol. 14, no. 1, p. 6, 2018.

[15] S. Ren, K. He, R. Girshick, and J. Sun, "Faster R-CNN: towards real-time object identification with region proposal networks," *IEEE Transactions on*

Pattern Analysis and Machine Intelligence, vol. 39, no. 6, pp. 1137–1149, 2016.

[16] J. Dai, Y. Li, K. He, and J. Sun, "R-fcn: Object detection via region-based fully convolutional networks," *Advances in neural information processing systems*, 29. 2016.

[17] J. Redmon, S. Divvala, R. Girshick, and A. Farhadi, "You only look once: unified, real-time object identification," in Proceedings of the 2016 IEEE Conference on Computer Vision and Pattern Recognition (CVPR), Seattle, WA, June 2016, pp. 779–788.

[18] W. Liu, D. Anguelov, D. Erhan, *et al.*, "SSD: single shot multibox identifier," in Proceedings of the European Conference on Computer Vision, Amsterdam, The Netherlands, October 2016, pp. 21–37.

[19] I. Bechar and S. Moisan, "On-line counting of pests in a greenhouse using computer vision," in Proceedings of the VAIB 2010-Visual Observation and Analysis of Animal and Insect Behavior, Istanbul, Turkey, August 2010.

[20] Y. Zhong, J. Gao, Q. Lei, and Y. Zhou, "A vision-based counting and recognition system for flying insects in intelligent agriculture," *Sensors*, vol. 18, no. 5, p. 1489, 2018.

[21] T.-Y. Lin, M. Maire, S. Belongie, *et al.*, "Microsoft coco: common objects in context," in Proceedings of the European Conference on Computer Vision, Zurich, Switzerland, September 2014, pp. 740–755.

[22] M. Everingham, L. Van Gool, C. K. I. Williams, J. Winn, and A. Zisserman, "The pascal visual object classes (VOC) challenge," *International Journal of Computer Vision*, vol. 88, no. 2, pp. 303–338, 2010.

[23] O. Russakovsky, J. Deng, H. Su, *et al.*, "Imagenet large scale visual recognition challenge," *International Journal of Computer Vision*, vol. 115, no. 3, pp. 211–252, 2015.

[24] X. Chen, Z. Wu, and J. Yu. "TSSD: temporal single-shot detector based on attention and LSTM," In *2018 IEEE/RSJ International Conference on Intelligent Robots and Systems (IROS)*, IEEE, pp. 1–9, 2018.

[25] W. Ding and G. Taylor, "Automatic moth identification from trap images for pest management," *Computers and Electronics in Agriculture*, vol. 123, pp. 17–28, 2016.

[26] A. Shrivastava and A. Gupta, "Contextual priming and feedback for faster R-CNN," in Proceedings of the European Conference on Computer Vision, Amsterdam, The Netherlands, October 2016, pp. 330–348.

[27] Y. C. Zhou, T. Y. Xu, W. Zheng, and H. B. Deng, "Classification and recognition approaches of tomato main organs based on DCNN," *Transactions of the Chinese Society of Agricultural Engineering*, vol. 33, pp. 219–226, 2017.

[28] L. S. Fu, Y. L. Feng, E. Tola, Z. H. Liu, R. Li, and Y. J. Cui, "Image recognition method of multi-cluster kiwifruit in field based on convolutional neural networks," *Transactions of the Chinese Society of Agricultural Engineering*, vol. 34, pp. 205–211, 2018.

[29] X. Wei, F. Liu, Z. Qiu, Y. Shao, and Y. He, "Ripeness classification of astringent persimmon using hyperspectral imaging technique," *Food and Bioprocess Technology*, vol. 7, no. 5, pp. 1371–1380, 2014.

[30] F. Liu and Y. He, "Classification of brands of instant noodles using Vis/NIR spectroscopy and chemometrics," *Food Research International*, vol. 41, no. 5, pp. 562–567, 2008.

[31] H. Wang, J. Peng, C. Xie, Y. Bao, and Y. He, "Fruit quality evaluation using spectroscopy technology: a review," *Sensors*, vol. 15, no. 5, pp. 11889–11927, 2015.

[32] I. Sa, Z. Ge, F. Dayoub, B. Upcroft, T. Perez, and C. McCool, "Deep fruits: a fruit identification system using deep neural networks," *Sensors*, vol. 16, no. 8, p. 1222, 2016.

[33] M. Martineau, D. Conte, R. Raveaux, I. Arnault, D. Munier, and G. Venturini, "A survey on image-based insect classification," *Pattern Recognition*, vol. 65, pp. 273–284, 2017.

[34] Q. Yao, J. Lv, Q.-J. Liu, *et al.*, "An insect imaging system to automate rice light-trap pest identification," *Journal of Integrative Agriculture*, vol. 11, no. 6, pp. 978–985, 2012.

[35] Y. Wang and X. Zhang, "Autonomous garbage identification for intelligent urban management," in Proceedings of the International Conference on Electronic Information Technology and Computer Engineering, Shanghai, China, October 2018, pp. 12–14.

[36] I. Rebai, Y. BenAyed, W. Mahdi, and J. P. Lorre, "Improving speech recognition using data augmentation and acoustic model fusion," in Proceedings of the International Conference on Knowledge-Based and Intelligent Information and Engineering Systems, Marseille, France, September 2017, pp. 316–322.

[37] Y. Guo, Y. Liu, A. Oerlemans, S. Lao, S. Wu, and M. S. Lew, "Deep learning for visual understanding: a review," *Neuro-computing*, vol. 187, pp. 27–48, 2016.

[38] X. Y. Zhu, Y. F. Liu, J. H. Li, T. Wan, and Z. C. Qin, "Emotion classification with data augmentation using generative adversarial networks," in Proceedings of the Pacific-Asia Conference on Knowledge Discovery and Data Mining, Melbourne, Australia, May 2018, pp. 349–360.

[39] X. Y. Zhu, Y. F. Liu, J. H. Li, T. Wan, and Z. C. Qin, "Emotion classification with data augmentation using generative adversarial networks," in *Proceedings of the Pacific-Asia Conference on Knowledge Discovery and Data Mining*, Melbourne, Australia, pp. 349–360, 2018.

[40] T. Luke, and G. Nitschke, "Improving deep learning with generic data augmentation." In *2018 IEEE Symposium Series on Computational Intelligence (SSCI)*, IEEE, pp. 1542–1547, 2018.

[41] N. Srivastava, G. Hinton, A. Krizhevsky, I. Sutskever, and R. Salakhutdinov, "Dropout: a simple way to prevent neural networks from overfitting," *Journal of Machine Learning Research*, vol. 15, pp. 1929–1958, 2014.

[42] J. Davis and M. Goadrich, "The relationship between precision-recall and ROC curves," in Proceedings of the 23rd International Conference on Machine Learning, Pittsburgh, PA, USA, June 2006, pp. 233–240.

[43]   A. Godil, R. Bostelman, W. Shackleford, T. Hong, and M. Shneier, "Performance metrics for evaluating object and human identification and tracking systems," NISTIR 7972, National Institute of Standards and Technology, Gaithersburg, MD, USA, 2014.

[44]   Z. Y. Liu, J. F. Gao, G. G. Yang, H. Zhang, and Y. He, "Localization and classification of paddy field pests using a saliency map and deep convolutional neural network," *Scientific Reports*, vol. 6, no. 1, 2016, *Article* 20410.

[45]   J. Li, H.-C. Wong, S.-L. Lo, and Y. Xin, "Multiple object detection by a deformable part-based model and an R-CNN," *IEEE Signal Processing Letters*, vol. 25, no. 2, pp. 288–292, 2018.

Chapter 26

A prioritized potential framework for combined computing technologies: IoT, Machine Learning, and blockchain

Deepshikha Agarwal[1], Khushboo Tripathi[2] and Kumar Krishen[3,4]

Abstract

In today's scenario, every organization is dependent on the use of computers for automating business and work. The data generated by the organization is huge and has great significance in analyzing the processes. It can be rightfully called as the lifeblood of any organization. The world of computing requires three technologies: Internet of Things (IoT), machine learning (ML), and blockchain. The confluence of these technologies is inevitable in the coming future due to the benefits which are involved in future applications. There is barely any activity today which is cannot apply the use of these three technologies e.g., healthcare, automation, education, etc. IoT can be defined as interconnection of various autonomous devices which are capable of communicating with each other. IoT requires an intermittent Internet connection and address for every device. The user of these devices can remotely monitor and manage by retrieving the information on a handheld device similar to the cellphone. This way, the devices are connected 24/7 and continuously generating data. Challenges of IoT involve the following: security, connectivity problems, and huge data. The devices can be made capable of taking intelligent decisions by incorporating Artificial Intelligence (AI) and ML technology. ML is a sub-branch of AI. It has got huge potential to detect the patterns and anomalies in the data which is generated by the wireless sensor nodes in IoT. The advanced decision-making process of ML has already influenced our daily routines, for example: banking, healthcare, gaming, transportation, and space exploration. Challenges faced by ML are the following: security, centralized architecture, and resource limitations. To cover the security aspect of these two technologies, blockchain technology is the perfect answer. It is a decentralized

[1]Department of IT, IIIT Lucknow, India
[2]Department of CSE, Amity University Haryana, India
[3]University of Houston, USA
[4]NASA Johnson Space Center, USA (Formerly)

peer-to-peer network which stores the records and transactions in blocks which cannot be altered. This technology secures the communication by eliminating the need for any trusted third party. The blocks are stored in such a manner which makes it impossible to hack or tamper the data by taking control of device or capturing the records. This chapter will present a comprehensive and quantitative analysis of the existing research and how these technologies can be a transformative impact for access to information by the users. The convergence of blockchain, ML, and IoT will provide scalable, secure high-level intellectual functioning that will be the new paradigm of digital information. This book chapter presents futuristic potential of convergence of three technologies and elaborate discussion of the past researches.

Keywords: Machine learning; Blockchain; Healthcare; Transport system

26.1   Introduction

The world has witnessed the use of three well-known technologies: Internet of Things (IoT), Artificial Intelligence (AI), and blockchain. Blockchain is a security-based mechanism which provides the services of greater trust, transparency, security, and privacy in business processes. This technology is based on the storing the ledger in distributed locations and hence greater level of security is ensured. IoT is also called as Internet of Devices which consists of interconnected autonomous devices. The devices are connected always and are accessible at any point of time. Such a network serves the purpose of remote accessing, monitoring, and management of resources in a controlled way. It is a visionary technology which will connect everything on the fly. Machines which can act intelligently and take decisions independently without human intervention are equipped with AI. Till now, researches were done independently in all the three technologies. But actually, IoT cannot be realized in its full capacity until it is combined with blockchain to ensure security of communication and data and AI to make autonomous intelligent decisions by identifying patterns and optimizing the resources [1]. These innovations combined together have the potential to change the future by improving business processes, creating new business models, and providing connectivity everywhere and all the time. In IOT network, large amount of data is produced. This data can be stored and managed efficiently using blockchain technology in combination with AI. This convergence will bring transformation in the way business models are incorporated, for example, autonomous agents like wireless sensors, automatic vehicles, intelligent cameras will be capable of making decisions autonomously without human help. People will be able to use them for high security money transactions using blockchain and will help in sustaining IoT networks with advanced features. Therefore, the convergence will help in improving management of data, security of data, and remote automation [2]. Figure 26.1 shows the general working procedures of the three technologies.

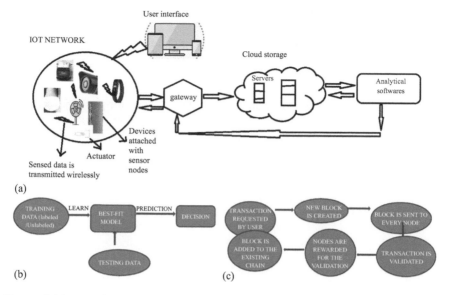

Figure 26.1   *Working procedures of the three technologies. (a) IoT networks. (b) Process of Machine learning (ML). (c) Creation of blockchain*

26.2   A review on combined technologies

The possibility of convergence of IoT and AI in future is presented in [3]. However, there are security issues if used in unethical way and may cause a treat to the system. Authors in [4] have presented the discussion focusing on the inclusion of AI into the IoT applications where significant coding effort is required. They have proposed AI stalk to decompose any complex AI application into simplified distributed modules using the IoT technology. In [5], the chapter proposes a water quality monitoring system which is based on IoT for monitoring water quality accurately in real time. These results are stored in a cloud database. The chapter [6] presents an overview of the blockchain technology and its implementation, infrastructure of IoT which is based on blockchain network and blockchain. However, no implementation has been discussed. Authors in [7] present a design concept for developing the IoT data management platform based on blockchain and smart contracts. By this method, they aim to achieve effective data management and ability to settle conflicts between untrusted Internet of Things (IoT) devices by providing security services. The chapter lacks any physical demonstration of the proposed system. In this demo [8], a blockchain-enabled IoT service layer platform based on one Machine to Machine (M2M) IoT standards and a blockchain hybrid application has been built by using Logchain which is suitable for IoT. Ref. [9] proposes a dynamic access control scheme in IoT networks to solve the problems of the existing access control method for direct data communication between devices. Ref. [10] covers all the major theoretical aspects

Table 26.1 Summary of literature survey

S. no.	Author(s)	Presented work	Research gap
[1]	Ashish Ghosh *et al.*	Presented the idea of convergence	No implementations done
[2]	Yun-Wei Lin *et al.*	Proposed AI talk to simplify complex AI modules	Does not present security issues
[3]	Hamza Khurshid *et al.*	Proposed water quality monitoring system based on AI and IoT	No implementation shown. Security features are not discussed
[4]	M. Singh *et al.*	Presents an overview of blockchain technology in IoT networks	Only theoretical concepts are shown
[5]	H. Cui *et al.*	Proposed a design concept for IoT data management platform based on blockchain and smart contracts	No physical implementation is discussed
[6]	C. Lee *et al.*	Developed a blockchain-enabled IoT service layer platform using Logchain	Not shown any use of AI or ML
[7]	D. Hwang *et al.*	Proposed a dynamic access control scheme in IoT networks	No implementation shown. Does not discuss the problems of big data, security
[8]	Ahmad Banafa	Book covers theoretical aspects of AI, blockchain, and IoT	Lacks discussion on the issues and challenges in the convergence
[9]	Z. Li *et al.*	Presented a prototype of fine-grained transportation insurance	Very few metrics are used in the calculation. Security breaches are not presented
[10]	K. Sharma *et al.*	Survey on the proposed applications of ML algorithms with IoT	ML is not considered
[11]	V. Porkodi *et al.*	Study to incorporate ML in IoT applications	Theoretical concepts only

of IoT, fog computing, AI, and blockchain technology. In [11], the authors have investigated the convergence of these technologies and presented a prototype of fine-grained transportation insurance. The use of AI helps in calculating correct premiums by assessing vehicles usage and driver's behavior using IoT data collected from mobile sensors. Author in [12] presented a survey on the proposed applications of ML algorithms with IoT. The study [13] also provides the idea of ML adoption in various fields of IoT applications. Table 26.1 shows a concise summary of this discussion.

26.3 Research gaps

Researchers have proposed several applications based on the convergence of the technologies. However, it suffers with several research gaps. The biggest gap is that of resources to handle such huge amount of generated data. Moreover, the success or failure of this convergence. The process of extracting meaningful information, analysis, storage is a very complex and complicated task. It involves lots of precision otherwise, the meaning inferred will go all wrong leading to incorrect and useless results, processing power and cost. There is a dire need for newer algorithms to bring compatibility between the technologies. All the existing algorithms in data mining and ML have to be made application specific. Generalized algorithms may not be able to give accurate answers. Complex adaptive AI systems may lead to self-sustaining malicious evolution of systems that can mimic a cancerous growth in the human body. Superior AI systems will be required to combat this dangerous situation. Another major concern is the weakness in the existing security measures in IoT systems. This concern arises from the fact that all the devices will be connected all the time through internet. Thus, the entire data will be sent over the insecure channel which may be watched by a hacker. This will expose the weakness of the system to the hacker and later on, passive attack from that hacker may sabotage the entire working of the network. Thus, mock attacks should be made on the AI system to existing loopholes and to close them from hacking attempt. The previous discussion, we have shown the proposed work of several authors, however, none of them have done any visible implementation of their prototype. Also, they are unaware of the security threats which their system may be vulnerable to.

26.4 Case studies

1. Facebook: It is a well-known social platform for making social relationships with different people and groups. It also allows chatting conversations, photo sharing, tagging functionality, and detection of inappropriate posts, pictures and videos. This is achieved using moderation and flagging by ML algorithms in detecting them. Those messages or content which is labeled as inappropriate are straightway blocked from viewing automatically by the ML model. It also uses ML to make the latest posts to be shown first on the page to the user. This needs identification of the time it was posted and to synchronize with the current time to identify as a latest post. In the future, Facebook aims at creating an amalgam of several ML algorithms for sorting queues and prioritizing posts based on number of times its shared, their severity, and the likelihood they're breaking the rules.

   Facebook uses an ML model named "WPIE," which stands for "whole post integrity embeddings" for assessing the posts and other content. The algorithms judge the type of content based on several points together by taking as input, posts, caption, image, or video. This means the algorithms judge various elements in any given post in concert, trying to work out what the image, caption, poster, etc., reveal together. The use of certain words in the caption (like "potent") might tip the judgment one way or the other. Figure 26.2 shows the prioritizing procedure used by Facebook drawn as a flowchart.

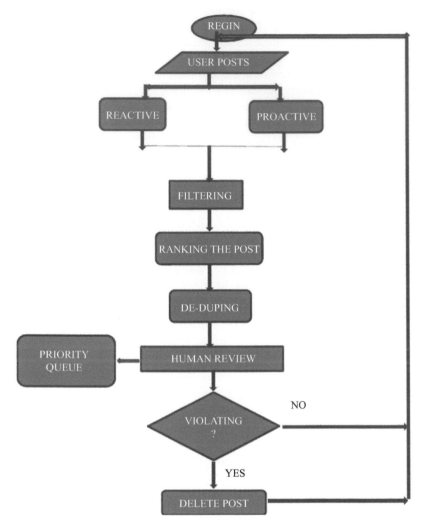

Figure 26.2   Flowchart for prioritizing procedure used by Facebook

2. Google Map: Google Map is a great utility application for people who are lone travelers. It provides features like fastest route, alternate routes, voice navigation, congestion on the road. It is said to employ ML models for prediction. Google has partnered with DeepMind, an Alphabet AI research lab, to improve the accuracy of its traffic prediction capabilities. Google Maps use memory to store the historical traffic patterns for roads over time and then analyze it to deduce important results for estimating the best route between a pair of destinations. This done by looking the traffic pattern at different times of the day along with the average speed of the traffic. The algorithms combine this

historical data with live traffic conditions to suggest the best route and estimated time to reach (ETA). It also accepts feedback, recommendations from the users, and local government guidelines to create a near-perfect solution. Incident reports from drivers over the Google feedback mechanism allow to quickly generate alerts and modify the navigation for alternate routes due to lane blockage or road damage, accidents etc. As a result, Google Maps automatically reroute to help in avoiding any traffic jams and get to the destination on-time.

26.5   Convergence of IoT, Machine Learning, and blockchain methods

The above discussions have led to the fact that blockchain, IoT, and ML are going to be the key technologies which will drive the next wave of the digital universe [14]. Imagine a smart home IoT network which consists of all tube lights, bulbs, fans, TV connected to each other. Let each of these devices has their own unique identity and works using blockchain. Blockchain identity means that the device is working on its own and is autonomous. Hence, by using smart contracts, mini payments can be made to the device to enable its working. In this way, any user can make payments to the device which will work according to the tariff charged. All these devices are connected in a peer-to-peer blockchain network and so they will also store data pertaining to their usage, their performance, failures. Here, ML can be used efficiently to increase and optimize the working of all the devices in the IOT network [15–17]. ML algorithms inside the device can use the data stored in the device to determine if any failure has happened and immediately suggest or take appropriate action to reduce the downtime. This would also allow real-time monitoring and maintenance of the IOT devices [16,18]. Additionally, ML can also improve the processing of ordering of replacement parts by precisely calculating the statistics. This kind of system can be realized for a commercially available building or rooms where investors can invest in the building and maintenance of these devices and they can earn their share on the profit of individual device.

This kind of convergence will be benefitting business models, commercial products and their services. This will largely be applicable on vehicles, industrial machines, CCTV cameras, etc. This will aid in the development of value-aided services to the user. These technologies also revolutionize analytics, storage and maintenance of Big Data database systems and their performance improvement [19]. This will also provide convenience and use-on-demand services.

26.5.1   Framework

Figure 26.2 displays the framework for the combined working of these three technologies. As can be seen, the framework can be defined to be working in three-level hierarchy. The first tier is the lowest level which comprise of the devices which are attached with sensor nodes capable of sensing and transmitting wirelessly. They can send or receive data packets. The user can access these devices through his user interface which is mostly mobile phone based browsing or

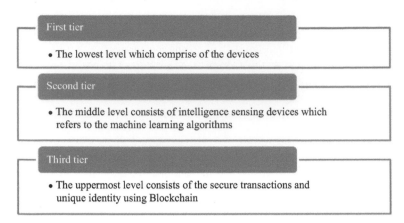

*Figure 26.3   Framework of levels of working concept of IoT devices, ML, and
blockchain*

accessing. The second tier or the middle tier consists of Intelligence in these devices. This refers to the machine learning algorithms which can be locally installed in these devices or there can be a central controller running the ML algorithms [20]. It can also be implemented using cloud infrastructure. These algorithms collect the data and analyze it for making predictions. For example, breakage in the refrigerator door lock or food items stored in the fridge getting stale. These predictions can be used to call for immediate corrective actions by putting off the refrigerator using a small attached electromechanical relay. The uppermost tier or the third tier consists of the secure transactions and unique identity using blockchain. Every connected device in the IoT network can become its own profit center by working autonomously. Any client can access these devices for personal usage and profit. The blockchain necessitates a smart contract binding these devices and the consumers [21]. Whenever a consumer wants to access the devices, he has to make a micro payment to the device to get the services. Once this transaction is validated, its added to the ledger and due to its transparent process, each of the members are aware of the transaction and the details. Figure 26.3 refers the framework concepts of computing technologies.

26.5.2   Futuristic applications for combined computing technology

The convergence of these technologies is going to build a revolution far beyond the human mind can encompass. Few applications which will be highly benefitted by this convergence are healthcare sector, transportation, education, banking, etc. The two most latest applications among them are discussed below. Figure 26.4 shows the convergence of the three computing technologies.

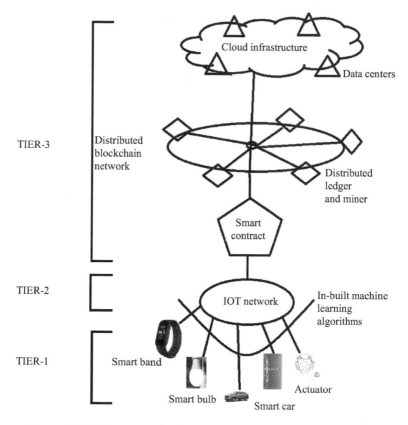

Figure 26.4   Framework of convergence of the three technologies

26.5.3   Issues in combined computing technologies

This convergence has the ability to create a future digital transformation which will change the look of the world. However, the realization of such a network needs some necessary points to ponder upon. The network should have all the necessary and sufficient infrastructure to support the Big Data which will be generated by IoT and blockchain technologies [22]. The blockchain technology is still in its infant stage and suffers with scalability and computation delay issues. To make the network fast, administrator must ensure hi-speed connectivity to transmit large amounts of data, hardware, and protocol changes in devices to cooperate together. Lots of funding is required by stakeholders to allow research for realizing the convergence and for the development of this network. Moreover, all the three technologies are currently working separately for different applications [23]. The convergence requires heavy changes in the protocol suites to allow compatibility between the flow of payload. Serious security concerns are also present in ML modeling, input data, and vulnerability of IOT devices. Security breach can cause complete failure of the system as everything is connected together and dependent for its working. Another very important aspect is due to its vastness, any failure in the system is going to lead to a heavy downtime and loss of revenue for the stakeholders. Single point of control and monitoring is dangerous for the automated system. This will also involve legal issues as several groups of people will access the network and share the services. Legal contract [24] can be self-executing smart contracts which maybe using AI for its automatic control and infrastructure. However, a smart contract is not alterable or stoppable once its executed. This could cause repairable damage in case of a bug or virus which gets inside the network. The larger convergent systems become, and the more autonomous they are, the more likely we are to be faced with deciding difficult questions. There will also be a requirement for higher bandwidth to support the simultaneous working of the technologies in every application. There would be a sudden rise in the duplicate packets passing through the bandwidth. This may give rise to confusion, congestion and crashing of the communication network. Fast and efficient processing needs to be done at the intermediate levels to lessen the burden on the network and allow reliable communication of the huge data.

On the basis of the above discussion, the key issues can be listed as the following:

- Interoperability
- Infrastructure
- Legal regulations
- Funding
- Governance
- Lack of expertise
- Scalability
- Latency, computation power

To deal with these hurdles, several steps can be ensured. First, adequate and targeted funding should be achieved as all technological research and development requires funding. Government should design the regularity rules for conglomeration of these different technologies together. Second, responsible ownership should be granted. For seamless working across different platforms, private and public partnerships should be invited. Lastly, there are severe ethical issues and protection and regulation requirements [25]. The regulations should be designed to cover the application and the way the emerging technology is used instead of technology itself.

26.6 Pioneering results for combined computing

26.6.1 *Impact of IoT, Machine Learning, and blockchain in intelligent transport system*

Road transportation is another important area which requires automated, intelligent, and secure working which includes traffic monitoring and accident alert

[21,26,27]. Consider a case where a car is moving at a fast speed on a national highway which is very less populated. There are very rare police vans or ambulances along the entire stretch of the highway. If the car suffers an accident on the highway, it will be a long time before anybody will be able to find out about the mis-happening and help may arrive after a long delay. To deal with any such situation, all the people travelling inside the car will be equipped with medical sensing devices. Even the vehicle will be attached with sensors to sense stress, strain in the vehicle. Once the vehicle suffers an accident, the sensors attached to the body will generate abnormal data which will be stored in the blockchain ledger using unique identity. The results will be analyzed by the ML software using sensing IoT devices on the cloud to assess the situation, the degree of damage and vital statistics of the people travelling inside the vehicle. In case, the situation is beyond control and needs immediate medical help, an alert will be generated by the software to the nearby police vans and hospital ambulance to reach to the crash site and look at the parameters from the ledger. In this way, fast identification can save lives in real-time. Pictorial representation is shown in Figure 26.5.

We have proposed an algorithm to show the convergence of the three technologies by using IoT data aggregation [28] as the first step then development of blockchain structure [29] of this IoT data and finally, applying unsupervised ML technique to predict severity of the accident for getting immediate and appropriate medical help.

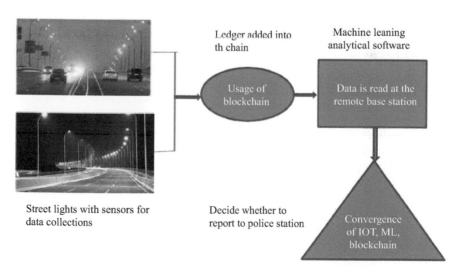

Figure 26.5   Pictorial representation of intelligent transportation system with computing technology

// CLUSTERING ALGORITHM FOR DATA AGGREGATION IN IOT
{n->Number of IOT nodes
Deploy the nodes randomly
        Set the node mobility parameters;
while Periodically
{ for each node
{ Send ("random messages to find the neighbors");
  Send (neighbor_count, residual_energy) to all neighbors;
  Determine Cluster_head = maximum (neighbor_count, residual_energy),
form a cluster within the range of this Cluster_head.;
}
Update the Cluster formation and heads
}
Cluster heads collaborate with the IoT nodes and aggregate the data received}

// CREATE BLOCKCHAIN STRUCTURE OF NEWLY RECEIVED DATA
FROM WEARABLE SENSORS AND CAR SENSORS
{ users:
        {users create transactions with their signatures with the IOT data received
from the cluster heads
        receive transactions, verify validity, forward to commissioners and butlers}
        butlers:
{ monitor transactions, store into their local pool, periodically synchronize
NTP time}
        $M = 1$, R = GetPreviousBlockRandomNum().
        If (first block of the tenure)
        then previous block = last valid special block of the previous tenure
        If (consensus -> genesis block || first block of the blockchain)
        then R-> 0
[GOTO 1] duty butler B_i :
        { picks transactions from the local pool, creates pre-block, sends to all
        commissioners
    cutoff time of block T_{cut} = GetPreviousBlockComfirmTime() + $M \times T_b$.
    commissioner :
    { verify validity
    If (agreed to produce the block)
    then send their signature on pre-block && current timestamp back to the
    butler }}
    duty butler :
    { if (collected at least$Nc2+1Nc2+1$ signatures from different commissioners)
    then serializes signatures into a string in ascending order of its timestamp and
    attach to the Pre-Header.
    R = GetPreviousBlockRandomNum()
    Final Header =R-value + block time
    If (block time < T_{cut})

then update signature in Pre-Header //to prove its work. GOTO 2
If (block time > T_{cut})
then block -> invalid block.
$R = (R + 1)modN_b$
$M = M + 1$. GOTO 1
[GOTO 2] // Valid block generated
    Butler B_R :
    { Final-Header sent to commissioners
    Release block to other nodes
    If (> half commissioners confirm receipt)
    then block enters the legal state with final confirmation
    if (Received valid block)
    then butlers and commissioners : delete the included transactions from their
    local pool, obtain R
    begin with the next round of consensus
    }

// APPLYING UNSUPERVISED MACHINE LEARNING MODEL OF
LOGISTIC REGRESSION TO PREDICT SEVERITY OF ACCIDENT
Get Block (values of X and Y)
Initialize X and Y values
store the error values
initializing learning rate alpha = 0.01 , e = 2.71828
    //Training for all values of X, Y and number of epocs
    Accessing index after every epoch
    // Make prediction
        double p = -(b0 + b1 * x1[idx]+ b2* x2[idx])
    //calculate the final prediction by applying sigmoid
        double pred = 1/(1+ pow(e,p));
    //Calculate error
    err = y[idx]-pred;
    // Update the values
        b0 = b0 - alpha * err*pred *(1-pred)* 1.0
        b1 = b1 + alpha * err * pred*(1-pred) *x1[idx]
        b2 = b2 + alpha * err * pred*(1-pred) * x2[idx]
        Print all the values b1, b2, b0 after every step
        error.push_back(err);
        }
    sort based on absolute error difference
    //Testing result
    double pred=b0+b1*test1+b2*test2; //make prediction
    if(pred>0.5)
    pred=1;
    else pred=0;
    }

26.6.2   Impact of IoT, Machine Learning, and blockchain in healthcare system

Healthcare is one of those fields which will always be needed to sustain healthy life and well-being of people. Now-a-days people are very aware of their health and want to stay fit and fine. Medical services and techniques have also evolved and advanced to a premium state. The healthcare sector covers medical illness, medicines, accidents and insurance [20]. There are also mobile-based applications which can access the monitoring devices attached to a person's body to measure real-time values for temperature, heartbeat, blood pressure, etc. Sometimes these devices are embedded inside the skin or they may be wearable in the form of a smart wristband. The attached sensors can relay the parameters to the mobile phone which is connected 24*7. These devices have unique blockchain ID and any new information which may indicate any abnormal difference in the reading of the patient will be stored in the ledger of the blockchain in a secure way. The ledger can be read by the ML software to carry out analytics and carefully identify the present condition of the patient. Based on the records, the ML software can immediately start a procedure to call the doctor or nearby ambulance in case any disorder is found. The doctor can access the ledger and see the reports and previous history to take measures. This method will allow fast identification, accurate prediction and will reduce the risk to the patient. It is typically suitable for elderly citizens and also critically ill patients. Pictorial representation is shown in Figure 26.6.

Shown below is the proposed algorithm for effective Intelligent healthcare services. The algorithm presents steps to aggregate data in IOT [28] network by selecting cluster heads, creating blockchain structure [29] of this data and then applying hybrid model of supervised learning which is improved further by using reinforced learning.

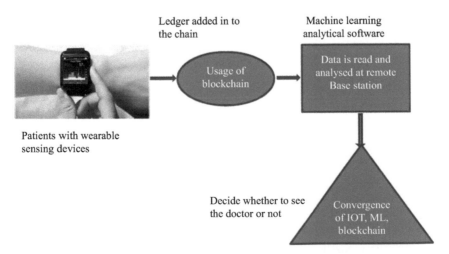

Figure 26.6   Pictorial representation of healthcare system with computing technology

// CLUSTERING ALGORITHM FOR DATA AGGREGATION IN IOT
{n->Number of IOT nodes
Deploy the nodes randomly
      Set the node mobility parameters;
while Periodically
{ for each node
{ Send ("random messages to find the neighbors");
    Send (neighbor_count, residual_energy) to all neighbors;
    Determine Cluster_head = maximum (neighbor_count, residual_energy),
form a cluster within the range of this Cluster_head.;
}
Update the Cluster formation and heads
}
Cluster heads collaborate with the IoT nodes and aggregate the data received}

// CREATE BLOCKCHAIN STRUCTURE OF NEWLY RECEIVED DATA
FROM SENSORS ATTACHED TO THE PATIENTS' BODY
{ users:
      {users create transactions with their signatures with the IOT data received
from the cluster heads
    receive transactions, verify validity, forward to commissioners and butlers}
    butlers:
{ monitor transactions, store into their local pool, periodically synchronize
NTP time}
      $M = 1$, $R = $ GetPreviousBlockRandomNum().
      If (first block of the tenure)
      then previous block = last valid special block of the previous tenure
      If (consensus -> genesis block || first block of the blockchain)
      then R-> 0
[GOTO 1] duty butler B_i :
        { picks transactions from the local pool, creates pre-block, sends to all
        commissioners
cutoff time of block $T_{cut} = $ GetPreviousBlockComfirmTime() $+ M \times T_b$.
    commissioner :
    { verify validity
    If (agreed to produce the block)
    then send their signature on pre-block && current timestamp back to the
    butler }}
    duty butler :
    { if (collected at leastNc2+1Nc2+1 signatures from different commissioners)
    then serializes signatures into a string in ascending order of its timestamp and
    attach to the Pre-Header.
    $R = $ GetPreviousBlockRandomNum()
    Final Header =R-value + block time
    If (block time $< T_{cut}$)

then update signature in Pre-Header //to prove its work. GOTO 2
If (block time $> T_{cut}$)
then block -> invalid block.
$R = (R + 1)mod N_b$
$M = M + 1$. GOTO 1
[GOTO 2] // Valid block generated
 Butler B_R :
  { Final-Header sent to commissioners
  Release block to other nodes
  If (> half commissioners confirm receipt)
  then block enters the legal state with final confirmation
  if (Received valid block)
  then butlers and commissioners : delete the included transactions from their
local pool, obtain R
begin with the next round of consensus
}

// APPLYING MACHINE LEARNING SUPERVISED MODEL WITH
REINFORCED LEARNING (Q BASED) OF LINEAR REGRESSION TO
DETECT THE DISEASE
 {
Get Block (x,y ,size of (x or y))
Input n -> no of data
For (i=1 to n)
 Read Xi and Yi
Initialize sum_X = 0, sum_X2 = 0, sum_Y = 0, sum_XY = 0
//Calculate Required Sum
 For (i=1 to n)
 { Sum_X = sum_X + Xi
 Sum_X2 = sum_X2 + Xi * Xi
 Sum_Y = sum_Y + Yi
 Sum_XY = sum_XY + Xi * Yi }
 //Calculate a and b of y = a + bx:
 b = (n * sum_XY - sum_X * sum_Y)/(n*sum_X2 – sum_X * sum_X)
 a = (sum_Y - b*sum_X)/n
// REINFORCED LEARNING FOR IMPROVING THE VALUES OF a and b
Associate a current state 's' to the calculated values
Observe whether the a and b agree with one of the action selection policies
Give positive or negative reward points 'r'
Update the Values of a and b for the state using these rewards
Try to attain maximum reward possible for the next state
set the state to the new state, and repeat the process until a terminal state is
reached
 }}

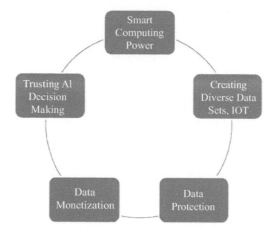

Figure 26.7   Application of IoT, AI, and blockchain

Expected outcome in both the application areas will be highly dependent on the machine algorithms used and implemented for further decisions using blockchain technology. With the rapid growth in blockchain technology in different areas of applications, the results are being reported in various research papers and articles [30–32]. In Figure 26.7, application of IoT, AI, and blockchain is presented [33]. The applications are followed by smart computing power, creating diverse data set, data protection, data monetization, trusting ML, and AI decision making.

26.7   Potential of computing technologies

Looking at the current scenario, the rapid growth in technology is dependent on different mechanisms and methods which can help in future. Still the research is continuing with the AI, ML, IoT, and blockchain technologies as on demand. The data storage and the use of data from storage are very important in technology and edge computing. The combined approach of all technologies together brings lots of appreciation in using of storage data. The blockchain is one of the concepts which really helps in storing the final information related to application areas. The above sections of transportation and healthcare system are the examples of storing intelligent information through IoT, ML, and AI techniques and then finally storing the data in blockchain concept. This is being implemented in C++, Java, and Python for achieving the outcome and good results. After study of literatures, here are some observations which has been implemented and proposed for near future optimistic results. Figures 26.8 and 26.9 depict the percentage of used each technology till date and further where research is needed as per increase of data in day-to-day life.

The rapid growth in connected devices in each application area are reported in [32, 34].

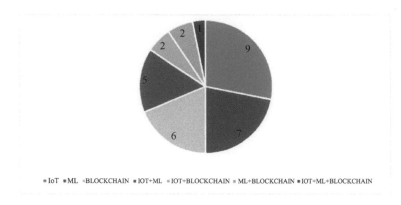

Figure 26.8   Percentage of used technology in current era

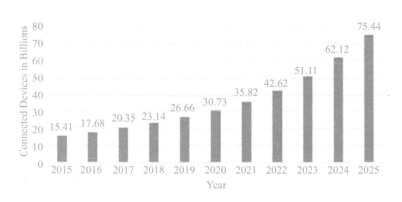

Figure 26.9   Growth of connected devices

However, there is still a lot of work to be done before we can effectively incorporate ML and blockchain to improve the performance together with IoT. The consensus algorithm and timestamp plus transaction data i.e. cryptographic hash of preceding blocks techniques are used in blockchain. The research in the area states that with reference to the number of blocks many parameters can be considered as throughput, simulation time, and energy efficiency with more futuristic metrics in each applications. The cryptographic hash function is useful for authentication and hence security of combined technologies is a challenge with the output metrics. One of the results is given as shown in Figure 26.10 which predicts that as per increase in number of blocks simulation time also increases. The other parameters have been evaluated and also are implemented

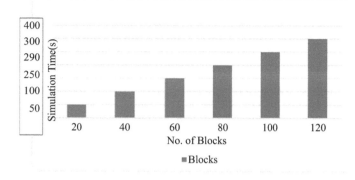

Figure 26.10   No. of blocks vs. simulation time

with new approach of storing and saving the information related to each field of application.

26.8   Future highlights

This section will present a comprehensive discussion on the future technology. The idea presented can be useful for global research.

Federation learning (FL) is a sub-branch of machine learning in which the model is developed not only by the training dataset provided by a single machine, rather multiple devices help in training the model. The dataset is dynamic and is fetched from varied sources. For example, a self-driven car will be able to get the best training if it receives the dynamic and distributed training from its fellow cars. This concept sounds very simple; however, it is a complex system where efficiency and cost are some of the greatest concerns. This learning requires data from different devices hence, security of individual donor machine may be compromised. They may suffer from denial of service attack. Moreover, inherent time delay is processing large pool of data may reduce the time efficiency of the overall system. Due to the cost involved, this learning is particularly preferred for wide-area, scalable IoT systems. However, due to its tremendous potential in creating better learned models, research should be focused on using FL in small IoT networks as-well. Figure 26.11 shows the development of FL model.

This model can be useful:

- for increasing the performance of the model;
- in building new and better applications in IoT;
- in merging Blockchain with IoT and ML.

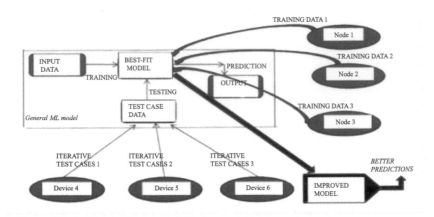

Figure 26.11   Development process of federation ML model

26.9   Conclusion and future scope

This chapter aims to cover the major aspects of the three recent technologies: IoT, ML, and blockchain. This work presents a comprehensive analysis of the existing research in computing technologies and a transformative impact on different applications like in healthcare and intelligent transport systems by using IoT, ML, and blockchain technologies together for accessing the useful information. The convergence of blockchain, ML, and IoT will provide scalable, secure high-level intellectual functioning that will be the new paradigm of digital information system. This convergence will bring a new definition to the services and applications provided for complete automation. Several issues are envisioned like data mining, data analytics, scalability, infrastructure development, funding issues, security threats are the challenging research areas in combined computing technology. However, with proper use of ML algorithms, IoT devices, blockchain technologies together with regulations and partnerships of private and public authorities challenging issues can be addressed in near future along with security issues. The chapter has shown how the convergence of the three technologies can be useful in healthcare and transportation system. Further research may be focused on the implementation of the systems. This would allow the understanding and building of numerous other smart applications like smart grid, smart structural monitoring, smart surveillance system, etc. to name a few. Complete implementation of these technologies will open doors to understand the potential in terms of design efficiency, energy usage, bandwidth requirement, dynamic application, effectiveness, real-time, correctness in detection, and security enhancements required by the system. With rapid analysis of all these parameters, the working efficiency can be enhanced to great extents.

References

[1] T.A. Balasubramanian, "The Convergence of IoT, AI and Blockchain Technologies", *IEEE India Info*, vol. 14, no. 1, 2019, pp. 58–62.

[2] J. Daniels, S. Sargolzaei, A. Sargolzaei, T. Ahram, P.A. Laplante, and B. Amaba, "The Internet of Things, Artificial Intelligence, Blockchain, and Professionalism", in: *IT Professional*, vol. 20, no. 6, pp. 15–19, 2018.

[3] A. Ghosh, D. Chakraborty, and A. Law, "Artificial Intelligence in Internet of Things", *IET*, Dec 2018,pp. 208–218.

[4] Y.-W. Lin, "AItalk: A Tutorial to Implement AI as IoT Devices", *IET*, May 2019, pp. 195–202.

[5] H. Khurshid, "Surface Water Pollution Monitoring Using the Internet of Things (IoT) and Machine Learning", *IET*, Nov 2020.

[6] M. Singh, A. Singh, and S. Kim, "Blockchain: A Game Changer for Securing IoT Data", 2018 IEEE 4th World Forum on Internet of Things (WF-IoT), Singapore, 2018, pp. 51–55, doi: 10.1109/WF-IoT.2018.8355182.

[7] H. Cui, Z. Chen, Y. Xi, H. Chen, and J. Hao, "IoT Data Management and Lineage Traceability: A Blockchain-Based Solution", 2019 IEEE/CIC International Conference on Communications Workshops in China (ICCC Workshops), Changchun, China, 2019, pp. 239–244, doi: 10.1109/ ICCChinaW.2019.8849969.

[8] C. Lee, N. Sung, L. Nkenyereye, and J. Song, "Blockchain Enabled Internet-of-Things Service Platform for Industrial Domain", in: 2018 IEEE International Conference on Industrial Internet (ICII), Seattle, WA, 2018, pp. 177–178, doi: 10.1109/ICII.2018.00033.

[9] D. Hwang, J. Choi, and K. Kim, "Dynamic Access Control Scheme for IoT Devices using Blockchain", in: 2018 International Conference on Information and Communication Technology Convergence (ICTC), Jeju, 2018, pp. 713–715, doi: 10.1109/ICTC.2018.8539659.

[10] A. Banafa, "16 IoT, AI and Blockchain: Catalysts for Digital Transformation", in: Secure and Smart Internet of Things (IoT): Using Blockchain and AI, River Publishers, 2018, pp. 113–120.

[11] Z. Li, Z. Xiao, Q. Xu, E. Sotthiwat, R.S. Mong Goh, and X. Liang, "Blockchain and IoT Data Analytics for Fine-Grained Transportation Insurance", in: 2018 IEEE 24th International Conference on Parallel and Distributed Systems (ICPADS), Singapore, Singapore, 2018, pp. 1022–1027, doi: 10.1109/PADSW.2018.8644599.

[12] K. Sharma and R. Nandal, "A Literature Study on Machine Learning Fusion with IOT", in: 2019 3rd International Conference on Trends in Electronics and Informatics (ICOEI), Tirunelveli, India, 2019, pp. 1440–1445, doi: 10.1109/ICOEI.2019.8862656.

[13] V. Porkodi, D. Yuvaraj, J. Khan, S.A. Karuppusamy, P.M. Goel, and M. Sivaram, "A Survey on Various Machine Learning Models in IOT Applications," in: 2020 International Conference on Computing and

Information Technology (ICCIT-1441), Tabuk, Saudi Arabia, 2020, pp. 1–4, doi: 10.1109/ICCIT-144147971.2020.9213819.

[14]   M. Keertikumar and M. Shubham, "Evolution of IoT in Smart Vehicles: An Overview", in: Proceedings of the 2015 International Conference on Green Computing and Internet of Things (ICGCIoT), Noida, India, October 2015, pp. 804–809.

[15]   N. Cam-Winget and Y. Jin, "Can IoT be Secured: Emerging Challenges in Connecting the Unconnected", in: Proceedings of the 53rd Annual Design Automation Conference (DAC '16), Austin, TX, USA, June 2016.

[16]   K. Tripathi and A. Jatain, "Real Time Challenges in Secure Internet of Things (RTCSIoT)", ACCT-2016, pp. 49–51, 2016.

[17]   A. Jain and K. Tripathi, "Biometric Signature Authentication Scheme with RNN (BIOSIG_RNN) Machine Learning Approach", in: International Conference on Contemporary Computing and Informatics (IC3I), IEEE, 10–12th Oct' 2018, 9007284, pp. 298–305.

[18]   P. Louridas and C. Ebert, "Machine Learning", *IEEE Software*, vol. 33, no. 5, pp. 110–115, 2016.

[19]   N. Fabiano, "Internet of Things and Blockchain: Legal Issues and Privacy. The Challenge for a Privacy Standard", in: Proceedings of the 2017 IEEE International Conference on Internet of Things (iThings) and IEEE Green Computing and Communications (GreenCom) and IEEE Cyber, Physical and Social Computing (CPSCom) and IEEE Smart Data (SmartData), Exeter, UK, 21–23 June 2017, pp. 727–734.

[20]   H.F. Atlam and G.B. Wills, "Intersections Between IoT and Distributed Ledger", *Adv Comput* 2019, pp. 1–41

[21]   M.M. Hossain, M. Fotouhi, and R. Hasan, "Towards an Analysis of Security Issues, Challenges, and Open Problems in the Internet of Things," in: Proceedings of the IEEE World Congress on Services IEEE, New York, NY, USA, June 2015, pp. 21–28.

[22]   S.M. Tahsien, H. Karimipour, and P. Spachos, "Machine Learning Based Solutions for Security of Internet of Things (IoT): A Survey", *J Netw Comput Appl*, vol. 161, 2020.

[23]   F. Liang, W.G. Hatcher, W. Liao, W. Gao, and W. Yu, "Machine Learning for Security and the Internet of Things: The Good, the Bad, and the Ugly", *IEEE Access*, vol. 7, pp. 158126–158147, 2019.

[24]   H.F. Atlam and A. Alenezi, "Blockchain with Internet of Things: Benefits, Challenges, and Future Directions", *Int J Intell Syst Appl*, vol. 10, pp. 40–48, 2018.

[25]   D. Strugar, R. Hussain, and M. Mazzara, "An Architecture for Distributed Ledger-Based M2M Auditing for Electric Autonomous Vehicles", in: Proceedings of the Workshops of the International Conference on Advanced Information Networking and Applications, Matsue, Japan, March 2019, pp. 116–128.

[26]   D. Agarwal, "Study of IoT and Proposed Accident Detection System Using IoT," *IOSR-JCE*, vol. 22, pp. 27–30, 2020.

[27] D. Agarwal, "A Comprehensive Transformative Effect of IoT, Machine Learning and Blockchain in Computing Technology", in: *Recent Trends in Blockchain for Information Systems Security and Privacy*, CRC Press, 2021, pp. 1–27

[28] J. Sathish Kumar and M.A. Zaveri, "Clustering Approaches for Pragmatic Two-Layer IoT Architecture", *Wireless Commun Mobile Comput*, vol. 2018, pp. 1–16, 2018.

[29] A.K. Tyagi, D. Agarwal, and N. Sreenath, "SecVT: Securing the Vehicles of Tomorrow using Blockchain Technology", in: *2022 International Conference on Computer Communication and Informatics (ICCCI)*, 2022, pp. 1-6. doi: 10.1109/ICCCI54379.2022.9740965.

[30] K. Christidis, and M. Devetsikiotis, "Blockchains and Smart Contracts for the Internet of Things", *IEEE Access* 2016, 4, pp. 2292–2303.

[31] F. Hussain, R. Hussain, S.A. Hassan and E. Hossain, "Machine Learning in IoT Security: Current Solutions and Future Challenges", *IEEE Commun Surv Tutor*, vol. 22, no. 3, pp. 1686–1721, 2020

[32] V. Astarita, V.P. Giofre, G. Mirabelli, and V. Solina, "A review of Blockchain Based System in Transportation", MDPI, Information 2020, December 2019, pp. 1–24.

[33] A.K. Tyagi, G. Rekha, and S. Kumari, "Applications of Blockchain Technologies in Digital Forensic and Threat Hunting", in: *Recent Trends in Blockchain for Information Systems Security and Privacy*, CRC Press, 2021.

[34] T. Alam, "A Reliable Communication Framework and Its Use in Internet of Things (IoT)", *Int J Sci Res Comput Sci Eng Inf Tech*, vol. 3, no. 5, pp. 450–456, 2018.

Chapter 27

Conclusion to this book

Amit Kumar Tyagi[1], Ajith Abraham[2], Farookh Khadeer Hussain[3], Habil Arturas Kaklauskas[4] and R. Jagadeesh Kannan[1]

As discussed in previous chapters, we can find out that the integration of these emerging technologies definitely will change the way of living, working in the next decade. But together these technologies get serious challenges like leaking of personal information, habits by IoT devices, require high energy for machine learning (ML) to refine big data, require more storage in cloud computing and many data center to store this data, security of this data by blockchain and providing authentication process to these integrated (ML + blockchain + Internet of Things (IoT)) systems, and many more. Hence, this section discusses few faced critical challenges in the integration of these technologies as:

27.1 Challenges in the integration of Machine Learning and IoT

Few challenges in the integration of ML/Artificial Intelligence (AI) and IoT can be discussed as:

(a) **Connecting gadgets**: We have the assignment of connecting the PCs and gadgets around us to the web these days. Fundamental gadgets including lights and temperature sensors convey over Bluetooth or ZigBee, yet both are guidelines that do not work on the web. Further developed mechanical machines conceivably impart through open platform communications (OPC) or exclusive attachment interchanges, however, with all their multifaceted nature, these gadgets can in any case not associate with the web. Organizations creating IoT gadgets are tending to this obstruction by utilizing

[1]School of Computer Science and Engineering, Vellore Institute of Technology, Chennai, India
[2]Machine Intelligence Research Labs (MIR Labs), USA
[3]Discipline (Software Engineering), University of Technology, Sydney, Australia
[4]Construction Economics and Property Management, Vilnius Gediminas Technical University, Lithuania

doors, otherwise called edge-based registering, to interface with cloud-based IoT stages. This makes it workable for systems to communicate information to the web. Be that as it may, interfacing systems is not as simple as refreshing programming; all things considered, it is an interest in retrofitting old gadgets, supplanting existing gear, and empowering a labor force to use this hardware. As current heating, ventilation and air conditioning (HVAC) frameworks from Honeywell and Johnson Controls are putting doors close to their current machine to machine (M2M) arrangements and web-based information to the web using MQ Telemetry Transport (MQTT), we see this simply starting to occur in numerous structures today. It is an advancement, over numerous years, not a quick redesign.

(b) **Data understanding:** The test of connecting products to the web has shrouded the way that the data passed on by their machines has not yet been gotten a handle on by a few organizations. A gadget that persistently streams voltage, temperature, battery, and erosion data is significant if the information cannot be deciphered (and to be perceived, information should be organized so it tends to be placed into a comprehended space model). Moreover, the information is futile without the opportunity to recognize results. This infers that we need information on how machines break down before we can chart what is happening. In the wake of interfacing hardware and sending information to an information lake, we need to stand by and see what's going on. This is the place where we can impact topic specialists, as they might have the option to give us more data. A PC with a lot of vibration, for instance, will before long breakdown. We additionally endeavored to apply prescient support, which is the thing that we have achieved, to connected entryways. In doing as such, we found that dampness and temperature among information focus, for example, engine temperature, RPMs, utilization every day, amperage load, stickiness, commotion decibels, opening velocity, geolocation, air particles, a season of the day, and encompassing temperature might be the best indicators of future issues. This equitable shows that understanding our piles of information requests that we utilize our inside abilities when preparing AI.

(c) **Training AI**: When we have acquired enough information to start actualizing AI, we show up at a preparation stage. This is extraordinary to each machine, representing variables, for example, the particular model, sorts of information, and potential impacts. To discover relations among data sources and results, we would then be able to utilize measurable methods with this data. No single model is appropriate for all cases of utilization; information researchers need to test different models to perceive what works. The impact of preparing guarantees that the calculations that work best to anticipate our system conduct are known to us. Shockingly, they will in any case be one-sided by this underlying arrangement of seed information. Thusly, we need to accomplish more on the off chance that we truly need to gain from systems. To accomplish genuine AI, we should represent more instances of machines working in genuine conditions, add new sensors for new data sources, and record new sorts of results. We need to re-run this model investigation again and again, endlessly, with each new case helping the AI models adjust and improve. For instance, we made a structure for understanding MRI checks and their ensuing conclusion. It has complex likelihood tables and numerical calculations with input factors and information to permit patients to be analyzed and treated all the more productively by doctors and radiologists. It at that point proceeds to take and case and figure out how to upgrade the probabilities when new factors, for example, offices and specialists are presented.

27.2   Challenges in the integration of blockchain and Big Data

Blockchain stockpiling limit and adaptability are as yet under discussion, as expressed, however, in the feeling of IoT applications, the character limit, and versatility impediments make these difficulties a lot more prominent. In this sense, blockchain may appear to be wrong to IoT applications, yet there are manners by which it is conceivable to completely ease or departure these limitations. This limitation is a significant snag to its consolidation into the IoT blockchain, where gadgets can create ongoing Gigabytes (GBs) of information or data (called Big Data). It is realized that some current blockchain usage can uphold only a couple of exchanges for every second, so this could be a likely bottleneck for the IoT. Moreover, the object of blockchain is not to store tremendous measures of data, for example, those created in the IoT. By joining these innovations, these worries can be managed. Presently, a ton of IoT information is put away and just a little part is valuable for separating data and creating activity. To decrease them, different methods have been recommended in the writing for separating, normalizing, and compacting IoT information. Inserted PCs, correspondences, and target administrations (blockchain, cloud) are remembered for the IoT, countless layers can profit by reserve funds in the measure of information produced by the IoT. The high volume of IoT information produced by transmission, handling assignments, and capacity can be facilitated by information pressure. Typical practices do not generally need extra, fundamental data, in contrast to odd information. To wrap things up, as the instance of Bitcoin-NG illustrates, blockchain could likewise be adjusted to expand data transmission and abatement the dormancy of its exchanges and, specifically, its agreement convention that causes its bottleneck, consequently empowering a smoother move to the IoT. Few popular challenges in the integration of Blockchain and IoT will be:

- **Security:** IoT frameworks need to determine security issues at various stages, however with extra multifaceted nature because of an absence of execution and raised heterogeneity of the stage. Moreover, the IoT situation includes a bunch of properties that influence wellbeing, for example, versatility, remote correspondence, or size. A careful IoT security investigation is done and several issues are found in [1,2]. The expanding number of IoT network assaults and their genuine ramifications make fabricating an IoT with more modern security unmistakably more fundamental. To give the genuinely necessary IoT security updates, blockchain is seen by numerous specialists as a key innovation. Notwithstanding, one of the vital difficulties of incorporating the IoT with the blockchain is the dependability of the information produced by the IoT. In any case, if data in the blockchain is as of now bad, blockchain can guarantee the information in the chain is perpetual and can recognize their changes. Degenerate IoT information may emerge from numerous conditions, aside from vindictive ones. The prosperity of the IoT design is influenced by a few components, for example, the climate, members, defacing, and the disappointment of the structures. Some of the time, the machines themselves and their sensors and actuators battle to work appropriately from the beginning. This condition would not be known until the gadget being referred to has been checked or it frequently works appropriately for some time and changes its conduct for reasons unknown (cut off, customized out of date quality, etc.).

Notwithstanding these cases, there are a few perils, for example, listening, trying to claim ignorance of administration, or force that can influence the IoT. Hence, IoT gadgets should be completely tried before their reconciliation with blockchain, and they should be put and epitomized in the perfect spot to stay away from actual harm, notwithstanding giving strategies to recognize framework disappointments when they happen. These gadgets are bound to be undermined because their constraints oblige firmware refreshes, keeping them from following up on potential bugs or breaks of security. Moreover, refreshing gadgets individually is additionally troublesome, as in worldwide IoT usage. Consequently, run-time refreshing and reconfiguration components should be situated in the IoT to keep it running over the long haul. Organization and firmware refreshes are permitted over the long haul by activities, for example, GUITAR and REMOWARE and are important to guarantee that the IoT is safely incorporated with the blockchain over the long haul. IoT and blockchain incorporation would likewise affect IoT correspondences.

To give secure interchanges, for example, transport layer security (TLS) or datagram transport layer security (DTLS), IoT application conventions, for example, constrained application protocol (CoAP) and MQTT right now utilize other security conventions. These safe conventions are mind-boggling and incredible, notwithstanding requiring brought together control and administration of key foundation, by and large with public key infrastructure (PKI). In the blockchain network, each IoT gadget will have its global unique identifier (GUID) and an unbalanced key pair introduced before it is associated with the organization. This will rearrange existing security conventions that as of now need to trade PKI endorsements and permit them to be utilized in lower-ability gadgets. "Filament" [3] is a critical IoT venture with the execution of a blockchain regarding security. Fiber is a product and equipment arrangement that gives Bitcoin-based installments and shrewd agreements with IoT highlights. Fiber frameworks have inserted crypto-processors that help five conventions: block name, tele-hash and savvy contracts running, and extra Penny back and Bittorrent conventions. Square name handles client character, while Tele-hash, the open-source execution of Kademlia DHT, offers securely encoded correspondences, and brilliant agreements characterize how a framework can be utilized.

- **Anonymity and privacy of data:** The issue of information security and secrecy, for example, in the e-health situation, is significant for some IoT applications to manage touchy information, when the gadget is connected to an individual. Blockchain is viewed as the ideal answer for tending to the administration of IoT character, yet there may be executions where, likewise with Bitcoin, protection should be ensured. This is the situation of a wearable with the capacity to veil the character of the individual while sending individual subtleties or keen vehicles that secure the protection of the courses of clients. The issue of information security in open and public blockchains has just been handled alongside the absolute most recent arrangements. Be that as it may, greater intricacy is associated with the issue of information security in IoT gadgets, as it begins with information assortment and proceeds to the correspondence and application levels. Frameworks need to be ensured so that information is secured and not reached by a third party without authorization, as it includes the reconciliation of cryptographic security programming into the gadget. These progressions should consider the limitations on machine assets and restrictions on monetary reasonability.

  A few frameworks have been utilized to make sure about correspondences utilizing encryption (IPsec, SSL/TLS, and DTLS). To implement these security instruments, for example, entryways, limitations on IoT gadgets regularly make it conceivable to utilize less confined gadgets. Utilizing cryptographic equipment could accelerate cryptographic exercises and forestall the overburdening of confounded ensured programming conventions. Information security and protection are key worries for IoT, and the issue of personality on the board in IoT can be lightened utilizing blockchain innovation. Another fundamental IoT work is a certainty, where blockchain joining can assume a job. The significance of trust in IoT frameworks is distinguished as one of the primary objectives to guarantee its viability. Information respectability procedures are another option in contrast to guaranteeing information access simultaneously, as they forestall the blockchain from over-burdening with the huge measure of IoT information created. This can bring about open administrations, yet with viable and confined admittance controls. MuR-DPA conveys dynamic information cautions and effective checks through open review confirmation. To wrap things up, there are information security laws, for example, the EU Data Protection Directives (EU-DPA), which should be modified to cover the new models that innovation makes conceivable. To guarantee information security in consistence with the law, these laws can be overwhelmed by actualizing the blockchain as a lawful structure.

- **Legal issues:** The possibility of an unregulated blockchain is important for its plan and mostly liable for Bitcoin's prevalence. As observed, blockchain, particularly in the feeling of virtual monetary standards, has carried with it a great deal of debate about legitimateness. The need, or possibility, to add control components over the organization has come as acknowledged, private and consortium blockchains. The IoT area, for example, the Data Protection Directive, is likewise influenced by the information security laws or guidelines of a nation. The greater part of these guidelines is getting out of date and should be refreshed, particularly with the rise of new troublesome innovations, for example, blockchain. Growing new laws and guidelines would make it simpler to ensure the security highlights of gadgets and in this manner, help to assemble the IoT network that is generally secure and trusted. Information security and information taking care of laws are as yet a gigantic obstruction to be handled in IoT in this unique circumstance and will likewise be a much more serious issue whenever utilized in blend with blockchain. As characterized, the non-appearance of guidelines makes drawbacks, as private key recovery or reset instruments or exchange inversion are not possible. Some IoT executions conceive a worldwide, remarkable blockchain for gadgets, yet it is indistinct if this sort of organization is proposed to be controlled by producers or accessible to clients. For this situation, it is normal that it would require a legitimate investigation. The fate of blockchain and IoT might be affected by these laws and, accordingly, the decentralized and free embodiment of blockchain could hypothetically be undermined by presenting a controlled, incorporated part.

- **Agreement:** With regards to IoT applications, the restricted asset nature of gadgets makes them unacceptable for direct support in agreement measures, for example, Proof of Work (PoW). As expressed, there is a wide assortment of propositions for agreement conventions, yet they are beginning by and large and have not been tried satisfactorily. Asset necessities rely upon the specific sort of agreement convention in the blockchain network. Arrangements regularly expect to designate these assignments to passages or some other unconstrained unit equipped for giving this usefulness. While there are endeavors to coordinate total blockchain hubs into IoT gadgets, mining is as yet a critical test in the IoT on account of its constraints, the users might be upheld by alternatively off-chain arrangements that move information outside the blockchain to lessen the high inertness in the blockchain. The IoT generally comprises of asset obliged applications, however, the IoT worldwide has a conceivably colossal figuring power, considering that by 2020 the quantity of gadgets in it is required to reach between 20 billion and 50 billion. Examination endeavors should be in zero on this district and exploit the appropriated idea of the IoT and the worldwide limit of the IoT agreement to adjust.
- **Energy:** Energy is a big concern for both technologies, i.e., for verifying blocks in blockchain (by miners) and making communications of IoTs for a long time, we want energy/power for running these integrated systems for a long time.
- **Scalability:** Scalability is the biggest issue towards IoT to trust on such devices over the Internet.
- **Standardization:** Till now, only a few companies have licenses to developed IoT devices, but no specific standard or procedure is followed to develop IoTs for today's applications.

27.3 Opportunities with Machine Learning, blockchain, and IoT

Each of the four domains of ML, IoT, cloud computing, and blockchain has massive scope for future research and implementation. There will be many opportunities with these technologies in near future [6–10]. The same opportunities we have discussed in this book and various developments on the existing applications for optimization and efficiency are discussed as below:

- **ML:** ML is a subset of AI. The impact of AI-related applications and implementations in our daily lives has emerged to a great extent such that almost every other sophisticated device in our surroundings involves some concept of AI in it. There are a plethora of opportunities for future research directions and enhancements in the field of AI. In applications of smart cities, Industry 4.0, data analytics-related concepts, AI can surely act as a bridging factor between different components and elements of automation and precision. AI algorithms and strategies can further be developed to ensure safety and security for data protection and even prevent small-scale identity thefts with the help of appropriate AI and ML algorithms. One of the possible applications and research domains of AI concerning the future would be the utilization of AI for performing vital and critical tasks to reduce the human interference required. Similarly, in the field of transportation, subjects of AI prove to help curate self-driven cars, automated trains and jetliners, and so on. These are some of the major domains and applications which open up various opportunities for extensive research and analysis [4].
- **IoT:** With almost every other device at homes, offices, and other environments are interconnected and linked to each other, IoT has been prominently visible in every major field. However, it also does possess several fields which can be further researched upon for improvisation and enhancement of the various IoT-related improvisations. Security and privacy of the large amounts of data which is generated by the nodes and devices in the framework must be protected from any sort of attacks and leakages and is of prime importance in the current world [5]. One of the other major research domains in IoT caters to that of maintaining the traffic congestion when transferring voluminous amounts of data between devices through networks. One of the other major concerns which need to be looked into is the high amount of energy consumption that is required during the utilization of IoT services. Hence, researches and developments on efficiently managing energy requirements have huge scope for future works.
- **Blockchain:** Blockchain is one of the popular technologies of this era, gained popularity for its concepts and security benefits. However, one of the major challenges faced by blockchain which can be extensively researched upon is the storage requirements for accommodating larger volumes of data. This is mainly because the storage needs which involve the encryption and authentication factors incorporate the entire blockchain. On similar grounds, one of the other areas which call for massive research opportunities is that of minimizing energy consumption while rapidly generating blocks for storing data [5]. One

of the other major concerns which require research is with regard to the scalability of the blockchain for extending its associated applications efficiently and reliably. Improvising and enhancing the above-mentioned features would provide a holistic perspective on blockchain.

27.4   Conclusion

ML, a subset of AI, becomes more powerful with Blockchain. Similarly, an IoT device's life increase when it integrates with Cloud computing for optimal storage. Hence, in this work, we have seen major evolutions in many sectors/applications with the integration of AI, blockchain, IoT, and cloud computing. This work provides several perspectives of advanced technology like AI, IoT, blockchain, and cloud computing which potentially help in various applications/sectors. In this work, we also discuss "how AI and Blockchain will help IoT in terms of architecture, system usage, security." So, with help of this combo (ML + blockchain + IoT + Big Data) will give much advancement in several fields and will be effective for many purposes in near future. The primary aim of this research is to give out brief usage of how AI and blockchain help potentially with IoT and challenges faced by AI and blockchain while incorporated with IoT. In summary, this work explains various aspects like AI and blockchain incorporating IoT in fields like agriculture, healthcare, military, education, customer relationship management (CRM), digital marketing, etc., and also the challenges that are faced while the integration of these technologies. This book also aims to other researchers out there who can potentially build various angles of AI and blockchain from this book and produce a better end product which is in a way helpful for society.

References

[1]   Tyagi, A.K., Nair, M.M., Niladhuri, S., and Abraham, A., "Security, Privacy Research Issues in Various Computing Platforms: A Survey and the Road Ahead", *Journal of Information Assurance & Security*, vol. 15, no. 1, pp. 1–16, 2020.

[2]   Tyagi, A.K. and Nair, M.M., "Internet of Everything (IoE) and Internet of Things (IoTs): Threat Analyses, Possible Opportunities for Future", *Journal of Information Assurance & Security (JIAS)*, vol. 15, no. 4, pp. 194–218, 2020.

[3]   Haenlein, M. and Kaplan, A., "A Brief History of Artificial Intelligence: On the Past, Present, and Future of Artificial Intelligence", *California Management Review*, vol. 61, no. 4, pp. 5–14, 2019. doi:10.1177/0008125619864925

[4]   Lee, S.K., Mungyu B., and Hwangnam, K., "Future of IoT Networks: A Survey", *Applied Sciences*, vol. 7, no. 10, p. 1072, 2017. https://doi.org/10.3390/app7101072

[5]   Porru, S., Pinna, A., Marchesi, M., and Tonelli, R., "Blockchain-Oriented Software Engineering: Challenges and New Directions", in: 2017 IEEE/ACM 39th International Conference on Software Engineering Companion (ICSE-C), 2017, pp. 169–171, doi: 10.1109/ICSE-C.2017.142.

[6] Tyagi, A.K., Agarwal, D., and Sreenath, N., "SecVT: Securing the Vehicles of Tomorrow using Blockchain Technology", in: 2022 International Conference on Computer Communication and Informatics (ICCCI), 2022, pp. 1–6, doi: 10.1109/ICCCI54379.2022.9740965.

[7] Deshmukh, A., Sreenath, N., Tyagi, A.K., and Eswara Abhichandan, U.V., "Blockchain Enabled Cyber Security: A Comprehensive Survey," in: 2022 International Conference on Computer Communication and Informatics (ICCCI), 2022, pp. 1–6, doi: 10.1109/ICCCI54379.2022.9740843.

[8] Tyagi, A.K. (ed.), *Data Science and Data Analytics: Opportunities and Challenges*, 1st edn, Chapman and Hall/CRC, 2021. https://doi.org/10.1201/9781003111290.

[9] Tyagi, A.K. and Abraham, A. (eds.), *Recent Trends in Blockchain for Information Systems Security and Privacy*, 1st edn, CRC Press, 2021. https://doi.org/10.1201/9781003139737.

[10] Kumari, S. and Muthulakshmi, P., "Transformative Effects of Big Data on Advanced Data Analytics: Open Issues and Critical Challenges", *Journal of Computer Science*, vol. 18, no. 6, pp. 463–479, 2022. https://doi.org/10.3844/jcssp.2022.463.479.

Index